The Charmed Circle
Joseph II and the "Five Princesses," 1765-1790

Central European Studies

Charles W. Ingrao, founding editor
Gary B. Cohen, editor
Howard Louthan, editor
Franz A. J. Szabo, editor
Daniel L. Unowsky, editor

The Charmed Circle
Joseph II and the "Five Princesses," 1765-1790

Rebecca Gates-Coon

Purdue University Press
West Lafayette, Indiana

Copyright © 2015 by Purdue University. All rights reserved.

Gates-Coon, Rebecca.
  The Charmed Circle: Joseph II and the "Five Princesses," 1765-1790 / Rebecca Gates-Coon.
     pages cm. -- (Central European Studies)
  Includes bibliographical references and index.
        ISBN 978-1-55753-694-5 (paperback)
        ISBN 978-1-61249-369-5 (ePDF)
        ISBN 978-1-61249-370-1 (ePub)
1. Joseph II, Holy Roman Emperor, 1741-1790. 2. Joseph II, Holy Roman Emperor, 1741-1790—Friends and associates. 3. Princesses—Austria—Vienna—Biography. 4. Austria—Court and courtiers—Biography. 5. Princesses—Austria—Vienna—Correspondence. 6. Women—Austria—Vienna—Correspondence. 7. Aristocracy (Social class)—Austria—Vienna—History—18th century. 8. Vienna (Austria)—Social life and customs—18th century. 9. Austria—History—1740-1789. I. Title.
  DB74.5.G38 2015
  943'.053092—dc23
  [B]
                        2014021340

Cover image: Carl Shütz (1745-1800). *Schloss Schönbrunn gegen den Garten. Wiener Strassenbilder im Zeitalter des Rokoko.* p. 20. 1914. Engraving. Print Collection, Miriam and Ira D. Wallach Division of Art, Prints and Photographs, The New York Public Library, Astor, Lenox, and Tilden Foundations.

To my family, immediate and extended.

Contents

Abbreviations	viii
Acknowledgments	ix
Preface	xi
Introduction	1
Chapter 1: Aristocrats: Ancestry and Posterity	11
Chapter 2: Court and Society	53
Chapter 3: Origins of *la société*	107
Chapter 4: 1765-1780: The *Damenkreis* during the Coregency	151
Chapter 5: 1780-1790: Politics under Joseph II's Sole Rulership	209
Chapter 6: Joseph II's Foreign Policy and the End of an Era	279
Chapter 7: Conclusion	331
Bibliography	343
Index	359

Abbreviations

EL	Eleonore Liechtenstein
FR	Franz Rosenberg
JII	Joseph II
JC	Josepha Clary
LK	Leopoldine Kaunitz
LL	Leopoldine Liechtenstein
ML	Moritz Lacy
MT	Maria Theresia
SK	Sidonia Kinsky

HA SB	Habsburgisch-Lothringische Hausarchive (12. Jh.-1918), Hausarchiv, Sammelbände
HHStA	Haus-, Hof- und Staatsarchiv
KA NL	Kabinettsarchiv, Staatsrat, Nachlaß Franz M. Lacy
KLA, FAR	Familienarchiv Rosenberg in the Kärntner Landesarchiv, Klagenfurt, Austria
LRRA	Lobkovicové Roudničtí, Rodinný Archiv, Nelahozeves, formerly at Žitenice
NM, RAŠM	Rodinný Archiv Šternberk-Manderscheid, Národní Muzeum, Prague
NRAS, DHP	National Archives of Scotland, Edinburgh, Douglas Home Papers
SOAL-D, RACA	Rodinný Archiv Clary-Aldringenů (Teplice), Státní Oblastní Archiv v Litoměřicích, Pobočka Děčín
SÚA, RAM AC Ústřední	Rodinný Archiv Metternichů, Acta Clementina, Státní Archiv, Prague
ZT	Zinzendorf Tagebücher, Reprosammlungen [microfilm], Kabinettsarchiv

Acknowledgments

During the early stages of this project I was assisted by several Short-Term Travel Grants from the International Research and Exchanges Board (IREX) for visits to archives in Litoměřice, Děčín, and Prague, for which I am grateful. The friendliness and professionalism with which I was treated there and in Vienna, Klagenfurt, Brno, and Edinburgh really cannot be overstated. The Liechtenstein archivist (Hausarchiv der regierenden Fürsten von Liechtenstein) of Vienna and Vaduz sent copies of additional materials relating to the lives of Leopoldine and Eleonore Liechtenstein, and the Hohenzollern-Hechingen archive in the State Archive of Sigmaringen, Germany provided supplementary documents pertinent to the lives of princesses Clary and Kinsky, members of that family prior to their marriages. I have met with kindness from so many individuals that it would not be possible to mention all of them here. I am particularly thankful for the Lobkowicz family's permission to access the Liechtenstein-Kaunitz correspondence in the Lobkowicz archives. I also wish to acknowledge Professor Derek Beales's kind assistance with source material at the outset of the study.

Preface

No Habsburg monarch has been treated by so many biographers as Joseph II, sometimes styled the "revolutionary Emperor." Over the more than two centuries since his death, however, a marked feature of the bulk of these biographies has been the instrumentalization of the emperor for the political agendas of the times in which they were written. Substantial studies based on significant archival research have, until recently, been few and far between, and the two most important—those by Henrik Marczali (1885-1888) and Pavel Mitrofanov (1907)—were more major studies of aspects of Joseph's reign rather than conventional biographies. In many respects, therefore, the recent completion of an extensive two-volume biography by Derek Beales is not only a milestone in the Joseph II historiography, but the most ambitious and exhaustive biography of the emperor ever attempted. Though Beales's work will no doubt serve as a standard reference work for all students of this monarch's reign for decades to come, there is nevertheless still substantial scope for scholarly engagement with many aspects of both his policies and his personality.

One of the many strengths of the Beales biography is its analysis of the curious mixture of affability and irascibility, of engaging warmth and contemptuous coldness, of touchiness and insensitivity of Joseph's personality. Among the sources used by Beales to illuminate this dimension of the study was the exchange of letters among five aristocratic women who formed Joseph's inner social circle for most of his adult life. This archival material has now been more exhaustively mined by Rebecca Gates-Coon in the volume to hand. What emerges is not only further revealing insight into the personality of Joseph II, but a richly textured study of aristocratic life in the Habsburg monarchy during the second half of the eighteenth century. Though the Habsburg nobility is receiving increasing attention in contemporary Habsburg historiography, this study of a unique group of noble women adds significantly to our understanding of the experience of noble life from a female perspective. It simultaneously sheds new light on court life under Joseph II, as well as uncovering the many layers of related topics, such as attitudes toward marriage and children, land-holding and privilege, and social habits and norms.

In addition to contributing to current debates on nobility and court life in the later eighteenth century this volume confronts us with the rather curious spectacle of reforming emperor finding social solace in a circle of women totally out of sympathy with his reforms, and of a group of high society ladies proud of their special relationship with a monarch of whose political engagement and personality they were highly critical. In analyzing why both parties would find the arrangement mutually beneficial, the author adds further depth to the portrait of Joseph II drawn by Beales. The pronounced strain of misogyny combined with the desperate need for some form of female companionship allowed an obviously very lonely and isolated emperor to find emotional fulfillment in this circle of acquaintances despite not taking any of the women's political or social views seriously. Although Joseph's association with the group he affectionately referred to as *"la société"* began with an unrequited romantic interest in one of its members, it remained entirely platonic—the emperor preferring to find fleeting sexual fulfillment with lower-class women or ladies of the theater. After the early death of two successive wives, Joseph remained a confirmed bachelor, and it is noteworthy that his two closest male associates, who also formed part of this exclusive social group, were life-long bachelors as well. But bachelorhood notwithstanding, in stark contrast to the court of Frederick II of Prussia, women—and women of suitable social status—were clearly so central to sociability in Joseph's mental universe, that the frequently reiterated rather severe but perceptive view of his brother and eventual successor, Leopold II, that these women were bigoted and knew as much about politics as about Chinese, never shook his commitment to them or his apparent need for them.

Equally intriguing is the ongoing commitment of these women to Joseph. None of their husbands played any important political role in the enlightened absolutist regime of the emperor, and the women apparently never overstepped the bounds of their association with him to attempt to further the political careers of their husbands—something which Joseph would in any case have never countenanced. Although the women frequently stressed that their association with a clearly difficult and frequently distressing emperor was motivated by a sense of duty, this study shows the degree to which it went well beyond that. On the one hand the ambivalent attitude of the women to Joseph did not lack genuine personal attachment. On the other hand, aristocratic women were as much custodians of family interests as their husbands, and of those interests the safeguarding of their status vis-à-vis the ruler and other elite families remained a paramount and ongoing concern. Thus, despite the fact that the women represented the apex of Viennese aristocratic society, they still desired and pursued the additional social capital that came with an intimate association with the monarch.

Franz A. J. Szabo
Editor

Introduction

In late eighteenth-century Vienna there existed a remarkable coterie of five aristocratic women, known to history as "the five princesses" (*die fünf Fürstinnen*), who achieved social preeminence and acclaim as close associates of the Habsburg "reform emperor" Joseph II: Princess Maria Josepha Clary (1728–1801); Princess Maria Sidonia Kinsky (1729–1815); Princess Marie Leopoldine Liechtenstein (1733–1809); Countess—subsequently Princess—Marie Leopoldine Kaunitz (1741–1795); and Princess Marie Eleonore Liechtenstein (1745–1812). Privileged and well connected, beneficiaries of the wealth produced by the Bohemian and Moravian estates of their husbands' families, these five individuals included among them two pairs of sisters, four cousins, and two sisters-in-law.

Four of the women were well acquainted as early as the mid-1760s. The group assumed a stable form by 1772, when Leopoldine Kaunitz returned to Vienna from Naples where her husband, son of state chancellor Wenzel Kaunitz, had held a diplomatic post. Her inclusion brought the number of female members to five. By this time, the emperor Joseph and two of his closest male associates, Field Marshal Count Franz Moritz Lacy (1725–1801) and Count Franz Xavier Orsini-Rosenberg (1726–1795), had become accepted members of the circle as well. Meetings of the group, for discussion of daily events, gossip, and sometimes literary matters (but never for card games), occurred with remarkable regularity throughout the 1770s and 1780s. During the Viennese social "season" (fall, winter, and spring), members of the group made their way several times each week to the inner city palace of one of the *Dames*, as group members called themselves. During the summer months, when the women dispersed to visit country estates in Bohemia and Moravia or to travel, members corresponded regularly. Sometimes special outings were arranged. When Joseph II undertook his many voyages, he sent letters and messages to these friends, both singly and as a group.

The women's adult lives coincided with exciting, restless years in the Habsburg monarchy, as both Maria Theresia and Joseph II implemented reforms that were intended to help the monarchy withstand threats to its stability and

2   ♦   The Charmed Circle

Artist unknown. The Roundtable of Emperor Joseph II (1741-1790). Oil, after 1790. Liechtenstein. Courtesy of The Princely Collections, Vaduz–Vienna.

From left to right: Countess Leopoldine Kaunitz *née* Princess Öttingen-Spielberg; Prince Franz Xavier Rosenberg Orsini; Princess Josepha Clary *née* Princess Hohenzollern-Hechingen; Emperor Joseph II; Princess Sidonia Kinsky *née* Princess Hechingen-Hohenzollern; Princess Eleonore Liechtenstein *née* Princess Öttingen-Spielberg; Princess Leopoldine Liechtenstein *née* Countess Sternberg; General Franz Lacy.

international stature from without and within. With assured access to the emperor and his closest advisors, the *Dames* were situated at the center of the political storm and enjoyed both a unique view of events and a chance to participate in public affairs—albeit informally and discreetly—as acknowledged friends of the emperor. Joseph and the women referred to their group affectionately as *la société*, *la compagnie*, or *nos Dames*. The group's composition remained fixed, and its solidarity endured, until Joseph II's tragic death in February 1790. Among the final letters composed by the zealous Habsburg reformer was a farewell to these trusted companions.

This study scrutinizes the activities of this select group of women during the "coregency" (1765–1780), when Joseph shared responsibility with his mother Maria Theresia, and during Joseph's decade as sole ruler (1780–1790) after Maria Theresia's death, years during which the women enjoyed their special position. When these women first entered adult life in the late 1740s and the 1750s, the monarchy had already faced and overcome a serious existential challenge, the War of the Austrian Succession (1740–1748). The 1750s, during which the older members of the group matured socially and secured their domestic establishments, that is, their positions as matrons in aristocratic houses, witnessed a renewal of hostilities with the Seven Years War (1756–1763), which postponed and altered Maria Theresia's incipient program of domestic reform but did not threaten the monarchy's survival. The late 1760s, 1770s, and 1780s, decades during which the women enjoyed their greatest influence and prominence, proved to be turbulent years for all social classes of the Habsburg monarchy. Controversial reforms in public affairs as well as changes in both the form and substance of court life begun under the aegis of the empress accelerated after Joseph II became her coregent in 1765. In the 1780s, after Maria Theresia's death left Joseph free to impose his own will as sole ruler, reforms became far more radical. Until the final dramatic collapse of his program, Joseph's attack on the entrenched interests of the Roman Catholic Church and on time-honored privileges of the nobility threatened to produce a "world turned upside-down," at least from the viewpoint of the monarchy's elite. These changes caused anxiety among segments of the multifarious nobility of the Habsburg monarchy but also produced an environment of creative ferment, unsettling for contemporaries and highly intriguing for subsequent historians.

During these decades prior to the advent of the French Revolution and subsequent French and Napoleonic Wars, the five *Dames* were as distinguished and eminent as it was possible to be for eighteenth-century women who conformed so unreservedly to the accepted practices of their class and station in life. Yet none of the *Dames* laid claim to intellectual prowess or to extraordinary beauty. They had entered their adult years as well-favored but conventional aristocrats and never overstepped customary boundaries of behavior that separated noteworthiness from notoriety. What, then, accounts for the formation of this rather improbable group, whose meetings were favored with the loyal presence of the sovereign and his closest male advisors? The emperor's association with the two men in the group, Field Marshal Lacy and Count Rosenberg, dated from his early adulthood. Their frequent attendance on the emperor excited little contemporary comment, although to the historian the regularity of these men's appearance at meetings of the *Dames* certainly underlines the significance of the group. An explanation for the position of the five women who were welcomed as companions by the irascible emperor on a daily basis for so many years is more difficult to come by. What manner of bond joined these five women with Joseph II? What function did the group serve for him? The women's roles as reputable matrons within ancient Bohemian families that belonged to the elite and powerful Habsburg court nobility may go far toward explaining the passionate interest with which the princesses approached the business of politics and their access to the emperor. But in what manner did these considerations inform the women's interactions with their imperial companion and their reactions to his ambitious reform program? How did they respond to important political events of the day and to the emperor's ambitious reform program? Scrutiny of the women's circumstances can serve as an intriguing case study in the activities of the Habsburg magnate class and the opportunities and constraints specific to aristocratic women. Yet external factors alone cannot account for the manner in which these women attained such favored status and, once arrived, managed to sustain their special standing within the emperor's inner social circle. How did individual temperament and personal circumstances work together to produce such a circle of associates? And how did the women themselves perceive their roles?

The five women have received no special attention from historians, except for an account of Eleonore Liechtenstein's life by the nineteenth-century historian Adam Wolf, published in 1875, which has particular value in offering excerpts (German translations of the French originals) from the correspondence of Eleonore and her sister Leopoldine Kaunitz.[1] In studies of Joseph II's life and reign one would expect to find extensive commentary on this set of friends who played such a unique role in his life. Most modern treatments do mention at least Eleonore Liechtenstein. But even descriptions of Eleonore's activities have been brief and approximate, and those concerning the group as a whole are even briefer. Such treatments have assumed that a mutual infatuation between Eleonore and the emperor was the group's sole motivator. Often they imply that Eleonore Liechtenstein and her husband Charles Liechtenstein simply made use of the emperor's favor to advance Charles's military career. Most descriptions are at best dismissive, at worst fanciful, for they have relied not on words of the women themselves but rather on a few oft-cited remarks of Maria Theresia, Joseph, and Joseph's brother Archduke Leopold (Joseph's successor as emperor) and on the historical tradition passed along from one biographer of Joseph to the next. Wolf's nineteenth-century biography, though not without error and though overly eager to disclaim on behalf of Eleonore and the other women anything more than a casual interest in political affairs, provides at least a useful corrective to these simplistic sketches; but the Wolf book appears to have been little known, or at least rarely consulted, by Joseph's earlier biographers. The latter have generally taken Joseph at his word. He claimed to pay little attention to the intellects of his women friends and repeatedly insisted that they could neither provide input nor have political influence. Thus Pavel Mitrofanov, in his classic study of Joseph II's reign, reports that in the circle of the five princesses politics was never discussed, since Joseph kept his work and his amusement completely separate from one another.[2] The biographer Fejtö too affirms that politics was strictly off limits when the emperor paid his visits to the circle of friends; "gossip and literary topics alone were tolerated within their circle, politics was banished from it." Karl Gutkas's 1989 biography, in a chapter on Joseph II's private life, offers no additional information.[3] With the work of Derek Beales in his fine biography of Joseph (volume 1 appeared in 1987 and volume 2 in 2009), Joseph's life has at last received a rigorous, painstaking reexamination.[4] Beales has sorted through the extensive, sometimes confusing documentary evidence concerning Joseph's views. The emperor's writings contain idiosyncratic admixtures of high-flown, almost manic prosody, self-righteous preaching, petty fault-finding, and earnest efforts to convey to contemporaries his own sense of urgency. They are the legacy of an individual who enjoyed impressing or startling his servitors but also took to heart his mission to carry out wholesale reform. A monumental product of careful research, Beales's biography of Joseph assesses the accuracy of descriptions of the emperor's reign that have long enjoyed currency among historians and offers corrections as needed. Among the many strengths of Beales's work is his attention to this group of women. Although the focus of the biography is the emperor himself, Beales's work draws upon a variety of primary sources, including letters of Eleonore Liechtenstein and her sister Leopoldine Kaunitz, and suggests both how important and how complex Eleonore's relationship with the emperor was.

The richest primary source for the current study is the correspondence of Eleonore Liechtenstein to and from her sister Leopoldine Kaunitz and to Eleonore's daughter Josephine Harrach. Additional correspondence of Leopoldine Kaunitz can be found in the Metternich family archive of the Státní Oblastní Archiv in Prague (Leopoldine Kaunitz's daughter was Clemens Metternich's first wife). Josepha Clary's letters to family and friends are held by the Státní Oblastní Archiv in Děčín, and these include some letters of her friends Leopoldine Liechtenstein and Sidonia Kinsky. A modest but valuable series of Leopoldine Liechtenstein's letters forms part of the Sternberg-Manderscheid collection of the archive of the Národní Muzeum in Prague. Only a few letters of Sidonia Kinsky were located for this study, and so it has been necessary to fill in the contours of her life from other sources. Fortunately the extensive Liechtenstein-Kaunitz correspondence in particular describes the activities of all five women and, perhaps even more important, reports their occasional disagreements. Apparently letters written by Joseph II to Eleonore Liechtenstein that were available in the Lobkowicz family archive when Adam Wolf composed his biography of Eleonore have been lost. But Eleonore described many of these in great detail in letters to her sister; frequently Eleonore copied into her letters Joseph's statements as direct quotes. A number of the emperor's letters to Leopoldine Kaunitz are extant, held with the Metternich family papers in the Státní Oblastní Archiv in Prague. Often Leopoldine herself then described (quite accurately) these same letters in her correspondence with her sister Eleonore. Materials relevant to the two nonimperial male members of the group—Count Moritz Lacy's *Nachlass* in the Haus-, Hof- und

Staatsarchiv in Vienna as well as Count (later Prince) Rosenberg's communications with his sovereigns in the Haus-, Hof- und Staatsarchiv and his papers in the regional archive in Klagenfurt—have been consulted as well.

Supportive primary sources include published memoirs and correspondence of contemporaries, such as Maria Theresia and her sons and daughters and the diaries of Count Karl Zinzendorf, still largely unpublished and held in the Haus-, Hof- und Staatsarchiv in Vienna.[5] Count/Prince Johann Joseph Khevenhüller-Metsch, who began a long career in high positions at court in 1742, kept diaries that are a rich source of information about court life until his death in 1776. Of Khevenhüller's compendious records, only the years 1750–1751, 1756–1757, 1760–1763, and 1768–1769 are missing, and all available years have been published. The women had far-flung family ties and acquaintances, close association with various Habsburg family members, and at least a passing acquaintance with most prominent individuals in the Vienna of their day. This being the case, resources that could provide additional detail concerning their adult lives, in the archives of Austria, the Czech Republic, and elsewhere in Europe, are virtually inexhaustible. It would be tempting and enjoyable to delve into the papers of every possible contact. Always one hopes to locate an additional collection of relevant correspondence, or just one more letter. It has been necessary to set limits for this study.

Although they are a fascinating and essential source of information that brings the historian very close to these women, the letters do have significant weaknesses as sources. Because the friends were together during many months of the year (at which time correspondence ceased), their shared environment enabled them to take much for granted in their letters, thus leaving much unstated. The dénouement of many tales is lacking. The letters describe activities and people who make an appearance and then disappear again without further mention when there is a break in correspondence. Reports concerning conversations of the group that were unmistakably and emphatically political in nature can be frustratingly vague; the women knew each other too well to bother with lengthy explanations. And while the activities of the women may be clearly described, their opinions and the grounds upon which they based their choices often have to be deduced indirectly, sometimes from recurring chance remarks. Assuredly the letters do not reveal all details concerning personal relationships. Some letters were written to be read by more than one person, and so discretion dictated a reserved tone and restricted content. In the case of these uniquely placed women, one additional reader might even be the emperor himself. Thus on 11 August 1781 Leopoldine Kaunitz wrote to Eleonore Liechtenstein, "I must not forget to warn you that while the Monarch is here, since I suspect he will be curious and since caution is always advisable, I will arrange my letters, whatever it costs me, so that he can read them. They will speak the truth in essentials, but I will not include all my thoughts, and you should not be surprised by the occasional odd turn of phrase."[6] At times one finds an additional, more confidential note accompanying the letter on a separate piece of paper, with a more frank assessment of a situation by the writer—but many such notes probably have not survived (in one case, for example, Leopoldine Kaunitz's letter to Eleonore Liechtenstein from Baden, dated 25 April 1779, begins "I must add a bit to what I wrote in my letter; since you will be showing it to my husband, I have not told you everything in it").[7] The women occasionally expressed concern that their letters might be opened and examined en route to their destination by the prying eyes of postal officials.[8] Finally, even from a distance of two hundred years the historian can detect much misinformation circulating by means of the letters, from the purported illness and death of someone who remained very much alive to false reports about the outcome of history-shaping battles (years later, for example, in August 1798, Josepha Clary reported that at the conclusion of the battle of the Nile a dying Nelson had received the sword of Napoleon, who according to news reports had been taken prisoner).[9]

In these decades prior to the French Revolution, the five women present a picture of quiet but unshakable confidence in themselves, their way of life, and their place within society. Despite serious concern about decisions taken by Joseph II and even real anguish over his religious innovations, they all played out their roles with eagerness and enthusiasm—even Eleonore Liechtenstein, who complained vociferously about the awkwardness of her relationship with the emperor. This study ends with the emperor's death in 1790, just as the French Revolution was assuming its more threatening form. Almost twenty-five years of warfare followed. Loss of life or limb among family members involved in the wars, financial exigencies on a scale previously unknown to the women, territorial and political changes that robbed many ancient families of wealth and time-honored position, the terrifying example of social revolution occurring in France—eventually the women would face all of these, as did all inhabitants of the monarchy from the most privileged to the least favored. The twilight years of the women were a period of international upheaval and domestic stagnation under the uncertain leadership of the sincere but timid Franz II (reigned 1792–1835), who acceded to the throne after the brief reign of Leopold II (reigned 1790–1792), Franz's father and the dead Emperor Joseph's brother. Only two of the *Dames* lived to see Napoleon pass the zenith of his power and one *Dame* alone was still alive when the Congress of Vienna met to make peace in 1815.

Because the focus of this study is the adult life of the princesses, all of whom married only once, they will generally be called by their married names. Their formal first names (minus the ubiquitous "Maria" or "Marie") will be used. The fact that two of the women shared the name "Leopoldine" has made it necessary to be almost pedantically exact in naming them; and when one adds the duplication and multiplication of names from older and younger generations of these families, the importance of special care and precision becomes obvious. All of the women had at least one informal moniker, a *Kosename* by which contemporaries of roughly equal social rank referred to them ("la Charles," "la Françoise," "la Clary," "la Kinsky," "la Kaunitz") but employing these repeatedly in an English text produces incongruous results. As for the women's relatives and associates, both French and German forms of names were sometimes used without system (Jean and Johann, Louis and Alois, and so forth), and selecting a single language for all would result in consistency but also awkwardness and some artificiality. In general, although not in every case, I have used the forms that appear most often in the primary sources. Thus Eleonore Liechtenstein's husband will be referred to as Charles, not Karl. Leopoldine Liechtenstein's daughter-in-law will be Caroline, although the form Charlotte appears as well. References to the group of women as a whole in the emperor's letters include a variety of cognomina, not all of them susceptible of interpretation: "the dear [*chère*] society," "our society," "the amiable fourteen," "the amiable plural," "the amiable corps of fourteen," "the five ladies," or, most often and most simply, "the society" or "our Ladies [*Dames*]."[10]

Finding English expressions for titles and ranks in the Habsburg monarchy and Holy Roman Empire can be problematic. Even more vexed is the question of geographic names for localities when over time both boundaries and official usages have changed. Although French was the language of polite discourse among the women and their friends, German or sometimes Latin place-names were generally used for territories within the monarchy (including Bohemia and Moravia) and the Holy Roman Empire. The practice here has been to use the German version as found in the primary sources, but usually with notation concerning subsequent or concurrent variant usage. Exceptions have been made when a particular form of the name has become part of standard English historical usage.

The terms "Habsburg monarchy" and "Habsburg lands" refer in this study to all territories under the direct control of the reigning Habsburg monarch, regardless of the actual form or technical legal status of the ruler vis-à-vis a given territorial entity.[11] The Holy Roman Empire will refer specifically to that juridical entity, a decentralized collection of secular rulers (princes, counts, knights), ecclesiastical dignitaries, and select towns, whose authority was limited at least in theory by their fealty to the Holy Roman Emperor himself. When contemporaries referred to "the Empire," they generally meant ethnically German lands that were part of the Holy Roman Empire but owed allegiance to the Habsburg emperor in Vienna only because he was their imperial overlord, not their direct ruler. Habsburg territory in modern Belgium is referred to interchangeably as Belgium and the Austrian or Belgian Netherlands. In keeping with much contemporary usage, and virtually all historical usage, Maria Theresia is the "empress" not because she held the office of female emperor (she did not) but because throughout most of her reign she was the wife or widow of an emperor. Joseph became emperor in his own right after his father died in 1765. In accordance with contemporary practice, historians refer to Joseph as "the emperor" beginning with his accession in 1765 even though so much of his work was done in his capacity as coruler and then sole ruler of Habsburg political entities over which he ruled directly, not merely as overlord and Holy Roman Emperor.

Notes

Translations are mine unless otherwise indicated. Punctuation is inconsistent in the original sources and has been amended in some cases to facilitate reading.

1   Adam Wolf, *Fürstin Eleonore Liechtenstein, 1745-1812: nach Briefen und Memoiren ihrer Zeit* (Vienna: Carl Gerold's Sohn, 1875). Wolf also produced a biography of the Habsburg archduchess Marie Christine.
2   Pavel Mitrofanov, *Josef II. Seine politische und kulturelle Tätigkeit,* vol. 1 (Vienna: C. W. Stern, 1910), 102-03.
3   François Fejtö, *Joseph II: un Habsbourg révolutionnaire,* new ed. (Paris: Quai Voltaire, 1994), 115-22, 219, 244. Fejtö, with admirable honesty, admits to some perplexity about Joseph's unusual social life in his chapter on Eleonore Liechtenstein, while affirming the importance of the emperor's choices; a Habsburg emperor, after all, could surely have formed relationships that would have proven gratifying in more conventional ways, and thus he could have avoided the emotional deprivation he most likely suffered in such a peculiar relationship. Paul Bernard, in *Joseph II* (New York: Twayne, 1968), 69-70, does not take into account the ongoing development of the group. Jean Bérenger, in *Joseph II: serviteur de l'état* (Paris: Fayard, 2007), 126, and Karl Gutkas, in *Kaiser Joseph II.: eine Biographie* (Vienna: Paul Zsolnay Verlag, 1989), 255, both characterize Eleonore Liechtenstein's relationship with the emperor as a means of advancing husband Charles's military career. These interpretations are standard statements in Josephine historiography but become suspect at once when the women's own words are examined.
4   Derek Beales, *Joseph II.* 2 vols. (Cambridge: Cambridge University Press, 1987-2009).
5   The Böhlau Verlag is publishing extensive portions of the diaries in Zinzendorf's original French, in the series Veröffentlichungen der Kommission für Neuere Geschichte Österreichs. The publications include valuable data concerning the political, social, and cultural circumstances in the lives of Zinzendorf and his contemporaries.
6   Lobkovicové Roudnickí Rodinný Archiv (LRRA), P 17/27, Leopoldine Kaunitz (LK) to Eleonore Liechtenstein (EL), Vienna, 11 August 1781.
7   LRRA, P 17/25, LK to EL, Baden, 25 April 1779.
8   In August 1778 Eleonore Liechtenstein was reluctant to record in her letter just what her opinions were concerning the peace negotiations then under way with Prussia to end the Bavarian war: "I dare not tell you what I think," she wrote to her sister Leopoldine Kaunitz, "for fear that my letters could be opened." In September 1778 Leopoldine Kaunitz informed her sister Eleonore that in a previous letter she had been obliged to omit much of what she had wanted to say since the letter would be sent by post rather than by a traveling acquaintance, "being afraid of the Empress's curiosity." LRRA, P 17/24, EL to LK, Eisgrub, 18 August 1778; P 17/24, LK to EL, 29 September 1778; P

17/28, EL to LK, [Mährisch] Kromau, 28 August 1782; P 17/28, EL to LK, [Mährisch] Kromau, 2 September 1782.
9 Rodinný Archiv Clary-Aldringenů (Teplice), Státní Oblastní Archiv v Litoměřicích, Pobočka Děčín [SOAL-D, RACA], carton 66, Josepha Clary (JC) to her son, 15 August 1798.
10 Literally, "la chere société," "notre société," "aimables quatorze," "l'aimable plurielle," "le corps aimable des quatorze," "des cinques Dames," "la société," "nos Dames."
11 Grete Klingenstein has aptly spoken of "the multinational, multiconfessional, multicultural, and multiconstitutional nature of the Habsburg monarchy." Grete Klingenstein, "Modes of Religious Tolerance and Intolerance in Eighteenth-Century Habsburg Politics," *Austrian History Yearbook* 24 (1993): 2. Useful discussion of terminology can be found also in the unpublished dissertation of Laura Lynne Kinsey, "The Habsburgs at Mariazell: Piety, Patronage, and Statecraft, 1620-1770" (Diss., University of California, Los Angeles, 2000), 26.

Chapter 1

Aristocrats: Ancestry and Posterity

The unique coterie to which the *Dames* belonged during their adult lives was made possible first and foremost by the distinguished heritage and elite status of the families with which each woman was associated. An aristocratic woman with the best chance for a prosperous, effective life was one whose house of origin was a successful collective entity and who married into an equally functional family, both houses being endowed with a strong will to survive and adapt to changing conditions. All five women enjoyed this advantage. Along with such a favorable position came the implicit but imperative obligation to safeguard and promote the long-term well-being of these families as well as to provide offspring for the next generation of each house. It has even been suggested that elite aristocratic women were in fact "career women," their profession being "dynasticism."[1]

    An aristocratic family was assumed to have traits that were transmitted from one generation to the next, both as physical characteristics and as aptitudes and attitudes. The Habsburgs themselves, most illustrious of aristocratic families, considered their family to possess certain unchanging, admirable qualities. In a letter to her son Archduke Ferdinand, rejoicing in the birth of his brother Grand Duke Leopold's fourth son in Tuscany in 1772, Maria Theresia expressed her hope that future Habsburgs would continue to serve their peoples as had their forebears, "all of them good, kindly princes, good Christians, good husbands, good fathers, loyal to their friends."[2] Referring to the Habsburgs' faithfulness to the Catholic Church, Maria Theresia reminded her daughter Maria Carolina, queen in Naples, to perform with exactitude her spiritual exercises during Lent, to lead her people in proper religious observance and "so as not to contravene the example of piety and faith that our house and that of Lorraine have always set," thereby earning divine approval and blessing.[3] The Öttingen-Spielberg family into which Leopoldine Kaunitz and Eleonore Liechtenstein were born had a strong Catholic tradition like the Habsburg sovereigns, and throughout their lives the two sisters viewed themselves as particularly called to defend the good cause of orthodoxy, which they supported, in Eleonore's words, "with the strength and spirit that is in our very blood."[4] The two Öttingen-Spielberg sisters also retained strong feelings about their family's association with southwestern Germany or "Swabia," even after years of residence in Vienna. Eleonore Liechtenstein frequently referred to her inborn Swabian nature, by which she meant a certain feisty obstinacy and down-to-earth hard-headedness. For their part, the Liechtensteins and Kinskys were known to have hot military blood. As an elderly woman, when Eleonore Liechtenstein observed her grandson Charles's youthful fascination with all things military, she concluded that his interest was hereditary, "a passion bred in the bone of the Liechtensteins."[5] Only a month later she noted his growing interest in horses and hunting and proclaimed, "it has to be conceded that this child is legitimate."[6]

The dual allegiance of women, to their birth families and to the families they joined by marriage, was not an exclusively female concern, since aristocratic men as well found it advantageous to foster strong ties with in-laws and collateral families. The welfare of families and of individuals required cultivation of a broad, dispersed nexus of supportive relationships. As a bride, each of the *Dames* had transferred much of her allegiance to her new family, to which her eventual offspring would belong. But she retained strong ties of interest, and in most cases affection, to her parents, to her siblings, and to her extended birth family. These preoccupations affected the responses of the princesses to political events and to the opportunities for action they encountered as individuals. Birth families (which will be considered first here) and husbands' families alike shaped the women's environment, their socioeconomic standing, and their sense of identity. As a corporate entity, the house both limited and empowered its members and adherents. In times of political vicissitude like the late eighteenth and early nineteenth centuries, family members were obligated to bestir themselves, to cobble together strategies for survival under fluctuating political, social, economic, and even juridical conditions; but the house's continued existence and the community of interests of its members also served as an intergenerational stabilizing force and a practical resource for individual aristocrats struggling to preserve their claims to social preeminence and exclusivity.[7] What was most important was the honor of the family—public comportment that upheld the family's reputation, that avoided behaviors deemed shameful and déclassé, that demonstrated a fine sensitivity to affronts to the dignity of both the family and its individual members, and that enhanced or at least preserved from diminution the family's rank and precedence within society, always by appropriately noble rather than ignoble means.[8]

Hohenzollern-Hechingen

Josepha Clary and Sidonia Kinsky were born into the Swabian Hohenzollern-Hechingen family in 1728 and 1729, respectively. All branches of the Hohenzollern family in existence in the eighteenth century traced their origins back to a single source, namely, the counts of Zollern, who built a fortress in the eleventh century on the Zollern mountain in the Swabian Alps.[9] During the thirteenth century a branch of the family established itself in Franconia, and thus originated those famous Hohenzollerns who later became electors of Brandenburg and produced Prussian kings and German emperors. The northern or Brandenburg Hohenzollerns chose Protestantism during the Reformation, while their Swabian kin, the ancestors of Josepha and Sidonia, remained Catholic. Because of a testamentary disposition from the fourteenth century, the nineteenth-century north German Hohenzollerns, by then eminently successful both politically and economically as kings of Prussia, were able to claim an ancient, residual right of succession to the lands of the Swabian Hohenzollerns.[10]

Under family head Karl (1558–1576), godchild of the Habsburg emperor Charles V and lord of the estates Haigerloch, Hechingen, and Sigmaringen, a true renaissance court flourished in Sigmaringen, which Karl's successors then tried unsuccessfully to maintain or even expand.[11] Upon Karl's death the three estates were distributed among his heirs. The Haigerloch line died out as early as 1634, but the Hechingen and Sigmaringen lines flourished, at least numerically, throughout the eighteenth century. The heads of both lines were elevated to the rank of imperial princes in 1623, as recognition for their support of the Catholic Habsburg cause in the confessional wars of the period. Technically these were sovereign rulers, recognizing no overlord other than the Holy Roman Emperor (thus *reichsunmittelbar*). Hohenzollern-Hechingen princes maintained Catholic orthodoxy on their lands and permitted no Lutheran congregations to form. Lands of the Swabian princes suffered from serious damage and bouts of the plague during the Thirty Years War. The princes found it increasingly difficult to claim effective political parity with neighboring rulers. It was the financial assistance of the northern branch of Hohenzollerns, led by the "Great Elector" of Brandenburg, that staved off bankruptcy in the Hohenzollern-Hechingen family during the seventeenth century. Financial arrangements made then and in subsequent years further validated these Brandenburg Hohenzollerns' claim to paramountcy within the entire Hohenzollern clan.[12]

Hermann Friedrich (1665–1733), father of Sidonia and Josepha, never became head of the Hohenzollern-Hechingen line, a position occupied by his older brother, Friedrich Wilhelm (1663–1735). Hermann Friedrich had at first entered the church but left with papal dispensation to found a family. After his first wife died leaving only a daughter, in 1714 he married Countess Josepha

Öttingen-Spielberg, with whom he had eleven children before his death, including Sidonia and Josepha.[13] Sidonia and Josepha were born in Freiburg im Breisgau (under Habsburg rule from 1368 to 1805, with several French interludes), where Hermann Friedrich, who was by then a general in the Habsburg army, served as military governor. The sisters and their other siblings were first cousins of Leopoldine Kaunitz and Eleonore Liechtenstein, both born Öttingen-Spielberg; the father of Leopoldine and Eleonore and the mother of Josepha and Sidonia were siblings.

When Friedrich Wilhelm's only son died without an heir in 1750, the family headship and property fell to the oldest brother of Sidonia and Josepha, Joseph Wilhelm (1717–1798). Joseph Wilhelm was careless with his money and loved a splendid court life, gambling, expensive travel, and hunting. His name is occasionally remembered because of his twelve-year association with Friedrich Wilhelm von Steuben (1730–1794), of American Revolutionary fame, who served as Joseph Wilhelm's *Hofmarschall* or chamberlain.[14] Although in his later years Joseph Wilhelm became attracted to many tenets of the French Enlightenment, including religious tolerance (to encompass the Jewish inhabitants of his lands as well as Protestants) and universal education, he was an unpopular landlord because his chronic financial neediness soured relations with his tenants. In the Hohenzollern-Hechingen family of the eighteenth century, careers in the church were especially attractive for younger brothers. Of six brothers of Josepha and Sidonia, three found places in the church, as canons at Cologne, Augsburg, and Elwangen and, in the case of the youngest brother Johann Karl (1732–1803), as a bishop. Two sisters were canonesses, at Hall and Buchau. Late eighteenth-century males of the Hohenzollern-Hechingen line also continued to serve as officers in the Habsburg imperial military. Despite this Swabian proclivity to support the Habsburg emperor, during the eighteenth century the Brandenburg Hohenzollerns assisted their less successful southern relations. Johann Karl, as prince abbot of Oliva, bishop of Kulm, and prince bishop of Ermland, advanced his career not through the assistance of the Habsburg emperors but through the patronage of the freshly minted kings of Prussia, his northern Hohenzollern relations. Since the Hohenzollern-Hechingen family head was proud but largely insolvent, the many siblings of Josepha Clary and Sidonia Kinsky were not loath to dun their well-placed married sisters for loans and preferment over the years.

Sternberg

In Leopoldine Liechtenstein's birth family, the Sternbergs, legend identified the Sternberg progenitor as Caspar, one of the "Three Kings" who visited Bethlehem after the birth of Jesus Christ. The star found on the Sternberg coat-of-arms was said to represent the famous star of Bethlehem.[15] There is some documentary evidence that the family was present in Bohemia by the mid-thirteenth century. Branches of the family could also be found in Moravia and Silesia. The Sternbergs boasted a clear line of descent from the late fourteenth century and were esteemed as one of the old Bohemian noble families that had achieved preeminence well before the confessional and political turmoil of the seventeenth century and had managed to hold its position thereafter. During earlier periods individual Sternbergs had been sympathetic to the Protestant cause in Bohemia. After the Protestants were defeated, a hallmark of the family was its generally tolerant Catholicism and its relative moderation. Though loyal to the Habsburgs, Sternbergs were not among the leaders in the Catholic retribution that swept over the land after the Protestants' defeat, and no Sternbergs were active in promoting confiscation of Protestant property or banishment. The family acquired the rank of imperial counts in 1661. By the mid-eighteenth century only the so-called Sternberg-Konopiště line of the family still existed.

The core of the Sternberg properties was Častolovice in East Bohemia and Zásmuk in Central Bohemia, the family's preferred country residence during Leopoldine's childhood.[16] The family head during the late seventeenth century, Leopoldine's great grandfather Adolph Wratislaw (died 1703), was a trusted friend of the Habsburg Emperor Leopold I. Adolph Wratislaw's elder son Franz Damian (1676–1723), Leopoldine Sternberg's grandfather and founder of the Damian branch of the Sternberg-Konopiště line, held various court positions but was plagued by a weak financial position and overwhelming debts. This being the situation, the achievements of his son Franz Philip (1708–1786), Leopoldine's own father, were all the more noteworthy. Franz Philip was an accomplished diplomat and courtier. He served from 1745 to 1748 as envoy representing the Bohemian electorate (held by the Habsburgs) in the imperial diet in Regensburg and from 1748 to 1764 as Habsburg ambassador to the Polish-Saxon court in Warsaw and Dresden, a period of service that encompassed important diplomatic activities incident to the Seven Years' War. Both Franz Philip and his wife Leopoldine, sister of the influential diplomat Prince Georg Starhemberg (1724–1807) who served as Habsburg ambassador to Portugal, Spain, and France and for several years as minister in Brussels, enjoyed the special regard and trust of Maria Theresia. Franz Philip ended his career as *Obersthofmeister* under emperors Joseph II, Leopold II, and Franz II. He was a polished, discreet individual, but his wife may have been the moving force behind the family's success; according to Baron Carl Joseph von Fürst, Prussian envoy to Vienna from 1752 to 1755, Franz Philip's intellectual gifts were less striking than those of his wife, who was equally involved in political affairs. Countess Sternberg was said to have taken part in the council meetings of the Saxon minister Brühl and to have had extraordinary influence at the court in Dresden.[17] The English minister in Vienna Lord Stormont (1727–1796) reported that she had intrigued on behalf of her brother Count Starhemberg when Maria Theresia was considering him as possible successor to

Chancellor Kaunitz in 1767. An alert, vigorous woman, she lived to the age of 87, and after returning to Vienna was active in many of the same social networks as her daughter Leopoldine Liechtenstein.[18] By the time daughter Leopoldine reached adulthood, her family had been accustomed for several generations to move comfortably in court circles in Vienna, familiar with the forms of public life, politically savvy, an influential but discreet presence in society.

With the assistance of his enterprising wife, Franz Philip placed his children in highly advantageous marriages. Leopoldine Liechtenstein's older brother, Christian Sternberg, effectively supported by his maternal uncle Prince Starhemberg, made a brilliant match in 1762, marrying Augusta, heiress to the Manderscheid-Blankenheim fortune and to "immediate" properties in the Eifel region (territory split today between Germany and Belgium), subject only to the Holy Roman Emperor, like property of the Hohenzollern-Hechingen and Hohenzollern-Sigmaringen families. The Manderscheid-Blanckenheim family, an ancient clan of the Holy Roman Empire, was facing extinction when Leopoldine's brother Christian Sternberg married his bride.[19] Intermarriage with exclusive old imperial families of the German lands by members of the Austrian or Bohemian nobility was an unmistakable sign of social advancement for the latter, helping to establish eligibility for exclusive *Stifte* (quasi-religious foundations of canons or canonesses attached to an abbey or cathedral) that required impressive pedigrees for admission. The final disposition of the Manderscheid property was not certain until many years after the marriage, in 1780, when Augusta's uncle died and she inherited the property.[20] Because of the lopsided nature of the marriage, with the Manderscheids in possession of great wealth and generally higher status, as part of the marriage negotiations Christian Sternberg and his parents agreed to add the bride's surname to their own, the family name becoming Sternberg-Manderscheid.[21] The Sternbergs had finalized the union of their older son with the Manderscheid heiress soon after daughter Leopoldine married the heir to the Liechtenstein family, likewise considered to be an excellent match since it was apparent as early as 1748 that Prince Franz Joseph I (1726–1781) would one day become head of the Liechtenstein family.[22] Leopoldine's three sisters also married into prominent families, Fürstenberg, Waldstein, and Lutzow. Her younger brother Gundaker (1737–1802) served in court positions and undertook several short-term diplomatic missions under Maria Theresia, Joseph II, Leopold II, and Franz II but did not marry.[23]

Öttingen-Spielberg

Leopoldine Kaunitz and Eleonore Liechtenstein hailed from the ancient Swabian family of Öttingen-Spielberg. They were daughters of Prince Johann Alois I von Öttingen-Spielberg (1707–1780).[24] As in the case of the Hohenzollern-

Hechingens, Prince Öttingen-Spielberg was a sovereign ruler within the Holy Roman Empire, recognizing no legal superior other than the Holy Roman Emperor. The girls' mother had died in 1745 shortly after the birth of Eleonore, the younger sister. Heads of the family during the two women's lifetimes were, successively, their father Johann Alois I, cousin Johann Alois II (1758–1797), and his son Johann Alois III (1788–1855). Leopoldine and Eleonore as well as their first cousins Josepha Clary and Sidonia Kinsky were distantly related to Maria Theresia, for the empress' grandmother, Duchess Christine Luise von Braunschweig-Wolfenbüttel, had been born an Öttingen princess.[25] The Öttingen-Spielberg sisters were also related to the Liechtenstein family, Eleonore's future in-laws, since their maternal grandmother had been a daughter of Prince Hans Adam von Liechtenstein.[26]

The early home of Leopoldine Kaunitz and Eleonore Liechtenstein was the town of Öttingen, today lying in the Donau-Ries district of Bavaria but in the eighteenth century part of an independent *Grafschaft* or county in the Swabian district (*Kreis* or "circle") of the Holy Roman Empire. Although family tradition extended the Öttingen line back to the tenth century and suggested a genealogical link to the imperial Hohenstaufen dynasty, firm documentary evidence of the Öttingen succession began in the early thirteenth century. The family's sixteenth-century head, Ludwig XV (1486–1557), converted to Lutheranism. For a time, his property was confiscated by Emperor Charles V, but the loss was not permanent. Ludwig's elder son remained Lutheran but the younger son returned to Catholicism. Each founded a line of the Öttingen family. The two lines split between them the town of Öttingen as well as the *Grafschaft* and governed the two portions separately. The senior Protestant line (called Öttingen-Öttingen) died out in 1731. The Catholic line formed three Catholic branches of the Öttingen family, Öttingen-Spielberg (the family of Leopoldine Kaunitz and Eleonore Liechtenstein), Öttingen-Wallerstein, and Öttingen-Baldern. They devised formulae for sharing the family resources. The Öttingen-Spielberg family head was elevated to imperial princely rank in 1734.[27] No branch of the larger Öttingen family was sufficiently powerful to play a major role in imperial politics during the eighteenth century. During the late eighteenth century the three Catholic branches lived amicably on a personal level, but they carried on expensive long-term lawsuits to finalize property distributions among them. The Öttingen-Baldern branch became extinct in 1798.

The mid eighteenth-century family head Johann Alois I, father of Leopoldine and Eleonore, was technically a wealthy man. His principal properties were Öttingen and Spielberg and the estates of Aufkirchen, Dürrwang, Mönchsroth, and Schwendi with inhabitants totaling 16,000 to 17,000. But Prince Öttingen-Spielberg's financial affairs were hopelessly encumbered by his ambitious land purchases and by the long-standing lawsuits that he pursued through the

Reichskammergericht (imperial court of justice) in Wetzlar, a notoriously slow-moving judicial organ of the Holy Roman Empire.[28] Management of the prince's finances was placed in the hands of a commission, under imperial oversight, in an attempt to safeguard the standing of the family as a whole. Long after Prince Johann Alois I died and the property had passed to the family of his brother, the Öttingen-Spielberg property remained burdened with debt and the family's financial situation was precarious. Despite straitened circumstances, the Öttingen-Spielberg family maintained its claim to the regard of peers and to access to positions commensurate with its high status.

Through marriage all five *Dames* joined families whose activities centered around the Habsburg court and who drew their wealth predominantly from the Habsburg crownlands of Bohemia and Moravia (alone among the five women Leopoldine Liechtenstein was born into one Bohemian magnate family and married into another). The status and interests of this powerful magnate class loomed large in the women's lives.

The seventeenth-century rebellion of largely Protestant Bohemia against the Habsburgs, which ended in defeat at the Battle of White Mountain in 1620, brought retribution in its wake with the forced re-Catholicization of Bohemia, Moravia, and Silesia, massive land confiscations, and emigration of many noble families. Generations of historians have focused their attention on these very real losses suffered by Bohemia. They have looked for evidence of the inexorable growth of Habsburg monarchical absolutism in the teeth of the Bohemian nobility's sullen resistance. More recent work, notably the pioneering study of R. J. W. Evans in 1979, has painted a more complex picture of the post-White Mountain Bohemian crownlands.[29] Careful study has demonstrated that even as the Bohemian and Moravian lands were drawn after their defeat into greater subordination and closer association with Vienna as a result of constitutional changes such as the *Verneuerte Landesordnung* (renewed land ordinance) of 1627 and other settlements, the Habsburg government found it expedient and even necessary to win the cooperation of Bohemia's great nobility in administering these territories. Increasingly as years passed the magnates of the crownlands dominated local and regional affairs and were even disproportionately represented in positions of importance in Vienna itself. Wealthy, ambitious, or merely fortunate families such as those joined by the five women became increasingly prosperous and influential, in contrast to most of Bohemia's lesser nobility. Through a variety of means, including timely reconversion to Catholicism, military service, skilled political services to the monarch, strategic amassing of confiscated lands, or simple dogged determination, great landowning families of Bohemia and Moravia, whether indigenous or transplanted, emerged and prospered during the century and a half that followed White Mountain.[30]

As Evans noted, this outcome was the result of a compromise, not a stable solution to Bohemia's problems. The sovereigns worked with and through regional and local administrative structures, ceding administrative powers to the nobility where doing so forwarded the goals of the central government in Vienna.[31] But the Habsburg government continued its drive to assert greater authority and draw increased income from the Bohemian crownlands, pushing forward measures that in the long term would strengthen central authority and the resurgent Catholic Church and would weaken entrenched regional and local interests and the dominance of the nobility and its representative bodies. More than a century after White Mountain, in 1741, as Maria Theresia's inheritance was contested by Prussia and its allies, many Bohemian aristocratic families again proved to be inconstant—behavior in striking contrast to the demonstrative loyalty of the Hungarian aristocrats to their Habsburg sovereign. Its cause defeated once again, Bohemia was subsequently integrated yet more fully into the monarchy as a Habsburg possession and was stripped of much of its fiscal autonomy. Its bureaucracy was reformed to better suit Habsburg goals and the power of its representatives (the estates) was further circumscribed. Yet once again, with remarkable speed most aristocratic families of the crownlands adjusted to changed conditions. Again *Kaisertreu,* in a matter of decades members of the Bohemian elite could be found in great numbers filling the offices of Habsburg administration in Vienna as before, not to mention regional positions of authority. The Bohemian magnate class had been integrated rather than alienated. Most individuals who had sided with the Bavarian Wittelsbach Emperor Charles VII, whose ineffective, war-filled reign lasted only until his death in 1745 and was followed by the election of Maria Theresia's husband Franz Stephan, were eventually amnestied by Maria Theresia. When the future *Dames* joined their new families as brides, Bohemian magnates and crown had already made their peace.[32]

Clary

The Clary family, more accurately Clary und Aldringen, which Josepha Hechingen-Hohenzollern joined by marriage in 1747, had acquired substantial property as a reward for military service to the Habsburgs in the seventeenth century and put down roots in Bohemia only since the Thirty Years War.[33] The family had come to Bohemia from the Trentino. Clary males had been stout warriors. The estate Teplitz (Teplice) in northwestern Bohemia was acquired by the family through a marriage alliance with the Aldringen family, recently arrived from Lorraine. Several years earlier Teplitz had been confiscated from the Kinsky family after the murder of its owner Wilhelm Kinsky (an associate of the famous and infamous commander Albrecht Wallenstein/Waldstein, as will be noted below) in 1634. The Clary family received imperial permission to add the name and arms of the Aldringen family to its own and thus became the Clary-Aldringen family. Josepha Clary's husband Franz Wenzel Clary inherited Teplitz in 1751 and was the first member of the Clary clan to reach the rank of prince, in 1767. A separate line of Clary counts also flourished during the eighteenth century.[34]

Although in earlier centuries Clary family members had distinguished themselves as soldiers, by the eighteenth century male family members of the princely Clary family were more likely to be civil servants or diplomats. The family's property at Teplitz, with its hot springs that were held to provide relief from rheumatism, gout, and sciatica as well as the pain of soldiers' gunshot wounds, attracted visitors from all over Europe. With time Teplitz became a social and cultural magnet, a circumstance that affected the character of the family, which assumed a somewhat cosmopolitan outlook.[35] Teplitz remained the property of the Clary family for centuries, until the end of World War II.[36]

Kinsky

In 1749 Sidonia Hohenzollern-Hechingen married into the Kinsky family (Kinský or Kinští in Czech), an old family indigenous to Bohemia and deeply attached to the land and its traditions.[37] Evidence of the family's residence in Bohemia extended back many centuries, before the formal conferral of diplomas of nobility and arms was established practice in Bohemia.[38] The name "Kinsky" was a modern rendering of the name and was not historically accurate, but by the eighteenth century it had been sanctioned by common usage. The original name Vchynice or Chynice referred to an ancient family fortress in the region of Litoměřice, owned until 1540 by the principal line of the Kinsky family. The family appended to its name also the designation Tetour z Tetova (Tettau), which was the surname of an eminent noble family of Bohemia with which the Kinsky family claimed kinship.[39]

Many Kinsky ancestors had been Utraquists during the Hussite wars. In the late sixteenth and early seventeenth century, they sided with the Protestant Bohemians in their struggle against the Habsburgs. Individual members of the family were known for their irascibility and hardihood, suited to the tempestuous times in which they lived. One Kinsky male had been a participant in the 1618 defenestration of Prague. Another fought on the Protestant side in the battle of White Mountain and fled before Karl Liechtenstein's harsh tribunal (described below) could execute him, ending his days as a scholar of sorts in Holland. Yet another was a compatriot of Wallenstein (Wilhelm Kinsky, mentioned previously). The heir to the family's estates and great grandfather of Sidonia's husband Wenzel Kinsky, who was himself Catholic, made overtures to both Catholic and Protestant sides during the Bohemian rebellion in 1618 and was saved from destruction at the hands of angry Bohemian Protestants only by the victory of the Habsburg cause in 1620. A man of intense temper, he was feared and disliked by many of his contemporaries when he died in 1626, but because of his services he and his successors enjoyed the gratitude and esteem of the Habsburg rulers. Most family lands that had been confiscated during the Bohemian uprising were returned to Kinsky ownership, with accruals from possessions of defeated Protestant noblemen.

Sidonia Kinsky's father-in-law Philip was a vehement, hot-tempered, yet talented individual. In the face of daunting odds, serving as Bohemian *Oberstkanzler*, he remained obstinately loyal to Maria Theresia's cause as she faced the contested succession to the crownlands of Bohemia, Moravia, and Silesia in 1740, and she grew to trust him. He was among the few advisors who enthusiastically supported her defiance of Frederick II. This was the individual to whom Maria Theresia addressed the oft-cited reproach in 1741, in the midst of the monarchy's crisis: "What crotchety behavior! And why all those grimaces, pray? Why do you discourage the poor queen, instead of offering advice and help?"[40] Maria Theresia indulged Philip Kinsky's moodiness and, according to report, even overlooked his tendency to spatter snuff on documents she passed to him for consideration, merely requesting that he not allow them to be "tabackig" when they were forwarded to the *Hofkanzler*. For all his loyalty to the throne, Philip himself represented a traditional, provincial Bohemian outlook, seeking to safeguard the interests of the Bohemian lands and giving secondary consideration to the Habsburg lands as a totality.[41] During the War of the Austrian Succession, he tried to minimize the war's cost to the Bohemian lands, supporting measures that would keep taxes moderate, limit military billeting, and protect Bohemia from actual hostilities as much as possible. After the war, Philip came to oppose the merging of Bohemia's administration with the Austrian, an early reform goal of Maria Theresia.[42] When his wishes were overruled, true to his irascible nature the indignant Kinsky retired from public life.

A family that occasionally produced bluff, even violent individuals, the Kinskys were considered to be courageous but not particularly sensitive or artistic. When a later Kinsky, Sidonia Kinsky's grandson Ferdinand, who became known to history as a patron of Beethoven, died in 1812, Eleonore Liechtenstein's daughter Josephine Harrach remarked in a letter to her mother that everyone had liked the young man, who had been thoughtful and generous; and she added rather unkindly that these winning traits in young Kinsky were difficult to explain unless he had inherited them through his Öttingen ancestors, that is, his grandmother Sidonia Kinsky, *née* Hohenzollern-Hechingen, whose own mother had been an Öttingen-Spielberg, "for this generosity comes only from his ancestors, not from his father or mother, nor from the Kinsky family, but solely from the kind old princess, and thus solely from the Öttingens."[43]

Liechtenstein

The Liechtenstein family, which Leopoldine Sternberg and Eleonore Öttingen-Spielberg joined through their marriages, was one of the Habsburg monarchy's wealthiest. Many theories and genealogical fantasies surrounded the origins and earliest activities of this powerful family.[44] One legend related that a sturdy Moravian villager plowing his field had found a solid nugget of silver (thus the name Liechtenstein, or light stone), which he, the founder of the family, employed to amass the first sizeable Liechtenstein fortune.[45] Enthusiastic genealogists claimed to trace the family to Roman times. Colorful stories and the enthusiasm of early generations of historians notwithstanding, the first credibly identifiable progenitor of the family was Hugo von Liechtenstein, a nobleman who owned property in Lower Austria in the twelfth century. Possibly the family's name derived from Hugo's acquisition, either through purchase or construction, of a fortress built on light, chalky rock (*lichter Stein*) near Maria Enzersdorf in Lower Austria. The Liechtensteins accumulated properties in Upper Austria, Styria, and the Tirol as well as Moravia and Lower Austria.[46]

Some Liechtenstein family members converted to Lutheranism, especially in the family's Feldsberg line, to which belonged the direct ancestors of the husbands of Leopoldine Sternberg and Eleonore Öttingen-Spielberg, with properties in Moravia near the border between southern Moravia and Lower Austria. Despite their disquieting and sometimes revolutionary social tenets, even the Anabaptists who settled on or near Liechtenstein properties were tolerated and protected by members of the Liechtenstein family, as were the Moravian Brethren, esteemed as industrious inhabitants.[47] The family head who led the Liechtensteins' return to Catholicism was Karl I (1569–1627), one of the most remarkable individuals ever produced by the family. Karl had been raised as a Protestant, but his dramatic conversion to Catholicism in 1599, followed several years later by the conversions of his two younger brothers Maximilian (1578–1643) and Gundaker I (1580–1658), put an end to the Liechtensteins' Protestant phase and returned both the family and the inhabitants of Liechtenstein lands to strict Catholic orthodoxy. Karl became a zealous and even ruthless protagonist of the imperial Catholic cause in predominantly Protestant Bohemia. He was elevated in rank from count to imperial prince in 1608, again followed by his two brothers in 1623. When the Catholic side emerged victorious in Bohemia after the battle of White Mountain, it was Karl I who presided over the harsh legal proceedings of 21 June 1621 in Prague, when 27 leaders of the Protestant cause were executed in the space of four hours.[48] Karl profited from advantageous acquisitions of confiscated Protestant properties, a circumstance that did not endear his family to the freshly defeated Protestants inhabitants of the Bohemian crownlands.[49] Acquisitive and not overly scrupulous, he was nevertheless a man of courage and of broad interests, initiating on a modest scale the art collecting pursued with great energy and dedication by later generations of Liechtensteins. In 1699 and 1712 the Liechtensteins purchased the estate Schellenberg and the *Grafschaft* Vaduz. In 1719 the family was able to convert these two purchases into the imperial principality of Liechtenstein.[50]

The most eminent eighteenth-century Liechtenstein, Joseph Wenzel, inherited enough wealth to support a lifestyle rivaling that of the Habsburgs and unimpeachable rank as prince of the Holy Roman Empire through his ownership of Liechtenstein. Josef Wenzel, who was head of the family when the two future *Dames* joined it by marriage, shaped the destinies of the Liechtenstein clan for several decades. Usually referred to simply as Wenzel, he embarked early on a military career in the Habsburg army, supported in his efforts to advance by none other than Prince Eugene of Savoy. His particular contribution was his work to reform the artillery in the Austrian army.[51] Wenzel's only son died in 1723 and, perhaps as a result, throughout his adult life Wenzel gave his attention to the interests of the larger Liechtenstein family. During the War of the Austrian Succession the Liechtensteins declined to recognize the Bavarian elector Charles Albert's claim to the Bohemian throne, even though the greater part of the Liechtenstein lands lay in occupied territory. Maria Theresia, who admired and respected Wenzel Liechtenstein, asked him to instruct young Archduke Joseph in military science and entrusted him with the honor of bringing from Parma to Vienna Joseph's new bride, the Bourbon Princess Isabella, in 1760. In this latter capacity, Wenzel Liechtenstein spared no expense, projecting a splendid public image as Joseph II's representative for the marriage by procuration in Parma. The husband of Leopoldine Sternberg and the future husband of Eleonore Öttingen-Spielberg, Wenzel's nephews Franz Joseph and Charles Borromaeus respectively, accompanied their uncle on this mission, during which the famous "golden carriage" of the Liechtensteins, originally constructed for the prince's ceremonial entry into Paris as Austrian ambassador, was much in evidence.[52] Wenzel Liechtenstein's ability to "represent," to use his wealth to create a spectacularly rich yet dignified public image, won the admiration of his contemporaries.[53]

After the death of Franz Wenzel in 1772 his nephew, Leopoldine's husband Franz Joseph, became the new Liechtenstein *Majoratsherr*. The *Majoratsherr*, with control of the splendid palaces and grounds of Feldsberg and Eisgrub, was a powerful economic and social force in the monarchy. Lesser members of the family (such as Eleonore's husband Charles Borromaeus) lived less liberally than the *Majoratsherr*, although their economic status remained extremely favorable.

Kaunitz

It was a thoroughly political family that Leopoldine Öttingen-Spielberg joined in 1761 when she married Ernst Kaunitz, eldest son of Chancellor Wenzel

Anton Kaunitz.[54] During the late sixteenth and early seventeenth centuries, Kaunitz ancestors had accumulated substantial properties in Moravia. The family as a whole had been drawn to Protestantism, especially to the Moravian Brethren. Family members participated in the anti-Habsburg rebellion of the early seventeenth century and consequently suffered the loss of much property. But Chancellor Kaunitz's great grandfather, Leo Wilhelm Kaunitz, orphaned offspring of the Protestant Kaunitz family, was very young when the events occurred and was raised as a Catholic. Thereafter the family distinguished itself by loyalty to Habsburg and Catholic causes.[55]

In the course of a few generations, the family moved from purely local recognition to international prominence. Wenzel Anton Kaunitz's grandfather Dominik Andreas (1654–1705) was a successful diplomat in the service of the Habsburgs. He arranged for the marriage of his youngest son Maximilian Ulrich to Maria Ernestine von Rietberg, heiress of the "free county" of Rietberg in Westphalia and several properties in Ostfriesland. To acknowledge the prestige and wealth of the Rietbergs, the Kaunitz family added the Rietberg name to its own, styling itself Kaunitz-Rietberg and combining the two coats of arms.[56] But Dominik Andreas's diplomatic career and many projects were expensive, and he left the family finances greatly weakened when he died in 1704. Thus it was left for Wenzel Anton's father, Maximilian Ulrich Kaunitz (1679–1746), to stabilize and promote the family's fortunes both through restraint in his own career goals (he served as governor of Moravia and undertook a few minor diplomatic missions but did not burden the family's finances) and through careful plans for his children. Of sixteen children born to Maximilian Ulrich and his wife only three, including the later chancellor Wenzel Anton and two daughters, outlived both their parents. In the long run this circumstance significantly lightened the family's financial burdens. A bright youngster, Wenzel Anton received careful and unusually rigorous tutoring at home and then enrolled at the University of Leipzig, highly esteemed as a center of learning in the first half of the eighteenth century. In 1736, he married Maria Ernestine Starhemberg (1717–1749), member of the powerful Austrian family. She died in her early thirties, having given birth to six sons (the oldest of them, Ernst, became Leopoldine's husband) and a daughter.

Leopoldine Kaunitz's father-in-law Wenzel Anton, the family's long-lived eighteenth-century scion (generally referred to as Wenzel, 1711–1794), achieved a position of unrivaled leadership under Maria Theresia, with substantial influence during Joseph II's sole rule as well. Wenzel Kaunitz's remarkable diplomatic career began in 1741 with his appointment as official messenger to the courts of Turin, Florence, and Rome to announce the birth of a male Habsburg, the future Joseph II. To raise funds for Wenzel's initial diplomatic posting, his father mortgaged an estate as collateral. There followed appointments to Brussels, to the peace talks following the War of the Austrian Succession, to Paris as ambassador, and finally to Vienna as Maria Theresia's state chancellor in 1753 at the age of forty-two. The most spectacular period of Wenzel Kaunitz's career unfolded during Maria Theresia's long reign. Over the years the list of accomplishments ascribed to his influence and intellect grew, beginning with the dramatic "reversal of alliances" of 1756 by which Austria dropped its venerable association with England and allied itself with the traditional enemy, France.[57] Kaunitz won the empress's complete trust, despite his far more tolerant approach toward confessional policy, his reputed skirt-chasing, and his personal idiosyncrasies. When Leopoldine married into the family, it had just reached the pinnacle of its power. In 1764, on the occasion of the Archduke Joseph's coronation as king of the Romans (a dignity which ensured his eventual succession as emperor), Chancellor Kaunitz and several other eminent aristocrats were elevated to the rank of prince of the Holy Roman Empire. The spectacular, long-term success of Leopoldine Kaunitz's father-in-law went far to shape the circumstances of Leopoldine's married life.

Noble status, with its ancient lineage and impressive pedigree, had to be accompanied by a noble lifestyle, funded by adequate economic resources. For families at the very top of the social scale, standards were high.[58] Those with estates in the Bohemian crownlands were fortunate. Taken as a whole, the lands of Bohemia and Moravia were considered to be a fertile area, with abundant meadows, forests, and farmlands. Bohemia in particular produced coal, tin, and even gold and silver in its mines. It had skilled workers who manufactured high-quality glass and porcelain products, and by the mid-eighteenth century textile production was growing. There was adequate rainfall, and rivers were available both for navigation and for mills. Czech inhabitants occupied the central and southeastern parts of the land and worked as farmers and artisans. The substantial German population, settled mostly in towns and in the border regions, worked in the mines, manufactures, and as minor officials. Some favored aristocratic families such as the Liechtensteins could draw upon auxiliary sources of income, such as proceeds generated by the credit market through loans to (or from) other prominent families or to the Habsburg government.[59] Still, the Habsburg monarchy, including the Bohemian crownlands, remained a fundamentally agriculture-based economy.

In the late eighteenth century the most secure way to hold together the wealth of a family and provide income for members was to incorporate lands and other tangible resources into legal entities that were protected from squandering by members, that is, to establish blocks of entailed property in a fideicommissum, which was held in trust for the benefit of the family according to rules that usually prescribed primogeniture.[60] Each of the families to which the individual *Dames* had linked their fortunes—Liechtenstein, Kinsky, Clary, Kaunitz—had established at least one fideicommissum, more or less extensive as family circumstances allowed. Property that was declared inalienable by this procedure could also include valuable objects the family had accumulated such as books, statuary, paintings, silverware, unique furniture, coins, and other curiosities from foreign lands or of ancient origins. In general, individual members enjoyed on their own behalf only the usufruct of the property. The fideicommissum assured an appropriate, that is, *standesmässig* livelihood and lifestyle for all branches and members while preserving intact the core wealth of the family. Used skillfully, the fideicommissum was a powerful economic tool. In theory the entailed property could not be mortgaged, placed under execution for debt, or have its value tapped in any significant way without the approval of a representative cross section of the larger family. In practice families could rely upon the acknowledged value of entailed property to make possible new acquisitions and the discharge of unavoidable obligations. The fideicommissum was also, most obviously, a means by which the landed nobility retained their all-important direct control of land.[61] When a house became hopelessly overextended, stringent measures did have to be taken, including appointment of curators to restrain the behavior of the *Majoratsherr* (or a headstrong heir), as happened in the case of Prince Johann Alois I Öttingen-Spielberg. Indebtedness was a problem for many families. In 1765, writing from Naples, Leopoldine Kaunitz commented on the tendency of noble families to ruin themselves financially, a trend she felt was growing. She noted with guarded approval that Joseph II, newly established as coregent after his father's death, was attempting to reduce government expenditures and would expect elite society to model itself after his behavior. She wrote to her sister, "The emperor's great retrenchment will not make residence [in Vienna] very pleasant in future." Elite society would have to become "simple in dress and equipage" in order to please the young regent. She concluded, "this will not result in a gay and brilliant court, but to speak the truth it will be the salvation of our nobility, which is bankrupting itself."[62]

Income of landowning aristocratic families came from both peasant or "rustical" lands (lands owned by landlords but controlled and worked by peasants) and the demesne, or "dominical" properties of the landlord (directly managed or rented out by the landlord), which typically were more profitable. Land registers recorded acreage and its status for the purpose of taxation. In the Habsburg monarchy rustical land officially used by peasant proprietors was often taxed at a higher rate, although in non-Hungarian regions even "noble" dominical land might be assessed some taxes. There was little incentive for a noble landowner to report the full extent of his property that might be liable for higher taxes, and so such records cannot provide an accurate, detailed picture of land distribution and its productiveness.[63] Families usually had properties of varying types in several jurisdictions, and more than one line of the family might control and actually benefit from that property. Additional sources of revenue were the individual contractual arrangements with tenants such as concessions for mills or breweries and inns. Both Bohemia and Moravia were areas where large landowners predominated, but few such families limited their possessions even to one region of the monarchy. Among the families examined here, only the Kinsky family had focused its possessions in this manner, owning property in Bohemia almost exclusively.[64]

The 1987 study by P. G. M. Dickson, *Finance and Government under Maria Theresia 1740–1780*, categorizes landowners of the Habsburg monarchy in the following manner: very large, a small group with annual revenues over 100,000 florins; large, with revenues from 10,000 florins to 100,000 florins, a group of landowners who might enhance their financial situation by holding high-paying offices with salaries of up to 30,000 florins; and middling landowners with incomes of 1,000 to 10,000 florins (comparable to large merchants and important officials without significant landholdings). The remaining socioeconomic groups, with incomes tailing off below 1,000 florins to 200 florins, were the traders, artisans, and professional middle classes and finally the peasants, artisans, and laborers, with incomes from 50 to 400 florins.[65] Ignaz De Luca, a contemporary (1746–1799, professor of political science in Linz, Innsbruck, and Vienna), categorized income roughly by rank, estimating that a princely family typically enjoyed an income of between 100,000 florins and 500,000 florins per year, and a family of counts usually had an income lying between 20,000 and 80,000 florins.[66] For both Bohemia and Moravia specifically, Dickson has sorted through the quagmire of primary evidence and secondary literature to compare approximate family incomes. Unfortunately the sources do not readily yield a clear picture of the relative wealth of aristocratic families. Reported incomes of noble families, and historians' painstaking efforts to assess the incomplete unstandardized data, provide only a rough sense of the relative economic strengths of these families.[67]

The Liechtenstein family had far greater resources and income than the Kinsky, Kaunitz, or Clary families. In Moravia alone, Prince Liechtenstein had a declared taxable revenue of 369,000 florins. In Habsburg lands and the empire as a whole, the Liechtenstein *Majorat* owned 24 towns, 760 villages, and 46 palaces.[68] Furthermore, as of the mid-eighteenth century, there were two Liechtenstein fideicommissa, the primary and more massive *Hauptmajorat* passing to the oldest son and family head (Leopoldine's husband and then her oldest son) and the *secundogenitur* that provided the wherewithal for a second son (Eleonore's husband Charles) to pursue an active career and, more importantly, establish a family. Sidonia Kinsky's husband inherited an excellent financial position in his possession of the principal estates of Böhmisch Kamnitz (Česká Kamenice), Mšeno, Choceň, and Rosice. Throughout his reign as family head, which lasted until his death in 1792, he continued to buy land, uniting the extensive Kinsky properties in Bohemia into a massive unit. He also purchased palaces in Prague and Vienna.[69] The Kinsky family, with a declared income of 165,000 florins as of 1756, was one of the wealthiest families within Bohemia proper. The Kaunitzes, with income derived from their Moravian lands that was ostensibly greater than Prince Clary's, although not approaching that of the Kinsky family, incurred heavy expenses under the headship of Chancellor Wenzel Kaunitz for building projects, art collection, princely representation, and the careers of the chancellor's five sons. The extent of the family's indebtedness did not come to light until after the death of both Leopoldine Kaunitz and her husband Ernst.[70] Finally, the Clary family's rank was more modest among Bohemian landowners than those of the Liechtenstein, Kaunitz, or Kinsky families, with reported income of 67,000 florins.[71] The family's most significant possessions remained the estate Teplitz, including within its boundaries just under fifty towns and villages, and the estate of Graupen (Krupka) with a few additional villages. Auxiliary sources of income for the Teplitz estate came from services rendered to visitors to the medicinal baths and rudimentary mining of brown coal.[72]

Likewise of great importance for the social standing of each of the five *Dames* were the choices, both fiscal and professional, made by their husbands as individuals and as public representatives of their families. Leopoldine Liechtenstein's husband Franz Joseph, who became head of the Liechtenstein family in 1772, was a sober individual and a good manager. He served in the military briefly as a young man and undertook several minor diplomatic assignments. Subsequently he demonstrated little interest in a military or political career but made a special effort to build the family's collections of engravings and other art works, an activity deemed appropriate and laudable by contemporaries. There is no evidence that his wife Leopoldine felt any anxiety about his behavior or his management of the family properties, nor did she concern herself with financial matters. Franz Joseph was a genial and generous host, esteemed by his friends, but not a political or social star. Although his health became a serious concern as early as 1777, his relatively early death was unexpected. In summer of 1781 he, Leopoldine Liechtenstein, and their second son Johann had traveled to Spa and Paris. Joseph II, who passed through Spa during their visit and wrote to Field Marshal Lacy from there on 20 July 1781, reported that Franz Joseph was in excellent spirits and his complexion was good.[73] But the prince was taken ill in Luxembourg, and even with the ministrations of three doctors in Metz, his condition failed to improve. After receiving his urgent message in Paris, Leopoldine hurried to Metz, arriving on 17 August at noon. By this time Franz Joseph had resigned himself to death, although he remained conscious and able to converse with her and his son Johann. The prince died on 18 August at 8:00 at night, leaving the eldest son Louis (Alois) as heir. Leopoldine Liechtenstein told her brother that near the end Franz Joseph had lamented, "With my fortune, and with 300,000 subjects, see what I am reduced to!" It particularly saddened him to die so far away from his lands.[74]

The husband of Josepha Clary, Franz Wenzel Clary (1706–1788), held the court position of *Oberstjägermeister,* or grand master of the hunt, during most of his active life.⁷⁵ For Prince Clary the court position offered a chance to serve his sovereign and to affirm his own status and the traditional fealty that formed the very core of noble identity. But the position provided few opportunities for its incumbent to distinguish himself—and Prince Clary was in any case not a man to dazzle contemporaries. A strong or even merely eccentric personality in such a position might have carved out a modest sphere of influence for himself despite the increasingly marginal nature of the job. The incumbent of this position had oversight over the imperial game preserves and had to organize imperial hunts, which could be important social occasions. Subordinate hunting staff fluctuated at around 200 employees.⁷⁶ The *Oberstjägermeister* enjoyed proximity to the rulers and to other powerful individuals. But there is no evidence that Franz Wenzel Clary took advantage of this circumstance. By an interesting coincidence, he was a notoriously poor shot and rather a hindrance to successful hunting. A querulous, fussy individual, he was not a welcome guest at the summer retreats of the aristocracy. When the Clary couple visited Feldsberg in summer 1778, Eleonore Liechtenstein, herself a guest, wrote to her sister that Prince Clary's imminent arrival was dreaded; he was "an insufferable man," especially difficult to tolerate during sojourns in the countryside. He never had success as a huntsman, Eleonore explained. Invariably either he could not hit his deer or no animal would make an appearance for him at all. The hunters at Feldsberg included other sportsmen and sportswomen of modest skill, but even they would be more successful than the *grand veneur*, Eleonore observed.⁷⁷

Reforms instituted by Joseph II as new coregent in 1765 would have annoyed a far more placid imperial *Oberstjägermeister* than Prince Clary. Joseph restricted local and regional imperial hunting activities and ordered the extermination of the wild boar population in the vicinity of Vienna because the animals damaged crops. The emperor described his changes jocularly as "a fearful reformation, Count Clary is in tears over it," noting on 19 October 1765 that the day's hunt had been a dreadful confusion, with too many people in attendance. Count Clary (not yet a prince) would be sick with anger. Prince Clary was an adequate court functionary but was also plaintive, dreary, and unexceptional in society, probably because as he aged poor health left him chronically in pain and despondent. He took his responsibilities seriously, as complaints made by Field Marshal Lacy to both Maria Theresia and Joseph II over the course of many years make clear. In 1766, as Lacy began to enjoy new property he had acquired at Dornbach just northwest of Vienna, he complained that Clary hampered him when, as proprietor, he tried to exercise his hunting prerogatives in the forests. Lacy requested, and Maria Theresia promised, that he should be free of this nuisance, "this horrid subjugation." As late as 1785, Lacy reported that Clary continued to hinder his (Lacy's) free exercise of hunting rights. Joseph agreed that Prince Clary had "a talent for going about everything wrongheadedly" and described the instructions he was giving the tiresome courtier (*secatore*) to free Lacy from ongoing vexation. When Lacy continued to expostulate about "this eccentric master of the hunt," Joseph promised to send orders to Prince Clary's subordinate, the *Forstmeister*, bypassing the obstreperous prince entirely. In fairness to Prince Clary, it should be noted that when Grand Duke Leopold visited Vienna in 1784 he found that Lacy insisted on his private hunting rights "with great rigor." Prince Clary died in June 1788 after suffering through many years of sickness and discomfort. Only a month after the ailing prince's death, Joseph suspended most operations of the imperial hunt altogether, requiring hunting employees to be retrained as forest personnel and footmen.[78]

Leopoldine Kaunitz's situation was unique among the five women because her husband was the eldest son of a brilliantly successful political father. According to the English travel writer Henry Swinburne (1743–1803), in his report of 1778 concerning Vienna, the elder Kaunitz's abilities completely overshadowed the personalities of his five surviving sons (the sixth son had died as a child) for whom, in Swinburne's opinion, the chancellor cared but little. They possessed few distinguishing characteristics: "the two eldest sons are *bornés*, but gentle, worthy creatures; the third and fourth absolute nonentities; the fifth a sad *roué*."[79] Grand Duke Leopold recorded the modest impression made on him by the Kaunitz sons when he visited Vienna in 1778. Leopold described the second eldest Dominik as a young man with little or no aptitude for political affairs and the younger Joseph Kaunitz as a youth with talent but without the inclination to exert himself. During his 1784 visit to Vienna, Leopold reported that Ernst Kaunitz was thoroughly inept and indolent, and again that Joseph Kaunitz was a man possessing "sufficient ability" but lacking prudence and good conduct, unable to apply himself seriously to any task.[80]

However disappointing his progeny may have been, like other heads of powerful families the chancellor was eager to acquire new honors for his family and to enhance its fortunes. He rejoiced in the successful military career of Franz Kaunitz, his third son, who rose to the rank of lieutenant field marshal (*Feldmarschall-Leutnant*) and master of ordnance (*Feldzeugmeister*). As a young man Ernst, together with his wife Leopoldine, traveled to Naples in 1764 as Austrian ambassador and served in that capacity until 1770. Briefly in 1769 Ernst also acted as Austrian representative in Rome during the election of a new pope. Both of these missions involved limited but substantive responsibility. Reports that preceded young Ernst Kaunitz to Naples described him as having an attractive build, full-sized and healthy, speaking French well and Italian a little, endowed with a good heart and average intelligence but little travel experience or education, and not given to excessive drinking or gambling. Ernst proved to be equal to middling efforts but lacked a bent for serious diplomacy or politics. As Leopoldine Kaunitz learned in Naples, her husband was not industrious. Particularly during these early years of her marriage Leopoldine worried constantly about Ernst's extravagance. He was unwilling to exercise restraint but afraid to contact his father as the couple's financial situation worsened. He shared the chancellor's fondness for attractive female singers and actresses but lacked the elder Kaunitz's sagacity. Ernst's clumsy romantic adventures in Naples were retailed as common gossip in Vienna and reached the ears of Maria Theresia. After his recall from Naples, Ernst served briefly as Moravian governor in Brünn (Brno), after which he and Leopoldine returned to Vienna. For all her apparent conservatism and loyalty to old friends, Maria Theresia shared her son Joseph's admiration for energetic, hardworking officials; and the easygoing Ernst never received important commissions during her reign or under her more demanding, austere son. Ernst Kaunitz held the post of court buildings inspector for many years (although, according to statesman and diarist Count Karl Zinzendorf, Ernst Kaunitz knew nothing about construction techniques, his father the chancellor being the true expert), and during the 1780s Joseph II finally conferred upon him the post of *Obersthofmarschall*, a position with which Ernst was at last content. The social position that Leopoldine Kaunitz built for herself and enjoyed after she and Ernst returned to Vienna was enhanced by her relationship with her father-in-law the chancellor, not by the career of her husband.[81]

Eleonore Liechtenstein and Sidonia Kinsky had active military spouses. In marked contrast to the well-organized and well-managed army that the Prussian king Frederick II inherited, preserved, and used to great effect against the Habsburg monarchy during his reign, Austrian military institutions of the period were in a state of what military historian Christopher Duffy has dubbed "perpetual but creative ferment," in spite of the generally conservative and even archaic outlook of much of the officer corps.[82] A series of motivated military leaders, coupled with the reforming inclinations of Habsburg sovereigns, brought about improvements in both internal organization and functionality on the battlefield, although the reputation of the Austrian army, especially its officer corps, never approached the luster of Prussian arms during the period.

Sidonia Kinsky's husband Prince Franz Ulrich entered the military comparatively late, at the age of 28. His father had wished him to choose an administrative career. When Franz Ulrich became family head, he followed his inclinations and joined the army. Under Maria Theresia and Joseph II, Prince Kinsky's career in the army followed what might be called a typical trajectory; given his social standing and strong commitment to the career, his achievements were solid but not extraordinary. Kinsky acquitted himself well in the Seven Years War and was awarded the *Ritterkreuz* in 1757 at the first awards ceremony of the Military Maria Theresia Order, newly created to reward valorous officers. For subsequent meritorious actions during the campaign of 1760 Kinsky received the higher-grade *Commanderkreuz* of the order in 1765.[83] Prince Kinsky appears to have borne with relative comfort his twin responsibilities as career military officer and family head. In 1772, after the death of Prince Wenzel Liechtenstein, who had been director of the artillery, Franz Ulrich Kinsky was appointed to replace him in that post.[84] During Kinsky's tenure, reforms spearheaded by Joseph II and Lacy reorganized the artillery to make its operations correspond more closely to standard military practices in the other branches of the military and to eliminate vestiges of its earlier special status. Joseph II wished to give the artillery a more standardized, less ambiguous or "obscure [*geheimnisvoll*]" standing within the military, as he explained to Lacy.[85] Kinsky was generally a team player, not sentimental about nonessential traditions. He left the military in 1778, then aged 52, and was awarded the rank of field marshal as recognition for his service to the artillery.[86] In retirement the prince focused his attention on managing the Kinsky properties until his death in 1792.

Eleonore Liechtenstein's husband Charles joined the military at the age of 17, conforming with contemporary practice. Like Kinsky, Charles served meritoriously in the Seven Years War. After the Austrian forces together with Russian troops occupied Berlin in October 1760, Charles had the honor of bringing official news of the sacking of the Prussian capital to the court in Vienna. According to family lore, it was then, at noon on 15 October, that Charles, who was making his colorful, ceremonial entry preceded by a dozen mounted trumpeters, first saw his future bride, the young Eleonore Öttingen-Spielberg, who was watching the procession from the window of a house on the Graben with her sister Leopoldine. By the end of the Seven Years War Charles had reached the rank of lieutenant general.[87] In contrast to Kinsky's smooth career, Eleonore's husband Charles, though heart and soul a military man, had a variety of misadventures during his military service. His wife Eleonore often found herself in an uncomfortable position, pressured by her marriage and loyalty to her husband on the one hand and her unusual friendship with his commander-in-chief Joseph II on the other. Piqued by real or imagined snubs and sensitive to a fault, Charles tendered his resignation from the military more than once, but his request to depart was never accepted by either Maria Theresia or Joseph II until Charles's final illness forced his withdrawal. Often Charles's problems resulted from a clash of wills between Joseph II, ostensible head of the military, and Maria Theresia who, despite her disclaimers, continued to influence virtually all decisions.[88] Charles's wife Eleonore took his part energetically, telling her sister Leopoldine Kaunitz that with his hot head and free spirit Charles was too honorable for the eighteenth century, when military advancement required an officer to be a skillful intriguer at court. For many years Charles hoped in vain for a promotion but was passed over while junior officers moved ahead of him. During the War of the Bavarian Succession of 1778–1779 (discussed in chapter 4), Charles Liechtenstein capably commanded a corps of troops stationed in a defensive posture near Leitmeritz (Litoměřice) in Bohemia, under Field Marshal Ernst Gideon von Laudon's leadership.

As the 1780s drew to a close, Charles Liechtenstein faced a more formidable challenge to his professional abilities with the outbreak of Joseph II's war with Turkey (described in chapter 6). Now 58 years old, Charles had expressed a wish to be active in the campaign and was taken at his word. His orders were to take the Turkish fortress of Dubicza (Dubica) and advance into Bosnia, and so he left Vienna for the front in March 1788. His troops attacked the Turkish fortress, breaching its walls. But the Turks repulsed the attack, and a three-month stalemate ensued. Finally Charles fell ill. In mid-July he was forced to relinquish his command to a successor (who quickly enjoyed greater success). Charles withdrew to Agram (Zagreb) in Croatia to convalesce. Nursed in Agram by Eleonore herself, who quickly joined him there and brought him back to Vienna still an invalid, Charles left the military a dying man but did at last receive the coveted promotion. He passed away in Vienna on 21 February 1789.

For men who chose a military career, the officer corps offered comradery and perhaps an enhanced sense of personal significance, even for aristocratic men who showed little aptitude for the few other spheres of activity open to men of their class. For females of aristocratic houses, a military husband or son could be a source of pride, a reassuring symbol of the enduring noble élan of the family. Drawbacks were equally obvious. Military life was grueling, not just for ordinary soldiers but for officers as well. Active service at training camps and in battle took its toll, even if severe injuries or death were avoided. Always present as well was the risk of venereal diseases, endemic among poorer, unattached female camp followers but a potential threat to upper class military personnel likewise, owing to their peripatetic and disorderly lifestyle. Charles Liechtenstein's weak health and mercury treatments suggest that he contracted a venereal disease as a young officer. Other explanations might account for his ill health and the remedies chosen by his doctors; but when Charles visited Italy for several months in 1783, Joseph II wrote to his brother Leopold in Tuscany that Charles's purpose in traveling was to hunt game birds and find a cure for his long-term venereal disease. Charles's behavior was secretive when he was queried about his plans at the time, but in a letter to Rosenberg the emperor scoffed at the possibility of other health concerns: "The farce that is being played out concerning Prince Charles is not to be believed. There has been yet another letter to Princess Françoise [Leopoldine Liechtenstein] expressing the greatest alarm about him, just as if he was suffering from a violent fever [*la fièvre chaude*] instead of the clap [*une pisse chaude*]." During an acute illness in 1784 Charles lamented the stories that were circulating about him. He expressed embarrassment, Eleonore reported to her sister; "they will say I'm the world's greatest libertine, but most assuredly they do me wrong."[89] Charles conceded only that there remained traces of an old infection. Syphilis and gonorrhea were certainly widespread, and not only in the officer corps (some historians believe that both Habsburg emperors Joseph II and Leopold II suffered from gonorrhea).[90]

Officers' wives had to contend with behaviors which, though long accepted as typical of the aristocratic officer corps, still occasioned anxiety and friction within families. Hard drinking and gambling were not rare. From the perspective of officers' wives and mothers, gaming and lavish, inconsequent spending were a greater threat than insobriety. An officer who was too careful with his money was not esteemed by fellow officers, for such caution could be regarded as déclassé and unworthy of a cavalier; and so even among married officers the military lifestyle could militate against rational management of a family's resources. Throughout her married life Eleonore Liechtenstein worried about her husband's penchant for gambling, a habit that approached the level of an addiction among officers seeking quick excitement. Gambling in the military was simply a more egregious form of practices that were rampant throughout elite society. Regulations to limit or prohibit games were largely ignored by officers.[91] During Eleonore's absences on the family estates in summers, while her husband remained alone in Vienna, his gaming increased. In September 1782, reporting Charles's activities to Eleonore, Leopoldine Kaunitz observed that while Eleonore was away Charles kept company with a motley assortment of individuals ("people none of us know, sportsmen, gamblers, bath attendants, a hodgepodge of types"). The situation was worrisome, she wrote, although these nighttime comrades dispersed like owls returning to their burrows when Eleonore came back to Vienna. Charles's urge to gamble surfaced at regular intervals throughout his adult life. Eleonore Liechtenstein found it expedient to appeal to "his honor and his duty to his children" at such times.[92]

Among the husbands of the five women, it is apparent, there were no professional standouts. As a matter of course the *Dames* supported the career choices of the husbands with whom fate, families, or personal inclination had indissolubly linked them. In so doing, these aristocratic wives were not following a romantic ideal of female domesticity and submission. They did not require to be sustained in their efforts even by romantic affection, much less passion. Instead they were motivated by desire to promote the welfare of their families, traditionally an imperative for all members of noble families, and by a more generalized but deeply engrained conviction, largely religious in nature, that specific duties were theirs, independent of affection or reward. All five women had certainly married well. But neither family position nor the professional activities of spouses can explain the five women's social success and their ongoing, ready access to Joseph II. Each woman's individual characteristics and social demeanor were unique, a crucial ingredient in the complex mix of personalities that comprised the *société*.

Oldest among the women was Josepha Clary. She and her sister Sidonia Kinsky, one year younger, were in their mid-thirties by 1765 when Joseph became emperor and coregent. Siblings from a numerous Swabian family, they had come to Vienna as young women and had been active at the youthful Maria Theresia's court. A reputed beauty during her younger years, Josepha Clary's most striking characteristic was her complaisance and thoughtfulness. Contemporaries prized and frequently praised her cheerful, friendly, outgoing personality. In 1770, the English traveler Lady Mary Coke described Josepha Clary as still "one of the prettiest & most Amiable Women I ever saw."[93] Josepha's friend Leopoldine Kaunitz called her "the kind, incomparable Princess." Josepha Clary's company, Leopoldine told her sister Eleonore Liechtenstein, was like "a sweet parfume that completely envelops you . . . This is not a form of ideal virtue that exists only in my imagination, it is her daily practice, always even-tempered, true to God and to her neighbors, exacting towards herself. Everyone respects her and everyone loves her, no one draws back from her. She inspires respect and trust." Josepha Clary's companionship was gentle and serene, Leopoldine Kaunitz affirmed, instilling "peace in my very soul."[94]

Count Karl Zinzendorf became acquainted with Sidonia Kinsky, Josepha Clary's younger sister, in 1761. Zinzendorf reported that Sidonia Kinsky was diminutive in stature.[95] Lady Mary Coke made the acquaintance of Sidonia Kinsky in Spa in 1764 and described her at various times as having "the most pleasing figure without being a regular beauty that I ever saw; & her manner extremely agreeable," a personage "more amiable and more agreeable then [sic] I can describe her," with a "figure . . . prettier then [sic] anything I ever saw; you will hear everybody say the same that I do."[96] According to Prussian envoy Fürst, in the 1750s Chancellor Kaunitz had been romantically interested in Sidonia Kinsky who, however, gave him no encouragement.[97] In 1776 Eleonore Liechtenstein made what was very likely an oblique reference to this earlier episode in commenting on the peculiarities of both Kaunitz and Sidonia Kinsky as she mused about each individual's unpredictable plans for visiting Laxenburg, the Habsburg summer retreat near Vienna: "It is no accident that in earlier times they suited each other, they have much in common in their eccentricity if not in their intellects."[98] A lavish hostess as a young wife in Vienna, Sidonia Kinsky nevertheless had an independent nature that grew more pronounced as she matured, and the other women reproached her when she failed to concert plans with the rest of the *Dames* in the group, preferring to remain for long periods at her suburban retreat in Weidlingau. Her friends referred to her, with a Voltairean twist, as the "Solitaire" of Weidlingau or "our Weidlingau hermit." According to Abbé Jean François Georgel, secretary to the French embassy who resided in Vienna during the early 1770s and claimed to enjoy a warm friendship with the five women and with Joseph II himself, Sidonia read widely and avidly.[99]

Next in age was Leopoldine Liechtenstein. The former Countess Sternberg had married at the age of seventeen, and so by 1765, though only in her early thirties, she too was an established matron. While her husband lived and served as head of the entire Liechtenstein clan, Leopoldine Liechtenstein's economic advantages as well as her social status outstripped those of her friends. Like Sidonia Kinsky, she was said to have attracted the admiring attentions of Chancellor Kaunitz in earlier years. An ambitious, somewhat imperious individual for whom occasional conflicts with both family and associates were inevitable (Georgel spoke discreetly of "the dignity of her bearing" and "her sedate, serious manner," which helped her to secure proper regard for her family's standing and did not detract from her "kind and benevolent" character), she was nevertheless a loyal and esteemed friend. She was the only one of the five women without a blood relationship to the others.[100]

Youngest in the group were Leopoldine Kaunitz and Eleonore Liechtenstein. In their early twenties during the mid-1760s, they had been married only a few years when the group formed. Concerning Leopoldine Kaunitz, a 1763 report that preceded her arrival in Naples in the company of her ambassador husband described her as a wealthy heiress who was well-educated and animated but not pretty ("non bella").[101] Abbé Georgel confirmed Leopoldine Kaunitz's unprepossessing exterior. Contemporaries generally acknowledged her sharp intelligence but also commented on her argumentativeness. She had, again according to Georgel, a "caustic turn of mind, without being spiteful"; during conversation, he noted, "a dispute sharpens her wit, and then a flow of words, each well placed, serves to pave the way for the triumph of her ideas."[102] Count Zinzendorf recorded in his journal many occasions when he and Leopoldine Kaunitz discussed a wide variety of topics, including economic policy and political theory. More than the other *Dames*, Leopoldine Kaunitz clearly relished the clash of ideas and interests that made the years of the coregency and the decade of the 1780s so turbulent, although she did not always applaud the course of events. Among the five women, Leopoldine Kaunitz was certainly of a more serious intellectual bent than her friends, for all her ostensible diffidence. Lady Mary Coke observed that Leopoldine possessed "an uncommon understanding."[103] In a letter to Josepha Clary in 1781, Leopoldine Liechtenstein referred to Leopoldine Kaunitz as "this pleasant savante and, even more, this godly woman."[104] She and her sister Eleonore Liechtenstein were very close. When Leopoldine Kaunitz died in 1795, Leopoldine Liechtenstein reported that the younger sister Eleonore was devastated, left with indelible memories of a sister who had also been like a mother to Eleonore. "Their mutual trust was limitless," Leopoldine Liechtenstein wrote to her brother, "and because of that there will be heartache throughout the rest of life for the one who remains."[105]

Concerning Eleonore Liechtenstein herself, junior member of the group, reports were uniformly and enthusiastically favorable with regard to both appearance and personality. Count Karl Zinzendorf, not easily pleased by his women associates, described Eleonore in his journal in 1772 as "a charming woman of many attainments."[106] The English traveler Wraxall wrote, "Her person is pleasing, and though her features cannot be esteemed regular, their expression is admirable. Her mouth is peculiarly beautiful, and over her whole figure is diffused an air of modesty, intelligence, and dignity, rarely blended in any woman. She possesses besides an enlarged and cultivated mind, a fund of amusing conversation, and powers of entertaining, as well as improving, very superior to the generality of her sex in Vienna."[107] According to Charles Greville, nephew of the British envoy in Naples Sir William Hamilton, Eleonore Liechtenstein was very handsome but "to the full as devout & strict as her sister." It was Eleonore Liechtenstein who first attracted the regard of Joseph II, which in turn led to the emergence of the group of *Dames* as a stable entity. The strong bonds of affection between the elder and younger pairs of sisters in the *société* were a force for the group's stability and longevity.

As aristocratic wives, the women assumed responsibility for the perpetuation of the family name and traditions into future generations. In particular, each hoped to raise a male heir for the house into which she had married. All of the women except Eleonore Liechtenstein were wives of family heads or of heirs to that position, a circumstance that only strengthened the imperative to raise to adulthood a healthy, functional son and heir. The importance of a male heir was so obvious that it scarcely merited comment beyond the occasional resigned sigh when a female child was born. Typical of this attitude was Leopoldine Kaunitz's remark to Eleonore concerning the birth of an infant daughter to an acquaintance in 1779—the birth was "a matter of little interest."[108] It was a rare family that was so blessed with both male progeny and the material wealth to forward their careers and marriages that it did not have to ration resources toward this end, since the loftier the social position of the family, the stronger and more insistent was the felt need to maintain living standards. Many of the most prestigious male career paths required a substantial outlay of financial resources at least initially, which second or third sons of even the richest families could find hard to muster, especially when much of the family's property was entailed and controlled by the family's head. Over time the establishment of multiple branches of a family and their provisioning with land and capital could deplete the resources of a family and imperil its socioeconomic status, resulting in a diminution of influence, opportunity, exercise of patronage, and reputation. Awareness of this exigency was one source of shared identity for members of all great houses. As Leopoldine Kaunitz had remarked to Eleonore Liechtenstein as early as 1766, the resources required to establish a son in a line of productive activity were greater than those needed to dower a daughter. Although Eleonore would certainly love a daughter just as well as any son and would not wish to be unjust, a son would necessarily draw upon more of the family's wealth, whereas a daughter from a family such as the Liechtensteins, Leopoldine asserted, would not need a large fortune to make her attractive in the marriage market.[109]

With the early birth of at least one healthy son, four of the five *Dames* were spared anxious preoccupation with this important task, at least until their children matured and their growing independence produced distractions of a different nature. The oldest of the women, Josepha Clary, lost her first son (born in 1752) at the age of 14, but a son born in 1753 as well as four daughters (1747, 1748, and 1755, and 1756) survived to adulthood. Sidonia Kinsky too produced the requisite offspring. The first and third Kinsky sons (born 1750 and 1752) soon died, but a middle son (1751) married and produced sons of his own to preserve the family name, and a healthy daughter followed (1754). Sidonia Kinsky's family thus consisted of only two children, but these included the all-important male and eventually his progeny as well.[110] Leopoldine Liechtenstein, in the compelling role of wife to the heir presumptive of the immense *Majorat* of the house of Liechtenstein, lost her first son (born 1752, two years after her marriage) before his second birthday as well as a second son (born 1758), who died just after his second birthday. But three sons (born in 1759, 1760, and 1762) as well as three daughters (born 1754, 1756, and 1768) reached maturity, for a total of six children.[111] Eleonore Liechtenstein gave birth to a daughter in 1763, and there followed a series of healthy sons in 1765, 1767, 1775, 1776, and 1780. She lost only one child, a son born in 1770, who died of measles during a minor epidemic in Vienna in 1773.[112]

Only for Leopoldine Kaunitz did the problem of the "succession" become an ongoing, recurrent source of anxiety. Married to the chancellor's eldest son and naturally eager for an heir, Leopoldine Kaunitz faced one disappointment after another, starting with the death of a premature baby girl in December 1767, while she and her husband were residing in Naples.[113] Still in Naples, in April 1769 the couple rejoiced over the birth of a healthy baby boy whom they named Joseph, an event much fêted by Maria Theresia and her daughter the queen of Naples. But the child died in Vienna five years later. A daughter born in 1773 also died at the age of five. Only the youngest daughter, born in 1775 (named Eleonore, the future wife of Clemens Metternich), survived to adulthood. Miscarriages and stillbirths occurred despite Leopoldine's efforts to observe the best practices of the day and all the precautions that were recommended by both doctors and lay contemporaries.[114] The health hazards of early childhood had to be accepted as part of the natural order in the eighteenth century. But Leopoldine Kaunitz mourned the loss of her young children deeply. In late July 1778, after her older daughter Françoise had died, Leopoldine Kaunitz described her own despair to her sister Eleonore: "For myself, I felt such shock, such despair that I cannot describe them; I mourned in her all my children . . . I cannot express how bitter my sorrow is." Father Ernst Kaunitz was in a pitiable state. "I did not know what to do with my husband, just consider, he has not been able to bring himself to enter the rooms where he will no longer find this little girl whom he loved so much." Little Eleonore, nicknamed "Lorel," also fell sick, devastating father Ernst, for whom the sick room was haunted by memories (although in the event this youngest daughter did recover): "he is terribly afraid of these rooms . . . I can only hope that time will heal him, but it passes slowly when one is unhappy. My God, if we had faith, if we loved God, we would not be so sad!" Leopoldine Kaunitz feared what the future might hold for her one remaining child Lorel. "If I had to judge the future by the past," she wrote, "I would not have a moment's peace, but I cannot believe that our gracious God wishes to take away all my children. I think instead that he will leave me this one, and so when there is no immediate danger . . . I manage to live from day to day and not to look ahead."[115] Josepha Clary reported Leopoldine Kaunitz's travails to her own husband: "she [Leopoldine Kaunitz] is being tested like refined gold, and I do believe that her soul is wholly pure and pleasing in the sight of God."[116] On the care and education of this one surviving daughter, Leopoldine Kaunitz lavished the attention that historian Ivo Cerman has described as characteristic of many Habsburg aristocratic families of the late eighteenth century who were influenced by educational ideals of the Enlightenment and particularly a growing cult of sensibility.[117] Leopoldine Kaunitz spent years searching for precisely the right preceptors and program for her daughter, often wishing that her own busy life would permit her to act as her own daughter's governess. Because of Leopoldine's misfortunes, it was doubly important from the larger Kaunitz family's perspective that the wife of Ernst Kaunitz's younger brother Dominik, Bernardine Plettenberg, should produce an heir. Here again there was but a single male, however, and two daughters. Bernardine herself died in 1779 after a troubled sojourn in the Kaunitz family, as will be noted subsequently (chapter 2). With time Leopoldine Kaunitz accepted her own uncomfortable situation, resigned to the paramount claims of this nephew to eventual headship of the family.[118]

Where healthy young male heirs were available, their education and establishment could be a worrisome procedure. Sidonia Kinsky and Josepha Clary, to all appearances, did not suffer from serious disquiet as these interesting future family heads matured into their roles. In a letter written in October 1772 to her friend Lady Mary Coke, Sidonia Kinsky reported with satisfaction that her son was about to make his *entrée* into the adult world. He would appear to advantage, she felt, "so far as substance goes, but less so with regard to externals, which unfortunately weigh so heavily for or against a person in this unjust world, where only the superficial attracts attention."[119] Josepha Clary, her husband Franz Wenzel, and their only son Johann Nepomuk enjoyed amicable relations, despite Prince Clary's notoriously irritable temperament. When by 1786 the prince's increasing age and ill health prevented him from making trips to Bohemia to oversee the family properties, Johann received from Prince Clary at first provisional and then permanent plenipotentiary powers to manage the estates and to make all decisions in routine matters, an arrangement "very well done in my opinion," Eleonore Liechtenstein remarked.[120] According to Eleonore, during the last two years before his death in 1788 Prince Clary had existed in a sort of second childhood in any case, "not to mention that he has been soft in the head all his life." As a widow Josepha Clary, concerned about her son's financial status, felt that her late husband's testamentary bequests for her were too taxing for the son and successor: "my benefactor . . . has done more for me than the circumstances of my kind son can well afford." Josepha Clary declared that she would have more than enough revenue and that "all this opulence would be odious to me."[121]

Some families bewailed a shortage of sons. Eleonore Liechtenstein and her husband Charles had too many, according to Eleonore. In July 1782, as she sought a new tutor for her boys, Eleonore Liechtenstein remarked, "My fertility in boys is certainly a disagreeable thing." As an adult, each son would require a dignified, *standesmässig* subsistence, consistent with noble status and free (at least to all appearances) of the taint of commerce or the professionalism found among doctors or scholars. Only for the two oldest sons did Eleonore and Charles Liechtenstein attempt to provide a well-defined career path, with minimal success. The eldest, named Charles after his father and other Liechtenstein forebears, would always have a vocation of sorts, as Eleonore noted, managing the wealth of this younger branch of the Liechtenstein family. "At least he has a future, he has house and home, but for these younger ones, who are doomed to perpetual bachelorhood, who must enter the church or the military, it is dreadful for in the end happiness and true virtue are found only in domestic life, and rarely with a canon or officer." Two days later Eleonore wrote, "If anyone were to ask me what I would wish to do [with five sons], I would answer unequivocally, establish the eldest in his household and as for the others, cobblers or husbandmen."[122]

These two oldest sons, Charles and Wenzel, remained a source of discomfiture to Eleonore even after they became adults. As early as summer 1779, Eleonore Liechtenstein criticized her oldest son Charles's character and development. "He has an insouciance, a lack of discipline that makes me tremble, shudder, break into a cold sweat, thinking of the consequences, in combination with the example of his father which is—almost as if it had been chosen from among a thousand—the one that is least suitable for him." In early August 1780 she wrote to Leopoldine Kaunitz, "my children have a mental laziness, an inattentiveness, a lack of discipline that one does not readily meet with in a family." Son Charles, she reported, disliked reading and thinking, and he spoke poorly every language he had studied.[123] In summer 1784, from intercepted mail, Eleonore Liechtenstein learned about young Charles's extensive debts and disreputable love affairs. While such gallantries were distasteful, families assumed that ill-assorted romantic affairs could be disrupted or would fade away with time if there was no threat of an actual mésalliance. Massive losses of money at the gaming table, on the other hand, could mean serious trouble. Unscrupulous individuals would readily help a foolish young heir borrow money and pursue his expensive adventures on the assumption that he would one day be his own master and repay their efforts. As Eleonore labored to uncover all her son's debts, her discouragement was profound. She wrote to her sister, "I am charged with a painful task, can it be that personalities so little like my own must be my deepest concern?"[124] Although her husband Charles suggested a military career, son Charles (in his own desultory fashion) and Eleonore both preferred a civilian post, perhaps leading to employment as a diplomat or administrator. Eleonore complained that her husband merely wanted to dispose of young Charles without much effort, "and since for a military career it is only necessary to obtain a uniform and dress him in it, this seems preferable to the bother, the travels, the recommendations that take time and cause annoyance."[125] Young Charles was sent with a private tutor to Leipzig and Göttingen, attended lectures by prominent scholars such as August Ludwig von Schlözer (1735–1809) and Johann Stephan Pütter (1725–1807), and returned home in 1787 after a "grand tour" through Germany, Holland, and England. Joseph II then smoothed the way for the young man to take a post in Brussels under the direction of Count Trautmannsdorf, then serving as Habsburg minister. Charles promised well in his new profession, as reported by Archduchess Marie Christine and her husband, Habsburg governors in Brussels. Traveling back to Vienna at the time of his father's final sickness and death in 1789, young Charles did not return to his post in Brussels because of growing unrest in the Austrian Netherlands (described in chapter 6). After Joseph II's death, Charles became a personal favorite of Leopold II, serving him as a sort of personal secretary.[126] But Leopold too soon died, in 1792. Married since January 1790 and the father of two small sons who were the all-important male Liechtenstein heirs for this younger branch of Liechtensteins, Charles now controlled considerable family wealth but had little to occupy his time. Under the new Emperor Franz, Charles appeared at court only twice weekly as chamberlain and easily dissipated his remaining energies in lighter pursuits and extravagances. Charles's final, and fatal, foolish act was his participation in a duel, an affair of "gallantry" that ended his life in December 1795. Eleonore and her sister had noted earlier signs of Charles's tendency to become involved in such competitive scrapes and, without really expecting to eliminate Charles's participation in these traditional displays of aristocratic "honor," they had hoped to persuade him to show restraint (in Leopoldine Kaunitz's words, "a well-bred, upright man is not readily found in a situation where he must fight"). Eleonore's despair over her eldest son's death was great.[127]

It was Eleonore Liechtenstein's dearest hope that her second son Wenzel would enter the church. Among aristocratic families who sent sons into the church, usually by way of membership in cathedral chapters, the ultimate goal was a bishopric. Not especially enthusiastic, Wenzel attempted to make a career in the church. As in the case of an aspiring diplomat like his older brother Charles, a young man with high hopes for church patronage required formal education. But as Wenzel matured it became apparent that he was singularly ill suited to an ecclesiastical career, being too fond of gaming and womanizing and generally uninterested in clerical matters.[128] Still, he was given a clerical tutor and was sent to Rome for training in the Collegium Germanicum, once an institution with strong Jansenist leanings but now viewed as generally orthodox.[129] From Rome Wenzel proceeded to Salzburg for seminary study. Eleonore's difficulties with this son were just beginning when Joseph II died. After many troubled years during which his behavior scandalized both clerical authorities and the Habsburg emperor himself, Wenzel traveled to Rome and secured from the pope his release from the minor orders he had taken. He then joined the military, where he served creditably.[130]

Eleonore Liechtenstein's remaining three younger sons, whose years of maturity extended well beyond the limits of this study, grew up without the distracting prospect of substantial inherited wealth. All three joined the military as young men, many years before their older brother Wenzel, a choice not surprising given the turbulent times, the Liechtenstein heritage, and these young men's positions within the family. Each son enhanced the family's traditional reputation by serving his emperor on the battlefield, all three of them apparently comfortable in following this typical Liechtenstein vocation. All Eleonore's military sons were wounded and imprisoned at times during the French wars. One son, Franz, died as a result of war injuries in 1793. Eleonore found some consolation in reports that the young man had died devoutly. When Eleonore's daughter-in-law consulted her concerning the education of children, Eleonore was reluctant to offer advice; as she wrote to her own daughter, "with regard to education, I have not been sufficiently fortunate to wish to be imitated or consulted."[131]

Like Eleonore, Leopoldine Liechtenstein produced the requisite male heirs but found them difficult to guide. Friction between Leopoldine Liechtenstein and her sons, particularly the eldest named Louis or Alois, was routine by the late 1770s, when Louis was in his late teens and early twenties. Eleonore described some of these conflicts vividly to her sister Leopoldine Kaunitz (it should be remembered that Eleonore had not yet faced similar issues of control and governance that made her miserable by the mid-1780s). She predicted difficulties for Leopoldine Liechtenstein. "All day long," she wrote to her sister, "I have before my eyes three young persons who will be capable of causing their parents many a sleepless night." Leopoldine Liechtenstein's sons, she wrote, were "quite ill-mannered." Eleonore had witnessed several scenes of argument and refractoriness toward their mother. These altercations had trivial causes, Eleonore reported. "They were about insignificant things, paltry matters, both sides became obstinate, each wanted to have the last word. . . . The truth is that young people cannot bear any form of restraint, be it ever so gentle, and today's charming morals only strengthen that spirit of independence even more." Subsequently Eleonore enlarged upon this theme, describing young Louis as "a sort of savage who cannot be tamed; nothing amiable, nothing agreeable in his manners or his intellect, no principles and no religion or morality, lazy, indolent, selfish, hard, and yet lax; he will always be led about by sycophants and lackeys." To an even greater extent than his younger cousin Charles, Louis occupied a particularly difficult position, a likely successor to enormous wealth yet subject to parental authority for the interim.[132]

When Leopoldine's husband Franz Joseph, the Liechtenstein paterfamilias, died in 1781, Leopoldine's acclimation to life as a widow was more than usually difficult if only because her position as wife of the Liechtenstein *Majoratsherr* had been so lofty. Her husband had been thoroughly reliable but her son Louis, now family head, was young and capricious. Eleonore believed that Leopoldine Liechtenstein's distress over her unfolding relationship with Louis was even greater than her grief over the loss of her husband. Commenting on Leopoldine Liechtenstein's situation, Leopoldine Kaunitz reasoned that conflict was inevitable: "as a rule, once sons are grown and become their own masters, their mother can no longer live in society with them, her role ends unhappily because she must act as mediator between father and son; but when the father dies, the son takes his place and the mother can only withdraw." Leopoldine Kaunitz sympathized with the widowed princess's difficulties. She wrote, "it is harsh and painful, these are the little daily deaths that Msgr de Fénelon describes." Initial decisions about what the family should do after Franz Joseph's death were made by Leopoldine Liechtenstein with Field Marshal Lacy as advisor, together with her rather reluctant brother-in-law Charles Liechtenstein, who became Louis's guardian. Leopoldine Kaunitz foresaw difficulties. "I am convinced," she wrote, "that this matter of succession is just the thing to create disorder when there is such a craving for wealth as at present." Charles was forced to run interference between Louis and his strong-willed mother Leopoldine as she faced the painful downward adjustment in her status and authority. Eleonore doubted her husband Charles's ability to manage money and noted that at heart he was not fond of the domineering Leopoldine Liechtenstein, who managed to exasperate him at every turn.[133] Charles wished to include Louis in all deliberations concerning family property, reasoning that the young heir would soon control the *Majorat* anyway. Lacy was stricter, uneasy about the welfare of the widowed mother.[134] Eventually, in 1782, Louis was declared to be legally of age, granted venia aetatis somewhat early. By then Charles Liechtenstein had indeed confused his accounts and owed repayments to the Liechtenstein *Majorat*, precipitating one more financial crisis among the many that he and his wife Eleonore faced over the years.[135]

Leopoldine Liechtenstein's third son Philip entered the military but had a relatively brief career. He served in the Turkish war but then spent much time abroad in succeeding years.[136] Philip suffered a serious illness in 1798 and recovered only gradually and partially. He died in 1802 just shy of his fortieth birthday, having reached the rank of lieutenant colonel. But the career of Leopoldine Liechtenstein's second son Johann, or Jean, proved to be the most spectacularly successful of any Liechtenstein of his generation. He entered the military with Field Marshal Lacy's support and patronage in 1782. His health was fragile, and in Joseph II's Turkish campaign of 1788–1789, during which his uncle Prince Charles Liechtenstein and the emperor Joseph himself both contracted their final, fatal illnesses, Johann too became ill, the first of many sicknesses he endured, usually after active participation in military campaigns. He was a brave officer, often seen in the midst of his troops during the hottest fighting (popular reports claimed he had 24 horses shot from under him over the course of his career) and able to make split-second decisions on the field of battle.[137] He served in important military and even diplomatic posts (he was Habsburg signatory to the Treaty of Pressburg in 1805) before he resigned from the military in 1809.[138] Leopoldine Liechtenstein's pride in her second son Johann was understandably great. Among the sons of the *Dames* Johann Liechtenstein and his achievements enjoyed the greatest renown.

Notes

1   Clarissa Campbell Orr, "Aristocratic Feminism, the Learned Governess, and the Republic of Letters," in *Women, Gender and Enlightenment*, edited by Sarah Knott and Barbara Taylor (New York: Palgrave, 2005), 308; M. L. Bush, *Rich Noble, Poor Noble* (New York: Manchester University Press, 1988), 97–100.
2   Maria Theresia. *Briefe der Kaiserin Maria Theresia an ihre Kinder und Freunde*, edited by Alfred von Arneth, vol. 1 (1881; repr., Osnabrück: Biblio Verlag, 1978), 146.
3   Rodinný Archiv Metternichů, Státní Ústřední Archiv, Prague, Acta Clementina (SÚA, RAM AC), 11/20. Letter of Maria Theresia (MT) to Maria Carolina, 9 February, no year.
4   LRRA, P 17/27, EL to LK, [Mährisch] Kromau, 11 July 1781.
5   LRRA, P 18/59, EL to Josephine Harrach, 25 August 1804.
6   LRRA, P 18/59, EL to Josephine Harrach, 19 September 1804.
7   Siegfried Grillmeyer, "Der Adel und sein Haus. Zur Geschichte eines Begriffs und eines erfolgreichen Konzepts" in *Elite um 1800: Erfahrungshorizonte, Verhaltensweisen, Handlungsmöglichkeiten,* edited by Anja Victorine Hartmann et al. (Mainz: Philipp von Zabern, 2000), 368–69.

8   A succinct description of the concept of "honor" can be found in Peter N. Stearns, ed., *Encyclopedia of Social History* (New York: Garland, 1994), in an article by Robert A. Nye entitled "Honor Codes," 325–27.
9   Sources for family history of the Hohenzollern-Hechingens: Fritz Kallenberg, ed., *Hohenzollern* (Stuttgart: Verlag W. Kohlhammer, 1996), 15–35; Detlev Schwennicke, ed., *Europäische Stammtafeln*, n. F., vol. 1, pt. 1 (Frankfurt am Main: V. Klostermann, 1998), tables 120–23.
10 Kallenberg, "Hohenzollern im Alten Reich," in Kallenberg, *Hohenzollern*, 62.
11 Karl Mors, *Hechingen und Burg Hohenzollern* (Sigmaringendorf: Verlag Glock und Lutz, 1989), 33–38.
12 Kallenberg, "Hohenzollern im Alten Reich," in Kallenberg, *Hohenzollern*, 60.
13 The remainder of this account concerning members of the Hohenzollern-Hechingen family draws on Michael Huberty, *L'Allemagne dynastique*, vol. 5 (Le Perreux: A. Giraud, 1976–1994), 71–72, 84–87, 96–101, 115–27.
14 Kallenberg, "Die Fürstentümer Hohenzollern im Zeitalter der Französischen Revolution und Napoleons," *Zeitschrift für die Geschichte des Oberrheins* 111, no. 2 (1963): 360.
15 Petr Mašek, *Modrá krev: minulost a přítomnost 445 šlechtických rodů v Českých zemích*, 2nd ed. (Prague: Mladá Fronta, 1999), 268. Family history of the Sternbergs is based upon Constant von Wurzbach, *Biographisches Lexikon des Kaiserthums Oesterreich* (1856–91; repr., New York: Johnson Reprint, 1966), 13: 266–89; Aleš Chalupa, "Familie der Grafen," in *Die Manderscheider: Eine Eifeler Adeslfamilie. Herrschaft, Wirtschaft, Kultur. Katalog zur Austellung, Blankenheim, Gildehaus, 4. Mai–29. Juli 1990. Manderscheid, Kurhaus, 16. August–11. November 1990* (Köln: Rheinland-Verlag, 1990), 83–87. Also *Die Wappen des böhmischen Adels*, Siebmacher's Wappenbuch, vol. 4, part 9 (1886; repr., facsimile production vol. 30, Neustadt an der Aisch: Bauer & Raspe, 1979), 172–73.
16 Chalupa, "Familie der Grafen," 84.
17 Eduard Vehse, *Geschichte der deutschen Höfe seit der Reformation* (Hamburg: Hoffmann und Campe, 1852), 14: 94.
18 Derek Beales, *Joseph II* (Cambridge: Cambridge University Press, 1987–2009), 1: 145–47; Wolf, *Marie Christine, Erzherzogin von Oesterreich* (Vienna: Carl Gerold's Sohn, 1863), 169–72.
19 Peter Neu, "Die Grafen von Manderscheid: ein historischer Überblick," in *Die Manderscheider: Eine Eifeler Adelsfamilie*, 27–28.
20 In discussing the marriage with his son, Franz Philip stressed Augusta's solid character. Augusta was acknowledged by all who knew her to have many merits, but possibly her appearance was not in her favor (Zinzendorf, ever blunt in his journal, described her as "extremely ugly" in April 1763). Haus-, Hof- und Staatsarchiv, Vienna, Zinzendorf Tagebücher, (HHStA, KA ZT), Band 8, 3 April 1763; Chalupa, "Familie der Grafen," 83–84.
21 Leopoldine's Damian branch of the family ended in the male line in 1847 when the only son of the Sternberg-Manderscheid couple died (Leopoldine's nephew). However, descendants of the Leopoldine branch successfully perpetuated their part of the family, weathering two world wars and multiple land confiscations to regain the family estates under the Czech Republic in 1989.
22 Gerald Schöpfer, *Klar und Fest: Geschichte des Hauses Liechtenstein*, 2nd ed. (Graz: Institut für Wirtschafts- und Sozialgeschichte, Karl-Franzens-Universität, 1996), 89.
23 Wurzbach, *Biographisches Lexikon*, 38: 282.

24 This account of the Öttingen-Spielberg family's history is based on the following sources (except where separately noted): *Die Wappen des hohen deutschen Adels* (J. Siebmacher's großes Wappenbuch; repr., Neustadt an der Aisch, Bauer & Raspe, 1974), vol. 4, pt. 2, 190–93; *Neue deutsche Biographie* (Berlin: Duncker & Humblot, 1953–2007), 19: 472–74.

25 Adam Wolf, *Fürstin Eleonore Liechtenstein, 1745–1812* (Vienna: Carl Gerold's Sohn, 1875), 10.

26 This relationship can be conveniently traced in William Addams Reitwiesner, *Matrilineal Descents of the European Royalty: a Work in Progress*, vol. 5, 5th ed. (Washington, DC: W. A. Reitwiesner, 1997), ACA 19, ACA 23, ACA 27. The women's mother, Theresia von Holstein-Wiesenburg, had been a daughter of Maria Elizabeth von Liechtenstein, who was herself a daughter of Prince Hans Adam von Liechtenstein.

27 Petra Ostenrieder, *Wohnen und Wirtschaften in Oettingen 1600–1800: Untersuchungen zur Sozialtopographie und Wirtschaftsstruktur einer bikonfessionellen Residenzstadt* (Augsburg: AV-Verlag, 1993), 98–99.

28 Wolf, *Fürstin Eleonore*, 4–7.

29 Robert John Weston Evans, *The Making of the Habsburg Monarchy, 1550–1700* (New York: Oxford University Press, 1979).

30 Evans, *Making of the Habsburg Monarchy*, 196–201.

31 Evans, *Making of the Habsburg Monarchy*, 232–34; Petr Mat'a, "Landstände und Landtag in den böhmischen und österreichischen Ländern (1620–1740). Von der Niedergangsgeschichte zur Interaktionsanalyse" in *Die Habsburgermonarchie 1620 bis 1740*, edited by Petr Mat'a and Thomas Winkelbauer (Stuttgart: Franz Steiner, 2006), 345–400.

32 Eugen Guglia, *Maria Theresia: ihr Leben und ihre Regierung* (Munich: R. Oldenbourg, 1917), 2: 316.

33 Sources for the Clary family's history include: *Neue deutsche Biographie*, 3: 262; Alfons Clary-Aldringen, *A European Past: Memoirs*, translated by Ewald Osers (London: Weidenfeld and Nicolson, 1978).

34 *Die Wappen des böhmischen Adels* (J. Siebmacher's großes Wappenbuch; repr., Neustadt an der Aisch: Bauer & Raspe, 1979), 30: 116–17; *Die Wappen des hohen deutschen Adels*, vol. 4, 2. Teil, 41–42.

35 Oldřich Pulkert and Jan Šaroch, "Beethoven in den böhmischen Bädern" in *Ludwig van Beethoven im Herzen Europas*, edited by Oldřich Pulkert and Hans-Werner Küthen (Prague: České Lupkové Závody, 2000), 333–35; Clary, *A European Past*, 6.

36 *Teplitz-Schönau* (Berlin-Friednau: Deutscher Kommunal-Verlag, 1930), 228–29.

37 Unless otherwise noted, the following summary of the history of the Kinsky family is based upon Josef Erwin Folkmann, *Die gefürstete Linie des uralten und edlen Geschlechtes Kinsky* (Prague: Verlag von Karl André, 1861).

38 Ivan Brož, *Velké postavy rodu Kinských*, 2nd ed. (Prague: Petrklíč, 2001), 8.

39 Folkmann, *Die gefürstete Linie*, 29–30; Otakar Odlozik, "The Nobility of Bohemia, 1620–1640," *East European Quarterly* 7, no. 1 (1973): 22–23; Jaroslav Macek, "Beethoven und Ferdinand Fürst Kinsky," in *Ludwig van Beethoven im Herzen Europas*, edited by Oldřich Pulkert and Hans-Werner Küthen (Prague: České Lupkové Závody, 2000), 219.

40 Alfred von Arneth, *Geschichte Maria Theresia's*, vol. 1 (Vienna: Wilhelm Braumüller, 1863), 223–24. No date provided, but presumably from mid-1741. This passage has been variously translated. The phrasing here is that found in Robert Pick, *Empress Maria Theresa: the Earlier Years, 1717–1757* (New York, Harper & Row, 1966), 71.

41 Egbert Silva-Tarouca, *Der Mentor der Kaiserin: der weltliche Seelenführer Maria Theresias* (Zurich: Amalthea, 1960), 98–99; Eugen Guglia, *Maria Theresia: ihr Leben und ihre Regierung,* vol. 1 (Munich: R. Oldenbourg, 1917), 70–71.
42 Brož, *Velké postavy,* 76–77.
43 LRRA, Q 1/66, Josephine Harrach to EL, Bruck, 14 November 1812.
44 Sources for this description of the Liechtenstein family's history are: Schöpfer, *Klar und Fest*; Evelin Oberhammer, "Viel ansehnliche Stuck und Güter: die Entwicklung des fürstlichen Herrschaftsbesitzes," in *Der ganzen Welt ein Lob und Spiegel* (Vienna: Verlag für Geschichte und Politik, 1990), 33–45; Wilhelm Pfeifer, *Das Fürstenhaus Liechtenstein in Nordböhmen,* Schriftenreihe des Bundes der Niederländer, Heft 16 (Böblingen: Niederlandverlag, 1984); Erich Kippes, *Feldsberg und das Haus Liechtenstein im 17. Jahrhundert: die Gegenreformation im Bereich der fürstlichen Herrschaft* (Vienna: Böhlau, 1996).
45 Another story described how an early Liechtenstein had traveled to Jerusalem with six snow-white stags in harness. Wurzbach, *Biographisches Lexikon,* 15: 112. In a more elaborate version of the story about discovery of silver, the villager unselfishly gave the stone to his emperor. Both texts available at: http://www.sagen.at/texte/sagen/liechtenstein/sagen_liechtenstein.htm ("Die Sage vom Liechtenstein" and "Die Sage vom lichten Stein"). Sources cited for digital texts: Friedrich Uhlenhut, ed., *Das Buch vom Liechtenstein, aus Anlaß des 70. Geburtsfestes Sr. Durchlaucht des regierenden Fürsten Johann von und zu Liechtenstein zur Belehrung und Unterhaltung der vaterländischen Jugend* (Vienna: Johann Preiss, n.d.); Dino Larese, *Liechtensteiner Sagen* (Basel: Friedrich Reinhardt, 1970), 7. In some versions of the story, the farmer continues to dig and ends up with a pile of silver stones.
46 David Beattie, *Liechtenstein: a Modern History* (London: I. B. Tauris, 2004), 8; Schöpfer, *Klar und Fest,* 20–23.
47 Volker Press, "Das Haus Liechtenstein in der europäischen Geschichte" in *Liechtenstein, fürstliches Haus und staatliche Ordnung: Geschichtliche Grundlagen und moderne Perspektiven,* edited by Volker Press and Dietmar Willoweit (Vaduz: Verlag der Liechtensteinischen Akademischen Gesellschaft; Munich: R. Oldenbourg, 1988), 28–29.
48 Beattie, *Liechtenstein,* 14.
49 Press, "Haus Liechtenstein," 49.
50 Oberhammer, "Viel ansehnliche Stuck und Güter," 43; Harry Schlip, "Die neuen Fürsten: zur Erhebung in den Reichsfürstenstand und zur Aufnahme in den Reichsfürstenrat im 17. und 18. Jahrhundert" in *Liechtenstein, fürstliches Haus und staatliche Ordnung,* 249–92; Schöpfer, *Klar und Fest,* 66; Hans Jürgen Jüngling, "Die Heiraten des Hauses Liechtenstein im 17. und 18. Jahrhundert. Konnubium und soziale Verflechtungen am Beispiel der habsburgischen Hocharistokratie," in *Liechtenstein, fürstliches Haus und staatliche Ordnung,* 332.
51 Press, "Haus Liechtenstein," 58; Harald Wanger, *Die regierenden Fürsten von Liechtenstein.* (Neustadt an der Aisch: Degener, 1995), 103; Rudersdorf, "Josef Wenzel von Liechtenstein (1696–1772)," in *Liechtenstein, fürstliches Haus und staatliche Ordnung,* 370–75.
52 The carriage and the prince made yet another appearance in Frankfurt in 1764, when Archduke Joseph was crowned Roman King. Wanger, *Die Regierenden Fürsten,* 105–06.
53 Rudersdorf, "Josef Wenzel von Liechtenstein," 371–75.
54 This description of the family history of the Kaunitzes draws on the following sources: Grete Klingenstein, *Der Aufstieg des Hauses Kaunitz* (Göttingen: Vandenhoeck &

Ruprecht, 1975); Franz A. J. Szabo, *Kaunitz and Enlightened Absolutism 1753–1780* (Cambridge: University Press, 1994), 7–11; Wurzbach, *Biographisches Lexikon*, 11: 59–86; Bronislav Chocholáč, "Die Wirtschaftslage der mährischen Herrschaften des Wenzel Anton Fürsten von Kaunitz-Rietberg," in *Staatskanzler Wenzel Anton von Kaunitz-Rietberg 1711–1794: neue Perspektiven zu Politik und Kultur der europäischen Aufklärung,* edited Grete Klingenstein and Franz A.J. Szabo (Graz: Andreas Schnider, 1996), 466–68.

55 Dušan Uhlíř, "Kaunitz und die böhmischen Länder" in *Staatskanzler Wenzel Anton von Kaunitz-Rietberg 1711–1794,* 488.

56 Uhlíř, "Kaunitz," 486.

57 Foreshadowing his grandson's later stance, Dominik Andreas Kaunitz had likewise favored more cordial relations with France. Szabo, *Kaunitz and Enlightened Absolutism,* 10.

58 H. M. Scott and Christopher Storrs, "Introduction: The Consolidation of Noble Power in Europe, c. 1600–1800," in *The European Nobilities in the Seventeenth and Eighteenth Centuries,* edited by H. M. Scott (New York: Longman, 1995), 1: 13.

59 See Herman Freudenberger, *The Waldstein Woolen Mill: Noble Entrepreneurship in Eighteenth-Century Bohemia* (Boston: Baker Library, Harvard Graduate School of Business Administration, 1963); Arnošt Klíma, "The Role of Rural Domestic Industry in Bohemia in the Eighteenth Century," *Economic History Review*, n.s. 27, no. 1 (February 1974), 48–56; Gustav Otruba, "Anfänge und Verbreitung der böhmischen Manufakturen bis zum Beginn des 19. Jahrhunderts (1820)," *Bohemia* 6 (1965): 230–31.

60 Hannes Stekl, *Österreichs Aristokratie im Vormärz: Herrschaftsstil und Lebensformen der Fürstenhäuser Liechtenstein und Schwarzenberg* (Munich: Oldenbourg, 1973), 29–30.

61 Christine Lebeau, *Aristocrates et grands commis à la cour de Vienne (1748–1791): le modèle français* (Paris: CNRS Éditions, 1996), 42–43.

62 LRRA, P 16/19, LK to EL, Naples, 15 November 1765.

63 This account draws upon the careful work of P. G. M. Dickson, *Finance and government under Maria Theresia, 1740–1780,* vol. 1 (New York: Oxford University Press, 1987), 78–114. Also Jerome Blum, *The End of the Old Order in Rural Europe* (Princeton, NJ: Princeton University Press, 1978), 22.

64 Eila Hassenpflug-Elzholz, *Böhmen und die böhmischen Stände in der Zeit des beginnenden Zentralismus: eine Strukturanalyse der böhmischen Adelsnation um die Mitte des 18. Jahrhunderts* (Munich: R. Oldenbourg, 1982), 335.

65 Dickson, *Finance and Government,* 1: 133.

66 Dickson, *Finance and Government,* 1: 37. Ignaz de Luca, *Topographie von Wien,* vol. 1 (facsimile reprint, Vienna: Promedia, 2003; first published Vienna: Thad. Edlen v. Schmidbauer, 1794), 21.

67 As reiterated by Dickson's summary, *Finance and Government,* 1: 113–14.

68 Dickson, *Finance and Government,* 1: 88; Wolf, *Fürstin Eleonore,* 19.

69 Folkmann, *Die gefürstete Linie,* 66–67.

70 Chocholáč, "Die Wirtschaftslage," 466–80.

71 Dickson, *Finance and Government,* 1: 92.

72 *Teplitz-Schönau,* edited by A. Worliczek (Berlin-Friedenau: Deutscher Kommunal Verlag, 1930), 25–26.

73 Rudersdorf, "Josef Wenzel von Liechtenstein," 379; HHStA, Habsburgisch-Lothringische Hausarchive, Sammelband (HA SB) 72/3, Joseph II (JII) to Lacy, Spa, 20 July 1781.

74 LRRA, P 17/27, Josepha Clary (JC) to Sidonia Kinsky (SK), included with letter of EL to LK, Kromau, 25 August 1781; NM, RAŠM, carton 93, Leopoldine Liechtenstein (LL) to brother, Stuttgart, 23 August 1781.
75 His appointment occurred in 1758. Johann Josef Khevenhüller-Metsch, *Aus der Zeit Maria Theresias: Tagebuch des Fürsten Johann Josef Khevenhüller-Metsch*, vol. 5 (Vienna: Adolf Holzhausen, 1911), 37, 28 May 1758.
76 The complex nature of many court posts has particularly interested historians in recent years. Martin Scheutz and Jakob Wührer, "Dienst, Pflicht, Ordnung und 'Gute Policey,'" in *Der Wiener Hof im Spiegel der Zeremonial-Protokolle (1652–1800): eine Annäherung,* edited by Irmgard Pangerl, Marin Scheutz, Thomas Winkelbauer (Innsbruck: Studien Verlag, 2007), 34–35; Jeroen Duindam, *Vienna and Versailles: the Courts of Europe's Dynastic Rivals, 1550–1780* (Cambridge: Cambridge University Press, 2003), 76; Leopold Joseph Fitzinger, "Versuch einer Geschichte der Menagerien des österreichisch-kaiserlichen Hofes," Session 17, March 1853, *Sitzungsberichte der Mathematisch-Naturwissenschaftlichen Classe der Kaiserlichen Akademie der Wissenschaft* 10 (1853), 300–403; Vehse, *Geschichte der deutschen Höfe*, 14: 75. Joseph II's changes are noted in T. C. W. Blanning, *Joseph II* (London: Longman, 1994), 107.
77 LRRA, P 17/24, EL to LK, Eisgrub, 1 August 1778.
78 HHStA, HA SB 16, "Relatione del Viaggio . . . 1784," 448–49; Pavel Mitrofanov, *Josef II. Seine politische und kulturelle Tätigkeit*, vol. 2 (Vienna: C. W. Stern, 1910), 613; HHStA, HA SB 7, JII to Leopold, 19 October 1765; HHStA, KA Staatsrat, NL, Lacy to MT, [late Dec. 1766,] Fasz. 3 carton 2; HHStA, HA SB 72–73, Lacy to JII (with JII's reply), Neuwaldegg, 21 July 1785, SB 72–73.
79 Henry Swinburne, *The Courts of Europe at the Close of the Last Century*, vol. 1 (first published 1841; London: H. S. Nichols, 1895), 334.
80 HHStA, HA SB 15 (held in SB 16), "Allegato di No. 3. Impiegati Principali a Vienna e nello Stato"; SB 16, "Relatione del Viaggio . . . 1784."
81 Bernardo Tanucci, *Epistolario. 1723–1768* (Rome: Edizioni di storia e letteratura, 1997), 12: 585, Tanucci to Charles III of Spain, Portici, 1 November 1763; HHStA, ZT, Band 31, 5 September 1786. LRRA, P 16/18, LK to EL, Vienna, 12 August 1763. Ernst Kaunitz received a salary of 36,000 florins as ambassador in Naples and a lump sum for expenses, but the amount was never enough for the couple. Wolf, *Fürstin Eleonore Liechtenstein*, 99; Chocholáč, "Die Wirtschaftslage," 477.
82 Christopher Duffy, *The Military Experience in the Age of Reason* (1987; Ware, Hertfordshire: Wordsworth, 1998), 53; Duffy, *The Army of Maria Theresa: the Armed Forces of Imperial Austria, 1740–1780* (New York: Hippocrene Books, 1977), 63.
83 Wurzbach, *Biographisches Lexikon*, 11: 295; Duffy, *Army of Maria Theresa*, 25–28; Duffy, *Austrian Army in the Seven Years War*, 95–96; J. Hirtenfeld, *Der Militär-Maria-Theresien-Orden und seine Mitglieder* (Vienna: Kaiserlich-Königliche Hof- und Staatsdruckerei, 1857), 201–04.
84 Rudersdorf, "Josef Wenzel von Liechtenstein," 372, 376; Duffy, *Army of Maria Theresa*, 108–09.
85 HHStA, KA Staatsrat, NL, fasc. 3 carton 2, JII to Lacy, 24 November 1770.
86 Edith Kotasek, *Feldmarschall Graf Lacy: ein Leben für Österreichs Heer* (Horn, Austria: F. Berger, 1956), 84. The reforms are described in detail in Alphons von Wrede, *Geschichte der K. und K. Wehrmacht: die Regimenter, Corps, Branchen und Anstalten von 1618 bis Ende des XIX. Jahrhunderts* (Vienna: L. W. Seidel: 1905), vol. 4, part 1, 5–9, 69–72.
87 Duffy, *Army of Maria Theresa*, 29; Wolf, *Fürstin Eleonore Liechtenstein*, 17.

88 Schöpfer, *Klar und Fest*, 91.
89 Duffy, *The Austrian Army in the Seven Years War*, vol. 1, *The Instruments of War* (Rosemont, IL: Emperor's Press, 2000), 187; LRRA, P 17/30, EL to LK, Vienna, 27 August 1784; HHStA, HA SB 8, JII to Leopold, Vienna, 13 October 1783; Familienarchiv Rosenberg in the Kärntner Landesarchiv, Klagenfurt, Austria (KLA, FAR), carton 77, fasc. 64–355a, JII to Rosenberg, Prague, 18 September 1784; HHStA, HA SB 9, JII to Leopold, Semlin, 29 July 1788.
90 Karl Gutkas, *Kaiser Joseph II.: eine Biographie* (Vienna: Paul Zsolnay, 1989), 449.
91 Duffy, *The Austrian Army in the Seven Years War*, 1: 185, 210–11; Duffy, *Military Experience*, 86.
92 LRRA, P 17/28, LK to EL, Vienna, 12 September 1782; P 16/22, EL to LK, [Gross] Meseritsch, 16 Sept. 1770; P 17/25, LK to EL, Baden, 8 October 1779.
93 Lady Mary Coke. *The Letters and Journals of Lady Mary Coke* (Bath: Kingsmead, 1889–1896), 3: 319, Vienna, 11 November 1770.
94 LRRA, P 17/24, LK to EL, Laxenburg, 9 August 1777 and 24 August 1777.
95 Haus-, Hof- und Staatsarchiv, Vienna (HHStA), Reprosammlungen [microfilm], Kammerarchiv, Karl von Zinzendorf, Tagebuch, Band 6, 11 March 1761.
96 Coke, *The Letters and Journals*, 1: 8, Lady Mary Coke to her sister the countess of Strafford, Lady Anne Campbell, Spa, 19 July 1764.
97 Vehse, *Geschichte der deutschen Höfe* (Hamburg: Hoffmann und Campe, 1852), 13: 276.
98 LRRA, P 17/24, EL to LK, Feldsberg, 5 July 1776.
99 LRRA, P 18/59, EL to LK, Kromau, 6 August 1777; EL to Josephine Harrach, s.l., s.d. [summer 1804]; Jean François Georgel, *Mémoires pour servir à l'histoire des événemens de la fin du dix-huitième siècle depuis 1760 jusqu'en 1806–1810 par un contemporain impartial (feu M. l'abbé Georgel)* (Paris: Alexis Eymery, 1817), 1: 317.
100 Vehse, *Geschichte der deutschen Höfe*, 13: 201–02; Georgel, *Mémoires*, 1: 318.
101 Bernardo Tanucci, *Epistolario. 1723–1768* (Rome: Edizioni di Storia e Letteratura, 1997), 12: 585, Tanucci to Charles III of Spain, Portici, 1 November 1763.
102 Georgel, *Mémoires*, 1: 318.
103 Coke, *The Letters and Journals*, 4: 24, Vienna, 8 February 1772.
104 Rodinný Archiv Clary-Aldringenů (Teplice), Státní Oblastní Archiv v Litoměřicích, Pobočka Děčín (SOAL-D, RACA), carton 64, Leopoldine Liechtenstein (LL) to Josepha Clary (JC), Spa, 14 July [1781].
105 Rodinný Archiv Šternberk-Manderscheid, Národní Muzeum, Prague (NM, RAŠM), carton 93, LL to her brother, Vienna, 14 March 1795.
106 HHStA, Zinzendorf, Tagebuch, Band 17, 7 May 1772.
107 N. W. Wraxall, *Memoirs of the Courts of Berlin, Dresden, Warsaw, and Vienna, in the Years 1777, 1778, and 1779*, vol. 2 (London: T. Cadell Jun. and W. Davies, 1799), 409; *Hamilton Letters: The Naples Dispatches of Sir William Hamilton*, edited by John A. Davis and Giovanni Capuano (London: I. B. Tauris: 2008), 13, Charles Greville to Hamilton, Vienna, 9 October 1769.
108 LRRA, P 17/25, LK to EL, Vienna, 19 August 1779.
109 LRRA, P 16/20, LK to EL, Naples, 29 April 1766; Scott and Storrs, Introduction, 25.
110 Reitwiesner, *Matrilineal Descents*, vol. 2, AKA 149–150.
111 Jacob von Falke, *Geschichte des fürstlichen Hauses Liechtenstein* (Vienna: W. Braumüller, 1868–1882), 2: 243–44.
112 *Briefe der Kaiserin Maria Theresia an ihre Kinder*, 1: 186, MT to Archduke Ferdinand, 24 February [1773].

113 LRRA, P 16/21, LK to EL, Naples, 18 January 1768; SOAL-D, RACA, carton 66, JC to daughter Countess Ledebur, Vienna, 13 January 1768.
114 During a pregnancy in 1777 Leopoldine Kaunitz reasoned that if she could at least reach the seventh month without mishap, "then the good Lord will take care of matters." Sadly, this pregnancy too ended soon after she penned this remark, while she was spending her semi-obligatory time with the court at Laxenburg. Most famously Maria Theresia spent years advising her daughter Marie Antoinette, wife of the French dauphin and eventual king, about facilitating and safeguarding a pregnancy. LRRA, P 17/24, Laxenburg, LK to EL, 15 August 1777; *Briefe der Kaiserin Maria Theresia an ihre Kinder*, 1: 183, MT to Archduke Ferdinand, 18 February 1773.
115 LRRA, P 17/24, LK to EL, Vienna, 25 July 1778; LK to EL, Vienna, 24 July 1778; LK to EL, Vienna, 25 July 1778.
116 SOAL-D, RACA, carton 54, JC to husband Prince Clary, Eisgrub, 26 July 1778.
117 Ivo Cerman, *Habsburgischer Adel und Aufklärung: Bildungsverhalten des Wiener Hofadels im 18. Jahrhundert* (Stuttgart: Franz Steiner, 2010).
118 Not surprisingly, given the fragile prospects for continuation of the family, Dominik Kaunitz briefly considered a second marriage after Bernardine's death in 1779, with potential partners including his niece Josephine Liechtenstein, Eleonore's daughter. In the event he remained a widow. The Moravian branch of the Kaunitz family came to an end only a few decades after Leopoldine's death when Dominik's son Alois died, leaving only daughters.
119 This son Joseph visited England with Sir Robert Keith as his escort in 1772 and called on Lady Mary. National Archives of Scotland, Edinburgh, Douglas Home Papers (NRAS, DHP), Papers of Lady May Coke, Box 197, fasc. 1, Sidonia Kinsky to Lady Mary Coke, Vienna, 21 October 1772; for the visit, Lady Mary's journal entries, 23 June through 8 July 1775.
120 SOAL-D, RACA, carton 54, authorization in document dated Vienna, 4 July 1786; legal transfer of authority, Vienna, 1 May 1787; LRRA, P 17/41, EL to Josephine Harrach, Vienna, 9 August 1786.
121 LRRA, P 17/43, EL to Josephine Harrach, Vienna, 21 June 1788; SOAL-D, RACA, carton 67, JC to daughter Countess Wilczek, 10 July 1788.
122 LRRA, P 17/28, EL to LK, 13 July 1782; EL to LK, Kromau, 9 September 1782; EL to LK, Kromau, 11 September 1782; Hassenpflug-Elzholz, *Böhmen und die böhmischen Stände*, 344–45.
123 LRRA, P 17/25, EL to LK, Kromau, 7 October 1779; P 17/26, EL to LK, Eisgrub, 2 August 1780; EL to LK, Kromau, 29 August 1780; P 17/28, EL to LK, Kromau, 12 August 1782; EL to LK, Kromau, 28 August 1782.
124 LRRA, P 17/30, EL to LK, Kromau, 19 July 1784 and 28 July 1784.
125 LRRA, P 17/29, EL to LK, Kromau, 18 August 1783. Duffy, *The Austrian Army in the Seven Years War*, 1: 176; Robert A. Kann, "Aristocracy in the Eighteenth Century Habsburg Empire," *East European Quarterly* 7, no. 1 (1973): 7; Hassenpflug-Elzholz, *Böhmen und die böhmischen Stände*, 352; Christine Lebeau, *Aristocrates et grands commis à la cour de Vienne (1748–1791): le modèle français* (Paris: CNRS Éditions, 1996), 69.
126 In this capacity Charles accompanied Leopold to the imperial coronation in Frankfurt and was sent to Paris to announce to the French court Leopold's accession. According to some contemporaries, Leopold made use of young Charles to arrange trysts with imperial paramours. In July 1791, hearing that Leopold intended to employ Charles Liechtenstein in state business (*affaires*) as well, Zinzendorf noted curtly, "what a choice." HHStA, ZT, Band 36, 13 July 1791.

127 LRRA, P 17/30, LK to EL, Vienna, 23 July 1784. The cause of the duel was identified at the time by family and associates as competition for the favors of a young Countess Czernicheff (from a Russian diplomatic family). Public opinion and later accounts, particularly the biographer Hilde Spiel, instead ascribed the tragedy to Charles's relationship with the wife of the eminent Jewish banker Nathan Arnstein, Fanny von Arnstein. HHStA, ZT, Band 40, 8 December 1795; Wolf, *Fürstin Eleonore Liechtenstein*, 202–03; Falke, *Geschichte*, 2: 251, 341–42; Hilde Spiel, *Fanny von Arnstein: a Daughter of the Enlightenment, 1758–1818*, translated by Christine Shuttleworth (New York: Berg, 1991), 136–45.

128 LRRA, P 17/29, EL to LK, Kromau, 12 August 1783.

129 Goethe mentioned him favorably in his "Italienische Reise" because it was through Wenzel Liechtenstein that Goethe was offered access to Roman aristocratic circles. Schöpfer, *Klar und Fest*, 92; Rita Krueger, *Czech, German, and Noble: Status and National Identity in Habsburg Bohemia* (New York: Oxford University Press, 2009), 50–51; LRRA, P 17/35, EL to husband Charles Liechtenstein, Vienna, 18 July 1788; Wolf, *Fürstin Eleonore Liechtenstein*, 203–04.

130 Wenzel fathered an illegitimate child in Salzburg, born in 1800. His conduct drew the unfavorable attention of Emperor Franz II. Release from the clerical profession, which required papal concurrence, came in 1804. Courageous as a soldier, Wenzel apparently also had a winning personality. Contemporaries recorded his presence at a surprising number of the seminal events of his day. LRRA, P 17/33, EL to LK, [Gross] Meseritsch, 29 June 1789, 14 July 1789, and 10 August 1789; *Europäische Stammtafeln*, edited by Detlev Schwennicke (Marburg: J.A. Stargardt, 1984), n.F. vol. 3, part 1, table 39; Falke, *Geschichte*, 2: 345–46; Wolf, *Fürstin Eleonore Liechtenstein*, 271.

131 SOAL-D, RACA, carton 65, JC to son Jean Nepomuk Clary, Weidlingau, 16 August 1794; Wolf, *Fürstin Eleonore Liechtenstein*, 243; Oskar Criste, *Feldmarschall Johannes Fürst von Liechtenstein: eine Biographie* (Vienna: Gesellschaft für Neuere Geschichte Österreichs, 1905), 17–18; Falke, *Geschichte*, 2: 350, 363; LRRA, P 18/52, EL to Josephine Harrach, Vienna, 25 October 1797.

132 LRRA, P 17/24, EL to LK, Feldsberg, 11 October 1777; P 17/26, EL to LK, Eisgrub, 23 July 1780.

133 LRRA, P 17/27, EL to LK, Vienna, 31 August 1781; P 17/27, EL to LK, Feldsberg, 19 September 1781; LK to EL, Vienna, 23 October 1781.

134 LRRA, P 17/27, LK to EL, Baden, 1 September 1781; EL to LK, Vienna, 28 August 1781; Vienna, 4 September 1781; Feldsberg, 30 September 1781.

135 Charles's early resignation of the guardianship resulted in a bonafide quarrel with Leopoldine Liechtenstein and Lacy, who took offense at the change. LRRA, P 17/27, EL to LK, Kromau, 2 August 1781; P 17/28, EL to LK, 8 [July 1782].

136 LRRA, P 17/46, EL to Josephine Harrach, Vienna, 27 August 1791.

137 Georg Schmidt, "Fürst Johann I. 'Souveränität und Modernisierung' Liechtensteins" in *Liechtenstein, fürstliches Haus und staatliche Ordnung: geschichtliche Grundlagen und moderne Perspektiven*, edited by Volker Press and Dietmar Willoweit (Vaduz: Verlag der Liechtensteinischen Akademischen Gesellschaft; Munich, Vienna: R. Oldenbourg Verlag, 1988), 387.

138 Criste, *Feldmarschall Johannes Fürst von Liechtenstein*, 26.

Chapter 2

Court and Society

The elite aristocratic class to which the five women belonged consisted of several hundred magnate families of economic weight and significant political influence within the monarchy, most of whom resided in the imperial capital of Vienna at least during the colder months of the year in order to enjoy the society of their peers and to live in proximity to the Habsburg court. The five *Dames* found themselves positioned at the very pinnacle of Viennese society. As the British envoy Sir Robert Murray Keith put it to Lady Mary Coke, a frequent visitor in the imperial capital, the women and their closest associates were "the first People in Vienna."[1] This was the environment in which the small *société* of the *Dames* flourished.

The European nobility as a social class, with the court aristocracies at its summit, has enjoyed a renewal of interest from historians in recent decades after a period of relative neglect following World War II. It can be argued that the seed for historians' recrudescent interest was planted quite early, in 1949, when Otto Brunner's *Adeliges Landleben und europäischer Geist: Leben und Werk Wolf Helmhards von Hohberg 1612–1688* looked at the complexities of the life and political and economic functioning of the nobility as a subject in its own right, instead of focusing on the growth of absolutism and central power.[2] Brunner's study of the minor nobleman and writer Wolf Helmhard von Hohberg in Lower Austria, drawing on a broad array of source materials, placed one seventeenth-century nobleman within a larger cultural and political context. Accepting implicitly the historiographical assumption that the trajectory of noble power and influence in early modern times was a simple downward slope toward the virtual extinction of local power and the triumph of monarchical absolutism, Brunner nonetheless moved beyond the simplistic portrayal of a political duel between local authority and central power to examine the actual life and the social and intellectual world of the nobility.

For several decades thereafter most historians turned their attention elsewhere, to the more numerous strata of society such as the peasants or nascent bourgeoisie or to other groups and themes that matched more closely the interests of Marxist historians or highlighted national themes more effectively than did the multiethnic, multinational European aristocracies. In their introduction to a collection of essays entitled *The European Nobilities in the Seventeenth and Eighteenth Centuries* (1995), H. M. Scott and Christopher Storrs date a rebirth of widespread interest in the nobility of Europe to the mid-1970s.[3] Initially these new efforts owed much to the groundbreaking theories of sociologist Norbert Elias, whose focus was the court nobility of absolutist France. Elias adopted the traditional storyline that posited a straightforward, unremitting weakening and "domestication" of the nobility in the evolving modern French state, but he also sought to bring sociological insights to bear on court life and the formative causes of aristocratic behavior.[4] Subsequent historians have cast doubt on the reality of this "taming" process described by Elias and in addition have focused on the remarkable resiliency of the nobility, which, contrary to the standard narrative, weathered ostensibly catastrophic changes and for some time resisted with considerable success the gradual erosion of its position. Jonathan Dewald's synoptic work entitled *The European Nobility, 1400–1800* (1996), a thoughtful synthesis of his own contributions to the historiographical debate and those offered during the early 1990s by other historians, demonstrates how judicious criticism and revision of earlier conceptions have helped to advance understanding of the nobility's place in European history.[5]

Heightened interest in the aristocracy of the Habsburg monarchy of the eighteenth century in particular can be dated from the appearance in 1975 of Grete Klingenstein's *Der Aufstieg des Hauses Kaunitz*, a careful, focused study of the family antecedents and education of Wenzel Kaunitz.[6] The tendency had long been to dismiss this group as a caste of closed-minded elitists in Vienna who, although active in the interests of their own families and class and in some cases superficially acquainted with fashionable literature of the Enlightenment emanating from France and northern Germany, were both disinclined and ill equipped to engage in a serious way with new ideas. Certainly there were strong elements of continuity from the social and intellectual world of one aristocratic generation to the next. Elite families continued to gather in the capital for traditional pleasures and entertainment. Social intercourse still provided the backdrop against which women and men watched for opportunities to promote the interests and fortunes of family and friends. Klingenstein's work, describing as it did the careful, diverse program of education that produced the progressive statesman Kaunitz, inspired the research of a new generation of historians who have uncovered evidence of both greater openness and deeper familiarity with ideas of the Enlightenment among families of the late eighteenth-century Habsburg elite. The recent work of Ivo Cerman and others concerning the intellectual life of the court aristocracy has described a cosmopolitan, literate environment in which the new currents of Enlightenment thought received serious consideration.[7] Literate, well-informed grandees were among those who congregated for the social season in Vienna. These magnates were often the individuals from whom top personnel who served as administrators and as shapers of policy were selected during both the coregency and Joseph II's sole rule, for the reforming Habsburg sovereigns required appropriately educated and socialized candidates to fill leadership positions in court and administration.

Vienna's population in 1764 was about 155,300. By 1783 it had reached more than 202,700. The concentration of people, buildings, vehicles, and commerce formed a stark contrast to conditions in the remainder of the Habsburg monarchy. The second most populous city, Prague, had a respectable 72,874 residents in 1784. All remaining towns had much smaller populations.[8] According to the English traveler Henry Swinburne, writing in 1780, the streets of Vienna, lined with high houses, were "crooked, narrow and indifferently paved, with many disagreeable smells."[9] The city, center of a vast empire, was nonetheless a lively, colorful metropolis, its innermost district boasting stately mansions of the most significant aristocratic families from both the monarchy and the Holy Roman Empire (Lobkowicz, Schwarzenberg, Windischgrätz, Dietrichstein, Esterházy, Batthyány, Daun, Khevenhüller as well as Liechtenstein, Kaunitz, Clary, and Kinsky). Its lush suburbs were dotted with summer palaces or *jardins*, as their owners called them, merging into the surrounding countryside. Only in Vienna was nighttime brightly lit, with 3,445 oil lamps burning from dusk until 1:00 a.m., placed on the streets in the late 1770s by the indefatigable reformer Joseph von Sonnenfels (1732–1817).[10]

In aristocratic Viennese society of the late eighteenth century, traditional family, class, and regional interests remained vitally important. As in earlier generations, the aristocracy that congregated in the imperial capital was multinational, multiethnic, and transnational. The monarchy's grandees still tended to cluster in approximate regional groups, however, for in social life as in political life, in many noble families regional loyalties could at times trump ties to the centralized Habsburg monarchy. Aristocrats themselves could readily distinguish ethnic differences, discerning linguistic variations even in the colloquial French patois that virtually all of them spoke socially. When Leopoldine Kaunitz's niece Thérèse Kaunitz was residing at her female foundation or *Stift* in Mons and wrote a letter to Eleonore Liechtenstein's daughter Josephine, Eleonore detected a distinctive "Flemish" turn of phrase: "It is a rather pretty letter, with that gay, light, Flemish style that our climate never produces."[11] And yet Thérèse was not a long-term resident of Mons. Even the flightiest and most insouciant groups within the Habsburg monarchy and the Holy Roman Empire were held to be more stable than members of external groups, especially the French aristocracy that visitors to Paris observed with a mixture of envy and disapproval. Friends in Vienna watched carefully as acquaintances returned from visits to Paris, to see if they had adopted affected, frenchified manners or lax moral behavior. Social circles in Vienna apparently agreed with the dictum of the Earl of Chesterfield, when he dispensed advice to his son prior to the latter's visit to German courts in 1752 after a sojourn in the French capital: "People who are lately come from Paris, and who have been a good while there, are generally suspected, and especially in Germany, of having a degree of contempt for every other place. Take great care that nothing of this kind appear, at least outwardly, in your behavior; but commend whatever deserves any degree of commendation, without comparing it with what you may have left, much better, of the same kind at Paris." Sidonia Kinsky's friends were relieved to find that she returned from a trip to Paris in the mid-1760s with laudably unaltered manners.[12] Always there was a presumption that the moral character and standards of the Habsburg monarchy's peoples were more solid, honest, and god-fearing than those of the irreligious French kingdom. Leopoldine Liechtenstein's father had cautioned Leopoldine's brother Christian to be careful about the company he kept as a young man staying in Paris in 1757; "I will not talk to you," wrote Leopoldine's father, Count Philip Sternberg, "about the seductive dangers that face young people in that land, I know that you have a great fund of religion."[13]

During the first half of her reign while her husband lived, Maria Theresia had sponsored a lively, gay court life. Josepha Clary and Sidonia Kinsky, oldest members of the group of *Dames*, had been participants. Apparently Count Emanuel Silva-Taroucca (1696–1771), early mentor of Maria Theresia, had deliberately made both his own wife and Josepha Clary available to the young Maria Theresia as acceptable companions.[14] Especially in the 1740s there had been musical and theatrical performances in which only the elite participated, sometimes joined by the archdukes and archduchesses. Rich pageantry had accompanied court-sponsored sleigh rides and carousels in the 1740s, 1750s, and early 1760s.[15] The names of the two oldest women, mentioned frequently in *Obersthofmeister* Khevenhüller's journal in early years, were joined by those of their younger cohorts by the 1760s. Maria Theresia's numerous family and congenial husband ensured that court life in Vienna in the early 1760s remained lively and attractive despite the war with Prussia, not yet concluded. The splendid celebration of the marriage of the heir to the throne, Archduke Joseph, with his beautiful bride, Isabella of Parma, in 1760 was one of Eleonore's earliest memories of her adult life in Vienna. Isabella had entered the city in a procession of nearly 100 coaches. Many years later, Eleonore described for her daughter her own excitement as she watched the splendid wedding from a gallery in the Augustinian church in Vienna: "For a pair of eyes that had seen nothing but the Visitation convent in Strasbourg, this was something quite dazzling."[16] Joseph's first wife Isabella died of smallpox in 1764. For Joseph's second marriage in January 1765 to Maria Josepha of Bavaria the rejoicing was somewhat less flamboyant.

All five *Dames* received initiation into formal and informal facets of court life through service as ladies in waiting (*Hofdame, Kammerfräule*) to Maria Theresia herself or to her mother, the widowed empress Elisabeth Christine of Brunswick-Wolfenbüttel (d. 1750). All five were likewise inducted into the honorary *Sternkreuzorden* or Order of the Star-Cross, a lineage-based female order under the patronage of the empress whose members gathered twice yearly on May 3 and September 14, generally in the Hofburg chapel. When Wenzel Liechtenstein traveled to Frankfurt in 1764 as royal commissioner for the election and coronation of Archduke Joseph as King of the Romans (a status that normally implied eventual election and elevation to the post of Holy Roman Emperor), Eleonore Liechtenstein and her husband Charles too attended in semi-official status, as honorary escorts (*Ehrencavalier* and *Ehrendame*). The young couple's function was to swell the ranks of dignitaries from the Habsburg court. Eleonore applauded Joseph's carriage and demeanor during these coronation ceremonies. She wrote to her sister Leopoldine Kaunitz, "the King was strikingly beautiful and acquitted himself with a charming grace and nobility; it seems to me that people here are very pleased with him."[17] But after attending the coronation, Eleonore was happy to escape the crowds and tumult, telling Leopoldine, "I have sworn that if I should live to see 20 more coronations I will never again attend one."[18]

Emperor Franz Stephan (formally Franz I) died in summer 1765 and Archduke Joseph succeeded him as emperor and coregent. Aging but still vigorous, Maria Theresia curtailed the more exuberant and costly court activities, with Joseph's enthusiastic concurrence. Sir Robert Murray Keith reported, "the present imperial reign has almost totally abolished those gaudy exhibitions [of earlier times], and instead of fifty days in the year in which every grandee was permitted, to give a full scope to the genius of his tailor, and clap upon his back the produce of a thousand acres, we have now but one solitary first of January, to air our finery, and kick up the dust of pageantry."[19] Most elaborate events at court now served some diplomatic purpose. The French chargé d'affaires reported that these changes were not favorably received by the interested public, which feared the inauguration of "a simplicity that is gloomy and too philosophical" to replace "the lustre appropriate for a great court," signaling the end of "charms and pleasures in the capital of a vast empire."[20] Count Franz Rosenberg was said to be a driving force behind efforts to simplify court life because he disliked encumbering clothes and rituals.[21] The venerable Spanish *Mantelkleid*, a complicated costume consisting of a heavy formal dress coat, hat, feather, harem trousers, and various additional encumbrances and appendages, was no longer worn for court festivities, for Joseph disliked its unwieldiness. Ceremonies through which membership in honorary orders were bestowed (for men the Golden Fleece was especially coveted), dear to the nobility, could not be wholly abolished, even if they were assigned lower priority in the court calendar by late eighteenth-century sovereigns. Additional service-oriented orders for men included the Maria Theresia Military Order and the Order of Saint Stephan, both founded by Maria Theresia, awarded for outstanding military leadership and political or diplomatic service to the monarch, respectively.

Although she willingly made concessions to her son that lessened the rigors of court etiquette, Maria Theresia was aware that a certain amount of imperial representation was useful and salutary. As long as the empress lived, the Habsburg court remained attractive if sedate, a magnet for the socially or politically aspiring. The empress explained her approach in advice to her daughter Marie Antoinette, the French queen, who had reported to her mother in autumn 1780 that because so many courtiers would soon be thronging Versailles, she planned to resume all the formalities of court life that had seemed unnecessary when fewer individuals were present. Maria Theresia applauded her daughter's resolve: "I am aware of all the tedium and emptiness, but believe me, when this is not done the difficulties that result are far more consequential than the little discomforts of ceremonial, especially there where you live, with a people that is so temperamental." Throughout her life, Maria Theresia cultivated cordial relationships with members of the most exalted families as well as with able if less socially prominent servitors. She was an active, loyal friend. She used social niceties quite deliberately to oil the machinery of state. Advice the empress offered in 1770, again to Marie Antoinette who was then the newly arrived French dauphine, characterizes this policy explicitly: "when one lives in such great retirement as to associate with only a few people, there will be (I must admit to my great regret, as you have seen here in recent times) many discontented, jealous, envious people, there will be vexations; but if one circulates more broadly in high society, as used to be the case here 15 or 20 years ago, then one avoids all these inconveniences." In so doing one felt better, body and soul (*pour l'âme et le corps*), she wrote, and the contentment and gaiety of one's surroundings were compensation for any extra effort. In a letter to Marie Beatrix of Modena, future wife of Archduke Ferdinand, Maria Theresia lauded simple social pleasures. She conceded that her son Ferdinand was an indifferent scholar, less diligent than Grand Duke Leopold, but predicted also that Ferdinand would be a congenial, amiable individual if Joseph's influence did not render him "philosophical," a devotee of "this so-called philosophy that consists in liking and enjoying nothing at all, neither theater, nor hunting, nor games, nor dance, nor conversation. I believe such people are to be pitied rather than imitated, for they have fewer pleasures by far."[22]

Even as age and ill health slowed her movements, Maria Theresia went to great lengths to gratify her close associates. In a letter from June 1780, again to daughter-in-law Marie Beatrix, the empress described her attitude toward a visit she planned to make to Field Marshal Lacy's suburban palace in Dornbach. The party would consist of two dozen persons. "I must admit," she wrote, "that in this heat I am afraid, but this is an event that was planned this past winter, and it is my only opportunity to oblige Lacy." She mentioned the situation to her daughter Marie Christine as well: "I am well, but weighed down by my thoughts and by the frailties of my corpulent condition—loins, legs, arms, hearing, eyesight, all of these together do not make for a pleasant assemblage of parts, and they hinder my movements constantly. The outing to Dornbach has worried me now for a full week, if I had not promised last winter I would not undertake it."[23] To all appearances Maria Theresia's interest in the great families who participated in the life of the court and the imperial capital was genuine. All five *Dames* were objects of her solicitude. The empress's attentiveness to the concerns of the families that formed the Habsburg court elite often came across as meddling. Yet she was able to hold their esteem and affection.[24] Maria Theresia felt deeply the loss through death of close friends and associates, a characteristic not noticeably prevalent among eighteenth-century royalty. In June 1772 she wrote disconsolately to Archduke Ferdinand, "In the past year and a half I have lost five friends who have left a great void and cannot be replaced at my age; these are Tarouca, Ulfeldt, Batthyany, [Wenzel] Liechtenstein, van Swieten and la Paar [Josepha Paar, born Öttingen, as noted previously, who was Maria Theresia's *Obersthofmeisterin*]."[25]

After Maria Theresia's death Joseph II, who had often expressed contempt for court formalities, further simplified the externals of court life. The traditional trappings seemed superfluous and burdensome to him, serving only to keep parasites and lazy social climbers occupied.[26] However, some forms of social gathering at court were still necessary. Even in the mid-1780s the infrequent "circle" or *appartement* could be a rather stuffy affair. For aristocratic women, this was the quintessential court event, a staged social setting that permitted the sovereign— and the sovereign's consort when present—to greet Vienna's elite (those whose lineage, ennoblement for services, or an acquired character such as officer status made them *appartementsfähig*) and perhaps to sit for a few games of cards with favored individuals. For her sister Eleonore's amusement, Leopoldine Kaunitz compared these circles or assemblages at court with large-scale imperial hunts after attending a gathering held by Joseph II for his brother Archduke Maximilian, archbishop-elector of Cologne, who visited Vienna in October 1785. "One might say that there are no two things more unlike than a circle and a hunt for game birds," Leopoldine wrote, "and yet I find many similarities; lots of people gather without really knowing why, one stands around for a long time and feels bored, one makes very disagreeable noises with voice and mouth without any purpose other than to make oneself heard; finally 2 or 3 birds make an appearance, they rush about hither and thither, everybody turns towards them, and usually one misses them for they are very difficult to catch."[27] Many Habsburg practices were adapted from the court at Versailles or, at greater remove, were channeled by way of the former Habsburg rulers of Spain. The publicity generated by Joseph II's changes has perhaps masked the strength of tradition and has led to exaggerations in historical treatments of Josephinian court life. As Jeroen Duindam has noted in his close study of ceremony at both the Habsburg and Bourbon courts, in actual practice continuities with the coregency were striking throughout most of Joseph's reign, particularly when the activities of other Habsburg family members are included in the picture.[28] As will be seen, Joseph preferred to project an air of informality and unconventionality in his social activities, visiting the gatherings of the aristocracy in a casual way that was a novel and interesting phenomenon for Viennese society. But Habsburg rulers had traditionally retained a greater degree of privacy in their personal lives than did the Bourbons. The court under Joseph II in the 1780s was not the attractive destination that it had been under Maria Theresia. She had possessed a winning personality that her son could not match; and this circumstance made the neglect of programmatic court activity a more serious omission for this introvert monarch than it would have been for a more convivial ruler. Still, although the old forms and pageantry of court life were little to the emperor's taste, he too used them skillfully and deliberately as tools of policy, to gratify foreign or domestic dignitaries.[29]

Throughout the 1760s, 1770s, and 1780s the five *Dames* participated actively in court events. Their husbands joined imperial hunts. As couples they attended court dinners, theatrical or musical offerings, and balls, as well as religious services and the obligatory *appartements*. At events sponsored by the court those aristocrats in attendance expected rank and favor to influence their reception; and if an individual or a family feared that it could be worsted in a competitive skirmish over status or recognition, its members might even prefer to absent themselves from an event entirely, so important was this symbolism.[30] Very often the *Dames* spoke of attending these events as a duty associated with social and family position. Compliance was owed both to family and to the monarchy. Infrequent but still regular visits to other Habsburg family members were also considered compulsory by the women. Interaction with the sovereign and other Habsburgs typically lacked the easy give and take of friendships with peers.

At lower levels of the nobility, simple ennoblement by the sovereign might be a straightforward reward for service or, indeed, it might accompany appointment to office, enabling a talented non-noble incumbent to function more effectively in a bureaucracy largely led by other noblemen.[31] Elite families and individuals could and did initiate requests for honors and elevations in rank, but their behavior had to be tactful, since too much eagerness was felt to be uncouth.

When wealthy Count Carl Joseph Palm reputedly paid 500,000 florins to induce Joseph II to grant him the rank of prince, tongues wagged. Writing to her sister, Eleonore Liechtenstein called the event "so ludicrous."[32] A popular story, retailed by Eleonore to her daughter, described the reaction of Chancellor Kaunitz to news of this elevation; Kaunitz had turned his head away and called for a glass of water.[33] Archduchess Marie Christine spoke disdainfully of the new prince in a letter to Josepha Clary. Palm had acquired an empty title, Marie Christine believed, for no one would forget who he really was and had always been.[34] At precisely this time Prince Esterházy too had arranged an elevation in rank for his family, newly linked with the Liechtensteins through the planned marriage of Leopoldine Liechtenstein's daughter Marie with the prince's grandson. Now all family members would be titled princes or princesses, not just the family's chief. Eleonore was sorry that Prince Esterházy's promotion in rank was paired with Palm's, "for he is in poor company." The interested public was aware that Prince Esterházy himself had paid several thousand ducats for the imperial boon, but this more predictable elevation was greeted with less indignation. Leopoldine Liechtenstein and her daughter Marie professed indifference to the change.[35]

When Josepha Clary's husband sought elevation to princely rank in 1767, Josepha feared that society would believe she and her husband were eager for the title. It was true, she noted with obvious satisfaction, that the change in status would be useful in future to her son (twelve years old at the time), but she herself certainly did not care how she was seated at formal dinners.[36] Joseph's sarcastic remarks as he considered the request of Josepha's husband suggest that her concern was well placed. Clary's application had spurred others to emulate his action. "Count Paar also desires this dignity," Joseph wrote to his brother Leopold, "and comparing his meritorious postal services [Johann Wenzel Paar held the post of *Oberster Reichs-Hof- und Generalpostmeister*] with those of Count Clary's hunts, and the illustriousness of each family, I find as much justification for one as for the other." Joseph went on to mock the services performed by the two courtiers. "Paar has watched over the precious lives of emperors, empresses, wives, archdukes during their many voyages. Clary on the other hand has preserved these same individuals from the murderous jaws of wild boars, and the deer from felled timber. Paar swears at the postilions and Clary at his huntsmen. Paar wears out the horses of the poor peasants [through obligatory relays]. Clary causes their fields to be grazed out and their vineyards to be ravaged." Joseph professed himself to be perplexed by the choice. "In other words *par nobile fratrum*, I do not know if Paar's merits in having done a great deal too little outweigh Clary's in doing too much, and if one or the other or both should be decorated with this grand title, which in attaching tassles to horses' harnesses makes it necessary for persons who dislike each other to call each other your lordship [*Euer Liebden*] and entitles wives to pass through doorways a few seconds sooner."[37]

Not all families wanted promotions in rank. Some were too proud of their ancient lineage and essentially too conservative to petition for elevation. For many others it was sufficient to maintain status and perpetuate the family line. The latter could be challenging tasks in themselves given changing circumstances and fashions.

Quite apart from formal functions sponsored by or for the sovereigns, aristocratic social life in the capital had a character of its own. Residences of great families in Vienna, often neither convenient nor comfortable for their inmates, made wonderful items of representation. Social intercourse was the setting for serious contests over status, always precarious for both individuals and families. Continual vigilance was needed. Families watched for opportunities and guarded members against insults, denigrations, and loss of prestige. Leopoldine Kaunitz expressed well in 1779 the restlessness of aspiring members of elite society. She wondered if life in the capital could ever be tranquil: "in theory it seems feasible to me and yet in practice it proves to be impossible because we do not have the courage to free ourselves from the many annoyances and constraints that are so wrongly called duties, because we cling to this existence more than we realize, unable to countenance being forgotten or pushed aside or left in ignorance of what is happening."[38] Returning to Vienna after visiting Eleonore Liechtenstein in the countryside in September 1778, Leopoldine Kaunitz found the bustling atmosphere overwhelming. She was perpetually rushing and yet accomplishing nothing, she complained, having insufficient time to do anything except to become annoyed. She urged her sister to prolong her rural retreat. "Oh, do not come here, dear sister," she wrote to Eleonore, "despite the pleasure I would have in seeing you again, it is too unhealthy; remain as long as you can in the countryside."[39] But Leopoldine Kaunitz clearly relished this active life, as did her friends.

Social life took its most basic form in the more or less stable groups of individuals who came together for dinner in the early to mid-afternoon. The English ambassador Keith left an amusing record of large dinner parties he sponsored in the carnival season (*Fasching*): "During the late carnival, I had the honour to feed, fatten, and stuff at my table, at least three hundred of the first lords and ladies of the Holy Empire. I went to work ably, for I laid the groundwork of their surfeits with beef, pudding, and potatoes, for the honour of Old England, building thereupon with all the ragouts, pies, and sauces of France; and finishing the superstructure with the jellies, ices, spices, and devildums of Italy. This succeeded to a wonder. Every guest smacked his lips and unbuttoned his waistcoat at the second course; and several ladies had their stay-laces cut open, in honor of my confections; so that in the space of six weeks I had the satisfaction to see that no less than three jaundices, five dropsies, and thirteen apoplexies amongst those great personages, were fairly and honestly laid to my door, and that of my kitchen. I need not add, that with so much well-earned glory on my side, I am not mean-spirited enough to grudge the melting of my last guinea." Husbands and wives often appeared at dinners as couples, but their choice of postprandial activity depended on individual preference. Attendance at a play or opera might follow in the early evening, and finally a visit to one of the semipermanent private "assemblies," typically at Chancellor Kaunitz's residence or that of Prince Colloredo, the imperial vice chancellor. Another English observer described these gatherings as follows: "Every night in the week there is an assembly somewhere. They begin about nine o'clock after the play, and people converse or walk about till eleven. Then comes supper, which is generally very splendid; indeed the great nobility live here in a style of magnificence, of which in England we have no idea."[40] An alternative destination could be one of the small informal evening gatherings or soirées held by prior arrangement at private residences. The small group might enjoy a late, light supper before adjourning and returning home perhaps around midnight.

Through their social contacts, the five women could meet all persons who were socially prominent as either residents of Vienna, including ambassadors, or as travelers passing through. Vienna's elite aristocracy hosted a variety of gatherings at which a lively exchange of news and views occurred, although these were not the fullblown "salons" of the classic French variety where individuals of many classes mixed indiscriminately as a matter of course. These gatherings attracted members of the most exclusive aristocratic society and often the "seconde noblesse" as well, or at least the fringes of these groups.[41] The older view of Viennese aristocratic life, which assumed that such gatherings lacked substantive intellectual content, has been significantly altered by Cerman's work, as noted previously, which confirms the functioning of highly literate groups of aristocrats.[42] By the 1780s young aristocrats were increasingly drawn to the more relaxed atmosphere and the greater variety of guests at gatherings of the lesser nobility, more attractive than the staid soirées of their elite elders.[43] At popular gatherings such as that of Fanny Arnstein, wife of the banker Nathan Adam Arnstein, one could meet artists and writers and Jewish or formerly Jewish members of the wealthy bourgeoisie. Eleonore deplored her two oldest sons' frequent visits to Fanny's residence in the 1780s. Additional broadly based and self-aware groups with progressive intellectual and artistic interests would soon appear in Vienna, including most obviously the gatherings of Caroline Greiner but also other hostesses.[44] While the younger generation was open to newly emerging elites, the generation of the *Dames* was slower to accept new groups. More palatable to the *Dames* was the interesting colony of outspoken Englishmen and women who visited or resided in Vienna. According to Leopoldine Kaunitz, as early as 1763 there were "a number of Englishmen, people with lively minds but who all speak French wretchedly."[45] Zinzendorf, in his journal, frequently mentioned the "flood of Englishmen" or a "host of Englishmen." Visiting Vienna in autumn 1769 Englishman Charles Greville found that his acquaintance with the Kaunitzes and the Liechtensteins opened doors to him virtually everywhere.[46]

At most gatherings, large and small, games of chance were popular as well as conversation; gambling was certainly not confined to military circles. Although the *Dames* did not play cards or gamble during their soirées with Joseph II, on other occasions they joined the games, as confirmed by Zinzendorf's diary, Lady Mary Coke's remarks, and the letters of the women themselves.[47] A study of the role of games of chance in eighteenth-century society by Thomas Kavanagh has noted its "ethos of bravura and conspicuously embraced risk" by means of which aristocrats could feign indifference to fate and fortune. Sir Keith reported to his sister in March 1773 that card playing was so widespread that when he made it clear in company that he was no gamester he was left largely to his own devices. Visiting Spa in summer 1781, Leopoldine Liechtenstein spoke almost with awe of the extravagant games of chance she observed: "one can scarcely speak of it without shuddering, seeing the tenacity and passion with which people lose immense sums. Reflecting on this, and also taking into consideration the indiscriminate company found here, can serve as an effective antidote for me, but this is not equally the case for many people." She noted that "the ruin of a young man can be a matter of a single day here."[48] The English visitor Nathaniel Wraxall observed an additional diversion. "Ladies who do not sit down to cards," he wrote, "frequently have on their lap a little box of old Lac, and employ themselves in untwisting gold thread, which by no means prevents conversation, as it only occupies the fingers." This was the fashionable pastime of "picking gold" or parfilage, which involved loosing the gold and silver threads from epaulettes, tassels, and other decorative trim on fancy clothing. The practice most likely came from the court in Versailles and fashionable Parisian circles. Lady Mary Coke reported that Josepha Clary had introduced this activity to her, it being "the fashionable imployment [sic] of the Ladys here when they are in Company." In 1777 Eleonore Liechtenstein recorded a visit to Baden with her husband Charles, during which, in an apparent reversal of roles, she read aloud and he picked gold ("I read [Tasso] and he picked gold [*parfilait*]").[49]

Balls also were standard evening social fare, particularly numerous during the carnival season. They could be long-winded affairs, lasting until 5 o'clock the following morning or later; Josepha Clary attended a ball hosted by Baron Fries in October 1777 that lasted until eight in the morning. As the *Dames* aged, they attended these events in the capacity of chaperone to marriageable daughters or simply as benevolent observers.[50] In 1779 Eleonore reported to Leopoldine Liechtenstein that, with her daughter Josephine nearly grown, she herself had joined the ranks of chaperones. Together with Josepha Clary, who had served as chaperone to her many daughters ("this disagreeable occupation") for fully eighteen years, Eleonore remained at the event until 4 o'clock in the morning. The same year Leopoldine Kaunitz lightheartedly described herself, dressed for a ball, as "a gothic figure set out to frighten the birds."[51]

The caustic remarks of Wraxall, visiting Vienna in the late 1770s, have been cited by generations of historians: "The Austrian ladies are by no means deficient in external accomplishments, mental and personal: they are in general elegant, graceful, and pleasing; but rarely do they possess a cultivated mind. The principal reading of a woman of quality, is such as tends to pervert and contract, rather than to enlarge and improve her understanding. Holy legends, lives of female saints and devotees, masses, and homilies, constitute her chief information. She knows little of Madame of Sevignè [sic], and less of Racine, Moliere, or Fontenelle. If she has perused the works of Cervantes and of LeSage, she has done much. With Saint Theresa and Saint Catharine of Sienne, she is familiar."[52] The entertainment value of Wraxall's remarks for his late eighteenth-century English readers was no doubt great, but the description is caricature rather than disinterested observation. Even the most cursory scrutiny of the correspondence of the *Dames* reveals a lively interest in both older and newer works of quality literature, secular as well as religious, and a healthy appetite for current, more ephemeral products of the press, the stage, and the evolving arts and sciences of the day. The women looked explicitly to the epistolary style of Madame de Sévigné as an ideal worthy of emulation.[53]

The women's adult years coincided with an upsurge in book and periodical production throughout the lands of the Holy Roman Empire, beginning in the 1760s. The multinational aristocratic public could obtain virtually any title from travel, from friends, or from agents who worked in foreign capitals, and gained increased familiarity with current literature through discussions at the informal gatherings that were so vital a part of Viennese social life. For the aristocracy, Maria Theresia's system of censorship was decidedly porous even before Joseph II liberalized regulation of both foreign and domestic publications (measures discussed in chapter 5). During the last years of her reign the empress, apparently spurred to act by conservative advisors and churchmen, did make an effort to tighten controls particularly over publications that explicitly discussed church law and doctrine.[54] But throughout the period the market for literature of all kinds was sufficiently robust that a publisher such as Joseph Thomas Trattner (1717–1798), who produced reprints (often unauthorized) of foreign works, could make a fortune in Vienna.[55] The women's letters demonstrate familiarity with popular works of the Enlightenment, including the principal *philosophes*. They appear to have deliberately avoided only those publications considered by contemporaries or confessors to be too strongly anticlerical or irreligious, a stance that may have been widespread among the Habsburg aristocracy. On many occasions the women (especially Eleonore Liechtenstein) let fall disparaging remarks about "philosophers" and "encyclopedists" in general, rather in the manner practiced by Maria Theresia. The women did not consciously seek to incorporate elements of a new Enlightenment ethos into their world view, as was apparently the case for some contemporaries.[56] Sons and daughters of the women certainly gave evidence of broad literacy and sophistication. In 1779, Leopoldine Liechtenstein's oldest son Louis, visiting his aunt Eleonore Liechtenstein at Mährisch Kromau (Moravský Krumlov), was enamored of the poetry of Albrecht von Haller (1708–1777). He could recite poems by heart and he spoke of many other authors he had read, some of whom Eleonore Liechtenstein felt were less worthy than Haller. Eleonore Liechtenstein ascribed to him a certain intellectual arrogance, a lack of firm principles and judgment. "I find in him," she wrote to Leopoldine Kaunitz, "great similarities with the Emperor in many matters." Eleonore Liechtenstein explicitly disclaimed any desire to have an aristocratic author among her sons; such activity, she felt, would be déclassé. Despite such dismissive remarks, the easy familiarity of all the women with the current works of both French and, to a somewhat lesser extent, German writers can be documented in their letters. Their facility with the French language greatly exceeded their knowledge of German. Both Eleonore and Leopoldine Kaunitz occasionally expressed frustration with their own inability to function well in German.[57]

A favorite diversion for all classes of Viennese society was attendance at theaters, where operas and plays provided edification, social and political commentary (usually oblique), and simply an opportunity for the populace to congregate. Theater attendance was a routine part of the *Dames'* lives when they resided in Vienna. Enthusiastic and opinionated, interested in both the substance of plays and artistic and personal aspects of theatrical life, the women critiqued performances in their correspondence, peppering their letters with theatrical allusions.[58] Theater was a potent form of mass media in late eighteenth-century Vienna, possibly eclipsed only by religious events of the church. Maria Theresia had famously remarked in 1759 to her theater director Count Giacomo Durazzo that theater was essential for the Viennese ("Spectacles müssen seyn"). According to Johann Pezzl, prolific author and publicist during Joseph II's reign, when a new play or opera was to be given, crowds of theatergoers created traffic jams, producing a cacophony that called to mind a hellish concert. Pedestrians were at risk on the Michaelerplatz because of the carriages, crossing from all directions, and one needed both a degree of hardihood and a nose that was not too sensitive to withstand the great crush of people and vehicles.[59]

After Emperor Franz Stephan died, Maria Theresia handed over to her new coregent Joseph the primary responsibility for the two court-sponsored Viennese theaters, the "Hofburg" theater or Burgtheater and the Kärntnerthor theater.[60] Throughout the coregency and also his decade of solo rule the emperor devoted much time and energy to theatrical affairs, adopting as his own goal the publicist Sonnenfels's promotion of German-language drama, particularly productions that were on an elevated moral level and could both entertain and edify. French productions were preferred by the aristocratic public as a group. Sidonia Kinsky and Leopoldine Liechtenstein were among those who lobbied for its continued support and promotion. According to Eleonore Liechtenstein, as early as 1768 the fate of French productions was the talk of the town. She found the excessive concern of some individuals—Leopoldine Liechtenstein, for one—to be ridiculous. Although as he grew older Chancellor Kaunitz seldom attended performances, he was distressed especially when Joseph II virtually assured the failure of French theater productions by prohibiting the lucrative theater casino that had financed them. But the emperor was earnest and persistent.[61] When Joseph was away from Vienna in May 1775, Marshal Lacy suggested to Maria Theresia that a French troupe of performers could be engaged to provide entertainment during the upcoming visit of Archduke Ferdinand and his wife. Maria Theresia replied that she dared not undertake such a move given the emperor's sensitivity on the subject.[62] In 1776 the emperor formally inaugurated his project to transform the Burgtheater into a "German national theater" for both plays and operas. He remained actively involved in the selection of repertoire, actors, and musicians thereafter and even to a remarkable extent in the editing and staging of performances. At times Joseph proved to be neither liberal nor tolerant with regard to the content of productions, particularly comedies, and he disliked portrayal of unseemly or suggestive situations. The emperor delegated some responsibility for active management of theatrical and musical performances to Count Rosenberg, who apparently shared Joseph's goal of elevating the moral tone of the stage.[63] Like her father-in-law and other aristocratic theater patrons, Leopoldine Kaunitz was skeptical of the efforts of the German writers, translators, and performers promoted by the court. She and the chancellor both judged a 1779 German performance of the opera *Zémire et Azor* to be unsatisfactory: "the Germans do not know how to do these things, there is slowness, dragging . . . I keep wishing to be backstage with a whip, to make everyone move faster."[64] It proved impossible to adhere to a purely German bill of fare, and for the regalement of important foreign guests at court both Italian and French productions were in fact staged. The emperor's additional decision to allow theaters to function in a variety of Viennese venues enlivened the theater scene in Vienna.[65] At the Leopoldstadt theater lighter productions were presented, often in the Viennese dialect of German. Leopoldine Kaunitz's description of her own experience at a performance featuring the folk character Casperl typified the ambivalence of educated Viennese; this was a type of entertainment "that I do not like at all," she wrote to Eleonore, "but still I had to laugh."[66] The *Dames* kept well abreast of theatrical news through their excellent contacts—Rosenberg, Chancellor Kaunitz, and the emperor, who found time to concern himself with theatrical affairs in Vienna even during his many trips and during military campaigns.[67]

In a journal recording his visit to Vienna with the French ambassador Prince Rohan in 1773–1774, Zorn von Bulach noted that attendance at the theater was a thoroughly social occasion in the capital. Through the windows in the *loges* one could espy one's neighbors and their activities. Joseph II and the theater-going public spent much of their time at the theater in conversation with friends and colleagues. The emperor himself would circulate to the various boxes, greeting his particular friends. Khevenhüller (Rosenberg's predecessor as theater manager) had observed with some asperity in 1772 that theater performances were becoming the chief source of entertainment for the upper class; "now they choose to do nothing but spend the evening hours until 9 or 10 at night in the houses of comedy." Even the emperor, Khevenhüller noted in his journal, appeared to pay little attention to the performances themselves. "Although the young master scarcely heeds the shows," Khevenhüller remarked, "they are useful to him since they give him an evening's entertainment and enable him to move around, visiting and gossiping with his lady friends in the *logen*."[68]

Amateur theatrical performances were staged in residences by groups of interested aristocrats, including the sons and daughters of Josepha Clary and Leopoldine Liechtenstein. Such performances were not open to the general public, and in this respect they bore little resemblance to professional playacting, which would have been déclassé in every respect. The marriage of Josepha Clary's son with the daughter of the Prince de Ligne, a passionate and gifted amateur, virtually guaranteed that Josepha's family would be active in dilettante dramatic productions, both in Vienna and at the Clary estate in Teplitz. Josepha permitted her children and their friends to stage performances in the family palace even during one of Prince Clary's serious illnesses, scandalizing her friends. While Eleonore Liechtenstein was in the country in summer 1780, Leopoldine Kaunitz accompanied Eleonore's daughter Josephine to such a performance in the Clary residence, persuading Sidonia Kinsky to attend as well. Leopoldine Kaunitz took seriously her role as chaperone at this event, assuring Eleonore that she had never left young Josephine's side. "I remained as close to her as to my own shadow," she told Eleonore, "and without being obvious about it, during the comedy I placed myself quite near to her, like a good *maman*." The hall had been hot and crowded, full of foreign dignitaries and assorted women, but the performance had been entertaining, starting after 8 o'clock and not finishing until 11 o'clock.[69] After Leopoldine Liechtenstein's son Louis married, he, his wife, and Leopoldine's daughter Marie sponsored and participated in many amateur theatrical performances. Leopoldine Liechtenstein disapproved of the involvement of her daughter and daughter-in-law in these productions that could bring them into contact with such a varied group of people.[70]

In addition to books and the theater, fashionable theories of popular science and pseudoscience were a topic of conversation in the monarchy's elite drawing rooms. A colorful assortment of scientific fashions flourished in Vienna as in Paris, attracting the attention of the *Dames* and their associates and typifying the eclectic curiosity of eighteenth-century minds. In summer 1783 a remarkable haze or mist spread over much of Europe, produced by eruptions of the Laki volcano in southern Iceland beginning 8 June. Eleonore Liechtenstein's son-in-law, residing with her and her daughter in Kromau, told Eleonore about speculation that this dry fog portended the approach of a comet in collision course with earth and thus the end of the world. Certainly, Eleonore noted, both the sun and the moon had taken on the color of blood. When to these symptoms one added other disruptions—"upheavals of the earth, of peoples, governments, religion"—such an outcome seemed possible.[71] The study of magnets and electricity attracted much attention, as did phrenology. The *Dames* pondered the ideas of Lavater and Mesmer but remained skeptical. Eleonore was particularly disdainful of the pseudoscientific activities of secret societies such as the Rosicrucians and Illuminatists, believing that they spread superstition and could be pernicious, endangering genuine religious faith.[72]

In contrast to the brisk tempo of life for residents in Vienna and the social rivalries of the winter "season," the warmer months brought a more leisurely pace to aristocratic life. During some portion of the late spring, summer, or early fall, members of most well-to-do families fled the capital for the fresher air of suburban residences or the rural pursuits of country estates in Bohemia, Moravia, Hungary, or other parts of the monarchy. Prominent, ambitious families were naturally disinclined to spend the cold months in the country; as Leopoldine Kaunitz remarked to Eleonore, when Eleonore traveled to Gross Meseritsch (Velké Meziříčí) in October 1765, nothing could be so melancholy as the countryside in winter.[73] But during the warm months, the palaces of central Vienna emptied. The husbands of all *Dames* except Leopoldine Kaunitz controlled substantial family properties. For these four women, summering on country estates, completely removed from Vienna, was an option. Regardless of individual circumstances, all of the *Dames* habitually followed this practice at least to some extent and either moved to the countryside for the summer and early fall or traveled away from central Vienna to the suburbs to visit Baden bei Wien or the country homes of relatives or friends. Year in and year out, this migratory pattern leant a characteristic rhythm to the activities of the women, including the meetings of their small *société*.

During Maria Theresia's reign the imperial family led the exodus from the Hofburg in central Vienna to Schönbrunn, located between the suburban villages of Meidling and Hietzing, where new imperial apartments were available from the mid-1760s (much of the enlarged palace had been completed as early as 1748).[74] When the weather was not unreasonably cold, Maria Theresia strongly preferred Schönbrunn, transferring both her work and her recreation there. At a further remove, and more exclusive in its admission of guests, was the imperial summer retreat at Laxenburg, to which a select group of families received invitations somewhat on the pattern of Louis XIV's famous court excursions to Marly.

Laxenburg, with its extensive park and buildings, had been a possession of the Habsburgs for many centuries. Maria Theresia adapted an additional building to accommodate her large family, so that both an "old" and a "new" palace (also called "der blaue Hof") were in use. After Franz Stephan's death in 1765, Laxenburg received few additional embellishments, and during his mother's lifetime the emperor expressed little interest in the locale.[75] As sole ruler Joseph made changes to the grounds, although apparently not, as some historians have suggested, in order to create a fashionable English-style garden like that of his friend Marshal Lacy in Dornbach (described below) to replace the formal French gardens constructed by his mother.[76] The emperor stayed at Laxenburg for portions of the summer and invited select court nobility, including the *Dames*, to visit for several weeks at a time as had Maria Theresia. With Rosenberg's help, the emperor established a new, more relaxed code of behavior and dress for Laxenburg. However, sojourns at Laxenburg could never be really relaxing for guests; they remained court events. In June 1786, completing her yearly sojourn, Eleonore remarked to her daughter that even after 23 years, she still found the visit nerve-wracking and peculiarly distasteful.[77] The emperor disliked the grandeur of Schönbrunn, although after Maria Theresia's death he occasionally used the facility for festivals. Instead, Joseph had a relatively modest house built for himself in the Augarten in Vienna as a suburban retreat. Nicknamed "Kaiserstöckl" or "Josephsstöckl," this became one of his favorite residences beginning in 1780.[78]

Like the heads of many aristocratic families, Chancellor Kaunitz owned an imposing suburban palace in Mariahilf near Schönbrunn. Ernst Kaunitz and his wife Leopoldine knew they would eventually inherit property from the chancellor but in the 1780s they acquired their own *jardin* as well, a purchase that seriously strained their finances. The Liechtenstein *Majorat* under the control of Leopoldine Liechtenstein's husband had a magnificent suburban palace in Rossau, north of Vienna's central district. Beginning in the late 1770s Sidonia Kinsky owned her own villa, the so-called "Huldenberg Landhaus" in Weidlingau, then a village west of Vienna but not far from Schönbrunn. An attractive structure designed for the Huldenberg family by Fischer von Erlach, the house had been the scene of significant events, such as Maria Theresia's greeting of Joseph II's second wife, Josepha of Bavaria, upon her arrival in 1765 (the bride was subsequently transported to nearby Schönbrunn). In 1770 Marie Antoinette had stayed here briefly before setting off on her journey to France to be the wife of the French dauphin, later Louis XVI.[79] Prince Kinsky's complaisance and financial support, which enabled his wife Sidonia to make the purchase and improve the grounds, earned high accolades from Sidonia's friends, for this property delighted the princess. Josepha Clary sent a message to Prince Kinsky via her own husband Prince Clary in which she waxed lyrical about Sidonia's happiness at Weidlingau: "it is the prettiest pathway I know to reach heaven, for in this way she has it both in this world and also in the next. She leads a life that is most Christian, innocent, and kind. She makes all those around her happy. The servants, her neighbors, her workers are all touched by her benevolent heart. Joy and serenity are reflected in every face. It is like the golden age . . . it must be admitted that we are very fortunate in our husbands."[80] Leopoldine Kaunitz wrote to Eleonore Liechtenstein that even kings could not be more generous than Sidonia's husband. According to Leopoldine Kaunitz, Prince Kinsky had allotted 3000 florins to his wife for expenses associated with Weidlingau, so that she would not have to draw upon her own capital. Visiting in September 1778, Leopoldine Kaunitz reported that Sidonia was as content as a queen, scarcely perturbed at all by the Bavarian "Potato War" that was then unfolding, pitting the monarchy against Frederick II and his allies (described in chapter 6).[81] Sidonia beautified the palace grounds, having completed by 1792 what Eleonore called a "small exotic grove."[82] For a number of years Sidonia also had at her disposal an apartment in the Belvedere palace.[83]

One of the women's favorite destinations during pleasant weather was the suburban property of Field Marshal Lacy at Dornbach, west of Vienna near the Wienerwald. Lacy lived at his residence in the central district only during the coldest months, moving both his household and his work to his "small country house" as early in the season as feasible.[84] Lacy continually embellished the modest baroque palace and the surrounding meadows and woods. His gardens gained some renown and attracted eminent domestic and foreign visitors. The natural-looking English style of garden was still comparatively rare in Vienna, quite different from formal French gardens that remained popular.[85] At Dornbach trees and paths were deliberately arranged in attractive ways, but there was no definite central focus or geometric design. Even Lacy's palace, though sumptuously appointed inside, did not occupy a prominent location in his garden. Outbuildings included a Chinese pagoda or pleasure house, a temple dedicated to the goddess Diana, and an entire "hamlet" or artificial village with at least seventeen (some visitors reported a higher number) exquisite little huts, each containing sofas, a table, a fireplace, and pleasant yet simple adornments. Here the field marshal entertained guests who came to see his creation. The park contained artificial ruins, statues, a pheasant garden, waterfalls, an orange grove and other fruit trees, a greenhouse, and ponds. One circular-shaped cluster of trees, accompanied by stone formations, was christened "tombeau de J. J. Rousseau," deliberately reminiscent of the grave site constructed by architect Hubert Robert. At its edge the park merged into the Wienerwald (to which much of it has returned today). Undoubtedly Lacy's visits to Spa, international gathering place of the aristocracy, in 1769, 1771, and 1774, had given him additional ideas.[86]

Lacy's was the second largest English garden in the monarchy, topped only by the Harrach family's garden in Bruck an der Leitha, property that was inherited by Eleonore Liechtenstein's son-in-law Johann Harrach as *Majoratsherr*.

One contemporary visitor described the wonderful surroundings at Dornbach as full of gently meandering paths and delightfully varied, irregularly shaped clearings, all surrounded by a profusion of trees and bushes. The natural array, it was reported, astonished and intoxicated the visitor.[87] Another observer, Joseph von Kurzböck, wrote in 1779 in his *Neueste Beschreibung aller Merkwürdigkeiten Wiens* that Lacy's palace, while not luxurious, was tastefully furnished and reflected the "philosophical" spirit of the proprietor. Kurzböck praised the skillful treatment of the landscape that allowed nature, unspoiled or enhanced with only the lightest touch, to speak directly to the observer. He noted with delight the shady paths, bright waterfalls, murmuring brooks, grottoes, and pavilions, as well as the adjacent territory that was suitable for hunting. The well-known Prussian writer Friedrich Nicolai, who visited Dornbach in 1781, declared himself at a loss for words to describe Lacy's exquisite property.[88]

In summer as in winter, the Liechtenstein *Majorat* invariably boasted the most impressive residences and accommodations for family members. This was true of the family's rural as well as urban and suburban properties. Among the Liechtenstein possessions was an estate complex along the border between Lower Austria and Moravia, conveniently situated roughly 50 miles from Vienna. Two particularly fine palaces were available, Feldsberg (Lednice) and Eisgrub (Valtice). Leopoldine Liechtenstein moved easily between Vienna and these country palaces at short notice, for specific engagements.[89] Often gatherings were organized around hunting, which attracted aristocratic males to the countryside. The landscape between the two Liechtenstein palaces included preserves and several large ponds that drew rich game for hunting parties. Leopoldine Liechtenstein acted as a sort of stage manager for the large assemblage of guests who came to Liechtenstein hunts, relishing her role and playing it well. Many men and not a few women were passionate hunters, although not all were proficient. Other men like Chancellor Kaunitz had little interest in the pursuit, which could resemble an organized slaughter. Concerning aristocratic hunting parties Wraxall reported, "I dare not relate what I have heard of the quantities of game, large and small, killed, or rather slaughtered in some of the shooting parties. Many hundred head of deer, hares, boar, and all kinds of wild fowl, are massacred by these relentless sportsmen; who estimate the diversion only by the multitudes which they destroy, and by the facility of the chace, if chace indeed it can properly be termed."[90] Sir R. M. Keith also disliked the preoccupation with hunting. In October 1773 he wrote to his friend Bradshaw describing an event he had witnessed at Austerlitz, "I hope you don't love hunting, and shooting, and coursing, and sniping, and toiling in mud and mire, for the honour of being the cook's purveyor. No; you are too much a man of sense and delicacy; and I am sure of your approbation when I confess that all the monsters of the forest were slaughtered by these dignified Nimrods, whilst I fetched a walk with fair ladies in the precincts of the shady grove, or, at most, was pleased to approve the labours of the chase from the windows of a gilded landau, in which a dame of quality sat by my side, and two angelic damsels vis-à-vis . . ."[91] Hunting was certainly not universally popular with women, a number of whom participated only in a restricted, staged manner. Often it was assumed that many would be more interested in promenades (generally by carriage) to savor the landscape. But some women joined in enthusiastically. At Feldsberg in 1780, Eleonore Liechtenstein reported to her sister that Josepha Clary's daughter Thérèse had wished to go hunting with the men. Her complaisant mother Josepha would have permitted the outing, but hostess Leopoldine Liechtenstein pronounced it unsuitable for Thérèse, presumably because the young woman would have lacked female companions. Thérèse did not go (and, according to Eleonore Liechtenstein, she was "a bit bad-tempered as a result").[92]

Leopoldine Kaunitz, not a fan of hunting, sent her sister a facetious account of a hunt at Feldsberg in September 1776. To her the hunt had been tiresome, although other participants said it was superb. She, hostess Leopoldine Liechtenstein, the French ambassador, and others had taken their places in an enclosed, elevated stand. There they had remained for four hours, with nothing to do but wait. Ten times the beaters forced boars out into the open. Each time a beast made itself visible the occupants of the shelter "saluted" it with haphazard gunfire, inflicting a few random injuries. At long last the hunt ended. The harvested game was exhibited before the hunters and huntresses, who were told that together with the other hunting parties at the event they had killed a numerous if motley assortment of wildlife. The participants received flattering, inflated reports concerning their individual successes and the quantity of game each had bagged. These reports were greeted with varying degrees of credulity by the hunters. Leopoldine Liechtenstein was delighted, quipped Leopoldine Kaunitz: "la Françoise [Leopoldine Liechtenstein] firmly believes she has shot all those."[93] In a published account of hunting at Feldsberg from roughly the same time period, the English doctor and visitor John Moore credited Leopoldine Liechtenstein with considerable skill as a markswoman.[94]

One of the most wrenching changes in Leopoldine Liechtenstein's life as she became a widow in August 1781 was her loss of access to, and control over, Feldsberg and Eisgrub, where she had reigned for decades as hostess (in a letter from Vienna to his brother in August 1772, enumerating the whereabouts of his absent friends, the emperor actually reported, "Princess Françoise reigns at Feldsperg," an apt description of Leopoldine's felicity when guests congregated).[95] Leopoldine Liechtenstein's friends watched with concern as she faced the difficult transition from proprietress of some of the most sumptuous residences in the Habsburg monarchy to dowager princess with reduced means. In the immediate aftermath of Franz Joseph's death, Eleonore Liechtenstein worried that Leopoldine had lost her sense of the practical. The new widow remarked rather languidly that she (Leopoldine) did not really know what her own resources would now be "but that she will certainly have enough. She will change her mind about that with time." In September Eleonore again remarked to her sister that Leopoldine Liechtenstein would have to adjust to her new situation; at some point she would have to face the fact that Feldsberg was no longer hers.[96] "My God, for the sake of her happiness I could wish that she was less fond of all these possessions," wrote Eleonore, "for little by little Louis [the eldest son and now the *Majoratsherr*] also is developing a taste for them, he is making plans; and is it possible to find one's bearings in a place where one was once mistress and where the person over whom one had authority has become master."[97] In summer 1782 Eleonore was still concerned about Leopoldine Liechtenstein's too active interest in Feldsberg and Eisgrub: "My God, the poor woman, she deludes herself and is becoming more and more embittered. . . . she simply cannot face the fact that all of this no longer belongs to her." Leopoldine Liechtenstein did find some consolation for her loss. She was wealthy enough as a widow to purchase a villa in the fashionable Viennese suburb of Hütteldorf, not far from her friend Lacy's Dornbach. But it was fitting that she died at her beloved Feldsberg, in June 1809.[98]

Prior to the death in 1771 of Emanuel Liechtenstein, father of both Franz Joseph and Charles Liechtenstein, Eleonore and her husband used Eleonore's own possession Gross Meseritsch (which they referred to as Meseritsch), on the Oslawa (Oslava) River, as their summer getaway, or they stayed at various palaces belonging to the Liechtenstein *Majorat*.[99] Eleonore once described Meseritsch as "a shabby nest," with its ancient palace that resembled "a veritable fortress."[100] She made infrequent visits, but they were extremely busy because of her status as actual proprietor.[101] After Emanuel Liechtenstein died, Charles inherited Mährisch Kromau, and the couple preferred that location.[102] Kromau, as the couple generally dubbed the locale, lay between Znaim (Znojmo) and Brünn, in hilly, forested country along the Oslawa River. Charles and Eleonore Liechtenstein made improvements to the palace grounds, employing Marcellus A. Isidore Canevale, who worked for the Liechtenstein family and other aristocratic families as well as for Joseph II.[103] Eleonore had a comfortable hunting lodge built for her husband at Zahradisch (Zahradište), less than eight miles northwest of Meseritsch. But Charles Liechtenstein preferred Vienna at all times of year and disliked the slow pace of life in the countryside unless good hunting was available. He visited Kromau only occasionally, although his wife wished he would stay longer, both for his health and for the sake of the family's finances; "he is one of those people who cannot bear to lose sight of the steeple of St. Stephan's," Eleonore wrote to Leopoldine Kaunitz in August 1779.[104]

Eleonore was conscious of the lesser appeal of the Kromau property by comparison with the estates of the *Majoratsherr* at Eisgrub and Feldsberg available to her sister-in-law Leopoldine Liechtenstein. From Kromau Eleonore could reach Feldsberg in a carriage ride of less than 4 ½ hours when the weather was good.[105] She returned from such visits feeling discontented and envious of her successful sister-in-law. Prior to visiting Feldsberg in June 1776, for example, she had spoken of her own summer residence cheerfully. Although Kromau offered no special amenities, Eleonore wrote to her sister, she found it a cheerful (*riant*) place and was never bored by her life there. Returning from Feldsberg some weeks later, she remarked ruefully that Kromau appeared ugly to her, with its rocky promenades surrounded by mountains, so inferior to the trails at Eisgrub, which was the most beautiful locale she had ever seen.[106] Nevertheless, Eleonore Liechtenstein was fond of Kromau, with its fresh air and the feeling of independence she enjoyed when residing there. Although the property passed to her eldest son with the death of her husband Charles in 1789, she cherished for the rest of her life the memory of summers spent there with her children.[107]

During the first few years of their marriage, Leopoldine Kaunitz and her husband Ernst had spent summers at the lesser Kaunitz palace in Jarmeritz (Jaroměřice nad Rokytnou), later reserved for the second son Dominik's family. Then the couple went to Naples on diplomatic assignment. Subsequently stationed in Brünn from September 1770 through November 1772, they were naturally drawn to nearby Austerlitz, where the host Chancellor Kaunitz attracted eminent visitors from many walks of life including, of course, the political. Visits to Austerlitz were pleasantly informal, even when Joseph II himself put in an appearance. "The Weather is very fine," the English visitor Lady Mary Coke reported from Austerlitz in September 1773, when both she and Leopoldine Kaunitz were among the guests, "and we amuse our selves perfectly well. Every body breakfasts in their own rooms in what manner they please; every kind of breakfast is ready at all hours: you have but to send for it. When that is over, you may stay in your own apartment, or go into the great room, where there is always Company and different employments, or you may go out in any manner you please. At two O'clock we dine and are generally twenty, and we have been two and twenty at table; sometimes two or three are absent." Several days later she continued, "Three of our company went off yesterday, but we had a recruit at night, and tomorrow all the Foreign Ministers are expected: they were to have come to-day, but the Empress has a drawing-room at Schonbrune, which they stay for." "We go out every day after dinner in open carriages; some times a coursing; some times to see the Gentlemen shoot, for I cannot otherwise partake of that amusement, tho' the Ladies here shoot as much as the Gentlemen, but it happens that those who are at Austerlitz are not very fond of it, so that they remain humble spectators like myself. Since the Princess Kinsky and the Princess Charles Lichtenstein have been here, we three generally go together. When we come home we walk in the Garden till it is quite dark, and then all the Company meets in the great room, where they make their parties at cards, chess, or if they prefer reading or working there are two other rooms light up for that purpose."[108] A month later Sir Keith too praised the informality of a sojourn at Austerlitz. To his friend Bradshaw he wrote in October 1773: "Our landlord, Prince Kaunitz, has read Rabelais, and made a proper use of his maxims. 'Sois heureux à la mode,' is the only rule laid down for everybody; and we were five-and-thirty masters and mistresses who adhered strictly to the letter of that golden law . . . In short, my journey to the country has done me good, to mind as well as body; and it has brought me into a closer connection with several valuable people, than all the frippery of town etiquette would permit me to form in the preceeding six months. That's the advantage of country living; and faith (between you and me) it is almost the only advantage which belongs to it."[109]

Once Leopoldine and Ernst Kaunitz had moved back to Vienna from Brünn, frequent journeys to Austerlitz lost their appeal. Instead, Leopoldine looked forward to visiting Baden bei Wien, a popular destination for Viennese of all classes that received six to eight hundred visitors yearly in the late eighteenth century (for longer stays, wealthy families traveled to Teplitz and Carlsbad or, most glamorous of all, to Spa in Belgium, which attracted 1000 guests yearly from all countries).[110] Her sister Eleonore too occasionally spent a few summer weeks at the spa town of Baden, a 2 ½-hour carriage ride south of Vienna, staying briefly with specific medical purposes in view for her husband or for herself. For Leopoldine Kaunitz, however, Baden took the place of a regular summer retreat since Austerlitz belonged to her long-lived father-in-law. Leopoldine Kaunitz found her stays to be both therapeutic and pleasurable. Although facilities at spas were generally segregated according to socioeconomic status and profession, social behavior was decidedly less formal than was the case in the capital.[111] Particularly happy at Baden in the summer of 1779, Leopoldine Kaunitz reminded Eleonore that the waters were said to be helpful against hypochondria; no gloomy thoughts were possible and one's blood circulated freely, in perfect equilibrium. A return trip for bathing in September of that year again enchanted her. She reported that every aspect of life in Baden pleased and contented her, even the air itself. "Baden is my Crumau [Kromau]," she wrote after a visit in 1781, "to me it offers the charm of freedom and repose."[112] Being so close to both Vienna and Laxenburg, however, Baden was not always a restful place. The same individuals who were active socially and politically in Vienna could continue their frenetic activity in Baden. Friends might travel out from Vienna on a day trip even if they did not choose to take the waters themselves. Leopoldine acknowledged that sometimes the social life was too intense. In a letter in May 1779 Eleonore commiserated with her, admitting that a during sojourn at Baden one was at the mercy of anyone who came for a visit.[113] Her occasional complaints notwithstanding, Leopoldine Kaunitz was a thoroughly sociable individual, avid for political news and social gossip. Baden was for her a valuable resource. She might have found lengthy stays in the countryside without the attractive presence of her father-in-law Chancellor Kaunitz to be tedious. Leopoldine and Ernst Kaunitz did not inherit Austerlitz until June 1794, when Leopoldine had less than a year to live.

Neither Josepha Clary nor Sidonia Kinsky had any great liking for the country estates of their husbands' families in Bohemia. As noted, during warm months Sidonia removed to her suburban villa. Her husband Prince Franz Ulrich Kinsky's preference for Prague and the Bohemian countryside left Sidonia in peaceful enjoyment of her residence at Weidlingau, often in the company of her unmarried sister, a canoness at Buchau. Josepha Clary joined them for weeks at a time. Josepha's husband Franz Wenzel Clary made extended summer journeys to the Clary estates in northern Bohemia. The Teplitz baths drew an increasingly cosmopolitan and illustrious society. Occasionally the spa town even took on political importance; for example, it was selected in October 1764 as the location to which Joseph II traveled to discreetly scrutinize one of his possible brides, Kunigunde of Saxony.[114] The spa attracted so many aristocratic guests that there was simply no space left in the palace, Prince Clary lamented in 1779.[115] His wife Josepha noted sympathetically that Teplitz would be a more pleasant place if all the visitors congregated simultaneously, so that they could entertain themselves while the master of the palace avoided seeing inconvenient visitors, "but to continually have company just when one thinks oneself alone is very disagreeable." Josepha Clary was invariably reluctant to journey to Teplitz.[116] In the 1780s, as Prince Clary's health failed, his wife tried to persuade him to take his cure at Baden and dispense with the long journey to Teplitz, an unmistakable sign that Josepha believed duty might otherwise require her to accompany her husband on the dreaded journey. In summer 1783, when the ailing Prince Clary again left for Bohemia and Josepha remained in Vienna, Eleonore remarked, "she must have a very decided aversion for Teplitz, for she is so strict with herself and so accustomed to making sacrifices in all matters. I hope he will return safe and sound, for otherwise she will reproach herself for the rest of her life." Daughter Thérèse took her mother's place as the prince's travel companion and nursed him during a serious illness.[117]

Even with all their advantages and resources, the *Dames* faced constraints that aristocratic society imposed on all female members. Young married women, and more particularly unmarried women who were in the marriage market, had to be especially discreet in their social relations. Their behavior, morals, and even their health received careful scrutiny from relatives, social connections, and the interested public.[118] Both in Vienna during the winter and at country residences in warmer weather, mature married women enjoyed greater freedom of association and outlets for independent activity. But they too needed to be circumspect. Visiting Vienna in the late 1770s, the Englishman Wraxall recorded his impressions concerning the mores and social behavior of women of his acquaintance.

"Gallantries here are covered with a mysterious veil, and assume the exterior of friendship," Wraxall wrote. "Unlike the fickle and libertine amours of Warsaw, or Petersburgh, they generally last for a quarter of a century, and are rarely broken off on either side. Slow in forming, they are still more slow in dissolving." Wraxall thought Maria Theresia was responsible in large part for this prudence. "The Empress," he observed, "rigidly virtuous in her own conduct, faithful to the marriage bed, and never suspected of female weakness, makes very little allowance for the indiscretions of others. She crushes every degree of libertinism beneath the weight of her displeasure. A woman of condition, if known to be frail, unless her frailty be confined to one lover, and managed with the utmost attention to privacy and decorum, is certain to receive an order to quit Vienna: perhaps she is obliged to languish out life in some obscure provincial town of Hungary, Austria, or other parts of her Imperial Majesty's dominions." Wraxall's portrayal of Maria Theresia's interference was thoroughly unflattering. "It is hardly possible to conceive how minute and circumstantial a detail her inquiries embrace, relative to the private conduct of her subjects of both sexes: their actions, amusements, and pleasures, even the most concealed, are constantly reported to her. She employs emissaries or spies, who omit nothing for her information . . . An illiberal superstition, rather than a rational disapproval of gallantry, on account of the private and political ills which it produces, actuate her in this rigorous proscription . . . In no European capital are so much decency, caution, and respect for appearances maintained, in all connexions of pleasure or attachment, as at Vienna. These attentions are indispensable, in order to avoid attracting the Imperial notice, always followed by reprehension or punishment." Elsewhere Wraxall remarked rather unchivalrously, "The superstition of an Austrian woman, however characteristic, habitual, and excessive, is by no means inconsistent or incompatible with gallantry: she sins, prays, confesses, and begins anew; but she never omits her mass, not even for her lover. Few of them touch meat either on the Friday or Saturday of every week, or during the whole period of Lent, and they confess frequently; if not from principle, yet from habit or from fear." Wraxall allowed that other factors could be at work. "I am inclined to believe," he mused, "that besides the restraints alluded to, neither the climate nor the air of Austria are favorable to violent passions of any kind. There is something phlegmatic in the constitution of the inhabitants, physical and intellectual, which is adverse to strong emotions."[119]

On balance, the behavior of the five *Dames* conformed to the dictates of society; and when it did not, they preserved appearances. The testimony of contemporaries about private lives of their acquaintances cannot always be accepted as conclusive because behavior could be so discreet as to escape detection completely, as the diarist Zinzendorf's case makes clear. More than once, aristocratic married ladies to whom Zinzendorf had been paying court proved to have already bestowed their extramarital favors elsewhere, unsuspected by him.[120]

Alternatively, irregularities might be simply overlooked. Norbert Elias, studying the behavior of the court nobility under "absolutist" monarchs, concluded that the nobility was inclined to regard strict monogamy as "bourgeois" behavior, its rules not fully binding even for female aristocrats.[121] Such generalizations should not be extended untested to the behavior of an entire group. Most aristocratic women were circumspect in their public actions, even after the inquisitive Maria Theresia's exit from the scene in 1780. It is clear, however, that many individuals did not remain quiescent in distasteful or tedious marriages and that a certain open-minded nonchalance toward the foibles of one's social peers was regarded as a sign of good breeding. When behavior gave rise to public scandal in a manner demeaning to the family and, in a more general sense, to elite society as a whole, or when transgressions could result in financial jeopardy for the family, sanctions certainly were applied by the concerned family or even the imperial court. Females in a family could be chastised more readily than males. The family head (and in some cases this would be the woman's husband) held the purse strings and could restrict a female family member's freedom of movement, oblige her to remove to a less convenient or less appealing residence, or even consign her to a convent. An errant woman might be denied access to her children, a form of leverage employed by Chancellor Kaunitz to restrain the love affairs and gambling of his daughter-in-law Bernardine, wife of Ernst Kaunitz's younger brother Dominik. Leopoldine Kaunitz herself, in letters to Eleonore, initially favored banishing her errant sister-in-law to a convent, as did Maria Theresia. Leopoldine eventually softened her stance ("this woman is mother of children, who should not be disgraced"). The elder Kaunitz transferred custody of Bernardine's children to their great aunt, his widowed sister Countess Questenberg. When the countess died in 1778, much responsibility for Bernardine's two daughters, though not for the son and heir, devolved upon Leopoldine Kaunitz. Bernardine's own travails ended soon with her death in 1779.[122]

Among the five women only the personal lives of Eleonore Liechtenstein and Leopoldine Kaunitz can be traced reliably. Their extant correspondence is extensive, and their confidence in each other was unlimited. But even here the record is unlikely to be complete. Certainly one major crisis in Eleonore Liechtenstein's married life occurred in 1764–1765, when she was both flattered and troubled by the attentions of Count Carl O'Donnell (1715–1771), a successful military commander of Irish origins who was decades older than Eleonore, considerably older than even her husband Charles Liechtenstein. Letters that Eleonore Liechtenstein had written to O'Donnell as well as the written statement she prepared for her confession at year's end, all obtained by her husband Charles, confirmed both her inclination for O'Donnell and her resistance to his blandishments. Charles Liechtenstein was sufficiently distressed by his young wife's behavior to consider separating from her. Writing from Naples Leopoldine Kaunitz warned her sister that O'Donnell was a seasoned roué. An affair with a relatively innocent younger man who showed regard for Eleonore's honor would be less dangerous, Leopoldine wrote; "when a woman lets it be known that she loves, from that moment she becomes very weak and has few defenses left to her . . . he [O'Donnell] would not be the man to fail to press his advantage or neglect an opportunity." What made O'Donnell's attentions especially unfortunate, according to Leopoldine Kaunitz, was "his reputation for conquest and amorous adventures." This was not someone for whom Eleonore should jeopardize the peace of her married life. Leopoldine Kaunitz's letters to Eleonore encouraged Eleonore to occupy her time fully, to renew her religious faith, to view her husband's jealousy as a sign of affection, to avoid solitary situations with O'Donnell so far as this could be done without exciting remark, and to do her duty as wife and Christian. Leopoldine admonished her sister, telling her that the two of them, Leopoldine and Eleonore, would be more culpable than other women if they transgressed because they had received a solid upbringing and were familiar with good principles. With the passage of time, Eleonore overcame her inclination for O'Donnell.[123] Her friendship with him eventually became casual and relaxed, and when O'Donnell died suddenly in March 1771 Eleonore mourned his passing sincerely.[124] A second and far more significant perturbation in Eleonore's married life was Joseph II's strong preference for her.[125] The efforts the emperor made to spend time with Eleonore launched the group that became "the Five Princesses," and so these events will be described in chapter 3.

Leopoldine Kaunitz reported her own brief adventure as a young woman while living in Naples, where her husband Ernst served as Habsburg ambassador. Early during her sojourn she had noticed that married women in Naples frequently had lovers who were on open and friendly terms with the women's husbands, a custom more widespread and accepted among Neapolitans than at home in Vienna. She wrote to Eleonore in May 1764 about a casual acquaintance with a gentleman she called "Monsieur Veri" (possibly Verri): "gallantry is indescribably common here . . . if you speak to someone two days in a row that is enough for him to be seen as your cicisbeo. That is what has happened to me . . . and neither he nor I were thinking of such a thing, as you can well imagine." Veri had offered to show her the antiquities of Rome when she and her husband visited the city. Rumors circulated concerning the pair. Several months later Leopoldine Kaunitz was mortified to discover that she had misjudged Veri's intentions; he was in fact offering himself as "Ami du Maison," as the party in such an arrangement was dubbed.[126] The sources are silent concerning possible romantic interludes later in Vienna for Leopoldine Kaunitz. More than the other four couples considered here, she and her husband Ernst Kaunitz moved from one residence to another in unison. Leopoldine often found herself thwarted in her own plans, usually because of a whim of her father-in-law Chancellor Kaunitz. But in addition,

Ernst Kaunitz simply preferred to remain in Vienna as did Charles Liechtenstein. In August 1780 Leopoldine Kaunitz remarked to Eleonore Liechtenstein, "as for him [Ernst], he has a decided aversion for the countryside, and he complains about people who spend time there and like it." "It is dreadful," she wrote in July 1781, "how he clings to this city of Vienna, and nothing anyone does can get him to part with it."[127] Because of experience with Ernst Kaunitz's infidelity in Naples, as will be noted below, Leopoldine adopted a pragmatic attitude toward her marriage. "I would wish," she wrote to her sister, "that my husband could have a younger woman for his wife, I am far too old and too worn out for him." She was sorry to be little more than Ernst's housekeeper, she said, "but matters being as they are, one has to try to keep things going as pleasantly as possible."[128]

Leopoldine Liechtenstein's relationships with her husband Franz Joseph and her friend Lacy, himself a male member of the *société,* are difficult to characterize. A friend of the family, Lacy was welcomed as a close associate by both Leopoldine herself and her husband throughout the latter's lifetime. A number of contemporaries as well as subsequent historians have assumed that Lacy and Leopoldine were joined in a long-term intimate relationship, and strong circumstantial evidence in Lacy's correspondence supports this assumption.[129] Zinzendorf noted in 1778 that his colleague Philip Sinzendorf had discussed with him the love affair of Lacy and Leopoldine Liechtenstein for two hours ("les amours" of the field marshal and "la Psse L.").[130] But according to witnesses the marriage of Leopoldine Liechtenstein and her husband was an unusually harmonious one.[131] Leopoldine Liechtenstein behaved so discreetly as to cause no serious consternation among her family and associates and to leave behind little evidence. A stable, exclusive extramarital relationship would in any case have raised few eyebrows in Viennese society.

Sidonia Kinsky lived mostly apart from her husband, who preferred his own interests and associates—male and female—in Prague. Standards applied to aristocratic wives and daughters were more rigorous than those for aristocratic men. For males casual encounters passed without remark, if reasonable discretion and moderation were exercised. Although longstanding, acknowledged liaisons (sometimes with social peers but more often with women of lower social rank) were noticed, they were greeted with indulgence and indifference. Maria Theresia's own husband Franz Stephan was known to have transgressed. Chancellor Kaunitz likewise publicly and flagrantly ignored Maria Theresia's strict code of conduct in his relationships with actresses and singers, and yet he retained her esteem.[132] Judged by contemporary standards, the chancellor was a benignant individual who looked after the professional interests of former favorites, whereas some aristocratic men, crudely domineering toward lower-class men in any case, were also careless or sexually predatory toward women of lower status.[133] In their wills, sons of both Eleonore Liechtenstein and Leopoldine Liechtenstein openly accepted responsibility for illegitimate offspring by women of lower status and made provisions for their care.¹³⁴ Prince Kinsky's particular liaison was with an aristocratic married woman, a Countess Wallis. Already in 1773, when Zinzendorf visited Prague, he had seen Kinsky and Countess Wallis together at dinners and on promenades. Zinzendorf described Countess Wallis as pretty, with beautiful eyes and "French" features (*figure françoise*). After visiting her, the usually critical Zinzendorf noted that she was a woman he could himself love, with her pleasing vivacity.¹³⁵ Whenever the prince came to Vienna, his wife Sidonia dutifully rearranged her own schedule to attend to his needs, but she was relieved that he rarely remained in town for long. Leopoldine Kaunitz described one such sojourn in August 1778, during the War of the Bavarian Succession, which threatened to bring hostilities to Bohemia. Visiting Sidonia at Weidlingau Leopoldine was pleased to see that Sidonia was taking in stride her husband's expected arrival in Vienna, although it obviously displeased her. Sidonia planned to return to the Kinsky residence in central Vienna briefly in order to receive him, after which she was hoping he would move on to Feldsberg, Kromau, and thence back to Bohemia. In October Leopoldine Kaunitz noted without further comment that since the military situation in Bohemia had improved, Prince Kinsky planned to return to Prague; Countess Wallis, Leopoldine added, had already done so.¹³⁶

Ernst Kaunitz, Leopoldine's husband, was an amiable but rather directionless man who indulged in several affairs early in his marriage when he and Leopoldine were stationed in Naples while he served as Austrian ambassador. He humiliated Leopoldine by his public courting of the opera singer Katharina Gabrielli, protégée of the elder Kaunitz. Young and idealistic, Leopoldine Kaunitz considered separating from her husband. Possibly after Archduchess Maria Carolina married the king of Naples, Leopoldine thought, Ernst could be assigned to some other diplomatic post and she herself could return to Vienna to live on her own, in a form of retirement. Then, she wrote her sister, she would take a modest apartment near Eleonore and keep a small domestic establishment; and when Eleonore was available the two sisters would visit the chancellor or attend the theater together. "What a release that would be," she concluded. Leopoldine guessed correctly that after Katharina Gabrielli there would be other escapades, but eventually she decided that her role as a member of the house of Kaunitz required her to protect Ernst's honor and particularly to conceal his foolishness from Maria Theresia. Leopoldine feared that if she ended her oversight over household finances Ernst would ruin himself and her.¹³⁷ A dramatic altercation that ended Ernst Kaunitz's relationship with Katharina Gabrielli was retailed in Vienna and beyond, as Josepha Clary's remarks to her daughter Countess Ledebur in December 1767 make clear. Countess Ledebur had heard the story even in Prague. Apparently while Ernst was away from Naples, the French ambassador had replaced him in Katharina's favor. Upon Ernst's return there had been a violent meeting of the three at which time the singer had received a blow from the blunt side of the French ambassador's sword. Details of the story were murky, but Katharina had departed for Turin and Ernst's romantic spree was at an end.[138] Chancellor Kaunitz admonished his son concerning the gossip ("the very shabby tale"). Ernst moved on to other romantic dalliances. During the rest of her married life, Leopoldine Kaunitz was never truly at ease about Ernst Kaunitz's judgment and conduct. However, her expectations after the Naples experiences were not high, and she was content with a friendly partnership. Already in 1769 Leopoldine Kaunitz wrote to Eleonore in a rather philosophical vein concerning Charles Liechtenstein's dalliances, arguing that with patience on the wife's part a marriage could accommodate the periodic transgressions of a husband.[139]

In 1781, while summering in Kromau and Meseritsch, Eleonore Liechtenstein came upon old personal papers of her husband Charles from the 1760s containing evidence of at least one significant extramarital affair on his part. Eleonore evinced no particular interest in Charles's early liaisons, but she did not want her daughter to see the letters. She and Leopoldine Kaunitz agreed to let the matter rest.[140] Eleonore had been aware of a second romantic interlude from the early 1770s, when Charles Liechtenstein was residing in Pressburg as military commander and Eleonore remained in Vienna. According to gossip, while in Pressburg Charles Liechtenstein began a relationship with Archduchess Marie Christine, whose husband Prince Albert was serving as governor. Charles Liechtenstein even reported to Eleonore that in an interview with him Maria Theresia herself had referred to his friendship with Marie Christine. From Brünn in July 1772, Leopoldine Kaunitz confirmed the "petite intrigue" between Charles and Marie Christine; Ernst Kaunitz too had heard reports. Leopoldine urged Eleonore to remain on good terms with Marie Christine, who could do Eleonore harm otherwise. Eleonore could at least depend upon Marie Christine to behave discreetly. If the situation became serious, Eleonore should feign total ignorance.[141]

Given the realities of domestic and social life—and the fact that most Catholic families could not countenance divorce and did not often resort to annulment—each aristocratic couple had to work out a modus vivendi, adjusting to the realities of partnerships that had often been planned by families with considerations of prestige and competitive advantage foremost in their minds. Observing the Prince de Ligne's interaction with his wife (who was a sister of Franz Joseph and Charles Liechtenstein), Count Valentin Esterházy reported to his wife from Marimont in 1784 that the pair got along well together by seeing each other as little as possible.[142] Tensions between husband and wife were eased somewhat by the substantial autonomy that older married and widowed aristocratic women enjoyed, exercising this freedom of action as a matter of course just as aristocratic males did, although women remained more mindful of appearances and the potentially censorious judgments of society at large than were their husbands and brothers. The most intimate aspects of family members' lives were generally shielded from direct public scrutiny and discussion by common custom and by mutual tolerance among members of the aristocracy.[143] Interestingly, although Josepha Clary was linked to a husband who was acknowledged by all her associates to be both dreary and irascible, a liability in society, it was she who may have had the most realistic approach to marriage among the *Dames*, and consequently the strongest, most durable friendship with her husband. She often expressed satisfaction and gratefulness for the affection and generosity of both her son and her husband. Josepha closed her letters to her husband Franz Wenzel with words of special endearment: "adieu, best friend, be assured that I love you most tenderly, and for life."[144]

One of the most important measures of a family's current status within aristocratic society was the nexus of relationships it established through marriage alliances for its young members. This "connubium," or circle of families with whom the family was deemed eligible to form marriage alliances, was of great importance to an aristocratic family and could be enhanced through the skillful use of contacts made at court functions and through daily social intercourse. Initial marriage and "establishment" of a son or daughter was an expensive, burdensome undertaking for many families. Where requisite family resources were not available for all offspring, they were expected to remain single. Every family member was entitled to maintenance, but not every individual received an equal chance to enjoy all that the aristocratic lifestyle could offer. Opportunities in aristocratic families were unevenly distributed according to gender and birth order. But financial standing was not the sole consideration. When a family gained access to increasingly exclusive and ancient connections from which its own members could select marriage partners, the improvement in status was a form of social capital for the whole family, to be husbanded, managed, and spent strategically.[145]

All of the *Dames* except Leopoldine Kaunitz, who died before her daughter chose a husband, were preoccupied at times with the promotion or arrangement of marriages for sons or daughters during the years when the *société* flourished. Although not behindhand in seeking advantages for their families, none of the five women had reputations as matchmakers. Decorum dictated reticence concerning the subject in public. When questioned about the marriage prospects of their sons and daughters the women demurred, responding that as parents they would not wish to influence or interfere with the choices made.[146] But the matter was far too important to be left to the whims of the young persons involved.

Sons and daughters of all five *Dames* married into richly propertied and appropriately pedigreed families, although in both branches of the Liechtenstein clan several remained single. Leopoldine Liechtenstein, energetic and ambitious, found an excellent match for her oldest daughter, also named Leopoldine, who married Charles Emmanuel, Landgrave of Hesse-Rotenburg (1746–1812) in 1771. Finding an appropriate alliance for the all-important oldest Liechtenstein son Louis, heir to the Liechtenstein *Majorat* and to leadership of the entire Liechtenstein clan, was an arduous process. Leopoldine Liechtenstein, widowed in 1781, and Lacy worked together. At first an intra-familial alliance was considered, a strategy that the Liechtensteins had employed in earlier generations to conserve wealth and bolster the family's position. In July 1780, when Louis was 21 years old, Lacy had suggested to Eleonore Liechtenstein that the young heir might marry his cousin Josephine, Eleonore's only daughter. Eleonore was dazzled by the prospect, despite her reservations about Louis's personality and character. She was willing to consider the marriage if her daughter showed any inclination "to undertake the difficult though brilliant course [*carrière*] that would open before her."[147] Louis's choice then fell elsewhere, and Eleonore remained rather wistful. The ultimate selection of Caroline (or Charlotte) Manderscheid (1768–1831) by and for Louis was universally applauded, however. The Manderscheids were a valuable connection, an old imperial family domiciled in the Eifel region. Having witnessed the prosperous outcome of her own older brother Christian Sternberg's alliance with Augusta, the Manderscheid heiress and Caroline's half sister, Leopoldine Liechtenstein was eager for a Liechtenstein alliance with the Manderscheids; as she commented, "with regard to the name, the alliance, and the chapters [Manderscheid daughters traditionally enjoyed placements at selective *Stifte* such as Thorn, Elten, Vreden, Essen, and St. Ursula] I know of nothing more distinguished."[148] When Leopoldine Liechtenstein visited Augusta's home in Blankenheim in 1781 and met the younger sisters, Leopoldine had been charmed by their attractiveness and piety. Together with her own mother, Countess Leopoldine Sternberg, Leopoldine Liechtenstein eagerly planned the meeting of her son Louis with Caroline Manderscheid, the elder of the two young women. The Liechtenstein-Manderscheid wedding took place at the Liechtenstein palace at Feldsberg in November 1783. Two months before Louis's marriage, Leopoldine Liechtenstein's youngest daughter Marie married the heir to the vast Esterházy fortune, Prince Nicholaus II, grandson to Nicholaus "the Magnificent" (patron of the composer Joseph Haydn). The alliance with the Esterházy family was announced with considerable éclat. But in September 1783, the two families solemnized Marie's marriage to young Nicholaus Esterházy in a small private service, more subdued than customary, because of the illness of the bride's mother Leopoldine.

Impressed with Leopoldine Liechtenstein's success in finding prestigious marriage partners for her children, Leopoldine Kaunitz nevertheless expressed uneasiness to her sister Eleonore. "I think," she wrote to Eleonore Liechtenstein, "that if matters turned out so successfully for me I would be dying of anxiety lest some horrible misfortune awaited me sooner or later."[149] Leopoldine Kaunitz's lighthearted remarks proved to be prophetic, for major difficulties would beset these splendid matches. Marie's marriage began under particularly difficult conditions. She was only fifteen years old, her groom eighteen. Almost at once after the wedding the young bridegroom departed on a journey. In his absence his widowed father, 45-year-old Prince Anton, became so infatuated with the bride that he wished to set aside the marriage and claim Marie for himself. Apparently the elderly Prince Nicholaus Esterházy and Leopoldine Liechtenstein worked together to avert such a catastrophe. The Esterházy family's squabbles, well-known at least among allied families, led Eleonore a few years later to describe the troubled family environment as "the sterile magnificence of Esterhaz." Archduchess Marie Christine mentioned the situation in her letter to Josepha Clary: "I pity her [Leopoldine Liechtenstein] for finding herself in the midst of this peculiar family." Marie's husband, young Prince Nicholaus, was profligate and became with time a notorious philanderer, extreme even in a somewhat lax age and society.[150]

The marriage of Louis Liechtenstein with Caroline Manderscheid, attended by such high hopes, apparently involved real affection. But Louis suffered from ill health throughout his adult life, despite visits to spas and the attentions of medical specialists. As early as the mid-1780s his condition was a cause for concern, given the need to produce an heir for the family. Louis never did achieve robust health, although he lived until 1805. He suffered from "fits" that included hallucinations and convulsions that could occur on the public streets. These were followed by days of total inactivity and despondency, a condition of *mélancholie* (presumably a form of clinical depression) that was treated by purgatives, blistering, and plasters, apparently in an effort to draw from the unfortunate prince any troublesome substances that might be causing internal imbalances or encumbrances. No heir resulted from the marriage.[151] From virtually the beginning of her marriage, Caroline found the imperious personality of her mother-in-law Leopoldine Liechtenstein to be irksome. Leopoldine worried when Caroline habitually skipped mass and frequented only the theater. Caroline followed no program of devotional reading, stayed late at balls, and, possibly the most wounding circumstance, rarely spent time with her mother-in-law. The young couple staged amateur comedies in their residence, an activity considered by the more staid individuals in society to be too risqué for a young wife. When questioned, Caroline responded that it was the responsibility of her husband Louis alone to regulate her behavior. But Louis did not concern himself. Letters Caroline wrote in the 1780s make it clear that she felt lonely and friendless in her new role. Returning to Vienna after visiting her sister in April 1789, she described her sadness: "I was so content, so happy, what a difference here, but I do not want to bore you with my melancholy, for I am so terribly sad; this always happens to me after I have spent time with people who are so dear to me."[152] Family and friends had cause for concern, for in the 1790s Caroline would give birth to two illegitimate children, a son named Charles Fribert in 1793 and subsequently a daughter, both fathered by a military officer, Franz von Langendonck.[153] There is no evidence that Louis reproached his wife for her extramarital relationship.[154] Leopoldine Liechtenstein's second son Johann did not marry until 1792, choosing 16-year-old Josepha Sophia von Fürstenberg-Weitra. The first child of Johann and his new wife was a girl, Leopoldine, born in September 1793. There was great rejoicing in the Liechtenstein family when a son, the future Louis II, was born to the couple in 1796. Additional sons and daughters followed.[155] Leopoldine Liechtenstein's youngest son Philip remained single.

For her middle daughter Antonia, judged to be somewhat disfigured after a bout with smallpox, Leopoldine Liechtenstein chose placement in an aristocratic female foundation or *Stift* rather than marriage. Membership in a *Stift* and the attendant benefits were reserved to the offspring of families whose lineage met certain prescribed norms. The female *Stift* was roughly comparable to institutions that served young male noblemen, but the latter were far more likely to lead to church careers than were their female counterparts. A daughter's eligibility for acceptance by a prestigious *Stift* was a valuable commodity in the marriage market, since such a bride improved the standing of the family into which she married as well as that of any future offspring. Aspiring aristocratic families in the Habsburg monarchy sought access to prestigious *Stifte* as part of their efforts to claim *Ebenbürtigkeit* or equality of birth with other ancient families in the Holy Roman Empire. The position as a *Stiftsdame* could serve as a temporary or permanent alternative to marriage, and aristocratic parents viewed the *Stift* as a satisfactory "establishment" for daughters. There were, after all, few other prospects for unmarried aristocratic women. A *Stiftsdame* or canoness could resign her position if an eligible marriage offered. Young women appear to have welcomed the opportunity, and parents had no need to coerce daughters into entering a *Stift*. Life as a canoness was rarely luxurious. However, it conferred recognized status, and daughters relished the relative independence their membership afforded them as single women. Canonesses had few religious obligations once a period of probation had been served. They enjoyed considerable freedom of movement, ready access to friends and relatives, and, to the extent that family finances and practical living arrangements permitted, a simplified version of the comforts to which they had been accustomed at home.[156]

The *Stift* at Essen chosen for Antonia by Leopoldine Liechtenstein was among the most exclusive in the Holy Roman Empire. Applicants had to prove descendance from counts or princes, not merely ennobled ancestors. If a controversy concerning these genealogical proofs arose, the Essen chapter appealed for adjudication to the equally elite male *Domstifte* in Köln and Strasbourg. During the seventeenth century, under Prince Hartmann (1613–1686), the Liechtenstein family had tried to place daughters in Essen. At that time, the Liechtenstein application had been rejected when the genealogical chart was deemed too "unknown" by examiners in Cologne (Köln) and Strasbourg. The Liechtenstein family's origins in Moravia were judged to be "ministerial," a result of their services on behalf of the imperial Catholic party there, and not equal to the most ancient military nobility of the Holy Roman Empire.[157] By the late eighteenth century the Liechtenstein family had become very powerful, with influence beyond the borders of Habsburg lands. Nevertheless, evidence suggests that Antonia was not immediately welcome at Essen. When her genealogical documents were presented to the *Stift* in 1770, the Liechtensteins were scolded for appending to them endorsements and signatures that did not conform to tradition in Essen.[158] Antonia gained admittance, however, and remained a canoness until the foundation's dissolution in 1803 when its property was absorbed into the kingdom of Prussia. As was common practice, Antonia acquired and held simultaneously a second position in another foundation, at Thorn.[159]

Like Leopoldine Liechtenstein, Eleonore Liechtenstein achieved impressive results from her first foray into the marriage market for her children. Eleonore had grown increasingly fond of her maturing daughter Josephine. During the summer of 1779, as Josephine approached marriageable age, Eleonore and her daughter particularly enjoyed their sojourn together in the country at Kromau. Eleonore wrote to Leopoldine Kaunitz, "She [Josephine] seems to be so content, so very gratified that I am convinced these are the best days of her life, at least with regard to the sort of happiness that never leads to regret and does not cause disquiet."[160] The following year at precisely the critical moment, when Josephine was seventeen years old, her health deteriorated. She suffered from weakness, dizziness, and general malaise. Eleonore restricted Josephine's appearances even among close friends and relatives, concerned for her daughter's well-being but worried also that reports would circulate and damage her daughter's chances in the marriage market.[161] An initial proposal from the Sinzendorf family was quashed by Josephine herself, who disliked the prospective groom. Charles and Eleonore Liechtenstein explicitly (and perhaps showily) refused to pressure their daughter. For their restraint they received praise from Maria Theresia herself, who took seriously the Habsburg monarch's traditional prerogative of finding for or against the projected alliances of the court aristocracy.[162] Another match was soon under consideration, this time with the heir to the Harrach family *Majorat*. Eventually Johann Harrach (1756–1829) was accepted, and the couple were married in January 1781. A particular ally in the business had been Countess Rosa Harrach, mother-in-law to Sidonia Kinsky's grown son Joseph and sister to the groom's father. In October 1781, Eleonore wrote to her sister Leopoldine Kaunitz from Feldsberg, "If by chance—though I do not suppose it—you should see Rose [Harrach], give her my regards, commend my daughter to her care, for it is she [Rose] who managed everything so now she must provide support and encouragement."[163] Josephine's marriage into the Harrach family, although carefully vetted and approved by family and friends, was not especially happy, at least initially. The Harrach family's religious traditions included a particularly austere form of Jansenism, which (as will be noted in chapter 4) was anathema to all five *Dames* and especially to convent-educated Eleonore Liechtenstein and her sister. Josephine found her mother-in-law, born a member of the powerful Dietrichstein family, to be overbearing, strict, and puritanical; but unlike Caroline Manderscheid, Josephine tried to comply with the older woman's demands. Johann's temperament disappointed Eleonore. She had recognized early a certain timidity in her future son-in-law and a tendency to hypochondria. Yet he was a solid young man, his family respectable and wealthy, and the advantages of the match had seemed overwhelming.[164] At Kromau Eleonore wrote to Leopoldine Kaunitz in July 1784: "My daughter has written me another pitiful letter from Vienna. Her husband has just left, I am sure that was very difficult, and she finds herself, she says, alone, deprived of everyone she loves, handed over to this mother-in-law whom she does not love. She says that the problem is the excessive weakness of her husband, who is unable to resist the slightest wish of his mother."[165]

Johann Harrach's father died in 1783, and so Eleonore's son-in-law inherited the Harrach family's rich possessions in Bohemia, Moravia, and Austria. As years passed the childless Harrach couple's situation had much in common with that of Josephine's aunt Leopoldine Kaunitz and husband Ernst, since the family headship was likely to pass not to their offspring but first to a brother and then to a nephew. Eleonore Liechtenstein grew ever closer to her daughter, who became a veritable friend and would fill the void created when Leopoldine Kaunitz died in 1795. Often discouraged when she considered the behavior of her own grown sons, in June 1785 Eleonore confided to Leopoldine Kaunitz, "So it is with children; those who survive kill you with worry, and those who do not will kill you with grief. Our gracious God knows what is needful for us." But her adult daughter was a source of pride to Eleonore. In 1789 she wrote, "I do not know how this good Pepie [Josephine] alone has escaped the plague of foolishness and misconduct that is the portion of my children." Leopoldine Kaunitz commiserated: "for a mother, daughters as they mature could be a great resource and yet it is daughters that we must give away, whereas sons remain to burden and embarrass us throughout our lives! It is certainly true that we are not in this world to please ourselves." In July 1782, after Josephine's marriage, Eleonore had written, "I miss my daughter terribly. It is a great sacrifice to give away one's children [in marriage] and the other side believes that a tremendous favor is conferred when they are taken off your hands." But son-in-law Johann Harrach would become a friend and even a source of financial assistance to Eleonore in years to come, during the darkest days of the French and Napoleonic wars.[166]

Eleonore Liechtenstein's eldest son Charles selected a bride without consulting his mother, deeply offending her. Eleonore began the search for a suitable bride when her husband died in early 1789 and young Charles became *Majoratsherr*. She noted eligible daughters from related and well-established families that in her view were worthy of a connection with the Liechtensteins. Eleonore focused her attention especially on her own Öttingen relatives and the Lobkowicz family, looking for discreet ways in which young Charles could meet the potential brides. Leopoldine Kaunitz had been sanguine about Charles's prospects in summer 1789. She wrote to Eleonore Liechtenstein, "he is too fond of you to take a wife without considering whether or not she will suit you, and I have a sufficiently high opinion of him to be convinced that in thinking about his choice he will ask himself 'but will she please my mother?'"[167] But Charles became acquainted with his future bride Maria Anna Khevenhüller-Metsch (1770–1849) in 1789 at the Viennese home of Countess Antonia Maria Zichy (1759–1809), formerly a Khevenhüller-Metsch and a cousin of the bride-to-be. Countess Zichy was the wife of Karl Zichy (1753–1926), a Josephinian reformer who enforced unpopular measures in Hungary.[168] A second cousin of Count Rosenberg, who as a male member of the *société* of the *Dames* was one of Eleonore's close friend, had married Maria Anna's sister. Although Rosenberg had been unenthusiastic about the connection when it concerned his own family, Eleonore now suspected his complicity in her son's case. She misprized the genealogical credentials of the Metsch family and was unimpressed by the Pressburg convent where the motherless bride had been educated. Most of all she feared that Countess Zichy would manipulate easygoing Charles.[169] Eleonore Liechtenstein's outbursts of indignation and near despair over the news continued for many weeks during the summer of 1789. She wrote Leopoldine Kaunitz, "Was any mother ever treated so thoughtlessly? I am to have nothing at all to do with the marriage other than to sign the contract as one of the witnesses. He writes to me in great haste by dispatch to give me news of the matter and to ask for my consent, which he knows I cannot refuse. What son would be satisfied with such a consent?" Charles's new link with Countess Zichy would be intolerable: "he is throwing himself into the power of this scheming Zichy woman, immodest and arrogant, who does not hesitate to take advantage of the complaisance and foolishness of a young man, to make him choose without thinking, without the advice of those whose province it is to guide him, a young woman of her [Zichy's] family, with whom she has caused him to fall in love. I am to give my consent so that as quickly as possible she [Zichy] can ensure the success of the deception she has practiced."[170] The marriage took place in Vienna in September 1789. Eleonore quickly grew fond of her new daughter-in-law, who was a loyal and loving friend after the early demise of Eleonore's son Charles and a devoted mother to Eleonore's grandchildren. Among Eleonore's remaining sons, as noted previously, only the third, Maurice, eventually married. His bride was Leopoldine Esterházy, granddaughter of Leopoldine Liechtenstein, a union promoted by Leopoldine's daughter Marie and favored by Eleonore.¹⁷¹ The younger sons remained bachelors and did not draw on the family's resources to establish households.

Where Eleonore had a superfluity of sons, Josepha Clary had a single son and many daughters. With fewer financial resources than her friends, Josepha nevertheless managed to achieve a "great marriage" (in the words of Sir Robert Murray Keith in his report to Lady Mary Coke in 1775) for son Johann in 1775 with a daughter of the Prince de Ligne, head of a prominent family with properties in Belgium.¹⁷² This connection became a source of worry, embarrassment, and entertainment for Josepha for the remainder of her life. Prince de Ligne was a likeable, occasionally brilliant individual who doted on his daughter Christine, Josepha Clary's daughter-in-law. Even before the French wars disrupted the prince's income in Belgium the Ligne family was a financial concern for Josepha Clary. Ligne was generous and even profligate, and Josepha's son had to pay for visits of the prince, his family, and his various hangers-on in Teplitz.¹⁷³ Once the unrest in Belgium became serious and French influence increased the prince, who remained loyal to the Habsburgs, lost access to his properties there, and with them his income.

In many families with a surplus of daughters, the strategy was to discourage some of them from marrying so as to minimize payment of expensive dowries. Good-natured Josepha Clary spent a full two decades searching for suitors for her young daughters, beginning in the 1760s (her oldest daughter married in 1766, and the youngest married in 1787). She eventually found suitable partners for all four, by dint of unremitting effort. With her sunny, easygoing, friendly personality, Josepha was an indulgent matron. As mother-in-law too, she kept her distance, sometimes clucking solicitously about the antics of her daughter-in-law as well as the almost equally forward behavior of her own married daughters but unwilling to cause discord by censuring them. To Eleonore Liechtenstein and Leopoldine Kaunitz and even to Leopoldine Liechtenstein, accustomed to stricter standards, the behavior of the Clary daughters seemed indecorous. Of the youngest daughter Thérèse, Eleonore Liechtenstein remarked, "she is pleasant but has an air of assurance and flirtatiousness that would not please me in my own daughter. Princess Clary has never been particular about this, and that is no doubt because she does not notice it."¹⁷⁴ But Josepha Clary's daughters were amiable and attractive, and their enthusiasms were characteristic of open-minded groups within the young Habsburg aristocracy of the late eighteenth century. The Clary family was well-to-do but could not offer large dowries. In spite of this constraint, each new family connection had to be respectable and prosperous. The Clary daughters married into the Ledebur, Chotek, Hoyos, and Wilczek families, all houses of high if not brilliant status. Josepha Clary's son-in-law Johann Rudolf Chotek (1748–1824), married to her daughter Maria Sidonia, served for many years as a prominent administrator under both Joseph II and later Leopold

II, an outstanding career that the diarist Zinzendorf (not entirely impartial) believed to have been abetted by the "intrigues" of Josepha Clary and Archduchess Marie Christine, working in concert.[175]

The marriage of the youngest Clary daughter Thérèse was long deferred. Her fate became a matter of concern for her parents. On 29 July 1778 Josepha Clary had lamented to her husband that the following day would be Thérèse's birthday: "22 years old and no establishment, fiat voluntas tua."[176] In October 1779 Maria Theresia offered to Josepha Clary a vacant place in the *Stift* at Nivelles in Belgium for Thérèse. Although Maria Theresia had such nominations in her gift, the Clary family's genealogical eligibility still had to be verified by the foundation. At Nivelles applicants typically had to demonstrate that their families had been noble as far back as great great grandparents. In 1761 Zinzendorf had observed in his diary that the genealogical proofs required for Nivelles were "diabolically difficult."[177] To Josepha's dismay, Thérèse's documentation appeared to be inadequate.

The situation was appalling, as Eleonore wrote to Leopoldine Kaunitz in July 1780. Josepha herself was at a loss ("she does not know which way to turn"). Several days later Eleonore added, "my God, I pity her, her situation is dreadful! But is it certain then that she cannot provide the [genealogical] proofs? does she have the documents, but they are deficient? For a genealogical table proves nothing, especially in the case of families that are little known and yet may still be noble." It was true, Eleonore noted, that Josepha could have the emperor override the objections of the *Stift*. "But I understand they are saying in town that the canonesses fear an [imperial] fiat, and have already lodged a protest against it, I do not know if this is true, what is annoying is that people are already starting to talk. What would she have done if this had happened with one of her older daughters [the married sisters]? Not one would have found an establishment."[178] Joseph II assured Josepha that he would investigate the problem and find a solution, but for the Clary family's reputation his intervention was bound to be a mixed blessing. The sovereign could apply pressure on the foundation and trump its objections to an applicant. But to accept help in the form of a fiat or *Machtspruch* from the sovereign would be to concede in the face of aristocratic public opinion that one's proofs had not been adequate. Although not rare in the late eighteenth century, such pressure and assistance from the ruler would still be viewed unfavorably by other noble families, as a despotic encroachment by the monarch on the corporate privileges of the nobility. Josepha's friends understood the seriousness of her predicament. Leopoldine Kaunitz reported Leopoldine Liechtenstein's reaction; "she would give two fingers off her hand, she says, to secure an establishment for Thérèse." The emperor did intervene in favor of Thérèse's admission, and apparently Josepha Clary was grateful. "I believe," wrote Eleonore Liechtenstein in July 1781, "that the emperor expedited matters but that they would have ended in success without him and would then have seemed less a result of [imperial] favor. But on the other hand, la Clary [Josepha Clary] would have been tormented for a longer period and would have faced more trouble and uncertainty."[179]

Once Thérèse's placement at Nivelles was secure, the fond Josepha, who had longed for this opportunity for her daughter, began to lament her daughter's departure for Nivelles.[180] But placement in the *Stift* undoubtedly preserved Thérèse's chances for marriage. Count Johann Joseph Wilczek (1738–1819), serving the Habsburgs in various posts in Milan and Thérèse's senior by twenty years, began expressing interest in marrying her as early as 1783. At her *Stift* Thérèse Clary frequently came into contact with Archduchess Marie Christine, who resided in Brussels at the time and frequently visited Nivelles. The archduchess promoted the match. The wedding took place in 1787, after Thérèse had resigned her position at Nivelles; but the marriage was of short duration, for Thérèse died in childbirth in 1790.[181]

Sidonia Kinsky had only a single son and daughter for whom establishments were needed, and for each an eligible marriage *partie* was forthcoming. In 1777 the sole surviving son, Joseph, married Rosa Harrach (1758–1814), a collateral relative of Eleonore's son-in-law and daughter of the Rosa Harrach who had promoted Josephine's marriage. Joseph Kinsky died in 1798. The couple produced two sons and two daughters. The oldest of these and heir to headship of the family was Ferdinand, born 1781, who in later years became one of Beethoven's patrons. As Beethoven scholars know, he died in 1812 after falling from his horse, even before his grandmother Sidonia Kinsky herself died, but not before he and his wife too had themselves produced sons to perpetuate the male line. Sidonia's daughter Maria Anna Kinsky was three years younger than her brother and made her debut at court in early 1773 at the age of nineteen, as Sidonia reported to Lady Mary Coke. Sidonia reported that Maria Anna was "delicate and not yet fully grown either physically or mentally, I could not be happier with her."[182] In 1778 Maria Anna married Count Rudolf Ferdinand Salburg (1732–1806), from a landed family of Upper Austria. When the union was announced, some witnesses felt that Maria Anna's interests had been sacrificed to preserve family resources for her brother. Certainly Count Salburg was more than twenty years his bride's senior, and the marriage removed her from her circle of relatives and friends in Vienna, to live near Linz. Many years later, in 1806, as a widow Maria Anna married a second time, the groom being Count Wenzel Sinzendorf (1755–1810) from a family with property in Lower Austria—to all appearances a long-standing attachment based entirely on affection.[183]

Only Leopoldine Kaunitz died before her turn came to play matchmaker. After Leopoldine's death in 1795, her sister Eleonore Liechtenstein felt responsible for the welfare of her niece, the intelligent, headstrong young woman "Lorel" Kaunitz. To the consternation of her close relatives, including Eleonore

Liechtenstein who tried to counsel her, from among a number of suitors Lorel eventually chose Clemens Metternich (1773-1859), whose family was a relative newcomer on the Viennese social scene. Bowing to the inevitable, Eleonore helped prepare her niece's trousseau and attended the marriage at Austerlitz on 27 September 1795. Metternich's immense political influence and power lay in the future. In the early years of their marriage, the eventual "coachman of Europe" and his bride Lorel found themselves snubbed by the bride's relatives and associates.[184]

It is clear that with so many family and personal interests livening the mix and with an environment that facilitated variation in place and pace of life, both society and court life in late eighteenth-century Vienna were thoroughly absorbing for all five *Dames*, who participated actively and energetically. The historian Padover's description of Viennese social life under Maria Theresia as "dull and petty" requires amendment, even for that earlier period. During Joseph II's sole rule in the 1780s dramatic changes added an extra fillip of liveliness and immediacy to everyday discourse.[185] This invigorating setting offered the five enterprising women a universe of opportunities for agreeable interactions with peers and for astute cultivation of the favor of influential groups and individuals.[186] The five *Dames* were consummate social creatures who moved skillfully among their peers at court functions and informal gatherings, representing and defending their personal and family interests amid the interplay of competition and cooperation that formed the core of daily life for the court aristocracy. Concurrently, in this busy, charged environment, and with many pressing demands on their attention, the *Dames* went about establishing and nurturing their improbable little *société*.

Notes

1 NRAS, DHP, papers of Lady Mary Coke, box 199, Sir Robert Murray Keith to Lady Mary Coke, Vienna, 5 January 1775.
2 Otto Brunner. *Adeliges Landleben und europäischer Geist. Leben und Werk Wolf Helmhards von Hohberg 1612-1688* (Salzburg: O. Müller, 1949). This was Otto Brunner's second major work. The first, a more theoretical treatise that appeared in 1939 entitled *Land und Herrschaft: Grundfragen der territorialen Verfassungsgeschichte Südostdeutschlands im Mittelalter,* had become problematic in postwar historiography because of its apparent espousal of National Socialist notions concerning "folk," culture, and the organic nature of the German body politic.
3 *The European Nobilities in the Seventeenth and Eighteenth Centuries,* ed. H. M. Scott, 2 vols. (New York: Longman, 1995).
4 Norbert Elias, *Die höfische Gesellschaft: Untersuchungen zur Soziologie des Königtums und der höfischen Aristokratie* (Neuwied: Luchterhand, 1969).
5 Jonathan Dewald, *The European Nobility, 1400-1800* (New York: Cambridge University Press, 1996), xiv-xvii, 4-7. Specialized studies of the aristocracy that have particular value for this study are Jeroen Duindam's *Vienna and Versailles: the Courts of Europe's Major Dynastic Rivals, 1550-1780* (Cambridge: Cambridge University Press, 2003), Hubert Christian Ehalt's *Ausdrucksformen absolutistischer Herrschaft:*

der Wiener Hof im 17. und 18. Jahrhundert (Munich: Oldenbourg, 1980), and Christine Lebeau's *Aristocrates et grands commis à la Cour de Vienne (1748-1791): le modèle français* (Paris: CNRS éditions, 1996). Two valuable studies focusing on the nobility of the Bohemian lands are Rita Krueger's *Czech, German, and Noble: Status and National Identity in Habsburg Bohemia* (New York: Oxford University Press, 2009) and Eila Hassenpflug-Elzholz's *Böhmen und die böhmischen Stände in der Zeit des beginnenden Zentralismus: eine Strukturanalyse der böhmischen Adelsnation um die Mitte des 18. Jahrhunderts* (Munich: R. Oldenbourg, 1982).

6   Grete Klingenstein, *Der Aufstieg des Hauses Kaunitz* (Göttingen: Vandenhoeck & Ruprecht, 1975).
7   Ivo Cerman, *Habsburgischer Adel und Aufklärung: Bildungsverhalten des Wiener Hofadels im 18. Jahrhundert* (Stuttgart: Franz Steiner, 2010).
8   Dickson, *Finance and Government*, 1:51-52.
9   Swinburne, *Courts of Europe*, 1: 351-52.
10 Gustav Otruba, "Verwaltung, Finanzen, Manufakturen, Gewerbe, Handel und Verkehr: technische gewerbliche Bildung und Bevölkerungsentwicklung," in *Österreich im Zeitalter des aufgeklärten Absolutismus*, ed. Erich Zöllner (Vienna: Österreichischer Bundesverlag, 1983), 142.
11 LRRA, P 17/27, EL to LK, Kromau, 20 August 1781.
12 Philip Dormer Stanhope Chesterfield, *The Letters of Philip Dormer Stanhope, 4th Earl of Chesterfield*, ed. Bonamy Dobrée (New York: AMS Press, 1932), 1751-1761, 5: 1872 (to his son, London, 11 May 1752); LRRA, P 16/19, LK to EL, Naples, 17 December 1765.
13 NM, RAŠM, carton 153, Franz Philip Sternberg to son Christian, Warsaw, 2 July 1757.
14 LRRA, P 18/61, EL to Josephine Harrach, Vienna, 15 July 1806, P 18/61.
15 Wolf, *Aus dem Hofleben*, 285-86.
16 LRRA, Q 1/63, EL to Josephine Harrach, Vienna, 6 October 1808.
17 LRRA, P 16/18, EL to LK, Frankfurt, 7 April 1764.
18 LRRA, P 16/18, EL to LK, Öttingen, 14 April 1764.
19 Sir Robert Murray Keith, *Memoirs and Correspondence* (London: Henry Colburn, 1849), 1: 443.
20 Qtd. in Jean-Paul Bled, Bled, *Marie-Thérèse d'Autriche* (Paris: Fayard, 2001), 399-400, message from M. Bérenger to the Duc de Choiseul, 3 December 1766.
21 Wolf, *Aus dem Hofleben*, 314-15.
22 HHStA, HA, SB 3, MT to Marie Antoinette, Vienna, 3 November 1780; Alfred von Arneth, ed., *Maria Theresia und Marie Antoinette* (Leipzig: K. F. Köhler, 1866), 8-9, 1 November 1770; *Briefe der Kaiserin Maria Theresia an ihre Kinder*, 3: 99-100, MT to Marie Beatrix, 27 November 1768.
23 *Briefe der Kaiserin Maria Theresia an ihre Kinder*, 3: 420, MT to Marie Beatrix, 5 June 1780; 2: 462-63, MT to Marie Christine, 3 June 1780.
24 Robert Pick, *Empress Maria Theresa: The Earlier Years, 1717-1757* (New York: Harper & Row, 1966), 226.
25 When Kaunitz fell ill in 1776, it was a matter of great concern to Maria Theresia: "Today I am going to pay a visit to Prince Kaunitz, who is completely out of danger. He had an inflammation of the lungs; Kestler has pulled him through by bleeding him twice." Maria Theresia, *Briefe der Kaiserin Maria Theresia an ihre Kinder*, 1: 132, MT to Ferdinand, 18 June 1772; 2: 31, MT to Ferdinand, 20 June 1776.
26 Beales, *Joseph II*, 1: 156.
27 LRRA, P 17/30, LK to EL, Vienna, 6 October 1785.
28 Duindam, *Vienna and Versailles*, 212.

29 Beales cites the comments of the Prince de Ligne, surely a competent source in this matter (*Joseph II*, 2: 132), who observed that the emperor "knew how to act the sovereign and put on display a fine court when it was absolutely necessary; and then he gave to that court, which normally had the atmosphere of a convent or barracks, the ceremony and dignity of a palace of Maria Theresia." Charles Joseph Ligne, *Mémoires et mélanges historiques et littéraires* (Paris: Ambroise Dupont, 1827), 1: 241.

30 Duindam, *Vienna and Versailles*, 181.

31 Franz A. J. Szabo, "Perspective from the Pinnacle: State Chancellor Kaunitz on Nobility in the Habsburg Monarchy," in *Adel im "langen" 18. Jahrhundert*, ed. Gabriele Haug-Moritz, Hans Peter Hye, and Marlies Raffler (Vienna: Austrian Academy of Sciences, 2009), 243-45.

32 LRRA, P 17/29, EL to LK, Kromau 29 July 1783; P 17/29, LK to EL, 26 July 1783.

33 LRRA, P 17/38, EL to Josephine Harrach, Kromau, 1 August 1783.

34 SOAL-D, RACA, carton 64, Archduchess Marie Christine to JC, 11 August 1783.

35 Count Fries, who received the rank of prince at this time also, was known to have purchased his honor dearly as well. LRRA, P 17/29, LK to EL, Vienna, 17 July 1783; EL to LK, Kromau, 21 July 1783; EL to LK, Kromau, 29 July 1783.

36 SOAL-D, RACA, carton 66, JC to daughter Countess Ledebur, Vienna, 24 January 1767.

37 HHStA, HA, SB 4, JII to MT, 31 January 1767; Alfred von Arneth, ed., *Maria Theresia und Joseph II.: ihre Correspondenz sammt Briefen Joseph's an seinen Bruder Leopold* (Vienna: C. Gerold's Sohn, 1867-68), 1: 1, 215 (partial text); François Fejtö, *Joseph II: un Habsbourg révolutionnaire*, new ed. (Paris: Quai Voltaire, 1994), 169; Karl Friedrich von Frank, *Standeserhebungen und Gnadenakte für das Deutsche Reich und die Österreichischen Erblande bis 1806, sowie kaiserlich österreichische bis 1823* ([s.l.] Selbstverlag, Schloss Senftenegg, Niederösterreich, 1967-1974), 1: 183.

38 LRRA, P 17/25, LK to EL, Vienna, 18 October 1779; Stekl, *Österreichs Aristokratie*, 138.

39 LRRA, P 17/24, LK to EL, 22 September 1778.

40 Keith, *Memoirs*, 1: 459-60, Sir R. M. Keith to Mr. Bradshaw, Vienna, 5 March 1774. Additional description (ascribed to R. Arbuthnot) cited in Keith, *Memoirs*, 2: 196; Joachim Schondorff, ed., *Aufklärung auf wienerisch* (Vienna: P. Zsolnay, 1980), 20-21.

41 Nicole Pohl describes the basic contours of what historians generally denominate the classic *salon* in "'Perfect Reciprocity': Salon Culture and Epistolary Conversation," *Women's Writing* 13, no. 1 (2006): 141-42.

42 Wraxall, *Memoirs of the Courts of Berlin, Dresden, Warsaw, and Vienna*, 2: 473. Zinzendorf, *Europäische Aufklärung zwischen Wien und Triest: Die Tagebücher des Gouverneurs Karl Graf Zinzendorf, 1776-1782*, vol.1, "Einführung," 170-76; Cerman, *Habsburgischer Adel*, especially 186-90.

43 Concerning this phenomenon, see Leslie Bodi, *Tauwetter in Wien: zur Prosa der österreichischen Aufklärung 1781-1795*, Schriftenreihe der Österreichischen Gesellschaft zur Erforschung des 18. Jahrhunderts 6, 2nd ed. (Vienna: Böhlau, 1995), 77; Wolf, *Fürstin Eleonore Liechtenstein*, 251.

44 James Van Horn Melton, *The Rise of the Public in Enlightenment Europe* (New York: Cambridge University Press, 2001), 216-19. In *Conservative Tradition in Pre-revolutionary France: Parisian Salon Women* (New York: P. Lang, 1999), Jolanta T. Pekacz makes the case that even French *salonnières* were a mostly conservative group, both politically and in the circumscribed roles they envisioned for themselves as women.

45 LRRA, P 16/18, LK to EL, Vienna, 21 November 1763.

46 HHStA, ZT, Band 22, 5 December 1777, 16 December 1777; William Hamilton, *The Hamilton Letters: The Naples Dispatches of Sir William Hamilton,* ed. John A. Davis and Giovanni Capuano (London: I. B. Tauris, 2008), 13, Charles Greville to Hamilton, Vienna, 9 October 1769.

47 In their letters the *Dames* mention games such as troisette (presumably tressette), whist, and hombre. Lady Mary Coke, *The Letters and Journals of Lady Mary Coke* (Bath: Kingsmead reprints, 1970), 3: 311-12, 1 November 1770; SOAL-D, RACA, carton 54, JC to her husband, June 1769; carton 66, Franz Rosenberg [FR] to JC, Pisa, 27 March 1795; HHStA, ZT, Band 21, Vienna, 7 May 1776; LRRA, P 17/24, LK to EL, Vienna, 1 September 1777; P 17/25, LK to EL, Vienna, 20 October 1779.

48 Kavanagh's particular focus is French practices. Thomas Kavanagh, "The Libertine's Bluff: Cards and Culture in Eighteenth-Century France," *Eighteenth-Century Studies* 33, no. 4 (2000): 510; Beales, *Joseph II*, 1: 158; Keith, *Memoirs*, 1: 367-68, Sir R. M. Keith to his sister, Vienna, 7 March 1773; SOAL-D, RACA, carton 64, LL to JC, Spa, 18 July [1781].

49 Wraxall, *Memoirs of the Courts of Berlin, Dresden, Warsaw, and Vienna*, 2: 240-41; Lady Mary Coke, *Letters and Journals*, 3: 316-18, 11 November 1770; 334-35, Vienna, [8] December 1770; LRRA, P 17/24, EL to LK, Baden, 7 September 1777. Among the papers of Madame de Deffand, reported in her published correspondence, is a poem explaining rather facetiously the attractions of the practice. The first stanza states:
    Vive le parfilage!
    Plus de plaisir sans lui!
    Cet important ouvrage
    Chasse partout l'ennui.
    Tandis que l'on déchire
    Et galons et rubans,
    L'ont peut encor [sic] médire
    Et déchirer les gens.
    Or, roughly translated:
    Long live parfilage!
    No more pleasure without it!
    This important work
    banishes boredom everywhere.
    While one tears to pieces
    both braids and ribbons
    one can also malign
    and tear to pieces other people.
M. de Saint-Aulaire, ed., *Correspondance complète de Mme du Deffand avec la Duchesse de Choiseul, l'Abbé Barthélemy et M. Craufurt* (Paris: Michel Lévy Frères, 1867), 2: 112.

50 The younger generation received preparation for such events at children's balls. In a letter to her married oldest daughter in 1767 the fun-loving Josepha Clary described with relish the dancing lessons of her younger daughters with "Vestris," quite possibly the famed dancer Gaëtan Appoline Balthazar Vestris, 1729-1808, routinely active in Paris but sojourning in Vienna in 1767. LRRA, P 17/24, LK to EL, Vienna, 8 October 1777; P 16/21, EL to LK, Vienna, 11 February 1768, P 16/21; SOAL-D, RACA, carton 66, JC to her daughter Countess Ledebur, 17 February 1767; Philip H. Highfill, *Biographical Dictionary of Actors, Actresses, Musicians, Dancers, Managers and Other State Personnel in London, 1660-1800* (Carbondale: Southern Illinois University Press, 1973-1993), 15: 147.

51 LRRA, P 17/25, EL to LL, Vienna, 30 July 1779; LK to EL, Vienna, 15 August 1779.
52 Wraxall, *Memoirs of the Courts of Berlin, Dresden, Warsaw, and Vienna*, 2: 239, 248-49. Grand Duke Leopold, in his "Riflessioni sopra lo stato della Monarchia" of 1778, found fault with both male and female education (as well as much else in Vienna). The latter produced young women of the "first" and "second" classes who were ignorant, knew nothing of running a household or educating children, and were ashamed of their own children, living only for pleasure. French educators were at fault for both sexes, as well as the constant balls, picnics, fireworks, horse races, and bad books, especially novels and excessively sentimental German poetry and books. Adam Wandruszka, *Leopold II., Erzherzog von Österreich, Grossherzog von Toskana, König von Ungarn und Böhmen, römischer Kaiser* (Vienna: Verlag Herold, 1963-65), 1: 357-58; Beales, *Joseph II*, 1: 326; Gutkas, *Kaiser Joseph II.*, 37.
53 Nicole Pohl notes that "regard for Mme de Sévigné was, with some exceptions, universal, as her conversational style was married with great wit and a sensibility that particularly appealed to eighteenth-century readers." Nicole Pohl, "'Perfect Reciprocity': Salon Culture and Epistolary Conversation," *Women's Writing* 13, no. 1 (2006): 145. LRRA, P 16/20, LK to EL, Naples, 27 May 1766; P 16/21, LK to EL, P 16/21, Naples, 3 January 1769; SOAL-D, RACA, carton 66, JC to her son Prince Clary, Weidlingau, 9 August 1797.
54 Ernst Wangermann, "Matte Morgenröte: Verzug und Widerruf im späten Reformwerk Maria Theresias" in *Maria Theresia und ihre Zeit: eine Darstellung der Epoche von 1740-1780 aus Anlass der 200. Wiederkehr des Todestages der Kaiserin*, ed. Walter Koschatzky (Salzburg: Residenz Verlag, 1979), 70-71.
55 T. C. W. Blanning, *The Culture of Power and the Power of Culture: Old Regime Europe 1660-1789* (New York: Oxford University Press, 2002), 141-42; Jean-Pierre Lavandier, *Le livre au temps de Marie-Thérèse: code des lois de censure du livre pour les pays austro-bohémiens 1740-1780* (Bern: Peter Lang, 1993), 138; Paul P. Bernard, *Jesuits and Jacobins: Enlightenment and Enlightened Despotism in Austria* (Urbana, IL: University of Illinois Press, 1971), 30; Franz A. J. Szabo, "The Cultural Transformation of the Habsburg Monarchy," *Studies in Music* 16 (1997), 44.
56 The letters of Eleonore Liechtenstein and Leopoldine Kaunitz contain many references to their reading, too frequent to be cited individually. Adam Wolf's biography of Eleonore notes the women's extensive reading. *Fürstin Eleonore Liechtenstein*, 28, 82, 94, 137, 244, 302, 330-31. For the aristocracy's attitude towards the religious criticism of the *philosophes*, see Cerman's summary, *Habsburgischer Adel*, 451.
57 LRRA, P 16/22, EL to LK, Kromau, 22 September 1779; Schöpfer, *Klar und Fest*, 92-94; Wolf, *Fürstin Eleonore Liechtenstein*, 201-02, 331; Falke, *Geschichte*, 2: 353-54.
58 As in the case when Josepha Clary quoted a passage from Destouches's "Le philosophe marié" in a 1794 letter to her son: "I know that in spite of my many faults you love me to distraction . . . There you have my old theatrical erudition," she joked. SOAL-D, RACA, carton 65, JC to son Prince Johann Clary, 21 June 1794.
59 Maria Theresia's remark cited in Peter Csendes and Ferdinand Opll, ed., *Wien: Geschichte einer Stadt*, vol. 2, *Die Frühneuzeitliche Residenz, 16. bis 18. Jahrhundert* (Vienna: Böhlau, 2001-2006), 523. Pezzl is cited in *Aufklärung auf wienerisch*, 19-29.
60 Verena Keil-Budischowsky, *Die Theater Wiens* (Vienna: P. Zsolnay, 1983), 57-58.
61 Eleonore's own husband, whom she did not mention, was also involved in the effort to save the French theater. Jean-Paul Bled, *Marie-Thérèse d'Autriche* (Paris: Fayard: 2001), 327; Vehse, *Geschichte der deutschen Höfe*, 13: 263-64; LRRA, P 16/21, EL to LK, Vienna, 19 October 1769; Cerman, *Habsburgischer Adel*, 194; Beales, "Mozart and the Habsburgs," 11.

62 Beales, *Joseph II*, 1: 235.
63 Johann Josef Khevenhüller-Metsch, *Aus der Zeit Maria Theresias. Tagebuch des Fürsten Johann Josef Khevenhüller-Metsch. 1774-1776 und Nachträge*, ed. Maria Breunlich-Pawlik and Hans Wagner (Vienna: Adolf Holzhausens, 1972), supplementary entries by the author's son, 1774-1775, 134; Beales, *Joseph II*, 1: 235; Gutkas, *Kaiser Joseph II.*, 163-64.
64 LRRA, P 17/27, LK to EL, Vienna, 15 October 1779. For Chancellor Kaunitz's stance, Szabo, *Kaunitz and Enlightened Absolutism, 1753-1789*, 205-08.
65 Beales, *Joseph II*, 2: 462-63; Keil-Budischowsky, *Die Theater Wiens*, 60.
66 LRRA, P 17/27, LK to EL, Baden, 29 September 1779.
67 The indefatigable imperial impressario sent instructions and comments to Count Rosenberg from the military front even during the difficult Turkish War, late in his reign. Helmut Reinalter, *Am Hofe Josephs II.* (Leipzig: Edition Leipzig, 1991), 43.
68 Anton Joseph Zorn von Bulach, *L'ambassade du prince Louis de Rohan à la cour de Vienna 1771-1774*, rprt. (Strasbourg: G. Fischbach, 1901), 11-12; Beales, *Joseph II*, 1: 314-16; Khevenhüller-Metsch, *Aus der Zeit Maria Theresias. Tagebuch des Fürsten Johann Josef Khevenhüller-Metsch* (Vienna: Adolf Holzhausen, 1907-1925), 7: 123-25, 20 April 1772.
69 LRRA, P 17/26, EL to LK, Eisgrub, 28 July 1780; LK to EL, Vienna, 26 July 1780; Oldřich Pulkert and Jan Šaroch, "Beethoven in den böhmischen Bädern" in *Ludwig van Beethoven im Herzen Europas*, ed. Oldřich Pulkert and Hans-Werner Küthen (Prague: České Lupkové Závody, 2000), 335.
70 Concerning amateur theatrical activities, LRRA, P 17/31, EL to LK, Kromau, 29 September 1785; P 17/29, LK to EL, Vienna, 15 September 1779; Schöpfer, *Klar und Fest*, 95; Stekl, *Österreichs Aristokratie*, 200-01; Franz Hadamowsky, *Wien, Theater Geschichte: von den Anfängen bis zum Ende des Ersten Weltkriegs. Geschichte der Stadt Wien* (Vienna: Jugend und Volk, 1988), 3: 566-68.
71 LRRA, P 17/29, EL to LK, Kromau, 15 July 1783; Richard B. Stothers, "The Great Dry Fog of 1783," *Climatic Change* 32, no. 1 (1996): 79-89; Manfred Vasold, "Die Eruptionen des Laki von 1783/84: ein Beitrag zur deutschen Klimageschichte," *Naturwissenschaftliche Rundschau* 57, no. 11 (2004): 602-08.
72 LRRA, P 17/25, EL to LK, Feldsberg, 22 August 1779; LK to EL, Vienna, 24 August 1779; Wolf, *Fürstin Eleonore Liechtenstein*, 336.
73 LRRA, P 16/19, LK to EL, Naples, 8 October 1765.
74 Eugen Guglia, *Maria Theresia: ihr Leben und ihre Regierung* (Munich: R. Oldenbourg, 1917), 2: 213.
75 Joseph Zykan, *Laxenburg* (Vienna: Herold, 1969), 33-34.
76 Beales, *Joseph II*, 2: 440-42.
77 Gutkas, *Kaiser Joseph II.*, 270; Reinalter, *Am Hofe Josephs II.*, 156-57; Wolf, *Fürstin Eleonore Liechtenstein*, 194.
78 Beales, *Joseph II*, 1: 197.
79 Hertha Wohlrab, *Penzing: Geschichte des 14. Wiener Gemeindebezirkes und seiner alten Orte* (Vienna: Jugend und Volk, 1985), 56-57.
80 SOAL-D, RACA, carton 54, JC to her husband Prince Clary, Eisgrub, 12 August 1779.
81 LRRA, P 17/25, LK to EL, Vienna, 28 October 1779; P 17/24, LK to EL, 24 September 1778.
82 LRRA, P 18/47, EL to Josephine Harrach, 18 August 1792.
83 NRAS, DHP, papers of Lady Mary Coke, Rose Harrach to Lady Mary Coke, 7 June 1771; Lady Mary Coke, *Letters and Journals*, 3: 470, Vienna, 24 October 1771. In *Histoire d'une grande dame au XVIIIe siècle: la Princesse Hélène de Ligne*, 2nd ed. (Paris:

Calmann Lévy, 1888), 316, 322-23. Lucien Perey reports that Joseph II made the apartment available to Sidonia Kinsky; but Rosa Harrach and Lady Mary ascribed the favor to Maria Theresia and are probably more reliable sources, being close friends of the princess (Perey also confuses some biographical details concerning Sidonia Kinsky).

84 Lacy's residence in the central city, Nr. 1-3 Seilerstätte (the so-called "Kommandantenhaus"), had been assigned to him when he became Daun's successor as president of the war council. Kotasek, *Feldmarschall*, 218-19.

85 Kotasek, *Feldmarschall*, 217-18.

86 Today the park contains Lacy's grave, for the elderly soldier was buried in his beloved Dornbach in 1801. Géza Hajós, *Romantische Gärten der Aufklärung: Englische Landschaftskultur des 18. Jahrhunderts in und um Wien* (Vienna: Böhlau, 1989), 32, 36, 42, 137-38, 150; Kotasek, *Feldmarschall*, 228-29.

87 Kotasek, *Feldmarschall*, 218.

88 Maria Auböck and Gisa Ruland, *Grün in Wien: ein Führer zu den Gärten, Parks und Landschaften der Stadt* (Vienna: Falter, 1994), 220.

89 The Lednice-Valtice Cultural Landscape has been designated a protected area in UNESCO's World Heritage program.

90 Alexander Novotny, *Staatskanzler Kaunitz als geistige Persönlichkeit: ein österreichisches Kulturbild aus der Zeit der Aufklärung und des Josephinismus* (Vienna: Hollinek, 1947), 106; Nathaniel W. Wraxall, *Memoirs of the Courts of Berlin, Dresden, Warsaw, and Vienna*, 2: 256.

91 Keith, *Memoirs*, 1: 445-46, Keith to Mr. Bradshaw, Vienna, 13 October 1773.

92 LRRA, P 17/26, EL to LK, Feldsberg, 30 September 1780. Horseback riding counted some Viennese women among its enthusiasts; but among the *Dames*, only for Sidonia Kinsky and Eleonore is there evidence of interest. LRRA, P 16/22, EL to LK, 16 October 1771; Lady Mary Coke, *Letters and Journals*, 3: 460-61, Vienna, [2] October 1771.

93 LRRA, P 17/24, LK to EL, Feldsberg, 26 September 1776.

94 John Moore, *A View of Society and Manners in France, Switzerland, and Germany*, 5th ed. (London: W. Strahan and T. Cadell, 1783), 2: 395-401.

95 HHStA, HA, SB 7, JII to Leopold, 27 August 1772.

96 LRRA, P 17/27, EL to LK, Vienna, 31 August 1781 and Feldsberg, 27 September 1781.

97 LRRA, P 17/27, EL to LK, Vienna, 31 August 1781; EL to LK, Feldsberg, 21 October 1781. For provisions for Liechtenstein widows, see Evelin Oberhammer, "Gesegnet sei dies Band: Eheprojekte, Heiratspakten und Hochzeit im fürstlichen Haus," in *Der ganzen Welt ein Lob und Spiegel* (Vienna: Verlag für Geschichte und Politik, 1990), 196-97; Falke, *Geschichte*, 2: 241.

98 LRRA, P 17/28, EL to LK, Kromau, 31 July 1782; P 17/42, EL to Josephine Harrach, Vienna 11 August 1787.

99 Wolf, *Fürstin Eleonore Liechtenstein*, 21.

100 LRRA, P 17/33, EL to LK, Meseritsch, 4 September 1789.

101 Eleonore's reports to her sister and daughter over the years mention a wide range of supervisory activities, with visits to groves and forests, wine cellars and granaries, granges. She was a sporadically diligent but mostly absentee landlady throughout her life. LRRA, P 17/27, EL to LK, Meseritsch, 10 August 1781; EL to LK, Meseritsch, 16 August, 1781; P 17/33, EL to LK, Meseritsch, 13 July 1789; Q1/62, EL to Josephine Harrach, Meseritsch, 5 September 1807.

102 LRRA, Q1/66, EL to Josephine Harrach, Vienna 23 October 1812. Mährisch Kromau has always to be distinguished from Böhmisch Kromau (Český Krumlov).

103 LRRA, P 17/25, EL to LK, Kromau 25 September 1779; Hajós, *Romantische Gärten*, 132.

104 LRRA, P 17/31, Meseritsch, 7 October 1785; P 17/25, EL to LK, Feldsberg, 20 August 1779; EL to LK, Kromau, 9 October 1779.
105 LRRA, P 17/25, EL to LK, Feldsberg, 22 October 1779.
106 LRRA, P 17/24, EL to LK, Kromau, 26 June 1776; EL to LK, Kromau, 16 July 1776.
107 LRRA, P 17/27, EL to LK, Kromau, 7 July 1781; P 17/24, EL to LK, 21 August 1777; Falke, *Geschichte*, 2: 360-61.
108 Lady Mary Coke, *Letters and Journals*, 4: 237-38, Austerlitz, 14 September 1773, 19 September 1773, 20 September 1773.
109 For Keith, by contrast, activities at Feldsberg and Eisgrub seemed stilted. Keith, *Memoirs*, 1: 445-446, Sir R. M. Keith to Mr. Bradshaw, Vienna, 13 October 1773; 2: 70-72, Sir R. M. Keith to Mr. Chamier, Vienna, 28 July 1776.
110 Christina Kröll and Hartmut Schmidt, "Bäderkunde und Badepraxis in der Goethe-Zeit," in *'Was ich dort gelebt, genossen–': Goethes Badeaufenthalte 1785-1823: Geselligkeit, Werkentwicklung, Zeitereignisse,* ed. Jörn Göres (Königstein: Athenäum, 1982), 38.
111 Zorn von Bulach, *L'ambassade du prince Louis de Rohan*, 67.
112 LRRA, P 17/25, LK to EL, Baden, 25 April 1779; LK to EL, Baden, 4 May 1779; LK to EL, Baden, 23 September 1779; P 17/27, LK to EL, Vienna, 22 September 1781.
113 LRRA, P 17/25, EL to LK, 1 May 1779; P 17/30, EL to LK, Vienna, 28 August 1784.
114 Gutkas, *Kaiser Joseph II.*, 61; Emilio Bicchieri, "Lettere famigliari dell'Imperator Giuseppe II a Don Filippo e Don Ferdinando Duchi di Parma, (1760-1767) con note e documenti," in *Atti e memorie delle RR. Deputazioni di storia patria per le provincie modenesi e parmensi* (1868), 4: 120-21, Joseph II to Philip, Duke of Parma, 28 September and 13 November 1764; Woldemar Lippert, ed., *Kaiserin Maria Theresia und Kurfürstin Maria Antonia von Sachsen. Briefwechsel, 1747-1772* (Leipzig: Königlich Sächsische Kommission für Geschichte, 1908), 235-38, Maria Antonia of Saxony to MT, 14 September 1764 and MT to Maria Antonia, 14 October 1764; Clary, *A European Past*, 8; Maria Theresia, *Briefe der Kaiserin Maria Theresia an ihre Kinder*, 2: 148, MT to Ferdinand, 2 October 1778.
115 SOAL-D, RACA, carton 54, JC's husband Prince Clary to JC, [Teplitz,] 4 August 1779.
116 For herself, Josepha clearly wanted nothing to do with the management of Teplitz, but she expressed satisfaction with its growing popularity. LRRA, P 16/22, EL to LK, Vienna, 7 August [1771] and Meseritsch, 23 October 1771; P 17/26, LK to EL, Vienna, 24 July 1780; P 17/29, EL to LK, Kromau, 20 August 1783; P 18/55, EL to Josephine Harrach, 5 August 1800; SOAL-D, RACA, carton 54, JC to husband Prince Clary, Vienna, 11 September 1781; Pulkert and Šaroch, "Beethoven in den böhmischen Bädern," 335.
117 LRRA, P 17/29, EL to LK, Vienna, 17 September 1783.
118 Single women attained to a somewhat greater freedom of movement when their families obtained for them a place, or prebend, at one of the exclusive *Stifte* or female foundations. A recent study of conditions in the *Stift* at Essen, where Leopoldine Liechtenstein obtained a place for one of her daughters, is revealing. Especially interesting are the comments found in Ute Küppers-Braun, *Frauen des hohen Adels im kaiserlich-freiweltlichen Damenstift Essen (1605-1803)*, ed. Alfred Pothmann and Johannes Meier (Münster: Aschendorff, 1997), 260-61, in letters of Jeannette Manderscheid, sister of Leopoldine Liechtenstein's daughter-in-law Caroline, dated 12 and 13 April 1771 and 20 June 1774.
119 Wraxall, *Memoirs of the Courts of Berlin, Dresden, Warsaw, and Vienna*, 2: 246-55.
120 A sensitive man, by 1810 Zinzendorf was disillusioned and embittered, speaking in caustic terms of the coarseness of married women. The Irish writer Melesina Trench

noted in the late 1790s that in Vienna's aristocratic circles women were not shunned for their transgressions: "those who are of notorious bad character are received in all societies with as much *empressement* as those of the very best conduct. The few really virtuous women do not make a class apart, but associate indiscriminately, and even form friendships, with those who are most notoriously otherwise . . . The best feature in the character of the society at Vienna is a universal appearance of good nature." HHStA, ZT, Band 55, 30 March 1810; Melesina Chenevix St. George Trench, *Journal Kept During a Visit to German in 1799, 1800* (London: Savill and Edwards, 1861), 57-58.

121 Norbert Elias, *The Civilizing Process*, first published in German in 1939, rev. ed. Erick Dunning et al., trans. Edmund Jephcott (Malden, Mass.: Blackwell, 2000), 155. This situation has much in common with Olwen H. Hufton's account for the west European aristocracy, *The Prospect Before Her: A History of Women in Western Europe* (New York: Alfred Knopf, 1996), 4: 146-50, not surprising in view of the links among Europe's multinational aristocracies.

122 HHStA, Grosse Correspondenz Kaunitz, G. C. 405 c, Wenzel Kaunitz to Countess Bernardine Kaunitz-Rietberg-Questenberg, Laxenburg, 7 September 1777; Wenzel Kaunitz to LK, 27 March 1779; LRRA, P 17/25, LK to EL, Baden, 25 April 1779.

123 Summarized in Wolf, *Fürstin Eleonore Liechtenstein*, 61-62, 66; LRRA, P 16/19, EL to LK, 29 October 1765, 2 December 1765; P 16/20, EL to LK, 21 April 1766, 5 June 1766, and 16 October 1766; P 16/19, LK to EL, Naples, 13 August 1765.

124 Lady Mary Coke, visiting Vienna in 1771, reported during O'Donnell's final illness that he was "look'd upon as an excellent Officer, & [was] amiable in every part of his Character." Wolf, *Fürstin Eleonore Liechtenstein*, 66. Lady Mary Coke, *Letters and Journals*, 3: 383-84, 24 March 1771.

125 Beales suggests that Eleonore may have had an affair also with Count Franz Rosenberg. Beales, *Joseph II*, 2: 21*n*16. While it is a possibility, there appears to be little evidence of this since a rather flippant closing to a letter (8 August 1780), cited by Beales ("Give my regards to Rosenberg, I love him as always even though I realize that it is the most unfortunate of passions") would hardly be the place for Eleonore to utter a serious *cri de coeur*. Such flamboyant closings can be found in a number of letters of the *Dames*, e.g., messages from Leopoldine Kaunitz and Eleonore Liechtenstein to Madame Burghausen, a mutual friend of the women. LRRA, P 17/24, LK to EL, 6 July 1776; P 17/24, EL to LK, 8 July 1776; P 17/26, EL to LK, 8 August 1780.

126 LRRA, P 16/18, LK to EL, Naples, 4 May 1764; *Aufklärung auf wienerisch*, 173-74; Wolf, *Fürstin Eleonore Liechtenstein*, 26.

127 LRRA, P 17/26, LK to EL, Vienna, 9 August 1780; P 17/27, LK to EL, Vienna, 21 July 1781.

128 LRRA, P 17/25, LK to EL, Vienna, 22 August 1779.

129 HHStA, NL, fascicle 3, carton 3, "Lettres aux dames." There are several documents but especially striking is letter no. 60, no date but apparently from 1766. The salutation begins "bonjour, ma belle et aimable Princesse" and what follows is explicitly a love letter.

130 HHStA, ZT, Band 23, 25 January 1778, Vienna.

131 HHStA, ZT, Band 7, 13 February 1762.

132 Wraxall, *Memoirs of the Courts of Berlin, Dresden, Warsaw, and Vienna*, 458; Vehse, *Geschichte der deutschen Höfe*, 13: 201-02.

133 Although neither Chancellor Kaunitz nor Leopoldine Kaunitz lived to see it, the chancellor's own grandson, Leopoldine's nephew Alois, apparently so far transgressed the rather liberal bounds of decency as to be banished from the capital for purchasing young girls of the lower middle class for his own pleasure, usually from quiescent parents. The

excesses of Prince Nicholaus Esterházy, Leopoldine Liechtenstein's son-in-law, were well known but they led to no penalties. Most historians have concluded that as time passed, and certainly by the time the Congress of Vienna convened in Vienna (when the last princess died), public standards of aristocratic behavior for both men and women had become less exacting. Susanne Feigl and Christian Lunzer, *Das Mädchenballett des Fürsten Kaunitz: Kriminalfälle des Biedermeier* (Vienna: Österreichischen Staatsdruckerei, 1988).

134 The many affairs of Eleonore Liechtenstein's bachelor sons with aristocratic women, beginning in the mid-1790s, were no secret in Eleonore's social circles. Ernst Kaunitz, despite his own checkered past, balked initially at accepting Clemens Metternich as his son-in-law because the young man was too "experienced." LRRA, P 18/50, EL to Josephine Harrach, 20 May 1795; P 18/54, EL to Josephine Harrach, 1799; P 18/59, EL to Josephine Harrach, spring and summer 1804; Q 1/62, EL to Josephine Harrach, summer 1807; Jean Mistler, *Madame de Staël et Maurice O'Donnell, 1805-1817, d'après des lettres inédites* (Paris: Calmann-Lévy, 1926), 19.

135 Possibly this was Maria Maximilian, born Countess Schaffgotsch, 1741-1818, wife of Count Franz Ernst Wallis. HHStA, ZT, Band 18, 10 August, 12 August, and 13 August 1773, Prague.

136 LRRA, P 17/24, LK to EL, Vienna, 5 August 1778 and 3 October 1778.

137 LRRA, P 16/20, LK to EL, Naples, 18 September 1766, 9 December 1766, and 23 December 1766.

138 SOAL-D, RACA, carton 66, JC to daughter Ledebur, Vienna, 26 December 1767; LRRA, P 16/21, LK to EL, Naples, 7 February 1767, 19 February 1767, and 10 March 1767.

139 HHStA, Grosse Correspondenz Kaunitz, G. C. 407 c, Chancellor Kaunitz to Ernst Kaunitz, 8 December 1767; Wolf, *Fürstin Eleonore Liechtenstein*, 86; LRRA, P 17/25, LK to EL, Vienna, 22 August 1779; P 17/32, LK to EL, Baden, 25 September 1786; P 16/21, LK to EL, Naples, 4 May 1769.

140 LRRA, P 17/27, EL to LK, Meseritsch, 8 August 1781; LK to EL, Vienna, 11 August 1781.

141 LRRA, P 16/22, EL to LK, Pressburg, 21 July; LK to EL, Brünn, 21 July 1772.

142 Valentin Ladislas Esterházy de Galántha, *Lettres du Cte Valentin Esterházy à sa femme, 1784-1792*, ed. Ernest Daudet (Paris: Plon-Nourrit, 1907), 47, Count Valentin Esterházy to his wife, Marimont, 29 September 1784.

143 Johannes Arndt, "Möglichkeiten und Grenzen weiblicher Selbstbehauptung gegenüber männlicher Dominanz im Reichsgrafenstand des 17. und 18. Jahrhunderts," *Vierteljahrschrift für Sozial- und Wirtschaftsgeschichte* 77, no. 2 (1990): 174.

144 SOAL-D, RACA, carton 54, JC to her husband Prince Clary, Vienna, 22 October 1776.

145 Hans Jürgen Jüngling, "Die Heiraten des Hauses Liechtenstein im 17. und 18. Jahrhundert. Konnubium und soziale Verflechtungen am Beispiel der habsburgischen Hocharistokratie," in *Liechtenstein, fürstliches Haus und staatliche Ordnung: geschichtliche Grundlagen und moderne Perspektiven*, ed. Volker Press and Dietmar Willoweit, 2nd ed. (Vaduz: Verlag der Liechtensteinischen Akademischen Gesellschaft; Munich: R. Oldenbourg, 1988), 333.

146 Eleonore Liechtenstein was particularly skeptical of her sister-in-law Leopoldine's disclaimers regarding her eldest son; "in the end she and the marshal [Lacy] will between them oblige the young man to do what they wish." LRRA, P 17/28, EL to LK, Kromau, 27 July 1782.

147 LRRA, P 17/26, EL to LK, Eisgrub, 26 July 1780; EL to LK, Eisgrub, 29 July 1780; LK to EL, Vienna, 9 and 14 August 1780.

148 NM, RAŠM, carton 93, undated letters to LL's "sister"; LL to her mother, Spa, 8 June 1781.
149 LRRA, P 17/29, LK to EL, Baden, 27 September 1783.
150 When the widowed Prince Anton Esterházy himself subsequently took a second wife (a Countess von Hohenfeld), this new alliance threatened the special status of Marie and young Nicholaus Esterházy, since an additional heir might be produced. Prince Anton's marriage remained childless. LRRA, P 17/40, EL to Josephine Harrach, Kromau, 11 June; EL to Josephine Harrach, 30 July 1785; EL to Josephine Harrach, Vienna, 3 August 1785 and 10 August 1785; SOAL-D, RACA, carton 64, Marie Christine to JC, 26 July 1785; Wolf, *Fürstin Eleonore Liechtenstein*, 185; LRRA, P 17/43, EL to Josephine Harrach, Vienna, 1 July 1788; P 17/31, LK to EL, Vienna, 13 October 1785; P 17/45, EL to Josephine Harrach, Vienna, 30 December 1790.
151 LRRA, P 17/32, EL to LK, Altenburg, 17 September 1786; P 17/33, EL to LK, Meseritsch, 31 LRRA, P 17/33, EL to LK, Vienna, 1 June 1791; P 18/51, EL to Josephine Harrach, 30 May 1796; NM, RAŠM, carton 93, LL to brother, Hütteldorf, 16 July 1792; Falke, *Geschichte*, 2: 280; Schöpfer, *Klar und Fest*, 96.
152 NM, RAŠM, carton 47, Caroline Liechtenstein (Manderscheid) to sister, Vienna, 16 April 1789.
153 Ferdinand Wilczek, "Ein genealogisches Rätsel aus der Biedermeierzeit," *Adler: Zeitschrift für Genealogie und Heraldik* 20, nos. 13/14 (1964): 161-63; Jaroslav Čelada and Oldřich Pulkert, "Beethovens 'unsterbliche Geliebte,'" in *Ludwig van Beethoven im Herzen Europas: Leben und Nachleben in den böhmischen Ländern*, ed. Oldřich Pulkert and Hans-Werner Küthen (Prague: České Lupkové Závody, 2000), 383-408.
154 After Louis Liechtenstein's death in 1805, his widow Caroline penned some bitter letters, apparently to Augusta Sternberg, explaining her feeling of alienation from the Liechtenstein family. NM, RAŠM, carton 47, Carolina Liechtenstein (Manderscheid) to sister, Baden, 15 September 1805; LRRA, P 18/52, EL to Josephine Harrach, Vienna, 14 August 1797.
155 According to report, *Majoratsherr* Louis himself was much gratified by this accession to the family. Schöpfer, *Klar und Fest*, 97; LRRA, P 18/51, EL to Josephine Harrach, 27 May 1796.
156 Concerning the attractiveness of life as a *Stiftsdame* for aristocratic women, see Küppers-Braun, *Frauen des hohen Adels*, 217, 265-68, 278-79, 286-88, 301.
157 Küppers-Braun, *Frauen des hohen Adels*, 275-77.
158 Küppers-Braun, *Frauen des hohen Adels*, especially 57-158, 296, 301.
159 *Die Manderscheider: Eine Eifeler Adeslfamilie*, 136; Küppers-Braun, *Frauen des hohen Adels*, 380-83.
160 LRRA, P 17/25, EL to LK, Kromau, 25 September 1779.
161 LRRA, P 17/26, EL to LK, Vienna, 10 July 1780; EL to LK, Kromau, 5 August 1780.
162 The work of Jeroen Duindam notes the longstanding assumption among both Habsburg and Bourbon monarchs that marriage alliances of court nobility were the legitimate concern of the ruler. Jeroen Duindam, *Vienna and Versailles,* 285-86; LRRA, P 17/26, LK to EL, Vienna, 20 July 1780; P 17/33, EL to LK, undated; P 17/26, LK to EL, Vienna, 22 August 1780.
163 LRRA, P 17/27, EL to LK, [Feldsberg,] 13 October 1781.
164 LRRA, P 17/27, EL to LK, Feldsberg, 16 October 1781; P 17/28, EL to LK, Kromau, 12 August 1782; P 17/29, EL to LK, Kromau, 18 August 1783.
165 LRRA, P 17/30, EL to LK, Kromau, 17 July 1784.

166 LRRA, P 17/28, EL to LK, Kromau, 21 July 1782; P 17/31, EL to LK, Kromau, 26 June 1785; P 17/33, EL to LK, Meseritsch, 4 September 1789; LK to EL, Vienna, 30 July 1789.
167 LRRA, P 17/33, LK to EL, Vienna, 19 July 1789.
168 Because of Karl Zichy's work in carrying out the Josephinian reforms in Hungary, Countess Zichy was sometimes called the "queen of Hungary" (*reine d'Hongrie*) by detractors. Wolf, *Fürstin Eleonore Liechtenstein*, 220.
169 LRRA, P 17/33, EL to LK, Meseritsch, 14 August 1789; Wolf, *Fürstin Eleonore Liechtenstein*, 217-18.
170 LRRA, P 17/33, EL to LK, Meseritsch, 14 August 1789, 17 August 1789, 28 August 1789.
171 Eleonore deplored what she called the "libertinage" of her sons, by which she meant not simply sexual license but more generally casual morals and religious attitudes. Maurice's engagement to Leopoldine Esterházy occurred after he returned from French captivity in November 1805, and the marriage was celebrated at the Esterházy palace in Eisenstadt in April 1806. LRRA, P 18/59, EL to Josephine Harrach, 18 July 1804; Q 1/69, EL to Maurice Liechtenstein, Vienna, 10 December 1803; P 18/60, EL to Josephine Harrach, Vienna, 16 October 1805; Falke, *Geschichte*, 2: 360-61.
172 NRAS, DHP, Lady Mary Coke's correspondence, box 199, Sir Robert Murray Keith to Lady Mary Coke, Vienna, 5 January 1775.
173 The death of his son Charles in 1792, fighting in the Austrian army against the French, was a terrible blow to the Prince de Ligne. The Ligne family's activities provided an endless saga of interesting and sometimes unedifying anecdotes. SOAL-D, RACA, carton 65, JC to son Johann Nepomuk, Vienna, 4 October 1784; Pasteur, *Le prince de Ligne*, 120, 149, 226, 231-32, 254-55, 257; Philip Mansel, *Prince of Europe: the Life of Charles-Joseph de Ligne, 1735-1814* (London: Weidenfeld and Nicolson, 2003), 144-49.
174 Eleonore found Thérèse Clary to be pleasant but too flirtatious. LRRA, P 17/24, EL to LK, Eisgrub, 21 July 1778; P 17/26, EL to LK, Feldsberg, 30 September 1780.
175 Ivo Cerman includes passages from letters of Josepha Clary's daughter Countess Chotek as well as her husband Count Johann Rudolf Chotek and brother-in-law Count Wilczek in Cerman, *Habsburgischer Adel*, especially 186-90.
176 SOAL-D, RACA, carton 54, JC to husband, Eisgrub, 29 July 1778.
177 LRRA, P 17/25, LK to EL, Vienna, 28 October 1779; HHStA ZT, Band 6, 7 November 1761.
178 The problem of missing documents on the Hohenzollern-Hechingen side was solved by testimony confirming that Josepha Clary was the full sister of Marie Christine Thun, whose son Count Sigismund Thun had been accepted as a member of the Knights of Malta. For the Clary side, where information concerning the Aldringen family was difficult to locate, Eleonore suggested enlisting the help of Count Leopold Clary, nephew of Josepha Clary's husband, whose family would likewise benefit from a favorable outcome. LRRA, P 17/26, EL to LK, Eisgrub, 29 July 1780; EL to LK, Eisgrub, 31 July 1780; LK to EL, Vienna, 2 August 1780; P 17/27, EL to LK, Kromau, 7 July 1781; SOAL-D, RACA, carton 66, JII to JC, Brussels, 25 June [1781]; Fürstlich Hohenzollernsches Haus- und Domänenarchiv, Staatsarchiv Sigmaringen, Depositum 39, Bestand HH1, Rubrik/Nr.: A491, attestation from reigning prince Joseph Guillaume de Hohenzollern-Hechingen, Sigmaringen, 14 July 1781 and Count Meinrad Hohenzollern, Chanoine Capitulaire de la Cathedrale de Constance, Veringue [Veringen], 14 July 1781.
179 LRRA, P 17/27, LK to EL, Vienna, 7 July 1781; EL to LK, Kromau, 11 July 1781.

180 LRRA, P 17/27, LK to EL, Vienna, 14 July 1781; LK to EL, Vienna, 21 July 1781.
181 SOAL-D, RACA, carton 64, Marie Christine to JC, 20 October 1783 and 7 November 1783. Marriage plans for Thérèse Clary and Wilczek were finalized in summer 1787, while Thérèse was still at Nivelles.
182 NRAS, DHP, box 197, Lady Mary Coke's correspondence, SK to Lady Mary Coke, Vienna, 21 October 1772.
183 HHStA, ZT, Band 23, Vienna, 18 February 1778; Band 51, 19 and 24 April 1806; Johann Siebmacher, *Die Wappen des Adels in Niederösterreich*, reprint of Siebmacher's *Wappenbuch* (Nürnberg, 1909) (Neustadt an der Aisch: Bauer und Raspe, 1983), vol. 26, part 2, 13, 154; Reitwiesner, *Matrilineal Descents*, vol. 2, AKA 190; LRRA, P 18/61, EL to Josephine Harrach, St. Veit, 20 August 1806. Some sources report that Maria Anna and Salburg divorced in 1789, but this appears to be incorrect. Lulu Thürheim visited the Salburg couple in 1805 at their estate Salaberg. Lulu Thürheim, *Mein Leben: Erinnerungen aus Österreichs grosser Welt, 1788-1819*, trans. René Van Rhyn (Munich: Georg Müller, 1913), 1: 101-02, 151-53
184 The outstanding debts left by father Ernst Kaunitz at his death caused something of a scandal. SOAL-D, RACA, carton 66, JC to son Prince Clary, Vienna, 9, 10, and 27 May 1797.
185 Saul K. Padover, *The Revolutionary Emperor, Joseph II of Austria*, rev. ed. (Hamden, CT: Archon Books, 1967), 65.
186 See Lawrence Klein's apt comments on this subject (in an English context), in "Gender and the Public/Private Distinction in the Eighteenth Century: Some Questions about Evidence and Analytic Procedure," *Eighteenth-Century Studies* 29, no. 1 (1995): 97-109. Michael E. Yonan, "Modesty and Monarchy: Rethinking Maria Theresa at Schönbrunn," *Austrian History Yearbook* 35 (2004): 26.

Chapter 3

The Origins of *la société*

In a remarkable letter written in summer 1775, Grand Duke Leopold scolded his older brother Emperor Joseph about the unsuitable company Joseph kept. Leopold's critique was direct and vivid: "that persons among the groups you visit informally dare to meddle by talking to you about political matters and accordingly if they are women to make wrongheaded objections . . . and even dare to scold you . . . or make impertinent remarks, and that you can allow this, tolerate it, and visit them again seems to me one of the most astonishing things in the world." Leopold advised Joseph to quash the impertinence of female friends "who argue about matters that they understand no better than Chinese. Pardon this digression," Leopold continued, "but I become angry when I think that after all the efforts you make, persons to whom you are particularly amiable cause you unpleasantness and are so materially wanting in respect." In a series of exchanges the brothers weighed the appropriateness of Joseph's attendance at the soirées of women who ventured to discuss politics with him. Three weeks later Leopold returned to his theme: "allow me to tell you that it is entirely up to you to prevent persons with whom you socialize from discussing political matters, by merely threatening in all seriousness to visit no more if they talk to you about politics, and by letting them know that their company is agreeable to you but by no means essential, and then simple ambition and fear of losing your company will cause them to change their tune at once."[1]

Convention frowned upon the overt involvement of women in politics. Most observers assumed, as did Grand Duke Leopold, that an upright, well-intentioned woman would abstain from politics voluntarily. The examples of two capable contemporary female rulers, Maria Theresia and Catherine II, demonstrated the aptitude of certain unusual women for positions of power. Nevertheless, popular conceptions affirmed that political and diplomatic functions, narrowly defined, belonged to the male sphere of action. Despite her unusual status as female ruler, Maria Theresia herself did not assume the fitness of other women for political roles. There were no substantive government posts for women, although female appointments such as *Obersthofmeisterin* to Maria Theresia, "aja" to imperial children or archducal grandchildren, or more commonly service as ladies in waiting at court, signaled high status and could bring the appointee some informal social or political influence. Although Joseph deplored the ready access to the empress that Maria Theresia's *Weiberhof* had in the final years of her reign, in general the empress was not given to discussing politics with the court ladies who surrounded her.[2]

As women, the *Dames* played no formal role in events, even though they were members of families belonging to the monarchy's social and political elite. Nevertheless, prominent families that spent the winter "season" in Vienna, as did the Liechtenstein, Kaunitz, Kinsky, and Clary families, were well-informed politically, and both male and female family members could be active, seeking to safeguard family interests and to solidify their status vis-à-vis the ruler and other elite families. Informal activities of women were recognized as legitimate and even essential. Influence wielded by women at the Habsburg court was likely to be of a subtle nature. Male Habsburgs, despite various romantic dalliances and liaisons, had no tradition of installing official mistresses or accepting direct female participation even in informal political councils. When the English traveler Nathaniel Wraxall described the relationship between Eleonore Liechtenstein and Joseph II, he stressed that Eleonore disclaimed "even the smallest political influence or credit with him [Joseph II]. I have heard her do so," wrote Wraxall, "as he, on his side, frequently cites a maxim from which no Sovereign should deviate. It is, that 'Princes never ought to allow a woman, let her merit or talents be what they may, to acquire an ascendancy over their affections, on account of the political consequences which almost always result from such a passion.'"[3]

Social and political roles for Europe's aristocratic women as individuals prior to the upheavals of the French Revolution and Napoleon lacked clear delimiters. Certainly these activities were subordinate to those of men, but their relatively casual, unstudied nature and the diversity of institutions of sociability afforded women considerable latitude. As Jerzy Lukowski has observed, "The most determined [women] simply had to do the best within the constraints of what social structures and conventions allowed."[4] Boundaries between the personal and the political, between the private and the public spheres, were indistinct and permeable.[5] By modern standards the interplay of diverse groups and individuals of both sexes with alternately consonant and clashing interests and a multiplicity of goals, all contained within a monarchical structure of government, was markedly political in nature. Politically astute women like Joseph's circle of *Dames* could see themselves as models of female discretion because their political participation was informal. In the competition for influence and good will at the Habsburg court and among aristocratic factions, talented women were valued assets and were acknowledged as such. To today's historians the political content of such informal activity is unmistakable (the historian Dena Goodman has written convincingly of a historiographical "false opposition" between the public and private spheres in the Old Régime).[6] To contemporaries, the women's unusual friendship with the sovereign and other high officials might be the subject of envy, since access to the imperial family and most specifically to the sovereign was always the most critical single factor in the political life of the Habsburg monarchy. However, if this activity remained within acceptable social norms and did not impinge upon *les grandes affaires* of direct governance and diplomacy, it was not deemed inappropriate or unseemly. Instead, what made Joseph II's *société* unusual in the eyes of contemporaries was the unchanging, exclusive composition of the group, the regularity of its gatherings over decades, and the reputation it acquired among the cognoscenti for frank, unrestrained conversation.

Like their menfolk, aristocratic women who were prominent at court articulated the views of their social class. In conversations with the emperor as with their social peers, in broad terms (and with allowance for some personal inclinations) the *Dames* and their closest social contacts could be expected to represent the interests of noble proprietors of the lands of Bohemia, Moravia, and Lower Austria. Given the ethnic and territorial diversity of the monarchy, there could be nothing resembling a single point of view and certainly no monolithic offensive or defensive posture of the nobility as a whole over against the monarch. Although there was skirmishing in the ongoing contest to define the boundaries of central power and noble authority, respectively, no Habsburg ruler—not even the iconoclast Joseph II, as will be seen—seriously sought to overturn the established social hierarchy in theory or to dispense with the support of its elite in practice.[7] After all, in the overwhelmingly agricultural economy of the Habsburg monarchy, sovereigns could ill afford to forgo the services of the principal landowning class.

In his early writings Joseph II spoke in dramatic terms of the need to humble the great families. In his "Rêveries," most likely composed in 1763 when he was 22 years of age, prior to his coregency, he declared that it would be desirable to "humble and impoverish the great seigneurs [*les grands*]," declaring that he did not "believe it is useful to have little kings and great subjects who live at their ease without concerning themselves with the prospects of the state." He pointed out that in the sweeping proposals he was setting forth "it is the seigneurs that I will take on [*que j'attaque*]." Nevertheless Joseph worked with these seigneurs and employed their sons in government posts.[8] In other documents, Joseph's statements are less strident. Although the emperor railed against unworthy, coddled aristocrats, crown and aristocracy including those troublesome "little kings" necessarily remained mutually supportive and cooperative in a fundamental sense. This was the case even though Habsburg sovereigns—and Joseph II most radically—introduced reforms that limited the power and income of privileged groups and their corporate institutions. For all his fulminations, Joseph himself appears to have subscribed to the commonplace assumption that the male progeny of great houses, if properly educated and motivated, were particularly and even naturally well suited to fill responsible positions in government. Instead of discarding the services of the group they regarded as natural leaders, he, Chancellor Kaunitz, and tacitly even Maria Theresia through her adept selection of enterprising "paladins" argued the need for greater professionalism and better education of the nobility. While professing egalitarianism with regard to birth in a manner typical of popular enlightened thought and publicizing his goal of appointing and rewarding individuals purely in accordance with their merit—surely intended as indirect criticism of wasteful practices he witnessed under his mother's rule—Joseph himself also explicitly expressed a preference for individuals of good family, "wellborn people," who were to be favored over mere careerists and upstarts ("gens de fortune"). Chancellor Kaunitz made use of similar language in his response to one of Joseph's early statements, a memorandum identifying defects in the existing Habsburg system of governance, when he affirmed the suitability of the eldest sons of "la Grande Noblesse" for high positions as statesmen, given proper preparation and attitude, while their cadet brothers should devote themselves to careers as military officers. During the coregency Joseph shared with his mother the authority to make decisions concerning personnel, although in military affairs his influence was preponderant. He found fault with virtually all his servitors, and even his most earnest, enlightened employees generally fell short of the emperor's exacting standards. But for top-level posts, civilian and military, he relied throughout his reign on available wellborn individuals.[9]

The older three *Dames*, Josepha Clary, Sidonia Kinsky, and Leopoldine Liechtenstein, came of age during a peaceful interlude that was relatively secure and stable for the elite of the monarchy, their adult years beginning after the time of dark desperation and heroic resistance in the early 1740s but well before the future emperor Joseph II had reached the age of political discernment. The three oldest future *Dames* married and established households in 1747, 1749, and 1750, respectively. Maria Theresia's reign had begun in 1740 with an existential crisis for her lands and her position. Newly ascended to the throne, the inexperienced ruler found her inheritance challenged in the War of the Austrian Succession (1740–1748) not just by Frederick II of Prussia and the Bavarian prince Charles Albert but also by Spain, France, and even Saxony-Poland. All of these were hoping to share in spoils left by the young queen's defeat. The elderly set of advisors that Maria Theresia had inherited from her father Charles VI confronted this crisis with her, mostly in a timorous manner. Maria Theresia faced down these threats, sacrificing most of Silesia but preserving intact the rest of her inheritance.

Peace did not last, it is true. In the "reversal of alliances" or "diplomatic revolution" of 1756 sponsored by Wenzel Kaunitz—soon to be Leopoldine Öttingen's father-in-law—the former enemies Austria and France made common cause against Prussia and England and were joined by Russia, Sweden, Saxony, and Spain. Threatened by an overwhelming coalition of powers, Frederick II carried out a preemptive strike against Maria Theresia, launching the Seven Years War, 1756 to 1763. In this second duel with Prussia, Maria Theresia tried but failed to win back the territory of Silesia that had been her only serious loss in the War of the Austrian Succession. The conflict damaged the monarchy, in particular undermining it financially. But this new war was one Maria Theresia had chosen to wage, not a fight for survival. When the two younger *Dames,* Eleonore Liechtenstein and Leopoldine Kaunitz, arrived on the scene in Vienna in the early 1760s, completing the numbers of the future circle of five *Dames*—and just as Archduke Joseph was receiving his earliest initiation into affairs of state—even the Seven Years War was winding down. While fraught with potential danger, this second war never engendered the sense of crisis experienced during the early 1740s. The monarchy had won its fight for survival. It was not again tested so seriously until the French wars of the 1790s.

During and after each military struggle, Maria Theresia undertook significant internal reforms to make her state better able to withstand the strain of extended military effort and expenditure. She had inherited a government near bankruptcy, a substantial portion of its revenues used to service an enormous debt rather than to pay for a strong army or other necessities. The goal of most reforms of the late 1740s and 1750s, guided by Count Friedrich Wilhelm von Haugwitz, was to safeguard the revenues of the central government, urgently needed for the military contests with Prussia, against interference from the regional estates by obtaining their approval for a larger multiyear tax levy and some taxation of the dominical lands of the nobility as well as the rustical lands of the peasants. There were many regional variations in these agreements, and few new procedures applied to Hungary, the Italian lands, and Belgium. But with more active central oversight over the collection of taxes, Maria Theresia's government increased its leverage vis-à-vis provincial officials and diets. These early reforms also saw the separation of judicial functions from administrative and financial management and the creation of a new governing body to guide policy in both the Austrian and Bohemian lands, the "Directorium in publicis et cameralibus." Haugwitz's reforms met with opposition from aristocratic landowners, even those closely allied with the court. "The loudest protests," remarked Maria Theresia in her "Political Testament," composed around 1750, "came from the court itself, from those who battened on my favor or who owed their riches and good name to the bounty and generosity of my ancestors."[10]

Before the end of the Seven Years War, a more extensive reorganization of central administration, sponsored by Wenzel Kaunitz, saw the creation of a *Staatsrat* or council of state with oversight over all non-Hungarian lands (in practice Hungarian affairs were also considered by this deliberative body) and the transformation of Haugwitz's "Directorium" into a "United Austrian and Bohemian Chancellery." These reforms, like the earlier ones, further limited the authority of the provincial estates. Again Maria Theresia was hoping to secure her tax base against the depradations of landowners who were dominant in the provincial bodies by guaranteeing to peasant households the minimum resources in land and other necessities to support a healthy economic existence. Maria Theresia's early reforms included ambitious measurement, registration, and categorization of both rustical and dominical properties in the "hereditary lands" (excluding Hungary, the Italian lands, and Belgium). The new regulations proved difficult to enforce. Maria Theresia's government moved cautiously, trying to obtain the consent of the important elites in her lands for changes she made.[11] Partial measures at best, these early measures did not seriously jeopardize her harmonious relationship with the monarchy's secular and religious elites; but neither did they effect more than incremental improvements in peasant conditions.

After the death of Franz Stephan, Holy Roman Emperor as well as Maria Theresia's husband and coregent, on 17 September 1765 Maria Theresia named her son Joseph, now himself emperor, to be her new coregent. Despite her expressions of sadness and apathy after her husband's death, Maria Theresia continued to control most political decisions as she had during her husband's lifetime. By virtue of his new status as emperor Joseph naturally took charge of specifically imperial affairs. Maria Theresia also granted him authority over the military, although here she continued to interfere. The new coregent quickly demonstrated an enthusiasm for his military role, an interest that continued throughout the coming decades. Writing to her sister Leopoldine Kaunitz, Eleonore Liechtenstein speculated at first that Maria Theresia would simply retire after Franz Stephan's death, relinquishing all power to her son. It soon became clear that Maria Theresia would do nothing of the sort. By late September 1765 Eleonore could report to her sister Leopoldine Kaunitz that Maria Theresia had decided to remain active but would appear in public less frequently.[12] Chancellor Wenzel Kaunitz continued to direct Habsburg foreign policy and also had great influence in domestic affairs. Kaunitz's star had been in the ascendant since the mid-1750s and he remained a powerful player for decades. He had often to mediate between mother and son.[13] Kaunitz's influence began to wane only after Joseph II became sole ruler in 1780.

The five women's unique political experience began during the early years of Joseph's coregency, in the late 1760s, although the group did not coalesce fully for several years. The coregency of the empress and her son differed in tone and substance from the earlier years of Maria Theresia's reign, when Franz Stephan had served as coregent. Relations between Maria Theresia and Joseph were rarely untroubled throughout fifteen years of collaboration. The coregency began relatively auspiciously. Joseph deferred to the empress's experience and position and acquiesced in her political choices. However, when the new emperor made proposals of his own, the divergences between the two rulers' conceptions of their roles and the policies they favored frequently led to conflict and tension. By the mid-1770s this situation had evolved into a fluctuating but essentially unending series of quarrels, as Wraxall noted: "The Emperor himself, her son, though possessing her warmest affection, associated to a participation in the Royal Authority, and declared Coregent of Hungary, Bohemia, and all the Austrian dominions, yet remains dependent on his mother. She preserves the supreme direction, and is regarded as the only efficient Sovereign. Even in the military department, which she has in some measure resigned to him, it may be questioned whether he can make any essential changes or regulations, without her consent and approbation. Conscious of possessing ability to govern, she will never commit the felicity and protection of her people, to other hands than her own."[14] Expressions of gracious (and probably calculated) self-deprecation notwithstanding, the empress remained confident in her own capacity and rectitude. She sought her son's input, but once decisions were taken, by and large she expected Joseph to concur and to rally support for them.

A detailed analysis of the differences in style and substance between the two rulers Joseph and Maria Theresia is beyond the scope of this study.[15] Joseph described himself, not always coherently, as a sovereign of a new type, one who would devote his whole being to the welfare of the state, whose actions would be wise and correct because they were based on rational consideration for the welfare of all his subjects. He wanted to apply his principles to the affairs of all social classes and regions equally, confident that the policies he adopted would promote the greater good of the state and thus the well-being of the greatest number of inhabitants. The state was an impersonal abstraction, but it was absolutely paramount in Joseph's mind. He preferred an autocratic approach to governing, soliciting input from underlings but not collegial discussion about policies. As will be noted subsequently, many of the emperor's goals corresponded to the ideals that much historiography of eighteenth-century Europe categorizes as "enlightened despotism," or alternatively "enlightened absolutism."[16] Maria Theresia admired the intellectual prowess of her son. Nonetheless she feared that, tempted by popular philosophical notions, irreligion, and a desire to appear clever and win acclaim, he would destroy both the moral and the material foundations of the monarchy, those characteristics that secured for it the loyalty of its varied subjects. She accepted existing differences between regions and between social groups, willing to adjust the treatment she accorded to each in order to retain support and tolerating a kaleidoscope of customs and legal systems while seeking to modernize these incrementally. Maria Theresia was a serious reformer, capable of endorsing radical policies in some areas (such as landlord-peasant relations, as will be seen). She sought counsel and consensus so far as possible, however. She was no despot, and she positively disavowed any association with Enlightenment thought, emanating from France or elsewhere.

To the empress's eager son, halfway measures and modest policies that resulted from accommodation to circumstances represented squandered time and resources.[17] For as long as Maria Theresia lived, Joseph II faced the frequent frustration of his own political goals. Tensions surfaced often between mother and son and were well known to the interested public ("the wrangling [*des brouilleries*] between him [Joseph II] and his mother," as Leopoldine Kaunitz characterized the episodes, adding "it is wrong of him to let the whole world know of it").[18] Disagreements plagued relations within the triumvirate of empress, emperor, and chancellor as well and undermined its effectiveness. Periodically a crisis or quarrel over policy would occur, and the diplomatic community and political elite in Vienna would be treated to the spectacle of a bickering trio. Joseph II or Kaunitz occasionally offered to resign his post, or Maria Theresia would signal her own supposed inclination to retire to a convent and leave Joseph in control. The roles of these three individuals, who were so often at loggerheads, have been variously characterized by historians. In matters of foreign policy many contemporaries expressed misgivings about the young emperor's ambitions and his longing to excel on the field of battle. Certainly Joseph was enthusiastic about all things military. In some of his writings he appeared eager to infuse a strong martial spirit into all his lands, making soldiers of ever greater numbers of his subjects. He urged introduction of systematic conscription and generally extolled the virtues of a military ethos in which efficiency and obedience were paramount.[19] Both he and Maria Theresia were fearful of the military prowess of Frederick II and apprehensive about expansive action by Russia or Turkey. In truth, during the coregency none of the three leaders was eager for armed combat, but Maria Theresia was the least likely to support an assertive policy in order to obtain additional territory. In her view the lesson to be drawn from the Seven Years War was that an aggressive foreign policy triggered unforeseen problems and wasted resources and human life.

Active in court and social life, the future *Dames* encountered each other regularly during the early 1760s, as noted in chapter 2, and could form solid friendships. Of special significance was the close relationship of four of the women, the sisters Eleonore Liechtenstein and Leopoldine Kaunitz and their cousins (also a pair of sisters) Josepha Clary and Sidonia Kinsky, with Maria Theresia's *Obersthofmeisterin* Countess Paar, who was a relative but also an early mentor for the four women in Vienna. Frequent visits to the countess brought all the women together except Leopoldine Liechtenstein. Leopoldine Liechtenstein and Eleonore were drawn together often through their marriages to two Liechtenstein brothers. Eleonore participated in Liechtenstein family gatherings where her sister-in-law Leopoldine Liechtenstein, wife of the older brother and future *Majoratsherr*, presided as hostess.

By the 1760s, Joseph II was visiting Countess Paar's residence with some frequency as well as fashionable soirées held by Sidonia Kinsky, Leopoldine Liechtenstein, and their close friend Princess Esterházy, but he also frequented the residences of other elite families. One of the young emperor's favorite diversions was to visit small groups composed of congenial friends from the top echelons of Viennese society, especially women. This interest manifested itself by the late 1760s, a conscious choice by Joseph and his own device.[20] One group with which the emperor associated during the coregency centered around Count Joseph Nicholaus Windischgrätz (1744–1802), his wife Countess Josepha Windischgrätz (born Erdödy, 1748–1777), and the official Count Philip Cobenzl (1741–1810). Individuals who visited the Windischgrätz gatherings sported viewpoints that were considered to be progressive within Vienna's social and political environment. These were representatives of Vienna's most literate aristocrats, seriously interested in the philosophical views and ethical systems postulated by French and German Enlightenment writers of the day.[21] Beales has suggested that the Windischgrätz group was the most "radical" or progressive coterie to which Joseph belonged. With regard to Countess Windischgrätz's early death, in 1777, Maria Theresia wrote to Marie Beatrix, wife of Archduke Ferdinand, that this was an especially great loss for the emperor, for whom the friendship had provided "trustworthy and tranquil company." Several additional aristocratic women were especially favored over the years.[22] The emperor generally restricted his social visits to the gatherings of the court aristocracy. His relationships with these highborn hostesses and other female associates were apparently platonic. Joseph's biographers have concluded that in all likelihood he confined his sexual relationships to women of inferior birth. According to his brother Leopold, observing Joseph's habits in later life, the emperor was actively promiscuous. During Maria Theresia's lifetime such tendencies may have been somewhat muted or partially concealed. Possibly the emperor sought to preserve appearances and so avoid Maria Theresia's censure.[23]

Joseph II made the acquaintance of Eleonore Liechtenstein as well as the other future members of the group of *Dames* as a matter of course at formal and informal gatherings of the court aristocracy. Eleonore mentioned meeting "le Roi," that is, Joseph, as freshly crowned King of the Romans, at Countess Paar's as early as September 1764, and during the following several years she noted his appearances occasionally.[24] Leopoldine Kaunitz and Eleonore discussed by letter the likelihood that the emperor, now again a widow, might take a mistress even in the face of Maria Theresia's displeasure.[25] By 1770 the emperor was calling upon Countess Paar at least once a week. In late 1770 Lady Mary Coke described Countess Paar herself as "a Charming old Lady [who] . . . has three Nieces [Leopoldine Kaunitz was residing in Brünn at this time], who She bred up, that I don't think can be matched in any part of Europe: the Princess Kinsky, the Princess Clary, and the Princess Charles Liechtenstein: they are all handsome, sensible, agreeable & the conduct of angels; they never fail going to her every evening, & often go no where else." Lady Mary Coke referred to these women as her own "three favourates." Countess Paar, according to Lady Mary, was "eighty-five years of age, but one of the finest old Ladys I ever saw."[26] In a letter dated 29 December 1770, Eleonore reported to her sister Leopoldine Kaunitz that the emperor frequently made visits of three or four hours at Countess Paar's residence.[27] The countess sickened and died in March 1771 at the age of 86, while Lady Mary was visiting Vienna. Lady Mary wrote: "I dined at Prince Kaunitz. Madame de Paar is still alive, but thinking her in the last agonies at two o'clock, the Bells were rung, which is usual here. I passed the evening with the Princess Esterhazy. A Lady told me that the Emperor is much hurt with the thought of losing the society of Madame de Paar's. I believe I told you he came almost every night, as all those Ladys are great favourates [sic]."[28]

Missing from these early reports were the names of Leopoldine Liechtenstein and Leopoldine Kaunitz. Leopoldine Liechtenstein's accession to the group soon followed naturally from her friendship with Eleonore and their shared Liechtenstein family ties. As noted previously, Leopoldine Kaunitz resided in Naples from 1764 to 1770, during which time she received her own political initiation of a less usual character. She and her husband Ernst Kaunitz experienced firsthand the vagaries of political life at the Neapolitan court. Like her ambassador husband Leopoldine Kaunitz had received an assignment before leaving Vienna for Naples, divulged to her during private conferences with Maria Theresia in 1763 and 1764. Leopoldine was to participate fully and designedly in Neapolitan court life and to remit to Maria Theresia candid reports about the young Neapolitan king Ferdinand, future husband of Archduchess Maria Josepha. Noncompliance with a request from the empress would have been awkward, and not only because of the empress's attractive but forceful personality. Leopoldine Kaunitz and the other women generally kept a discreet, respectful distance from the empress, rarely broaching political topics and generally acting as socially subordinate acquaintances. As representatives of prominent court families, the women were naturally eager to win the empress's approval. Leopoldine Kaunitz's selection was flattering to her, clear evidence that the empress considered her a suitable candidate for such a sensitive assignment, and Leopoldine's availability for the job as Ernst's wife undoubtedly played a role in the couple's selection for the Naples mission, in conjunction with Ernst's status as the chancellor's eldest son. A year later, when the empress asked both

Leopoldine Kaunitz and Eleonore to travel to Innsbruck from Naples and Vienna, respectively, for Archduke Leopold's wedding, to swell the ranks of court cavaliers and ladies in attendance, both would demur because of the expense, but with trepidation. It was never easy to disappoint the empress.[29]

King Ferdinand was only thirteen years old when Leopoldine and Ernst arrived in Naples. The Habsburg bride selected for Ferdinand, Archduchess Maria Josepha, died before she could set off from Vienna in 1767. With the toughness of a *Realpolitiker*, Maria Theresia was already planning the substitution of Maria Josepha's younger sister Maria Carolina as Maria Josepha lay dying ("I expect her death at any moment. . . . Now it is necessary to provide another bride for the King of Naples").[30] Archduchess Maria Carolina arrived in Naples in late spring of 1768, and the Kaunitzes celebrated her coming with an extravagant *Fest*. Gold and silver medallions to commemorate the marriage were distributed among the populace.[31] Now Leopoldine's job was to relay confidential reports about the young queen's behavior as well as the king's antics. By mail Chancellor Kaunitz directed the couple—Leopoldine as well as ambassador Ernst—to behave discreetly and to cultivate the favor of the powerful minister Bernardo Tanucci (1698–1783) and his wife so that the young queen too would gain the confidence of this powerful pair. As the chancellor reminded them, the Kaunitz couple's task was delicate. Ernst had to send accurate reports concerning conditions at the Neapolitan court to which Maria Theresia had sent her daughter as a young bride, a deplorable environment by Viennese standards. At the same time he had to preserve a decorous tone so that his missives would offer acceptable reading for Maria Theresia herself even when they were addressed to the chancellor. What occurred in Naples became gossip in Vienna, the chancellor warned the couple. Ernst's wife Leopoldine too was to exercise good judgment ("all conceivable prudence"). "Tell Leopoldine," the chancellor instructed his son, "that I am asking her to be especially careful to avoid laying herself open to reproach for outbursts and a quick temper, given that nothing enhances the wit and charm of a woman so much as gentleness and an even temper, and nothing makes her so odious as the opposite."[32]

Unfortunately during their years in Naples Leopoldine and her husband failed to ingratiate themselves with the local nobility. Leopoldine was not easygoing and genial. As noted in a previous chapter, Ernst Kaunitz soon discredited himself in a clumsy and scandalous love affair with the singer Katharina Gabrielli. He joined with gusto in the juvenile pranks of King Ferdinand, indulging in behavior that was considered to be inappropriate for an imperial ambassador. Chancellor Kaunitz scolded his son, warning him that his escapades were the talk of Vienna.[33] In reports to Maria Theresia Count Rosenberg, who became well acquainted with Kaunitz couple in the course of his own Italian missions, wrote disparagingly about Ernst, observing that he lacked firmness of character. The

Naples assignment was challenging, Rosenberg conceded, and an Austrian ambassador who hoped to influence the boorish young king of Naples needed strong powers of persuasion. Concerning Leopoldine, Rosenberg was at first more sanguine. He found her to be devout, well educated, and well behaved. "She has piety, wit, is well-read, and has a certain naiveté that I liked," Rosenberg reported. Only Leopoldine's foolish displays of jealousy over her husband's extramarital adventures had been unfortunate. Grand Duke Leopold, who accompanied Maria Carolina to her new post in Naples in spring 1768 and remained with her there for six weeks, sent Maria Theresia thoroughly unfavorable accounts of the Kaunitz couple, observing that they were disliked and that Maria Carolina had adopted the unattractive practice of speaking loudly in German to the Kaunitzes, apparently under the impression that Italian courtiers would not understand her words. A competent female confidante for the new queen would be difficult to locate, Leopold acknowledged; even Leopoldine Kaunitz did not have the requisite skill for the position. In the final weeks of his visit Leopold was at pains to soften his remarks about Ernst Kaunitz, assuring Maria Theresia that Ernst was a trustworthy envoy. But Maria Theresia reported to Rosenberg that she had no confidence in Ernst Kaunitz and not a great deal in Leopoldine, who was quick-witted but spoke indiscreetly; "they have not had the good fortune to make themselves liked, much less esteemed."[34]

Leopoldine Kaunitz found her role in Naples highly distasteful. She could not condone the conduct of the lively Maria Carolina. Leopoldine soon came to realize that her unfavorable reports were not especially welcome in Vienna. Coregent Joseph visited Naples in spring 1769, charming Leopoldine Kaunitz during his stay with his informality and impartiality. He sent back to Vienna glowing reports concerning the queen and the status quo in Naples, contradicting Leopoldine's more critical observations (admittedly Joseph may have penned his optimistic assessment with public relations in mind).[35] As was her practice in such matters, Maria Theresia sent copies of her own private correspondence with her daughter Maria Carolina to Leopoldine Kaunitz, betraying Maria Carolina's trust and compromising Leopoldine Kaunitz's position in an effort to enlighten Leopoldine concerning the young queen's manner of reasoning. Leopoldine was required to compile detailed lists of candidates for Maria Carolina's ladies in waiting, describing the characteristics of the women, the strength of their loyalty to the king of Spain (who exercised enormous influence over his son Ferdinand) or to the Neapolitan minister Tanucci, and their suitability as confidantes for the queen. With all of these requests Leopoldine Kaunitz dutifully complied. But Queen Maria Carolina quickly became acclimated to her new position. She ascertained that unfavorable reports were reaching Vienna and readily guessed their source, although Maria Theresia had promised Leopoldine strict confidentiality. Naturally the queen grew to distrust and dislike

Leopoldine.³⁶ To make this bad situation worse for Leopoldine, Maria Theresia proved difficult to please. The empress complained to Eleonore and indirectly to Countess Paar that Leopoldine Kaunitz's reports were infrequent. She told Eleonore that the Kaunitz couple spent too much money, a charge aimed particularly at Ernst after his special mission to the papal election in Rome. Eleonore comforted Leopoldine, assuring her (correctly) that Maria Theresia would not remain indisposed toward her.³⁷ Maria Theresia was loyal to her servitors, even those who were unable to give satisfaction. The empress's friendly interest in Leopoldine's activities endured even though the Kaunitz couple's presence in Naples was no longer useful. Maria Theresia condoled with Leopoldine as the latter recovered from a miscarriage, offering motherly advice and the assurance that "another time things will go better, this first sacrifice you have made to God will bring to you a blessing for another time." The empress rejoiced with Leopoldine over the birth of Leopoldine's son in 1769 (christened Joseph, he died after the family returned to Vienna, in March 1774).³⁸

It was a politically experienced, chastened, and relieved Leopoldine Kaunitz who moved with her husband from Naples to Brünn in September 1770. There from 1770 to 1772 Ernst served as Moravian *Landeshauptmann* or governor, as had his grandfather many decades earlier. Ernst found little to occupy his time in this assignment. Both he and his wife wished to return to Vienna. Leopoldine remarked in a letter to Eleonore that Ernst would happily accept a job as imperial housecleaner in order to escape Brünn.³⁹ Chancellor Kaunitz lobbied the empress for a post for his son but was forced to report to Ernst that the empress could offer only the position of superintendent of buildings. This should be satisfactory, the elder Kaunitz felt, since Ernst would retain his current salary; but Leopoldine's sentiments were to be considered as well ("Therefore you must not speak of this to anyone but your wife . . . Send me a response at once, however, so that if, contrary to my expectations, this seems unsuitable to you, either yourself or your wife, I may keep the empress from committing herself").⁴⁰ This court post brought Ernst and Leopoldine back to Vienna at last, and there they remained. The department of buildings and public works, which grew from 42 employees in 1748 to about 100 in 1780, was a substantive if scarcely central operation in the imperial household and its director could expect to travel and exert himself from time to time.⁴¹ But Leopoldine Kaunitz was ashamed of the appointment and worried that Joseph II would view it as a sinecure. "I will admit to you," she wrote to her sister, "this position that has been conjured up just so that it can be said that we have one makes me thoroughly embarrassed." Her fears were reasonable, as Joseph's letter to his brother Leopold makes clear: "Just think that by dint of begging Prince Kaunitz has obtained for his son Ernst, whom you know, the post of director of buildings . . . You can imagine how much he knows about this and what kind of job he will do."⁴²

Joseph II's predilection for Eleonore Liechtenstein developed while her sister Leopoldine was absent from Vienna. Evidence suggests that the emperor's strong attachment dates approximately from his extended conversation with Eleonore at a court ball in January 1771, just after her husband Charles had been bypassed in that year's massive military promotion. Maria Theresia had already done her best to soothe the feelings of the Liechtenstein couple. In an hour-long conversation with Eleonore, Joseph too attempted to justify the sovereigns' inaction in the matter.[43] At the ball Joseph conversed apart with Eleonore for a full hour. Derek Beales's biography of Joseph II has provided the most authoritative interpretation available concerning Joseph's state of mind during this period. Beales describes the ensuing relationship with Eleonore as "the most intense affair" of the emperor's life and dates the height of the emperor's infatuation to the years 1771 and 1772.[44] Like her sister Leopoldine Kaunitz, who normally exerted a calming influence on her sister and was a proponent of caution and forbearance, Eleonore's husband Charles was away from Vienna, serving as military commander in Pressburg. Despite his exalted imperial position, or perhaps because of it, Joseph proved to be an awkward suitor for Eleonore's favors. Not disguising his inclination, Joseph tried to be with her as much as possible, at small social gatherings and during her carriage rides with her friends in the Prater and Augarten parks. He confided to Eleonore that Maria Theresia teased him about his partiality. It appears that when Eleonore returned to Vienna in July 1772 from the countryside, the emperor declined to attend a gathering at Leopoldine Liechtenstein's residence where Eleonore was present simply because he wished to confound his mother the empress.[45] However, Joseph's importunities were impossible to misinterpret, even if Eleonore often exclaimed over the peculiarity of his behavior. As early as August 1771 Eleonore confided to her sister that her own husband Charles would not care for the discussions she was having with the emperor.[46]

During the period of Joseph II's strongest fascination with her, Eleonore came to expect regular marks of distinction from him—his visits, his special eagerness to converse with her—and was even somewhat piqued when these were not forthcoming. The private exchange between Eleonore and Joseph that took place during a visit to Dornbach in July 1772, noted by several of Joseph's biographers, was typical of the mixture of gallantry and clumsiness in the emperor's personality. Rather fatuously the emperor remarked to Eleonore that in a sense he regarded her as if she were his wife. One was not really in love with one's wife, he explained, yet one took an interest in all that pertained to her. Eleonore reported her own reply to her sister. She had told the emperor that, although she was flattered by his attention and by the consideration he showed her, she failed to follow his abstruse reasoning. She would prefer, she said, that he have less regard (*bontés*) for her and greater consideration for her husband Charles.[47]

Eleonore's responses to Joseph in these early years of their relationship were moderate in tone and occasionally oblique. She was in no position to insult with impunity a Habsburg emperor, whatever her inclinations may have been. Beales is surely correct in surmising that Joseph II hoped to persuade Eleonore to be his mistress.[48] Quite possibly the emperor initially found Eleonore's generally courteous responses encouraging.

Eleonore wrote confiding letters to Leopoldine Kaunitz, detailing episodes in her new friendship with the emperor. The two women's letters provide a relatively straightforward record of the relationship from Eleonore's point of view, although not all circumstances are fully clarified by the correspondence (e.g., Joseph's proposal to station Charles Liechtenstein—and thus very likely Eleonore as well—in Belgium).[49] Leopoldine cautioned her sister about the special connection with the emperor. She pointed out the drawbacks to a liaison with any ruler and particularly with this reputedly misogynistic emperor. As early as 1768, when Eleonore had reported her suspicion to Leopoldine Kaunitz that Joseph II had at last chosen a female favorite, Leopoldine responded that particularly in view of Maria Theresia's likely displeasure she herself would not wish such a fortune to be bestowed on her worst enemies "for it would be very awkward and very dangerous to find oneself placed between the mother and the son."[50] Leopoldine Kaunitz believed the emperor would end up despising Eleonore should she accede to his wishes. There was also the probability that envy and spite would be visited upon any woman occupying the position of favorite. The dictates of religion and morality proscribed such an adventure.[51] There is no evidence in Eleonore's letters or in reports of contemporaries that she considered gratifying the emperor. Concerning the relationship, the contemporary Wraxall wrote, "Flattered as she [Eleonore] unquestionably is with the partiality, and gratified by the attentions of the first Crowned Head in Europe, she has invariably acted with such caution and regard to her own honor, as to maintain unsullied the purity of her character. No one ventures to suppose, and still less to assert, that she has yielded to him any thing inconsistent with the strictest virtue. She is the object of his affection and friendship; not his mistress."[52] Grand Duke Leopold, an ill-humored observer of the emperor's small circle of women friends during a visit to Vienna in 1778 (in his peculiar, private record entitled "Stato della famiglia"), claimed that Eleonore was in love with Joseph.[53]

Eleonore's own extensive comments throughout the 1770s indicate that she was flattered by the imperial attentions rather than moved by them. Eleonore recognized the complexity of her situation, for the emperor had the power to influence the standing of her family without risking serious public censure or indignation. These inbred, almost instinctive concerns of a young aristocratic matron were precisely the complicating factors that apparently deterred Joseph's brother, the more circumspect Leopold, from forming liaisons with women from highly connected and powerful families in Florence. Eleonore's disinclination, the cautionary advice of her sister Leopoldine Kaunitz, and her own estimation of the discomforts that awaited the recipient of special favors from a moody, capricious sovereign all tended to thwart Joseph's romantic plans. An additional reason for Eleonore's caution was the sensitivity and jealousy of her husband Charles, who became aware of the emperor's interest in his wife and expressed resentment. Eleonore prudently restricted the amount of time the emperor could interact with her in the absence of a witness to his words and actions. She insisted that letters written by Joseph should be of such a character that she could comfortably show them to her husband, and by and large she enforced this rule. She shared many of the letters she received from the emperor with Leopoldine Kaunitz (and in subsequent years with the other three women who made up the group of *Dames* as well).

From his post in Florence, Grand Duke Leopold learned very early about Joseph's growing friendship with Eleonore Liechtenstein, his contacts with her close friends, and presumably other social forays made by the emperor as well. His correspondence with Maria Theresia may have been a source of information or, even more likely, reports came from his own contacts in Vienna. Not all of the brothers' private correspondence has been preserved. One revealing exchange occurred as early as February 1772. Joseph apparently felt called upon to reassure Leopold. He was, the emperor reported, perfectly easy in his mind, distributing his evenings equitably among several coteries, "that is to say, either at the home of Princess Esterházy, Madame Tarocca, Madame Rose Harrach, or Princess Kinsky." He described the "exclusive company" at Sidonia Kinsky's gathering: "present yesterday were the husband and wife, Madame Kaunitz, Princess Charles Liechtenstein, Princess Clary, Prince Kaunitz, Rosenberg, Braganza, and myself. We conversed for more than two hours, and that is harmless [*innocent*]."[54] In mid-March 1772 Leopold wrote that he had been startled by some of Joseph's disclosures (apparently written in cipher) but had eventually concluded that a particular relationship described by Joseph had ended. Leopold wrote, "I am pleased that it is all broken off for a hundred thousand reasons, it is a bad bit of goods that one cannot approach or come in contact with in any manner without getting stung and doing oneself great harm without even realizing it."[55] In subsequent letters Joseph sent additional reassurance to Leopold that his relationship with the individual named in earlier letters was no longer romantic; they merely conversed lightheartedly. A few weeks later the subject was canvassed yet another time. Joseph once more assured his brother of his own perfect equanimity. While Maria Theresia was at Schlosshof, he reported, he was at leisure in Vienna. He left his residence only in the evening, to take walks, visit the theater, or attend some informal gathering. The capital was empty, with everyone summering in the countryside. "For my part, I am retrogressing greatly in gallantry," Joseph declared; he was once again becoming indolent, he assured his brother. Association with women was intolerable for a rational man in the long run; "and I can declare," he continued, "that often the choicest, wittiest remarks turn my stomach." Later letters returned to the topic, with Joseph stressing his adherence to his customary routine: "the reports I sent you are no longer realities, the illustrious Princess has been absent more than three months [Eleonore remained in the countryside] and I have not the slightest news from her just as she knows nothing of me."[56]

In the exchange between the brothers in 1775 noted at the beginning of this chapter, Leopold's language still conveyed urgency but his focus had shifted. His concern extended to all of the emperor's interactions with favored female friends, not just Eleonore Liechtenstein. In a previous missive Joseph had praised his particular friend Countess Windischgrätz, contrasting her rational views with the *déraison* of other women. She was an open-minded woman, accessible to reasoned arguments, "and there are not many among the sex, said to be so enchanting, who are like this, they insist upon having their way always." Joseph professed himself disillusioned with women and as free from partiality as a newborn; "the moment of folly that I mentioned to you recently has passed completely . . . I have no wish to make love, nor do I want to attempt to make new acquaintances." He was content to sleep alone, finding his situation convenient and commodious.[57] Leopold's warnings continued. A ruler of Joseph's age, Leopold affirmed, should be very careful around women and avoid even the appearance of favoritism to individuals or groups. Joseph's peace of mind and reputation were at stake, wrote Leopold, but there were more serious risks as well; "an infinite number of persons who seek to seduce or connive at the seduction of employees and especially heads of government, as soon as they perceive or suspect that you favor the company of some woman, will not fail to profit from this, hoping to use the woman to seduce or dominate, and in this way you can be induced to cut a poor figure or make mistakes, or act unjustly." The ruler had to remain impartial and indifferent. The more Joseph imagined himself to be invulnerable, the more problematic was the company he had apparently chosen for himself.[58]

Joseph tried to explain to Leopold how he interacted with his women friends. He conceded that to form a serious attachment would be a misfortune (*le comble du malheur*). He found it amusing to listen to women as they described their trivial schemes and aired their sophistries and prejudices. When confronted with the fallacies in their ideas, they became fretful and tried to change the subject; "every time you bring reason to bear to prove matters are otherwise, then as soon as they realize this, so to speak, they become angry, look for another argument, seize on some word, in other words they turn the conversation in a completely different direction in order to win their case." Leopold claimed to be appalled by Joseph's remarks, presumably responding to reports from his contacts in Vienna. Joseph countered that, while he appreciated Leopold's concern, he needed to cultivate social relationships or he would be always alone. He was single, he reminded Leopold. He had tried chasing common women (*les filles*), but that strategy resulted in health problems "and you experience such a great emptiness." He preferred to get what pleasure he could from his immediate environment, "to take what profit one can, to laugh about the rest, and to try to spend a few hours each evening diverted from work."[59] Still unsatisfied, Leopold continued to expostulate. Joseph, he declared, should not permit his acquaintances to become meddlesome or insolent.[60]

The intensity of the relationship between Eleonore Liechtenstein and the emperor lessened with time. It appears that Joseph himself moderated his behavior by late 1772. Leopoldine Kaunitz moved back to Vienna, again providing daily counsel to her sister; and eventually Eleonore's husband Charles also returned to Vienna from Pressburg, soon to take up a new post as military commander for Lower and Upper Austria. As early as December 1773 Joseph was reporting to Marshal Lacy, who was absent from Vienna, his pleasure with the circle of *Dames* as a stable group and, most strikingly, the frequency of the gatherings: "meanwhile our little meetings [*sociétés*] continue 5 times a week, I always find there the pleasure and serenity of good, reliable company." Several days later Joseph reiterated his satisfaction. "The amiable, good princesses are pleased to meet 5 times per week." Joseph attended gatherings regularly, he told Lacy, and he could not be happier with the situation.[61] The course of the friendship between Eleonore and Joseph II remained unpredictable because of the emperor's prickly personality and Eleonore's excitable, outspoken nature. Throughout their years of association, periodic misunderstandings troubled the relationship. Sometimes Eleonore found the emperor's intense interest in her to be irksome, almost tyrannical and at times ridiculous. In summer 1779, when she was slow to inform the emperor of her latest pregnancy, his fussiness annoyed her. Eleonore had initially told him casually that she was indisposed with a cold, "a slight rheumatism." His response had been "a dissertation of two pages about my health which has been declining by his calculation for about two years, my extraordinary thinness, my despondency and melancholy that he perceives quite clearly." The emperor recommended consultations with two or three skilled doctors and absolute compliance with their dictates. When Eleonore announced her pregnancy at last, Joseph's melodramatic response exasperated her; "it is incredible, as you say, to react so keenly to such thoroughly ordinary matters, completely natural, a pregnancy, a minor indisposition . . . and to be indifferent, hard, pitiless concerning what is more vital and consequential." Joseph offered fulsome, personal advice to his close friends on a variety of topics. Eleonore described a letter she received from him in October 1779 as "a treatise on education, on the duties of a mother." Joseph probably believed he had produced "a document full of eloquence," Eleonore remarked, but the result of his effort was a mere jumble of words. "I find that the confusion and muddle in his ideas increase daily."[62]

Particularly troubling to Eleonore on a personal level was an incident that occurred near the end of the coregency in early 1780, as the emperor returned from Russia, where he had conferred with Catherine II. He insisted upon stopping at Kromau to visit Eleonore, bringing with him his traveling companion General Browne. The emperor persisted in this plan in spite of Eleonore's concern about its propriety ("extremely embarrassing and unpleasant") and about the probable annoyance of Maria Theresia, who wished Joseph to return directly to Vienna. Eleonore was also reluctant to permit Joseph to see her daughter Josephine at this juncture because of Josephine's problematic health. Eleonore wished to travel to Feldsberg, where she could receive the emperor's visit without embarrassment. But Josephine's governess vetoed that proposal for it would have involved Josephine's appearance among the guests at Feldsberg and "it would not be advantageous for my daughter to be seen at a time when people might notice something peculiar about her." Eleonore remained at Kromau but considered the emperor's behavior capricious and selfish. She suspected that it was her opposition to his plan that strengthened the emperor's resolve to proceed. The visit took place on a rainy 19 August. Joseph arrived with his companion, and the trio attempted with limited success to make a wet, dismal day enjoyable through dining and conversation about the recent Russian trip.[63] An awkward episode, the visit passed without serious mishap. The ease with which an imperial visit to Eleonore in Kromau could be planned and carried out attests to Eleonore's autonomy as an aristocratic matron during her summer sojourns. Surely flattered to receive an imperial visit, she remained apprehensive about the public impression such a visit would make. Neither she nor the emperor attempted to disguise Joseph's movements. After Joseph's visit to Kromau, Eleonore's sister Leopoldine Kaunitz suggested that Eleonore had overreacted to a situation that did not merit such concern.[64]

During the autumn following Joseph's visit there occurred the most significant quarrel the two friends ever had, and by comparison Joseph's untoward summer appearance at Kromau paled in significance. The problem was Charles Liechtenstein's plan for construction of a military barracks in Vienna. Maria Theresia had endorsed the initiative, but Joseph's military council, the *Hofkriegsrat,* had not, and it issued a reprimand, backed by imperial authority. As she often did, Eleonore interpreted the emperor's actions as an intentional insult and humiliation to her husband and indirectly to herself. She railed against the mistreatment she believed Charles received regularly from Joseph. In characteristic manner, Charles Liechtenstein informed his wife that he wanted no interference from her in his difficult relationship with the emperor. Charles sent a reminder to Eleonore by way of her sister: "He says that you must absolutely resolve to tell him [Joseph II] firmly that you will not take part in such discussions and that you wish him not to speak to you about anything that concerns your husband."[65] As always, the episode was eventually smoothed over by the principal participants. Charles acknowledged the authority (and thus the reproof) of the *Hofkriegsrat*, which was the principle stressed by Joseph; but the barracks was built just the same. The exchanges that resulted from this incident illustrate well the emperor's mode of reasoning with his irate friend Eleonore, an approach that infuriated her. He urged Eleonore to cultivate a tranquil spirit by viewing such mundane occurrences in perspective, without exaggeration. She should not torment herself by analyzing each event in microscopic detail; and she should trust her friend Joseph, "who, for such a long time and in spite of everything, has remained unfailingly attached to you . . . you will certainly do me justice some day, even if the present moment is not yet favorable." He added the lighthearted menace of another visit to her in the countryside, certain to exasperate his friend further.[66] From Eleonore's point of view the quarrel had been serious, an episode that could have signaled the end of her special relationship with the emperor and potentially, by extension, an end to the *société* as well. In advising Eleonore, Leopoldine Kaunitz noted the possibility of such a falling-out and cautioned her sister to moderate her responses. Leopoldine Kaunitz mentioned possible repercussions that had always to be a concern in a personal relationship between sovereign and subject: "Another thought also suggested by his character is that if one makes him feel too much to blame, it will render him irreconcilable, I do not mean as so-called friend but rather as master; concerning the former, let it pass, but the latter situation would be unfortunate for your husband."[67]

In this case as in others Eleonore Liechtenstein professed not to believe the emperor's disclaimers and his convoluted professions of innocence (he pleaded reasons of state and claimed to make only dispassionate decisions that promoted the general good). In all likelihood, the episode was merely a byproduct of Joseph's ongoing conflict with Maria Theresia. As ever the emperor remained confident that any misunderstandings between himself and Eleonore would be temporary.[68] It is not surprising that the bluff, uncomplicated Charles Liechtenstein found court life treacherous as he sought to reconcile his dual allegiance, to both emperor and empress. For Joseph a misunderstanding with the Liechtenstein couple, while important in its effect on his personal happiness, was not the all-consuming issue that it seemed at first to Eleonore and her husband. Maria Theresia herself interpreted the episode as yet another contest between herself and the emperor. Eleonore eventually conceded the role played by tensions between mother and son. Eleonore wrote, "She [Maria Theresia] is reported to be in a very bad humor, she said to my husband, it is not you that this matter concerns, it is against me that the blows are directed, the poor woman, to what a state she has been reduced!" Over a month later Eleonore added that Maria Theresia's role had been unworthy of her; the empress deserved the son she had.[69]

Joseph II retained a special regard and admiration for Eleonore Liechtenstein throughout the rest of his life. The emperor rarely blamed himself for their tiffs. A noteworthy exception occurred once in October 1773 when, after a misunderstanding, he confessed to Leopoldine Kaunitz that he realized he was not a person who could readily give and receive love.[70] Eleonore interpreted as personal slights various incidents that were the result of Joseph's thoughtlessness or the peculiar and unfortunate dynamics of his relationship with his mother Maria Theresia. The emperor claimed to be surrounded by intrigues concocted by the empress's particular favorites and, by extension, the empress herself. Mother and son were unable to find an enduring modus vivendi, a system of joint rule that would have assured comfort for themselves, tolerable effectiveness for their retainers, and a pleasant environment for friends such as the *Dames*.

The emperor's friendships with the other four *Dames* developed naturally in the course of his association with Eleonore Liechtenstein. Unwilling to encourage exclusive meetings with the emperor, Eleonore could converse with him in relative comfort within a small circle of intimate friends. Joseph's romantic interest undoubtedly added piquancy to the group's activities in its early years. In his brief biography of Joseph II, Paul Bernard depicts the group during its entire existence as an appendage of Joseph's relationship with Eleonore and his desire to spend time with her under socially acceptable conditions.[71] In the narrowest sense this is a valid observation: the group of five women and the emperor with his two male friends would not have formed and flourished without Joseph's special interest in Eleonore. However, the emperor's affinity with each of the other four women took on a momentum of its own. These *Dames* too came to feel a proprietary interest in the group and a sense of entitlement, each woman expecting from the emperor both friendship and communication quite apart from Eleonore's special status. In the view of Eleonore's biographer Adam Wolf, a fonder, more honorable friendship (*zarter und edler*) than the one that united the members of this little group could scarcely be imagined.[72] For their gatherings in Vienna, the group generally came together sometime between eight and ten o'clock in the evening. During the emperor's absences from Vienna, all five *Dames* received letters from him from time to time. Their expectations were high. While the emperor was traveling in Russia in 1780, for example, Leopoldine Kaunitz reported to Eleonore, "I have received from the Emperor a letter from Zamosc dated the 5th [August], I do not know how he finds the time but they [the letters] are plentiful, as you say, this proves at least that we are of some usefulness to him; la Kinsky [Sidonia Kinsky] has received one, a copy of which she has sent to la Clary [Josepha Clary], where he speaks with concern about the illness of the young prince [Sidonia's son]." Josepha Clary's own letter from the emperor did not meet her high expectations, being insufficiently lively and personal.[73]

Always the primacy of the group's female contingent was indisputable; *la société* could assemble and function without the presence of its two nonimperial male members but not without females. As noted previously, the two male members of the group, Field Marshal Lacy and Count Franz Rosenberg, were long-time close associates of the emperor, who valued their companionship as well as their service. Lacy and Rosenberg were already regular participants by the time Leopoldine Kaunitz arrived back in Vienna from Brünn, their presence welcomed by the women.

Like Charles Liechtenstein, Count Moritz Lacy had begun his military career as a young man, at 18 years of age. He was something of an outsider, coming from an Irish family that had been in Russian service. Of less exalted social origins than many of his colleagues, junior officer Lacy proved to be diligent and enterprising, attentive to detail and exacting in his expectations of his officers and himself. In the multinational Habsburg officer corps he found opportunities to excel.[74] Lacy's actions in the War of the Austrian Succession and the Seven Years War highlighted his talent as leader of fast-moving, relatively small groups of soldiers. He early won the favor of Prince Joseph Wenzel Liechtenstein, director of the Habsburg artillery, who supported Lacy's career and welcomed him as an associate of the Liechtenstein clan. Thus Lacy naturally became a close friend of Leopoldine Liechtenstein, as she joined the Liechtenstein family by marriage.[75] He also received important support from his influential commanding officer, war council president Field Marshal Daun. Most important, Lacy attracted the favorable attention of his sovereign Maria Theresia and subsequently Joseph II. Lacy's dramatic rise to favor and influence, while unusual, was not unique; Laudon, reputedly Lacy's rival, also advanced rapidly, moving from major to full general in five years.[76] Lacy's culminating achievement was his appointment to be Daun's successor as president of the *Hofkriegsrat* in 1766, a position he held until 1773.

At the height of his powers Lacy was a veritable workhorse, regularly laboring fourteen hours a day to reform the staff system, modernize uniforms, eliminate the corruption that was endemic in the supply system, and generally oversee even the most minute aspects of the whole ungainly, outmoded Habsburg military. Lacy introduced the Prussian-style cantonal system of military recruitment and conscription in many regions of the monarchy.[77] He resigned his post in autumn 1773 in favor of Field Marshal Andreas Hadik, possibly finding it too difficult to please Joseph, head of the Habsburg military forces and jealous of his own authority, and simultaneously his mother Maria Theresia, still much interested in military affairs. Lacy spent time at Spa and in southern France for his health. After his return in 1774, he remained his sovereigns' most influential advisor in military affairs as a *Staats- und Konferenzminister*, even though he was no longer willing to serve as president of the war council.[78]

Lacy's relationship with Maria Theresia was closer than Joseph himself realized, for the two of them carried on a pithy private correspondence to which Joseph had no access. Maria Theresia, inclined to conceal from her son the extent of her interference, urged Lacy to disguise his letters to her as correspondence with

Leopoldine Liechtenstein.[79] But Lacy was also close to Joseph. Wraxall spoke highly of Lacy's appearance and character in the late 1770s: "With Marshal Lacy I have the honor to be acquainted, and to meet him sometimes in private society. He is now approaching towards his sixtieth year; but, it is impossible not to perceive, that when young, he must have been very handsome. In his person he is tall and thin; his complexion sallow, and his features small. He has the figure, deportment, and manners of a man of quality; but, there is in them still more of the courtier and the gentleman, than of the soldier. Grave, and somewhat distant on first acquaintance, he becomes afterwards pleasing and communicative. He speaks French with equal ease and elegance; entertains magnificently, and his table is served with no less delicacy than profusion." Lacy remained an attractive figure even as he aged. "Though now advancing fast to old age, he preserves a youthful appearance; and though he has been six times wounded by musket-ball, he enjoys perfect health; all the bullets having been extracted, without injury to his constitution. In his youth, he sacrificed to pleasure and dissipation; but at present he lives retired, mixes little with the gay world, and passes the evening of an active life, in the enjoyment of a dignified repose. Possessed of an immense fortune, partly transmitted to him by descent, and partly acquired in the course of long and honorable service; he uses it as one, who while he knows the value of riches, is nevertheless superior to them. Of an elevated mind, above the little arts of intrigue, or of Court cabal; he is not less respected than beloved, by the Sovereigns whom he serves."[80] In July 1780, after some time spent with Lacy at Eisgrub, Eleonore characterized Lacy as a singular individual who brooked no opposition and disliked being asked probing questions. He was discreet to a fault, impenetrable, entirely self-controlled, and fastidious. As to fussiness about his person, Eleonore wrote, "I assure you that he is scarcely second to your father-in-law [Chancellor Kaunitz, who had a reputation for eccentricity and foppishness] and he likes hearing about death and illness just as little [as Kaunitz]." Despite these oddities, Eleonore found him agreeable when part of a small, intimate group, fair-minded, cheerful, and capable of responding to genuine affection.[81] Wraxall believed Lacy to be "equally formed for the Cabinet and the drawing-room, as for the field," a personage who enjoyed "the most distinguished place in the Emperor's confidence and affection, that Prince visits him at all hours, converses with him on matters of business while the Marshal is dressing, and consults him on every point. Nor is it only on military or political subjects, that Joseph applies to him for advice and assistance. Lacy is the depository of his most secret thoughts; participates his [sic] domestic troubles; and soothes him in those moments of dejection, disappointment, and chagrin, to which a divided sovereignty is peculiarly liable."[82]

With these personal assets, Lacy excelled as both courtier and officer, a complex, multifaceted man. He maintained ties with old military friends, especially officers who, like him, had Irish roots.[83] But he also had a private side that included love of gardening and the beauty that it produced. Each year Lacy added embellishments to the grounds of his estate at Dornbach. He was at ease in the company of women as well as men. Lacy enjoyed collecting fine wines and learning about special cuisine. He was a connoisseur of dogs and horses. He was familiar with literature of the Enlightenment and was known to be much taken with the ideas of Rousseau.[84] Lacy did not react well to criticism, even (or especially) from his imperial masters. Maria Theresia worked hard to soothe his feelings when she had to differ with him. In 1769 she reminded him that it was a mark of her affection that she spoke frankly and expected him to reciprocate.[85] She could jest with him (when he inquired about her health, she scribbled "ill weeds grow apace"), and she confided to him her worries about her son and other thorny issues. She presented him with gifts of fine tobacco and went to considerable trouble to visit his suburban villa.[86] Lacy had to maneuver constantly between mother and son, a difficult and sometimes impossible task. Joseph's esteem and friendship for Lacy, unpredictable in their manifestations like all the emperor's relationships, were also strong. When Joseph's older daughter Thérèse (Maria Theresia) died, it was Lacy who comforted the emperor, to Empress Maria Theresia's satisfaction.[87]

Although as a young man his name was connected with several prospective brides, relatively early in life Lacy decided to forego marriage.[88] Very likely a major factor in this decision was his weak financial position at the time. In common with his contemporaries, Lacy believed substantial wealth was a prerequisite for establishment of a proper aristocratic household. An itinerant mercenary at the beginning of his career, Lacy had no wealthy relations upon whom he could draw for assistance. In 1761, congratulating Leopoldine Liechtenstein's husband Franz Joseph and the Liechtenstein family upon the marriage of Franz Joseph's brother Charles with Eleonore, Lacy remarked that he himself was a confirmed bachelor in spite of attractive and tempting examples of conjugal happiness. He had considered marriage, he explained, but what would have been "a pardonable folly" in a young man would be ridiculous at his own advanced age (he was then 36 years old).[89] Several years later, writing to his nephew Captain Stuart to caution him against an imprudent marriage, Lacy dilated on the financial challenges. Unless a military officer had supplemental income or property, Lacy wrote, marriage was an indiscretion that would lead to misery for both the officer and his bride.[90] In 1774, when both Maria Theresia and Joseph II suggested that Lacy should bring back a bride from his trip to France, Lacy pointed to Joseph's own example, noting that after two attempts the emperor himself seemed peculiarly reluctant to attempt a third marriage.[91] Lacking wife and family, Lacy nevertheless knew how to make and retain close friends. His special relationship with Leopoldine Liechtenstein has been mentioned. As Lacy left for Spa in 1773,

Leopoldine Kaunitz told Eleonore that Leopoldine Liechtenstein was to be pitied because she had few other close associates; "the sweetness, the pleasure of her life has been in this friendship."[92] It is interesting that Maria Theresia herself had given an oblique nod to the special relationship between Lacy and Leopoldine Liechtenstein in directing Lacy to send his communications with her under cover of Lacy's own correspondence with "our mutual friend Princess Françoise," as previously mentioned.[93] Lacy was especially fond of Leopoldine Liechtenstein's second son Johann, a promising young officer. After her husband's death, Leopoldine Liechtenstein resided during the warmer months in a villa not far from Lacy's suburban home in Dornbach.[94]

Many contemporaries saw in Lacy an artful courtier whose polished ways and subtle intrigues were designed to retain the favor of the monarchs and to exclude rivals. Lacy's secretiveness and his access to information unavailable to others probably formed part of his attractiveness for Leopoldine Liechtenstein who, according to her circle of acquaintances, relished having access to confidential, privileged information. Lacy had a polished but somewhat unapproachable personality, exhibiting his undeniable charm only to his select companions and his sovereigns. He never won the favor of the broader public. Eleonore Liechtenstein combined lukewarm praise of Lacy's intellect with sharp observations about his secretiveness and exclusiveness: "It is unfortunate that he is so unsociable and taciturn and that because of this very few people can know him." Throughout Lacy's career, there were individuals in his environment who quietly hoped for his demotion or fall from favor. Leopoldine Kaunitz's father-in-law Chancellor Kaunitz was among Lacy's detractors, disliking Lacy personally and criticizing his ideas.[95]

Like Lacy, Count Franz Xavier Orsini-Rosenberg was a bachelor.[96] He came from a landed Styrian family with estates based at Rosegg, not far from Klagenfurt. Visiting Vienna in 1773, Lady Mary Coke praised him: "He is one of the most Amiable sensible Men I ever knew: among other talents he has that of languages beyond anybody, and has as much knowledge of English as I have: the accent is the only thing that wou'd make you know him for a foreigner."[97] Maria Theresia sought Rosenberg's help in the most sensitive situations of her reign; the biographer of Joseph's brother Leopold, Adam Wandruszka, dubs Rosenberg the "fire brigade" (*Feuerwehr*) of the Habsburg family.[98] Rosenberg's career began in 1742, when at 19 years of age he served the Hungarian ambassador in London, a post that brought him valuable experience in view of the importance of the English alliance during the War of the Austrian Succession. Rosenberg began his own independent service as Habsburg ambassador in Copenhagen in 1754. During the Seven Years War, he was ambassador in Madrid. He next served as minister and advisor to Grand Duke Leopold in Florence from 1766 until 1770, where he helped Leopold introduce reforms in the Tuscan administration. Twice Maria

Theresia sent him to Parma to restrain the political meddling and extravagant lifestyle of her married daughter Amalia, even asking Rosenberg to check with the royal couple's doctor about private aspects of their marriage.[99] The empress sought Rosenberg's opinion when important appointments were made. Maria Theresia's confidence in Rosenberg was almost limitless, but she was aware of a few shortcomings. When Archduke Maximilian traveled through Germany to Belgium and France in 1774 with Rosenberg as his chaperone, in her instructions Maria Theresia urged her son to rely upon his mentor Rosenberg. The empress wrote, "I have known Rosenberg for forty years, he has served me everywhere to my satisfaction and thus merits my trust. In the most difficult and critical circumstances he was responsible for advising and supporting Leopold and his wife [in Tuscany], for establishing his [Leopold's] reputation, for ensuring their well-being and that of their lands. You cannot be unaware that he is liked and esteemed by the discerning public, just as he has been in foreign countries where he has served, which is clear proof of his character and personal merit. You should consult him concerning everything and follow his advice." But, she added, "He is not sufficiently particular, and this is the only matter concerning which I have less confidence in him than in all other points. He is but too indulgent, amiable in society, with an easygoing politeness."[100] In 1777 Joseph II appointed Rosenberg to the post of *Oberstkämmerer*.

Rosenberg was something of an epicure, harboring few political ambitions. Wraxall offered the following observations: "[Rosenberg] . . . is one of the most pleasing noblemen of the Imperial Court; who, under a cold exterior, conceals qualities equally solid and ingratiating. Polished in his manners, cultivated in his understanding, and highly acceptable to his master; if he possessed ambition equal to his talents, it is probable that he might act a conspicuous part on the political theatre. But, his love of pleasure, joined to the indolence of his temper, will retain him always in the shade."[101] In 1780, when Archduchess Marie Christine selected the personnel that she and her husband Prince Albert would need as they became Habsburg governors in Brussels, she requested the services of Rosenberg as her principal minister. Joseph II vetoed the choice. He explained to Leopold that Rosenberg was too complaisant and unenterprising.[102]

Like Lacy, Rosenberg pursued discreet romantic liaisons. According to some modern-day accounts, Rosenberg had an Italian mistress, "Madame Lucrezia," who resided at Rosegg, where Rosenberg completed construction of a new palace in 1780; she was thus the namesake of Rosenberg's newly renovated palace there, "Lucreziana." More plausibly, perhaps, the name may have referred to the Roman heroine Lucretia or to the Roman epicurean poet Lucretius or, alternatively, to another estate Rosenberg had owned while living in Florence.[103] Rosenberg was an active and progressive, if generally absent, landlord who favored the expansion of free trade and was a strong though undogmatic proponent of physiocratic views. On his Styrian lands he attempted to introduce smelting ovens, which did eventually produce some metal for production of coins in Salzburg but were not a financial success. Rosenberg was conversant with the latest works of the French Enlightenment and economic theory.[104] Throughout the late 1770s and the 1780s Rosenberg acted as the emperor's chief advisor and manager for court theatrical productions, but Joseph's own active interest in theatrical activities robbed the post of independent authority. To the emperor, Rosenberg was a trusted servitor rather than a mentor and advisor, as Lacy was. Chamberlain Khevenhüller noted that Rosenberg's jovial humor made his company attractive to his sovereigns.[105]

When remarking upon the attendance and membership of the two men in the group, the *Dames* characterized their presence as a valued resource. Sometimes a calming influence or even a constraining force in conversations about sensitive topics was needed (Lacy), sometimes leavening and a lighter touch (Rosenberg). Almost always the men were urgently solicited by the women to act as backup and reinforcement in the job of diverting and occupying the emperor. Rosenberg served as a conduit for communication when the emperor himself did not initiate arrangements for a meeting. Often it was Rosenberg's responsibility to inform one of the women (many times this was Leopoldine Kaunitz) that Joseph was likely to desire a gathering of the group on a given evening. All available members, including Lacy, would then be summoned with suggestions concerning location and other circumstances. When Joseph traveled, messages for Eleonore and for all the women were frequently passed to them within the emperor's letters to Lacy and Rosenberg, in addition to the missives sent by the emperor directly to the women.[106]

Only once, and briefly, when Leopoldine Kaunitz returned to Vienna from Brünn, was there a real possibility of a change of personnel within the little *société*. Having taken a dislike to Leopoldine Kaunitz during his visit to Naples, Joseph worried that her unwelcome influence in the group would force him to withdraw. The Kaunitz couple's transfer to Vienna was bringing an unpleasant accretion to the little society ("the coterie of Princesses"), he reported to Leopold; "as for her, I find her as ugly as she is insufferable, and yet her sister Princess Charles dotes on her." Joseph was annoyed by the intrusion ("a rather sharp-tongued recruit"). At this juncture, Lacy suggested an alternative candidate for inclusion in the group, Leopoldine Liechtenstein's sister Princess Fürstenberg.[107] But Leopoldine Kaunitz was duly assimilated, no doubt owing to the preference of Eleonore. It seems likely that Leopoldine Kaunitz then helped Eleonore and the emperor to moderate the tone of their interactions, just as she helped them reconcile specific differences in subsequent years. Joseph's dislike for Leopoldine Kaunitz gave way to warm regard in the coming years.[108]

The emperor, mainspring of the group and its raison d'être, was a talented, entertaining conversationalist, a trait rare in a reigning sovereign, as biographer Bérenger observes.[109] Swinburne described the emperor's conversational skills in the late 1770s: "His manners are easy, his conversation lively, voluble, and entertaining; running rapidly from one subject to another, and displaying frequently a vast variety of knowledge. Perhaps he manifests too great a consciousness of possessing extensive information; and he may be reproached likewise with frequently anticipating the answers of the persons with whom he converses. A mixture of vanity and of impetuosity conduce to this defect." Swinburne reported that the emperor could talk "freely and merrily. One is apt to expect more from an Emperor and to forget that he is one. His accent is rather harsh and nasal. His French is very good, except a few Germanisms."[110]

Joseph's brief marriage to Isabella of Parma, dead of smallpox just prior to her twenty-second birthday after giving birth to the couple's second daughter (who also died), was felt by some contemporaries to have softened his nature at least temporarily. That marriage might have improved his political instincts as well as his social skills if Isabella had lived longer.[111] Joseph had also been fond of his younger sister Archduchess Maria Josepha, who died of smallpox in October 1767, and of his only surviving daughter Theresia or Thérèse, who died in 1770. The loss of these female connections surely affected him deeply. His unchivalrous behavior toward his second wife, Maria Josepha of Bavaria, excited public comment and opprobrium. Leopoldine Kaunitz and Eleonore had approved of Joseph's selection of the Bavarian Maria Josepha, unenthusiastic as it was. They had preferred her to a princess from Saxony or Modena. But as early as December 1764 Leopoldine had expressed pity for the bride-to-be in view of the likely coldness of her future husband Joseph.[112] After Maria Josepha's death Joseph frequently proclaimed that he was perfectly satisfied with his single status. His preoccupation with the issue is striking but not difficult to understand given his status as eldest son and ruler. Maria Theresia famously shared her joy over the birth of Leopold's first son in early 1768, publicly announcing to the audience at the Burgtheater (apparently in Viennese dialect) that "Der Le'pold hat an Buam," Leopold has a little boy! Eleonore happened to be in attendance on that evening and reported the incident to her sister Leopoldine.[113] In a letter to Leopold written in June of the same year, Joseph set the tone from which he rarely deviated in later years, urging Leopold to continue the good work, producing children whose existence protected Joseph from demands that he marry a third time ("the obligation of having a wife, a role I detest").[114] In 1771, reporting symptoms of his own ill health to Leopold (hemorrhoids being the chief complaint), Joseph reaffirmed his contentment as a bachelor, "not having a wife—what would such a poor creature do with a sour recluse [*hibou*] and I with a family." In a remark to Lacy, sent during a visit to Leopold's numerous family in 1775, Joseph again mentioned his good fortune in having a brother who saved him from the annoyance of producing a family of successors: "that is my situation, and I can assure you . . . that I enjoy my freedom to the fullest."[115]

The emperor did remain friendly with women and social groups outside the small circle of *Dames*. His relationship with Count and Countess Windischgrätz has been mentioned. Swinburne noted that on those evenings of the week when he did not meet with his five special friends, Joseph might pay a brief visit to Princess Esterházy or Madame de Burghausen, both of them friends of the *Dames*. Joseph put in appearances at social gatherings of Chancellor Kaunitz. The emperor did not visit any single group or house to the exclusion of all others even in later years, a practice that would have occasioned resentment. He could be awkward with women, sometimes offending them with his sarcasm, coldness, and feigned indifference. Despite his conversational skill, the pleasant, warm expressions he included in his letters to individual women he seemed unable to use in the discourse of everyday life with them.[116] As early as 1774, Joseph wrote to Leopoldine Kaunitz in truly graceful terms describing his eagerness to return to the gatherings of the *société*, to "these precious evenings, when the heart is worn on one's sleeve [*le coeur est sur les levres*], and reserve is left at the door."[117] Extant letters and notes from the emperor to Leopoldine Kaunitz over the course of many years contain repeated expressions of affection and regard, too frequent and diverse to be self-serving flattery and certainly not the products of romantic infatuation.[118]

Each woman in her own way relished the special status that participation in the *société* conferred. In keeping with her position as daughter-in-law to the chancellor, Leopoldine Kaunitz was acutely attuned to political events.[119] She was always near the center of activity while her father-in-law the chancellor lived, with ready access both to him and to the emperor. She enjoyed the confluence of officials and other personages who waited upon her, hoping for access to the emperor or to the chancellor. In August 1777, for example, when Joseph had just returned to Vienna from a trip to France Leopoldine Kaunitz was visited by several foreign ministers who dropped by her residence hoping to encounter the emperor.[120] Leopoldine Liechtenstein, secure in her lofty position as the respectable wife of the Liechtenstein *Majoratsherr*, also set great store by her membership in the unique group of *Dames* because it gave her access to privileged sources of information. Leopoldine Liechtenstein's friends often had occasion to note her penchant for secretiveness and her cageyness in retailing news she obtained. In large and small ways Leopoldine Liechtenstein communicated this attitude to her associates, withholding political news until she could retail it comfortably and in strict privacy.

When discord erupted within the group, Josepha Clary generally played the role of peacemaker. Her soothing influence was needed. Leopoldine Liechtenstein (not to mention the courteous Lacy) was guarded in her speech, but other group members were at times outspoken. Eleonore had a particularly forthright nature, unable to restrain herself in conversation even when aware that topics were sensitive. Cheerful and lighthearted without being a foolish woman, Josepha relished the liveliness of the high-powered group just as she delighted in her role as matron to her dutiful son and brood of personable daughters. The other four women were always glad of her company, and so was the emperor. Freshly arrived in Prague in late October 1771 to tackle famine conditions (described in chapter 4), he reported to Maria Theresia that affairs were in a deplorable state but that he had not yet turned to the business at hand or gone anywhere "except yesterday after 9 o'clock, when my council meeting was finished, I visited mistress of the hunt Princess Clary, who is only passing through, other than this I have seen neither women, nor men, nor troops, nor opera."[121] Writing to Leopoldine Kaunitz in May 1779, as she took her cure in Baden, the emperor complained about "the persecutions I have to endure from Prince Clary [Josepha's husband]," lamenting "the effects this has on our *société*." Prince Clary's bad humor communicated itself to his wife, the emperor wrote, who in turn passed it along to her friends; "and thus through a sort of electricity I find myself receiving the jolts that this man's insupportable character can produce at any moment, and there I am, a participant in a sense in the marital difficulties of this wretch." But the emperor did not contemplate ending his friendship with Josepha Clary nor, it appears, did he reproach her for the inconvenience.[122]

By contrast, Josepha's sister Sidonia Kinsky grew increasingly irascible and independent-minded as years passed. Sidonia's insouciance sometimes inconvenienced the other women. After a frustrating day during which, because of Sidonia's carelessness, the women had failed to contact the emperor concerning evening plans, Leopoldine Kaunitz wrote to Eleonore comparing Josepha—good, conciliatory, to all appearances an angel—with her wayward sister Sidonia. Happy was the person who sought to follow in Josepha's footsteps, observed Leopoldine, "but in truth her sister is not only far from this, but takes another path entirely." A month later Leopoldine Kaunitz had additional misadventures to report when Sidonia, serving as the designated hostess for an evening gathering, had gone off to a fireworks display with the emperor and the Duke of Braganza without informing Leopoldine Kaunitz and Josepha, who sat waiting alone until 10 o'clock for the group's return.[123]

Brief quarrels aside (and sometimes interfamilial incidents or jealousy caused friction between Leopoldine Liechtenstein and Eleonore Liechtenstein), the friendship that united all five women endured. In Vienna in June 1775, Eleonore Liechtenstein ended a letter to her sister Leopoldine Kaunitz with a special message summarizing her affectionate feelings for all the *Dames*, who were together in Laxenburg: "tell them each one individually and all together, how much I love them, it is thus that I love them, it is the whole *société* and each member of which it is composed that I love, and this friendship forms an essential part of my happiness."[124] The Englishman Wraxall described the functioning of the full complement of *société* members as he observed it in the late 1770s in his memoirs. As many as four evenings a week, Wraxall reported, Joseph II was in the habit of visiting "a little circle chiefly composed of females," most prominently Princess Charles Liechtenstein but also her sister Countess Kaunitz, the Princess Francis Liechtenstein, Princess Kinsky, and Princess Clary. "Marshal Lacy," he added, "who has been attached near twenty years to the Princess Francis Lichtenstein, is generally admitted into this select society; and Count Rosemberg [*sic*], the Lord Chamberlain, is likewise, sometimes, of the party . . . The persons above named [the five *Dames*, Rosenberg, Lacy], meet alternately at one another's houses, to which Joseph repairs with the utmost privacy, unattended and alone. I know that he himself constitutes its principal entertainment and occupation. He talks, and the ladies listen. Lacy, as well as Rosemberg, are probably too experienced Courtiers, to invade this prerogative." Wraxall confirmed that the group's principal diversion was conversation. "Cards are never brought, for the Emperor dislikes them. The last time that he ever sat down to play, was in 1764, after his coronation at Francfort. It is true that the ladies, desirous of varying the evening amusement, attempted, some time ago, to introduce a book, by way of change; but, the experiment did not succeed. Joseph prefers conversation."[125] In his journal, it is interesting to note, *Obersthofmeister* Khevenhüller alleged that the emperor did not know how to play cards properly and so eventually banned all games of chance at court gatherings.[126] On at least one occasion Joseph II himself suggested that the group should try reading together. Leopoldine Kaunitz reported in November 1774 that as the emperor passed along to her a brochure entitled "Plan d'économie politique dédié à Mr. Turgot" he proposed that the group select a specific title to read together during the coming winter evenings, saying "with great urgency that he wished us, la Clary [Josepha Clary] and me, to make a decision about the reading material." When Josepha Clary and Leopoldine Kaunitz could not make up their minds, the emperor suggested "le voyage de Solander" (by Swedish naturalist Daniel Solander, 1733–1782). Leopoldine worried that this selection was too long but also feared that too much dissension would cause the reading project to be dropped altogether—as apparently happened.[127]

Over time the group's members adopted a familiar, stylized mode of communication about their daily plans. Upon encountering one of the *Dames*, Joseph's regular greeting was *was machen wir?*, that is, "what are we going to do?"—his mode of asking where and when the group would come together next. To make a gathering possible, one of the women had to keep her residence "open" to company, with household staff ready to greet visitors. The remaining *Dames* could then attend other social events during a portion of the evening, confident that the emperor would find the group assembled at the customary hour should he choose to visit. So long as the emperor was in town, the group met even when several of its members were absent or unavailable, although it functioned best when all were there to contribute. Leopoldine Kaunitz described in detail a fatiguing evening that she and Josepha Clary suffered through in October 1780, trying to amuse Joseph. Conversation was dull ("an incredible aridity") and the evening dragged on; "we try just about every topic, it is like being forced to stroll for 2 hours in a chamber that is 6 feet long and 3 feet wide."[128] Leopoldine Kaunitz expressed relief that Eleonore and especially Leopoldine Liechtenstein would soon be returning to town, "and then there will be a greater number of us."[129]

The emperor's forthright reliance upon this group of women for companionship is remarkable in view of the disdain he continued to express for women in general. As noted previously, in conversation and correspondence with other men Joseph belittled women as a group. In 1768 he described his interactions with women as necessarily frivolous; he had found that to please them one had only to amuse them, "the rest follows easily." Their behavior was capricious, shaped solely by vanity, he asserted. He told Leopold in June 1772 that the coquetry of women and their desire to be considered attractive were beyond belief; "one could write volumes about the silly things that are said and done."[130] Years later in 1787 he derided the new Prussian king Frederick William when the latter established his "official" mistress in great comfort, and at great cost ("that is paying dearly for the same pleasure that one could have at a much better price").[131] Joseph's peculiar, brusque manners sometimes alienated female acquaintances; and the puzzled reactions of these friends, particularly Eleonore Liechtenstein, to his eccentric social sorties no doubt added to his frustration.

All evidence suggests that the emperor was a hard worker, even though, as Beales notes, few contemporaries gave him credit for his industry. He cast himself in the role of a stoic philosopher-king whose goals, ostensibly iconoclastic and wicked but actually enlightened, were certain to cause clucking consternation among befuddled conservative spirits.[132] Conversing with the *Dames*, the emperor liked to shock, to irritate or rile, to make paradoxical statements or let drop ingenious aphorisms. When he was surly or merely drowsy, the group humored him and made allowances. As a young man he struck contemporaries as inordinately ambitious, anxious to make a name for himself, and so long as Maria Theresia lived he complained of the galling constraints she imposed. In a letter to Lacy in 1773 he wrote that he preferred to take risks, to obtain great results or suffer complete defeat as ruler, rather than to move forward cautiously.[133] The difficulty of his position during the coregency may explain in part his ungracious behavior as a young ruler. His own ambitious domestic and military goals eventually brought him to grief; but even then, although he lost the facile, cheerful optimism of his earlier days that had persisted even as he complained that he was overburdened and misunderstood, particularly during Maria Theresia's lifetime, he invariably blamed circumstances and contemporaries for his failures rather than any overreaching on his own part.

Joseph prided himself on his ability to separate his personal life from his métier as ruler, making fulsome statements about his own objectivity, rectitude, and rationality. The diarist Zinzendorf recorded a conversation he had with his colleague Count Philip Sinzendorf, who noted how systematic Joseph II tried to be in all his actions. According to Sinzendorf, Joseph's intent was to remain emotionally unmoved by anything that was said to him in a social setting (nothing would ever "render him either hot or cold"). Zinzendorf remarked that such uprightness did the emperor honor.[134] But Joseph's wish to demonstrate his devotion to the abstract ideal of the state that he served led to uncompassionate and probably counterproductive treatment of individuals. His demands on his officials and servants were unrelenting. When Lady Mary Coke and several of the *Dames* were visiting Austerlitz in September 1773 and the emperor too made a brief appearance at the palace out of regard for the chancellor, Lady Mary noted: "He [the emperor] looks well, and does not seem to have suffered from the hardships he voluntarily undergoes in all his journies, but I cannot say so much for poor General Pellegrini, who seems at least ten years older since I saw him. 'Tis one of the few things in the Emperor that I cannot reconcile with that superior understanding that he shews in almost everything else. Why harrass and wear out his officers and attendance for no one purpose? If there was a war the fatigues and hardships are necessary, and must be bore as well as they can; but to wear people out in order to inure them to hardships seems to me ill understood. He never lies in a bed during all the time of his journey. He carries with him the case of a matrass and pillow case; those at the place where he stops are filled with straw and laid upon the ground, upon which his Majesty sleeps. Those who attend him are obliged to sleep in the same manner, and as some of them are older then [*sic*] him, they are, of consequence, less able to bear constant fatigues and hardships, especially when they last for four or five months together."[135]

There is no reason to doubt the sincerity of the emperor's intentions, but he could not always live up to the lofty ideal of a dispassionate, purely rational sovereign. Paul Bernard has described the emperor's personal intervention in judicial proceedings, occurring even as Joseph insisted that under his scepter reason alone ruled. As Bernard aptly puts it, the emperor had a "strongly developed tendency to look upon his prejudices as having normative value."[136] The emperor noisily sought to eliminate favoritism in his dealings with families of the court aristocracy, traditionally a cosseted group. Hoping to demonstrate impartiality, he seemed simply heartless. The emperor's high ideals should have precluded the granting of imperial favors to any of his special friends; but behaviors entrenched in the very nature of court life could not be transformed by the actions and willpower of one eager monarch. Despite his high-flown rhetoric, the emperor let his personal preferences affect many decisions. As his biographer Beales has noted, Joseph was aware of this circumstance and was rather ashamed of himself.[137] Certainly the *Dames* expected to reap some tangible benefits from their special status with the emperor. Their requests were comparatively modest. In 1772, when Eleonore urged the emperor to bestow the Order of the Golden Fleece upon her brother-in-law Ernst Kaunitz and the emperor complied, the personal favor was in reality neither arbitrary nor shocking, given the circumstances. The occasion was the birth of a first child to Maria Carolina, queen of Naples, where Ernst had served as ambassador (as described in chapter 4), and the award gratified Ernst's father, the chancellor. The emperor had shown the *Dames* (Leopoldine Kaunitz was not present) his list of nominations for the "Toison," which included also the son of imperial Vice Chancellor Colloredo. Eleonore remarked to her sister that selection of Ernst Kaunitz was reasonable: "the comparison of fathers, of sons, all is in your favor. You have 2 ambassadorships [Naples and Rome], you concerned yourselves with the marriage of the queen whose lying-in is celebrated through the promotion." When the emperor granted her request, Eleonore pronounced him "charming . . . amiable."[138]

When their requests were not granted, the *Dames* were frankly indignant. In October 1777 Eleonore wrote in some disgust to her sister about the emperor's indifference to his friends' interests, pointing out that Joseph was surely very confident of his friends' regard, to judge from his cavalier treatment of them. It was always the same dreary routine, Eleonore sighed, and the *Dames* had long ago discovered "that this society is of no use to us, that it leads nowhere, that it brings us almost no pleasure."[139] At times the emperor made a great show of his impartiality. When the slow working of the Holy Roman Empire's judicial organs produced a judgment unfavorable to Prince Johann Alois Öttingen-Spielberg, the father of Leopoldine Kaunitz and Eleonore and a debtor consumed by a veritable *Prozesswuth* (the prince conducted lawsuits against relatives and neighboring landowners that could not be resolved in his lifetime), Joseph explained in a note to Leopoldine Kaunitz that he could not influence the actions of the imperial commission that had assessed Prince Öttingen-Spielberg's financial situation; he could only assure her that he would promote any informal concessions that might be procured for her father. "That is all I have been able to do," Joseph concluded, "please be just, I beg you, to the emperor, who can do nothing about the constitution of his Empire, and to Joseph, who can do nothing about the fact that he is emperor."[140] The *Dames* did their part through careful management of the public face of Joseph's regard for them. In August 1780, when the emperor, recently returned from Russia, did not come to the theater where so many personages had gathered hoping to see him, Leopoldine Kaunitz confessed that she was glad to have attended herself. If the emperor had not made an appearance, at least no one could accuse the *Dames* of holding him back from attending ("I was glad to be there so that no one could even dream that it was we who kept him away").[141]

The *Dames* did sometimes feel that the emperor's behavior toward them was more than usually unyielding, a byproduct of his effort to demonstrate that no tangible advantage to family or associates could result from their close association with him. In October 1775, Eleonore Liechtenstein remarked to her sister that Joseph behaved more churlishly toward herself and her husband Charles than toward total strangers, just to prove that she and Charles had no special influence with him.[142] Beales concludes with reason that the emperor's interaction with the *Dames* "gives the lie to his constant assertions, accepted by some historians, that private considerations never affected his public actions."[143] Joseph tried but failed to live up to his ideal, a circumstance worthy of remark chiefly because he made rather overblown, pompous claims about his own objectivity and invulnerability to prejudices that shackled inferior intellects. He compensated for his occasional shortcomings through ostentatious nonchalance at some times and by arbitrarily refusing to please his public, and his particular friends, at other times. In any case he did not make wholesale concessions to the wishes of his friends. When Leopoldine Kaunitz sought the position of *Hofmarschall* for her husband Ernst, Joseph diplomatically absolved himself of responsibility for the choice. He wrote to Leopoldine that he was uncertain of Maria Theresia's plans and could not encourage Ernst to ask for a position that might not be available. No decision concerning the post was to be expected soon.[144]

His disclaimers notwithstanding, the emperor confided to the *Dames* matters of state that went far beyond the boundaries of typical social conversation in the Habsburg capital. Joseph never conceived of his evening gatherings as a forum for discussion of policy matters or for airing the contents of briefings from his advisors. A visitor at a gathering in 1773, Count Valentin Esterházy found that politics was not discussed and that Joseph broke off the conversation when the subjects of politics, religion, or government administration were broached. Certainly Eleonore's biographer Adam Wolf subscribes to this view.[145] Nevertheless, the women's correspondence tells a different story and attests to repeated, virtually continuous disclosures by the emperor concerning both policies and the persons who executed them. Unfortunately for historians, during the winter months, when the group met most frequently, all members resided in Vienna and written correspondence was largely unnecessary. The best evidence remains the letters produced when Eleonore Liechtenstein tarried on her country estates in late autumn, after the other women had returned to Vienna and to their regular evening meetings with Joseph. The following description by Leopoldine Kaunitz of a letter she received from the emperor is but one of many that could be adduced as evidence of the emperor's forthcoming attitude toward his friends: "I have received two letters about which I have much more to tell you, but it will be quickest to send you the originals after I have answered them, the one from the Emperor is 4 pages, I had to read it at least twice to understand it properly, it contains arguments about Silesia and the Code Theresien and the Promised Land, similar to what you have already received, and then some things along the lines of the trick he [Joseph II] played on the Prussian general who wanted to see him."[146]

Quite possibly the emperor's indiscretion began simply as an inclination to display quickness of mind or to surprise and shock his female listeners. Many contemporaries assumed that the group's discussions were frank and substantive in nature. Prince de Ligne, who recorded that he had been present at gatherings, professed himself to be astonished by the frankness of the women's remarks. He had heard statements that were truly impolitic [*inconvenable*], he averred.[147] Joseph's brother Leopold, ever censorious and even contemptuous of the emperor's social habits, was certain that all manner of political affairs were discussed by the group. The women, he observed during his visit to Vienna in 1778, were impudent and brazen, scolding the emperor who, besotted and gullible because of his attraction to Eleonore, meekly accepted their verbal abuse ("they scold him and say all sorts of impertinent things"). The imprudent women then bragged openly about their favored access to political information.[148] In his description of Marie Christine, also in 1778, Leopold remarked that this sister, always interfering in public affairs and seeking to influence the emperor, deliberately and designedly courted the ambitious *Dames* and *Obersthofmeisterin* Countess Chanclos (successor to Countess Paar in that position), a practice that Leopold found disgusting.[149] The Zinzendorf diaries, by contrast, are silent about such unattractive behavior on the part of the *Dames*. Zinzendorf frequently recorded the substance of his interactions with Eleonore, Leopoldine Kaunitz, and Josepha Clary, and he was not a man to whitewash the failings of his contemporaries.

Historians have documented amply Joseph's unattractive characteristics—his arrogance and hastiness, his occasional petulance, his intellectual superficiality. Positive traits that sprang from his earnest desire to be a rational, effective, fair-minded, and industrious ruler were also unmistakable. The fondness Joseph felt and expressed, after his own fashion, for this unique circle of *Dames* exposes one of the peculiarly attractive sides of his personality. Despite the ostensible oddness of such a selection of individuals—three of the *Dames* were many years older than Joseph and to all appearances staid, mature society matrons unlikely to attract the favorable notice of an aspiring iconoclast—the social dynamics of this particular circle of friends suited Joseph II. Adding to the peculiarity of this group was the circumstance, noted rather bluntly by Joseph's biographer Padover, that Joseph as coregent "disliked everything his mother represented and reacted against all who were attached to her"; and yet these women, and particularly the two oldest sisters, were certainly associates of his mother though not confidantes.[150] The *société* proved to be a happy combination of personalities and interests. The proficiency of the *Dames* in meeting the emperor's needs for companionship, honed by lengthening experience, enabled them to retain his favor and preserved the viability of the group. Both Lacy and Rosenberg were more astute and disinterested than the average courtier and were individuals with broad interests, familiar with the latest topics and literature of the day. Neither was an uncritical admirer of the emperor or of his plans and methods; but both were tactful and discreet. That these talented, influential men repeatedly chose to be present at gatherings of the group throughout the years of its existence speaks to the importance they ascribed to this constellation of individuals, and no doubt also to enjoyable hours of companionship.

Throughout her life, even as she aged, the empress Maria Theresia retained an unaffected, intuitive interest in and sympathy for many of the friends and advisors who surrounded her. Joseph II's personality was quite different. Already as coregent his manners could be churlish and impatient when his subjects, or events, did not bend to his will, and these same characteristics manifested themselves even in purely friendly exchanges. Maria Theresia's biographer Guglia suggests that it was Joseph's lukewarm, largely theoretical interest in the affairs of others, male or female, that left him with only a small circle of persons whom he cared for and trusted, and even these limited feelings were fragile and easily disrupted.[151] This meant that individuals with whom he was genuinely comfortable, such as his circle of *Dames*, were doubly important to him, and the relative ease and comfort he felt in the company of the *Dames*, after his initial infatuation with Eleonore Liechtenstein had passed, undoubtedly goes far to explain the longevity of the *société*. That there were hazards attendant upon an association involving such disparities in power and influence was a truth acknowledged implicitly and at times explicitly by each of these matrons of highly placed aristocratic houses. But the association was flattering to the women and greatly valued by them.

From casual, mundane beginnings and the routine if unusually persistent infatuation of the young emperor Joseph for an attractive young woman of aristocratic birth, this oddly assorted *société* evolved naturally, becoming the most memorable episode of five women's lives and a comfort, even a form of congenial refuge, for the emperor. A pleasant glimpse of the everyday intercourse and banter of the group in its mature form appears in Leopoldine Kaunitz's letter to Eleonore on 15 August 1779, when Leopoldine, the emperor, and Chancellor Kaunitz had attended a performance at Schönbrunn. Before parting from Leopoldine, the emperor asked "so what shall we do tomorrow [*was thun wir denn morgen*]? my God, I do not know, perhaps go to Prince Colloredo's, I replied. No, he said, we must plan something, we shall go to la Kinsky's [Sidonia Kinsky]. Very well, with all my heart, at what time? About 5 o'clock, all right, and so we parted from each other, and I too must part from you for I have not another minute." The following evening, Joseph and Leopoldine Kaunitz had visited Sidonia Kinsky at Weidlingau as planned. At length, when conversation lagged and it was time to break up the gathering, the emperor and Leopoldine Kaunitz returned to Vienna together in the emperor's carriage. Leopoldine's own empty carriage preceded them, her servant holding up a lantern in the dark, rainy night. Leopoldine's words conveyed both pride and pleasure. The procession, she wrote, "had a thoroughly imperial air."[152]

Notes

1. HHStA, HA SB 7, Leopold to JII, 30 July [1775]; Leopold to JII, 21 August 1775; JII to Leopold, 11 August 1775.
2. Robert Pick, *Empress Maria Theresa: the Earlier Years, 1717-1757* (New York: Harper and Row, 1966), 127. In his biography of Maria Theresia Edward Crankshaw spoke of the empress as a "man's woman." Edward Crankshaw, *Maria Theresa* (New York: Atheneum, 1986), 110.
3. Wraxall, *Memoirs of the Courts of Berlin, Dresden, Warsaw, and Vienna*, 2: 411.
4. Jerzy Lukowski, *The European Nobility in the Eighteenth Century* (New York: Palgrave Macmillan, 2003), 39, 177-78.
5. Duindam, *Vienna and Versailles*, 234-42.
6. Dena Goodman "Public Sphere and Private Life: Toward a Synthesis of Current Historiographical Approaches to the Old Regime," *History and Theory* 31, no. 1 (1992): 2 and especially 14. The elusive concepts of "public" and "private" and definitions of political culture and public opinion, compared and contrasted with institutions of *sociabilité* as these pertain to European political life prior to the French Revolution, have generated lively discussions among historians, beginning particularly with Jürgen Habermas's *Strukturwandel der Öffentlichkeit: Untersuchungen zu einer Kategorie der bürgerlichen Gesellschaft,* published in 1962. See also Philippe Ariès and Georges Duby, eds., *A History of Private Life*, vol. 3, *Passions of the Renaissance*, trans. of *Histoire de la vie privée,* 1986 (Cambridge, MA: Belknap Press, 1989), especially in Ariès' introduction to the volume as a whole, 19.1-11, Roger Chartier's introduction to the first section, 15-19, and Yves Castan's "Politics and Private Life," 21-67.
7. Scott and Storrs, Introduction, 36-41.
8. Beales, "Joseph II's 'Rêveries',." in *Enlightenment and Reform in 18th-Century Europe* (London: I. B. Tauris, 2005), 158-81. More extensive explanation in Beales, "Joseph II's 'Rêveries'," *Mitteilungen des Österreichischen Staatsarchivs* 33 (1980): 146-47.
9. With regard to attitudes towards education and employment of the nobility see especially Szabo, "Perspective from the Pinnacle," 239-60; Friedrich Walter, *Männer um Maria Theresia* (Vienna, A. Holzhausen, 1951); Beales, *Joseph II*, 1: 173-74, 190; *Maria Theresia und Joseph II.: ihre Correspondenz sammt Briefen Joseph's an seinen Bruder Leopold*, 3: 335-61, "Denkschrift des Kaisers Joseph über den Zustand der österreichischen Monarchie"; Adolf Beer, ed., "Denkschriften des Fürsten Wenzel Kaunitz-Rittberg," *Archiv für österreichischen Geschichte* 48 (1872): 1-162.
10. Qtd in Jean-Paul Bled, *Marie-Thérèse d'Autriche* (Paris: Fayard, 2001), 141.
11. Charles W. Ingrao, *The Habsburg Monarchy, 1618-1815*, 2nd ed. (New York: Cambridge University Press, 2000), 168-69.
12. LRRA, P 16/19, EL to LK, Meseritsch, 25 September 1765.
13. Bled, *Marie-Thérèse*, 187.
14. Wraxall, *Memoirs of the Courts of Berlin, Dresden, Warsaw, and Vienna*, 2: 340-41.

15 The first volume of Derek Beales's biography of Joseph II, subtitled *In the Shadow of Maria Theresa, 1741-1780* (1987), is far and away the best resource.
16 Beales, *Joseph II*, 2: 652-65; also Beales, "Was Joseph II an Enlightened Despot?," in *Enlightenment and Reform*, 262-86; Blanning, *Joseph II*, 82-84.
17 Blanning, *Joseph II*, 56-91.
18 LRRA, P 17/24, LK to EL, Vienna, 26 June 1776.
19 Szabo, "Prolegomena to an Enlightened Despot?" in *Politics and Culture in the Age of Joseph II*, edited by Franz A.J. Szabo, Antal Szántay, and István György Tóth (Budapest: Institute of History, Hungarian Academy of Sciences, 2005), 16-17; Ingrao, *Habsburg Monarchy*, 192; Beales, *Joseph II*, 1: 188.
20 This was definitely not, as was sometimes the case, an effort to mimic the misogynist Frederick II. Joseph's admiration for the military prowess and organizational skills of Frederick II was a source of uneasiness for Maria Theresia. Gutkas, *Kaiser Joseph II.*, 43; Beales, *Joseph II*, 1: 154-55, 323-25; LRRA, P 16/21, EL to LK, Vienna, 30 March 1767.
21 As examined in Ivo Cerman, *Habsburgischer Adel und Aufklärung: Bildungsverhalten des Wiener Hofadels im 18. Jahrhundert* (Stuttgart: Franz Steiner, 2010).
22 Two additional women of whom Joseph II became fond were the Marquise d'Herzelles, who cared for Joseph's little daughter Thérèse but left Vienna in January 1770, after the death of her charge, and Countess Thérèse Kinsky, born Dietrichstein. *Briefe der Kaiserin Maria Theresia an ihre Kinder*, 3: 272, MT to Marie Beatrix, 7 April 1777; Beales, *Joseph II*, 1: 202, 323-24.
23 Beales, *Joseph II*, 1: 335; 2: 429-30; Harke de Roos, *Mozart und seine Kaiser* (Berlin: Ries und Erler, 2005), 30-36.
24 LRRA, P 16/18, EL to LK, Vienna, 29 September 1764.
25 LRRA, P 16/21, LK to EL, Naples, 13 February 1768 and 19 March 1768.
26 Lady Mary Coke, *Letters and Journals*, 3: 311, 1 November 1770; 336-37, 15 December 1770.
27 LRRA, P 16/22, EL to LK, Vienna, 29 December 1770.
28 Wolf, *Fürstin Eleonore Liechtenstein*, 108; Lady Mary Coke, *Letters and Journals*, 3: 381, 21 February 1771.
29 Maria Theresia's request had been unequivocal and so was her response: "I am not happy that I will not see persons at Innsbruck as I would have hoped." When Maria Theresia wished Eleonore Liechtenstein and her husband to travel to Paris with Marie Antoinette, who was to marry the heir to the French throne, the Liechtenstein couple declined with greater decisiveness, Eleonore because she would have been outranked at festivities by the Princess of France and Charles because he felt that his age and elevated rank made such a role unseemly. SÚA, RAM AC, 11/20, MT to LK, Schönbrunn, 29 June 1765; LRRA, P 16/18, LK to EL, 29 March 1764; SÚA, RAM AC, 11/20, MT to LK, Vienna, 17 January 1765; LRRA, P 16/19, LK to EL, Naples, 9 April 1765 and 10 August 1765; LRRA, P 16/21, EL to LK, Vienna, 21 December 1769.
30 KLA, FAR, fasc. 64-355a, MT to Rosenberg, Schönbrunn, 15 October 1767.
31 Wolf, *Fürstin Eleonore Liechtenstein*, 93.
32 HHStA, Grosse Correspondenz Kaunitz, G. C. 405 c, Chancellor Kaunitz to Ernst Kaunitz, Vienna, 21 May 1768.
33 HHStA, Grosse Correspondenz Kaunitz, G. C. 405 c, Chancellor Kaunitz to Ernst Kaunitz, 8 December 1767.
34 KLA, FAR, carton 77, fasc. 65-362, Rosenberg to MT, Florence, 19 April 1768; fasc. 64-355a, MT to Rosenberg, 8 April [1768]; Wandruszka, *Leopold II.*, 1: 208-18.
35 HHStA, HA SB 4, JII to MT, 10 April 1769.

36 SÚA, RAM AC 11/20, MT to LK, 24 September [no year]; MT to LK, 12 January 1769; KLA, FAR, fasc. 70-377, letter from secretary Pichler to Rosenberg, Vienna, 11 April 1768.
37 LRRA, P 16/21, EL to LK, Vienna, 4 July 1768; EL to LK, Vienna, 2 September and 2 November 1769.
38 In another communication Maria Theresia expressed appreciation for Leopoldine Kaunitz's reports and enclosed an ornamental snuffbox. The empress added a personal note: "I would not be sorry to hear that your son has been weaned, I think that he is sapping your strength too much, and I would be glad to learn that you are pregnant again." SÚA, RAM AC, 11/20, MT to LK, 21 January [1769]; MT to LK, 15 December [no year].
39 LRRA, P 16/22, LK to EL, Brünn, 4 January 1772.
40 HHStA, Grosse Correspondenz Kaunitz, G. C. 405 c, Chancellor Kaunitz to Ernst Kaunitz, Vienna, 26 October 1772.
41 Duindam, *Vienna and Versailles*, 76.
42 LRRA, P 16/22, LK to EL, Brünn, 29 October 1772; *Maria Theresia und Joseph II.: ihre Correspondenz sammt Briefen Joseph's an seinen Bruder Leopold*, 1: 387, JII to Leopold, 17 November 1772.
43 Wolf, *Fürstin Eleonore Liechtenstein*, 106-07.
44 Beales, *Joseph II*, 1: 325.
45 LRRA, P 16/22, EL to LK, 5 July and 11 July 1772.
46 LRRA, P 16/22, EL to LK, 19 August 1771.
47 LRRA, P 16/22, EL to LK, 11 July 1772. Beales (*Joseph II*, 1: 328-29) has discussed in some detail this odd exchange between Joseph and Eleonore Liechtenstein, described by Eleonore in her letters to Leopoldine Kaunitz.
48 Beales, *Joseph II*, 1: 330.
49 Wolf, *Fürstin Eleonore Liechtensten*, 135-36.
50 LRRA, P 16/21, LK to EL, 13 February 1768, Naples.
51 Leopoldine's extensive advice is succinctly recapitulated in Wolf, *Fürstin Eleonore Liechtenstein*, 130-31.
52 Wraxall, *Memoirs of the Courts of Berlin, Dresden, Warsaw, and Vienna*, 2: 410.
53 The text of Leopold's remarkable document is related in Wandruszka's biography *Leopold II.* (Vienna: Verlag Herold, 1963), 1: 332-55.
54 HHStA, HA SB 7, JII to Leopold, 26 March 1772; *Maria Theresia und Joseph II.: ihre Correspondenz*, 1: 365-66.
55 HHStA, HA SB 7, Leopold to JII, 16 March 1772.
56 HHStA, HA SB 7, JII to Leopold, 20 April 1772; 13 July 1772; 17 Nov. 1772.
57 HHStA, HA SB 7, JII to Leopold, 16 Feb. 1775.
58 HHStA, HA SB 7, Leopold to JII, 3 March 1775.
59 HHStA, HA SB 7, JII to Leopold, 13 March 1775 and 11 August 1775.
60 HHStA, HA SB 7, Leopold to JII, 21 August 1775.
61 HHStA, KA NL, fasc. 3, carton 4, JII to Lacy, 27 December 1773; JII to Lacy, 1 January 1774.
62 LRRA, P 17/25, EL to LK, Kromau, 20 September 1779, 29 September 1779, and 3 October 1779; Feldsberg, 22 October 1779.
63 LRRA, P 17/26, EL to LK, Eisgrub, 28 July 1780 and 29 July 1780; Kromau, 15 August 1780; 19 August 1780.
64 LRRA, P 17/26, LK to EL, Vienna, 12 August 1780, 14 August 1780, and 18 August 1780.
65 LRRA, P 17/26, LK to EL, Vienna, 10 September 1780.

66 LRRA, P 17/26, EL to LK, Feldsberg, 22 October 1780. Eleonore cited the emperor's message in this letter to her sister.
67 LRRA, P 17/26, LK to EL, Vienna, 26 October 1780.
68 SÚA, RAM AC, 11/22, JII to LK, 2 September 1780. In a rather sardonic message to Leopoldine Kaunitz the emperor wrote, "Give my regards to your sister, at another time I shall take my revenge for her malicious, ironical letter."
69 In October 1771 Eleonore Liechtenstein had reported to her sister that Maria Theresia and Joseph were said to be quarreling constantly, with military promotions as one source of discord. LRRA, P 16/22, EL to LK, 1 October 1771; P 17/26, EL to LK, Kromau, 9 September 1780; P 17/26, EL to LK, Feldsberg, 25 October 1780.
70 LRRA, P 16/23, LK to EL, Vienna, 8 October 1773; P 17/25, EL to LK, Kromau, 9 October 1779.
71 Paul P. Bernard, *Joseph II* (New York: Twayne, 1968), 69-70.
72 Wolf, *Fürstin Eleonore Liechtenstein,* 140.
73 LRRA, P 17/26, LK to EL, Vienna, 12 August 1780.
74 Jean-Michel Thiriet, "Comportement et mentalité des officiers autrichiens au XVIIIe siècle," *Mitteilungen des Österreichischen Staatsarchivs* 33 (1980): 129; Duffy, *The Austrian Army in the Seven Years War,* 1: 159; Duffy, *Army of Maria Theresa,* 34; Duffy, *Military Experience in the Age of Reason,* 138; Franz-Lorenz von Thadden, *Feldmarschall Daun: Maria Theresias größter Feldherr* (Vienna: Verlag Herold, 1967), 159-60.
75 Kotasek, *Feldmarschall Graf Lacy,* 229; Wolf, *Aus dem Hofleben Maria Theresia's: nach dem Memoiren des Fürsten Joseph Khevenhüller* (Vienna: Carl Gerold's Sohn, 1858), 10-11.
76 Lacy's biographer Edith Kotasek concedes that Lacy viewed Laudon's successes and popularity with a jaundiced eye, although military historians have debated the seriousness of the purported quarrel as a factor in the military's evolution during the period. Kotasek, *Feldmarschall Graf Lacy,* 59; Nathaniel W. Wraxall, *Memoirs of the Courts of Berlin, Dresden, Warsaw, and Vienna, in the Years 1777, 1778, and 1779* (London: T. Cadell Jun. and W. Davies, 1799), 1: 336-37; Duffy, *Military Experience in the Age of Reason,* 143-44.
77 Duffy, *Army of Maria Theresa,* 35; Nosinich, "Kaiser Josef II. als Staatsmann und Feldherr," pt. 2, 409.
78 Kotasek, *Feldmarschall Graf Lacy,* 119-20.
79 Beales, *Joseph II,* 1: 403.
80 Wraxall, *Memoirs of the Courts of Berlin, Dresden, Warsaw, and Vienna,* 1: 332-33.
81 LRRA, P 17/26, EL to LK, Eisgrub, 31 July 1780.
82 Wraxall, *Memoirs of the Courts of Berlin, Dresden, Warsaw, and Vienna,* 1: 334-36.
83 Rupert S. Ó. Cochláin, "The O'Donnells in Austria," *The Irish Sword* 5, no. 21 (1962): 199.
84 Kotasek, *Feldmarschall,* 217, 228-29.
85 HHStA, KA NL, carton 2, fasc. 3, Lacy to MT, Vienna, 29 January 1769.
86 HHStA, KA NL, carton 2, fasc. 3, Lacy to MT, Vienna, 31 March 1771; Guglia, *Maria Theresia,* 2: 280.
87 Kotasek, *Feldmarschall,* 239.
88 Kotasek, *Feldmarschall,* 227.
89 HHStA, KA NL, carton 3, fasc. 3, Lacy to Franz Joseph Liechtenstein, 12 April 1761.
90 HHStA, KA NL, carton 3, fasc. 3, Lacy to nephew Captain Stuart (who wished to marry), 1 Dec. [1768].
91 HHStA, KA NL, carton 4, fasc. 3, Lacy to JII, Marseilles, 17 February 1774.

92 LRRA, P 16/23, LK to EL, Vienna, 20 October 1773; Beales, *Joseph II*, 1: 223-24.
93 HHStA, KA NL, carton 2, fasc. 3, MT's reply to Lacy's letter of 5 Jan 1771 and MT to Lacy, 18 April [1778].
94 Kotasek, *Feldmarschall*, 229-30.
95 LRRA, P 16/20, EL to LK, Vienna, 17 February 1766; P 16/22, 13 Dec. 1771; P 17/25, EL to LK, Feldsberg, 11 September 1779; Kotasek, *Feldmarschall Graf Lacy*, 71, 80.
96 Wolf, *Fürstin Eleonore Liechtenstein*, 119.
97 Lady Mary Coke, *Letters and Journals*, 4: 276, Florence, 8 December 1773.
98 Wandruszka, *Leopold II.*, 1: 174.
99 Vehse, *Geschichte der deutschen Höfe*, 14: 105-11; Hans Pawlik, *Orsini-Rosenberg: Geschichte und Genealogie eines alten Adelsgeschlechts* (Klagenfurt: Geschichtsverein für Kärnten, 2009), 118-21; Rolf Kutschera, *Maria Theresia und ihre Kaisersöhne: ein Beitrag zum Habsburgerjahr 1990* (Innsbruck: Wort und Welt, 1990), 191, 195; Guglia, *Maria Theresia*, 2: 266-67.
100 *Briefe der Kaiserin Maria Theresia an ihre Kinder*, 2: 326-27, MT to Archduke Maximilian, undated instructions (April 1774).
101 Wraxall, *Memoirs of the Courts of Berlin, Dresden, Warsaw, and Vienna*, 2: 412; Zinzendorf, *Europäische Aufklärung zwischen Wien und Triest: die Tagebücher des Gouverneurs Karl Graf Zinzendorf, 1776-1782* (Vienna: Böhlau, 2009), vol. 1, "Einführung," 161-62.
102 HHStA, HA SB 7, JII to Leopold, 14 Nov. 1780.
103 Zinzendorf, *Europäische Aufklärung zwischen Wien und Triest*, vol. 1, "Einführung," 185-86.
104 Pawlik, *Orsini-Rosenberg*, 122-23; Zinzendorf, *Europäische Aufklärung zwischen Wien und Triest: die Tagebücher des Gouverneurs Karl Graf Zinzendorf, 1776-1782*, vol. 1, "Einführung," 185-86; Wandruszka, *Leopold II*, 1: 173-75.
105 Khevenhüller-Metsch, *Aus der Zeit Maria Theresias: Tagebuch des Fürsten Johann Josef Khevenhüller-Metsch. 1774-1776 und Nachträge*, ed. Maria Breunlich-Pawlik and Hans Wagner (Vienna: Adolf Holzhausens, 1972), 49; Pawlik, *Orsini-Rosenberg*, 123.
106 Numerous letters from Joseph II to both Lacy and Rosenberg: HHStA, HA SB 72; KLA, FAR, carton 76, fasc. 64-352.
107 HHStA, HA NL, JII to Leopold, 17 Nov. 1772; KA NL, fasc. 3, carton 4, JII to Lacy, 27 December 1773; JII to Lacy, 1 January 1774; Lacy to JII, s.d., c. February 1774.
108 Wolf, *Fürstin Eleonore Liechtenstein*.
109 Jean Bérenger, *Joseph II: serviteur de l'état* (Paris: Fayard, 2007), 110.
110 Swinburne, *Courts of Europe*, 1: 351, Vienna, 12 September 1789.
111 Beales, *Joseph II*, 1: 82.
112 LRRA, P 16/18, LK to EL, Naples, 16 October 1764 and 4 December 1764.
113 Guglia, *Maria Theresia*, 2: 274n1. Guglia reported that he was unable to find the source of the quotation, noting that Arneth simply stated that the quote was well known. Alfred von Arneth, *Geschichte Maria Theresia's* (Vienna: Wilhelm Braumüller, 1863-1879), 7: 567n667. LRRA, P 16/21, EL to LK, Vienna, 18 February 1768.
114 HHStA, HA SB 7, JII to Leopold, 11 June 1768.
115 HHStA, HA SB 7, JII to Leopold, 8 August 1771; KA NL, carton 2, fasc. 3, JII to Lacy, Florence, 10 June 1775.
116 Reinalter, *Am Hofe Josephs II.*, 153.
117 SÚA, RAM AC, 11/22, JII to LK, s.d., s.l. The letter is undated, but the emperor had conveyed to Leopoldine Kaunitz the good news that her brother-in-law Franz Wenzel Kaunitz, military officer, would become proprietor of a regiment (a prize valued by

Chancellor Kaunitz, the general's father). The former proprietor, Count Aynse, died in August 1774 and Franz Wenzel became his successor in September 1774.

118 A marginal note on the fair copies of this collection of letters in the Metternich family archives, apparently an assessment of their possible value for publication, even suggests that some are love letters. A close reading of Joseph's rather inflated prose, coupled with some attention to the context, rules out this possibility. SÚA, RAM AC, 11/22, marginal comments at the beginning of fair copies, "Correspondance de l'Empereur Joseph II avec Mad. la Comtesse de Kaunitz-Rietberg *née* Princesse d'Oettingen."

119 Zinzendorf recorded lively exchanges. For example, in 1771, "Spoke at length with Madame Erneste Kaunitz about the defects of the government of Moravia, of which she is making quite a study"; in 1775 "Madame de Kaunitz told me about the conversation between Prince Louis and Monsieur de Malesherbes which is, she says, in the newspapers." HHStA, KA ZT, Band 16, 2 June 1771; KA ZT, Band 20, 19 December 1775 Vienna.

120 LRRA, P 17/24, LK to EL, 6 August 1777.
121 HHStA, HA SB 4, JII to MT, Prague, 22 October 1771.
122 SÚA, RAM AC, 11/22, JII to LK, 5 May 1779 (billet).
123 LRRA, P 17/24, LK to EL, Vienna, 29 June 1776 and 10 July 1776.
124 LRRA, P 16/23, EL to LK, Vienna, 28 June 1775.
125 Wraxall, *Memoirs of the Courts of Berlin, Dresden, Warsaw, and Vienna*, 2: 412-13.
126 Khevenhüller-Metsch, *Aus der Zeit Maria Theresias*, 6: 149, 28 October 1765.
127 LRRA, P 16/23, LK to EL, Vienna, 1 November 1774.
128 LRRA, P 17/26, LK to EL, Vienna, 30 October 1780.
129 LRRA, P 17/26, LK to EL, Vienna, 1 November 1780.
130 *Briefe der Kaiserin Maria Theresia an ihre Kinder,* 2: 228-29, JII to Leopold, 28 July 1768; 37, 16 June 1774; 374, 13 July 1774.
131 HHStA, HA SB 9, JII to Leopold, 8 Feb. 1787.
132 Beales, *Joseph II*, 1: 311-14.
133 HHStA, HA SB 72, JII to Lacy, 2 July 1773; cited in Beales, *Joseph II*, 1: 315.
134 HHStA, KA ZT, Band 23, 25 January 1778.
135 Lady Mary Coke, *Letters and Journals*, 4: 237, Austerlitz, 11 September 1773.
136 Paul P. Bernard, *The Limits of Enlightenment: Joseph II and the Law* (Urbana, IL: University of Illinois Press, 1979), 123.
137 Beales, *Joseph II*, 1: 225.
138 LRRA, P 16/22, EL to LK, 15 June 1772.
139 LRRA, P 17/24, EL to LK, Feldsberg, 9 October 1777.
140 SÚA, RAM AC, 11/22, JII to LK, undated note.
141 LRRA, P 17/26, LK to EL, Vienna, 22 August 1780.
142 LRRA, P 16/23, EL to LK, Feldsperg, 25 October 1775.
143 Beales, *Joseph II*, 1: 334.
144 SÚA, RAM AC, 11/22, JII to LK, s.d., s.l. (billet).
145 Valentin Ladislas Esterházy de Galántha, *Lettres du Cte Valentin Esterházy à sa femme, 1784-1792*, 163-64; Wolf, *Fürstin Eleonore Liechtenstein*, 140.
146 LRRA, P 17/25, LK to EL, Vienna, 16 September 1779.
147 Cited in Lucien Perey, *Histoire d'une grande dame au XVIIIe siècle. La Princesse Hélène de Ligne* (Paris: Calmann Lévy, 1888), 318.
148 Wandruszka, *Leopold II.,* 1: 346. This 1778 document and Leopold's observations from his 1784 visit are in HHStA, HA SB 15 and 16.
149 Wandruszka, *Leopold II.*, 1: 350.

150 Padover, *The Revolutionary Emperor,* 60.
151 Eugen Guglia, *Maria Theresia: ihr Leben und ihre Regierung* (Munich: R. Oldenbourg, 1917), 2: 254.
152 LRRA, P 17/25, LK to EL, Vienna, 15 and 16 August 1779.

Chapter 4

1765–1780: The *Damenkreis* during the Coregency

When coregent Joseph visited Naples in 1769 he stayed with Leopoldine Kaunitz and her husband Ernst, the Habsburg ambassador, at their residence. Leopoldine wrote enthusiastic letters to her sister Eleonore, extolling the virtues of this future ruler of Habsburg lands. He would be a true father to his country, Leopoldine asserted. Although Joseph could be eccentric in his personal behavior (almost as idiosyncratic as her father-in-law Chancellor Kaunitz, Leopoldine suggested), his grateful subjects would have every reason to esteem him as overlord. Eleonore's response was skeptical. She wrote, "you are right about many matters. I hope that you will never be undeceived with regard to others."[1] But many contemporaries predicted a golden age of prosperity and rationality as Leopoldine Kaunitz had, and Eleonore too hoped for good leadership from the emperor. In summer 1773, when she read Albrecht von Haller's *Usong*, Eleonore Liechtenstein was convinced that the author was depicting the character of Joseph II. Coregent Joseph appeared to contemporaries to have enormous promise as future solo ruler.[2]

In retrospect, given the frenetic pace of change during the 1780s under Joseph's sole rulership, contemporaries would remember the coregency as a period of stability. However, these years witnessed the launching of many policy initiatives that claimed the attention of the *Dames* and the interested public at large. The women interpreted the decision-making process throughout these years in personal terms, as a mix of conflict and concord obtaining between two loci of power, Maria Theresia and her son Joseph. This was an accurate assessment, for always at least these two principals were involved in policymaking. But the voice and authority of Leopoldine Kaunitz's father-in-law the chancellor were likewise powerful even in matters unrelated to foreign policy, which was Kaunitz's specialty par excellence. In military affairs, nominally under Joseph's exclusive control but attracting the active interest of Maria Theresia as well, *société* member Lacy too was an important player, initially as president of the war council and then as an advisor (technically a "conference minister") with strong but subtle influence. Both of these men were the soul of discretion, but the women's peculiarly close association with both men, joined with the women's constant intercourse with the emperor himself and ongoing friendship with Rosenberg, permitted the *Dames* to distinguish shifting alignments and tensions among chief shapers of policy.

During the first dozen years of the coregency the Habsburg monarchy was at peace, and its sovereigns could focus their attention on the most pressing domestic issues. Very early during the coregency Maria Theresia and Joseph II turned their attention to the lot of the tax-paying peasantry, an area of vital concern to all landowning families of the monarchy and so to the *Dames* as well. The empress and her coregent were in agreement about the need to protect the monarchy's tax base. Both had concluded that exorbitant demands of landlords for peasant dues and services were siphoning off resources urgently needed by the state. These depredations could so debilitate the rural population that it could neither pay taxes nor sustain a robust increase in numbers, which eighteenth-century "populationist" theory held to be desirable. Maria Theresia's earlier reforms for various regions of the monarchy, begun prior to her husband's death under the aegis of Count Haugwitz and subsequently recast as time, experience, and local conditions dictated, had been primarily fiscal and administrative both in focus and substance. New county or district commissioners had been appointed to represent Vienna's interests vis-à-vis provincial and landlord agents. Directives prohibiting the seizure or exchange by landlords of highly productive rustical lands and annexation of the better quality acreage to the dominical property more directly controlled by the landlord (and generally taxed at a lower rate or not at all) were on the books. Such regulations had not been rigorously enforced.[3] Now more ambitious and increasingly aware of the need for agricultural reform, the central government sought to regulate effectively the compulsory labor or "robot" owed by rustical peasants to their landlords. Previous reforms in this area too had fallen short. The goal was to define the maximum amount of labor and dues that could be required of peasants through formulae based on the amount of land peasants controlled or the state taxes they paid. The government focused its attention on rustical lands, since regulating practices on dominical lands controlled directly by landlords appeared to be unfeasible politically. In 1767, in spite of the opposition of Hungarian landlords, Maria Theresia promulgated regulations (the so-called *urbarium*) limiting compulsory labor by peasants in the Hungarian kingdom who farmed rustical lands and restricting other coercive practices used by landlords to extract additional profit from tenants. Regulations for Transylvania and the Habsburg-controlled remnants of Silesia followed in 1769 and 1771, then for Bohemia and Moravia in 1775 (considered in greater detail below), and Styria and Carinthia in 1778. By the time Maria Theresia died in 1780, most regions had received new labor regulations.[4]

These regulations, modest though they were, subjected landlord-peasant relations to increased scrutiny in a manner not seen under earlier Habsburg rulers. But the reforms were difficult to achieve and the process consumed attention and resources throughout the coregency. Agricultural conditions in Bohemia and Moravia in particular, where most lands of families of the *Dames* lay, were of special importance to the central government, since these were among the most fertile and potentially productive regions of the monarchy, once Silesia had been lost to Prussia. Planning for urbarial reform in the Bohemian crownlands had begun by the late 1760s. But it was a famine during the years 1770–1772 that focused the government's attention on deplorable conditions there. There were crop failures over much of Europe, but among the Habsburg possessions the hardest hit were Bohemia and Austrian Silesia. Moravia and Lower Austria also suffered much. In early August 1770 the government imposed a prohibition on grain exports from these areas, soon expanded to apply to the entire monarchy. Many inhabitants fled from the Bohemian lands to Hungary and Lower Austria. The government distributed grain stores of the military to the populations in stricken areas, but relief was meager and slow in coming.[5] In an attempt to expedite relief efforts, Joseph traveled to Bohemia in late October 1771 and did his best to alleviate suffering. But the situation did not really improve until a good harvest in 1772 eased shortages. Even before his efforts to fight hunger, the emperor had made a favorable impression on rural inhabitants during travels through Bohemia and Moravia. Sometimes, as in Moravia in 1769, he had engaged in popular symbolic gestures that demonstrated his sympathy and regard for the laboring peasant population, climbing down from his carriage to take a turn plowing peasant fields along the way. Zinzendorf recorded in his diary in 1773 that he had seen a monument between Wischau (Vyškov) and Rausnitz (Rousínov), not far from Brünn, erected by Prince Wenzel Liechtenstein to commemorate imperial plowing on Liechtenstein lands that had occurred on 19 August 1769. The marker's inscription was rendered in Czech, German, and Latin. Zinzendorf dismissed the whole as "a monument without taste or grace."[6] Joseph's visit to Bohemia during the height of the famine further increased his popularity. His efforts to combat the famine made a favorable, lasting impression and won the affection of the humbler denizens of rural Bohemia.

Once the worst of the emergency had passed, it was possible to tackle the regulation of Bohemian agrarian labor practices in earnest, a matter of grave import and daunting complexity. Unfortunately, the divided counsels of Maria

Theresia, Joseph, and their advisors yielded slow, tentative results. The government had fumbled, casting about for remedies that would be acceptable both to landlords and to tenants. Maria Theresia advocated a remarkably radical change in traditional landlord-peasant relationships, an approach that would offer peasants control of land parcels distributed under hereditary tenure, with compulsory labor commuted to payments. Few historians have portrayed Maria Theresia as an exemplar of enlightened absolutism; and the empress herself ascribed no part of her motives for assuming such a stance to fashionable Enlightenment thought.[7] But if adopted in toto, her plan would have ended most forms of servitude for the peasant inhabitants, generally by converting these requirements to cash equivalents to be remitted to landlords. The emperor, by contrast, favored labor agreements reached voluntarily between landowners and their tenants, estate by estate. But initial attempts to have landlords reach voluntary new agreements with their peasants in this manner, as endorsed by Joseph and by Bohemian landed interests, progressed very slowly. Maria Theresia then urged instead the imposition of uniform maximum limits on robot requirements, based on size of the peasants' holdings and taxes owed. Acceptance of these norms was to be obligatory for landlords.[8]

The government eventually had recourse to a relatively modest reformation of the system of compulsory labor rather than its abolition. After much discussion and hesitation, which in reports to his brother Leopold the emperor ascribed to Maria Theresia's timidity and vacillation, a relatively modest *Robotpatent* was issued for Bohemia and Moravia in August and September 1775, with further elaborations in 1777. The patent categorized peasant tenants according to the resources in land and equipment at their disposal and specified maximum labor requirements for each group. Peasants could choose the new regulations or they could bide by their old obligations. Choices were to be made within a year. The difficult task of interpreting and implementing the patent's instructions and applying them to each estate was entrusted to commissioners assisted by district captains. Implementation of the reforms was a protracted, difficult business, and as with earlier measures, lax enforcement proved to be the patent's weakness. But the regulation brought some relief to the peasants of Bohemia and Moravia.[9]

During the years immediately after the new regulation was published, as Joseph's biographer Beales has noted, in contested cases the emperor generally assumed a more conservative stance than did Maria Theresia, just as he had when plans for the reform were initiated.[10] Even Joseph's most astute biographers have found it difficult to unravel the tangled course of events surrounding changes in Bohemia's urbarial system in the mid 1770s. The relative positions of the empress and her coregent seem paradoxical in that the empress wished to push agrarian change further and faster than did her ostensibly reform-minded son. During much of the decade, as the issue was debated, Joseph reproached Maria Theresia for advocating radical reforms that would disrupt the monarchy's functioning and destroy the livelihood of the landed classes.[11] Maria Theresia and her advisors, the emperor complained, wanted a "general upheaval . . . wrecking fortunes"; "she says that I have abandoned her, that I have joined the opposition, essentially that I have allowed myself to be won over, and seduced, to oppose her, by God knows whom, that my social contacts [*sociétés*], even my servants have influence over my views, when they are different from hers." Maria Theresia's ideas were too radical, "too ruinous," championed only by herself and a few councilors. Her ongoing attempts to incorporate more ambitious changes would bring about utter chaos in the countryside, "in short, overturning the Robot Patent published a year ago . . . she would like to abolish servitude, arbitrarily regulate contracts and rents that the peasants who lease lands to work have paid their landlords for centuries." She had no regard at all for the landowners, Joseph wrote his brother, and these stood to lose at least half of their revenues. She accused Joseph of letting his friends sway his views.[12]

There is no evidence of direct influence on the emperor from the *Dames* or other specific associates with landholdings in Bohemia and Moravia. Evidence concerning specific discussions of the topic in the *société* is unfortunately scant, although some contours of the *Dames*' stances can be traced. Urbarial reform was a process of many years, not the result of individual events that could have elicited dramatic responses during a few soirées. Certainly many contemporaries with material interests at stake must have voiced alarm concerning the reforms and counseled moderation. In view of his many statements in favor of rural reform and the ambitious changes he introduced only a few years later as sole ruler, it is scarcely credible that the emperor actually preferred the status quo and shared the conservative goals of more intransigent Bohemian landowners, although it must be conceded that in a letter to his brother Leopold in January 1777 he recited in his own critique precisely those views espoused by the Bohemian nobility.[13] The historian Joseph Karniel has suggested that Joseph impeded plans for a more sweeping reform of peasant conditions because he wished to enact an even greater transformation that would include religious tolerance. Therefore, as a young ruler eager to make a name for himself he was waiting until, as sole ruler, he would be able to claim full credit for a radical masterstroke.[14] At least two historians, Fejtö and Blanning, have suggested that the emperor's opposition to his mother's plans for rural reform came in part from the simple fact that they were hers.[15] Joseph's own words indicate that his concern about the impact of rapid change on the state's overall strength but even more specifically on funding and supplying the military was a long-term, consistent preoccupation for him and went far to shape his outlook.[16] Admittedly Maria Theresia, who had herself survived a military crisis of major proportions early in her reign, was in a position to recognize this necessity as well. As soon as 1778 Joseph did make use of his expensive army in an effort to lay claim to Bavarian lands, straining the monarchy's finances. The possibility of such an enterprise was certainly present in his mind in earlier years, if not the specifics of the Bavarian plan itself, and international events were unpredictable in any case. Joseph can perhaps be taken at his word: as he told his brother Leopold, he feared the disruptiveness of the empress's wish for a thoroughgoing rural transformation.

The empress persevered with her more radical approach on several state-administered estates beginning in 1775, introducing a system devised by *Hofrat* Franz Anton Raab (1722–1783) whereby all robot labor was indeed ended and both dominical and rustical land was parceled out among the peasant population including new settlers, who were especially encouraged and received additional assistance. The tenants worked the land under hereditary leases nearly equivalent to ownership and owed the landlord (the state in this case) only rent in the form of cash or produce. The landlord took over responsibility for paying taxes from these accumulated peasant fees. The peasants made additional payments to the landlord proportional to the labor they had previously owed and the land they now controlled.[17]

Greatly complicating the process of reform was the peasant unrest that erupted in the Bohemian crownlands during the mid-1770s and recurred sporadically for several years. Confusing reports about the unrest and rumors about government measures to combat it were difficult for contemporaries to sort out, and these are a challenge for historians as well.[18] Certainly the Habsburg government had dickered too long over urbarial reform. Much of the delay—though surely not all—probably did result from the empress's efforts to conciliate many points of view, as her son plaintively argued. On the other hand, Maria Theresia was perhaps correct in holding Joseph's earlier visits to Bohemia partially responsible for raising peasant hopes to unrealistic levels, albeit unintentionally. Furthermore, the fact that new regulations were being prepared could not remain unknown in the countryside. Rural life had its own complexities, with the inhabitants' concerns varying according to location and socioeconomic status. To preserve rural peace, the government needed to move expeditiously to eliminate uncertainty about the future. It did not do so, and the combustible mixture of harsh conditions and heightened expectations produced serious peasant unrest in Bohemia beginning in March 1775. The Bohemian peasants claimed that the emperor (or occasionally the empress, in some versions) had promised them in 1771 that robot would be abolished entirely. They insisted that the relevant proclamation must have been suppressed by landlords. They professed loyalty to the sovereigns and promised to obey any orders that came directly from Vienna—but not from landlords or provincial officials, whom they distrusted. In many areas the peasants refused to work until a genuine imperial patent should prescribe their duties. This directive had to be either the older patent supposedly granted by the emperor in the course of his ministrations during the famine or a new one favorable to the peasants which imperial authorities rather than landlords were to enforce. For their part, landlord and provincial authorities urged the peasants to carry on with their traditional tasks until an imperial commission arrived to adjudicate disputes. Local estate officials worried not just about restoring order but also about inducing the recalcitrant peasants to work the fields and plant the year's crops, absolutely essential for the rural economy. Estate officials and district administrators reported the resurgence of identifiably Protestant groups, who refused to make customary payments to Catholic priests. Accounts sent to Vienna contained references to activities of the "Lämmelbrüder" or neo-Adamites, a persistent sect of Bohemian and Moravian religious dissidents whose activities were sure to alarm the staunchly Catholic Maria Theresia, already worried about enticements offered to her subjects by the more tolerant Prussian king Frederick II, who might tempt her Protestant subjects to leave Habsburg lands entirely. As Karniel has demonstrated, Habsburg leaders were aware of the ease with which external powers (most obviously tolerant Prussia but also Russia, in the case of Orthodox subjects) might attract the favorable notice of discontented Habsburg subjects. Neither naive nor ignorant, the empress understood the political complexities that resulted from the great ethnic and confessional diversity in her lands; but her solution, the old, familiar approach that had been applied repeatedly with limited success by her predecessors, was to assimilate all groups of subjects within the Catholic Church by persuasion if possible and by force if not, so far as was humanly possible.[19]

The uprising began in northern and eastern Bohemia and spread quickly. Groups of peasants moved from village to village, persuading or coercing the inhabitants into joining forces against the landlords and their representatives. The Bohemian lands of the Clary and Kinsky families and also some Liechtenstein property in Bohemia were impacted by the peasant uprising. The peasant population in Moravia was considered to be more tractable, but even here there was unrest as the summer months passed in 1775. In July disturbances occurred in Meseritsch, Eleonore's property, where peasants demanded the "golden patent" about which stories circulated throughout the regions of unrest. Written in gold lettering, this imperial patent was said to prescribe large reductions in peasant robot.[20] In Mährisch Kromau the timely appearance of soldiers preserved order. Some unrest was reported on the Kaunitz estate at Austerlitz (Slavkov), but a more serious and potentially dangerous situation could be found at Jarmeritz, where Leopoldine Kaunitz's brother-in-law Dominik Kaunitz was sufficiently concerned about the surly peasant population to remove his wife and children from the estate.[21] Whenever district commissioners or their representatives became fearful that trouble was brewing in specific Bohemian or Moravian locales, they requested and received detachments of soldiers to quash the renitents. In meting out punishments, local authorities generally tried to distinguish leaders from followers and also from those who had been coerced into joining forces with the rebels. But officials deliberately used exemplary punishment to frighten the populace at large. Floggings were administered as well as execution by hanging in the case of ringleaders. The peasant unrest in Bohemia and Moravia as well as the harsh reactions of both landlords and the government in Vienna laid bare the foundations of compulsion and brutality that undergirded the agrarian system of production. Peasant unrest, when it took on serious proportions, was a fearful matter that had to be treated as a weighty affair of state. Peasant refractoriness terrified the wealthy families for whom the peasants were expected to labor. But peasant refusals to sow fields were not purely matters of income for the privileged. Delays could jeopardize the food supply of the entire population. Both government and estate officials quickly took alarm. When real danger threatened, members of favored socioeconomic groups experienced an almost visceral reaction; suppression of the unrest then had priority over all other concerns among both the reform-minded and traditionalists.

Given the high stakes involved in such crises, the Habsburg government had no wish to publish details concerning its internal weaknesses to the world at large, to its rival Prussia, or even allies. Habsburg fears were well-founded, for economic hardship in combination with Habsburg intolerance toward the tenacious if camouflaged Protestant presence in Bohemia did increase Habsburg vulnerability to interference by interested parties beyond Bohemia's borders.[22] The Saxon ambassador in Vienna, Gustav Georg Völkersahn, relayed reports to his government about the situation in the countryside but found news difficult to obtain. He had heard that Eleonore Liechtenstein's husband Prince Charles was having difficulty with the peasants in Meseritsch. According to report the peasants had surrounded the palace until they were warned away by soldiers. They had not only refused to cultivate their own fields but had threatened to burn the landlord's crops. Völkersahn wrote that he could not report the prince's response to the difficulties because reliable information was so hard to come by. News was withheld especially from foreigners (Saxony shared a border with Bohemia, and the Saxon government had received alerts concerning conditions near that border, whereas news from Moravia and other interior areas was vague).[23] Correspondence that passed between the French ambassador in Vienna, Breteuil, and his superior Vergennes in Paris confirmed that the government in Vienna was trying to underplay the seriousness of the problem and any damage likely to result to the monarchy's economy.[24] In a letter to her sister from Laxenburg in June, Leopoldine Kaunitz noted that her associates there lowered their voices when they spoke of the revolt in Moravia. The situation was terrible for those whose possessions lay entirely in the affected areas (essentially the case for Leopoldine's branch of the Kaunitz family, although the Kaunitzes also claimed land in the Holy Roman

Empire) for, as Leopoldine Kaunitz remarked, it portended a long-term, substantial loss of revenue. No doubt among close acquaintances the fears of the affected landowners were well aired. After a visit to Leopoldine Liechtenstein's husband Franz Joseph in August, Zinzendorf recorded in his diary that Countess Sternberg (Leopoldine Liechtenstein's mother or possibly her sister-in-law) had remarked that she wished to have the unruly peasants drawn and quartered (*écarteler*).[25] Modest reforms, landlord pressure, sporadic repression, and the passage of time eventually put an end to the widespread peasant refractoriness.

Given the available evidence, it cannot be said that the *Dames* took a consistent interest in the practical details of estate management or rural conditions, although it is clear that they along with their fellow landowners viewed the government's rural initiatives with mistrust. In orderly aristocratic households matters of estate management, while overseen by the male family head, were handled by employees with specialized expertise in agricultural production. Any substantial changes in agrarian conditions were certain to disconcert the *Dames* and their families, however. Although not a topic for polite table conversation, agrarian relations and the government's efforts to relieve the famine and to regulate peasant services and payments necessarily claimed their attention. In October 1773 Sidonia Kinsky reported to Leopoldine Kaunitz that her (Sidonia's) husband and other Bohemian landowners were angry about Count Hatzfeld's "lamentation" concerning the "urbaria," probably a reference to reform-minded Hatzfeld's outspoken criticism of the disproportionate workload of many Bohemian peasants. Count Karl Friedrich von Hatzfeld (1718–1793), a member of the *Staatsrat*, together with Franz Anton von Blanc (1734–1806), an enthusiast for urbarial reform who had Maria Theresia's support, favored changes that moved well beyond the voluntary work agreements between landlords and their tenants. Like Maria Theresia and Raab they favored mandatory, objective norms specifying an absolute maximum of three days of robot per week. Echoing the alarm voiced by the emperor and others, Leopoldine Kaunitz reported that some landowners expected to lose half of their revenues, others more likely a third, if the government actually pushed forward its strict regulation of labor.[26]

Instructions for urbarial reform eventually reached local officials, impacting the lives of individual landowners and tenants. Summering on her estates in 1777, Eleonore Liechtenstein found herself obliged to cooperate with a regulatory commission ("this accursed commission of the district captain") that would specify labor requirements of inhabitants in both Kromau and Meseritsch. Her responses to this situation are illuminating. While her lack of enthusiasm was patent, Eleonore's attitude during the process was not inflexible or obscurantist. Certainly she voiced the sentiments of most landowners: "what can I tell you about the countryside here unless I speak of grain, crops, taxation, chicanery of the Court and departments, injustice against the landlords, impertinence of subjects, in sum an infinite number of such concerns."[27] Particularly irksome to Eleonore in 1777 were peasant claims to forest products ("great claims on timber, God knows what will occur to them after the 60 questions they will be asked," she wrote to Leopoldine Kaunitz).[28] But even here her remarks were relatively moderate. Eleonore's references to disputes over forests—and the fact that she found the entire process troublesome but not a serious economic threat—bring to mind the historian Karl Grünberg's description of the Bohemian and Moravian peasants' pressing need for kindling and pasturage. Access to forests could be contested by landlords and used as leverage against tenants since it was based on traditional usages alone in many cases. Generally remaining unregulated, these perquisites could become bargaining chips.[29]

Two years later, in 1779, Eleonore was again dealing with the commission. It was difficult to find news with which to fill her letters, Eleonore told her sister, for she was busy tending to very tiresome matters. She was incensed by the treatment meted out to the landlords by the government but was convinced that the practical experience she gained would prove valuable; "the more one is bamboozled [*chicané*], the more it is necessary to have a fundamental understanding of one's business affairs and to keep a close watch on them." The commission was also investigating a quarrel of longer standing involving restless inhabitants of the Liechtenstein village of Hosterlitz (Hostĕradice) in southern Moravia, "a case . . . that is one of the most disagreeable one can have with one's subjects."[30] An assessment of arrangements made in southern Moravia with landlords such as Eleonore and her husband would require detailed examination of estate operations. Eleonore's expressions of distaste for regulatory procedures did not convey much anxiety about the ultimate results and certainly not implacable hostility. Apparently she rather readily came to terms with the new requirements and found the actions of the *Kreishauptmann* Baron Kaltschmied (who may have been quite favorably disposed toward her and other landlords) to be reasonable. She judged him to be "a very worthy man, very decent, very sensible, but it requires heavy labor to sustain a conversation with him all evening and throughout supper."[31] Pressure from the government, the threat and reality of peasant unrest, the relative moderation of the reforms, and the likelihood that as in the past enforcement of new regulations would be relatively ineffective or at least lenient all played a role; but no doubt so did Eleonore's own awareness of serious defects in rural labor relations.

As noted previously, after conversations with Joseph II years earlier in Naples, Leopoldine Kaunitz had predicted that the emperor would introduce salutary changes by means of which all subjects, even the poor, would receive justice. He would moderate the overmighty position of the prominent and the wealthy without behaving harshly toward any group. Leopoldine had looked ahead to these imperial actions with optimism, applauding in advance the fairminded changes that Joseph would make.³² She and the other *Dames* were not without sympathy for the rural poor. From her estate in Meseritsch in October 1771, Eleonore Liechtenstein had reported much misery among the inhabitants; the harvest that year had been even worse than the one in 1770, and no abatement in state taxes had been granted. Leopldine Kaunitz too had noted with concern the onset of famine conditions in the countryside from Brünn.³³ In 1772 Eleonore learned of epidemic disease in Moravia and reported the troubling news to her sister.³⁴ And it should be noted that while the women themselves evinced little enthusiasm for the new regulations, there were a number of enterprising Bohemian landlords among their acquaintance, including first and foremost Chancellor Kaunitz, who perceived value in altering rural labor relations and who by the mid-1770s were introducing significant reforms on their private estates, emulating the actions taken on royal lands and moving well beyond robot regulation to actual commutation and subdivision of properties.³⁵ The women's jaundiced attitude toward rural reform in the 1770s resulted in part from their membership in a class that depended upon the labor of the agrarian masses and feared the uncertainty of innovation. But it also reflected a basic pessimism about attempts to remedy en masse the complex defects entrenched within rural labor relations. The reforms of the 1770s in fact brought about no quick solution to rural problems, and ill will lingered among and between landlords and peasants of the Bohemian lands in the coming years even after significant unrest ended and the urbarial regulation was fully introduced. Both landlords and peasants made peace with the new regulations grudgingly, by one means or another. In their awareness of the diversity and complexity of rural conditions and the difficulty of effecting improvement, the *Dames* no doubt resembled Joseph II; but the emperor did not share their pessimism concerning the possibility of an eventual substantive transformation, as time would tell.

In the course of the 1780s, religious reforms introduced by the emperor would become a serious concern of the *Dames*, and their disapproval would be evident to the emperor himself. With occasional exceptions, during the coregency the government's religious policy was not a source of special anxiety for the women. This was true even though by the end of Maria Theresia's life and reign, principles and objectives that would shape the Josephinian reforms had been formulated at least in part by a number of the empress's advisors, especially Chancellor Kaunitz, and by Joseph himself.

During Maria Theresia's long reign, external forms of baroque Catholicism still flourished, observances inherited from previous Habsburg reigns. Broadly conceived, baroque piety was the predominant form of Catholic religious and artistic expression in the Habsburg monarchy from roughly 1600 to 1780. This was a demonstrative, triumphant response of the Roman Catholic Church to the Protestant Reformation in Austrian and Catholic German lands, characterized by deliberate restatement of Catholic doctrine and bolstered by a rich array of religious expression including pilgrimages, processions, and devotional exercises, most of these being openly and intentionally popular, communal experiences. This was religion that appealed to the believer's senses as much as to his or her intellect. Adoration of the Eucharist, veneration of the Virgin and saints, and collective, public, dramatic demonstrations of faith elicited an emotional response from the faithful. By the mid-eighteenth century, however, there was occurring also a gradual but accelerating trend toward alternate approaches conveniently referred to by some historians as "reform Catholicism," a trend influenced by both secular and Christian Enlightenment thinkers with largely practical objectives as well as by more conservative theologians who wished to purify church practices. Catholic reformers took the church to task for its overemphasis on externals of religion, for its overmighty stance toward the state and stultifying effect on both economic and intellectual life, for its inattention to vital but prosaic parish work.[36]

The published works of such disparate reform Catholics as the French theologian François de Salignac de La Mothe-Fénelon (1651–1715) and the Italian reformer Ludovico Antonio Muratori (1672–1750) became increasingly well known in Vienna during Maria Theresia's reign and were common currency by the time significant reforms were undertaken during the coregency. The writings of Fénelon popularized a moderate form of Catholic Quietism. Although elements of Fénelon's thought had proved controversial and were deemed not wholly orthodox, his ideas were popular among literate Catholics of the eighteenth century, and they were frequently cited by the *Dames*. The reform Catholic ideas of Muratori were also highly regarded in Vienna, where even the imperial family read his publications, which identified what he considered to be the abuses of baroque worship, such as excessive veneration of saints and relics.[37] Muratori advocated a moral rebirth among Catholics, a deepening of the inward spiritual life. He sought a reduction in the number of religious holidays (some reductions were in fact made by Maria Theresia prior to the coregency, in cooperation with the pope), greater use of the vernacular during Mass so that ordinary parishioners could understand the service, restrictions on pilgrimages and processions, and fewer distracting practices such as the Marian cult that deflected worshippers' attention from God and Jesus Christ. Particularly popular among many of Muratori's followers was the distaste he expressed for the Society of Jesus, or Jesuits. Muratori's proposals found support among several Austrian bishops by the mid-eighteenth century.[38] His ideas also suited Catholic rulers such as the Habsburgs, with their conviction that the entrenched position of the church, its claim to a significant proportion of the country's manpower and wealth (particularly in its monasteries, convents, and foundations), and its adherents' excessive expenditures of time and money on church rituals, pilgrimages, and celebrations penalized the economies of Catholic lands vis-à-vis their Protestant neighbors. In their moderate Viennese form, the ideas of Fénelon and Muratori were acceptable to all but the most conservative Catholic factions.

Already in Maria Theresia's early years, and more markedly during her coregency with her son, the government claimed the authority to regulate those church activities that bore directly upon the material welfare of society. Maria Theresia's predecessors also had tried to regulate their subjects' religious lives in ways that would benefit the state, so the empress's actions, although more systematic and far reaching, were not unprecedented.[39] During the 1750s and 1760s Maria Theresia enforced a number of administrative and fiscal changes to the benefit of the state, some with papal cooperation and some without but most under the increasingly ambitious guidance of Chancellor Kaunitz and eventually with the enthusiastic concurrence of the young coregent Joseph.[40] In this effort the government enjoyed considerable support not only from proponents of secular doctrines generally ascribed to the Enlightenment but also from yet another specific group of Catholic reformers, the Jansenists, who were inspired by ideas that originated with the mid seventeenth-century Dutch theologian Cornelius Otto Jansen (1563–1648). Jansenism emphasized mankind's sinful nature and the need for efficacious grace in the Augustinian tradition. The French monastery at Port Royal had served as the seedbed of the movement. Doctrinal differences with Catholic orthodoxy eventually led to schism, with the establishment by Jansenists of a separate church in Utrecht, dubbed the Little Church, and with publication of the papal bull *Unigenitus* in 1713 that proscribed principles of the French Jansenist theologian Pasquier Quesnel concerning the nature of grace and free will. For many reform-minded Catholics who themselves had no wish to part company with the Catholic Church, elements of Jansenism remained attractive and even necessary, a corrective to existing church abuses. No longer a vital intellectual force in France by the mid-eighteenth century, Jansenism played a significant role in shaping reform Catholicism in the Habsburg monarchy under Maria Theresia, having reached Habsburg lands by way of the Netherlands. In common with Gallicanism, Austrian Jansenism stressed the rights of local bishops and national churches over against the papacy, thus in many cases providing theological support for an increased state role in religion. Many Jansenists were willing to endorse state efforts to reform the church and abolish baroque practices. The Jansenists' aptitude for literary expression of their beliefs made them valuable allies for governments that sought church reform; but many Jansenists were otherwise fundamentally nonpolitical.[41]

In Habsburg lands Jansenists regarded themselves as devout Catholics, although their most vocal adherents were detested by more traditional Catholics such as the *Dames*. In practical terms Austrian Jansenists decried the Catholic Church's deviation from the simpler practices of early Christianity. They espoused a more personal, simple, sober form of Catholicism that, as critics were quick to note, showed certain affinities with Protestantism. They supported restrictions on monasticism and favored lay reading of the Bible. They stressed the need for genuine repentance if a priest was to grant absolution in the confessional, an approach that resulted in greater strictness. Jansenists condemned a variety of popular and lucrative practices of the clergy, such as simultaneous private masses celebrated at multiple altars.[42] Pilgrimages, veneration of religious statues, relics, and holy places, as well as popular cults such as the devotion to the Sacred Heart of Jesus were suspect. In common with other reformers, Jansenists generally opposed what they viewed as the pernicious, corrupting influence of the Society of Jesus and accused its members of falsely exaggerating the individual's capacity to effect his own salvation. Conscientious Jansenists viewed with disfavor what they considered frivolous recreation, such as theater and dance. In the earlier years of Maria Theresia's reign, Jansenism in its stricter forms had only moderate appeal for the aristocracy and the populace at large. But Jansenist ideas attracted favorable notice from intellectuals, from some members of the clergy, and the literate middle class.[43] By the 1760s, prelates with Jansenist leanings had reached influential positions in the monarchy. They were active even as confessors to the Habsburg family, replacing Jesuits in that important function. In these roles during the 1760s and 1770s the increasing reliance upon Jansenist clerics may well have contributed to a trend toward a more personal, inwardly focused religion among families of the Habsburg elite, who rejected radical French Enlightenment attacks on religion but were disposed to seek greater personal meaning in religious practices.[44]

Evidence suggests that particularly after her husband's death Maria Theresia herself was attracted to a more somber, ascetic, internalized form of Catholicism although many elements of baroque Catholicism remained in her approach, especially in the importance she ascribed to symbolic, outward, communal displays of faith. She sponsored the translation of Jansenist literature from French to German, thus favoring the broader transmission of Jansenist ideas. Such works contained no tales about miracles, no litanies, no legends about saints; their focus was texts from the Bible. One scholar, Peter Hersche, has even suggested that Maria Theresia herself could reasonably be denominated a "moderate Jansenist" or "philojansenist."[45] As Grete Klingenstein has argued, during Maria Theresia's reign the reform movement within Catholicism itself was gradually shifting the focus of religious life from the church's corporate, political activities to the beliefs and practices of individual believers. Even the pious Maria Theresia was affected by the simpler, more internalized ethos that increasingly influenced Catholic reformers of the late eighteenth century.[46]

In many of Maria Theresia's reforms, and in some of her attitudes, the growing Jansenist influence certainly can be discerned. Maria Theresia was both a fervent Catholic and a practical ruler. In her "Political Testament" from about

1750 she had argued with regard to religion in her hereditary lands that owing to the generous support of her forebears Catholicism was flourishing. Far from needing additional pecuniary assistance, religious authorities had not used their worldly resources wisely and should not receive more. Her words conveyed an unsentimental view of the Catholic hierarchy.[47] Austrian Jansenism's willingness to support the authority of the state in its contests with the pope or ultramontane bishops was naturally attractive to Maria Theresia and later to Joseph II as well. This statist approach was championed in the work of "Febronius" (actually Johann Nicholas Hontheim, auxiliary bishop of Trier), who in 1763 published his controversial *Von dem Kirchenstaat und der rechtmässigen Gewalt des Papstes*. The document made a strong case for the powers of the secular ruler, defining the pope's primacy narrowly and reserving extensive authority to general councils and national synods. In the late 1770s Febronius was obliged to recant, under pressure emanating especially from the church hierarchy in Vienna. But in the meantime his ideas had circulated broadly within the monarchy because Maria Theresia, counseled by her confessor Ignaz Müller, provost of the Viennese convent of Saint Dorothea and a cleric of Jansenist leanings, refused to interdict circulation of the controversial publication despite its condemnation by the pope in 1764.[48] Both "Febronianism" and Jansenism, though not identical in purport or in the supporters each attracted, contributed powerful arguments toward the cause of an enhanced regulatory role for the state in religious matters. Both approaches deemed advantageous to Catholicism many regulations that had as their practical end result a more frugal, streamlined church that promoted the state's material interest rather than Rome's.

Like Maria Theresia, the *Dames* approached religion with a mixture of deference to traditional authority and practical independence of mind. Leopoldine Kaunitz and Eleonore Liechtenstein had received their early education at the Visitation convent of St. Stephan in Strasbourg and the experience remained a formative influence in their lives as adults. All five *Dames* appear to have been devout but not uncritical Catholics. For many aristocratic men and women, unstudied acceptance of the forms and dogma of the religion they had inherited no doubt afforded adequate spiritual sustenance. Looking back in 1801, Zinzendorf thought that even Maria Theresia's children, who included the prelate Archduke Maximilian, seemed to approach religion as actors. "Why is it that all of the children of Marie Therese, who is considered to be such a religious Princess, have themselves so little religion?" he wrote. "It is because they have never heard tell of the moral foundations [*morale*] of religion of the heart. They have been brought up merely to become good playactors." Zinzendorf believed the church had been wrong to condemn proponents of "mystic" theology such Fénelon, Quesnel, and Jansenism in general.[49] Zinzendorf, it should be remembered, was a convert from Protestantism to Catholicism early in his adult life but was never fully at ease as a practicing Catholic. The more flexible outlook of well-traveled or broadly educated associates of the women such as Count Zinzendorf, Chancellor Kaunitz, the Prince de Ligne, and the emperor himself added some diversity to the intellectual environment of the *Dames*.[50] Among individuals with whom the women had contact on a regular basis, Gottfried van Swieten (1733–1803), son of Maria Theresia's famous doctor and court librarian under Joseph II, held views that clearly diverged from the mainstream of Catholic thought, but even he was neither a religious radical nor an atheist.[51] The letters of the *Dames* testify to the women's familiarity with dissident views of Catholicism and the competing world views of the Enlightenment and thus suggest a more deliberate choice in favor of traditional orthodoxy.

The Protestant visitor Wraxall's observations about the women of Vienna were wide of the mark for the *Dames* when he asserted, "Very little of the exterior of devotion is . . . visible among women of condition: it interrupts no pleasures of society or conversation; it neither mixes with their discourse, nor tinges their manners: they reserve it for the altar, or the confessor."[52] Among the *Dames* outward signs of religion—its practices, customs, and ceremonies—were not lacking, and their statements confirm that they sought to be inwardly mindful of religious precepts in their daily activities. On their menfolk religion may have rested somewhat more lightly, with observances more perfunctory and less systematic but still conformable to accepted practice. Charles Liechtenstein's approach to religion was probably typical of many of his contemporaries. From his military camp in Leitmeritz (Litoměřice) in May 1778, Charles thanked Eleonore for her prayers, pilgrimages, and great devotion, all undertaken in an effort to secure divine protection for him on the field of battle; but he urged her not to torment or fatigue herself in these efforts, for he would willingly leave the future to God's mercy and will. Occasional jocose expressions he used in his letters suggest an easygoing, comfortable approach (e.g., his valedictory to Leopoldine Kaunitz in February 1764, "Adieu dear sister, I am yours as Calvin is the devil's. Charles").[53]

Throughout lives that contained not just the pleasures of privilege but also personal heartaches and cataclysmic public events (these arrived particularly after Joseph II's death, with the wars of the French Revolution and Napoleon) the *Dames* relied upon the time-tested dictums of religious consolation that had sustained generations before them. Expressions of traditional religious faith appear frequently in the women's correspondence, at times explicitly drawn from the writings of Fénelon. Typical was Leopoldine Kaunitz's comment after the illness of her only surviving child, "Lorel" (Eleonore, later the wife of Clemens Metternich) in July 1778. "The good Lord never sends us more than we can bear," she wrote to Eleonore, "we have only to trust in him and he will send nothing except that which is for our own good, if we do not make it worse ourselves—yet another truth that must not be forgotten especially in present circumstances." And in August she continued in the same strain when concerns about the War of the Bavarian Succession were also troubling her, referring to "God who permits evils for our own good, and who will provide the means for our salvation in the midst of all contingencies if we let him, if we trust in him, if we surrender ourselves to him."[54] Her sister Eleonore responded with similar observations.

The women complied with the devotional requirements of the church calendar, conforming to accepted observances of Christmas, Easter, Pentecost, Corpus Christi, and holy days sacred to the Virgin Mary and the apostles. On a daily basis they reported attending mass and often vespers at nearby churches. They submitted willingly to rigorous auricular confession, seeking seclusion in advance for meditation and prayer and often preparing a careful written record of their actions and thoughts. In 1770, Lady Mary Coke noted Sidonia Kinsky's intense devotion: "The Princess Kinsky is so devote [*sic*], that it was with some difficulty I persuaded her to let me set with her two hours this evening. She has been in retreat since Thursday, & is not to appear again till after Christmas" (Lady Mary wrote on 22 December).[55] The *Dames* accepted the guidance of family priests, who helped them maintain equilibrium in their spiritual lives and bolstered their loyalty to orthodox belief. These family chaplains recommended appropriate reading material and warned them about problematic titles or authors. Like Maria Theresia, Eleonore Liechtenstein and Leopoldine Kaunitz professed to set great store by regular reading of pious Catholic authors. Maria Theresia urged her adult children to read only those items approved by their confessors, even if a questionable title seemed merely entertaining and harmless. "This compliance is the least one can do for the sake of preserving one's peace of mind during a time when so many dangerous books flood the lands," she wrote.[56] Yet like Maria Theresia, the women did read interdicted books.[57] In April 1770 Leopoldine asked her sister to send to her in Naples the current list of prohibited books, since Leopoldine thought she might herself have acquired some of them and she did not want them confiscated when she moved to Brünn.[58] Leopoldine's attitude was not unusual. Even under Maria Theresia, censorship that effectively restricted the publications available to the population as a whole was easily circumvented by individuals with sufficient money or connections, who could obtain virtually any book they desired. Although Maria Theresia admonished even her grown sons to restrict their reading to appropriate materials, this did not always mean traditional, papal-approved titles. Despite the reputation of the monarchy under Maria Theresia's rule for piety and prudery, its upper crust was able to retain a degree of sophistication and cosmopolitanism. This practical, relaxed deference toward outward forms was adopted deliberately by active, ambitious members of the elite. An attitude that combined practicality and piety did not seem cynical to contemporaries; there was considerable variation among individuals and families in their approach to religious observance during this period of creative ferment.[59]

Changes that affected the Catholic Church during the coregency were much more moderate than those later enacted with considerable éclat by Joseph II, more a matter of "tilt" than a full change of course, as historian T. C. W. Blanning aptly notes.[60] Until the final years of the coregency, religious policy was not a significant source of controversy for the *société* or for the public at large. Maria Theresia's reforms have been variously assessed by historians. Most, though by no means all, studies of the subject have dated the beginnings of Josephinian religious reforms or "Josephinism" to Maria Theresia's reign. An important pioneering treatment of the reforms by Ferdinand Maass, who focused his attention narrowly on church-state relations, contended that Maria Theresia, a traditional Catholic who lacked religious insight and was unable to foresee the consequences of her actions, unthinkingly exploited privileges initially granted by the pope, urged to action by Chancellor Kaunitz. Already, under the guidance of her unprincipled chancellor, Maria Theresia had initiated the process by which in coming decades the Habsburg government would undermine church authority.[61] Other historians have seen the empress as an astute and pragmatic yet also sincere reformer. Thus Blanning argues that it is "quite wrong to suppose that she was a Catholic of the old school, a weak and foolish woman led astray by the devious and cynical Kaunitz, as used to be supposed."[62] Scrutiny of Maria Theresia's actions has convinced many historians that although she and even Kaunitz initially sought to obtain papal consent or at least acquiescence for contemplated changes, they concluded that the papacy was unequal to the task of reforming the church.[63] Recent studies have also noted that like other lands of Europe the eighteenth-century Habsburg monarchy too provided a hospitable environment for home-grown reformers of various stripes: traditional pious Catholics who nevertheless acknowledged the church's need for internal reform, groups with greater or lesser Jansenist leanings (including such individuals as Maria Theresia herself, who was especially critical of the condition of Catholic education), progressive statesmen such as Chancellor Kaunitz, freemasons with generally tolerant if sometimes inchoate outlook, and earnest, utilitarian statists such as Joseph II himself.[64] All of these overlapping groups, then, contributed to the environment in which were taken the decisions of Maria Theresia with her coregent Joseph and her chancellor Kaunitz.

The increasingly acute and portentous contest between the Habsburg government and the papacy for jurisdiction and income was less visible to the public than specific reforms introduced by the empress to alter popular Catholic practices. During her reign Maria Theresia curbed what she saw as particularly objectionable abuses in traditional customs. In doing so she further expanded the government's role in regulating her subjects' religious lives, an approach that would be adopted with great vigor by her successor Joseph. As noted previously, she limited the number of religious holidays, initially reducing some traditional celebrations to "half" holidays, with inhabitants expected to return to their work after religious observances. Quiet but stubborn popular resistance to such changes persisted for many years.[65] The number and exuberance of religious processions was reined in. As early as 1752, the use of trumpets and drums in the liturgy had been curtailed. Particularly after Franz Stephan's death, the court's own ceremonial visits to convents and to individual churches, traditional since the reign of Ferdinand II and typically associated with church festival days, gradually diminished in number. Prior to Franz Stephan's death the court had attended about 78 solemn services in various churches per year (and according to the historian Schmal, in 1758 the court made fully 120 ceremonial visits and pilgrimages to churches and cloisters). After Franz Stephan's death, with Joseph installed as coregent, the number of visits dropped to a third of the previous average from 1766 to 1773 and dwindled to just a fifth from 1773 to 1780.[66] The Corpus Christi procession remained the most elaborate display of the church year. Zinzendorf reported that in the Corpus Christi procession of 1761 the imperial family and all prominent male and female members of the court had participated, with each holding a torch and proceeding to the Saint Stephan's cathedral. The procession in this imperial form dated from the sixteenth century and served as a public affirmation of the ruler's lesser authority, inferior to that of the king of heaven. By the advent of Joseph's reign even the magnificence of this remaining procession had been restrained.[67]

The empress suppressed or restricted a number of hoary folk practices: excesses in religious folk drama, in New Year celebrations, the ringing of church bells to ward off storms, sale of chapbooks with fanciful content, and clerical trade in candles, amulets, and consecrated rosaries. By the mid-eighteenth century many of these practices were viewed as outmoded expressions of baroque piety at best and superstitions at worst by the educated public, even the strictly orthodox. Maria Theresia tried to temper the populace's fear of ghosts, witchcraft, and magic. As her son would do with such enthusiasm in later years, she issued decrees intended to improve the moral tone of her subjects' lives: instructions for appropriate behavior on Sundays and church festival days, exhortations to industrious work, and decorous respect for social rank.[68] She restricted collective pilgrimages to popular shrines in an effort to minimize the loss of labor and the diversion of money into nonproductive causes, although outright prohibitions came only later, during Joseph's sole rule.

The single most dramatic religious reform during Maria Theresia's reign, the abolition of the Society of Jesus in Habsburg territories in 1773, actually caused little consternation in court circles, including the little *société* of *Dames*. The possibility had been bruited in the monarchy and elsewhere in Europe for many years. Reformers throughout Europe had been highly critical of the Jesuits, arguing that they were hungry for power and willing to use lies and deceit to maintain their authority.[69] Theologians with Jansenist leanings had naturally been the sharpest critics, but the need for reform was openly canvassed among individuals of many schools of thought. Earlier in Maria Theresia's reign the Jesuits were excluded from their traditional influence at the University of Vienna and from their authority as censors, as part of efforts to limit the influence of the church over education. In the late 1760s, as the issue attracted public attention after the Society's expulsion from France, Naples, Parma, and the Spanish and Portuguese empires, Leopoldine Kaunitz expressed relative indifference to the fate of the Jesuits. She considered them to be intolerant and self-serving, although they had performed services useful to society and were now being unfairly blamed for sins they had not committed. The church would be able to maintain itself without the order, she was convinced. After all, twelve poor fishermen had been sufficient to lay its foundation.[70]

The pro-Jesuit Pope Clement XIII died in February 1769.[71] In May 1769 a new pope was selected, the Franciscan Cardinal Ganganelli, or Clement XIV, who was known to be critical of the Jesuits. Ernst Kaunitz had been sent to Rome from his ambassadorial post in Naples to serve as Austrian envoy for the election but in this post he had possessed neither power nor influence. The Habsburg government took no formal position either for or against preservation of the order but rightly assumed that the new pope would abolish it. The first copies of the decree abolishing the Society reached Vienna at the end of August 1773. The government immediately seized Jesuit property, and it was only several years after the abolition, as the financial ramifications associated with the Society's demise became clear, that there was consternation among some elite families because the Jesuits had been involved with them in credit dealings that were now taken over by the government.[72] In the early 1770s, there were roughly 1,900 Jesuits living in Habsburg lands. 343 Jesuit houses were duly closed. Former members of the Society who could not be absorbed into active positions within the church hierarchy as priests, teachers, or confessors received modest pensions.[73] The dissolution of the Society was the subject of discussion and considerable condoling with worthy ex-Jesuits, but it did not cause much soul searching, being the stuff of parlor conversation instead. In September 1773, as she visited Austerlitz (a sojourn during which Sidonia Kinsky and Eleonore Liechtenstein also put in appearances), Lady Mary Coke reported: "I arrived at seven O'clock in the evening, and was carried into a great room where I found all the Company assembled; some at cards: others setting round a table listening to one who was reading the Pope's Bull, which is just arrived, to put in execution his orders against the jesuits."[74] Pope Clement XIV died 10 September 1774. Rumors circulated that he had been driven mad by remorse about the Jesuits' fate or had been poisoned by ex-Jesuits. Zinzendorf recorded the gossip in his diary in 1775. Returning from a gathering at Princess Esterházy's residence, where Joseph II had also made an appearance, Zinzendorf recorded Rosenberg's remarks about the dead pope, "who died mad, driven to distraction by the injustice he was forced to commit against the Jesuits by the king of Spain." Rosenberg had observed also that the Jesuits had played a vital role in education, now suffering from their absence. "He sang the praises of the Jesuits."[75]

Other religious orders faced new limitations during Maria Theresia's lifetime. From the government's point of view, religious orders were problematic if only because their loyalties so often crossed political boundaries. Critics contended that they drained the monarchy's financial resources, manpower, and potential for population growth and for expansion of the economy through their promotion of celibacy and a contemplative lifestyle.[76] Restrictions were placed on money brought to these institutions by new members of orders and by the bequests of older members or well-wishers. Regulations restricted the activities monasteries and convents could engage in for income. The minimum age for entering orders was raised to 24.[77] In August 1771, after new reports surfaced concerning abuses, cloister prisons were abolished. These reforms, important for those whom they affected directly, caused little public stir. Historians have apportioned responsibility for these changes variously among the three chief players, empress, emperor, and chancellor. The empress gave them her cautious, sometimes hesitant endorsement. They received enthusiastic support from coregent Joseph and Chancellor Kaunitz, who had earlier introduced such measures in Lombardy.[78]

During Joseph's decade of sole rule, as will be seen, the *Dames* would become greatly exercised over the government's tolerance policies for Protestants and Jews. While she lived, Maria Theresia acted as a brake on change in the monarchy's treatment of these groups even as the chorus of supporters of confessional tolerance grew among academics, publicists, reform Catholics, and political leaders including Kaunitz and the coregent Joseph.[79] Of all religious issues with which they had to deal during the coregency, tolerance of alternative, non-Catholic sects and religions was the topic that separated Maria Theresia and Joseph II most starkly and bitterly, setting the stage for quarrels viewed at close quarters by the *Dames* but known also to the interested public. Recalling her own near annihilation by attacks initiated by the Protestant Prussian kingdom at the beginning of her reign, Maria Theresia viewed her Protestant subjects as a potentially hostile political force within her realm and apparently believed that political stability was tenuous unless virtually all inhabitants subscribed to a single religion. This conviction made her particularly sensitive to reports of overt Protestant activity among renitent Bohemian peasants in the 1770s, as noted previously. The dynasty's historical identity was closely linked to the defense of Christianity against Islam and of Roman Catholicism against Protestantism, although in practice, and for reasons of historical development and political expediency, limited religious pluralism obtained in some territories of the monarchy. Maria Theresia had started her reign with harsh measures against the Jews resident in Prague, whom she suspected of disloyalty and wished to expel from the city. Only the unwillingness of the Bohemian estates to comply with Maria Theresia's draconian directives had blocked their full implementation.[80] During the coregency, despite the urging of Kaunitz and Joseph and obvious economic advantages, the empress still could not bring herself to reduce the disabilities that burdened the monarchy's non-Catholics in any meaningful way. For practical reasons she assumed a more lenient stance toward Protestants in specific cases as the years of her reign passed; and she accepted the presence of Protestants in her army, including its officer corps. But the empress was troubled by the pragmatic and humanitarian arguments put forward by Chancellor Kaunitz and, more vociferously, by her son Joseph, both of whom urged her to grant limited toleration or at least to overlook minor transgressions by peaceful, productive Protestant groups. She asserted that the souls of her subjects were her responsibility and required the enlightenment of the true Catholic faith.

For coregent Joseph the persistence of Protestantism within the population after so many generations of conversion efforts underscored the need for broader confessional tolerance. When in 1777 the reports from Moravia describing thousands of crypto-Protestants who had declared themselves Hussites or Lutherans reached Vienna there ensued a dramatic long-distance quarrel between the empress and Joseph, then absent on one of his trips to France. He lobbied vigorously for tolerance in this case. His letters urged the empress to judge her subjects by their usefulness to the state, not their religion. A government could not save these souls against their wills, he wrote. In essence, Joseph recapitulated many of the rational, utilitarian arguments of the English, French, and German Enlightenment. In one of his less strident epistles, Joseph II wrote, "For me tolerance simply means that in purely temporal matters . . . I would employ, I would allow to have lands, trades, to be burghers, those who are capable and who would bring profit and industry into the lands."[81] Maria Theresia, already disconcerted by what she saw as her son's indifference to both principles and practices of Roman Catholicism and willing to enforce compliance on her subjects through forceful measures, chose her own course. She directed the Catholic clergy to try persuasion first. Thereafter recalcitrants were to be transported to Transylvania, since the legal system there required the empress to tolerate a plurality of religions in any case. Outraged by her decisions, in his response Joseph II asked for permission to resign his post as coregent or at least to publicize his own disapproval. Maria Theresia was angered when the Moravian Protestants had the audacity to send representatives to Vienna with a petition addressed directly to Joseph. Kaunitz, looking for a practicable middle course, tried to persuade Maria Theresia to approve a form of tacit tolerance for reasons both of state and of Christian charity, accepting the Protestants' private worship as a de facto usage without bestowing on it official encorsement, always with the stated hope of their eventual voluntary conversion to Catholicism. Maria Theresia softened her harshest measures only temporarily, unwilling to sanction genuine, public freedom of worship for her Protestant subjects or to give tacit approval to tolerant treatment.[82] In the end, after agonizing over the proper course to follow, she heeded the warnings of conservative churchmen, especially Vienna's archbishop Migazzi, and reaffirmed her intolerant policies. These were still in place when the empress died.[83]

During the coregency, Joseph's personal religious practices provoked unfavorable comment and some ill will among tradition-minded contemporaries. He had signaled his confrontational approach at once upon becoming coregent. According to custom, Maria Theresia and Franz Stephan had regularly traveled to Klosterneuburg for the feast day of Saint Leopold on November 15. Joseph undertook the journey in 1765 but took with him only male courtiers. Breaking with tradition, he omitted much of the expected ceremonial. He did not appear at the yearly public prayers held at the plague column on the Graben in Vienna, a custom of several generations' standing. He also reduced the pageantry involved in the traditional annual Easter week visits of the imperial family to various churches.[84] Many Viennese disliked these changes. In 1771 Maria Theresia enumerated to her friend the *marquise* d'Herzelles what the empress perceived to be Joseph's many religious shortcomings. Not only was he loudly critical of the clergy and the church's authority but also he was personally slipshod in his practices, rarely confessing, rarely attending mass, engaging in no spiritual reading or conversation.[85] Observers believed that Kaunitz's skepticism, cosmopolitan manners, and contempt for many forms of etiquette were a significant influence on the young ruler. Even so, it appears that most observers expected that the emperor's program of reforms, once he had complete authority and the responsibility that went with it, would be moderate. Wraxall wrote hopefully about prospects for change and credited Joseph with diligent practice of his faith. "I have reason to think," he wrote, "that his [Joseph's] religious opinions are by no means contracted or illiberal. The bigotry and superstition which for ages have been hereditary in the House of Austria, and which still survive in all their force in Maria Theresia, will probably be extinct in her successor. But, I am far from meaning to insinuate that he is therefore tinctured with infidelity, deism, or any of the doctrines inculcated at Ferney, and at 'Sans Souci.' . . . Joseph, though no bigot, is a Catholic, convinced of the truths of the Christian Religion, and conforming to its injunctions in his practice. He not only confesses regularly, but as soon as he rises, he never fails every morning to offer up his prayers to God, kneeling; as he does in the same posture before he retires to rest. I cannot err in this fact, which I derive from an eye-witness of the highest rank, who would neither flatter nor deceive." Wraxall's comments encapsulated the views held by contemporaries, including the *Dames*, concerning the emperor's religious beliefs while Maria Theresia lived.[86]

Potential and actual changes in the government's stance toward the church were at times the topic of conversation at gatherings of the *société* prior to Maria Theresia's death, despite the moderate nature of reforms enacted during the period. Joseph rehearsed for the *Dames* arguments that affirmed the wisdom of introducing limited religious tolerance as a state policy. In an undated letter from the emperor to Leopoldine Kaunitz, probably written during the final years of the coregency when he was preoccupied with the resurgence of Protestantism in Bohemia and Moravia as well as a religious dispute then taking place at the university and seminary in Brünn (its dénouement is described in chapter 5), the emperor assured Leopoldine Kaunitz that religion was in his heart, his head, and in his total being and that he would not be disconcerted by "Molinists" or Jansenists; these were mere butterflies (or moths, *papillons*), he wrote, that would singe their wings against Joseph's own *lumière*. Surely these creatures could be transformed into industrious silkworms (*bons vers rampans à soye*), producing an abundant harvest "in the administering of the holy religion, and in the education of the young." The emperor chided Leopoldine Kaunitz for being "anxious and too fearful." Maria Theresia was known to defend the practice of forcible conversion to Catholicism on occasion. Possibly Leopoldine Kaunitz had done likewise in her conversation or correspondence with the emperor and had prompted this response.[87]

Throughout the years of the coregency, Eleonore Liechtenstein and Leopoldine Kaunitz occasionally lamented what they saw as a decline in traditional moral and religious fervor. Their criticisms extended to what they viewed as lax government oversight and lukewarm support for the traditions of the church. The culprits themselves in the women's view might be Protestant-leaning Jansenists or disciples of the philosophes; in their eyes these groups were equally unworthy and indeed not always distinguishable, as both were felt to undermine the unity and strength of the true religion. In late 1780, about a month prior to Maria Theresia's death, Leopoldine Kaunitz was indignant to learn that the Jansenist Philibert (pen name for Jean-Antoine Gazaignes, canon of Saint-Benoît, 1717–1802, author of the *Annales de la société des soi-disants jésuites* that began appearing in 1764) had come to Vienna, hoping to collect information for additional volumes of his publications.[88] He was reported to be gathering a list of complaints of governments and individuals against ex-Jesuits. Leopoldine Kaunitz argued that reasonable people should have nothing to do with him, if only because he was such a fanatic. However, even while disapproving of the project (as "thoroughly objectionable"), Chancellor Kaunitz had invited Philibert to dinner. Leopoldine Kaunitz suggested that Eleonore should caution her sister-in-law Leopoldine Liechtenstein, who might otherwise unwittingly lend her prestige to this vagabond ("a horrible schemer") by receiving him socially. Cardinal Migazzi had protested Philibert's presence in Vienna but his arguments had been ineffective;

"this Cardinal is unfortunately of such negligible stature that whatever he does for a cause is almost certain to harm it."[89] Although she was displeased, Leopoldine Kaunitz was not especially alarmed about the situation. The excitement concerning Philibert soon subsided, but Leopoldine took this opportunity to lament the general deterioration of behavior, "that everything goes so clearly from bad to worse, everywhere one looks one sees that justice, virtue, religion are so thoroughly undervalued, one becomes hardened to it." She added, "it is quite sad to have to be a witness to all of this, I will at least try to be a participant as little as possible." She noted that the French ambassador in Vienna took no interest in Philibert, only the Viennese themselves; "it is here [among the Viennese] that he has found support, as for me, I cannot help saying along with Moses that I had rather be despised and exiled with the people of God than heaped with honors among the Egyptians."[90] Leopoldine Kaunitz did not single out the coregent for criticism in such a case. Discussions concerning religion apparently remained muted during the coregency. They would acquire greater urgency very soon after the empress's death.

During the coregency foreign policy, like domestic, was of necessity a team effort of empress and coregent, guided by Chancellor Kaunitz. The *Dames* watched, appraised, apostrophized, and applauded or lamented. Until the final years of the coregency, Habsburg enterprises appeared to enjoy considerable success. In 1769 Zips, a small territory held by Poland but claimed as part of the Hungarian kingdom, was occupied by Habsburg forces at Joseph's behest while the Polish government was preoccupied with Russian incursions into its territory. Russia's growing presence in Poland, an area which the Habsburg government preferred to view as a neutral buffer zone, finally induced Maria Theresia, at the prompting of Kaunitz and Joseph II and apparently somewhat against her will, to join in the first partition of a portion of Poland's territory in 1772. The empress realized that otherwise Prussia and Russia would simply carve up the land without her participation. From the empress's point of view, this acquisition of Polish Galicia was a mixed blessing, for in it resided many diverse religious populations, most strikingly Jewish, Orthodox, and Protestant.[91] Maria Theresia brooded about the Polish partition from time to time for the rest of her life and expressed regret for her participation. Many contemporaries assumed that Joseph was the active party in the Polish partitions. Leopoldine Kaunitz told her sister later, in 1778, that her father-in-law Chancellor Kaunitz had selflessly permitted some blame to fall upon himself rather than to expose to public view circumstances that would have exonerated him personally.[92]

According to the Prince de Ligne, during a gathering of the *Dames* with the emperor that occurred soon after the Polish partitions when the conversation turned upon the recent hanging of a thief, one of the women had remarked, "How was it possible for Your Majesty to condemn him after having stolen Poland?"

The emperor had responded that his mother the empress, who was respected by the *Dames* and attended mass fully as often as they did, had been perfectly willing to take her share of Poland; "I am merely the first of her subjects."[93] The Prince de Ligne was capable of stretching the truth for the sake of entertainment and the details of his stories may be unreliable. However, this tale does suggest that the *Dames* spoke their minds freely concerning the affair. Four of the five women hailed from small imperial principalities in Swabia. Their families were likely to view with unease the aggressive behavior of larger powers and the apparent disregard for international norms and borders. In this case, the Holy Roman Emperor himself was one of the plunderers. Although they were loyal transplants to Habsburg soil, the *Dames* could not be indifferent to these circumstances and probably viewed the matter somewhat as Maria Theresia did, accepting the inevitability of partition but regarding the act also as a violation of international standards of behavior. Leopoldine Liechtenstein too had a stake in the security of lesser polities because of her family's marriage ties to the Manderscheid family and the minuscule principality of Liechtenstein.[94] On another occasion, according to Zinzendorf's diary, in a gathering at Chancellor Kaunitz's residence Leopoldine Kaunitz praised a Polish nobleman of her acquaintance for dressing in traditional Polish clothing.[95] In this case, Leopoldine Kaunitz's gesture may have signaled concurrence with the approach favored by both her father-in-law the chancellor and by Maria Theresia, both of whom preferred a gradualist approach toward Galicia and a relatively loose incorporation of this new peripheral possession into the monarchy, in contrast to the emperor's insistence on immediate assimilation and conformity with other Habsburg territories. Joseph wished to transform the province at once to match usages in the hereditary territories, eliminating even traditional Polish clothing and customs and making Latin the administrative language. In the newly acquired territory, officials were required to "dress German" (*deutsch kleiden*), although as a conciliatory gesture toward old customs noblemen who were accepted into the new Polish contingent of the expanded noble Hungarian bodyguard would dress in traditional costume as "ulanen."[96]

In 1774 when a conflict between Russia and Turkey ended with the treaty of Kuchuk-Kainarji, Joseph II successfully asserted the monarchy's claims against Turkey to acquire another territory, the Bukovina, officially annexed in 1775. Again the monarchy acquired additional land without bloodshed or great expense, although Joseph's reputation as a pacific ruler suffered.[97] The coregency's only serious armed conflict, the War of the Bavarian Succession in 1778–1779, was a less fortunate venture. Claiming portions of Bavaria or trading faraway Belgium for nearby Bavarian territory was an idea that had been taken under consideration by past generations of Habsburg sovereigns. Kaunitz had noted Bavaria's potential attractiveness as an accretion to Habsburg possessions as early as 1743, and Joseph himself had raised this issue already in the 1760s.[98] The death of Bavaria's Wittelsbach elector Maximilian Joseph at the end of 1777 appeared to offer a favorable opportunity. Habsburg legal scholars had prepared formal arguments for immediate occupation of portions of the kingdom. Briefly it appeared that Maximilian Joseph's successor, Elector Palatine Charles Theodore, was amenable to a possible trade of portions of Bavaria in exchange for Belgium. With an enthusiastic Joseph urging immediate action and Kaunitz only somewhat more cautious, a preemptive occupation of some Bavarian territory was planned in the hope that the monarchy could gain this advantage without provoking armed intervention.[99] Maria Theresia feared a hostile international response but reluctantly agreed to the strategy. In January 1778, after pressuring Charles Theodore for his explicit consent, Joseph ordered Habsburg troops into Bavaria to assert the monarchy's claim over significant portions of its territory. Unfortunately Joseph's move received no endorsement even from his supposed ally France, the best persuasive efforts of Kaunitz and Marie Antoinette notwithstanding. The Duke of Zweibrücken, new heir presumptive after Max Joseph's death, opposed the plan and sought help from Frederick II of Prussia, who was joined by Saxony, former Habsburg ally. The emperor together with Lacy traveled to the northeast of Bohemia to lead the war effort against Frederick. Joseph sent General Laudon with a second Habsburg force to the northwest to face off against the Prussian troops of Prince Henry on the Moravian border.

For several months the course that events would take appeared uncertain as the sides traded accusations, claims, and offers. As late as mid-June 1778, the emperor apparently hoped that Frederick II would eschew armed conflict and accept a settlement permitting the Habsburg monarchy to retain much of the territory it claimed.[100] These hopes were dashed when the Prussian king and his brother Prince Henry massed forces to enter Bohemia and Moravia in early July. As Prince Henry's invasion began, Laudon, fearing that his own forces were inadequate, retreated with scarcely a struggle and opened the way for Prussian troops to move in the direction of Prague. For his part the emperor, assuming an active role as commander for the first time in his life, became unnerved, possibly realizing in full only now the horrors that war could bring both to his troops and to the affected populations (he described the waging of war to his brother Leopold as "a dog's life," *un métier de chien*).[101] During July Joseph sent frantic, despairing reports to his mother in Vienna, suggesting that the Austrian army was in dire straits. Initially calm and prepared to accept the fortunes of war with courage as she had in her youth but uneasy about the justice of her cause, Maria Theresia now feared the worst and in mid-July, scarcely two weeks after the beginning of hostilities, she sought to open peace negotiations directly with Frederick II, sending a special envoy, Baron Johann Amadeus Thugut (1736–1818), to Frederick's military camp to offer sweeping concessions and bypassing and humiliating her son. The negotiations went nowhere, but Joseph's understandable displeasure led to the most serious foreign policy rupture between mother and son that occurred during the coregency. With some assistance from Kaunitz Maria Theresia continued at intervals to pursue accommodation with Frederick during the remainder of the campaign season, in a less dramatic but equally fruitless manner.[102]

Joseph's personal fortitude was never in question, and he recovered his composure in short order. However, his initial discomfiture at the front exacerbated the government's worst weakness in this crisis: the divided councils and indecision of the governing triumvirate of empress, emperor, and chancellor.[103] Wraxall quoted an Austrian officer as saying "We are sacrificed, counteracted, and dishonored. How can it be otherwise? The Empress, we are not ignorant, only wishes for peace. The Emperor breathes war, but knows not how to conduct it, though he aspires to superintend all the operations in person. Prince Kaunitz fluctuates between both; desirous of repose, yet anxious to gratify a Prince whose passion is ambition, and who may soon become his sole master."[104] With an essentially defensive strategy, the Habsburg forces held their position. But the public, enthusiastic at the war's outbreak, grew disillusioned when results proved to be meager. Neither the Prussians nor the Austrians were able to gain a decisive advantage in the field, despite constant maneuvering, and so the armies remained in place as autumn approached, foraging for supplies and plundering the Bohemian countryside. Frederick was the first to begin withdrawing some of his troops from Bohemia, a source of some satisfaction to the Habsburg side. Both sides drew back the bulk of their forces in October. Then haggling over peace terms began in earnest, punctuated by minor skirmishes among the remaining troops in the field. Joseph, whose will never failed after his initial panic, effectively raised the specter of a renewal of hostilities in 1779 and actually planned for that eventuality, thereby shoring up the Habsburg position in negotiations. In the treaty of Teschen in May 1779, brokered with the assistance of France and Russia (and thus signaling Russia's increasing influence in imperial affairs), the Habsburg monarchy gave up its claim to Bavaria except for some land on the right bank of the Inn River, named the Innviertel by Joseph. Frederick received additional concessions attractive to him, in particular recognition of Prussia's claim to Ansbach and Bayreuth.[105]

An inglorious episode for both sides, the war received derisive bynames—dubbed the "potato war" by the Prussians and the "plum war" by the Austrians owing to the hungry armies' preoccupation with foraging. The Austrian side could be relieved that the redoubtable armies of Frederick II and Prince Henry had been faced down through a well-conceived defensive strategy. In view of the ambitious initial goals, however, the interested public was not impressed. Battle casualties had been relatively few, but many lives had been lost in both armies to malnutrition and disease. Joseph believed that the monarchy's ability to hold off the Prussians (to the extent that it was not the result of his own prodigious efforts, that is) was owing to Lacy's skill as a strategist in selecting unassailable positions. Uncharacteristically generous, Joseph bestowed on Lacy as a lifetime yearly pension the 24,000 gulden that had been Lacy's field pay.[106] Critics were less pleased about Lacy's influence over Joseph II. According to Wraxall, as of November 1778, political and military opinion in Vienna roundly condemned Joseph and also Lacy for their inactivity and ineptness in the conduct of the campaign of 1778, even though the Habsburg position had improved by then. Joseph had let rich provinces of his Bohemian crownlands suffer under Prussian troops without defending them or at least inflicting damage upon the retreating armies. Critics alleged also that Joseph's attempts to direct operations personally had nullified the good military sense of his general Laudon, who might have moved against Prince Henry's troops. They blamed Lacy for limiting the success of a promising offensive action suggested by Laudon early in the campaign by failing to send reinforcements when requested. Maria Theresia did not share this negative assessment of Lacy's performance; and Lacy's biographer Kotasek, while faulting him for permitting the untested Joseph II to panic, exonerates Lacy otherwise, attributing the outcry against him to his unfortunate reputation as a shrewd courtier. In fact, the criticism was valid only in part. Laudon, who was a general favorite with the public, had shown himself to be overly cautious at critical moments during the campaign. As for Joseph, the Viennese public concluded that, eager to claim new territory, he had pressured his mother to make the attempt and then, when forced to fight, lost his courage on the battlefield. They judged his talents as a commander to be mediocre at best, even after he recovered his nerve.[107]

In the end the Bavarian war amounted to very little, the Austrian side under the extended cordon system having remained in a defensive posture. It had revealed the weakness of the Habsburgs' French alliance for all to see and had enhanced the standing of Russia, which had influenced the calculations of both sides without actively supporting or opposing either. That Joseph made the attempt (and would again try in the 1780s) to acquire Bavarian territory was easily understood by contemporaries and even more so by subsequent historians; a successful venture could have greatly enhanced the Habsburgs' position in southern German lands. Instead, the failed Bavarian episode further solidified Joseph's reputation as an aggressor who would seize any ostensibly easy advantage that offered. Joseph apparently did believe, as the historian Blanning has noted, that a successful state was one that expanded, but certainly he was not alone in this conviction among eighteenth-century rulers.[108] After the crises over Poland and the Bavarian war, the princelings and other small sovereigns in the empire naturally viewed Joseph as an unpredictable and ultimately unreliable source of support. For them the further weakening of imperial institutions conjured up a future of peril rather than opportunity. At the beginning of the coregency, as freshly minted Holy Roman Emperor, Joseph had tried without success to reform the sluggish, complex institutions of the empire. By 1778 he had largely discounted the value of his role as emperor. Possibly he found that the power and influence that he wielded was "too subtle and indirect" for him, as Blanning puts it. After this failed attempt at imperial reform he consistently and openly placed the interests of the Habsburg monarchy ahead of those of the empire. His standing within the Holy Roman Empire naturally suffered.[109]

Most of the limited military action of the Bavarian war took place in summer and early fall 1778, when the *Dames* were dispersed to country residences or the Vienna suburbs. Their extensive correspondence from the period merits special attention, even though their soirées with Joseph were largely in recess, for the letters afford detailed evidence of the reactions of each *Dame* to the course of events as well as a clear measure of the status of their friendship with Joseph as of 1778. By the time war broke out, the *société* of five women, Rosenberg, Lacy, and the emperor had withstood the test of time. Its members knew each other well. Three of the women had unique sources of information about the Bavarian campaign: Eleonore Liechtenstein from the letters of her husband Charles who was with Laudon's army, as well as frequent letters and notes sent by Joseph, who corresponded directly and frequently with her during these months from the battlefield; Leopoldine Kaunitz from her proximity to her father-in-law Chancellor Kaunitz who periodically confided in her; and Leopoldine Liechtenstein from letters of Marshal Lacy and her eldest son Louis, who was serving with Lacy's army. Joseph and Lacy in turn received news concerning the *société* from their respective female correspondents (apparently these letters have not been preserved). Interestingly, Maria Theresia herself passed along to the emperor detailed updates concerning the well-being of these special friends, even when the bulk of her letters were full of news about diplomatic concerns and war preparations. Thus in May 1778 she reported having seen Josepha Clary, who had informed her that Eleonore was recovering from a serious "fluxion." Subsequently Maria Theresia reported that Eleonore's children had been ill as well and that Leopoldine Kaunitz had just lost her elder daughter to "la scarlatine" (probably scarlet fever).[110] As so often, the richest source of information is the correspondence between Eleonore Liechtenstein and Leopoldine Kaunitz, but interpretation of these letters is no straightforward matter. Portions of them were clearly written for consumption by more than a single recipient, while other passages were just as obviously private, sometimes explicitly so, particularly where Eleonore Liechtenstein described the contents of letters from the emperor. At times the sisters expressed concern that letters in transit through the post could be opened and read. At other times, they made statements that, it seems evident, they hoped would reach and persuade additional influential associates. Their letters were full of speculation about both domestic politics and military strategy. Eleonore Liechtenstein expressed the wish her sister could come visit her in Kromau, where they would converse to their hearts' content "about current events, about the individuals who direct them, about the motives that make them act." Subject matter for discussion seemed inexhaustible, Eleonore observed, "so plentiful that I cannot speak about it for I do not know where to begin."[111]

Eleonore contrasted the detailed and frank reports she received from the emperor with the reticent and altogether more professional tone of correspondence from her husband who was also with the army and whose letters were "always so brief and so circumspect that one learns nothing."[112] A striking characteristic of the emperor's messages to Eleonore (as described by her, since the letters themselves apparently have not survived) as well as to his mother the empress was their frequent, abrupt changes in mood from one day to the next. Early in the campaign, as noted previously, the emperor was barely able to fight off panic. Some of his messages seemed indiscreet, given the army's vulnerable position and Eleonore's peculiar situation as wife of a commanding general. Joseph II detailed his fears, exhaustion, and general anxiety over the responsibility he bore for the war. Eleonore reported to her sister that Joseph and his officers were on horseback from 2 o'clock in the morning to as late as 9 o'clock at night. She felt that the emperor had received more than sufficient chastisement for any excessive exuberance or ambition he had displayed prior to the conflict. She wrote,

> His situation is dreadful . . . I scarcely dare repeat what he told me, he seemed so frightened and apprehensive. He assured me repeatedly that it is not for himself personally that he fears, but that there are grounds for concern when (not to mention the troubles and fatigues of body and soul) he considers that the monarchy's fate depends upon him, that he has the King of Prussia with a superior force arrayed against him, at any moment the alarm of battle, the Marshal who could let him down at any moment, Laudon who can no longer gallop a horse, Prince Albert laid low with a fever and in any case mostly without experience, and he himself who has never even seen the enemy, it seems to me that at this point he would sacrifice a great deal to have peace back again.[113]

These lamentations and the panic they conveyed also in letters to his mother from the battlefield were precisely what prompted the empress to send Baron Thugut as a unilateral peace emissary to Frederick's military camp, for Joseph's messages had convinced her that disaster was imminent. Possibly the empress should have known better; Eleonore's interpretation of Joseph's mood and the situation he faced was more accurate. She believed Joseph would change his tune at once if he could achieve a single victory, and he would quickly forget the evils of his current situation.[114] Nonetheless, even with the insight of a close friend ("who knows him better than we do," she intoned) Eleonore was disappointed and alarmed, virtually willing the emperor through her own steadiness to demonstrate firmness of character. "He does not have resolve and presence of mind in critical moments (this is what my husband has to the highest degree without possessing that rational intellect that dazzles so)," she wrote. "I confess to you . . . that I am quite worried about the outcome of all this."[115] Believing that, having committed to war, the emperor should make the best of circumstances, she urged him to put aside exaggerated fears. She quoted with approval Chancellor Kaunitz's words, "the wine has been poured, one must drink it." Eleonore's letters called on the emperor to be courageous. "Today I wrote him a letter full of courage and elevated sentiments, and as if I was persuaded that he had an infinite quantity of these." Simultaneously with her receipt of Joseph's jeremiad, Eleonore had received a dispassionate, sardonic letter from her husband Charles, calm and collected at his post with Laudon, in which Charles deplored the panic in Prague caused by news of Prussian troop movements (he dismissed the uproar as "a pretty mess," *le joli vacarme*).[116] Admittedly Charles did not have such great responsibility weighing upon him as did the emperor.

Initially Eleonore had been enthusiastic when the Habsburg government had moved to claim Lower Bavaria, like the other *Dames* and the broader public, all of whom presumably speculated as did Maria Theresia, Joseph, and Kaunitz that this valuable territory could be acquired at minimal cost. She grew impatient with the Habsburg army's purely defensive posture and the enemy's depredations in Bohemia. A counterthrust across the border into the territory of Prussia's ally Saxony was needed, she thought, advancing as far as Magdeburg ("by this means we could regain Silesia"). Informed by mid-August about Maria Theresia's unilateral efforts to negotiate peace, Eleonore easily guessed what Joseph's reaction would be ("quite a state of rage"), and her opinion of Maria Theresia plummeted.[117] Even as the military situation appeared to improve in late August, Eleonore continued to receive disquieting messages from the emperor. He complained that Lacy wished for peace at any price and was ill-humored and taciturn, while Field Marshal Laudon was obsessed by fear of defeat and could undertake no action. Still, the emperor was no longer distraught and his letters sounded more amiable: "He ends by charging me with a thousand compliments for my fine sister whom, he says, I love with all my heart."[118] Eleonore Liechtenstein was visiting at Eisgrub in late August when reports that the Prussian king was already withdrawing caused jubilation. "I . . . learned before leaving Eisgrub the news that the King has left his camp, everyone rejoices over it, it is ascribed to his unfavorable position, to the advantages of ours, it is seen as the equivalent of a victory that we owe not to the shedding of blood but to the skill of our maneuvers." When Eleonore, playing devil's advocate, ventured to suggest to the company at Eisgrub that previous negotiations could be a factor in Frederick's movements as well, "I was bidden to keep silent."[119]

Before long the emperor's messages grew calmer. Eleonore quoted to her sister a passage from the emperor's letter of 18 September: "Give my regards to your dear, good sister. Ah if Frédéric, tired of the terrible weather and beset with his ailments, should choose to move to his winter quarters and undertake nothing further, how pleased I should be to come see you again, truly the only thing that I miss and that grieves me." As the war wound down, Eleonore longed to hear that the monarchy's army had seized the initiative and was chasing Prince Henry all the way to Berlin. As for King Frederick, she wrote to her sister, "why is he allowed to move peacefully away into Silesia?"[120] Some historians, it might be noted, have asked the same question.[121] As the Prussian armies retreated in earnest in October and Joseph's own forces moved into winter quarters, the emperor actually expressed some elation. Certainly he did not brood over the fact that the original goals of the conflict had extended far beyond defense of Bohemia. Eleonore was quick to note that in the emperor's earlier, apprehensive missives there had been no such braggadocio. Though ever the sympathetic friend, after this war Eleonore Liechtenstein remained convinced that Joseph's aptitude for military command was modest.

With the campaign season ending the emperor continued to report to Eleonore the precautions he was taking against his wily foe. Having traveled to Sadova to check the health of his brother Archduke Maximilian, for example, the emperor wrote to Eleonore from Gitschin (Jičín) on 26 September, and she recorded his words for her sister: "In addition I have much to do. The King is still at the furthest edge of Bohemia, encamped on a very high mountain; he has detached the hereditary Prince of Brunswick towards Niess with a corps, which could be a matter of concern for Moravia, and another corps towards Lusatia." He explained his reasoning.

> I am being very careful not to do anything hasty, so as not to rush headlong to some disturbance and miss being where the attack could occur . . . Nevertheless since passage by way of Lusatia remains what I fear the most, I will have a part of the reserve artillery and five batteries of grenadiers march to Sobotka to have them near our positions. As for Moravia, if it becomes more serious, it is the corps of Jacquemin that is assigned to that and which, positioned near Königgrätz [Hradec Králové], is already on the route, but I must await the latest news; and all hastiness in making great decisions is just as dangerous as tardiness and irresolution are detrimental when the moment for decision has come. Adieu.[122]

Eleonore described Joseph's explanations rather sarcastically to her sister: "If he [Frederick II] had not so thoroughly devastated the countryside that he occupied, if the season was not so far advanced, if we had magazines or enough time to establish them, in sum if there were not 50 thousand *ifs*, we would be able, it is said, to act offensively, and even with success [*opérer même avec succès offensivement*]. That word must have startled him [Joseph], and in truth it is not our way." The emperor still experienced anxious moments, since even after Frederick's withdrawal from Bohemia some maneuvering and skirmishing took place throughout the winter. Eleonore described the emperor's fluctuating moods and, in the process, made clear the remarkable frequency of his wartime letters: "I will tell you about some passages from [the letter] I have just received from my Correspondent who, extraordinary circumstance, has gone eight days without writing to me . . . it seems to me that his mind is in a ferment, which always happens at the beginning of a new action, subsequently things will go better; there we are on our high horse."[123]

Eleonore was well-disposed toward the emperor and longed for victory. But she, along with much of public opinion, was not pleased with the prosecution of the war and was pessimistic about the future: "to feel so proud after having been plundered displeases me greatly, for as to taking revenge next year that will be out of the question, since I believe everyone has had enough of this." She told her sister, "just between the two of us, and speaking in confidence [*bien bas*] our manner of waging war, however canny and glorious it is said to be, does not please me in the least. We have losses in the millions and ruined lands, and if someone now should come to sack and plunder us, we would be in a pretty state." Because of her low opinion of the emperor's performance as commander, Eleonore worried when both Lacy and Laudon proved to be reluctant to commit to participation in a possible future campaign. Joseph, she told Leopoldine Kaunitz, did not have military talent. The prospect of a second season during which Joseph would make all decisions on his own ("where he will want to do everything himself without giving ear to anyone . . . he, who with all his bustle attends only to details without any larger plan and who nevertheless resents others when they fail to do things because he has forbidden them") was thoroughly disheartening.[124]

While Eleonore was summering in the country, her sister Leopoldine Kaunitz watched events unfold from the center, in Vienna. At times Leopoldine obtained confidential information about conditions at the military front from her father-in-law the chancellor (among the benefits of "the trust he places in me," as Leopoldine described their relationship).[125] On 18 July 1778, for example, during the critical early stage of the war, while attending as usual one of the chancellor's evening gatherings, Leopoldine Kaunitz witnessed his concern as he was suddenly called away to Schönbrunn. When he returned, she seated herself by his side and did her best to discover the state of affairs, as she told her sister. The chancellor complained that he and Maria Theresia were being kept completely in the dark about events on the military front. Since departing for the front, the emperor had not once sought Kaunitz's advice. Leopoldine was actually reassured by the chancellor's complaints because, as she wrote her sister, she then understood that his bleak humor resulted from pique rather than dismay over news of a military setback. Kaunitz repeated his complaint months later, telling Leopoldine Kaunitz, "I would not be able to tell you positively where the army of the King is, nor that of the Emperor, nor that of Prince Henry, nor Laudon." The chancellor's comments about the conduct of the war were blunt: "my father-in-law thinks that we make war in an appalling manner, that we have neither heart nor head, that we have let pass by the best opportunities for attacking the two armies . . . he has told my husband that he no longer knows whom to trust, that he is deceived on all sides, that his position is dreadful." Leopoldine Kaunitz was convinced that the confusion in Vienna was a result of Joseph's desire to control and direct every aspect of both the war and the eventual negotiations for peace. She noticed that at social gatherings her father-in-law carefully avoided conversation with foreign ambassadors, apparently because he was embarrassed about his own ignorance. Leopoldine Kaunitz tried rather tentatively to mend matters for the absent emperor, "for as you know I am always advocate for our Chief [Joseph]." She suggested to Kaunitz that the emperor

> wrote so little because he knew that women cannot always keep secrets. He would be wrong, he [Kaunitz] told me, she [Maria Theresia] has kept many important ones for me, and he [Joseph] ought to know that what passes through my hands is not noised about. He [Kaunitz] even gave me to understand that he feels offended, given that the Emperor, after having shown so much confidence in him prior to departing, has not given even a sign of life since then and has not asked his advice concerning a single action, even though circumstances have changed greatly.[126]

Leopoldine Kaunitz sent candid reports to her sister. Cautioned by her husband Ernst Kaunitz, she warned Eleonore not to mention the chancellor's remarks when visiting at Feldsberg, where a numerous company was gathered, or even to the other *Dames*. Her husband, she explained, venerated both the emperor and his father the chancellor and feared to speak of any possible disharmony between them. She herself doubted that the emperor had any idea of Kaunitz's discontent. She enjoyed political discussions with her sister and was annoyed by her husband's timorousness. "I have reread my letter to no purpose," she wrote. "I can find not a syllable that could not be read by the Emperor himself, it seems to me, but it is also true that he would himself be able to see some things that it would not be good for him to learn about from others . . . if I dare not tell you what I know, what I conjecture, what I think, I had rather not write to you."[127] Information shared between two *Dames* generally did circulate to all five women eventually. Two months later, Leopoldine Kaunitz asked Eleonore, again residing at Feldsberg, to caution Leopoldine Liechtenstein about the French ambassador, who would soon arrive there. The ambassador's object in conversation, she speculated, would be to learn from Leopoldine Liechtenstein the sentiments of Marshal Lacy and thus to detect any serious discord in the Austrian government. Eleonore agreed to pass along the warning.[128]

Leopoldine Kaunitz may have been aware as early as mid-July that some form of unusual peace initiative was under way, although she certainly did not know that Maria Theresia would send an emissary to initiate talks unilaterally.

Leopoldine Kaunitz wrote to Eleonore: "something deep in my soul tells me that too many people do not really want war for it to continue, I feel convinced that overtures will be made, that negotiations will resume, that the best course will eventually be chosen, and that, without having done ourselves much harm, we will finish this campaign season and we will not then renew the campaign." Learning of the emperor's crisis of confidence at the front Leopoldine Kaunitz urged her sister, possibly at the chancellor's suggestion, to embolden the emperor: "when you write to him, inspire him with that noble courage that must be his virtue at the moment. I am not speaking about personal bravery, he has too much self-respect to lack or fail to demonstrate that; but a certain pride that is appropriate at the present moment, that has nothing of fanfare but manifests confidence that ten thousand good troops, loyal and brave as his are, can hold their own against a greater number of Prussians." Again, more urgently, a week later Leopoldine Kaunitz wrote, "In God's name, encourage the Emperor so that even a defeat will not cause him to lose his head, this is of the greatest importance."[129] Early in the conflict Chancellor Kaunitz had expressed misgivings to his daughter-in-law about Lacy's ascendancy over Joseph, blaming the marshal for discouraging the emperor. According to Leopoldine Kaunitz, the chancellor believed that Lacy's approach was self-serving. Lacy would exaggerate obstacles, dampening the spirits of those who served with him; "proof of this . . . is that no one likes to serve under him, he demoralizes, he discourages everyone, never has he been able to give pleasure and satisfaction to his subordinates." Having painted such a gloomy picture, Lacy could later claim he had foreseen any misfortune that occurred. Leopoldine had suspected, however, that some of the chancellor's remarks might be veiled criticisms of the emperor himself.[130] When details about Thugut's secret mission to the Prussian king and Maria Theresia's plea for peace on virtually any terms became known and publicly canvassed Leopoldine was disgusted, pronouncing Thugut's mission "humiliating." A few days later she reported without enthusiasm, "They are working hard on the peace; my father-in-law said to me that when one does not know any better how to wage war it is necessary to think of peace." Her sister agreed that with her immoderate desire for peace the empress risked jeopardizing the monarchy's military forces and its bargaining position.[131]

Throughout the jockeying for position that preceded the war as well as the conflict itself, on both the Prussian and the Austrian sides publicists offered competing justifications for their sovereigns' positions, in some cases directly sponsored by those sovereigns themselves. Leopoldine Kaunitz in particular found these disquisitions highly engrossing, whether they were semiofficial publications or anonymous broadsides. At the outset, the Habsburg side had cited leaderless Bavaria's temporary status as a lapsed imperial fief to justify its occupation.[132] Other European rulers as well as the politically savvy public considered the Habsburg arguments to be weak and largely obsolete. Nevertheless, Habsburg legal experts labored to make a respectable case founded on imperial law while the emperor himself hoped to render all arguments moot by presenting the empire and especially Prussia with a fait accompli by his occupation of Bavarian territory. Writers employed by Chancellor Kaunitz laid out the strongest case they could to justify Habsburg initiatives. In mid-July Leopoldine Kaunitz learned that a "manifesto" of the Prussian king had appeared in Vienna ("entitled, if I remember correctly, motives that have prompted His Prussian Majesty to oppose the seizure of Bavaria"). This publication was probably the *Exposé des Motifs qui ont engagé Sa Majesté le Roi de Prusse à s'opposer au démembrement de la Bavière* (July 1778) by Prussia's Count Ewald Friedrich Hertzberg. Unable to lay hands on it immediately (and her sister Eleonore clamored for it from her rural exile in Eisgrub), Leopoldine Kaunitz received her first assessment of the document indirectly, from the English ambassador Keith who, with diplomatic tact, managed to make clear his admiration for the text without praising it directly. Finally, by the first week in August Leopoldine obtained the entire document. Critiquing its contents, she argued that the extensive documentation offered to justify Prussia could just as easily serve to demonstrate "that we have done everything [possible], and perhaps even too much, to have peace."[133]

The Austrian counterstatement was slow to appear, and Leopoldine Kaunitz worried that it would be poorly written. Finally in late September the Habsburg answer was published, most likely the *Réponse au Mémoire pour servir de suite à l'Exposé des motifs qui ont engagé S. M. le roi de Prusse à s'opposer au démembrement de la Bavière*, published in Vienna by Trattner. Pleasantly surprised by the publication's quality, Leopoldine sent a copy to her sister. The manifest was judged by readers to be a masterpiece, Leopoldine reported, "for its simplicity and clarity, for the noble moderation with which the situation is shown in its true colors." Leopoldine was especially impressed with "the happy turn of phrase we have been able to give to our humiliating negotiations and to the inordinate desire for peace expressed by the Empress." She believed that the publication vindicated Austrian policies on a number of fronts, "by tacitly making clear that even if there were plans for aggrandizement on our part in the seizure of Bavaria, it is above all the coming aggrandizement of the house of Brandenbourg that has forced us to counterbalance with our forces there [presumably a reference to Prussian claims on Ansbach and Bayreuth]." Leopoldine described for her sister the chancellor's delight with this finished product. "My father-in-law is very pleased with himself, he is just like a boy who has done his school assignment well, it gives him an almost childlike pleasure when his efforts succeed." The length of the document deterred some readers. At 44 pages, it was double the length of the Prussian justification.[134] Eleonore's letter with her reaction to the Austrian publication crossed paths with her sister's, since Leopoldine Liechtenstein had already sent a copy to Eleonore. Eleonore's praise was at first lukewarm: "it is an intimidating object to contemplate, and certainly very few people will read it; everything is already so well known that there is nothing left to learn. My sister-in-law [Leopoldine Liechtenstein] tells me that it is very well done, that it will do honor to the Prince [Kaunitz], who has known how to respond and use the circumstances advantageously." Several days later Eleonore was less critical, possibly in deference to her sister's enthusiasm. "Today we have finished the manifest in fine form [*glorieusement*]," Eleonore wrote. "Certainly it will do great honor to your father-in-law; there is throughout skillfulness, extensive research, politics; such an immense opus, I would prefer to be a galley slave than to undertake production of such a work."[135]

Leopoldine Kaunitz relished the war of words and was now curious to learn how the Prussian king would respond further. The sisters and Leopoldine Liechtenstein swapped additional publications, including two entitled *Abgemüßigte einstweilige Vorlegung der jetzigen Lage der Bayerischen Erbfolge-Strittigkeiten* (Necessary provisional exposition of the current state of the Bavarian succession disputes) published in Regensburg in September and the *Journal der Operationen der combinirten Königlich-Preußischen und Churf. Sächsischen Armee, unter Commando Seiner Königlichen Hoheit des Prinzen Heinrich von Preußen* (Journal of the operations of the combined royal Prussian and prince-electoral Saxon armies under the command of his royal highness prince Henry of Prussia). In her letter Eleonore referred specifically to Prince Henry's journal from his camp at Nimes, a masterful diary extract recounting the activities of the two armies, "excellently composed and just right for hiding their errors and highlighting their advantages, something that we are far from doing."[136] Leopoldine Kaunitz, as an enthusiastic partisan, quarreled with the ambassador from Holland Count Degenfeld when the latter found Austrian publications "too biting." Leopoldine argued that after all the injurious and unfair documents Prussian writers had produced, "we should be able to permit a publication . . . [in this case from the pen of *Hofrat* Sonnenfels] in which there is piquancy and sense." The discussion had remained civil (not "excessively sharp"), Leopoldine Kaunitz assured her sister, "but there is always some skirmishing [*de la petite guerre*]."[137]

While the conflict lasted, Leopoldine Kaunitz longed for an active military strategy, as did Eleonore. "The Nuncio told me the other day that this campaign has certainly been inglorious for the King," she wrote in October, "I think that this '*in*' is suitable for us also, for it was glorious for us only at that moment when he was retreating on all sides and everyone supposed that we would be pursuing him." Leopoldine tried to stifle her impatience, resolving to stop worrying about the war entirely: "I have made a resolution, which I undoubtedly will not keep for long, to let them make war and a truce, and even peace without me, for in the end all of this will happen without anyone's consulting me."[138] She even grew critical of her father-in-law's apparent passivity during peace negotiations, fearing that he would not defend the monarchy's interests with vigor. The chancellor still seemed discontented, convinced that both he and Maria Theresia had been shunted aside by the emperor throughout the episode. Leopoldine Kaunitz feared that he would take his cues from Maria Theresia, who had proved to be temperamental and unreliable in this crisis. "Let him be exiled," she wrote, "disgraced to the extent they wish, I could accept all that, but for him to countenance a dishonorable peace, that I could not bear."[139]

Leopoldine Liechtenstein received reports about the campaign from Marshal Lacy, as Eleonore reported to Leopoldine Kaunitz. Leopoldine Liechtenstein's concerns were twofold, for the fortunes of the monarchy's armies and for the personal well-being of her son Louis and the marshal, whose health was fragile and who quickly became discouraged about the course of the war. Eleonore described one of Lacy's dismal letters to Leopoldine Kaunitz in September 1778:

> La Françoise [Leopoldine Liechtenstein] sent me yesterday, always as a great secret, a letter from the Marshal . . . I cannot describe to you the tone of sadness and discouragement that permeates it, it is as if this is not the same man that we know . . . he says quite clearly that if he once comes back home, nothing in the world will bring him to venture out again, and as for the coming campaign, he will not be part of it. I wrote to la Françoise that in God's name he [Lacy] must not tell this to the army, for if the King learned of this, it would give him courage for the future or would at least make the peace more difficult for us.

When Eleonore visited her sister-in-law in Feldsberg, Eleonore had to choose her words carefully as they discussed the war because Leopoldine Liechtenstein feared the army's lackluster performance ("this miserable inaction") would tarnish Lacy's reputation.[140] Leopoldine Liechtenstein believed that with his selfless exertions Lacy would ruin his own health. She faulted the emperor for his oblique responses and demurrals when newspaper accounts praised his and Lacy's leadership: "she finds, and it is really true, that this modesty is poorly placed. In fact her real grievance is that he never sends any word to them about it at all." The situation tormented her because she was aware that Lacy was less popular than Laudon, who also enjoyed the support of Chancellor Kaunitz. Leopoldine Liechtenstein's unhappiness filled her letters to Eleonore. "La Françoise is still preoccupied with the subject that means everything to her and that animates her, as you have put it . . . she believes that the public is terribly unjust towards him, that his conduct receives nothing but criticism." Leopoldine Liechtenstein was convinced that the campaign would cost Lacy his life or force him to seek a healthier climate far away. Her resentment was lively ("I have received today a long letter from la Françoise, who seems to me still very bitter towards the Emperor").[141]

Leopoldine Liechtenstein's solicitude for Lacy's reputation was warranted. When Leopoldine Kaunitz wrote to her sister describing "what they are saying in Vienna and especially what people are complaining about," she confirmed that public opinion was insisting that Laudon had been trammeled by Lacy's caution and jealousy. Unlike Eleonore and Leopoldine Kaunitz, Leopoldine Liechtenstein spoke respectfully about the army's defensive posture, which she judged to be the result of Lacy's sage advice. Visiting Feldsberg in October, Eleonore found Leopoldine Liechtenstein's continuous complaints about the emperor's treatment of Lacy tedious. Eleonore reported, "she is terribly angry with the Emperor . . . when she gets started on that and with praises of the Marshal, which is the usual refrain, she is indefatigable, I received my fill this afternoon; but who among us is without a small share of weakness or absurdity?"[142]

Leopoldine Liechtenstein's dissatisfaction with her friend the emperor had an additional, more personal source during the late 1770s. In October 1777, when Eleonore arrived for a visit at Feldsberg, she had found Leopoldine Liechtenstein incensed over what she held to be spiteful imperial treatment of a close relative. Leopoldine's younger sister Josepha (1735–1803) was the wife of Karl Egon I, Prince Fürstenberg (1729–1787), serving as Bohemian governor in Prague since 1771. Prince Fürstenberg shared many of Joseph's ideas about reforming agriculture and rural conditions and like Chancellor Kaunitz had introduced robot commutation and subdivision of land on his estates.[143] But by the late 1770s the prince's personal extravagance had left him deeply in debt and in general he had forfeited the emperor's regard. Leopoldine Liechtenstein, wrote Eleonore to her sister, was greatly agitated, unable to advise Princess Fürstenberg because of the risk of imperial reprisals. Eleonore herself had found the situation disquieting. "All of this makes you fear repercussions affecting yourself"; "not the least indulgence" could be expected after a friendship of so many years' standing. According to Eleonore, Leopoldine Liechtenstein pronounced herself delighted to be away from Vienna and offered unusually sharp judgments (she was "deeply offended") concerning "his conduct, his personality, his manner of behaving with us, the role we play."[144] The resentment felt by Leopoldine Liechtenstein, usually such a staunch friend to the emperor, did not soon fade. During the 1778 crisis Prince Fürstenberg proved to be unenthusiastic about risking war over the succession to Bavaria, presumably because Frederick's warlike response was likely to target Bohemia. When the Prussian invasion began, Emperor Joseph felt that Fürstenberg's openly unhelpful attitude had fed into the undignified panic that gripped parts of Bohemia, especially Prague.[145] Fürstenberg became persona non grata for the emperor, who expressed his displeasure publicly. Joseph's animosity eventually drove Fürstenberg from office in 1782, after Fürstenberg transgressed yet again by opposing publication of Joseph's patent introducing religious toleration in Bohemia (described in chapter 5).[146]

As the campaign of 1778 neared its end, Lacy's letters to Leopoldine Liechtenstein included content very likely intended for broader consumption, with the public spin he wished to place on events. Apparently Leopoldine Liechtenstein had expressed to him some disappointment about the campaign, suggesting that it had ended prematurely and had brought little gain to the monarchy. Lacy replied rather sharply (according to Eleonore), "'You are certainly hard to satisfy, do you not remember the trouble and endless difficulties we had during the last war in entering, in sustaining ourselves in the country you would like us to penetrate now when we are alone whereas the King still has allies, not to mention his personal superiority, that of his army; do you not remember that not two months ago you believed Prague and half of Bohemia to be lost, and nevertheless we have managed to reach the point of chasing them out?' Those were just about his exact statements," Eleonore reported. Leopoldine Liechtenstein had also sent Lacy a list of purported deserters, which he had declared to be an exaggeration.[147]

Josepha Clary was a loyal Habsburg subject with a habitually optimistic outlook. For her and her family, however, the Bavarian war was a calamity. During the 1778 campaign, the maneuvers and skirmishing of the Prussian and the Habsburg armies took place on Bohemian soil, principally in the north where lay the property of Josepha's family. The vulnerability of the Clary family fortunes colored Josepha Clary's entire experience of the war. During the earlier Seven Years War, the spa town and Clary manorial seat at Teplitz had been declared neutral ground so that officers from both the Prussian and Austrian armies could recuperate there, although even then the Prussians had raided the area to capture Austrian officers.[148] Events of 1778 were far more frightening to the Clary family. As early as May 1778, Charles Liechtenstein reported to his wife from his post at Leitmeritz that Prince Clary was removing furnishings from his palace in Teplitz, expecting a Prussian invasion.[149] Prussian troops arrived in the summer. Josepha wrote anxiously to her husband that it appeared the Habsburg leadership was not even considering defending Bohemian territory, "that they will hand over our unfortunate lands to him [Frederick II]."[150] The population of Prague became nervous about a possible Prussian attack, as noted previously; word spread that the emperor might choose to leave undefended even that city. Both the Prussian and the Austrian armies, stationary in northern Bohemia, foraged for supplies in the countryside. Looting by Prussian armies in northern Bohemia damaged property and crops on Clary lands, particularly as the Prussians began to retreat in the autumn.[151] A major Clary income source, the sale of timber to Saxons over the border, was cut off during the hostilities, a loss also experienced by Leopoldine Liechtenstein's sister and brother-in-law, the Waldsteins, with estates at Komotau (Chomutov).[152]

Frightened and embittered, Josepha Clary blamed the chancellor and, through him, the emperor personally for having involved the monarchy in a profitless conflict. As in other similar cases, Leopoldine Kaunitz angrily told her sister that history would ultimately exonerate the chancellor. Contemporaries could not see clearly the "many things that we cannot understand at present."[153] Over Joseph's role, or at least over open criticism of his role, a serious if temporary rift opened between Leopoldine Kaunitz and Josepha Clary. Under the mistaken impression that Leopoldine Kaunitz shared her sentiments, Josepha contrasted Joseph's modest abilities with the military prowess of Frederick II. When Leopoldine reacted indignantly, Josepha reminded her that the offending remarks were purely private, made to a friend to whom Josepha had believed she could talk politics frankly. With Josepha and her husband facing financial ruin, Leopoldine Kaunitz found herself in a perplexing situation, as she explained to Eleonore: "They [the Clary couple] do not know where to find the money to live, just thinking about it takes one's breath away . . . despite all her virtue she cannot keep herself from holding him [Joseph] responsible as the instrument of all this, for she said to me again yesterday, and when I consider that it is the whim of a sovereign that is reducing us to misery."[154]

Josepha Clary and Leopoldine Kaunitz quickly became reconciled, but the episode reflected tensions among interested parties during the military campaign and the growing concern of the public at large.[155] To add to the bitterness of Bohemian landowners, rumor had it that the Archduchess Marie Christine was improperly influencing prosecution of the war, wishing to protect her husband's interests in Saxony even while Saxony was allied with Frederick against the Habsburg cause. According to Wraxall, writing soon after the war, "The Emperor her brother has experienced not less the effects of the Archduchess's interposition, during the progress of the last campaign, in a manner which must have occasioned him the deepest mortification. No one here doubts, that the resolution taken not to render Saxony the seat of war, as in sound policy the Austrians ought to have done; was principally, if not wholly, due to her tears and entreaties, which the Empress could not behold unmoved. Perhaps," he added darkly, "Joseph may at some future day resent and punish an interference, so incompatible with his objects of ambition."[156] Instead of Saxony, the Habsburgs' own Bohemian lands and the property and inhabitants of families such as the Clary had borne the brunt of the fighting. Leopoldine Kaunitz reported to Eleonore a story she had heard about Marie Christine's excessive partiality to the cause of Saxony as well as her unseemly eagerness to bring Albert home quickly and safely. "Mme. Marie even reached the point of saying that if it was necessary to sacrifice three districts [*cercles*] of Bohemia, they would have to be given up." According to Leopoldine, "Mme de Chanclos responded quite well: it is all very well for Your Royal Highness to be giving what does not belong to you."[157] The chancellor himself told Leopoldine Kaunitz that he feared naysayers such as the archduchess and others would further undermine the empress's confidence, telling her that "our

Lord God cannot bless us, for it is an unjust affair." Leopoldine Kaunitz was reluctant to credit rumors about Marie Christine's disloyalty ("she would be the first of her house to betray the interests of her family, this alone makes me think it cannot be"). Leopoldine did dislike Marie Christine's influence on Rosenberg, who was "so fawning that it is incredible, he sees only through the eyes of Mme Marie and speaks only according to her orders, to such an extent that I believe he thinks peace is essential at any price." Rosenberg, for his part, insisted that the archduchess was blameless. Leopoldine Kaunitz wrote, "I do not know when I will manage to control my temper. Yesterday unfortunately I quarreled with him and asked him if he was so blinded by *Frau* Marie that he was determined to sell us out to Saxony, he swore to me that she does not meddle in anything except to lament about her dear husband."[158]

The Clary family's experience of the "potato war" was more immediate than that of luckier landowners, even in Bohemia. Leopoldine Kaunitz told Eleonore that it was terrible to see the Clary family facing ruin, "people who are ruined, who have known abundance, who were fond of it, who enjoyed it, now at present without a sou and for the future thoroughly disordered financially." Prince Clary and his wife Josepha wept over their devastating losses in a scene that Leopoldine Kaunitz found unforgettable. The couple was bewildered, uncertain where to turn to meet daily household expenses; and as yet they did not know the full extent of their losses.[159] The massive damage to the Clary properties prompted Maria Theresia to bestow upon the family a gift of 1000 ducats. Leopoldine Kaunitz reported the donation to Eleonore in October, noting that the sum was not really sufficient to mend the situation but was certainly large enough to be embarrassing; and for this generosity the couple was obliged to be ostentatiously grateful. Prince Kinsky, Sidonia's husband, also assisted the Clary couple, Leopoldine Kaunitz added; "Kinsky [Sidonia Kinsky's husband], who has made them a loan under his name for 50 thousand florins, transfers to them together with his credit 10 thousand florins," a more appropriate gesture "that pleases me and is honorable and a real service."[160]

Aware of the resentment felt toward the emperor by both Leopoldine Liechtenstein and Josepha Clary during the summer and autumn of 1778, Leopoldine Kaunitz predicted uncomfortable moments ("torture") for the evening gatherings of the *société* during the approaching winter; "my God, I think to myself, what will become of us this winter?"[161] The two offended *Dames* felt that the emperor should have acknowledged their concerns. He should, they believed, have expressed sympathy with Josepha Clary's losses and at least mentioned the presence of Leopoldine Liechtenstein's eldest son Louis at the front. Such gestures made both to Josepha and to Leopoldine Liechtenstein (and Lacy as well) could solve all problems at once, Eleonore remarked, "but what can be done with this Emperor who does not think of anything and whom you cannot persuade to do anything directly; as you say, this is preparing for us a charming winter." Both her own husband Charles and the emperor would require constant soothing, she foresaw. "What a winter, dear sister!" Eleonore exclaimed. With "all our *Dames* embittered, there will be talk of a new campaign, there will be talk of a bad peace, one will not know what to wish for, or rather to fear."[162]

Sidonia Kinsky alone among the five *Dames* appears to have taken even military perils in stride, content to remain peacefully on her property at Weidlingau. According to Leopoldine Kaunitz, Sidonia was tranquil even though lands belonging to the princely line of the Kinsky family were threatened by Prussian troop movements. In late September 1778, after a visit to Sidonia at Weidlingau where they viewed the adjacent parkland with its deer, Leopoldine reported that Sidonia was perfectly happy, "as contented as a queen, worried very little about what happens beyond her horizon, which Germans so aptly call the *Gesichtskreis*." About a week later, Leopoldine Kaunitz again remarked upon Sidonia's remarkable equanimity. Only her sister Josepha's plight disturbed Sidonia. Josepha spoke of retiring to a small village after placing her youngest daughter Thérèse in her *Stift* and selling or renting out the Clary residence in Vienna.[163]

Despite tensions, dire predictions, and the conflicting interests of its members during the war, the *société* survived and continued to function. Prior to Maria Theresia's death in late 1780, several additional foreign policy initiatives greatly interested the *Dames*. The Habsburg government did not take a clear position regarding the American Revolution that had begun in 1775, focusing narrowly on the conflict's potential to distract for many years at least two great powers, England and France. For a time it appeared that the Habsburg government might act as mediator in the peace negotiations. Kaunitz and the emperor spent time and energy considering a strategy, but in the end they remained inactive.[164] Eleonore condemned this lassitude after receiving one of the emperor's letters. As she saw it, the Prussian king took France's part, the Russian empress sided with the English, and the Habsburg emperor as usual could not decide what to do.[165] A second initiative, the election of Archduke Maximilian Franz, Joseph II's youngest brother, as coadjutor of Cologne (and subsequently Münster) in August 1780, was successful, a significant diplomatic achievement. The election was sponsored and ultimately secured by Maria Theresia and was recognized as her accomplishment by the cognoscenti in Vienna, although many outsiders assumed that this move was one more example of Joseph's aggressiveness toward the empire.[166] The election virtually guaranteed Max Franz's eventual elevation as archbishop and elector of Cologne and bishop of Münster, when the current prelates should die. Maria Theresia had pressured the archduke to choose a career in the church, after which she brooded sadly about his fate. Leopoldine Kaunitz empathized with the emperor's frustration about the empress's irresolution. To make matters worse, Max's selection as coadjutor was announced and celebrated prematurely in

Leopoldine Kaunitz's view, so the empress had risked public embarrassment if plans went awry and the courier brought bad news. "This is really rather childish," she wrote to Eleonore, "for if it were to fail, which is certainly not impossible, how foolish we would look!" Maximilian's election did strengthen Habsburg influence in the Holy Roman Empire, and Leopoldine Kaunitz expressed satisfaction with this feat, since "in reality it is nevertheless true that this time the opposition of the king of Prussia was of no use, and that is itself a victory."[167]

An additional foray into foreign policy, this one Joseph's own project, fired the imaginations of the *Dames* during the coregency, when he visited Catherine II in Russia during the summer months of 1780. Joseph's goal was to lay the groundwork for a Russo-Austrian alliance to bolster the Habsburg position over against Prussia, which was then allied with Russia, to neutralize the potentially meddlesome activity of Russia itself within the territories of the Holy Roman Empire, and to line up support for his own foreign policy goals. The Habsburg monarchy's alliance with France had proved to be a disappointment, most recently during the Bavarian war. Chancellor Kaunitz, belatedly informed of Joseph's travel plans, agreed that the possibility was worth exploring. Maria Theresia too reluctantly gave her consent for the journey.[168] The emperor spent much of late spring and summer traveling in Russian territory, often in the company of Catherine. The two leaders did not see eye to eye concerning the goals of a potential alliance, each conjuring up quite different programs of aggrandizement. Catherine's wish to expand southward would involve additional incursions into Turkish territory, whereas Habsburg interests seemed best served by maintenance of a functional if weak Turkish regime to the south rather than a strong, expansionist Russia as immediate neighbor. Catherine was willing to support Habsburg gains in the Balkans against the Turks, but the value of these territories for the monarchy appeared uncertain. Joseph's principal aim was in any case Russian cooperation in countering Prussia's enmity. The two leaders speculated freely about schemes involving mutual assistance or guarantees but reached no firm agreement at this time.[169]

Early in the trip, from Mogilev, the emperor sent a letter to Leopoldine Kaunitz describing the town as "a wretched Polish city, dirty, poorly built, of which history would never take note." However, his impressions of the power and extent of the Russian empire were mostly favorable.[170] Letters came to Eleonore Liechtenstein as she stayed at Kromau or Feldsberg (she then passed the letters on to Leopoldine Kaunitz in Vienna) from Petersburg, Moscow, Riga, extolling the Russian empress, her court, and her lands, and discursing at length on elements of Russia's expansionist policy. The emperor appeared to be full of enthusiasm for all things Russian; and although some of this fulsome praise was probably for the benefit of Catherine's agents, who were likely to intercept his mail, Joseph was impressed by his potential ally. Eleonore described the text of one of these enthusiastic letters from early August 1780, in which Joseph praised Riga (Eleonore noted that it pleased him "like everything Russian"), dilating on its commerce, its institutions, its bridges.[171] It was after this visit with Catherine, as Joseph returned to Vienna, that he made his awkward visit to Eleonore in Kromau. His conversation at Kromau was naturally full of his impressions of Russia. "He seems to me enchanted with his trip," Eleonore wrote. He had enjoyed meeting Catherine; "he finds her very agreeable, gay, witty, and she has had the skill, which I think is relatively easy especially when one is as adroit as she is, to convince him that he is pleasing to her when she finds him agreeable."[172] Letters that passed between Maria Theresia and Marie Antoinette during Joseph's journey captured the mixture of interest and anxiety that the trip produced among close observers, particularly those invested in the faltering French alliance. Regarding Joseph's long trip Marie Antoinette remarked, "I am doubtful that there is anything to be gained from this Empress; but since my brother is intelligent and prudent, I am sure that he will do no harm, and that those who come after him will not outshine him." Maria Theresia subsequently reported to her daughter, in comments almost certainly intended for dissemination in French government circles, that Joseph seemed content with his journey but by no means blind to reality. The two sovereigns, she wrote, had not closed any deals. Joseph had merely acted to eradicate Russian prejudices against the Habsburg lands.[173]

As noted in an earlier chapter, immediately after the emperor's Russian trip and his visit to Kromau there occurred the quarrel between Eleonore and the emperor over Charles's plan, endorsed by Maria Theresia, to build a military barracks in Vienna. Through the intercession of Leopoldine Kaunitz, Leopoldine Liechtenstein, Josepha Clary, and Lacy, amicable relations were restored for the winter "season."[174] The ill will generated by that dispute, which was a serious conflict from Eleonore's point of view, eventually dissipated. The alarms of the Bavarian war too receded into the past. The little coterie survived and resumed its accustomed routine gatherings with the emperor.

Maria Theresia's death on 29 November 1780 transformed the political scene in Vienna. During the coregency the empress's strong personality and her distrust of her son had caused her to cling to authority. Her chancellor, Kaunitz, was an elder statesman with extraordinary acumen but also a healthy ego. He had been a trusted advisor to the empress and was accustomed to deferential treatment. Joseph had been the junior member of this triumvirate, although as years passed he had demonstrated a growing independence of mind. During the coregency the emperor could propose measures and influence policy, but he could rarely act without interference and criticism from the empress.

During this first period of association with the emperor the *Dames* esteemed him because of his position, admired his agile mind, and valued their privileged relationship with him. They made allowances for his moodiness and found their interaction with him stimulating. Eleonore's expressions of frustration notwithstanding, all five *Dames* appear to have regarded the emperor as desirable company, sincere if also prickly and unpredictable. Maria Theresia and even Chancellor Kaunitz worried about Joseph's insensitivity toward people around him. Concerning the likely results of this imperial indifference, Kaunitz wrote to Maria Theresia discreetly but pointedly in September 1779, "Some day one will have just what one deserves, which is to say, not a single friend and for servitors, rascals or vile spirits, what a prospect."[175] The empress accepted imperfections in herself, in her officials, in government, in society. Not so her son. During the Bavarian war Eleonore remarked upon the emperor's intolerant attitude, "the bad opinion he has of all those who do not understand or guess his views, who do not approve them, or who do not succeed. With him it is necessary to be perfect, he cannot make use of the services of people in whom he has detected a flaw."[176] Describing Joseph II's irritability and despondency in May 1779, she exclaimed: "What a future! He will become a true misanthrope [*Menschenfeind*], he will make himself hated, and will hate everyone." Three months later she wrote, "In truth this prince has a bad character, and a constant desire to be malicious, and such is our sovereign and our daily and particular company?"[177] At times Eleonore had personal grievances that added sharpness to her criticism, but in more sedate and moderate ways the other women seconded her views. They too experienced firsthand the emperor's thoughtlessness and brusque remarks. Josepha managed to shrug off the emperor's rudeness toward her own husband, the *grand veneur*. She assured Prince Clary that what he perceived as insults from the emperor were not to be taken personally. He could scarcely expect better treatment after witnessing the emperor's behavior to his mother the empress, she remarked in August 1778. If the prince could not overlook occasional rudeness toward himself, he should simply give up imperial service to preserve his peace of mind.[178]

The *Dames* realized that Joseph's position was irksome to him. Even the most minute matters, such as the granting of an annuity to a favored individual by Maria Theresia, led to conflict between mother and son over finances. As late as August 1780, only two months before Maria Theresia's death, when the empress fretted over Joseph's displeasure about pensions she had awarded, Leopoldine Kaunitz noted the unfortunate effects of this friction and acknowledged the emperor's predicament. "One must admit," Leopoldine wrote, "his role as Emperor is neither pleasant nor easy, for I believe that sometimes she does need to be restrained, I would only wish that he would not make her angry, for it is true that we are the victims of it . . . I anticipate many rows, and there would be an element of surprise and contrivance, quite novel and worthy of the cleverness of the Emperor, if they could amicably sort out all the matters with which they must deal."[179] Commiserating with each other, Leopoldine Kaunitz and Eleonore frequently employed metaphors about stormy weather in describing their own situation when the emperor's doldrums made evening conversations difficult to sustain. But at times one also catches a glimpse of that more attractive side of the emperor's personality that won for him loyalty from some subordinates and could make him a congenial friend with whom to discuss issues of the day. In September 1777, at a time when the Bavarian war was still in the future, Eleonore was surprised by the emperor's candor in describing his aspirations, his self-doubts, and his fear of failure. He described to her his eagerness to be a great military commander and his discouragement as he realized that all his preparations could be wasted time; "while you sacrifice the pleasures of life in rushing about, you will never be a great general and you risk weakening a friendship that is essential to your happiness." Eleonore remarked to her sister that although the emperor was being intentionally gallant, there was an honesty in his admission that she had never before encountered.[180] In an undated note in Leopoldine Kaunitz's papers, apparently written after one of their particularly lively disputes, the emperor sent Leopoldine Kaunitz a friendly and very human apology: "it is true that I may have said too much yesterday."[181]

Notwithstanding the friendly consideration the *Dames* demonstrated for the emperor and the satisfaction they derived from their status as favored friends, in sober moments these close observers expressed concern about his fitness for political leadership. They concluded that Joseph lacked firmness, both in his general principles and in the goals he pursued, despite his single-minded devotion to the welfare of the state. Blanning observes that Joseph II often wrote in a "characteristically over-excited, almost manic" style (mentioned with reference to a circular of 1781), and evidently his conversation could be equally frenetic. As Adam Wolf notes, the emperor appeared to court contradiction from these friends at times, although he was usually patient with the result.[182] The women, like many subsequent historians, detected a fickleness in his reasoning and a disposition to adopt and justify paradoxical positions. According to Leopoldine Kaunitz, whereas many rulers feigned virtue, the emperor longed to be thought wicked (*méchant*).[183]

In October 1777 Leopoldine Kaunitz remarked—no doubt half in jest—that she wished she had not come to know the emperor quite so well, even though "there is still a good heart, enveloped in a quantity of sophisms and notions that really are not sound."[184] A month before Maria Theresia's death, in a situation where Leopoldine Kaunitz believed the emperor to have made an unwise decision (a case involving her brother-in-law Charles Liechtenstein's subaltern Auernhammer), Leopoldine wrote that she had observed a thousand times that the emperor's personality was shaped by "contradiction," such that if one stressed a point and adduced arguments in support of one's position, this merely provided him with another occasion to respond with sophisms that were persuasive to no one else; and thereafter he could never be moved from his position—an interesting parallel to Joseph's own descriptions of the *déraison* of women.[185] While some contemporaries remarked upon the mercurial thought processes of the interesting young coregent, as sole ruler he would often demonstrate an unfortunate rigidity of approach. Biographer Jean Bérenger, comparing Joseph with his mother, suggests that, conservative though she was, Maria Theresia was too intelligent to ignore the evolving conditions in her environment, and so she managed to adapt in modest, practical ways to new ideas of Catholic reform and even the Enlightenment.[186] The idealistic but inflexible Joseph, by contrast, would later come to grief when his wishes were frustrated by stubborn reality.

Bon gré mal gré the monarchy had come through this period of dual rule unscathed, relatively prosperous, and in possession of a respectable, if hardly spectacular, international status. At least one of Joseph's biographers, Karl Gutkas, argues that the compromises that Maria Theresia and Joseph were forced to make during the coregency, the balance between his urge to accelerate and her braking efforts, served the monarchy rather well.[187] This was not the view of contemporaries, who could not always be certain who was running the government. The Bavarian war made particularly obvious the confusion that reigned among the makers of policy, visible not just to the initiated such as the *Dames* but also to the public at large. Not surprisingly, historians have found it difficult to apportion credit or blame for Habsburg policies during the coregency. The respective roles of Joseph II and Kaunitz can be particularly difficult to characterize, since each man was given to dressing up his proposals in phrases that were alternately pompous or sardonic, and often hyperbolic. Maria Theresia too voiced her anxiety in exaggerated tones. Sadly, the coregency frustrated and embittered both Maria Theresia and Joseph, two of the most earnest, hardworking, and talented individuals the Habsburg dynasty had ever produced.

Over the course of the coregency, Joseph became exasperated, even frantic, about government by "bumbling discussion," as Blanning characterizes Joseph's opinion of his mother's regime.[188] He longed to replace Maria Theresia's overlapping councils and informal advisors with a more autocratic style of governance. Unfortunately, the coregency left this monarch-in-training with awkward, ingrained habits of inconsistency, impatience, and arrogant contempt for opinions that differed from his own. Maria Theresia had sensed both the difficulties of her son's position and his weaknesses. In 1775, herself exasperated by the emperor's continuous criticism, she wrote to Count Mercy, Habsburg ambassador to France, that if she exited the scene her son would find ruling without her quite another proposition: "Once in charge, he will see the difficulties and will no longer be able to hide behind me."[189] With knowledge of hindsight it is obvious that during the period the empress's presence and authority, while disagreeable, had also absolved her son of ultimate responsibility for events, and he enjoyed a less careworn existence while under her tutelage. When an outcome was disappointing, he was not fully answerable. In the War of the Bavarian Succession, the emperor's eager quest for "glory" and new territory was not blocked by Maria Theresia; and after he launched the army in a war of aggrandizement, he expressed surprise, indignation, and self-pity as he faced the horrors consequent upon the decision to make war.

For all her hesitancy and *scrupules* (as the *Dames* referred to the empress's increasingly frequent crises of conscience) Maria Theresia's steady hand and practical sense were sorely missed after she passed from the scene. A remarkable woman concerning whom historians and storytellers have said much, Maria Theresia awaits her own meticulous modern biographer who can sort through both the historical record and the myths about her to provide an accurate assessment of her reign. The uncomfortable coregency had lasted for fully fifteen years. Joseph's role as coregent was not ideal preparation for his future job as sole ruler. The *Dames* were correct in fearing the results of Joseph's ingrained habits of thought and action; these would prove to be no help to him at all when he became his own master. The *Dames* viewed him with fondness, but also with anxiety. Eleonore Liechtenstein pronounced her judgment of Joseph's character with bluntness: the emperor, with many excellent qualities and much goodness, was "not well-suited to rule."[190] A group of individuals who associated daily with Joseph II, often seated by his side, the *Dames* looked ahead with misgivings to the emperor's inevitable accession to power.

Notes

1 LRRA, P 16/21, LK to EL, 9 April 1769; P 16/22, LK to EL, Naples, 10 February 1770; and EL to LK, Vienna, 8 March 1770. Reported by Eleonore Liechtenstein's biographer Adam Wolf and most recently in Beales, *Joseph II*, 1: 310.
2 LRRA, P 16/23, EL to LK, Meseritsch, 23 October [1773].
3 William E. Wright, *Serf, Seigneur, and Sovereign: Agrarian Reform in Eighteenth-Century Bohemia* (Minneapolis: University of Minnesota Press, 1966), 33-36.
4 Standard treatments of the subject are Wright, *Serf, Seigneur, and Sovereign* and Karl Grünberg, *Die Bauernbefreiung und die Auflösung des gutsherrlich-bäuerlichen Verhältnisses in Böhmen.* (Leipzig: Duncker & Humblot, 1894).
5 Gutkas, *Kaiser Joseph II.*, 128-29.
6 HHStA, KA ZT, Band 18, 17 September 1773.
7 Franz A. J. Szabo, "Ambivalenzen der Aufklärungspolitik in der Habsburgermonarchie unter Joseph II. und Leopold II.," in *Ambivalenzen der Aufklärung: Festschrift für Ernst Wangermann*, ed. Gerhard Ammerer and Hanns Haas (Munich: R. Oldenbourg, 1997), 26.
8 Analysis of the process can be found in Beales, *Joseph II*, 1: 346-58 and Szabo, *Kaunitz and Enlightened Absolutism*, 170-80.
9 Bled, *Marie Thérèse*, 347; Wright, *Serf, Seigneur, and Sovereign*, 50-54; Beales, *Joseph II*, 1: 352.
10 Beales, *Joseph II*, 1: 357-58.
11 Bled, *Marie-Thérèse,* 344; Beales, *Joseph II*, 1, 346-49, 356.

12   HHStA, HA, SB 7, JII to Leopold, 16 January 1777.
13   Wangermann, "Matte Morgenröte," in *Maria Theresia und ihre Zeit: eine Darstellung der Epoche von 1740-1780 aus Anlass der 200. Wiederkehr des Todestages der Kaiserin*, ed. Walter Koschatzky (Salzburg: Residenz Verlag 1979), 67-68.
14   Joseph Karniel, *Die Toleranzpolitik Kaiser Josephs II.* (Gerlingen: Bleicher, 1985), 204.
15   Bled, *Marie Thérèse,* 349; François Fejtö, *Joseph II: un Habsburg révolutionnaire*, new ed. (Paris: Quai Voltaire, 1994), 157; Blanning, *Joseph II*, 50-51.
16   For Joseph's views during the early years of the coregency concerning the paramount role of the military within society see Franz A. J. Szabo, "Competing Visions of Enlightened Absolutism: Security and Economic Development in the Reform Priorities of the Habsburg Monarchy after the Seven Years War," in *Miscellanea fontium historiae europaeae: Emlékkönyv H. Balázs Éva történészprofesszor 80. születésnapjára*, ed. János Kalmár (Budapest: ELTE, 1997), 191-200.
17   Wright, *Serf, Seigneur, and Sovereign*, 60-61.
18   Zinzendorf's diary entry of 16 August 1775 does not tally with other accounts but does suggest that in his tactics if not in his long-term goals, the emperor was making common cause with the noble landowners of Bohemia. HHStA, KA ZT, Band 18, 15 August 1775; Wright, *Serf, Seigneur, and Sovereign*, 51-52.
19   Karniel, *Die Toleranzpolitik Kaiser Josephs II.*, 184-207, 241-42.
20   *Prameny k nevolnickému povstání*, 707, 715. This document collection contains a number of reports from Bohemian lands of the Clary and Kinsky families.
21   LRRA, P 16/23, LK to EL, Laxenburg, 30 June 1775; *Prameny k nevolnickému povstání*, 733; Vladimír Bystrický, "Zprávy vyslanců Rýnské Falce a Bavorska ve Vídni o nevolnickém povstání v Čechách roku 1775," *Sborník archivních prací*, 42 no. 1 (1992): 30 (1 July 1775, Vienna).
22   Karniel, *Die Toleranzpolitik Kaiser Josephs II.*, 184-86.
23   *Prameny k nevolnickému povstání*, 806.
24   *Prameny k nevolnickému povstání*, 810-17, reports from July and August 1775.
25   LRRA, P 16/23, LK to EL, Laxenburg, 30 June 1775; HHStA, KA ZT, Band 18, 4 August 1775.
26   LRRA, P 16/23, LK to EL, Vienna, 20 October 1773; Alfred von Arneth, *Geschichte Maria Theresia's*, 9: 356; Emil Niederhauser, *The Emancipation of the Serfs in Eastern Europe*, trans. Paul Bődy (Highland Lakes, NJ: Social Science Monographs, Boulder, Colorado, 2004), 72.
27   LRRA, P 17/24, EL to LK, Kromau, 30 July 1777 and 2 August 1777.
28   LRRA, P 17/24, EL to LK, Kromau, 30 July 1777.
29   Karl Grünberg, Karl, *Die Bauernbefreiung und die Auflösung des gutsherrlich-bäuerlichen Verhältnisses in Böhmen* (Leipzig: Duncker und Humblot, 1894), vol. 2, esp. 284-89. Noted also by Moriz Robert von Bauer, *Die Landwirtschaft in Mähren vor Aufhebung der Untertänigkeit, 1781-1848* (Diss., Ludwig-Maximilians-Universität, Munich, 1907), 58-59.
30   LRRA, P 17/25, EL to LK, Kromau, 27 August 1779 and 28 August 1779.
31   LRRA, P 17/25, EL to LK, Kromau, 27 August 1779.
32   LRRA, P 16/22, LK to EL, Naples, 10 February 1770.
33   LRRA, P 16/22, EL to LK, Meseritsch, 15 February and 23 October 1771; LK to EL, 15 February 1771, Brünn.
34   P 16/23, EL to LK, 31 May 1772, Vienna.
35   Szabo, *Kaunitz and Enlightened Despotism*, 174-76.

36 This summary relies in large part upon discussions in Kerstin Schmal, *Die Pietas Maria Theresias im Spannungsfeld von Barock und Aufklärung: religiöse Praxis und Sendungsbewußtsein gegenüber Familie, Untertanen und Dynastie*, Mainzer Studien zur Neueren Geschichte 7 (Frankfurt am Main: Peter Lang, 2001), esp. 25-28.
37 Gutkas, *Kaiser Joseph II.*, 155.
38 Peter Hersche, *Der Spätjansenismus in Österreich* (Vienna: Österreichische Akademie der Wissenschaften, 1977), 50-64.
39 Virginia Ruth Mosser, "Strange Mercies: The Search for Miracles in the Habsburg Monarchy from the Reign of Leopold I to Joseph II (1658-1790)" (Diss., University of Virginia, 1998), 35.
40 Szabo, *Kaunitz and Enlightened Absolutism*, 220-28.
41 Blanning, *Joseph II*, 43.
42 Hersche, *Der Spätjansenismus*, 368-70.
43 Hersche, *Der Spätjansenismus*, 231.
44 Ivo Cerman, *Habsburgischer Adel und Aufklärung: Bildungsverhalten des Wiener Hofadels im 18. Jahrhundert* (Stuttgart: Franz Steiner, 2010), 450-51.
45 Hersche, "War Maria Theresia eine Jansenistin?," *Österreich in Geschichte und Literatur*, 15, no. 1 (1971), 14-25; Hersche, *Der Spätjansenismus*, 148-62; Schmal, *Pietas Maria Theresias*, 191-95.
46 Klingenstein, "Modes of Religious Tolerance and Intolerance in Eighteenth-Century Habsburg Politics," *Austrian History Yearbook* 24 (1993): 1-16.
47 Maria Theresia, *Politisches Testament*, ed. Josef Kallbrunner (Vienna: Verlag für Geschichte und Politik, 1952), 38.
48 Dries Vanysacker, *Cardinal Giuseppe Garampi, 1725-1792: an Enlightened Ultramontane* (Brussels: Institut Historique Belge de Rome; Turnhout: Brepols Publishers, 1995), 159; Paul P. Bernard, *Jesuits and Jacobins: Enlightenment and Enlightened Despotism in Austria* (Urbana, IL: University of Illinois Press, 1971), 12-14; Elisabeth Kovács, *Ultramontanismus und Staatskirchentum im theresianisch-josephinischen Staat: der Kampf der Kardinäle Migazzi und Franckenberg gegen den Wiener Professor der Kirchengeschichte Ferdinand Stöger* (Vienna: Wiener Dom-Verlag, 1975).
49 HHStA, KA ZT, Band 46, 30 July 1801. Also in Zinzendorf, *Wien von Maria Theresia bis zur Franzosenzeit: aus den Tagebüchern des Grafen Karl von Zinzendorf*, trans. Hans Wagner (Vienna: Wiener Bibliophilen Gesellschaft, 1972), 50.
50 Beales, "Christians and '*Philosophes*': the Case of the Austrian Enlightenment," in Beales, *Enlightenment and Reform in Eighteenth-Century Europe* (London: Tauris, 2005), 60-89; Philip Mansel, *Prince of Europe: the Life of Charles-Joseph de Ligne, 1735-1814* (London: Weidenfeld and Nicolson, 2003), 200-01.
51 Ernst Wangermann, *Aufklärung und staatsbürgerliche Erziehung: Gottfried van Swieten als Reformator des österreichischen Unterrichtswesens 1781-1791* (Vienna: Verlag für Geschichte und Politik, 1978), 14.
52 Wraxall, *Memoirs of the Courts of Berlin, Dresden, Warsaw, and Vienna*, 2: 248.
53 LRRA, P 16/13, Charles Liechtenstein to EL, Leitmeritz, 29 May 1778; P 16/18, note from Charles Liechtenstein to LK, Vienna, 27 February 1764.
54 LRRA, P 17/24, LK to EL, Vienna, 26 July 1778; LK to EL, Vienna, 16 August 1778.
55 Lady Mary Coke, *Letters and Journals*, 3: 340, Vienna, 22 December 1770.
56 *Briefe der Kaiserin Maria Theresia an ihre Kinder*, 1: 24, MT to Leopold, Innsbruck, s.d. (end of August 1765); Schmal, *Pietas Maria Theresias*, 84-86.
57 Maria Theresia's own devotional books, and those she urged upon her children, were sometimes on the papal index of prohibited books because of perceived Jansenist leanings, and her husband Franz Stephan had found quietist strains of the Catholic faith

attractive although he was also punctilious in outward observances. Hersche, *Der Spätjansenismus*, 150-51; Wandruszka, "Die Religiosität Franz Stephans von Lothringen" *Mitteilungen des Österreichischen Staatsarchivs* 12 (1959), 169-73.
58 LRRA, P 16/22, LK to EL, Naples, 17 April 1770.
59 Hersche, *Der Spätjansenismus,* 233-34.
60 Blanning, *Joseph II*, 48-49.
61 Ferdinand Maass, *Der Josephinismus: Quellen zu seiner Geschichte in Österreich in 1760-1790*, vols. 1-2 (Vienna: Verlag Herold, 1951-1953).
62 Blanning, *Joseph II*, 45.
63 Wangermann, "Josephinismus und katholische Glaube," in *Katholische Aufklärung und Josephinismus,* ed. Elisabeth Kovács (Vienna: Verlag für Geschichte und Politik, 1979), 335-36.
64 Beales, *Joseph II*, 2: 68-71; Wangermann, "Josephinismus und Katholischer Glaube," 332-33.
65 Hans Hollerweger, *Die Reform des Gottesdienstes zur Zeit des Josephinismus in Österreich*, ed. Bruno Kleinheyer and Hans Bernhard Meyer (Regensburg: Friedrich Pustet, 1976), 60, 69, 75.
66 Gutkas, "Kirchlich-sozialen Reformen," in *Österreich zur Zeit Kaiser Josephs II.: Mitregent Kaiserin Maria Theresias, Kaiser und Landesfürst, Ausstellung, Stift Melk, 29. März–2. Nov. 1980* (Vienna, Amt der Niederösterreichischen Landesregierung, Abt. 3/2, Kulturabt., 1980), 175; Schmal, *Pietas Maria Theresias*, 185-86.
67 Zinzendorf, *Aus den Jugendtagebüchern: 1747, 1752 bis 1763*, ed. Hans Wagner, Maria Breunlich, and Marieluise Mader (Vienna: Böhlau, 1997), 201, 571.
68 P. G. M. Dickson, *Finance and Government under Maria Theresia, 1740-1780* (New York: Oxford University Press, 1987), 1: 139.
69 Andreas Laun, "Die Moraltheologie im 18. Jahrhundert unter dem Einfluss von Jansenismus und Aufklärung," in *Katholische Aufklärung und Josephinismus,* ed. Elisabeth Kovács (Vienna: Verlag für Geschichte und Politik, 1979), 282-84.
70 LRRA, P 16/21, LK to EL, Naples, 26 September 1768 and 18 April 1769.
71 Abolition had already taken place in other countries. Measures taken in some lands had been abrupt and even brutal. Harold Action, *The Bourbons of Naples, 1734-1825* (London: Barnes and Noble, 1974), 118; Gutkas, *Kaiser Joseph II.*, 153.
72 In other towns of the monarchy the procedure took more time, as bishops chose to confer with the government before proceeding. Gutkas, *Kaiser Joseph II.*, 153; Kovács, "Josephinische Klosteraufhebungen 1782-1789," in *Österreich zur Zeit Kaiser Josephs II.*, 170.
73 Gutkas, *Kaiser Joseph II.*, 153; Beales, *Joseph II*, 2: 274.
74 Lady Mary Coke, *Letters and Journals*, 4: 235, 9 September 1773.
75 HHStA, KA ZT, Band 20, Vienna, 9 December 1775.
76 Many of the more serious measures were tested first by Habsburg authorities in Milan.
77 Kovács, "Josephinische Klosteraufhebungen 1782-1789," 171; Gutkas, *Kaiser Joseph II.*, 157.
78 Szabo, *Kaunitz and Enlightened Absolutism*, 222-23.
79 Szabo, *Kaunitz and Enlightened Absolutism*, 251.
80 Bled, *Marie Thérèse*, 167-69.
81 *Maria Theresia und Joseph II.: ihre Correspondenz*, 2: 152, JII to MT, Freiburg, 20 July 1777.
82 Guglia, *Maria Theresia*, 2: 338-42; Szabo, *Kaunitz and Enlightened Despotism*, 247-57; Beales, *Joseph II*, 1: 470-73.

83 Wangermann, "Matte Morgenröte," 69; Peter F. Barton, "Evangelische Christen der Toleranzzeit bauen Gemeinden in Österreich," in *Im Lichte der Toleranz: Aufsätze zur Toleranzgesetzgebung des 18. Jahrhunderts in den Reichen Joseph II., ihren Voraussetzungen und ihren Folgen* (Vienna: Institut für Protestantische Kirchengeschichte, 1981), 237.
84 Gutkas, *Kaiser Joseph II.*, 84; Wolf, *Aus dem Hofleben*, 310-11.
85 Cited in Beales, *Joseph II*, 1: 205.
86 N. W. Wraxall, *Memoirs of the Courts of Berlin, Dresden, Warsaw, and Vienna*, 2: 431.
87 SÚA, RAM AC, 11/22, JII to LK, s.d., s.l.; Peter F. Barton, "Toleranz und Toleranzpatente," in *Im Zeichen der Toleranz: Aufsätze zur Toleranzgesetzgebung des 18. Jahrhunderts im Reiche Joseph II.* (Vienna: Institut für Protestantische Kirchengeschichte, 1981), 253.
88 François-Xavier Feller, *Biographie universelle, ou dictionnaire historique des hommes* (Paris: J. Leroux, 1848), 4: 58.
89 LRRA, P 17/26, LK to EL, Vienna, 18 October 1780.
90 LRRA, P 17/26, LK to EL, Vienna, 21 October 1780.
91 Karniel, *Die Toleranzpolitik Kaiser Josephs II.*, 171.
92 For example, Blanning, *Joseph II*, 131; LRRA, P 17/24, LK to EL, Vienna, 11 August 1778.
93 Qtd. in Lucien Perey, *Histoire d'une grande dame au XVIIIe siècle: la Princesse Hélène de Ligne* (Paris: Calmann Lévy, 1888), 318.
94 Consternation was widespread within the Empire. Karl Otmar Aretin, *Das Alte Reich, 1648-1806* (Stuttgart: Klett-Cotta, 1997), 3: 180-83.
95 HHStA, KA ZT, Band 19, 29 April 1774.
96 Franz A. J. Szabo, "Austrian First Impressions of Ethnic Relations in Galicia: the Case of Governor Anton von Pergen," *Polin: Studies in Polish Jewry* 12 (1999): 53-54, 59-60; Horst Glassl, *Das österreichische Einrichtungswerk in Galizien 1772-1790* (Wiesbaden: O. Harrassowitz, 1975), 100, 107; Beales, *Joseph II*, 1: 363-64; Franz A. J. Szabo, "The Center and the Periphery: Echoes of the Diplomatic Revolution in the Administration of the Habsburg Monarchy, 1753-1773," in Marija Wakounig, Wolfgang Mueller, and Michael Portmann, eds., *Nation, Nationalitäten und Nationalismus im östlichen Europa: Festschrift für Arnold Suppan zum 65. Geburtstag* (Vienna: LIT Verlag, 2010), 9-10.
97 Paul P. Bernard, *Joseph II and Bavaria: Two Eighteenth-Century Attempts at German Unification* (The Hague: Martinus Nijhoff, 1965), 23; Blanning, *Joseph II*, 130-31.
98 Bernard, *Joseph II and Bavaria*, 7-11.
99 Bernard, *Joseph II and Bavaria*, 69-70.
100 Bernard, *Joseph II and Bavaria*, 106.
101 HHStA, HA SB 7, JII to Leopold, 18 July 1778.
102 Bernard, *Joseph II and Bavaria*, 123-25.
103 Bernard, *Joseph II and Bavaria*, 133.
104 Wraxall, *Memoirs of the Courts of Berlin, Dresden, Warsaw, and Vienna*, 2: 209-13.
105 Beales, *Joseph II*, 1: 421.
106 Kotasek, *Feldmarschall*, 152, 162, 168.
107 Beales, *Joseph II*, 1: 414-19.
108 Blanning, *Joseph II*, 152-53.
109 Blanning, *Joseph II*, 147-51; Gutkas, *Kaiser Joseph II.*, 428.
110 HHStA, HA SB 4, MT to JII, 6 May 1778; 15 May 1778; 29 May 1778.
111 LRRA, P 17/24, EL to LK, Kromau, 10 October 1778.

112 LRRA, P 17/24, EL to LK, Eisgrub, 27 July 1778. Charles Liechtenstein's letters to EL from 1778 are found in P 16/13.
113 LRRA, P 17/24, EL to LK, Eisgrub, 18 July 1778.
114 LRRA, P 17/24, EL to LK, Eisgrub, 18 July and 24 July 1778.
115 LRRA, P 17/24, EL to LK, Eisgrub, 28 July 1778.
116 LRRA, P 17/24, EL to LK, Eisgrub, 28 July and 30 July 1778.
117 LRRA, P 17/24, EL to LK, Eisgrub, 13 August and 18 August 1778.
118 LRRA, P 17/24, EL to LK, Kromau, 19 August 1778.
119 LRRA, P 17/24, EL to LK, Kromau, 21 August 1778.
120 LRRA, P 17/24, EL to LK, Kromau, 23 September 1778.
121 Bernard, *Joseph II and Bavaria*, 123.
122 LRRA, P 17/24, EL to LK, quoting JII's letter, Kromau, 30 September 1778.
123 LRRA, P 17/24, EL to LK, [Kromau], 8 October 1778.
124 LRRA, P 17/24, EL to LK, [Kromau] 2 October 1778; 6 October 1778; Feldsberg, 13 October 1778.
125 LRRA, P 17/24, LK to EL, Vienna, 18 July 1778.
126 LRRA, P 17/24, LK to EL, Vienna, 18 July 1778; 22 July 1778; 26 July 1778; 19 September 1778; 2 October 1778.
127 LRRA, P 17/24, LK to EL, Vienna, 18 July 1778.
128 LRRA, P 17/24, LK to EL, 22 September 1778; EL to LK, Kromau, 23 Sept. 1778.
129 LRRA, P 17/24, LK to EL, Vienna, 20 July 1778; 26 July 1778; 8 August 1778.
130 LRRA, P 17/24, LK to EL, Vienna, 26 July 1778.
131 LRRA, P 17/24, LK to EL, 16 August 1778 and 19 August 1778; EL to LK, Kromau, 22 September 1778.
132 Bernard, *Joseph II and Bavaria*, 15, 18-19; Michael Hochedlinger, *Austria's Wars of Emergence: War, State and Society in the Habsburg Monarchy 1683-1797* (London: Pearson Education, 2003).
133 LRRA, P 17/24, LK to EL, Vienna, 15 July 1778; EL to LK, Eisgrub, 18 July 1778; LK to EL, Vienna, 15 July 1778 and 3 August 1778. The publication, 21 pages in length, is cited in *Der Bayerische Erbfolge-Krieg 1778/1779 oder Der Kampf der messerscharfen Federn* (2007) by Jürgen Ziechmann, who has compiled a list of almost fifty contemporary publications, signed or anonymous, that appeared prior to and during the war (205-10).
134 LRRA, P 17/24, LK to EL, 25 September 1778.
135 LRRA, P 17/24, EL to LK, Kromau, 26 September and 30 September 1778.
136 LRRA, P 17/24, EL to LK, Kromau, 3 October 1778.
137 LRRA, P 17/24, LK to EL, [Vienna,] 3 October 1778.
138 LRRA, P 17/24, LK to EL, 9 October 1778 and 12 October 1778.
139 LRRA, P 17/24, LK to EL, 14 October 1778.
140 LRRA, P 17/24, EL to LK, Kromau, 22 and 26 September 1778 and 10 October 1778.
141 LRRA, P 17/24, EL to LK, Kromau, 28 September 1778 and 30 September 1778.
142 LRRA, P 17/24, LK to EL, 5 October 1778; EL to LK, Feldsberg, 18 October 1778; Christopher Duffy, "The Irish at Hochkirch, 14 October 1758," *The Irish Sword* 12, no. 48 (Summer 1976): 220.
143 Szabo, "Perspective from the Pinnacle," 253.
144 LRRA, P 17/24, EL to LK, Feldsberg, 9 October 1777 and 11 October 1777.
145 LRRA, P 17/24, LK to EL, Vienna, 29 July 1778.
146 Joseph Karniel, *Die Toleranzpolitik Kaiser Josephs II.*, trans. Leo Koppel (Gerlingen: Bleicher, 1985), 367; *Die Fürstenberger: 800 Jahre Herrschaft und Kultur in Mitteleu-*

ropa, ed. Erwein H. Eltz and Arno Strohmeyer (Korneuburg: Ueberreuter, 1994), 281; Beales, *Joseph II,* 2: 188-89.
147 LRRA, P 17/24, EL to LK, Feldsberg, 15 October 1778 and 16 October 1778.
148 Christopher Duffy, *The Austrian Army in the Seven Years War* (Rosemont, Ill.: Emperor's Press 2000), 1: 169.
149 LRRA, P 16/13, Charles Liechtenstein to EL, Leitmeritz, May 22, 1778.
150 SOAL-D, RACA, carton 54, JC to her husband, 30 July 1778.
151 *Briefe der Kaiserin Maria Theresia an ihre Kinder,* 2: 148, MT to Ferdinand, 2 October [1778].
152 LRRA, P 17/24, EL to LK, Eisgrub, 24 July 1778.
153 LRRA, P 17/24, LK to EL, Vienna, 11 August 1778.
154 LRRA, P 17/24, LK to EL, 24 September 1778.
155 LRRA, P 17/24, LK to EL, Vienna, 11 August 1778.
156 Wraxall, *Memoirs of the Courts of Berlin, Dresden, Warsaw, and Vienna,* 2: 335.
157 LRRA, P 17/24, LK to EL, 29 September 1778.
158 LRRA, P 17/24, LK to EL, 25 September 1778, 29 September 1778, 10 October 1778.
159 LRRA, P 17/24, LK to EL, 24 September 1778. Much later, the Napoleonic wars saw Bohemian and Moravian territory become the battlefield for conflicts on a much larger scale. Most famously, Kaunitz property was the scene of the momentous Battle of Austerlitz in 1805.
160 LRRA, P 17/24, LK to EL, 5 October 1778.
161 LRRA, P 17/24, LK to EL, 24 September 1778.
162 LRRA, P 17/24, LK to EL, 2 October 1778; EL to LK, Kromau, 30 Sept. 1778 and Feldsberg, 13 October 1778.
163 LRRA, P 17/24, LK to EL, 24 September 1778 and 2 October 1778.
164 Beales, *Joseph II,* 2: 105.
165 LRRA, P 17/25, EL to LK, Kromau, 9 October 1779.
166 Beales, *Joseph II,* 1: 430-31.
167 LRRA, P 17/26, LK to EL, Vienna, 9 August 1780 and 23 August 1780.
168 Beales, *Joseph II,* 1: 431-32; Gutkas, *Kaiser Joseph II.,* 216.
169 Beales's account admirably sorts out the many issues involved. Beales, *Joseph II,* 1: 431-38.
170 SÚA, RAM AC, 11/22, JII to LK, Mogilow [Mogilew], 3 June 1780.
171 LRRA, P 17/26, EL to LK, Kromau, 8 August 1780.
172 LRRA, P 17/26, EL to LK, Kromau, 19 August 1780.
173 HHStA, HA SB 3, Marie Antoinette to MT, 13 July 1780; MT to Marie Antoinette, Schönbrunn, 31 August 1780.
174 LRRA, P 17/26, EL to LK, Feldsberg, 23 October 1780, 25 October 1780, and 31 October 1780.
175 Karajan, Theodor Georg von, *Maria Theresia und Joseph II. während der Mitregentschaft: ein Vortrag gehalten in der feierlichen Sitzung der Kaiserlichen Akademie der Wissenschaften,* ed. Theodor Georg von Karajan (Vienna: K. K. Hof- und Staatsdr., 1865); "Beilagen," Kaunitz to MT, 18 September 1779, response to a message from MT, 39.
176 LRRA, P 17/24, EL to LK, 10 October 1778.
177 LRRA, P 17/25, EL to LK, 22 May [1779]; EL to LK, Eisgrub, 15 August 1779.
178 SOAL-D, RACA, carton 54, JC to her husband Prince Clary, Eisgrub, 16 August 1779.
179 LRRA, P 17/26, LK to EL, Vienna, 14 August 1780.
180 LRRA, P 17/24, EL to LK, Baden [bei Wien], 13 September 1777.
181 SÚA, RAM AC, 11/22, JII to LK, note, s.l., s.d.

182 Blanning, *Joseph II*, 61; Wolf, *Fürstin Eleonore Liechtenstein*, 140.
183 LRRA, P 16/23, LK to EL, Vienna, 16 October 1773.
184 LRRA, P 17/24, LK to EL, Vienna, 16 October 1777.
185 LRRA, P 17/26, LK to EL, Vienna, 26 October 1780.
186 Jean Bérenger, *Joseph II: serviteur de l'état* (Paris: Fayard, 2007), 548.
187 Gutkas, *Kaiser Joseph II.*, esp. 455.
188 Blanning, *Joseph II*, 60.
189 Marie-Antoinette, *Correspondance secrète entre Marie-Thérèse et le Comte de Mercy-Argenteau, avec les lettres de Marie-Thérèse et de Marie-Antoinette,* ed. Alfred von Arneth and A. Geffroy (Paris: Firmin-Didot, 1874-1875), 2: 330, MT to Count Mercy, 4 May 1775.
190 LRRA, P 17/24, EL to LK, Feldsburg, 13 October 1778.

Chapter 5

1780–1790: Politics under Joseph II's Sole Rulership

Joseph II was deeply shaken by the death of his mother Maria Theresia in November 1780. After an evening gathering held many months later, in August 1781, at the residence of Leopoldine Liechtenstein, Eleonore Liechtenstein scoffed at the emperor's recollections of his mother's death and his depictions of the melancholy and desolation he experienced upon his return to an empty Vienna after his travels. Leopoldine Liechtenstein had just lost her husband, who died during a trip to Spa and Paris. As Eleonore explained, the emperor claimed to be sympathetic, describing "what it cost him in coming back to no longer find his mother, who was always the one object that made him return with pleasure, and then the details about her death, about his difficulty in putting a brave face on what he suffered. My sister-in-law claims that she saw a tear on his cheeks, I think it was perspiration, I did not see this precious tear, and I do not believe it was there."[1] Joseph's biographers have affirmed that his sorrow was unfeigned. Once the sharpest grief subsided, however, he approached his role as sole ruler with enthusiasm, hope, and resolution, understandably relieved to be free of the empress's overbearing presence.[2] Full responsibility now rested with him. He was no longer the restive son pushing against restrictions imposed by his mother. He could undertake the reformation of government and society that the empress's authority had hindered. Maria Theresia had bequeathed to Joseph a stable and relatively prosperous realm. In the early 1780s, fresh to his task, the emperor was optimistic about prospects for reform, professing to believe that he could overcome opposition through rational argument and the demonstrable correctness of his principles.

For several months, the newly independent sovereign made few changes, creating an illusion of continuity with Maria Theresia's reign.[3] A flurry of activity succeeded this initial lull, accompanied by a barrage of edicts, as the enterprising emperor embarked on a course of relentless reform and innovation. Joseph worked incessantly, as Zinzendorf's diaries from the 1780s make clear. Contemporaries complained that he introduced changes too rapidly, without proper preparation, and then failed to follow through or to adapt them to real conditions. In observations recorded during a visit to Vienna in 1784, Joseph's brother Leopold remarked several times that Joseph was unaccustomed to systematic labor. The emperor liked to issue orders, Leopold observed, without concerning himself much with their execution.[4] By contrast, Joseph's attention to some details of his subjects' daily lives seemed excessive to many contemporaries. In the words of the historian Blanning, the emperor was "a terrible busy-body who could not mind his own business." He was in a hurry. During his ten years of sole rule he issued 6,206 decrees, twice the number published during the previous forty years under his mother.[5] An idealist who knew that the monarchy stood in need of improvement on many fronts, once Joseph had determined that a particular course of action was theoretically correct he was likely to disregard practical difficulties and usually declined to compromise. Joseph found it difficult to maintain even a show of respect for those whose opinions differed from his own. To his brother Leopold he frequently remarked that, regardless of distraction or resistance, he would invariably persist in the approach he had chosen ("always just proceeding on my course"). Branding his critics as obscurantist or merely ignorant, he generally conflated "natural law" with state law and assumed that state interests should be the highest priority of his subjects without exception.[6]

During most of his decade as sole ruler, Joseph did not enjoy robust health. Of relatively small and delicate frame, he often drove himself to exhaustion, particularly during his travels, which were extensive and frequent. By 1782, he reported to his brother Leopold that he had lost much of his hair, and he eventually resorted to a wig.[7] Contemporaries found the emperor's appearance far from prepossessing by the mid-1780s. His skin took on a red-brown tinge and his cheeks sagged. Leopold reported in 1784 that Joseph was worried about his health, which had suffered from multiple bouts with "the French sickness."[8] Leopold believed that Joseph's stern, unyielding approach to governing exacerbated the pressures on his health. An impatient, driving man, Joseph was persuaded that his servitors never worked with sufficient vigor and he became frustrated and ill tempered. Leopold found Joseph's complaints and self-pity tiresome.[9]

Increased power and freedom of action in no way lessened the emperor's irascibility vis-à-vis even his closest associates. Those who worked in direct contact with him, including Lacy, Rosenberg, and three husbands of the *Dames* who continued to serve at court or in the military—Prince Clary, Ernst Kaunitz, and Charles Liechtenstein—frequently found attendance on their impatient sovereign to be taxing. Joseph liberated himself almost entirely from the tutelage of Chancellor Kaunitz, who grew bitter and critical as he found himself pushed to the sideline.[10] Late in 1783, the emperor issued a circular (his so-called "pastoral letter"), publicly excoriating state employees for their laxness and demanding unquestioning obedience to all his directives.[11] When Leopold visited Vienna in 1784, he found widespread discontent among employees because of the constantly changing orders, criticisms, and threats. According to Leopold, employees at all levels realized that they could never labor hard enough to suit their imperial taskmaster.[12]

During the decade Ernst Kaunitz served both as Joseph's *Obersthofmarschall* and as director of buildings and public works. In the past the latter employment had required only moderate exertion. But under Joseph II there were few sinecures. Leopoldine Kaunitz knew that her husband lacked the expertise and physical capacity to master the complex tasks and extensive travel Joseph required of him. In mid-July 1783 she described for Eleonore Ernst's responsibility for all court buildings of the hereditary lands. The emperor was treating Ernst well, Leopoldine wrote, "but I am afraid that this expansion of his employment will force him to be always on the road." Two days later she wrote that she feared imperial ruses (*pièges*), whereby the emperor would manipulate Ernst as a means of entrapping and punishing other employees. The physical challenges of the position were too great for her husband; "it is moreover such a vast area . . . construction works in the sea at Trieste and Fiume, etc., dikes and bridges on the Danube, Prague, Brünn, Gratz, etc., how can anyone be responsible for all that, how can one be answerable for all that?"[13] Many years later, during Leopoldine Kaunitz's final illness in 1795, she confided to Zinzendorf her belief that the onset of her husband Ernst's deafness could be traced to the physical hardships of his employment under Joseph II, his "zeal for the service of Emperor Joseph."[14] The peevish imperial master of hunts Prince Clary had his own difficulties with the emperor. On 18 August 1783 at a service at the Schottenkirche marking the second anniversary of the death of Leopoldine Liechtenstein's husband Franz Joseph, Leopoldine Kaunitz found Josepha Clary in tears and learned that Prince Clary had left town early in the morning, without attending properly to his duties as master of the hunt or seeking the requisite imperial permission to absent himself. Leopoldine feared a rupture: "it is certain that something has happened and that he has received an affront from the Emperor today."[15]

Prince Charles Liechtenstein's difficulties with his imperial commander, mentioned earlier, likewise continued although after Maria Theresia's death he no longer struggled with the complexities of a dual allegiance. For Charles a military career represented traditional, personal service to his prince, and he easily took offense when he felt slighted. Thus in 1783, when he received no summons to participate in military training camps and judged that he would receive no responsible post in the event of military action, Charles sought an audience with the emperor and asked for permission to travel in Italy for four months. Charles made his request even in the face of an ongoing crisis with Russia over Catherine's annexation of Crimea (noted below) that could have required a military response. Such an impulsive exit by a senior military officer excited comment. Josepha Clary considered Charles's action to be an act of folly, "a terrible blunder." Unsurprisingly, Joseph was perplexed at least initially. He told Ernst Kaunitz that he pitied Eleonore, whose fortunes were linked with such a muleheaded individual (*une si mauvaise tête*).[16] As noted in chapter 1, Charles hoped this trip to Italy would be therapeutic. His poor health was owing at least in part to earlier bouts with venereal disease, and Charles did not publicize this more serious purpose in traveling.

Eleonore routinely assumed that the emperor deliberately slighted Charles as imperial revenge for some action or statement of her own that caused displeasure. But Joseph II's rudeness was felt broadly and almost at random by his servitors, including top military commanders, who were noblemen sensitive to any impairment of their honor. The emperor appeared to take pleasure in dressing down his generals and humiliating them in front of their subordinates.[17] Eleonore blamed the emperor for malice where none was really present, only an ingrained insouciance regarding the feelings of others, or at most overzealousness in fending off possible accusations of favoritism toward friends and toward the privileged orders. In summer 1781 Leopoldine Kaunitz quoted to her sister a note from the emperor that ended with the pleasant comment that nowhere could one be as comfortable as with friends. "O God," exclaimed Eleonore with characteristic energy, "he [the emperor] a friend, he to profane this sacred name, if friends were like him, one would have to forsake the world entirely, one would need to hide in the trees, it would be better to live with bears and lions."[18] The times when the emperor seemed to ignore or even avoid these special friends generally proved to be the result of simple thoughtlessness or preoccupation with political issues. This was a predictable feature of his fickle temper, Eleonore wrote in 1781, "which comes from the inconsistencies in his character, and the lack of feeling that animates his actions." A year later, from her tranquil residence in Kromau, Eleonore noted phlegmatically, "The conduct of the emperor is singular, neither his attentions nor his neglect are of any greater significance one than the other, so long as we have nothing for which to reproach ourselves."[19]

This was a hustling, forceful individual with whom the *Dames*, Lacy, and Rosenberg met for conversation and companionship. But in written communications, Joseph continued to express graciously his appreciation for the personal interest all the women took in him. From Pisa in January 1784, in a letter to Lacy that was intended for the women as well, Joseph complimented his friends in Vienna as he described Angelika Kauffman, a painter from southwest Germany with whom he became acquainted in Rome. Among several artists he had met, she in particular had pleased him. "She is a pleasant and excellent Swabian," he wrote, "it seems that a special destiny interests me in the females of that country, and it has been my good fortune to encounter only those who do not abuse my weakness for them." Joseph instructed Lacy to tell the *Dames* "that I know well that they have no need of me, but that for my part I need their society like daily bread."[20]

As Joseph assumed full power in late 1780, the meetings of the *société* continued without interruption. The mood of these gatherings grew somewhat more sober now. Joseph was in deadly earnest about his role as sovereign, keen to remedy the monarchy's deficiencies. Paradoxically, with Maria Theresia's brooding presence removed, much of the lightheartedness of Joseph's social forays also seemed to evaporate. Maria Theresia had grown increasingly somber in her assessments of her son, her expressions of disapproval ever more plaintive as she approached the end of her life. Although she lacked her son's facile intelligence, the empress had possessed some strengths that her son did not have, including a practical outlook that acknowledged and forgave shortcomings of both officials and subjects and a winning personality. She had bequeathed to her son a monarchy that had grown more prosperous during her reign of forty years. If she had been very cautious, she had also been realistic. But less than a year after Maria Theresia's demise, noting sadly how few people noted the name day of "the great Maria Theresia, so grand, so noble, so good, so beneficent," Leopoldine Kaunitz wrote to her sister, "If anyone thinks of it, I do not know, but it is scarcely spoken of, she has passed away, she can no longer help anyone, and how happy one was to please her!"[21]

In August 1781 Leopoldine Kaunitz remarked to Joseph that she had liked him better as coregent, "as a poor young hereditary prince."[22] However, there was no slackening in the women's enthusiasm for their special imperial affiliation. Pleasure fairly radiates from the pages of Leopoldine Liechtenstein's letters to Josepha Clary (and intended for broader circulation) from Spa during her family's visit there in summer 1781, where she enjoyed the special attentions of the emperor. Her sojourn had coincided with Joseph's own visit to Belgium, and as a close associate, she had basked in the glow of the emperor's fame and initial popularity there. At Spa Leopoldine Liechtenstein first received a surprise visit from Joseph's Belgian representatives, Archduchess Marie Christine and her husband Albert. Spa was buzzing with gossip about the activities of these newsworthy guests, Leopoldine reported. At the Vauxhall gaming tables crowds grew as the presence of these personages in Spa became known. Several days later Leopoldine reported with obvious relish the special visit her household received from the emperor himself. Joseph had arrived unexpectedly early, a practice he particularly enjoyed, entering the city on foot and ahead of his equipage, which had been damaged en route. His first stop was at the house occupied by the Liechtenstein family (Leopoldine, her husband Franz Joseph, and her two older daughters). The emperor accepted an invitation to dine informally, "absolutely as a family party [*absolument en famille*]," as Leopoldine reported. Leopoldine had been at church when the emperor arrived, and although she had heard the stir of excitement, she had dutifully remained in the church until the service ended ("as for myself, who think that God must come before all else, I finished hearing my mass, right to its finish"). She had then hurried back to her lodgings to greet the emperor, who inquired with interest about the rest of Leopoldine's family and applauded her plan to visit Paris. She and her party tried to calm and placate the enthusiastic crowds that gathered to see this interesting visitor: "they are already coming from everywhere to attend us, in order to know what they can do for His Majesty, it is difficult to make them understand that they should remain calm and omit all manner of display."[23]

When Grand Duke Leopold visited Vienna in 1784 and recorded his observations, he found the *société* little changed from his earlier visit of 1778. Leopold's distaste for the association was likewise unchanged. The group was Joseph's only routine social outlet, Leopold recorded with disgust. The emperor attended no balls or festivals. Typically Joseph took leave of Leopold each evening after theater performances had ended around 9:30 to meet with the *Dames*. At these gatherings the emperor declaimed to the women, monopolizing the conversation to the exclusion of all others including Lacy and Rosenberg. The women were bigoted and elderly, Leopold wrote (by this time the oldest women of the group, Josepha Clary and Sidonia Kinsky, were in their mid-fifties), and they loved to talk about politics and policy and to offer advice. Unflattering as always in his observations, Leopold reported that Joseph was dissatisfied with this group, as he was with all his contacts. Leopold's comments about his brother's activities had their customary jaundiced tone; but possibly Joseph was not especially gallant in his observations and let drop snide remarks about his staid circle of friends for Leopold's amusement.[24]

As Joseph's reforms moved forward, within the circle of *Dames* the optimistic Josepha Clary and politically savvy Leopoldine Liechtenstein were most receptive to Joseph's viewpoint or at least were willing to express complaisance during gatherings. Josepha was a friendly soul, eager to please the emperor. Leopoldine Kaunitz once remarked that Josepha worried constantly lest the group should do too little for the emperor whereas Leopoldine Kaunitz herself was cautious about doing too much and inadvertently loosing a stream of imperial mockery upon all the *Dames*. Thus in an episode in October 1781, Josepha had worried needlessly about the emperor's supposed aloofness ("the alleged sulking"), fearing that the *Dames* had somehow given offense. Again in summer 1782, when the group did not see the emperor for an extended period, Josepha was afraid the emperor was angry with his friends. In Leopoldine Kaunitz's words, "she [Josepha Clary] wore herself out in examining her conscience to determine if we have not done, or said, or written something."[25]

Leopoldine Liechtenstein was the most flexible in outlook among the women, willing to consider newly fashionable ideas and influenced and informed by her close friendship with Lacy, the enthusiast for Rousseau.[26] Her friends noted that in most situations she accepted changes as they came. She was also the least constrained in her friendship with the emperor, deliberately discounting the awkward fact of his exalted position. In late August 1782, sympathizing with the emperor after lengthy state visits by Russian dignitaries had exhausted him and an eye infection had plagued him, Leopoldine Liechtenstein invited Joseph (sending word by way of Josepha Clary) to relax at Eisgrub for several days virtually as a private individual: "all of us together would do our best to forget that he is a sovereign and that there are any other [people] in the world." Although sometimes the emperor visited and dined with group members quite informally Eleonore, more traditional in outlook than her sister-in-law, was surprised and perplexed by Leopoldine Liechtenstein's forwardness. "It is a lovely thing to have a warm heart," she commented to her sister. "She does all this with the best possible intention, but how can one say such things?" Leopoldine Kaunitz, less apprehensive, replied that Leopoldine Liechtenstein surely was jesting when she made her proposal, and the emperor would have taken it in that spirit.[27] In a fundamental sense Eleonore's viewpoint was more realistic, for the relationship between the *Dames* and the emperor was a thoroughly unequal one, as Lacy's cautionary remarks reminded them. When in summer 1781 Eleonore was particularly annoyed about the emperor's treatment of her husband Charles, Lacy had urged her to remain even-tempered: "he said, what would you do, he is your master, your possessions and your children are under his rule."[28] More than once the women cited Lacy's remark concerning friendship with members of the imperial family, "one should not fraternize [*se familiariser*] with lions."[29] But Leopoldine Liechtenstein was an enterprising woman, energetic and open to new impressions. Eleonore sent to her sister one of Leopoldine Liechtenstein's letters from her trip to France with the comment, "she has an unusual talent for stamping her personality on objects and events, and for describing them with admirable clarity and system, she would be capable of producing journals superior to many that we have."[30]

At times Leopoldine Kaunitz and Eleonore were sharp critics of the emperor's policies. Leopoldine Kaunitz happily engaged in the cut and thrust of political debate, both in gatherings of the *société* and other social settings. Throughout the decade Zinzendorf continued to report lively exchanges he had with Leopoldine Kaunitz in his diary. On several occasions in 1783, for example, he commented almost at random: "I talked with Madame de Kaunitz about abolition of tariffs"; or again, "Madame de Kaunitz pitched into me vigorously about the criminal code. . . . Madame de K. described to us the distribution of alms to the poor, which took place today for the first time"; or again in July 1785, "At the lord chamberlain's [Rosenberg] . . . Madame de Kaunitz talked about freedom of commerce among nations."[31] Of the five *Dames*, Eleonore remained the most resolutely conservative in outlook. She detested the Encyclopedists and spoke scathingly of the perfidy of fashionable modern writers.[32]

As he had been during the coregency, the emperor was regular in his attendance at evening gatherings even when only one or two of the women were available in Vienna. Having no established summer residence away from Vienna, Leopoldine Kaunitz frequently found herself providing conversation and company for the emperor without the group's full contingent of members. She did her best to call in reinforcements, urging Sidonia Kinsky and Josepha Clary to drive into town from Sidonia's summer retreat at Weidlingau and sending messages to Lacy and Rosenberg. The emperor was a persevering visitor. For example, he responded amicably after calling in vain at Leopoldine Kaunitz's residence one night in August 1781: "I [Leopoldine] was at my father-in-law's [Chancellor Kaunitz], where I spent the evening; during this time the Emperor stopped twice at my door around 8 o'clock and before 10, and so this morning I sent him my apologies in the most ridiculous note, telling him at the same time that I was going to Weidlingau . . . He sent me back a very nice card that I will take to the *Dames*, in which he says that he did not know la Clary [Josepha Clary] was at Weidlingau and that he will try to see them [referring to Sidonia Kinsky as well] if he can."[33] Typical of Leopoldine Kaunitz's occasional predicaments was her good-natured lament in October 1785: "As for myself, it is truly a misfortune, it is I who have to stand in for the society." She marveled at the emperor's constancy: "it must bore him to death, what can one say when everything has been said . . . I know that in his place I would not hold out." One evening she had been completely alone with Joseph and Rosenberg, but the next evening proved to be "more brilliant" because Josepha Clary and Lacy arrived "to offer us reinforcements."[34] Leopoldine Liechtenstein was a particularly valuable resource for the group, indefatigable, sophisticated, and invariably able to suggest lively topics of conversation. Leopoldine Kaunitz referred to Leopoldine Liechtenstein in September 1785 as the "mistress of the soirées" and Eleonore, preparing for her own return to Vienna from Meseritsch a month later, was glad to learn that Leopoldine Liechtenstein too would be back in the capital; "it is she who is the mainstay, not only the most solid but also the most useful." Since the emperor had come to power, Eleonore wrote, she herself and the remaining *Dames* had become like the oracles that lost their force with the birth of Jesus Christ.[35]

The *société* remained an implausible, idiosyncratic group. The emperor had banished from his court not only his dead mother's female friends (to end what he called "the false Spirit [*faux Esprit*] of this Republic of women," a decision that, as he put it, caused "a great outcry . . . I do not concern myself at all") but also his sisters.[36] He lacked an empress to assume those functions that normally pertained to female members of ruling families. Often he relied on the *Dames*, especially Eleonore Liechtenstein and Leopoldine Kaunitz, for practical assistance at important court events. During the festivities attendant upon state visits, occasional ceremonies and celebrations, and the court's summer visits to Laxenburg, the emperor assumed that the *Dames*—together with other court ladies, of course—would be among the participants, and they viewed this activity as obligatory. In summer 1784 Leopoldine Kaunitz described prospects for her stint in Laxenburg as being rather like death; the time would infallibly come but the actual date remained unknown and was sure to be a disagreeable surprise.[37] Occasionally the emperor showed some sheepishness about his dependence on this oddly assorted coterie. In September 1785, as Eleonore was about to leave Vienna for a visit to Feldsberg, where Leopoldine Liechtenstein was hosting a select group of men and women to enjoy hunts, scenery, and gossip, Eleonore asked the emperor good-humoredly to furnish her with a few tidbits of news to take to the assembled society. Joseph's irritated response had been that he knew nothing himself (possibly the issue in question was Joseph's renewed attempt to acquire Bavarian land and Frederick II's response, described in chapter 6).[38] About a week later, Eleonore told Leopoldine Kaunitz that Lacy had managed to spoil an entire evening's conversation by cautioning the emperor about his disclosures to the women ("because he said to the Emperor that he was telling us too much, and to us [he said] that we ought to be more circumspect").[39] The women held their peace quite deliberately—if with difficulty—when they could sense the futility of inquisitiveness or familiarity. What the *Dames* regarded as prudence and discretion was interpreted by Leopold during his visit in 1784 as incapacity and vacuousness. Leopold believed the women were incapable of making use of any confidential information they might receive from Joseph. And for Leopold this was the sole advantage of his brother's association with the odd little group.[40]

More so than in earlier years, the women had to tread softly. In summer 1781, for example, Leopoldine Kaunitz noted that the emperor seemed restless and obstinate, and so it was not a good time to put forward ideas that contradicted his.[41] The women carefully concealed their disappointment if the emperor failed to appear as expected at a gathering. In summer 1786, when after a break in the visiting routine Rosenberg alerted Leopoldine Kaunitz that the emperor would soon visit, she remarked to her sister (Eleonore Liechtenstein was absent in Kromau) that she was curious as to how the evening would go; "I confess that after such a long absence without any mark of regard, despite the intimacy with which we are honored, I am curious about the soirée . . . you can well imagine that we will be gentle and submissive, like dogs that are made to dance on a rope."[42]

While Maria Theresia lived, those individuals close to the throne, and probably a significant proportion of the monarchy's population at large, entertained high if somewhat indistinct hopes for the future reign of the ambitious young sovereign, as noted previously. It could be argued that at least in part it was owing to Maria Theresia's restraint on Joseph during the coregency that observers were so favorably impressed and optimistic about his wisdom and capacity to rule. As the 1780s began Joseph was popular with all classes of his subjects. He took part in their lives in demonstrative ways. His presence and assistance at emergencies such as floods or fires in Vienna was a typical and traditional gesture often made by both sovereigns and paternalistic landowners. But Joseph went further, traveling extensively throughout his lands and publicizing his concern for even minor injustices committed by his officials. He accepted petitions for redress from his subjects without exception, from every corner of the monarchy. In Vienna, even the lowliest of inhabitants could seek an audience with the emperor.

Joseph II's reign conformed in many particulars to the political classification many historians have christened "enlightened despotism." The ascription seems indisputable, even though there exists no unanimity of opinion concerning the functional reality of enlightened rulership. The designation implies that a given ruler is actuated by laudable motives, whereas it has also been argued that the public "enlightened" postures and actions of three prominent candidates for the accolade, Catherine II, Frederick II, and Joseph II himself, merely served to mask innovations intended to suppress domestic dissent and to promote military strength and relative economic and diplomatic clout vis-à-vis neighboring states.[43] If as the emperor sought increasingly tight control over his subjects a principal goal of his efforts was to increase the military might of his lands, he also bolstered his reform plans with arguments that were strongly infused with humanitarian language and goals. Joseph believed that in the hands of a rational, selfless ruler such as himself the welfare of the state was identical with the welfare of all its subjects, and so he pushed aside, restricted, or put an end to intermediate authorities, both groups and individuals, that interfered with the central government's direct link to all subjects of the monarchy. He discountenanced those groups that claimed a separate corporate identity or legal status, such as the nobility, the church, the traditional regional administrative bodies if they functioned semi-independently and represented the interests of the nobility, and even guilds, local civic and charitable groups, and masonic orders. These diluted the subjects' loyalty to the state. When status and property were at stake, such groups seemed likely to look to their own interests, not the state's. The emperor sought also to unify the many diverse traditions and legal systems of the monarchy's territories that impeded the expanding power of a unitary state.

Joseph achieved many successes through unremitting labor and initially by winning support for elements of his agenda among the populace at all levels.[44]

But a reform program that attacked the interests of so many powerful groups was bound to encounter resistance. By the end of his reign, the emperor had weakened his position and jeopardized his entire reform program through an ambitious foreign policy that limited his ability to respond to discontent in his own lands, provoked by his fast-paced and occasionally very unpopular reforms. He had alienated or disillusioned many of his close advisors and servitors and not only churchmen and noblemen but also wide, vocal swathes of the population, a result both of his own miscalculations and of the sheer force of adverse circumstances.[45]

Less than a year after Joseph became sole ruler, he took two dramatic actions that disconcerted the *Dames*. Through a series of decrees, mostly published in 1781 and 1782, he eased censorship of published materials; and he granted toleration to Protestant and Greek Orthodox subjects (though by no means equality with Catholics), together with limited emancipation for Jews.

As noted previously, prior to these changes Vienna had not been a hermetically sealed intellectual environment devoid of entertaining, enlightening, and controversial publications. Certainly the Englishman Wraxall had been devastating in his assessment of the situation in the late 1770s: "It is hardly credible how many books and productions of every species, and in every language, are proscribed by her [Maria Theresia]. Not only Voltaire and Rousseau are included in the list, from the immoral tendency, or licentious nature of their writings; but many authors, whom we consider as unexceptionable or harmless, experience a similar treatment." Books treating religion or morals could also receive harsh and often arbitrary treatment, Wraxall reported,

> A sentence reflecting on the Catholic religion; a doubt thrown upon the sanctity of some hermit or monk of the middle ages; any composition in which the pleasures of love are warmly depicted; for I by no means mean to speak of those licentious writings which it is the duty of every government to suppress; in a word, any thing where superstition is attacked or censured, however slightly, attracts immediate notice, and is instantly prohibited under severe penalties.... The far greater number of those books which constitute the libraries of persons distinguished for taste and refinement, not merely in France or England, but even in Rome or Florence, are rigorously condemned, and their entry is attended with no less difficulty than danger. It is indeed true, that notwithstanding every prohibition, knowledge pierces, and gradually diffuses itself over the Austrian dominions. But its progress is necessarily proportioned to the impediments in its way. On application to the literary inquisitors or censors, who regulate this branch of internal police, almost any work may likewise be procured, though not without trouble, expence, and delay. Leipsic, Paris, or the Hague, to one or other of which places recourse must usually be had, are distant. The indolence natural to the human mind, frequently prevents such an exertion, and extinguishes the feeble spark of desire to receive improvement.[46]

But Joseph II himself had observed in a memorandum as early as 1765 that every book banned by the Austrian censors could be obtained in Vienna, and from the beginning of his coregency he had argued for some liberalization of censorship policies. Under Maria Theresia's oversight and particularly after the death in 1772 of Gerhard van Swieten, who as head of the censorship commission had exercised restraint, the commission's pronouncements had been unpredictable particularly with regard to literature that had a tincture of political content. The commissioners had tried to gauge the likely reaction of both the empress and her coregent to specific decisions they took and had abandoned any attempt to apply objective systematic guidelines.[47] Even with these limitations, both quantitatively and qualitatively the 1760s and 1770s had been a period of growth and ferment in the monarchy's publishing industry, especially for the periodical press. Newspapers were becoming popular in Vienna, as were reading rooms or the *Lesekabinett*, as founded initially by the successful publisher Trattner in 1776, where subscribers had access to an array of newspapers, journals, and books.[48]

Relaxation of censorship was striking evidence of how optimistic and self-confident the emperor felt early in his reign. He was convinced that even in the face of ill-intentioned publicity his own views, based on rational state interests, would prevail and be persuasive to reasonable subjects. He expected the greater freedom of the press to work to his own advantage as he initiated his program of far-reaching reforms. A freer press would make possible the dissemination of arguments in favor of his measures in the face of conservative opposition. The new censorship regulations were complex and necessarily remained in a state of flux as Joseph's specific directives and their interpretation by designated personnel affected enforcement. As with earlier regulations, the directives drew a distinction between popular and scholarly books.[49] Popular books received closer examination but were no longer subjected to a critical parsing, sentence by sentence. Scholarly books were generally exempt from review. Baron Tobias Philip Gebler (died 1786), supporter of reforms as a member of the *Staatsrat* and himself a playwright, reported to Christoph Friedrich Nicolai (1733–1811, editor of the popular and progressive *Allgemeine deutsche Bibliothek* in Berlin) in 1783 that there was now virtually no book that was not openly for sale in Vienna.[50] Joseph's new regulations explicitly ended the scrutiny of books transported by foreign visitors into the monarchy, a practice that had embarrassed progressive thinkers in the monarchy during his mother's reign. The emperor also permitted the reprinting (essentially pirating) of all foreign books by the monarchy's own publishers, so long as the titles were not found on a much abbreviated list of prohibited books.

To head his censorship commission Joseph selected Gottfried van Swieten, who also served as director of the emperor's education commission. This younger Swieten's intellectual views were broad for his time, as noted previously. He had served as the monarchy's envoy in Warsaw and Berlin and later became director of the Habsburg court library. While stationed in Berlin Swieten had served as Chancellor Kaunitz's literary agent. He had supplied Kaunitz with the latest literature of the French Enlightenment and also erotica. At times conspicuously pedantic, Gottfried Swieten was said to imitate the chancellor's personal idiosyncrasies. But Swieten had a genuine love for literature and for the open discourse advocated by Enlightenment authors. Throughout the decade he fought for the intellectual rights of writers, a cause generally despised and derided by Joseph.[51]

In theory, the censors were now authorized to permit publication of materials on virtually any topic that was not directly offensive to morality or religion. The person of the emperor himself and his associates could be held up for criticism and even ridicule. The censorship changes released a flood of publications aimed at the public at large, many of them ephemera, which the *Dames* read as avidly as did the rest of literate Vienna. The popular appetite for news and controversy appeared to be insatiable, the mood of the reading public almost euphoric. Joseph's censorship reforms produced a heady atmosphere for both writers and readers. For several years the Viennese public greeted virtually any publication with enthusiasm, regardless of its merit.[52] Along with the rest of the reading public the *Dames* puzzled over the identity and motives of authors of anonymous publications, and rightly so: according to recent conclusions of Ernst Wangermann in his study of publishing in the 1780s, many publications had been commissioned or at least countenanced by interested religious or secular leaders, including the emperor.[53] Even as the *Dames* were themselves caught up in the *Lesesturm*, they quickly and frequently expressed misgivings about the long-term effects of unrestricted authorship. Almost immediately the women worried about possible consequences of casual criticism, fearing a loss of dignity and control for those in authority. In conversations with Swieten about censorship practices one evening at her father-in-law's gathering, Leopoldine Kaunitz challenged the wisdom and justice of the new liberal approach. Swieten himself conceded that looser censorship would result in the publication of calumny and fabrications, she reported to Eleonore later. These, he had remarked, could not be avoided, but anyone would be free to refute the lies. Leopoldine had controlled her temper and her tongue but believed that giving free rein to libel was like tolerating the activities of a pickpocket, "as if someone was at liberty to take my purse or watch, and I then [had] permission to demand its return." She had limited her criticism to publications containing anonymous denunciations (which the new regulations did seek to discourage), "wherein now one is entitled to make false attacks on persons who are named publicly while remaining anonymous oneself."[54]

The novelty of the new freedom of the press began to wear off by 1784 and 1785, and public excitement subsided somewhat.[55] Meanwhile, these censorship reforms offered a generous supply of conversation topics for meetings of the *société*.

The emperor feigned indifference to publications that commented on him and his policies positively or negatively, ostentatiously dismissing them as trivial distractions for lesser intellects. At a gathering in mid-1782, when Eleonore observed to Joseph that newspapers and brochures were praising his actions, he scolded her for assuming that he would care, declaiming, "It is a matter of complete indifference to me whether they speak well or ill about me, some will relish it, to others the taste will be sour, if only one has nothing for which to blame oneself, for peace of mind is a possession they can neither give nor take away." A general silence had ensued among the assembled friends, and Joseph's bad humor cast a pall on the rest of the evening's communications, according to Eleonore. In his report in 1784, Grand Duke Leopold testified that the emperor cared very much about what was said and written concerning him and that he habitually hired writers to respond to criticisms.[56]

Among the changes in censorship, the area attracting the most notice from contemporaries such as the *Dames* was the altered treatment of religious publications, a stunning volte-face for Joseph's subjects. Because Joseph's second major reform of his early reign, the toleration edicts that eased restrictions on non-Catholics to make his lands less hostile to all productive subjects, so quickly followed censorship reforms, in the minds of the *Dames* and much of the reading public at large the two innovations were closely linked. Uncensored publications soon appeared that subjected all aspects of the Catholic religion to unwonted public scrutiny. It had been understood in government circles during the coregency that both Joseph II and Chancellor Kaunitz considered greater toleration for the monarchy's religious minorities not only as a prerequisite for robust economic growth but also as an important strategic tool to safeguard the monarchy's international position. Such a change would enable the monarchy to fend off blandishments of tolerant Prussia that could weaken loyalty to the dynasty. Greater tolerance would both placate and gratify the leaders of an increasingly ascendant Russia, which was otherwise in a position to make use of the divided loyalties of Orthodox coreligionists within the monarchy's borders. While the details of suggestions made by Joseph as well as Kaunitz during those years could not be known outside government councils, Joseph's likely future approach to the problem of religious diversity had been evident to the public. During trips to other countries he had visited churches of various faiths and especially in Amsterdam he had noted explicitly the prosperity of Holland's tolerant society.[57] As noted in chapter 4, religious tolerance had been discussed by the *société* during the coregency when Maria Theresia and Joseph had quarreled over the proper response to a significant Protestant resurgence in Bohemia and Moravia in 1778–1779. Joseph had gone to considerable lengths to justify his position. In a lengthy message that referred to the previous evening's lively ("fameuse") discussion, Joseph recited the considerations that caused him to favor at least limited toleration for recognized Christian sects. The emperor had affirmed that he was a loyal Catholic ("I am nonetheless orthodox"). He argued that if people clung to false beliefs it did not follow that they could be converted by force. Covert Protestants mocked the Catholic sacraments, he wrote, and tended to be irreligious themselves, with no prescribed practices or discipline and with each family defining its own religion. It was best for the government to know who these people were, to categorize them clearly as Lutherans, and to let them listen to their Lutheran sermons and sing their Lutheran hymns openly on Sundays, so they could be monitored. Dropping all subterfuge, they were more likely to be influenced by the good example of Catholics. "Here is the scenario as I envision it, I speak not of public worship but of private tolerance," Joseph wrote. He believed his soul would not be damned because he preferred such an approach to force or expulsion. Even in the less strained environment prior to Maria Theresia's death, apparently Leopoldine Kaunitz had expressed some exasperation with his stance; and in this case she had left the emperor abruptly without saying goodbye, "thinking," Joseph surmised, "I do not need to bid him good night, the Devil will do that."[58]

The "Edict of Toleration" for Protestant and Orthodox subjects now officially permitted them to build unobtrusive churches and schools, to worship freely in private, and to enjoy many civil liberties on an equal footing with Catholics. Catholicism remained the preferred religion, alone enjoying the full endorsement of the state. In separate regulations, Joseph also broadened the choices available to Jews for jobs and education. Although the goal was assimilation, economic gain for the state, and greater control over poor Jewish itinerants of uncertain domicile and livelihood, these toleration decrees (which varied by region) for the Jews were generous and progressive by contemporary standards, a novel measure that garnered both praise and criticism and apparently was regarded with some distaste by much of the population at large, including the *Dames*.[59] Learning about the new regulations concerning the Jews while staying in Spa, even Leopoldine Liechtenstein wrote disparagingly to Josepha Clary, "Here then is the project put in motion for conversion of the Jews, which is likely to bring about suppression of the Catholics, it seems to me."[60] The new measures taken together reversed the policies of generations of Habsburg rulers who had made only grudging, pragmatic concessions to non-Catholic groups.

The *Dames* fretted about Joseph's handling of the two related issues, censorship and religious toleration. Both of these were major initiatives that could not be enacted through one-time, all-encompassing legislation; and throughout the decade the continuing evolution of Joseph's policies, together with inconsistent enforcement, kept both issues well to the fore in the minds of the public and the *Dames*.[61] As observant, traditional Catholics the women had some reason to be perplexed by the new regulations. Joseph's dramatic loosening of censorship in so many areas did smooth the way for favorable publicity for the emperor both domestically and internationally. However, for the clergy of the Catholic Church censorship actually became somewhat stricter.[62] Outright attacks on the validity of the Christian religion and publications that were overtly disrespectful of its fundamental tenets remained prohibited, with the boundaries separating the acceptable from the unacceptable being naturally a subject for debate. But Catholic publications themselves were strictly monitored because the emperor wished to exclude some works that inveighed against his more rational approach to Catholicism. Works by Catholic clergymen that disputed the government's religious reforms might be prohibited, as might the more traditional baroque expressions of Catholic piety that were now branded as old-fashioned or superstitious, such as tales concerning miracles and relics or guides to liturgical practices that Joseph considered to be outmoded and unsuited to an enlightened age. By contrast, religious works that supported Joseph's overall goals—those with Jansenist leanings, those that asserted the validity of state or conciliar claims against papal power—were freely permitted. The creeds, practices, ceremonies, and hierarchy of the Catholic Church all became popular topics for critical publicists. A veritable sea change had occurred, clearly separating the coregency from Joseph's decade of sole rule. Hailed by progressive groups within the monarchy and throughout Europe as an overdue unfettering of the popular press, for more conservative individuals and possibly for much of the monarchy's aristocratic elite as a group, the government's altered stance toward the Catholic Church was disquieting and not altogether welcome.[63]

From the outset, the *Dames* questioned not only the wisdom of the toleration edicts but also the emperor's authority to promulgate and enforce them. Eleonore's chagrin was apparent in her remarks to her sister in September 1781. "My husband tells me," she wrote, "that the emperor has already signed on the 14th a terrible decree concerning liberty of religion, I expect that soon he will issue one to prohibit us from being Catholics." To the sisters Eleonore and Leopoldine, liberty for non-Catholic sects necessarily implied restrictions on Catholicism. They believed that Joseph was sacrificing the interests of the Catholic Church to his own vision of a powerful state. Because the emperor expected the bishops in his lands to obey his injunctions even in the face of papal opposition, both Eleonore and Leopoldine Kaunitz believed that Joseph's actions threatened the unity of the Catholic Church. Rosenberg summarized the situation for Eleonore: the bishops were exhorted "to take back the power and authority that is rightfully theirs and which the court of Rome usurped during the dark ages, and . . . in case of opposition on their part the Emperor will be obliged to make use of the power God has given him to compel their obedience." "And thus," Eleonore wrote to her sister, "the court of Vienna no longer recognizes the Pope, the unity that is the basis of religion, the leader of the church, just as J. C. was leader of the Apostles, in a word no more religion [is recognized]. My God, what have we come to? It makes you tremble, you dare not think any more. God is always merciful, but when such great wrongs have been committed, such great injuries to the church, what is one to expect?"[64] A year later in summer 1782, by which time Joseph's religious reform program was accelerating dramatically, Leopoldine Kaunitz expressed similar frustration: "I assure you, dear sister, that I could weep when I see this destruction of our faith: everything is tolerated, everything is allowed, is approved except for the one catholic religion. Neither the Jews nor the Lutherans are being reformed, but we ourselves, we are to be taught a different law." She was deeply disappointed in Joseph, and she feared the future. "As for me," she wrote, "the emperor deceived me so much at the beginning, for I was far from foreseeing all that is happening, that I could wish he would deceive me still. But I admit to you, but to you alone, who know him, I fear that he realizes only too well what he is doing, that is to say what he is doing in these temporal days, but he does not realize what the consequences will be for eternity, and he even judges poorly concerning the consequences in these days; for the harshest, most violent, most self-interested pope, the most fanatical monks have never harmed sovereigns as have enlightened people [*die aufgeklärte Völker*]." The monarchy faced critical times, Leopoldine wrote. "Great revolutions have been made by unbelievers or heretics. Who was Cromwell? And in France, let him take note of what the Calvinists did, and in the end that League that opposed Henry IV was Catholic, but as soon as he himself became Catholic they yielded to him, whereas the English beheaded their king who was Protestant as they were, because he was enlightened [*aufgeklärt*]. What country is more peaceful than Spain?"[65]

The *Dames* drew their own conclusions about Joseph's motives and character, often uncomplimentary. They were certain that the emperor simply sought fame and notoriety as a progressive or even radical ruler. When in the course of his visit to Spa in 1781 the emperor consented to dine with the notorious *Abbé* Raynal (1713–1796), among others who were guests of the Prussian Prince Henry, Eleonore and her sister viewed the incident as an open disavowal of traditional religion. Eleonore wrote, "like you, I was quite shocked that the *abbé* Raynal was admitted to Prince Henry's dinner . . . It is in large part self-consciousness and fear of being ridiculed by these so-called *grands esprits* if he [Joseph II] should show them that he has religion. All of this proves that he has but little, yet is his character susceptible of becoming anything? He has never had a feeling for which he did not blush and which he did not disavow as the case arose; this is a wretched man, and by dint of destroying the small amount of feeling that he has, he will finish by becoming a monster." Deploring the fact that Raynal was permitted by Habsburg authorities to remain in Brussels, Josepha Clary described him to her husband as "an insupportable windbag, a man 72 years old" who attempted to imitate Voltaire. Leopoldine Liechtenstein, not easily ruffled, encountered Raynal in Spa as the emperor did and dismissed him as just one of "the troublemakers." (She also met Baron von Grimm, 1723–1807, "a learned man . . . in a very regular correspondence with the Empress of Russia, who they say writes volumes to him.")[66]

When as a byproduct of Joseph's new Russian alliance Grand Duke Paul's young sister-in-law, Princess Elisabeth of the house of Württemberg, was brought to Vienna later in 1781 as the future bride of Archduke Franz, who was Joseph's nephew and heir after Leopold, Josepha Clary worried about the impact of the new fashion of tolerance and the emperor's intentions concerning the religious instruction of the Protestant princess. She reported to her husband that the charming little princess had been raised as a Lutheran but had a Catholic mother. The latter, Josepha remarked, probably had few strong religious convictions since she was willing to abjure her own faith or at least permit her children to be raised as Lutherans. Josepha reasoned, "one must hope that tolerance will not be pushed so far that they will not have her convert, but in these enlightened times one must not count on anything."[67] When it appeared briefly that preparations for reception of the princess at the Visitation convent in Vienna had been suspended, Eleonore at once concluded (erroneously) that the princess would never become Catholic; "indeed one dares not dwell on all these thoughts at all." It was necessary, she wrote, to commit the situation to God's providence, "but it makes one tremble, especially with six children."[68]

Joseph's tolerance decrees were just the beginning of his program to reform church-state relations. At least initially, his broad goals were similar to those of his predecessor, Maria Theresia: the emperor wanted a more frugal Catholic Church that tended the spiritual health of parishioners without devouring the monarchy's wealth, deterring skilled workers from settling within its territories, or obstructing the population's increase. It is possible to find economic and political factors influencing many of his choices, as Joseph himself stated.[69] Far more than his mother, Joseph identified as nonessential to the true faith any practices that might cause economic loss to the state or weaken its cohesion. In his view, the international character of the Catholic Church and its claim to autonomy within the state—a claim with which, as Joseph could easily see, a Protestant ruler such as Frederick II or an Orthodox ruler such as Catherine II did not have to contend—impeded his efforts to augment and centralize state power. The scope of Joseph's claims expanded as years passed. He asserted his government's authority over the clergy, requiring bishops to swear allegiance to the crown, prohibiting the publication of papal bulls without government consent and ordering suppression of the bulls *Unigenitus* (directed specifically against Jansenists) and *In coena Domini* (authorizing the pope to require the removal from power of heretical rulers), restructuring the boundaries of parishes to make them more rational and efficient. The emperor regarded the priesthood as an appropriate vehicle both for educating good Catholics and for molding dutiful subjects. He expected parish priests to serve as conduits for information from the government as well as channels of grace for believers; it has been argued that he viewed the clergy as a form of religious civil service for his own employment as well as that of the church. Increasingly he made use of Catholic priests' ready access to the ears of his subjects to broadcast new injunctions and to enjoin obedience to the state's edicts from the pulpit of the church. As early as 1782 parish priests were specifically required to read the texts of new laws to their congregations.[70] Some reforms took on the nature of "Catholic puritanism." Others appeared to promote secular authority in areas of life previously held to be spiritual matters, such as the "Ehepatent" or marriage law of 1783, which was part of Joseph's larger reform of civil law. The new law declared marriage to be a civil contract and thus within the purview of civil law (Joseph allowed Catholic subjects to regard marriage as a sacrament as well and to be guided in matters of church marriage law by bishops with jurisdiction within the monarchy, who while vested with the authority to pronounce on disputed matters were at liberty to seek papal guidance).[71] Regulation of ceremonial aspects of church life became increasingly detailed and intrusive in the eyes of many contemporaries. Joseph received enthusiastic support in his reforms from Chancellor Kaunitz, whose critical attitude toward the Catholic hierarchy, somewhat muted while Maria Theresia lived, became particularly pronounced during the 1780s.

The religious reforms produced contentious discussions in the evening gatherings as did no other issue, for this was an area of policy concerning which the *Dames* often spoke their minds. As Leopoldine Kaunitz put it in 1782, "With this *seigneur* one must at least have nothing to regret; let us reserve our determination and our opposition for the important matters that concern our God and his religion."[72] For the *Dames* and their contemporaries, few areas of public and communal life could arouse greater interest and passion than religion—both because of the faith and convictions involved and also because religious institutions were so deeply and fundamentally embedded in society, affecting the political, social, and economic standing of all inhabitants. Many historians regard Joseph II's religious reforms as the most far-reaching and lasting of his policies, altering both religious and social institutions.

Only Eleonore and Leopoldine Kaunitz left detailed evidence of their personal reactions to religious policies of the 1780s. The views of the other women can be deduced from their friends' comments and from their own actions. Strong censure came from Leopoldine Kaunitz and Eleonore Liechtenstein, whose strictures were frequently seconded by Josepha Clary and her sister Sidonia Kinsky. Josepha Clary's amiability made her a moderating influence in the *société* but her views on religious questions were generally conservative, traditional, and not easily altered, as experience demonstrated. Leopoldine Liechtenstein, always discreet, kept her own counsel, but her friends judged her to be more moderate than they were themselves and accepting of change in general. Her friend Lacy, the consummate courtier, preferred to avoid sensitive topics altogether during evening gatherings. Leopoldine Kaunitz described a gathering in early October 1785 when Joseph had seemed to be in a reasonably good humor "even though we argued a bit over tolerance, theology, Blumauer's confession of faith [ex-Jesuit poet and Josephinian censor Alois Blumauer published in 1782 his *Confession of Faith of a Catholic Searching for Truth*]. The marshal [Lacy] was present, but whether he is there or not one cannot dissemble with regard to certain truths when the occasion arises." Rosenberg, described in earlier years by the papal nuncio as a devout Catholic who adhered to traditional values, was a loyal Habsburg servant as his own long, solid career attested. He was thoroughly acquainted with progressive ideas of the Enlightenment but his enthusiasm for Joseph's religious policy was not unbounded. Soon after the edicts of toleration were published, he had reported to Leopoldine Kaunitz "that these patents concerning religion are having a very bad effect in the provinces, that people are frightened and in despair, and that in general there is a prodigious amount of discontent." Apparently, like many contemporaries, Rosenberg ascribed primary responsibility for the new religious measures to the influence of Leopoldine's father-in-law Chancellor Kaunitz.[73]

The *Dames*, while not uncritical of contemporary religious leaders, argued—as had Maria Theresia—that society owed outward respect to representatives of the church. At the same time, in the field of religion as elsewhere the women did enjoy the public repartee. They eagerly discussed controversies that swirled around the religious reforms and swapped news of fresh publications. Leopoldine Kaunitz and Eleonore were avid readers of the serial publication *Wöchentliche Wahrheiten für und über die Prediger in Wien* (weekly truths for and about preachers in Vienna) edited in Vienna by Leopold Alois Hoffmann (1759–1801), published from May 1782 until June 1784 and popularly known as the *Predigtkritik*. Its essays subjected the homilies of Viennese sermonizers to public criticism by enthusiastic reformers. These reviews were a popular sensation, trenchant criticisms of clerics being a novelty highly valued by the public. Both Joseph II and his censorship commission were disposed to favor and promote the publication, which was in turn vehemently denounced by Vienna's Archbishop Migazzi.[74] The anonymity of contributors fueled lively rumors among the reading public and lent an air of intrigue and mystery to the publication, which had genuine entertainment and often educational value for the Viennese. Leopoldine Kaunitz relished the witty critiques she found in the journal, her occasional expressions of indignation or outrage notwithstanding. She sent her own penetrating observations to her sister.[75] The sisters exchanged assessments of outstanding or inferior sermons in much the same way that they critiqued current theatrical productions.

In the women's view, publications that supported unwise Josephinian reforms were too plentiful and alarmingly popular. Leopoldine Kaunitz objected to a publication authored by Hoffmann entitled *Zehn Briefe aus Österreich an den Verfasser der Briefe aus Berlin* (Ten letters from Austria to the author of the letters from Berlin), which appeared in 1784. Hoffmann's publication was written in response to a recent anonymous publication entitled *Briefe aus Berlin über verschiedene Paradoxe dieses Zeitalters* (Letters from Berlin about various paradoxes of this age), itself a reply to Viennese author Johann Friedel's panegyric of Joseph II published in the previous year and entitled *Briefe aus Wien*. The *Briefe aus Berlin* had criticized not the goals of Joseph II's religious reforms but rather the intolerance the emperor evinced toward those who opposed his views. In some respects a sophisticated commentary on the state of affairs under Joseph, the *Briefe aus Berlin* had compared the rather narrowly circumscribed public discourse in the Habsburg capital with the freedom of expression that obtained in Berlin. In Vienna, the author argued, only those authors who, however pitiful and unworthy their style of writing, supported the religious reform program, denounced and held up to ridicule the monks, conservative clergy (especially Archbishop Migazzi), and other targets of reformers, and unstintingly heaped praise on the emperor actually enjoyed real freedom from censorship. According to Grand Duke Leopold, Joseph permitted its reprinting but was irked by the *Zehn Briefe* and himself commissioned the first responses, including the clumsy production of Hoffmann so disliked by Leopoldine Kaunitz. Certainly Hoffmann's approach was straightforward and undiscriminating. He excoriated former Jesuits, the archbishop, and anyone who opposed Joseph's reforms. He lauded authors who, even if not always talented, sought to make Joseph's religious reforms understandable to an unschooled public.

At a soirée in early August 1784 Leopoldine Kaunitz complained to the emperor that Hoffmann expected "to act as the reformer of Austria without any other vocation except his impertinence, that this is just as it is among the Quakers, each individual so moved who raises his voice is listened to." She believed that the censorship commission was condoning what amounted to libel.[76] She conceded ruefully that the public had little interest in tracts offering a reasoned defense of established beliefs and practices. Such publications had no shock value and were frequently tedious. Leopoldine acknowledged that reformers had gained the upper hand in the publicity battle through their greater skill and intellectual rigor, but she was unwilling to ascribe this ascendancy to the correctness of their views. Visiting Vienna in 1784, Grand Duke Leopold, a supporter of many of the emperor's religious reforms, drew similar conclusions; he saw only books that criticized religion and heard only discussions about topics such as the abolition of auricular confession and the marriage of priests.[77]

Two conservative publicists who labored to produce readable materials and whose work was known to the women were Patrizius Fast (1726–1790), rector at the Metropolitankirche in Vienna, and a Belgian ex-Jesuit, François-Xavier

Feller (1735–1802), who was critical of Jansenist beliefs and supported the growing resistance to them in Belgium.[78] Also noted in the women's letters were Joseph Pochlin (1741–1796) and Joseph Schneller (1734–1802), who actively defended both traditional practices and former Jesuits, who were still a target of reformers and progressives after suppression of their Society.[79] Among the women's own close associates were additional individuals who entered the lists on behalf of traditional theology, practice, and church hierarchy. The *Dames* viewed these with forthright but not uncritical admiration. Virtually every reform measure promulgated by Joseph II drew a protest from conservative church leaders, especially Vienna's Archbishop Migazzi, mentioned previously, and the papal nuncio Giuseppe Garampi (stationed in Vienna until 1785).[80] Earlier in his career Migazzi himself had been a reformer, credited with strengthening the influence of Jansenism in the monarchy. With advancing age Migazzi seemed determined to oppose all change. He became a spokesman for orthodoxy, reacting to the onslaught of imperial decrees with brittle defensiveness. The emperor embarrassed Migazzi publicly by requiring him to relinquish his second bishopric at Waitzen (Vác) in Hungary, which he held simultaneously with that of Vienna. Leopoldine Kaunitz acknowledged Migazzi's hard work for pious causes but recognized also his disappointing lack of acuity and rhetorical skill: "The cardinal came to me this morning . . . God has given him many talents, but it is true that certain of them were not accorded him . . . it is also true that if there were more coherence in what he says, more dignity in what he does, they would never have dared to humiliate him as they have."[81] These were hard times for nuncio Garampi and other "ultramontanists" as well. A familiar friend of the women, Garampi had been a devotee of Muratorian Catholicism, thus a moderate reformer. He too had viewed with sympathy some Jansenist teachings about the value of the inner life of faith. Joseph II had met Garampi in 1769 when he visited Rome during the papal interregnum, and Garampi had made a favorable impression on the emperor. Garampi was a genial man, a skillful diplomat with well-honed social skills. During the coregency, in his efforts to protect the authority of the pope and the nunciature in Habsburg lands, Garampi sometimes played off Maria Theresia against her wayward son, a circumstance naturally resented by Joseph. After Maria Theresia's death, Garampi found himself forced onto the defensive by the emperor's new initiatives.[82]

Leopoldine Kaunitz and Eleonore believed traditional Catholics were being actively persecuted, as did Migazzi and other like-minded individuals. Already in summer 1781 Leopoldine Kaunitz reported that an especially well-reasoned publication defending the former Jesuits had been prohibited simply because the censors disliked its content.[83] At a soirée in July 1784, Josepha Clary exhibited a list of books circulating in Bohemia that named religious titles "that are to be suppressed and their reprint forbidden, as being full of superstition and counter to enlightened notions [*wider der erleuchteten Begriff*] of religion." Leopoldine Kaunitz admitted that many of the publications listed were completely without value, as one could easily see by scanning the titles; but, she added indignantly, there were also standard works concerning Catholic doctrine and catechism. The women had remonstrated with the emperor. "We said things fitting and right about the matter," she explained, "but such as we have already said as often as the paternoster, it does not matter."[84] In fall 1785, noting the many book announcements in the *Wiener Zeitung*, Eleonore observed that it could not be by chance that so many attacked traditional Catholicism and were penned by authors with Jansenist, progovernment leanings. "Certainly since the origins of Christianity," she wrote, "there has never been a time so dangerous and so difficult for religion as that in which we live." Eleonore mentioned with horror, but also with obvious interest, a title she had seen advertised that denigrated "everything, religion, mystery, worship, invocation of the saints, and then specifically each priest, each curate, each preacher."[85]

Rather than attacking non-Catholic contemporaries, the women reserved their bitterest scorn for Catholic publicists who, in the women's view, threatened the unity of the Catholic Church from within through their corrosive critiques. Over the course of their correspondence Eleonore Liechtenstein and Leopoldine Kaunitz criticized and condemned by name the leading lights of late eighteenth-century reform Catholicism in Habsburg lands, all of whom at one time or another enjoyed the favor and patronage of the emperor and his reform-minded associates: Wittola, Blarer, Rautenstrauch, Zippe, Eybel. These individuals had careers that spanned the reigns of both Maria Theresia and Joseph II and had been favorably regarded even by the empress at least temporarily. Although the *Dames*, as was their habit, referred to all of the writers as Jansenists, these reformers did not share one common viewpoint. In evening gatherings with the emperor, the women made clear their distaste for specific views they ascribed to each individual.

Provost Mark Anton Wittola (1736–1797), born in Silesia, was a writer of Jansenist inclination who had enjoyed the patronage of Maria Theresia. He had worked as a censor but eventually came to grief when he approved an anti-Jesuit publication by the French Jansenist Philibert, mentioned in chapter 4. Garampi and Migazzi had complained to Maria Theresia, and she had dismissed Wittola.[86] From 1784 to 1789 Wittola published the reformist *Wiener Kirchenzeitung*. He criticized the papacy and the Jesuits. He considered monks to be apologists for superstition, but his goal was to reform the monastic orders rather than abolish them. He favored tolerance for non-Catholics, arguing that if the church had acted to correct abuses instead of persecuting Lutherans, the sect would have faded away. On some issues Wittola actually took a moderate position, not the extreme Jansenist stance so hated by the women. For example, he favored fasting in moderation rather than total elimination of the practice and also voluntary celibacy, whereby a priest who found himself no longer suited to celibacy could be laicized.[87]

Melchior Blarer (1729–1796), also scorned by the women, was a radical Jansenist priest of Swiss origin, a restless individual who worked for several years training priests in Brünn and Vienna. In 1782 he incurred Archbishop Migazzi's wrath by ostentatiously refusing to celebrate mass when he felt himself to be unworthy (an unorthodox stance adopted by some Jansenists implying that the priest's state of grace could affect the efficacy of the sacrament). He openly criticized the manner in which priests collected payments for private masses while neglecting to minister to parishioners, arguing that these practices violated the teachings of the early church. During summer 1782 the women were appalled to learn that the emperor had offered Blarer the post of palace chaplain at Laxenburg (secondary sources mention Schlosshof rather than Laxenburg).[88] Josepha reported to Leopoldine Kaunitz that Blarer had celebrated mass in the emperor's presence ("his disgraceful spectacle of ostentation and impertinence with the Holy Mass"). "You can see, then, how he [Joseph] permits himself to be led about by these people . . . This news has simply stupefied me," Leopoldine Kaunitz told her sister, "I am deeply saddened by it."[89]

Eventually Joseph II and Blarer's other supporters in Vienna lost patience with the wayward priest's peculiarities. Blarer left Vienna in early summer 1783 and spent two years traveling. Returning to Brünn and Olmütz, he again antagonized the Catholic hierarchy and was arrested as a disturber of religious peace and brought to Vienna. This episode ended Blarer's career prospects in Vienna, since the emperor obliged him to sign a "revers" promising never to return. Leopoldine Kaunitz reported events in October 1785 to Eleonore: "They report that Plorer [sic] was seen here . . . la Françoise [Leopoldine Liechtenstein] said so, and I confirmed this, but the Emperor claims that he was only at the police station, where he was led (perhaps for questioning but he did not say that) and from there he sent him away back to Switzerland." She continued, "It must be, then, that the Emperor's eyes have been opened with regard to him, but will he not also see that those who favored him are not more worthy than he is, and that a Vitola [sic], a Braunauer, a Vanswieten, in appearing to be less mad, are but the more dangerous, for they act according to the same principles."[90] A rumor circulated that the emperor had been induced to act against Blarer by the ex-Jesuit chaplain Canal, house chaplain to both the Kaunitz and the Liechtenstein families, who had applied pressure through a "Princess Liechtenstein" (presumably Eleonore, who had a more active relationship with Canal than did Leopoldine Liechtenstein).[91]

Franz Stephan Rautenstrauch (1734–1785), abbot of the Benedictine monasteries of Braunau/Broumov and Břevnov in Bohemia, helped the emperor revamp the education of Catholic priests. His most noted contribution was elaboration of a plan for the emperor's "general seminaries," state-run institutions that Joseph inaugurated in 1783 to take over the training of priests from bishops and monasteries. Since the church was the principal provider of popular education in the Habsburg monarchy, Joseph set great store by an educated and enlightened clergy. As will be noted below, these new institutions were highly controversial, detested by conservative Catholics who believed that they inculcated a spirit of rationalism or naturalism, intentionally undermined papal authority over the clergy, and weakened confidence in traditional church doctrine and law.[92] Leopoldine Kaunitz was contemptuous of the work of Rautenstrauch, whose commission was "the poisoned source that will entirely destroy religion in our lands, such that if it continues on in this way, someday perhaps they will seek that religion of old but will no longer find it." Rautenstrauch died in late September 1785 while traveling in Hungary to organize new seminaries. Cheerfully, and a bit unfeelingly, the women observed that Rautenstrauch was now accountable before his God.[93]

Rautenstrauch was only 51 years old when he died. Rumors circulated that he had been poisoned.[94] In meetings with the emperor in October 1785 the *Dames* rejoiced openly over Rautenstrauch's demise. Their jubilation ended abruptly when Joseph announced to them that his choice of Rautenstrauch's successor would also displease them. Joseph named Augustin Zippe (1747–1816), director of the seminary in Prague, to replace Rautenstrauch as advisor on religious education. According to his biographers, Zippe (sometimes spelled Cippe or Cyppe in sources) had served in earlier years as deacon and school director in Böhmischkamnitz (Česká Kamenice), where he enjoyed the support of landlord Prince Franz Ulrich Kinsky, Sidonia's husband. Zippe's efforts to assist the parish poor were said to have put an end to begging there. Zippe had no personal contacts with the more radical Jansenist reformers, but his ideas showed the influence of Enlightenment thought.[95] Josepha Clary took alarm at once, certain that Zippe shared Rautenstrauch's Jansenist principles. At another gathering several days later lively disputes continued, during "an evening even more stormy concerning this matter of Zippe," as Leopoldine Kaunitz reported to her sister. Unaware that Zippe had already been definitively selected, Leopoldine Kaunitz had read to the emperor the preface to Zippe's published sermons, "a thoroughly Jansenist tirade, where he praises the *monseigneurs* of Port Royal as restorers of morals, which laxism had destroyed, and he refers to the provincial letters [of Blaise Pascal] as if citing Saint Peter." Joseph had listened angrily and then remarked, "very well, we will see what Zippe can do." The women realized then that the appointment had already been finalized. "The lamentations of la Clari [Josepha Clary] went on and on," Leopoldine Kaunitz wrote, "as for me I decided to remain silent; when the evil has been done one must endure it and keep still."[96]

Leopoldine Kaunitz and Eleonore also found fault with the publications of Joseph Valentin Eybel (1741–1805), professor of canon law in Vienna from 1773 to 1779. According to Ignaz de Luca's *Das gelehrte Oesterreich* (1776), Eybel served as tutor to sons of Prince Kinsky, Prince Clary, and Count Ernst Harrach and thus in all likelihood taught the future husband of Eleonore Liechtenstein's daughter Josephine.[97] During the empress's lifetime Eybel's Jansenist and Febronian views had alarmed conservative clerics such as Migazzi and Garampi. During the 1780s Eybel served as an agent in Joseph's dissolution of monasteries, a program described below. In his pamphlet *Was ist der Papst?* (What is the pope?) in 1782, one of several contentious publications penned by Eybel, he described the pope as a mere president under the republican constitution of the church. Other brochures publicized and interpreted Joseph's new marriage law, regulations concerning monastic orders, and other sensitive topics. In 1784 Eybel produced a controversial brochure that declared auricular confession to be contrary to the spirit and teachings of the early church. Eybel's publications eventually drew papal censure. His provocative works made popular reading in Vienna.[98] Throughout the 1780s Jansenist publications remained a particular concern for the women, a veritable bête noire. Given their outlook, the women's discomfiture over the publication of Jansenist-leaning notices and reviews in contemporary newspapers and journals was no doubt a rational response; for as the specialist on Austrian Jansenism Peter Hersche has suggested, the most effective means by which Jansenist views were spread among the populace was in all likelihood the written word. Jansenism's attractiveness lay in its reasoned prose, not the appeal to the senses through music, theater, and art that had been the mainstay of traditional baroque Catholicism.[99]

Secular advisors of the emperor who were involved in implementing religious reforms, such as Friedrich Binder (1708–1782) in the *Staatsrat* and Franz Josef von Heinke (1726–1803), also came in for criticism from the *Dames*. When Binder died in mid 1782, Leopoldine Kaunitz and Eleonore Liechtenstein visualized the judgment that faced those who attacked and weakened the one true church, much as they would greet Rautenstrauch's demise several years later. Leopoldine Kaunitz wrote to her sister, "Poor Binder will see now at the day of reckoning what politics is, and how inconsequential it is, and that there is only the eternal king, who makes a reckoning concerning what one has done for him, each of us according to the station in which he has placed us."[100]

During her summer stay at Kromau in 1781, Eleonore Liechtenstein discovered for herself just how widespread the feared Jansenist tendencies had become. During the final years of Maria Theresia's reign, in conjunction with the establishment of a new Moravian bishopric at Brünn (Brno), the university and seminary at Olmütz had been transferred to Brünn. With Maria Theresia's blessing the seminary received new teachers who were distinctly progressive, including the Jansenist Blarer. However, the more conservative archbishop of Olmütz, Count Anton Theodor von Colloredo, retained oversight over the seminary. After Maria Theresia's death, the seminary's director, Count Anton Maria Vetter, archdeacon in Brünn, tried to eliminate elements of Jansenist teachings from the curriculum. The result was a public quarrel involving additional bishops, the *Staatsrat*, and the emperor himself. Joseph eventually removed conservative clerics such as Vetter from any role at the seminary. The quarreling among both religious and secular authorities was a major factor in Joseph's decision to issue a more general regulation, dated 25 April 1781, prohibiting all future discussion of the contentious papal bulls *Unigenitus* and *In coena Domini*. The regulation also forbade discussion of Jansenism or Molinism in universities.[101]

As it happened, the Jansenist scandal in Brünn reverberated in diminutive Kromau, less than thirty miles away. To her consternation, Eleonore found reason to doubt the orthodoxy of the local Paulist monastery. She reported to her sister in July 1781 that the monks supported Blarer and opposed Vetter. They approved of all the government's reform measures, even concessions to the Jews and also the silence enjoined by Joseph with regard to the offending papal bulls. Eleonore had initially considered the monks to be "too simple, too little educated, so to speak, not to be orthodox." When she had mentioned the government's innovations they had indicated their approval, and Eleonore thought at first that the monks were merely being respectful or politic. However, Eleonore reported, "this bull, which they assured me had not been accepted anywhere, showed me the situation clearly." Finally, Eleonore said, she decided to avoid religious discussion altogether "because the dispute was becoming bitter and was not going anywhere at all." The monks criticized the lifestyle of the archbishop, especially his attendance at the theater (as frowned upon by stricter Jansenists), "so contrary and forbidden in the early church," and also his "little gallantries, and that with one hand he gives his arm to the ladies, and with the other he blesses the people." The Kromau monastery's provincial, Eleonore conceded, was himself a worthy man, not easily deceived by fashionable ideas, and he assured her that even if the bark of Saint Peter received some jolts, there would be no shipwreck. Eleonore concurred but was worried that the Jansenist blight was spreading and could lead astray individuals of weak or uncertain faith. Three days later she softened her critique somewhat, concerned lest she might misrepresent the monks and especially the provincial, "who really is a fine, worthy man, full of good sense and decency, and who does not have the aspect of a Jansenist." Eleonore still hesitated to speak frankly to the Paulist monks about her apprehensions, fearing that her words might be quoted in some publication.[102]

Leopoldine Kaunitz's response to Eleonore's problem with her monks in Kromau was a veritable litany of the tenets of orthodox Catholicism. "I would wish" she wrote,

> that they should know that you are of another opinion, that you think there must be unity in the church, that it cannot subsist except in subordination to a head, that if the monarch is set up as judge in dogmatic matters then we are

establishing royal primacy as in England, and that in matters of faith and dogma a papal bull is obligatory for all Catholics, who cannot wait upon the sanction of the sovereign . . . Luther too talked of nothing but the primitive church that he wanted to restore. The true, the only church is that which has always subsisted, that was transmitted to us living by our fathers; which in conformance with different times and manners has eased the rigor of its outward discipline, but which has never, whatever has been attempted against it and no matter how it has been persecuted and oppressed, wavered in the smallest way in its beliefs, which are pure and without blemish as received from Jesus Christ.[103]

Traditional Catholics generally associated Jansenism with heresy and schism. Another despised phenomenon likewise tainted with heresy for some conservatives was freemasonry. Historians usually depict mainstream freemasonry as an outgrowth of the secular Enlightenment. In an idiosyncratic apposition of ideas, Leopoldine Kaunitz and Eleonore Liechtenstein ascribed to it a variety of disparate, unattractive, and often contradictory features, including but not limited to secularism and loose living. Like a number of their contemporaries, they appear to have regularly confounded freemasonry and Jansenism, both of which in their view might undermine Catholic faith.[104] The popularity of freemasonry among male friends, including husbands and eventually sons, worried the women, although a number of their close associates such as Rosenberg, Lacy, Chancellor Kaunitz, and the emperor himself were not lodge members.[105] Observant Catholic men clearly found it possible to reconcile fashionable freemasonry with their faith. While belonging to a masonic lodge did not mean one was less a Catholic, such activity did suggest an inclination to favor toleration of competing beliefs and, in the case of a number of freemasons, active and specific support for the emperor's new tolerant policies toward Protestants and Jews.[106]

Freemasonry's heyday occurred during the first years of Joseph's sole reign. In 1785 Joseph II imposed tighter controls on lodge activities, limiting the number of lodges, requiring registration of their members and activities, and obliging those in Habsburg lands to be independent of foreign lodges. Some members then resigned, including Ernst Kaunitz and Prince Albert, for example, or they simply lost interest; and freemasonry's popularity declined.[107] As years passed, the women remained disdainful of masonic activities of close associates, but they came to regard freemasonry simply as pernicious frivolity that could encourage careless libertinism (by which they understood not simply sexual license but also a certain free-thinking stance toward morality) and irreligiousness, not as a serious heresy.[108]

Joseph's attempts to mandate change in popular religious usages frequently enjoyed only moderate success. Unpopular reforms were implemented halfheartedly or incompletely by reluctant priests and an unenthusiastic populace. Joseph intended to simplify religious practices and cleanse them of baroque flamboyance, superstition, and excessive expense in time and resources.[109] Regulations prescribed what was permitted in church music; liturgy; the use of amulets, images, rosaries, and relics; the collection of offerings; the ornamenting of main and side altars; and the use of decorative lamps. Other decrees mandated removal of decorative clothing and trinkets from religious statues. Joseph further reduced the number of religious holidays from 42 to 27 per year. He limited the number of candles that could burn on altars. The ringing of church bells (*Wetterläuten*) in stormy weather was prohibited as a superstition.[110] None of the changes were likely to be attractive to a majority of Joseph's subjects. The emperor's approach was largely practical, without systematic theological foundation. The emperor took little interest in the niceties of theological quarrels. Many reforms occurred as a practical result of specific practices or incidents that were brought to the attention of the emperor and his advisors and were deemed unacceptable.

As early as 1782 Leopoldine Kaunitz reported that the emperor was closing contemplative chapels and converting them to alternative uses. She had mixed feelings. "I do not approve of this," she wrote to her sister; but she added, "I do not care for them because I have always liked to pray collectively." The benefits of prayer, she affirmed, should be shared, with individuals joining in communal devotional practices.[111] In 1785, the closures included the Nikolaikapelle in Hütteldorf, where Leopoldine Liechtenstein owned a summer villa. Finally shut down in 1787, the building was slated to be demolished once the value of its construction materials had been assessed and a buyer for them located. Leopoldine Liechtenstein learned of the planned destruction and purchased the materials for 300 florins, their assessed value. The Lower Austrian government turned over this money to the Hütteldorf parish. But Leopoldine then gave the chapel itself back to the parish, which restored it and years later placed it back in service. Thus, according to local historians, one of the oldest ecclesiastical structures in the region was saved from destruction through Leopoldine Liechtenstein's efforts.[112]

For the *Dames*, as for many Catholics and generations of Habsburg rulers, journeys to Marian shrines, particularly Mariazell in Styria, were a cherished religious custom. During the eighteenth century, on average more than 150,000 people visited the shrine of Mariazell each year.[113] Maria Theresia had received her first communion at Mariazell as a child in 1728 and had visited the shrine eight times during her life, her final two pilgrimages taking place in 1757 and 1769. Even Joseph II made six visits in the course of his life. Mariazell occupied a special place in the religious life of the Habsburg lands. Many reform-minded clerics tolerated this traditional expression of piety. Maria Theresia's confessor Ignaz Müller had been willing to accompany her on her pilgrimage to Mariazell in 1769 even though he was openly critical of pilgrimages and similar practices. As Joseph began his sole rule in 1780, the number of pilgrims varied between 170,000 and 190,000 yearly. Pilgrims sought the Mariazell Virgin's intercessory prayers for a broad array of concerns. The shrine was not noted for any single type of miraculous intervention, although many women and couples who hoped for fertility in marriage visited, as did individuals with afflictions of the eye. The Habsburgs and wealthy aristocrats brought lavish gifts (often liturgical objects) to be stored in the shrine's treasury, while more humble suppliants might bring simple votive paintings or designs etched on wood. Aristocratic and royal pilgrims normally did not cover the entire distance to the shrine on foot, as did ordinary pilgrims. Pedestrian groups required at least four days of walking to reach Mariazell from Vienna, pausing in the course of these seven- or eight-hour days of exertion to rest at various chapels along the way. Most pilgrims made the journey in summer or fall, at which time grateful tradesmen in the small town of Mariazell did a brisk business.[114]

Earlier Habsburg governments, including Maria Theresia's, had imposed restrictions on mass pilgrimages. By the 1750s pilgrimages were a target of reformers who felt that, quite aside from the antiquated religious customs associated with them, they were accompanied by too much disorderly entertainment such as dancing, gaming, and other dubious pastimes. When in 1772, still during Maria Theresia's lifetime, pilgrimages that required overnight stays were forbidden, the journey from Vienna to Mariazell was excepted.[115] But all such mass movements, inherently rather disorderly, were naturally a target of Joseph's reforms. In 1783, Joseph finally prohibited the popular mass processions from Vienna to Mariazell, ending the shrine's special status. He cited the wasted time, the expense, and the dissolute behavior of some pilgrims on overnight travels. Joseph's prohibition of all mass pilgrimages did not affect the *Dames* personally but was discountenanced by them. The *Dames* were persuaded that the emperor scoffed at individuals who undertook pilgrimages. Still, even in 1783 clerics at Mariazell understood him to say that he did not wish to forbid the act of pilgrimage but rather to restrict its unseemly flamboyance. In 1786, 90,000 pilgrims reportedly made their way to the shrine, evidence of the tenacity of this beloved practice even in the face of imperial ambivalence.[116]

The *Dames* traveled to Mariazell regularly during both the coregency and the 1780s. They spoke of how their visits offered them solace as they faced personal difficulties. They described the journey itself and even the mountainous terrain with affection, as being healthful and invigorating. Leopoldine Kaunitz's observations to Eleonore in 1779 were typical: "I was very content with my devotions, or I should say, with the Blessed Virgin, it is so good to be in this chapel. I prayed with my whole heart for you and for all your children."[117] Aware of the emperor's somewhat cynical view of shrines and fearing future prohibitions, Leopoldine Kaunitz took her daughter along to Mariazell in summer 1782, hoping to impress upon Lorel's memory the image of this cherished shrine. Leopoldine Kaunitz wrote: "It is an outing of five days that will do her good, and I can at least be certain that she has seen Mariazell. One can be sure only of what one has already done, and not of what one will do; especially in these times more than ever one can say that what now exists will not exist always." Afterwards, Leopoldine Kaunitz wrote to her sister conveying something of her satisfaction with her visit as well as her gratification in observing the persistent traditional piety of other pilgrims. Arrived at Mariazell, she and her daughter had gone to bed early, for by 5 o'clock in the morning "the processions were singing with all their might. Since harvest is past, this is the season when they come in the greatest numbers." Pilgrims journeyed from Brünn and localities in Bohemia. "I was most comforted to see that the so-called Enlightenment [*Aufklärung*] has not yet reached them."[118] It should be noted that even with advancing age the women undertook this fatiguing trip. Leopoldine Liechtenstein was honored at Mariazell as a particular benefactress because she had obtained from Joseph concessions concerning daily services that were technically restricted by new regulations. Eleonore remarked to her daughter after a visit to the shrine as late as 1804 that she was repeatedly mistaken for Leopoldine Liechtenstein, to her own embarrassment: "Did I tell you that at Mariazell they always mistake me for Princess Françoise [Leopoldine Liechtenstein] and that at the benediction they say a paternoster and an ave for the illustrious patroness of this devotion, and all this because she told them that she had obtained permission from Emperor Joseph for them to hold the benediction each day at Mariazell." Eleonore had explained that she was instead Princess Charles Liechtenstein, to no avail; "they just do not understand."[119]

Quite a stir was created in the *société* in summer 1782 when the women learned that the emperor himself planned to travel to Mariazell. The *Dames* could not believe Joseph was sincere. Eleonore was struck by the public impression this news could make: "What will they say, those of the little church [Jansenists], the *philosophes*, the *Aufklärer*? In the end they cannot put their trust in him." But she was skeptical about the emperor's motives. "What a man!" she wrote to her sister, "may God enlighten him! Maybe there is after all some religious sentiment contained in this singular action." Eleonore assumed that the emperor was seeking a cure for his persistent eye infection, "finding that human remedies were of no help."[120] But according to Leopoldine Kaunitz, common talk of the town had it that the emperor was going to Mariazell to plunder its treasury. Leopoldine Kaunitz told her sister that Joseph would not steal petty property from one specific church. Instead, he might publish an edict "by which he appropriates to himself all treasures of the church." Her father-in-law Chancellor Kaunitz, she reported, was dumbfounded by news of the intended pilgrimage. Josepha Clary's reaction was straightforward, charitable, and jubilant: "since she has a lovely, kind soul, she saw nothing but good, and she cried bravo." Leopoldine Kaunitz was less sanguine; "if this man merely wished to soothe the more sensible persons among his subjects, if he makes use of this sanctuary only to lay hands on it more boldly, woe to us, woe to him, and I swear to you that I will become melancholy, misanthropic, I would want to hide myself away and neither hear nor speak to anyone."[121]

In the event, the eager women were disappointed, for the trip to Mariazell was countermanded. Joseph reported to Leopold that he (Joseph) had planned to travel by horseback with his brother Maximilian. When the weather was poor, Joseph had simply changed his mind. Rosenberg confirmed this explanation. Eleonore learned about the cancellation in Kromau before Leopoldine announced the news to her. "So there it is, nothing has come of this singular journey. Where were you the livelong day, dear sister, that you did not know about the new change. My husband let me know on the same day as your last letter, and our good Clary [Josepha Clary] who never knows anything, wrote about it to Françoise [Leopoldine Liechtenstein]." Accounts varied, however. "No one knows the reason that prevented his going," wrote Eleonore to her sister. "He will give you one after his fashion, since you are going to be with him; he has already said to la Clary what he always says, what are we going to do?" When, as predicted, Joseph II did speak with Leopoldine Kaunitz at a gathering soon after the episode, to her he seemed uncomfortable. "He did not want to talk about Mariazell," she wrote. "I think he is embarrassed, both for having wanted to go and for not having gone."[122]

The subject continued to fascinate. When Joseph was involved in a serious hunting accident in the Brigittenau near Vienna in summer 1784 and was so nearly mauled by a stag that his clothing was torn, Josepha Clary urged him to call for a celebratory service of thanksgiving (*Te Deum*). He showed the *Dames* the remnants of his torn cloak, and they tried to persuade him to send the remnants to Mariazell or possibly donate them to the Loretto chapel in the Augustinerkirche in Vienna. The latter was the site where traditionally the hearts of deceased Habsburg rulers were preserved. Joseph had quite recently caused the chapel to be moved from its central position within the church and had visited the newly reopened site the previous Saturday. He rejected the women's suggestions, and again the friends concluded that he was scornful of such pious exercises.[123] Still, the emperor did visit Mariazell in 1786, bringing back chaplets and devotional images for the *Dames*, Lacy, and Rosenberg.[124]

Reforming the monarchy's religious orders had been a goal of Maria Theresia, as noted previously, and the need for change had been widely recognized during the coregency.[125] Now, moving beyond the restrictions and investigations of troubled individual institutions that were instituted during Maria Theresia's reign, Joseph issued orders for actual dissolution of many convents and monasteries in 1781–1782. At first the emperor's target was the contemplative orders, faulted for their failure to contribute actively to the well-being of the state.[126] Soon the dissolutions included even large houses involved in teaching and other social services. Not initially characterized by ambitious, overarching goals, the closure program evolved into a source of revenue to foster improvements in parish life that Joseph believed the church needed—a greater number of well-trained secular priests, the establishment of new parishes where needed, and the improvement of pastoral care in existing parishes. Joseph briefly considered, and rejected, the simple expedient of expropriating what he deemed to be excess church property and applying it to these practical religious purposes. Instead a state-run religious fund (*Religionsfond*) was established to manage the confiscated property for the church. The central religious commission (*Geistlicher Ökonomat*, later called the *Geistliche Hofkommission*) oversaw these reforms. The proceeds from sales were used first to provide pensions for secularized members of former monastic houses who were unsuited to work as parish priests. The surplus would support additional parish priests and curates. Just as earlier during urbarial reforms of the coregency the emperor had wished to focus on each estate individually, so his approach to monastic reform called for assessment of the situation of each monastery, case by case. In May 1783 a second wave of dissolutions began, continuing to 1787. In all, 700 to 800 convents, monasteries, and other religious foundations were abolished, roughly one third of the monarchy's total.[127]

Planning for a third wave of dissolutions to begin in 1791 was nullified by the emperor's deteriorating health and subsequent death but also by the difficulty of providing sustenance for so many secularized monks and nuns. Wealth flowing into the Religionsfond had seemed ample at first. But the closing of monasteries did not produce adequate resources when so many of their former residents had to be pensioned. The reorganization of parishes proceeded hastily, with plans expanding over time even though the planners were not well-informed about available resources. Initially some monastic institutions had been targeted because they were financially weak and hopelessly in debt. As time passed it became clear that more money was needed for the emperor's parish plans; and by 1785 Joseph and his advisors were deliberately targeting rich monasteries and convents for liquidation. Now the emperor argued that any church property beyond the minimum needed to provide for its priestly hierarchy and their pastoral functions was rightfully at the state's disposal. The emperor did not expropriate church funds and cynically apply them to other purposes, to support unrelated programs. He did claim the authority to allocate resources in a manner that accorded with his own convictions.[128]

The women did not share the emperor's low opinion of cloistered life. Apparently none of the *Dames* felt personally called to become nuns, although there were aristocratic women who found convent life attractive. Maria Theresia, distraught after her husband's death, was only the most eminent among those who expressed longing for spiritual retreat and retirement. There is no evidence that she ever took practical measures to carry out such a plan once she overcame the initial shock of her husband's death. In any case, withdrawal to a convent would not have obliged her to take the veil.[129] For Leopoldine Kaunitz and Eleonore, early experiences at the Visitation convent of St. Stephan in Strasbourg had been formative and apparently positive. The Strasbourg convent was a significant force in the promotion of special devotion to "the Sacred Heart of Jesus" at mid-century. For reformers in Vienna this was an arcane, Jesuit-supported cult, a practice not in harmony with progressive goals and spurned by the Sorbonne in Paris and especially by religious thinkers with Jansenist leanings.[130] The *Dames* did not mention this cult in their letters, but they did follow some traditional and popular practices (e.g., Leopoldine Kaunitz in particular mentioned more than once her own observance of the "six Sundays" of Saint Gonzaga, and the women mention also seeking the Porziuncola Indulgence).[131]

All five *Dames* had friendly contacts with the Visitation convent in Vienna, which sheltered Archduke Franz's young bride, Elisabeth of Württemberg, upon her arrival in Vienna and was selected by Josepha Clary to care for and educate her granddaughters after the death of their mother, Josepha Ledebur, in 1778.[132] The plans that Joseph endorsed for the education and acculturation of Elisabeth at the Visitation convent contained remarkably favorable assessments of the likely effect of convent life on the princess, even beyond preparing her for conversion to Catholicism. The document "Reflexions sur le futur établissement de l'archiduc François de Toscane avec la Princesse Elisabeth de Württemberg" was not composed by the emperor but he sent the report to Leopold and also to Elisabeth's family. In his accompanying letter to Leopold dated 16 August 1781, cited at length in Beales's biography, the emperor wholeheartedly endorsed education at the convent, which would give the archduke a highly esteemed, well-educated wife. The plan itself praised the religious education the princess would receive. She would have before her "a continual example of wise instruction and the example of young persons of the first nobility who are educated there to perfection." The convent environment would be pleasant and salubrious, with easy access to "society that is most sought after and closest to the capital." The residents of the convent itself included "persons of the greatest merit and very agreeable, reasonable company."[133] These sentiments certainly clashed with many of the emperor's more general remarks about cloistered life per se. Quite possibly the *Dames* had a direct or indirect influence on the emperor's assessment of the Visitation nuns and their institutions. The women would have spoken in favor of selection of the Visitation convent; and the emperor certainly found the behavior and intellectual liveliness of his *Dames* to be congenial.

Joseph's dramatic closures of so many convent and monasteries unsettled the *Dames*, although like most contemporaries they conceded the need for reform. Probably he enjoyed the sensation and consternation his announcements caused in the small *société*. In September 1783, Joseph told the group that he had received petitions from nuns in three local convents of Augustinian nuns at

Himmelspforte, at St. Jakob auf der Hülben, and at St. Lorenz am Fleischmarkt. The case of the "Lorenzerinnen" generated particular interest among the *Dames*. Eleonore relayed to her sister the emperor's report to their small gathering, "that upon a single petition there were more than twenty or thirty signatories who stated that they had taken their vows before the age prescribed at present, that they were compelled, that they have complained to no avail for many years, and so to satisfy them each has been asked [to state] her choice, to be submitted signed and sealed, and then according to the number who wish to remain one, two, or three convents will be retained, he finds this device to be excellent, fair, and flawless." Eleonore described Leopoldine Liechtenstein's reaction: "Françoise remarked concerning this that it was dreadful, that she would have them flogged, and such nonsense." Eleonore had remained silent but meditated a form of sabotage. "I thought perhaps this was something to report to the Superior of the Laurentzen," she wrote, "for an ambush is being laid to ruin them, but on the other hand I do not know her and God knows if as a result of my good intentions I could find myself involved in a horrid mishmash."[134] Joseph wrote to his brother Leopold describing his plans for these three convents and added, "This has caused a great sensation among the good souls, and it seems that they have been busily altering the high opinion that they had of the happiness and satisfaction enjoyed in the monastic orders."[135] Of just under 200 nuns in the three convents, almost all eventually chose secularization rather than transfer to another convent of uncertain location, possibly in part because they knew that closure of their convents in Vienna was a certainty.[136] These convents had substantial property and had established schools. When the property of the Saint Jakob convent was dispersed in 1784, Josepha Clary asked the Lower Austrian government for permission to acquire the prized *Marienbild* of the convent, especially loved by the nuns and an object of veneration for Josepha Clary herself—possibly in order to transfer it to Vienna's Visitation convent.[137]

In an effort to make the parish the sole focus of religious life, Joseph prohibited public religious services in the remaining convents and monasteries.[138] The emperor did allow some exceptions when petitioned by his friends concerning the activities of favored groups such as the nuns at the Visitation convent. This convent was never a target for dissolution and even received permission to recruit additional nuns from sister convents outside the monarchy (Leopoldine Kaunitz remarked to Eleonore, "I assure you it seems something of a miracle").[139] But Leopoldine Kaunitz felt hypocritical and angry as she found herself pleading with the emperor on behalf of Vienna's Visitation convent when the residents wished to celebrate the festival of Saint Jane de Chantal, one of the order's founders. She told her sister, "you will understand and feel just how difficult it was for me to speak to him about a permission that he has no authority to give, and to talk to him without irritation." She had hesitated, "but finally I reminded myself so forcefully that the church is being persecuted, that we are living among unbelievers from whom we must obtain as a grace the exercise of our religion, that I made my first attempt several days ago with such an air of unconcern that there was truly some duplicity in it." She failed to persuade the emperor, who would permit the convent to acknowledge publicly only the festival of Saint Francis de Sales. Leopoldine Kaunitz had expostulated: "My God, Your Majesty, surely we are still tolerated, and indeed that is nothing evil." The emperor merely responded that he feared setting an inconvenient precedent for other convents, "and then I kept quiet," Leopoldine added.[140]

From her vantage point in Kromau, Eleonore Liechtenstein witnessed close up the dismay that spread at the local Paulist monastery during summer 1782 as the monks learned of the government's actions against monasteries.[141] A government commission tasked with closing the Kromau monastery did not arrive until August 1786 and then acted as humanely as possible, Eleonore reported. There were few great spiritual lights among the monastery's residents, she admitted. It was nevertheless wrong for the government to lay hands on this property; "it is an act of the greatest violence to drive away clerics against whom there have been no complaints, to take over properties that they have received from their founders, and to deprive the entire land of the spiritual succor that they provided." The government's plan was to convert the Paulist building in Kromau into a factory. Eleonore Liechtenstein tried in vain to preserve the church building as a second parish church or "a German congregation [*filiale*]," which she was convinced the town of Kromau desired.[142]

The diligent emperor also found time to regulate the quasi-religious female collegiate foundations or *Stifte* in Habsburg lands, valued so highly by noble families especially as "establishments" for surplus female offspring. As noted previously, several of these foundations were important to the *Dames*. Josepha Clary's daughter Thérèse was a *Stiftsdame* at Nivelles in Belgium until her marriage to Count Johann Wilczek in 1787. Leopoldine Kaunitz's elder niece, granddaughter of the chancellor, was canoness at Mons until her marriage to Count Rudolf Wrbna in 1785, and the younger Kaunitz niece, who was offered a vacant prebend by Joseph II in December 1780, remained a canoness until her death in 1805.[143] (The *Stifte* of Leopoldine Liechtenstein's daughter, at Essen and Thorn, lay outside the purview of Joseph's reforms for Habsburg lands as did Buchau, the *Stift* of Maria Anna Hohenzollern-Hechingen, sister of Josepha Clary and Sidonia Kinsky.) New regulations for Belgian *Stifte* were published on the emperor's behalf on 22 April 1786 by his representatives, Marie Christine and Prince Albert. The reforms were not radical. They diluted the religious elements of life at the foundations while leaving their social exclusiveness unimpaired. Residents no longer served as *Chorfrauen,* and other obligatory religious exercises were strictly limited. Residency requirements were made uniform, and no absences could last more than four months each year. Payment of an individual woman's prebend was made contingent upon her compliance with the rules. The minimum age for entry was raised to eighteen, and the traditional probationary period was eliminated entirely. Simple, standardized dress was required in public and at services. The popular practice of holding more than one prebend simultaneously was prohibited. Canonesses received explicit permission to enjoy secular amusements such as theatrical performances and balls in their locales, if they were properly chaperoned.[144] Apparently in discussions with Leopoldine Kaunitz the emperor argued that his reforms would make these institutions more serviceable and practical. Preserved among the billets penned by the emperor to Leopoldine Kaunitz was one explaining that he was sending her a copy of his new regulations for canonesses, a note beginning "Madame I wish to be blameless [*blanc . . . comme la neige*] in your eyes." In the message the emperor conceded that elderly canonesses might find it difficult to adjust their mode of living.[145] Marie Christine herself criticized the new provisions in her letter to Josepha Clary on 30 April 1786. Josepha had reported to the archduchess that her daughter Thérèse Clary was returning to her *Stift* after a period of absence. Marie Christine replied, "she will find her chapter distressed by the new regulations. I am sure that if the Emperor saw the grief he causes to both old and young he would not have done this thing or he would exempt them, for here all the freedom he gives them on the one hand and takes away on the other is useless to them." Marie Christine spoke of "general affliction" among the canonesses.[146]

With his plan in 1783 to establish state-approved "general seminaries," Joseph took from the bishops and religious orders their traditional role in training young priests and substituted new uniform institutions that were to prepare priests more adequately for useful work in their parishes, as envisioned by the emperor and his advisors. The curriculum would be tailored to meet both the needs of the church and the requirements of the state, to promote the general good of the population. Convinced of the legitimacy of his actions, Joseph nevertheless found that many of his subjects viewed this change as unwarranted interference by the state in yet another area of religious life.[147] The *Dames* loathed the new institutions. Leopoldine Kaunitz told Eleonore that Josepha Clary "has made me sad to the depths of my soul, she holds that it is truly lucky that we will not be seeing him [the women were visiting the chancellor and would not meet with the emperor], that religious affairs are going as badly as possible, that everything that is done concerning the new seminary will bring about the total destruction of religion in our land."[148] The seminaries became a particularly sensitive topic for the *société*. Leopoldine Kaunitz wrote to Eleonore on 22 July 1783 that Joseph had been with the group at Leopoldine Liechtenstein's residence the previous night but that she and Josepha had been afraid to speak their minds: "my fear, my terror, my revulsion increase continually, I saw the same thing on la Clari's [Josepha

Clary] face, we said nothing that could have even the most remote relationship to internal arrangements."[149]

Joseph's reform of the monarchy's charitable institutions further enhanced the role of the parish while also increasing the scope of the government's presence in subjects' everyday lives. The changes relegated to the sidelines those intermediary agents, traditionally active in charitable work, who were neither state employees nor parish priests. Joseph had inherited a decentralized system of relief for the indigent, the needy sick, and the aged population of the monarchy, a kaleidoscope of services offered by benevolent monastic orders, town and parish officials, landed proprietors, and kindly (or intimidated) individuals who offered handouts and shelter to beggars. Sometimes local officials simply moved panhandlers and indigents across jurisdictional lines in the notorious *Bettlerschub*, a bid to avoid the expense of supporting those who could not establish a claim to assistance through local birth or long-time residence. Authorities in Vienna in the 1780s in particular were contending with growing urban poverty.[150] The emperor's objective was greater centralization and efficiency through functional specialization of relief. Charity was to be a public function, overseen by the government even as it was administered by the church. His first program of centralized almsgiving in Vienna, under a relatively traditional system managed by the abbot of the Schottentor monastery, proved to be only a stopgap measure. Both Leopoldine Kaunitz and Eleonore pledged support for the "Liebesammlung" of the Schottentor abbot for only a year at a time, on the assumption that these arrangements were unlikely to endure (in Eleonore's words, "since things are so changeable in this world, . . . for this will soon be abolished, and then they will demand [payment] by right as revenue, whereas by remaining uncommitted, one can see at least how the matter fares and how it is managed").[151]

Eleonore's caustic remarks in her letter from Kromau in July 1781 afford a glimpse of the difficulties Joseph faced as he began to centralize and standardize charitable practices in his disparate lands. A new imperial patent concerning *hôpitaux* (asylums for the infirm), Eleonore reported to her sister, apparently pertained to the capital's institutions only, and more specifically to Vienna's *Findelhaus, Waisenhaus, Krankenhaus, Arbeitshaus*. The Bohemian chancellery had received a copy of the complicated instructions without understanding its limited application. Bewildered but afraid to ask for clarification, the chancellery had simply sent the entire project "en bloc" to the *Landeshauptmann*, who passed it on to each district captain, "and so finally it has arrived to disrupt our hospital in Kromau, and so forth and so on." Especially troublesome was the accompanying series of questions about local conditions that had to be answered and submitted by local officials. These, Eleonore Liechtenstein felt sure, would lead to mischief and government meddling.[152]

Reforms carried out by Count Johann Nepomuk Buquoy (1741–1803) on his own estates in southern Bohemia after the famine of the early 1770s had attracted the approving attention of the emperor. At a soirée in August 1782, the emperor outlined his own evolving plans for subsuming all the monarchy's privately supported *hôpitaux* that cared for the indigent elderly under more centralized, supervised management. Leopoldine Kaunitz described her own reaction and Josepha's. "Poor creature that I am, my hair stood on end at these words more than at a shot fired from a canon. These are the hospitals for the elderly, on whom they wish to bestow the pleasant liberty of being once again a charge on society in return for a few additional kreutzer beyond what they currently receive." She and Josepha had remonstrated. "We spoke like two Cassandras on the subject . . . demonstrating how those who have no children will be . . . robbed and poorly cared for in their decrepit condition; apparently it has been decided, the administration of all these hospitals will consume half the revenue." Josepha had voiced exasperation that was apparently felt by others, exclaiming "but, oh my God, is it not possible to correct abuses without destroying the entire thing?"[153] Eleonore regretted the change, which she felt would deprive infirm people of comfort and would be a spiritual loss to anyone who currently supported such a foundation, "for it is disinterested, it continues always the same, so many have taken a share in it, and it brings comfort to both young and old." Eleonore Liechtenstein's own preference was to encourage and expand private institutions in their traditional form.[154]

Joseph summoned Buquoy to Vienna to organize a new citywide charitable system, a centralized "institution" for the poor.[155] By 1783 the emperor was ready to abolish the charitable lay brotherhoods that had been attached to individual monasteries or churches. He pooled their resources to form parish-based brotherhoods that would support the new *Institut der thätigen Liebe des Nächsten* (roughly the "institute of active neighborly love") on Buquoy's model, focusing first on Vienna. Fines collected by local governments for a variety of transgressions as well as some money from abolished monasteries were also earmarked for the institutions. The emperor ordered that alms boxes be set up in private residences, the proceeds to be collected weekly and delivered to the institute. From these accumulated funds meager alms payments were distributed by parish clergy. The clergy were to exhort their parishioners to participate in the new charitable system. The popular journal *Wöchentlichen Wahrheiten* added its voice to the official chorus of encouragement. At the same time, Vienna's residents were prohibited from dispensing charity on their own or through unapproved channels. A similar approach with some adjustments was mandated for large population centers outside Vienna. The new dispensation resulted in a transformation of poor relief.[156] In summer 1783, Eleonore Liechtenstein reported from Kromau that the local confraternity of St. Anne, with its small fund from legacies left mostly by townspeople, had been informed "that no other confraternities are approved any longer except the *Liebs-Verein*, they are exhorted to establish that, and their meager resources are taken from them, remonstrances have availed them nothing."[157]

The *Dames* noted with disapproval the emperor's confiscation of the separate funds of the time-honored "court alms" and the "fund for converts" (*Hofalmosen* and *Convertiten Cassa*). The latter had been used by earlier Habsburgs to support converts to Catholicism, but in more recent reigns both funds had often been diverted to favored individuals who suffered from nothing worse than genteel poverty. Joseph merged these specialized funds with the general resources for charity. Josepha raised the issue at a soirée in October 1785. "Yesterday the questioned was raised, it was la Clari [Josepha Clary] who began, about an unpleasant matter concerning what are called the 'court poor' [*die Hofarmen*] and the Convert Fund," Leopoldine Kaunitz wrote her sister; "these are people who according to the system that has been established are not eligible for pensions, and who without being beggars are truly poor. As these people came at the beginning of the month to receive their little pittance at some place unknown to me, it was announced to them that they would receive nothing and that they were to go to their parish, and that they would be treated as provided for by the institute." The change caused pain and dismay, Leopoldine reported: "these are widows, poor spinsters, and among the converts some people of no means, for what can one do with eight kreutzer, and the majority of them will not receive even that." According to Eleonore, who had spoken with Buquoy himself, Joseph had long meditated making this specific change. Buquoy had opposed the action, arguing that the fund for converts succored poor if not actually destitute individuals.[158]

To systematize all charitable work Joseph aimed to segregate sick individuals from those who were merely needy. In the past these groups had often been collected almost indiscriminately in such institutions as existed. In August 1784 a large new general hospital opened in Vienna, equipped to handle all routine sicknesses and situated where there had previously been a large poorhouse. Despite its mammoth, impersonal proportions, the hospital did offer opportunity for the exercise of private charity, since wealthy individuals could fund beds in the hospital and pay the expenses of the sick persons who used them. Such beds sported a plaque on which the arms of a noble benefactor could be displayed. Separate facilities to treat special populations such as foundlings, invalid soldiers, and pregnant women were established. A new building, the *Narrenturm* (or "lunatics' tower," locally dubbed "Kaiser Josephs Guglhupf"), accommodated the mentally ill.[159]

To wealthy aristocrats such as the *Dames* who assumed that the personal nexus associated with the bestowal of largesse was essential to the comfort they offered the poor and the sick, these well-intended but abrupt initiatives to reorganize all charitable work appeared grotesque.[160] Eleonore Liechtenstein observed in connection with the shelters for the infirm that both those who dispensed and those who received alms were accustomed to a personal touch that was missing from the new arrangements. The *Dames* had doubts about the stability and long-term viability of the new institutions as contrasted with time-tested older methods by which families and corporate groups had dispensed alms as a matter of obligation, tradition, and habit. These criticisms proved to have some merit. After its rousing inauguration and the initial infusion of monies, the new poor relief system was chronically short of funds. Eleonore's daughter reported in August 1783 that Buquoy's "institute" in Königgrätz (Hradec Králové) had very nearly caused a disturbance when contributions fell off and assistance dwindled; "the institution . . . almost produced a rebellion among the poor who, having relied upon the initial arrangement, found themselves without resource when the enthusiasm of the rich diminished."[161] The hastiness of so many changes in poor relief and the inevitable proliferation of amendments and additions to the original regulations caused donors to postpone commitments.

Joseph packed a great many religious reform initiatives into the first few years of his reign. Alarming reports about the emperor's objectives soon reached Pope Pius VI in Rome from Archbishop Migazzi and papal nuncio Garampi. Some of Joseph's actions, particularly his unilateral appointment of abbots in Austrian Lombardy, threatened both the pope's authority and his income. The pope's discomfiture led to the most dramatic religious event of Joseph's reign: the journey of the pope to Vienna in 1782. Informed of the pope's intention to visit, Joseph was not pleased but, as etiquette required, he issued a formal invitation on 11 January 1782.[162] The pope arrived in Vienna on 22 March and stayed until 22 April, his visit encompassing Holy Week. His public appearances in Vienna attracted masses of spectators. Ambassadors and envoys residing in Vienna—representatives from France, Spain, Venice, Portugal, Sardinia, Naples, Russia, Prussia, Palatinate, Parma, Lucca, Genoa, England, Hannover, and Holland—paid their respects to him formally. From the various provinces of the monarchy bishops and archbishops converged on Vienna, as did foreign guests who timed their visits to the capital to correspond with the pope's presence. With his pleasing appearance and personality (he was described by contemporaries as a handsome and imposing figure) the pope planned to show himself to the populace liberally. He hoped that a strong and positive popular reaction to his own presence as head of the church would pressure Joseph into moderating his attack on monasteries and dissuade him from making unauthorized appointments to high church offices. The pope's visit reached its climax on Easter Sunday, 31 March, with high mass at St. Stephan's cathedral. In a final major ceremony on 19 April, the pope created four new cardinals.[163]

Despite his popular success, the pope left Vienna disappointed with his limited ability to influence policy. However, he maintained a public show of friendliness and respect for the emperor, even affirming publicly and explicitly Joseph's good standing as a Catholic. More than one historian has argued that Joseph's eagerness for this papal endorsement was less evidence of an imperial triumph than a demonstration of Joseph's urgent need for a testimonial from his papal guest, whose visit had certainly won for him the affection of the Viennese. It has even been suggested that the concession made by Joseph in order to obtain this public affirmation—upon their request, Hungarian bishops were explicitly permitted to continue deriving their powers of dispensation from the pope—actually recast Joseph's reforms into a program over which the pope retained some residual authority.[164] Emperor and pope parted company on the outskirts of Vienna at Mariabrunn, site of a shrine esteemed by the *Dames* and a convent that was destined to be shut down in the course of Joseph's reforms.[165] Throughout the papal visit, Joseph too was careful to exhibit before the broad public a respectful and friendly demeanor toward the pope, although in their private conferences he exasperated the pope with his intransigence on all but minor issues. In a letter to Leopold the emperor described how he and the pope had staked out their positions, exchanging notes in mid-April: "finally today He [the pope] has given birth to a document, and I shall give birth to a response. All that I can tell you so far is that these offspring will never marry each other."[166] To his circle of friends and associates, Joseph spoke sarcastically about the pope's visit, and he permitted the press to do the same. Still, the two leaders avoided a schism, and in late 1783 Joseph paid a return visit to the pope in Rome.[167]

Chancellor Kaunitz's behavior during the papal visit excited comment. Owing to Joseph's recurrent eye infection, the chancellor played a particularly active role.[168] The pope made a special effort to communicate with him, judging that Kaunitz was the author of a number of Joseph's most radical reforms. According to public report (not confirmed by the participants themselves), the pope's visit to Kaunitz at the chancellor's palace in Mariahilf in mid-April proved awkward. Kaunitz, it would appear, intentionally ignored rudimentary rules of etiquette: leaving to his sons Ernst and Franz Wenzel the chore of greeting and taking leave of the pope outside the palace; dressing informally; neglecting to bend the knee or kiss hands; abruptly and designedly replacing his own hat on his head at the very minute the pope did so. The pope was unable to hide his discomfiture but, recalling Kaunitz's well-known sensitivity concerning sickness and death, he remarked to the chancellor in parting that, since Kaunitz had reached an age when his mortal end could not be long deferred, he (the pope) would pray for Kaunitz, a boon that would surely benefit the chancellor's immortal soul. Possibly Kaunitz's health, not then at its best, was a factor in the chancellor's eccentric behavior. In any case Kaunitz used his influence to stiffen Joseph's resistance to the pope's demands, composing memos that warned the emperor against backsliding.[169] During his sojourn in Vienna the pope also visited Rosenberg, bedridden with a serious illness. The pope gave the lord chamberlain a beautifully ornamented memento of their meeting. According to report, the irascible cleric Blarer, not yet fallen from imperial favor and serving as director of the Vienna seminary, caused a scandal when, kept waiting for his papal audience, he began to abuse the pope volubly. Gossip had it that the emperor, who was determined to preserve outward respect and civility toward the pope, required Blarer to leave Vienna within 24 hours. At a soirée with the *Dames* in July 1782, however, Joseph refuted this popular account.[170]

The scheduled events of the papal visit included several occasions when court ladies were allowed to pay their respects. The *Dames* seized these opportunities, heedless of the likely impatience or ridicule of emperor or chancellor. Zinzendorf reported one of these occasions when about fifty ladies gathered, with Josepha Clary at their head, to kiss the pope's slippers and to listen while Leopoldine Liechtenstein delivered an address to the pope ("Princess Françoise harangued him"). The pope visited the Liechtenstein picture gallery on 15 April, at which time the entire Liechtenstein clan assembled to greet him.[171] Archduchess Marie Christine's correspondence with Josepha Clary in April 1782 attests to Josepha's great pleasure in seeing the pope but also to both women's understanding of complex papal-imperial relations. Marie Christine wrote, "I am quite glad that you are content with the pope"; but also, "God grant that all will be well and justly resolved if only so that this burdensome and troubling uncertainty does not continue." A great prince could not simply withdraw orders he had so publicly issued, Marie Christine conceded ("is not able, after having pushed forward so openly, to retract and make changes"). Great tact was needed "to preserve the honor of both the one and the other," Marie Christine wrote, "but I fear the excessive enthusiasm of the Viennese may do more harm than good to his [the pope's] cause, and I see that you share my sentiment concerning this."[172]

In his letter of 22 April 1782 to his brother Leopold, Joseph described his own relief over the pope's departure: "during this last week in particular the thing has become almost unbearable in view of the scheming and wheedling which he injects into his negotiations and all his conversation, and the truly ridiculous enthusiasm that has seized especially the women."[173] Joseph's report to Mercy affirmed the emperor's satisfaction with his personal success in turning events to his own profit. "It was not easy to accomplish on this occasion many objectives that are so nearly contradictory among themselves," he wrote, "to send the pope back as he came, yet to avoid any rupture or disagreeable sensation, to offer him a means of appearing to have achieved something, to convince the public of our good union and friendship, and to engage the Pope to offer a public testimony, spoken and written, of the inviolate and flawless state in which he has found religion in my states." Understandably Joseph felt entitled to gloat. "To manage all that took not a little composure, patience, and German persistence against all the great and small stratagems employed by an Italian from Rome who came thoroughly prepared," reported Joseph. The pope had tried to establish a damaging precedent with every word spoken and asked questions in excruciating detail on every topic. But Joseph was pleased: "in short all went well and it has ended more favorably than I had even dared to hope."[174]

With the *Dames*, Joseph delivered himself of witty aphorisms about the papal visit. Enchanted with the pope's geniality, the women were not equally satisfied with Joseph's behavior. Leopoldine Kaunitz reported to Eleonore Joseph's description of a communication he had received from the pope several months after the visit: "He said he had received a letter of four pages from the pope. The tone in which he said this, adding that he had answered it on the spot, gave me a horrible feeling." Very likely this was the pope's letter of August 1782, which prompted Joseph in his reply, distinctly sarcastic, to make mention of the supposed advisors of the pope who had unwisely endorsed the papal visit to Vienna. These same "advisors," Joseph had pointedly commented, had now induced the pope to write—or were writing for him—the letter Joseph had just received, protesting the confiscation and use of church property for ends that the emperor for his part deemed appropriate.[175]

As previously noted, a particular concern for the women throughout the decade was their fear that Joseph would too often allow his own decisions to be influenced by his desire for éclat and favorable mention by publicists of the Enlightenment.[176] In various missives to Leopoldine Kaunitz intended to justify his policies the emperor frequently incorporated references to an "être supreme," the "supreme being" often cited by such writers. But the emperor was no free thinker. Joseph apparently remained orthodox in his own theological outlook and personal practice of the Catholic faith, as even the papal nuncio conceded. Most of Joseph's biographers have been persuaded that the emperor remained a sincere Catholic, his church reforms being driven by political and practical rather than theological considerations.[177] Careful historians have found evidence that in the course of the 1780s the emperor embraced a somewhat more conservative approach. The historian Peter Barton has drawn attention to the limited, unstable, and increasingly restrictive nature of toleration in both principle and practice as granted by Joseph II and to Joseph's explicit affirmations in both formal and informal statements that Catholicism alone was the true faith.[178] When the emperor learned that conversions to Protestantism were more numerous than expected, as early as 1782 he made such conversions more difficult. Individuals who sought to identify as Protestant were required to submit to a six-week course of indoctrination in Catholic theology.[179] Historian Ernst Wangermann has noted that in the course of the decade Joseph's stance on both tolerance and censorship hardened somewhat, particularly after publications that smacked of deism or skepticism began to appear in significant numbers.[180] Barton notes that, according to his brother Leopold, Joseph was uncomfortable about the disrespect for religion that, in Leopold's view, had resulted from Joseph's own lax attitude toward Catholicism. Barton further suggests that after 1785 Joseph even permitted Vienna's Archbishop Migazzi, outspoken opponent of the emperor's reforms, to affect his (Joseph's) decisions.[181] Possibly the emperor was influenced by the admonitions of the *Dames* and other like-minded conservative contemporaries. Joseph's own relatively traditional beliefs concerning religious doctrine surely played a role as well. As Barton has concluded, there is every reason to assume that, just as the words of his various promulgations repeatedly affirmed, Joseph did sincerely desire the reconversion of straying Protestants to his own Catholic faith.[182]

In evening gatherings and in the women's correspondence throughout the 1780s the religious changes were constantly analyzed, debated, and assessed by the women. In some cases the women questioned not so much the emperor's goals—for example, few open-minded Catholics of the period denied that some monastic reforms were needed, nor did the *Dames*—as the emperor's right to act unilaterally.[183] And they concluded with considerable dismay that the central point of contention, with far-reaching consequences, was the emperor's authority to impose his will on the church.

In secular matters too, Joseph pushed forward a broad, disjointed program of reforms, eliciting spirited reactions from his friends. Again the women greeted many initiatives with understated, or unstated, skepticism. Their responses were not simply the result of an ingrained, unintelligent obstructionism. They had come to regard Joseph as an ardent but incautious and unpredictable ruler, an impression he reinforced with strident, hyperbolic proclamations about his intentions. Clearly they feared the consequences of the speed—more accurately the haste—with which the emperor sought to transform not only religious practices but also the inherited economic and legal systems as they functioned in the Habsburg monarchy of the late eighteenth century. Not a leveler whose goal was an egalitarian society, Joseph did want his government to provide effective protection to all productive subjects and enable those who were diligent to prosper within the status assigned to them (as he and contemporaries believed) by birth, providence, and individual circumstances. In return he expected to obtain from subjects their loyalty to the state and their best productive efforts. In his efforts to exclude from political power all intermediate authorities that were not agents of his centralized government, Joseph eroded first and foremost the prestige, legal and economic status, and political influence of the nobility, plainly a matter of consequence for the *Dames*.

To effect the changes he desired, Joseph continued to rely heavily on aristocrats in top government positions, making use of the talents of the lesser nobility as well. Qualitative changes in the nature of civil service including the introduction of yearly *Conduitenlisten* assessing performance and a meticulously graded, impersonal system of pensions made such employment a less obvious choice for the tradition-minded aristocrat. In most cases, Joseph's reforms increased uniformity of administration and judicial practice throughout Habsburg lands. Generally such changes restricted the autonomy of his servitors, whether noble or commoner. Aristocratic candidates of previous generations had preferred assignments that provided opportunity to display noble élan. Joseph was more interested in public-spirited, well-trained, diligent employees, who would adopt the interests of the state wholeheartedly as their own, following the imperial example.[184]

Through extensive administrative reforms Joseph sought to make regional and local governments throughout his disparate lands as alike as possible in structure and function. Inherited constitutions and legal codes very often served to enshrine the special position of the privileged orders of clergy and nobility, a situation that, in contrast to his Habsburg predecessors, Joseph was not willing to accept. In spite of the firsthand knowledge about local conditions he gathered through personal travel, the emperor's measures accommodated differences among the histories and usages of various regions only when absolutely necessary. Where he could not bend to his will the local and regional institutions filled with representatives of the nobility, he ignored them.[185] Administrative reform was particularly challenging in the kingdom of Hungary where Joseph offended the sensibilities of the Magyar nobility by refusing to convoke the Hungarian diet and rejecting the Hungarians' request that he undergo the traditional coronation ceremony as king of Hungary, a ritual during which he would have sworn to uphold the traditional Hungarian constitution. He redrew the historic boundaries of Hungarian counties without regard to his subjects' sentiments, disrupting established power relationships and clientage systems of the Hungarian nobility. He installed royal commissioners to oversee his new district governments. He initiated a census of the kingdom's entire population, a practice new to Hungary and feared by the peasants as a prelude to rigorous military conscription and by the Hungarian nobility as an attack on the *insurrectio* that had traditionally served to justify the nobility's exemption from most taxes. Joseph required mastery of German as an administrative language for all government employees in the Hungarian kingdom, with varying but tight deadlines for different levels of administration and in no case allowing more than three years for instruction.[186] These Hungarian reforms were to pave the way for the greater uniformity that the emperor envisaged for all regions of the monarchy over time, but in Hungary they were seen as a particular affront. Although the emperor was aware of the momentous nature of the Hungarian reforms, he underestimated the active resistance that they would eventually face and that would frustrate his plans. As Leopoldine Kaunitz observed to her sister in 1783, "The Emperor himself says that this constitutes a total upheaval and there will be a great deal of noise and many malcontents."[187] In an unmistakable, dramatic gesture, Joseph transferred the various crowns and insignia of Habsburg territories, including the crown of Saint Stephan so cherished by the Hungarians, from regional repositories to the *Schatzkammer* in the Hofburg for safe keeping. Leopoldine Kaunitz went to see the Hungarian crown after its arrival in May 1784 and pronounced it to be the most attractive of all regalia on display.[188] Finally, in 1787 Joseph extended his centralizing administrative reforms to Lombardy and even to the Belgian provinces, long a bastion of independence and a peculiarly inhospitable environment for Joseph's initiatives, as time would tell.

Indefatigable, the emperor also embarked upon a major reform of legal codes and judicial practices. The need for change had been recognized early during Maria Theresia's reign. In 1753 she had established a *Kompilationskommission*. It had labored for many years, trying to specify legal procedures for the monarchy's territories and to produce civil and criminal codes that would at least enumerate extant laws, without at first attempting to modernize them. A cumbersome and unsatisfactory draft of a civil *Codex Theresianus* appeared in 1766. A criminal code was actually published in 1768, the so-called *Nemesis Theresiana*, which simply collected and described existing, but often outmoded, laws and penalties. Its detailed illustrations of draconian physical punishments offended many and were considered to be an embarrassment to the monarchy; and at the end of Maria Theresia's reign there was general agreement that more far-reaching reform was needed.[189] In 1776, with the enthusiastic backing of Joseph, Maria Theresia had agreed to prohibit torture as an instrument of investigation and punishment.[190]

Soon after Joseph assumed full power in 1780 he drew upon the work of the commissions from his mother's reign first to reform the administration of justice, the goal being greater uniformity throughout the monarchy. Of special importance was his establishment of clear, rational procedures for legal appeals. Organizations that had exercised authority outside the justice system of the state, most notably the church and noble landlords, were restricted in their functions or stripped of them entirely. The emperor wanted to eliminate the multiplicity of lower courts staffed by untrained or biased personnel, including those serving in manorial courts. Noble landowners were now required to employ legally trained, qualified personnel if they wished to exercise judicial authority on their lands.[191] Before many years of his reign had passed, the emperor set out to completely overhaul the monarchy's laws themselves. Devising new legal codes required much time and effort. Both civil and criminal law remained in flux throughout Joseph's reign. The emperor promulgated new regulations and then amendments to those new regulations with great speed and unpredictability. Commissions attempting to organize and publish these decisions in a systematic way had to train their sights on a moving target. The emperor worked to enlist public opinion in favor of his new measures, encouraging or actively supporting publications that aimed to defend the new measures and persuade the public of their wisdom.[192]

For civil law, a new *Allgemeines bürgerliches Gesetzbuch* was compiled for the Austrian and Bohemian lands, taking effect at the beginning of 1787. The new code curtailed some practices that had favored noble landowners and had directly or indirectly buttressed their extensive control over economic resources. The emperor even considered abolishing entail, an important legal tool (as noted earlier) of aristocratic families that preserved their property as an entity across generations. In the event, he merely made establishment of new *fideicommissa* more difficult. Hardly revolutionary, this move was nevertheless one of a number of strategies the emperor employed that would in the course of time make control of productive land more broadly available to its actual cultivators. The emperor strengthened the rights of all offspring in a family, including in many cases those who were illegitimate, thus again chipping away at legal practices that helped privileged families to build, protect, and monopolize their corporate wealth.[193] More arcanely, provisions also restricted the corporate authority of the nobility to effectively limit ownership of land to fully recognized members of a given noble provincial diet. Lands held by both nobles and commoners could now be freely passed to new owners regardless of status. Newly prescribed procedures left little discretionary authority to judges, under the assumption that enlightened laws were universally and uniformly applicable and required no gloss. In case of uncertainty, the sovereign was to be the arbiter.[194]

During fall 1785 provisions of a new criminal code that was in preparation were discussed at the soirées. Leopoldine Kaunitz reported the discussion to her sister, who was then staying in the countryside: "We are going to see appear very shortly the new criminal code, what I have heard saddens me, there is dreadful cruelty and yet to no purpose, it makes the guilty person miserable while neither reforming him nor deterring others, this makes for suffering to no purpose, for in practice that is tantamount to impunity." The women judged a number of the provisions to be unnecessarily harsh. Leopoldine Kaunitz was resigned to the changes but believed that in this case the emperor had at least listened to objections raised by the *Dames*. "But what can we say other than jeremiads, only too happy if it can be with us as it was with this Prophet, whom Lorel [Leopoldine Kaunitz's daughter] has just been reading about, when the King and other mighty men, tired of hearing him, cast him into a cistern full of mud . . . one must admit that even if our words accomplish nothing, at least he [Joseph II] attends to them with patience and constancy."[195]

The new criminal code was not formally published until 1787, but many of its provisions were introduced earlier. It confirmed the exclusion of manorial courts from jurisdiction over criminal cases. It officially abolished the death penalty but the punishments that replaced death were specified primarily with deterrence as their object, not humanitarianism. Joseph favored sentencing delinquents to useful physical labor, preferably onerous and carried out in public to serve as a warning. The sight of convicts undergoing punishment would have a salutary effect on the public, he believed, and at the same time this labor would be beneficial to his state. For serious crimes, prisoners were sent to tow barges in Hungary, a punishment that resulted in death for most within a few months. Thus although he had greatly restricted the death penalty even before abolishing it (except in cases of emergency such as a popular uprising) in the late 1780s, the emperor substituted deliberately harsh treatment that often led to death. Flogging and branding were also favored practices. After conviction for premeditated murder, a condemned criminal was handled so roughly that he was likely to die of his treatment. Such ruthless punishment was a hallmark of the Josephinian justice system; the *Dames* had rightly feared this outcome. At least one historian has concluded that the emperor's harsh directives concerning barge-hauling "reveal a mind which by any standards was not entirely normal."[196] As in civil law, the reformed procedures afforded judges little discretionary authority.[197]

A prominent murder case that occurred in summer 1782 afforded the public an early glimpse of the harshness of Josephinian justice. A coachman, Josef Wiesenthaler, murdered his fiancée. Convicted, he was subjected to reformed criminal procedures that already invoked the death penalty only in rare cases. Wiesenthaler was branded, flogged, exhibited publicly, imprisoned, and for several consecutive years severely flogged again on each anniversary of his crime. Eventually he was sent to haul barges. Leopoldine Kaunitz believed the death penalty was more appropriate and actually more humane. Appalled by what she witnessed, in two separate letters Leopoldine Kaunitz reported events to her sister Eleonore: "Today you would have seen [had you been here] played out under our windows the first example of the new mode of punishing criminals guilty of the worst crimes: it is the coachman who murdered his mistress. I do not know what to say to you, I mistrust my emotions, and perhaps my spirit of contrariness . . . I find that they have managed to inspire compassion for this monster, and yet that he is even so not punished as he ought to be." A week later she reported, "This miserable coachman is not dead. He was aware that he was not condemned to death, but from what people say he definitely wishes he had been. His sentence, when you read it, is like a bad novel. I would have preferred to have him drawn and quartered . . . I cannot describe to you the many things to which he is condemned. I do not see how he can be useful to society. He will excite compassion and even in a theatrical play compassion for a monster is a great flaw." Leopoldine Kaunitz denounced these proceedings unequivocally. "Such proceedings pain me in a way that I cannot describe. It turns my stomach, unnerves me, it seems dreadful, and I can assure you that without being cruel I would be tempted to attest by laws both divine and human that the penalty of death is more appropriate, more just, more serviceable to the rest of society and even for the guilty than this new criminal code, the like of which has been known only in Russia."[198]

Joseph wished to streamline his judiciary and ensure that subjects were treated in a professional, impartial manner; but the emperor's haughty, imperious manner frequently caused contemporaries, the *Dames* among them, to question his fairness toward his administrators, and even his judgment. The historian Mitrofanov cites many contemporary reports of Joseph's biting tongue and his unwillingness to accept any blame for miscarried policies.[199] In 1782 Joseph learned that Hungarian courts had convicted a group of Gypsies of cannibalism, using harsh methods of interrogation and torture to obtain confessions and ordering executions. Joseph initially told the women that he knew nothing about the investigation and that he had sent an urgent inquiry to Hungary. By mid-1783 Joseph had clarified the situation to his own satisfaction, as he explained at an evening gathering. There had been no cannibals ("the cannibals were not cannibals at all"), he said, and he was ashamed that courts were capable of rendering such a verdict during his reign. The hardiest individuals among the accused had withstood torture, maintaining their innocence. Only these were still alive and were being held in prison. Joseph's doctor Brambilla had examined the prisoners and found clear evidence of mistreatment. Joseph expressed utter contempt for the officials involved. But Leopoldine Kaunitz was skeptical of Joseph's statements; "the fact is that he is angry about these judges and the entire procedure and feels some sort of shame, I do not know just what, that anthropophagi were to be found among his subjects."[200] Thus Joseph's reputation for habitual ungraciousness toward his officials could at times undermine the enlightened message he no doubt intended to send.

Joseph's legal reforms, civil and criminal, undermined the status of traditional corporate entities in Habsburg society such as the nobility by eliminating both laws and procedures designed to secure or promote their interests, in theory applying all legal provisions equally to all classes of subjects. However, delinquents of noble status were actually singled out for especially severe treatment.[201] Joseph argued that society and the state had a right to expect responsible moral behavior from noblemen, who continued to enjoy advantages denied to other classes of subjects. Among prisoners convicted of lesser offenses who could now be seen sweeping the streets of Vienna in broad daylight to the disgust or edification of the interested Viennese public were members of noble families. This practice of humiliating delinquents of all social classes in public venues was roundly condemned by Leopoldine Kaunitz, who was revolted by the sight in Vienna in August 1782 and feared a coarsening of public life. She wrote to Eleonore Liechtenstein, "People talk of nothing but the street sweeping. All letters are full of this. For my part, it feels to me just as if I were one of the people who are exposed. I cannot tell you how much I find this ill-advised and even unjust for those who are not great criminals." Delinquents were subjected to indignities by the populace. "The women abuse them with all possible insolence."[202] In the stratified society of the Habsburg monarchy that the emperor had inherited, it was felt by the public at large as well as the affected aristocracy that sweeping the street with shorn head was punishment that carried greater humiliation and loss for a nobleman than for a vagrant. Owing to collective norms observed by the nobility public disgrace of a nobleman shamed entire families and their associates and allies. When even noblemen faced public excoriation, the symbolism was powerful. In general Leopoldine Kaunitz believed the public punishments mandated by the new regulations simply resulted in contempt for delinquents of all classes or, worse yet, elicited sympathy for their plight. In meetings of the *Staatsrat*, Chancellor Kaunitz and council member Count Hatzfeld also had warned that if punishments were made too oppressive and visible the public would feel pity for criminals.[203]

Joseph wished to be known as a ruler who never interfered in the functioning of his state's judicial system. Such a stance on the part of the sovereign was in his view important evidence of rational, enlightened rule. His self-proclaimed adherence to this principle of noninterference won plaudits from his visiting brother Leopold in 1784, a rare compliment.[204] The emperor was eager to demonstrate that justice in his lands was no respecter of social standing or estate and that the state-run judiciary had the authority and also sufficient prestige and power to impose punishment as necessary even on members of the monarchy's favored families. Offending noblemen would no longer receive more lenient treatment than their less fortunate fellow countrymen under Habsburg judges. In a number of celebrated cases delinquents of noble status received harsher treatment at the hands of the emperor. He intervened actively in their cases and his severity was deliberate and unrelenting. The emperor claimed to place all subjects on an equal footing, but noble status had become an aggravating factor in legal procedures, particularly those that came to the attention of the emperor himself.

In his eagerness to demonstrate that his mightiest subjects would be answerable for their wrongdoing the emperor sometimes acted too hastily, drawing conclusions based on partial evidence. One such case involved Leopoldine Liechtenstein's eldest son Louis (Alois), whose reckless driving resulted in an accident in the Prater in 1787. The historian Paul Bernard has examined the case and has found that because of the emperor's meddling, Louis did not enjoy due process.[205] A more widely publicized case involving the emperor's own secretary Valentin Günther, a nobleman, was bungled through the emperor's interference and haste in 1782. Accused of espionage, Günther was arrested, dismissed from his post and, along with his mistress Eleonore Eskeles, who was a popular Viennese hostess, banished from Vienna, all without credible evidence of wrongdoing. The emperor took a personal interest in the case but was unable or unwilling to specify charges and then allow the interrogation and other due process to run its course. Leopoldine Kaunitz was critical: "But it is certain that this should have been handled differently from the beginning. One ought never to begin by exposing people publicly [*prostituer*] without convincing evidence." At a soirée in mid-August Günther's case had come up for discussion, and Leopoldine reported to her sister the emperor's vague pronouncements concerning Günther's status. "He cannot be convicted of jobbery and the like," she wrote, "but he has been very careless and I think he [Joseph] said suspect, or he has dubious associates." Leopoldine had remarked that if Günther was innocent he should receive public vindication. Joseph's response was ambiguous: "la Clary [Josepha Clary] claimed to know that he [Günther] would be sent to Galicia, and I [thought he would be sent] to Gratz, he [Joseph] repeatedly said no and nothing more." A week later, conversation returned to Günther. When the emperor reported that the case was closed, Josepha Clary quipped cheerfully that Günther was thus exonerated. Again Joseph's reply was enigmatic. Although nothing definite could be proved against Günther, the emperor said, not all suspicion had been removed. Eventually Günther, no longer welcome in Vienna even though he had been convicted of no wrongdoing, was given a post in Hermannstadt (Sibiu), and there he was obliged to remain. Apparently Eleonore Eskeles was eventually permitted to return to the capital and was at last fully rehabilitated under Joseph's successor Leopold II.[206]

Several prominent criminal cases occurred in 1786 in which the emperor's influence increased the harshness of the judicial outcome for noblemen. All attracted unfavorable comment from the *Dames*. The case of Lieutenant Samuel Székely, a nobleman convicted of stealing funds from the noble Hungarian bodyguard in which he served as bookkeeper under Prince Nicholaus Esterházy, was mentioned more than once in the women's correspondence. Eleonore was dismayed by the sight of Székely being exposed in the stocks in Vienna in June 1786. Székely was eventually exonerated under circumstances that were not clear to contemporaries. Eleonore reported to her daughter that in addition to a form of pardon Székely had received 100 ducats. He was permitted to leave the capital and subsequently could reside anywhere he chose with the exception of Vienna or Buda (even though he was no longer held guilty of any crime). The case had been controversial and had unleashed a minor but quintessential Josephinian *Broschürenflut*.[207] In another notorious case, a Count Podstatzky-Liechtenstein (from a family that originated in Tyrol, without close ties to the two Liechtenstein *Dames*) was convicted of helping to forge banknotes to cover his gambling losses. Eleonore reported to her daughter in early June 1786 that Podstatzky's sentence of several years' imprisonment in a fortress was under appeal. However, it appears that under specific orders from the emperor Podstatzky was sent to pull barges later that year. He was reported dead by 10 January 1787.[208] The case of Franz Zahlheim, a nobleman who murdered a distant female relative for her money, was the most notorious. This instance proved to be the last time that

Joseph approved enforcement of the death penalty. The execution was carried out publicly on 10 March 1786, and the procedure included the application of hot pincers and breaking on the wheel as prescribed by old legal codes. Zinzendorf reported in his diary that an immense crowd had attended the mid-morning execution. No doubt the Viennese were horrified by the event, but some were apparently also highly diverted. Later in the day when Zinzendorf met with the emperor, Joseph told Zinzendorf that he (the emperor) was displeased with his Viennese subjects.[209]

Joseph's most dramatic nonreligious domestic reform was his "Emancipation Patent," which eliminated the vestiges of serfdom in Bohemia in 1781 and in Inner Austria and Galicia in 1782. Decrees for Transylvania and Hungary followed in 1783 and 1785, respectively. The patent declared that peasants were free to buy and sell their "rustical" land as well as to move, marry, or change their occupations without obtaining the permission of their landlord, merely informing him of their intentions. Limits were placed on the punishments that could be levied by proprietors and manorial courts.[210] The practical value of these decrees for the peasants of Bohemia and Moravia, where the *Dames'* families held land, was substantial since it gave rural inhabitants some leverage against the countervailing power of large landowners acting in concert to control the labor market. Also important was Joseph's expansion of the "Raab" agrarian system, favored earlier by Maria Theresia, to all state-administered lands (cameral estates, lands of royal cities and towns, some church lands, ex-Jesuit lands). The program was to serve as an attractive model for Bohemia's private landowners. The peasants of state-controlled lands could commute their compulsory field work for the landlord, or robot, into a fixed payment. The government's agents parceled out dominical land that had been worked by robot and allow the peasants to control and cultivate it for a fee. With laudable exactitude, the emperor mandated that contracts be drawn up and examined estate by estate, again adopting the careful but time-consuming process he had advocated during the coregency. Programs of this nature were introduced on state properties throughout the hereditary lands. There was some confusion and discontent among the peasants affected, for whom modest changes to improve their lot were disappointing.[211]

In 1784 the nightmarish news of a major, bloody peasant revolt in Transylvania, led by individuals who insisted that they were acting according to the emperor's wishes for reform in the countryside, caused widespread anxiety among all landowners. As in peasant unrest of the previous decade, the legendary imperial patent written in gold letters made its appearance. The emperor ordered forceful suppression of the Transylvanian rebellion, and its leaders were publicly tortured and executed. To the rank and file of participants he granted amnesty. But already by 1784 active planning had begun for a new, ambitious initiative to reform the monarchy's entire agricultural sector. Abolition of serfdom and recasting of labor relations on state-controlled lands had been only the beginning. Joseph planned to introduce a new system of taxing the land that in combination with commutation of most peasant labor obligations into cash payments could be expected to reduce the income of large landowners significantly. Measurement and registration of land would prepare the way for equitable taxation of both rustical and dominical lands. As a preliminary step it was necessary to assess the value of all parcels of land according to their quality and the income they had produced in recent times. Taxes would be assessed according to the land's productive value regardless of the social status of its owners or the arcane legal status of the land itself, a radical approach certain to meet with opposition from noble landowners. During previous land registrations, landlords had omitted to declare much property, avoiding taxation entirely. The new assessment was to remedy this deficiency as well.[212]

During the 1770s and early 1780s voluntary commutation of robot and distribution of land parcels had been adopted in the Bohemian crownlands by a number of landlords who were convinced of its economic value and overall benefits (these included, as mentioned previously, Chancellor Kaunitz and Leopoldine Liechtenstein's brother-in-law Prince Fürstenberg). These landlords had been willing to introduce change on their lands prior to Joseph's coercive measures of the 1780s.[213] The forced pace of Joseph's program now provoked resentment and fear among virtually all landowners, who apparently believed that not only their economic power but also their social prestige were threatened by Joseph's initiatives and who certainly feared the emperor's likely future plans for change on private lands. The efficacy of previous Habsburg attempts to reform agrarian conditions had been blunted by such landlord resistance, and the success of the emperor's ambitious new program was thus by no means certain.

Using a cumbersome, controversial procedure that strained the monarchy's supply of trained (and untrained) surveyors, land measurement began. It made slow progress. Nevertheless, Joseph moved forward with additional plans for introduction of the bold new tax system dubbed the "rectification," a sort of physiocratic single tax on land. He appointed a central commission, chaired by Count Zinzendorf, to oversee the measurement of land, computation of taxes, and subsequent introduction of the new system. Plans specified that, when the new cadaster was completed and robot commuted, peasants living on rustical land could be obliged to pay no more than 30 percent of their total annual income in taxes, of which 12 percent would go to state coffers and 18 percent would fall to landlord, church, and local officials combined. Since field robot previously used by landlords to work their dominical lands would be commuted to annual payments, the landlord would have to hire workers if he faced a labor shortage. Observers predicted that where compulsory labor was no longer available and wage labor either too costly or too scarce, many landlords would be forced to lease or sell dominical land and its appurtenances to local peasants or perhaps to new settlers. This was precisely the outcome deemed most desirable by the emperor and his advisors. Noble proprietors anticipated, and noisily predicted, a precipitous decline in their incomes, some fearing a loss of as much as half.[214] Opposition to the system of taxation was virtually universal among the landowning nobility, and the prospect of a new system of taxation unnerved many peasant farmers as well. Once again there was unrest among peasants, some of whom alarmed landowners by refusing to pay any taxes at all under the mistaken impression that even greater relief would be forthcoming. Faced with so many complications Joseph formally inaugurated the new tax in 1789 but pushed back its full implementation until late 1790, hoping that work on the new cadaster would be finished by that time. The final patent actually exempted dominical lands from new labor and service limits imposed on rustical lands, a significant concession to unhappy landowners.[215]

Leopoldine Kaunitz, with her customary mental energy and interest, worked to understand the implications of the many changes of the 1780s for Kaunitz lands. She predicted dire consequences for landowners. Although Chancellor Kaunitz was among the more progressive Bohemian landlords, Leopoldine Kaunitz reported that the Kaunitz steward Röper was alarmed by Joseph's expansion of the Raab program that had initially commuted robot on state lands only. Röper reported in summer 1783 that the peasants on Kaunitz lands were now expecting new regulations with more favorable terms; "he does not know what to do with our peasants, those who had rented the *Mayerhöf* [farm operations leased to tenants, possibly as part of reforms on Kaunitz lands] have relinquished all of them, and at present one finds oneself without livestock and very nearly without robot . . . ; according to him, and he is right in this, the Raab system will bring our total ruin and is an instrument of despotism unheard of in any land."[216] Leopoldine Kaunitz struggled to make sense of Joseph's "rectification." Years later, in 1789, she reported to her sister that many proprietors refused to plan for the coming changes, speculating that Joseph (by then clearly ailing) would be dead before implementation could be achieved, "and that his successor will ordain something completely different." But Leopoldine believed that some change was inevitable. Even if there was a new sovereign, she argued, it would be necessary to institute the new system "because the peasants are so determined to do no more robot that by one means or another we must come to terms, so as not to lose everything." Leopoldine reported her progress: "I am very busy with my projects and plans for the rectification; we have to imagine ourselves transported to Calabria, where so much has been turned upside down by an earthquake, and we must make our arrangements, no doubt poorly but as well as we can, because those who do not make plans will perish completely and be reduced to beggary."[217]

As was her practice, Eleonore continued to spend many weeks each summer on her husband's estate Kromau and occasionally at Meseritsch, where she was proprietor in her own right even after her husband's death. Throughout the period, including times of minor peasant unrest such as the summer of 1782, she exhibited considerable sangfroid. When Leopoldine Kaunitz voiced concern that Elenore "could find the affairs of Moravia as well in a distressing condition, with regard to both religion and preservation of peace," Eleonore merely replied that her locality was quiet and she had received no news concerning the rest of Moravia. "The subjects here [Kromau] and at Meseritsch are calm," she observed.[218] Like her sister Leopoldine, Eleonore too educated herself concerning robot abolition, directed in Moravia by Baron Anton Kaschnitz under the oversight of Count Zinzendorf's commission in Vienna.[219] She too was pessimistic about the program's likely consequences for private lands. "It will never be possible to draw from the lands the income they yield now, but worst of all, those who will lease the lands, be they communities, individuals, outsiders, will not keep their commitments; it requires very little knowledge to be convinced of that, but also experience in general proves it, no one so far has benefited from the new system."[220] She reported with disgust that in addition to general rumors about a radical administrative reorganization of Moravia, she had heard that a new district captain would be stationed in Meseritsch. This would be a nuisance for her socially and "then also a rather dangerous spy, occasion for additional complaints from the subjects, and, if I should not furnish this gentleman with all that he needs, an opportunity to haggle with me, and yet there is no way around it, these people never pay, and how can one ask them to?"[221] Eleonore did not trust Kaschnitz, who was charged with directing both the robot abolition on state lands and the eventual "rectification" on all Moravian lands. "He is a clever man, this Kaschnitz," she wrote, "and you would not believe the talent he has for persuading and the ease with which he removes and resolves all the objections that one raises." Despite his efforts at reassurance, Eleonore remained uneasy; "at base this is a man whose many schemes I distrust and who describes them all in the most specious manner. Only time will reveal the truth."[222]

Like other observers, Eleonore noted that Joseph's impatience to complete the land surveys and rectification was resulting in mistakes, lack of uniformity, and inequities. In summer 1786 the district commissioner and his bailiff told her that the "rectification" was becoming increasingly muddled, with valuations fluctuating erratically from one locale to another. He reported that "they are setting the tax rate higher than the value, this alone proves that the thing cannot work; they are no longer abiding by the patent, each province has operated differently, there is no agreement among them." It was a veritable tower of Babel, she concluded.[223] In summer 1789 Eleonore supervised arrangements in Meseritsch, trying to assess the loss of income to both Kromau and Meseritsch. "You are likely to know more about the rectification, dear sister, than I do, although I am sitting right in the middle of it," she wrote to Leopoldine Kaunitz. Eleonore tried to spur her estate inspector to greater activity: "in vain have I spoken to him of coming to terms with the subjects, of projects to provide for cultivation, for assessments to ensure a better yield for certain poor-quality fields, either through leasing them out or through farming them myself, which may not prove profitable for me in view of the great expenses of farming at present." The inspector was stalling for time. "He does not seem at all worried, or in a hurry," Eleonore wrote, "he says he will wait until the tax rate is finally determined, and only then he will be able to begin dealing with the peasants. Here, although they are doubly burdened, they do not complain, and through it all the district captain is charged with inducing them to see reason."[224]

In addition to Joseph's grand initiatives to restructure agricultural labor and taxes, lesser imperial reform efforts designed to improve practices reached rural retreats such as Meseritsch. These projects required the participation of landed proprietors in practical ways. In July 1789 Eleonore described preparations for a village competition to reward the local producer of the finest colt or foal. The contest was a response to the emperor's directive that peasants' mares should be serviced by stallions from imperial stud farms, a cause particularly dear to the emperor because he needed remounts for his military. Eleonore wrote to her sister, "Here we are involved in the greatest adventures." There was to be a horse market, she reported, in the course of which prizes would be distributed. A communal celebration would be staged, and "the awards will be made with great fanfare at the bottom of the square to the sound of drums . . . They wanted me to take my place right there in the middle of all this commotion, and I leave it to you to judge . . . how well that would suit me. So I have decided to flee and I shall settle myself at Zahradišt [the Liechtenstein hunting lodge]." Her two eldest sons would remain behind and participate in the ceremony, Eleonore explained.[225]

By 1789, when the new tax system was to be officially inaugurated, opposition to the land reforms had reached fever pitch among landlords and among some mistrustful peasants as well. Even soft-spoken Josepha Clary, in a letter to her daughter in 1788, had referred to "this terrible Rectification, which will abolish all our contracts and upset all economic plans."[226] Unfortunately, harvests in both 1788 and 1789 were poor. Traveling to Meseritsch in June 1789, Eleonore reported to her sister that she had never seen the crops in such deplorable condition ("in many areas you can spare yourself the expense of harvesting"), although closer to her own estate the situation was less dire.[227] Land prices fluctuated dramatically because excessive amounts of acreage flooded the market, no longer deemed profitable by owners. Potential purchasers of land were wary, uncertain about what the future would bring. Sales of state lands drove down prices.[228] From her son-in-law Count Harrach Eleonore received reports "that the rush to sell these lands is incredible, it is, he says, like the partition of Poland and, he adds, the proverb will be confirmed, easy come, easy go." In particular, friends of Kaschnitz were obtaining land on the cheap. Harrach was not confident that even depreciated land was a wise purchase. "He thinks that even if there is any advantage to be had," Eleonore reported, "the wise Leopold [certain to be Joseph's successor] will immediately take this away from us; Harrach himself does not want to make any acquisition of this kind, even if he should receive it as a gift, he says."[229]

Joseph's efforts to reshape agrarian relations unnerved and finally enraged landowners. The disapproval of the *Dames* was persistent but quiet, no doubt muted by their personal association with the author of the disruptive changes. Joseph's hasty, rigid approach to reform went far toward alienating those noble landlords and others who might otherwise have been his supporters.[230] It was not economic ruin alone that many noble families feared. Also vital to their way of life was the existing social nexus, the "social prerogatives and respect due the lords" that were both product and proof of the "social gap" between them and their tenants, in the words of historian William Wright.[231] Not only would the reforms limit the lords' income and diminish their power and prestige, but under Joseph's new procedures the entire tax system, including allocation, collection, and remittance to government coffers, would operate without landlord direction or influence. Joseph's agrarian reforms raised resistance not just among traditionalists who might oppose virtually all change but also among reformers who favored a less state-centered approach that retained at least a modest role for the inherited feudal society of estates. Initially enthusiastic about Joseph's reforms, the relatively liberal Zinzendorf openly objected to the "rectification" because, unlike earlier reforms, it made no attempt to compensate landowners for their lost property rights. Joseph removed Zinzendorf from his position on the tax regulation commission. The Austrian-Bohemian chancellor Chotek, Josepha Clary's son-in-law, refused to approve the new regulations in January 1789, choosing instead to resign.[232] In relinquishing his post Chotek cited concerns about his health and his eight children (Josepha Clary's grandchildren), but he was known to have withheld his support for the tax reform.

Taken together, Joseph's secular reforms were far from compassing the destruction of the privileged Habsburg nobility or the social hierarchy it dominated. A recent description of the emperor's initiatives as mature ruler affirms that it was "never his intention, at any stage, to attack noble privilege or noble dominance of society, administration, and the military as such" but rather "to subordinate the nobility's interests to those of the state overall."[233] The work of R. J. W. Evans and others has argued that the goal of eighteenth-century century Habsburgs, including reformers Maria Theresia and also Joseph II himself, was not an end to aristocratic power but rather its redirection, redistribution, and harnessing for purposes of government deemed useful by these sovereigns and their advisors.[234] The importance of the matter cannot be overstated, particularly as it relates to the affairs of Bohemian aristocratic families such as those of the *Dames* and their close associates. Joseph II could not simply put an end to aristocratic power, thus sacrificing the support of his most powerful subjects and their usefulness in the administration of his lands. It is unlikely that such a purpose was ever seriously considered by the reforming emperor. Instead, he hoped to have the skilled assistance of a reformed aristocracy, not completely lacking autonomy as a group but cooperating with him to realize goals deemed rational and desirable by the energetic emperor. Seen in this light, the emperor's caviling against useless elites takes on a somewhat different meaning. Joseph spoke of himself as the servant of the state and believed he had sacrificed his comfort and personal inclinations for it. He expected comparable devotion from his noble subordinates. The newly reformed and rejuvenated nobility, like the reformed church, was to serve the interests of a rational, enlightened state.

Certainly among representative members of the Habsburg aristocracy in Vienna there could be found individuals such as the elder Kaunitz, Zinzendorf, and Swieten whose skills and commitments met Joseph's exacting standards. The emperor appreciated talent and industry as had his mother Maria Theresia. But where she had been peculiarly skillful in cultivating ties of loyalty and affection with her most talented servitors through rewards both tangible and intangible, the emperor's behavior toward wellborn retainers was often highhanded and capricious, particularly during the early years of his reign.[235] As familiars of the emperor and as active participants in Viennese society, the *Dames* took the measure of both Joseph's reforms and of these personal provocations. The emperor, harsh and disrespectful at times toward high officials both civilian and military, left the impression that he was unwilling to consider viewpoints that did not strictly coincide with his own. Significant portions of the nobility in his lands therefore resented him as a putative despot who demanded obedience where the late eighteenth-century Habsburg nobility continued to expect reciprocity and a mutual regard between crown and nobility to buttress the privileged status of both. From this still powerful though disparate noble class, many of its members alienated through the cumulative effect of his actions, the emperor met with obstruction and eventually effective resistance, an outcome highlighting the fact that at base late eighteenth-century rulers of the Habsburg monarchy could not forego with impunity the fundamental support of its aristocracy.[236]

Not long after Joseph II's death, as she learned with dismay about the growing social turmoil in revolutionary France, Eleonore Liechtenstein proclaimed in a letter to her daughter, "I love my religion and my station in life [*état*], and I had rather lose my life than the one or the other."[237] These words encapsulated her own enduring priorities and those of the other *Dames*. Joseph's domestic reforms had touched and changed virtually every institution dear to the hearts and vital to the interests of his *Dames*, and to most of the Habsburg aristocracy. Personally well disposed toward their emperor and gratified by his attention, the women were nevertheless sharply critical of measures that Joseph deemed vital to the welfare of his state. Throughout the 1780s the *Dames* remained deeply apprehensive about the consequences of his most ambitious measures.

Notes

1. LRRA, P 17/27, EL to LK, Vienna, 31 August 1781.
2. HHStA, HA SB 7, JII to Leopold, 11 December 1780 ("little by little," Joseph wrote to his brother Leopold, "I am preparing minds for the very necessary changes than I have been considering for a long time").
3. Gutkas, *Kaiser Joseph II.*, 224-25.
4. Wandruszka, *Leopold II.* (Vienna: Verlag Herold, 1965), 2: 94-95.
5. Blanning, *Joseph II*, 62, 66.
6. Henry E. Strakosch, *State Absolutism and the Rule of Law: the Struggle for the Codification of Civil Law in Austria 1753-1811* (Sydney: Sydney University Press, 1967), 120.
7. HHStA, HA SB 8, JII to Leopold, 14 November 1782.
8. This detail appears in the Italian edition of Wandruszka's biography, *Pietro Leopoldo: Un grande riformatore* (Florence: Vallecchi, 1968), 477 (text of "Cose particolari").
9. Wandruszka, *Leopold II.*, 2: 93-95; HHStA, HA SB 16-1, "Relatione del Viaggio . . . 1784," 400-01.
10. Bernard, *Jesuits and Jacobins*, 113.
11. Beales, *Joseph II*, 2: 345-52.
12. HHStA, HA SB 16-1, "Relatione del Viaggio . . . 1784," 379.
13. LRRA, P 17/29, LK to EL, Vienna, 17 July 1783 and 19 July 1783.
14. HHStA, KA ZT, Band 40, 5 January 1795.
15. LRRA, P 17/29, LK to EL, Vienna, 18 August 1783.
16. SOAL-D, RACA, carton 54, JC to her husband Prince Clary, Weidlingau, 27 August 1783. The emperor's statement was reported by Josepha.
17. Strakosch, *State Absolutism,* 129.
18. LRRA, P 17/27, EL to LK, Kromau, 2 August 1781.
19. LRRA, P 17/27, EL to LK, [Feldsberg,] 13 [October] 1781; EL to LK, Kromau, 14 September 1782.
20. HHStA, HA SB 72-3, JII to Lacy, Pisa, 27 January 1784.
21. LRRA, P 17/27, LK to EL, Vienna, 14 October 1781.
22. LRRA, P 17/27, LK to EL, Vienna, 18 August 1781.
23. SOAL-D, RACA, carton 64, LL to JC, Spa, 7, 14, 18, 19, and 21 July 1781.
24. HHStA, HA SB 16-1, "Relatione del Viaggio . . . 1784," 55, 67-69.
25. LRRA, P 17/27, LK to EL, Vienna, 14 October 1781; P 17/28, LK to EL, Vienna, 25 August 1782.
26. Lacy demonstratively walked beside his coach during a Swiss journey, evoking Rousseau's praise of walking in the *Confessions*. Géza Hajós, *Romantische Gärten der Aufklärung: Englische Landschaftskultur des 18. Jahrhunderts in und um Wien* (Vienna: Böhlau, 1989), 42-43.
27. Wolf, *Fürstin Eleonore Liechtenstein,* 182; LRRA, P 17/28, EL to LK, Kromau, 28 August 1782; LK to EL, Vienna, 31 August 1782.
28. LRRA, P 17/27, EL to LK, Kromau, 2 August 1781.
29. For example, LRRA, P 17/27, EL to LK, Kromau, 7 July 1781.

30 LRRA, P 17/27, EL to LK, Kromau, 30 July 1781.
31 HHStA, KA ZT, Band 28, 30 October 1783 and 6 October 1783; Band 30, 28 July 1785.
32 According to Zinzendorf, in April 1763 Sidonia Kinsky loaned him a copy *of La nouvelle Héloïse*. Zinzendorf read it with interest and they discussed its contents at Kaunitz's soirées. The princess' reactions are not recorded. Karl Zinzendorf, *Aus den Jugendtagebüchern: 1747, 1752 bis 1763*, ed. Hans Wagner, Maria Breunlich, and Marieluise Mader (Vienna: Böhlau, 1997), 318-19.
33 LRRA, P 17/27, LK to EL, Vienna, 16 August 1781.
34 LRRA, P 17/31, LK to EL, Vienna, 10 October 1785.
35 LRRA, P 17/31, LK to EL, Baden, 19 September 1785; EL to LK, Meseritsch, 17 October 1785.
36 HHStA, HA SB 7, JII to Leopold, 3 January 1781.
37 LRRA, P 17/30, LK to EL, Vienna, 26 May 1784.
38 This was most likely a reference to developments in foreign affairs, with tensions high over Frederick II's sponsorship of the *Fürstenbund*. LRRA, P 17/31, EL to LK, Eisgrub, 13 September 1785.
39 LRRA, P 17/31, EL to LK, Kromau, 26 September 1785.
40 HHStA, HA SB 16-1, "Relatione del Viaggio . . . 1784," 55, 67-69. On Joseph's attitude towards advisors, Strakosch, *State Absolutism*, 102-03, 114.
41 LRRA, P 17/27, LK to EL, Vienna, 20 August 1781.
42 LRRA, P 17/32, LK to EL, Vienna, 31 August 1786.
43 Charles Ingrao, "The Problem of 'Enlightened Absolutism' and the German States," *Journal of Modern History* 58, Supplement: Politics and Society in the Holy Roman Empire, 1500-1806 (December 1986), S167. As noted in chapter 4, Beales's biography considers the issue at some length.
44 Carl von Hock and Hermann Ignaz Bidermann, *Der österreichische Staatsrath, 1760-1848* (Vienna: H. Geyer, 1879, repr. 1972), 160-66.
45 Blanning offers a brief summary of this vexingly complex issue. Blanning, *Joseph II*, 101-03.
46 Wraxall, *Memoirs of the Courts of Berlin, Dresden, Warsaw, and Vienna*, 2: 250-52.
47 Bernard, *Jesuits and Jacobins*, 25-27.
48 Joyce S. Rutledge, "The Delayed Reflex: Journalism in Josephinian Vienna," in *Studies in Eighteenth-Century Culture*, vol. 9, ed. Roseann Runte (Madison, WI: University of Wisconsin Press for the American Society for Eighteenth-Century Studies, 1979), 80.
49 Frank T. Brechka, *Gerard van Swieten and his world 1700-1772* (The Hague, M. Nijhoff, 1970), 126-27; Bernard, *Jesuits and Jacobins*, 25.
50 Cited in Beales, "Christians and '*Philosophes*': the Case of the Austrian Enlightenment," in *Enlightenment and Reform in Eighteenth-Century Europe*, 74.
51 Ernst Wangermann, *Aufklärung und staatsbürgerliche Erziehung: Gottfried van Swieten als Reformator des österreichischen Unterrichtswesens 1781-1791*, ed. Erich Zöllner (Vienna: Verlag für Geschichte und Politik, 1978), 7, 10-11; Wangermann, "Das Bildungsideal Gottfried van Swietens," in *Gerard van Swieten und seine Zeit*, ed. Erna Lesky and Adam Wandruszka (Köln, Graz: Böhlau 1973), 175-76.
52 Leslie Bodi, *Tauwetter in Wien: zur Prosa der österreichischen Aufklärung 1781-1795*, 2nd ed. (Vienna: Böhlau, 1995), 80; Bernard, *Jesuits and Jacobins*, 65.
53 Wangermann, *Die Waffen der Publizität: zum Funktionswandel der politischen Literatur unter Joseph II.* (Vienna: Verlag für Geschichte und Politik, 2004), 17-18.
54 LRRA, P 17/29, LK to EL, Vienna, 1 July 1783.
55 Bodi, *Tauwetter*, 166.

56 LRRA, P 17/28, EL to LK, 7 July 1782; Bodi, *Tauwetter*, 157; Wandruszka, *Leopold II.*, 2: 92.
57 Joseph Karniel, *Die Toleranzpolitik Kaiser Josephs II.* (Gerlingen: Bleicher, 1985), 320.
58 SÚA, RAM AC, 11/22, JII to Leopoldine Kaunitz, s.d., s.l. Certainly these arguments closely resemble those he used with Maria Theresia to justify his attitudes towards the Moravian Protestants in 1777, described in chapter 4. Beales, *Joseph II*, 2: 176-77.
59 These complex changes in Habsburg policy are described in Beales, *Joseph II*, 2: 177-93, 201-13.
60 SOAL-D, RACA, carton 64, LL to JC, Spa, 9 June 1781.
61 Karniel, *Die Toleranzpolitik Kaiser Josephs II.*, 29.
62 Blanning, *Joseph II*, 161-62.
63 Cerman, *Habsburgischer Adel und Aufklärung*, 450-51.
64 LRRA, P 17/27, EL to LK, Feldsberg, 19 September 1781 and 23 September 1781.
65 LRRA, P 17/28, LK to EL, Baden, 27 July 1782 and 7 August 1782.
66 LRRA, P 17/27, EL to LK, Meseritsch, 10 August 1781; SOAL-D, RACA, carton 54, JC to husband Prince Clary, Weidlingau, 1 August 1781 and carton 64, LL to JC, Spa, 14 July 1781.
67 SOAL-D, RACA, carton 54, JC to husband Prince Clary, Weidlingau, 13 August 1781.
68 LRRA, P 17/27, EL to LK, Feldsberg, 18 October 1781.
69 The essay of Rudolph C. Blitz, "The Religious Reforms of Joseph II (1780-1790) and Their Economic Significance," in the *Journal of European Economic History* 18 no. 3 (Winter 1989): 583-94, overstates the case but is a useful reminder that Joseph's concerns were as much practical as ideological in nature.
70 Beales, *Joseph II*, 2: 314-16; Strakosch, *State Absolutism*, 144.
71 Strakosch, *State Absolutism*, 83; Hock, *Der österreichische Staatsrath*, 240.
72 LRRA, P 17/28, LK to EL, Baden, 8 July 1782.
73 Vanysacker, *Cardinal Giuseppe Garampi*, 170; LRRA, P 17/31, LK to EL, Vienna, 8 October 1785; P 17/27, LK to EL, Vienna, 11 August 1781. Rosenberg's remarks are recorded by Leopoldine Kaunitz.
74 Bernhard M. Hoppe, *Predigtkritik im Josephinismus: die 'Wöchentlichen Wahrheiten für und über die Prediger in Wien' (1782-1784)* (St. Ottilien: EOS, 1989), 110, 330-32, 412; Wangermann, *Die Waffen der Publizität*, 84-87. In May 1784 Joseph II sent Leopoldine Kaunitz a French brochure entitled "Lettre d'un Evèque à la Duchesse sur l'importante question s'il est permis d'exposer à la censure publique les excès dans lesquels tombent les ministres de la religion," which Leopoldine told her sister was "fort janséniste." If the emperor assumed Leopoldine would find the arguments persuasive, he was mistaken. More likely he anticipated with some pleasure that lively conversations would result. LRRA, P 17/30, LK to EL, Vienna, 22 Mai 1784.
75 For example, she excoriated a contributor's critique of indulgences. LRRA, P 17/28, LK to EL, Baden, 27 July 1782.
76 LRRA, P 17/30, LK to EL, Vienna, 2 August 1784. Wangermann, *Die Waffen der Publizität*, 96-102.
77 HHStA, HA SB 16-1, "Relatione del Viaggio . . . 1784," 390.
78 In an attempt to counter the Josephinian publications, the priest Patrizius Fast started his own periodical, the *Katholische Prüfung der wöchentlichen Wahrheiten der Predigtkritiker in Wien*. One of his closest supporters was Joseph Pochlin, also mentioned by the women. Pochlin was the author of the "Vösendorf sermon," particularly criticized by the *Wöchentliche Wahrheiten*. The *Journal historique et littéraire* (1773-1794) of Feller, opposing the Jansenist journals, was subsidized by Rome. Manfred Brandl,

Marx Anton Wittola: seine Bedeutung für den Jansenismus in deutschen Landen (Steyr: Wilhelm Ennsthhaler, 1974), 75; Hoppe, *Predigtkritik*, 335-40; Vanysacker, *Cardinal Garampi*, 272.

79 Manfred Brandl, *Die deutschen katholischen Theologen der Neuzeit* (Salzburg: W. Neugebauer, 1978), 2:187, 222. When Leopoldine Kaunitz died, Zinzendorf reported that she had left a legacy for the Jesuits by way of Schneller, to be received by the Society if it was reconstituted within twelve years of her death (and if not, the sums would be given to the Ursulines and the Salesians). HHStA, KA ZT, Band 40, 3 January 1795.

80 Hoppe, *Predigtkritik*, 314.

81 LRRA, P 17/31, LK to EL, Vienna, 28 October 1785.

82 Vanysacker, *Cardinal Garampi*, 115, 158-59; Hersche, *Der Spätjansenismus*, 343-45.

83 LRRA, P 17/27, LK to EL, Vienna, 8 August 1781; Strakosch, *State Absolutism*, 143.

84 These were publications of a former Jesuit school attached to the church in the Annahof, which served as a model *Normalschule* for the education initiatives of Maria Theresia and her protégé Johann Ignaz von Felbiger. LRRA, P 17/30, LK to EL, Vienna, 26 May 1784.

85 LRRA, P 17/31, EL to LK, Meseritsch, 17 October 1785.

86 Hersche, *Der Spätjansenismus*, 256; Hersche, *Die deutschen Domkapitel im 17. und 18. Jahrhundert.* (Bern: [s.n.] 1984), 2: 201.

87 Gutkas, *Kaiser Joseph II.*, 160; Hersche, *Der Spätjansenismus*, 268.

88 Hersche, *Der Spätjansenismus*, 276-78; Hoppe, *Predigtkritik*, 332; LRRA, P 17/28, EL to LK, 7 July 1782 and 24 July 1782.

89 LRRA, P 17/28, LK to EL, Baden [bei Wien], 22 July 1782.

90 LRRA, P 17/31, LK to EL, Vienna, 5 October 1785.

91 Charles H. O'Brien, "Jansenists and Josephinism: 'Nouvelles ecclesiastiques' and Reform of the Church in Late Eighteenth-Century Austria," *Mitteilungen des Österreichischen Staatsarchivs* 32 (1979): 143-64. O'Brien cites letters of Schwarzl to Dupac from 1785 and 1787.

92 Wangermann, "Josephinismus und katholische Glaube," in *Katholische Aufklärung und Josephinismus,* ed. Elisabeth Kovács (Vienna: Verlag für Geschichte und Politik, 1979), 335-37.

93 Beda Franz Menzel, *Abt Franz Stephan Rautenstrauch von Břevnov-Braunau* (Königsteiner Institut für Kirchen- und Geistesgeschichte der Sudetenländer, 1969), 174-75; LRRA, P 17/31, LK to EL, Vienna, 6 October 1785.

94 Menzel, *Abt Franz Stephan Rautenstrauch*, 136.

95 Wolf, *Fürstin Eleonore Liechtenstein*, 165; *Allgemeine deutsche Biographie*, ed. Historische Commission bei der Königl. Akademie der Wissenschaften (Leipzig: Duncker & Humblot, 45: 358; Anton Weiss, *Geschichte der Theresianischen Schulreform in Böhmen: zusammengestellt aus den halbjährigen Berichten der Schulen-Oberdirektion 17. September 1777-14. März 1792* (Vienna: Carl Fromme, 1906), 1: 23, 72, 327; Hersche, *Der Spätjansenismus*, 199; Jaroslav Lorman, "The Concept of Moral Theology of Augustin Zippe, a Moral Theologian at the Turn of the Epoch," in *The Enlightenment in Bohemia*, ed. Ivo Cerman, Rita Krueger, and Susan Reynolds (Oxford: Voltaire Foundation, University of Oxford, 2011), 216; Cerman, *Habsburgischer Adel und Aufklärung*, 212, 214.

96 LRRA, P 17/31, LK to EL, Vienna, 17 October 1785 and 20 October 1785.

97 Ignaz de Luca, *Das gelehrte Oesterreich* (1776), 115.

98 Kovács, "Beziehungen von Staat und Kirche im 18. Jahrhundert" in *Österreich im Zeitalter des aufgeklärten Absolutismus*, 49-50; Brandl, *Marx Anton Wittola*, 57.

99 Oszkár Sashegyi, *Zensur und Geistesfreiheit unter Joseph II.: Beitrag zur Kulturgeschichte der habsburgishen Länder* (Budapest, Akadémíai Kiadó, 1958), 176-94;

Beales, *Joseph II*, 2: 90-99; Hoppe, *Predigtkritik*, 405-06; Hersche, *Der Spätjansenismus*, 230-31, 353-54.
100 LRRA, P 17/28, LK to EL, Vienna, 21 August 1782.
101 Hersche, *Der Spätjansenismus*, 297; Beales, *Joseph II*, 2: 84-86.
102 LRRA, P 17/27, EL to LK, Kromau, 4 July 1781, 7 July 1781, and 11 July 1781.
103 LRRA, P 17/27, LK to EL, Vienna, 7 July 1781; Hersche, *Der Spätjansenismus*, 223.
104 Tadeusz Cegielski, "Au zénith du siècle des lumières: le jansénisme à la cour pontificale, impériale et dans les loges maçonniques: esquisse de la problématique," in *Le jansénisme et la franc-maçonnerie en Europe centrale aux XVIIe et XVIIIe siècles*, ed. Daniel Tollet and Pierre Chaunu (Paris: Presses Universitaires de France, 2002), 217-19.
105 Beales, *Joseph II*, 2: 535.
106 Karniel, *Die Toleranzpolitik Kaiser Josephs II.*, 403-04.
107 LRRA, P 17/29, LK to EL, Vienna, 21 August 1783; Gutkas, *Kaiser Joseph II.*, 326; Wolf, *Fürstin Eleonore Liechtenstein*, 169.
108 Charles Liechtenstein and Ernst Kaunitz and his brother belonged to the lodge "Zur gekrönten Hoffnung" in Vienna or the Brünn lodge "Zur aufhebenden Sonne." Beales, "Mozart and Habsburgs," in *Enlightenment and Reform*, 102-03; Alexander Novotny, *Staatskanzler Kaunitz als geistige Persönlichkeit: ein österreichisches Kulturbild aus der Zeit der Aufklärung und des Josephinismus* (Vienna: Hollinek, 1947), 152; Wolf, *Fürstin Eleonore Liechtenstein*, 169.
109 Wolf, *Die Aufhebung der Klöster in Innerösterreich, 1782-1790* (1871; repr., Vienna: Geyer, 1971), 106-07; Gutkas, "Die kirchlich-sozialen Reformen," in *Österreich zur Zeit Kaiser Josephs II.: Mitregent Kaiserin Maria Theresias, Kaiser und Landesfürst* (Vienna: Amt der Niederösterr. Landesregierung, 1980), 175.
110 Rolf Kutschera, *Maria Theresia und ihre Kaisersöhne: ein Beitrag zum Habsburgerjahr 1990* (Innsbruck: Wort und Welt, 1990), 165; Hertha Wohlrab, *Penzing: Geschichte des 14. Wiener Gemeindebezirkes und seiner alten Orte* (Vienna: Jugend und Volk, 1985), 92-93.
111 LRRA, P 17/28, LK to EL, Vienna, 25 August 1782.
112 Accounts concerning these developments vary. According to one report, Leopoldine's interest in the building stemmed at least in part from the proximity of her own property, for which the chapel formed a scenic backdrop. Gerd Pichler, Alice Kaltenberger, and Michaela Müller, *Die Nikolaikapelle im Lainzer Tiergarten in Wien*, Wiener Archäologische Studien (Vienna: Forschungsgesellschaft Wiener Stadtarchäologie, 2002), 4: 20-21; *Topographie von Niederösterreich*, 4: 437 (Vienna: Verein für Landeskunde von Niederösterreich, 1896), 4: 437.
113 Schmal, *Pietas Maria Theresias*, 170-71, 201; Laura Lynne Kinsey, "The Habsburgs at Mariazell: Piety, Patronage, and Statecraft, 1620-1770" (Diss., University of California, Los Angeles, 2000), 185, 300; Robin Okey, *The Habsburg Monarchy from Enlightenment to Eclipse* (New York: St. Martin's, 2001), 5.
114 Gutkas, *Kaiser Joseph II.*, 114; Renate Zedinger, *Hochzeit im Brennpunkt der Mächte: Franz Stephan von Lothringen und Erzherzogin Maria Theresia*, Schriftenreihe der Österreichischen Gesellschaft zur Erforschung des 18. Jahrhunderts, no. 3, ed. Moritz Csáky (Vienna: Böhlau Verlag, 1994), 121-22; Schmal, *Pietas Maria Theresias*, 170; Vehse, *Geschichte der deutschen Höfe*, 14: 140; Kinsey, "Habsburgs at Mariazell," 21, 118, 245.
115 Kinsey, "Habsburgs at Mariazell," 133, 156-58, 179, 183; Gutkas, "Die kirchlich-sozialen Reformen," 175; Schmal, *Pietas Maria Theresias*, 156-57.

116 Hans Hollerweger, *Die Reform des Gottesdienstes zur Zeit des Josephinismus in Österreich*, ed. Bruno Kleinheyer and Hans Bernhard Meyer (Regensburg: Friedrich Pustet, 1976), 342-43; Helmut Eberhart, "Magna Mater Austriae: zur Wallfahrtsgeschichte von Mariazell von der Gründung bis in das 19. Jahrhundert," in *Schatz und Schicksal: Steirische Landesausstellung 1996: Mariazell und Neuberg an der Mürz, 4. Mai bis 27. Oktober,* ed. Ileane Schwarzkogler (Mariazell: Kulturreferat der Steiermärkischen Landesregierung, 1996), 32-33.

117 LRRA, P 17/25, LK to EL, Vienna, 14 September 1779.

118 LRRA, P 17/28, LK to EL, Vienna, 16 August 1782 and 31 August 1782.

119 LRRA, P 18/59, EL to Josephine Harrach, 25 August 1804.

120 LRRA, P 17/28, EL to LK, Kromau, 14 August 1782.

121 LRRA, P 17/28, LK to E, Vienna, 12 August 1782 and 14 August 1782.

122 LRRA, P 17/28, LK to EL, Vienna, 16 August 1782; HHStA, HA SB 8, JII to Leopold, 12 and 15 August 1782; LRRA, P 17/28, EL to LK, Kromau, 17 August 1782; LRRA, P 17/28, LK to EL, Vienna, 18 August 1782.

123 By an unfortunate coincidence, a second hunting accident occurred in the Brigittenau a few weeks later, when Joseph inadvertently shot and killed a young man. LRRA, P 17/30, LK to EL, Vienna, 30 July 1784 and 4 August 1784; Felix Czeike, *Wien: Kunst, Kultur und Geschichte der Donaumetropole* (Köln: DuMont, 1999), 119-22; Beales, *Joseph II*, 2: 427.

124 HHStA, KA ZT, Band 31, 18 October 1786. There were other shrines in which the women took an interest. Mariaschein on the Clary family's Teplitz estate was one of these. It has been argued that these local and regional shrines had "the cultural and political side effect of fragmenting, rather than unifying, Habsburg culture." SOAL-D, RACA, carton 54, JC to her husband, Vienna, 11 September 1781; SOAL-D, RACA, carton 76, JC to her son, 10 August 1796; Virginia Ruth Mosser, "Strange Mercies: The Search for Miracles in the Habsburg Monarchy from the Reign of Leopold I to Joseph II (1658-1790)" (Diss., University of Virginia, 1998), 31, citing in turn Victor L. Tapié, *Rise and Fall of the Habsburg Monarchy* (New York: Praeger, 1971), 132.

125 Wangermann, *Die Waffen der Publizität*, 59.

126 Hock, *Der österreichische Staatsrath*, 416.

127 Beales, *Joseph II*, 2: 284-87.

128 Kovács, "Josephinische Klosteraufhebungen," in *Österreich zur Zeit Kaiser Josephs II.*, 171-72; Kutschera, *Maria Theresia und ihre Kaisersöhne*, 165; Hock, *Der österreichische Staatsrath*, 399-400, 419-24.

129 Küppers-Braun, *Frauen des hohen Adels*, 200; Guglia, *Maria Theresia*, 2: 227.

130 Eleonore Liechtenstein and Leopoldine Kaunitz retained ties with the Visitation convent in Strasbourg and sent rich votive objects to help embellish the cathedral. In 1792, the silver, gold, and copper ornaments found in St. Stephan's and the convent were confiscated by French revolutionary authorities. M. Barth, "Das Visitandinnen-Kloster an St. Stephan zu Straßburg 1683-1792," *Archiv für elsässische kirchengeschichte* 1 (1926): 239-42, 249-54, 260-62, 265, 269; LRRA, P 17/25, LK to EL, Baden, 2 October 1779; LRRA, P 18/47, EL to Josephine Harrach, 26 September 1792.

131 LRRA, P 17/26, LK to EL, Vienna, 14 October 1780; LRRA, P 17/30, LK to EL, Vienna, 30 July-1 August 1784. Eleonore remarked in 1782 that the Porziuncola observance would occasion "all sorts of lovely brochures." LRRA, P 17/28, EL to LK, Kromau, 31 July 1782.

132 It served as a place of refuge for Strasbourg nuns who fled France after their convent was dissolved in 1792. Anna Coreth, *Liebe ohne Mass: Geschichte der Herz-Jesu-Verehrung in Österreich im 18. Jahrhundert* (Maria Roggendorf: Salterrae, 1994), 139.

133 Beales, *Joseph II*, 2: 126n54; *Joseph II. und Leopold von Toscana; ihr Briefwechsel von 1781 bis 1790*, ed. Alfred von Arneth (Vienna: W. Braumüller, 1872), 40, JII to Leopold, 16 August 1781; also Joseph II's "Réflexions," 328-31.
134 LRRA, P 17/29, EL to LK, Vienna, 30 September 1783.
135 HHStA, HA SB 8, JII to Leopold, Vienna, 13 October 1783.
136 Gerhard Winner, *Klosteraufhebungen in Niederösterreich und Wien* (Vienna: Verlag Herold, 1967), 178-86; Wolf, *Fürstin Eleonore Liechtenstein*, 166.
137 This may have been the convent's revered Madonna of white stone, with scepter and rose—a statue that was moved to Vienna's Visitation convent—or possibly an illustration of it. The convent's statue of Saint Jacob was carried out in procession from the convent on the day of its closing by the superioress herself and was transferred to Vienna's Ursuline convent. SOAL-D, RACA, carton 64, JC to the K.K.N.Ö. Landesregierung, Vienna, 13 March 1784; P. Hugo Pfundstein, P. Hugo, *Marianisches Wien: eine Geschichte der Marienverehrung in Wien* (Vienna: Bergland, 1963), 67-68; Theodor Wiedemann, "Zur Geschichte des Frauenklosters St. Jakob in Wien," *Berichte und Mittheilungen des Alterthums-Vereines zu Wien* 32 (1906), 53-86; Gustav Gugitz, *Österreichs Gnadenstätten in Kult und Brauch* (Vienna: Hollinek, 1955), 1: 15-16.
138 Kovács, "Josephinische Klosteraufhebungen," 171.
139 LRRA, P 17/31, LK to EL, Vienna, 5 October 1785.
140 LRRA, P 17/29, LK to EL, Vienna, 2 August 1783.
141 LRRA, P 17/28, EL to LK, Kromau, 24 July 1782.
142 LRRA, P 17/32, EL to LK, Kromau, 27 August 1786 and 29 August 1786; Wolf, *Fürstin Eleonore Liechtenstein*, 110.
143 SÚA, RAM AC, 11/22, JII to LK, 7 December 1780.
144 Pierre Auguste Florent Gérard, *Histoire de la législation nobiliaire de Belgique* (Brussels: A. Vandale, 1846), 1: 95-100.
145 SÚA, RAM AC, 11/22, JII to LK, s.l., s.d.
146 SOAL-D, RACA, carton 64, Marie Christine to JC, 30 April 1786.
147 Strakosch, *State Absolutism*, 138-41.
148 LRRA, P 17/29, LK to EL, Vienna, 19 July 1783.
149 LRRA, P 17/29, LK to EL, Vienna, 22 July 1783.
150 Dickson, *Finance and government,* 1: 131; Bernard, "Poverty and Poor Relief in the Eighteenth Century," in *State and Society in Early Modern Austria,* ed. Charles W. Ingrao (West Lafayette, II: Purdue University Press, 1994), 238-43.
151 LRRA, P 17/29, EL to LK, Kromau, 16 August 1783; Martin Scheutz, "Demand and Charitable Supply: Poverty and Poor Relief in Austria in the 18th and 19th Centuries," in *Health Care and Poor Relief in 18th and 19th Century Southern Europe*, ed. Ole Peter Grell, Andrew Cunningham, and Bernd Roeck (Burlington, VT: Ashgate, 2005), 62.
152 LRRA, P 17/27, EL to LK, Kromau, 21 July 1781.
153 LRRA, P 17/28, LK to EL, Vienna, 18 August 1782.
154 LRRA, P 17/28, EL to LK, Kromau, 21 August 1782.
155 Bernard, "Poverty and Poor Relief," 244-45; Fred Hennings, *Das josephinische Wien* (Vienna, Munich: Herold, 1966), 69.
156 Kovács, "Josephinische Klosteraufhebungen," 171; Gutkas, "Die kirchlich-sozialen Reformen," 175; Bernard, "Poverty and Poor Relief," 245-46; Hoppe, *Predigtkritik*, 309-10.
157 LRRA, P 17/30, EL to LK, Kromau, 22 July 1784.
158 LRRA, P 17/31, LK to EL, Vienna, 17 October 1785; P 17/31, EL to LK, Meseritsch, 21 October 1785.

159 Gutkas, *Kaiser Joseph II.*, 360; Robert Waissenberger, "Das josephinische Wien," in *Österreich zur Zeit Kaiser Josephs II.*, 141.
160 Strakosch, *State Absolutism*, 144.
161 LRRA, P 17/29, EL to LK, Kromau, 16 August 1783.
162 *Joseph II. und Leopold von Toscana: ihr Briefwechsel,* 1: 82, JII to Leopold, 7 March 1782.
163 Gutkas, *Kaiser Joseph II.*, 294, 299-300; Hanns Schlitter, *Die Reise des Papstes Pius VI. nach Wien und sein Aufenthalt daselbst: ein Beitrag zur Geschichte der Beziehungen Josefs II. zur römischen Curie,* Fontes Rerum Austriacarum, Dipomataria et Acta 47 pt. 1 (Vienna: F. Tempsky, 1892), 13; Kutschera, *Maria Theresia und ihre Kaisersöhne*, 164.
164 Jean Mondot, "L'année 82 ou la fin de l'état de grâce. Le désenchantement du monarque et le commencement de la politique," *Das achtzehnte Jahrhundert und Österreich: Jahrbuch der Österreichischen Gesellschaft zur Erforschung des Achtzehnten Jahrhunderts* 22 (2007): 139-41; Wangermann, *Die Waffen der Publizität*, 78-82.
165 Gutkas, *Kaiser Joseph II.*, 266; Vehse, *Geschichte der deutschen Höfe*, 14: 184.
166 Schlitter, *Die Reise des Papstes Pius VI.*, 61.
167 Kovács, "Am Schisma vorbei. Zu den Ergebnissen der Reise Pius' VI. im Jahre 1782," *Österreich in Geschichte und Literatur* 28, no. 3 (1984): 153; J. Nosinich, "Kaiser Josef II. als Staatsmann und Feldherr. Österreichs Politik und Kriege in den Jahren 1763 bis 1790; zugleich Vorgeschichte zu den Kriegen Österreichs gegen die französische Revolution," *Mitteilungen des K.K. Kriegs-Archivs*, 1883, 137.
168 Schlitter, *Die Reise des Papstes Pius VI.*, 64.
169 Schlitter, *Die Reise des Papstes Pius VI.*, 58-60, 78-80; Kutschera, *Maria Theresia und ihre Kaisersöhne*, 164; Wolf, *Marie Christine, Erzherzogin von Oesterreich* (Vienna: Carl Gerold's Sohn, 1863), 1: 196; Hennings, *Das josephinische Wien*, 77-78; Gutkas, *Kaiser Joseph II.*, 299.
170 Johann Ferdinand Gaum, *Des heiligen Vater Pabsts Pius des Sechsten Reise von Rom nach Wien* (Vienna: s.n., 1982), 143, 145; LRRA, P 17/28, EL to LK, [Vienna,] 7 July [1782].
171 HHStA, KA ZT, Band 27, 25 March 1782; *Wiener Zeitung*, 17 April 1782.
172 SOAL-D, RACA, carton 64, Marie Christine to JC, 16 April 1782.
173 *Joseph II. und Leopold von Toscana: ihr Briefwechsel,* 1: 103, JII to Leopold, 22 April 1782.
174 *Correspondance secrète du comte de Mercy-Argenteau avec l'empereur Joseph II et le prince de Kaunitz*, ed. Alfred Arneth (Paris: Imprimerie Nationale, 1889-1891), 1: 99, JII to Mercy, 27 April 1782.
175 LRRA, P 17/28, LK to EL, Vienna, 18 August 1782; Kovács, *Der Pabst in Teutschland: die Reise Pius VI. im Jahre 1782* (Munich: R. Oldenbourg, 1983), 147-48; Schlitter, *Pius VI. und Josef II. von der Rückkehr des Papstes nach Rom bis zum Abschlusse des Concordats: ein Beitrag zur Geschichte der Beziehungen Josefs II. zur römischen Curie von 1782 bis 1784,* Fontes Rerum Austriacarum. Dipomataria et Acta 47 pt. 2 (Vienna: F. Tempsky, 1894), 52-53; Ferdinand Maaß, *Der Josephinismus: Quellen zu seiner Geschichte in Österreich 1760-1790*, Fontes rerum Austriacarum, 2. Abt., Diplomataria et acta 72 (Vienna: Herold, 1953), 2: 390-91, JII to Pius VI, Vienna, 15 August 1782.
176 Noted by other contemporaries as well. Karniel, *Die Toleranzpolitik Kaiser Josephs II.*, 327.
177 Gutkas, *Kaiser Joseph II.*, 45; Fejtö, *Joseph II.*, 250-51.

178 Peter Barton, "Der lange Weg zur Toleranz," in *Im Lichte der Toleranz: Aufsätze zur Toleranzgesetzgebung des 18. Jahrhunderts in den Reichen Joseph II., ihren Voraussetzungen und ihren Folgen* (Vienna: Institut für Protestantische Kirchengeschichte, 1981), 15.

179 Beales, *Joseph II*, 2: 190-95; Blanning, *Joseph II*, 74 (for Joseph's religious outlook); Barton, "Der lange Weg," 14-15.

180 Wangermann, *Die Waffen der Publizität*, 112-14.

181 Barton, "Evangelische Christen der Toleranzzeit bauen Gemeinden in Österreich," in *Im Lichte der Toleranz: Aufsätze zur Toleranzgesetzgebung des 18. Jahrhunderts in den Reichen Joseph II., ihren Voraussetzungen und ihren Folgen* (Vienna: Institut für Protestantische Kirchengeschichte, 1981), 237; Wangermann, *Wappen der Publizität*, 113. Also mentioned by Beales, *Joseph II*, 2: 60.

182 Barton, "Toleranz und Toleranzpatente in der Donaumonarchie," in *Im Zeichen der Toleranz: Aufsätze zur Toleranzgesetzgebung des 18. Jahrhunderts im Reiche Joseph II.* (Vienna: Institut für Protestantische Kirchengeschichte, 1981), 265.

183 Wangermann, *Die Waffen der Publizität*, 66.

184 Johann Christoph Allmayer-Beck, "Die Träger der staatlichen Macht: Adel, Armee und Bürokratie," in *Spectrum Austriae*, ed. Otto Schulmeister with Johann Christoph Allmayer-Beck and Adam Wandruszka (Vienna: Herder, 1957), 264.

185 William D. Godsey, Jr., "Adelsautonomie, Konfession und Nation im österreichischen Absolutismus ca. 1620-1848," *Zeitschrift für historische Forschung* 33 no. 2 (2006): 219-20.

186 Beales, *Joseph II*, 2: 366-70.

187 LRRA, P 17/29, LK to EL, Vienna, 14 August 1783.

188 LRRA, P 17/30, LK to EL, Vienna, 27 May 1784.

189 Beales, *Joseph II*, 2: 59-61; Hock, *Der österreichische Staatsrath*, 42-48.

190 Beales, *Joseph II*, 1: 236-38.

191 Pavel Mitrofanov, *Josef II. Seine politische und kulturelle Tätigkeit* (Vienna: C. W. Stern, 1910), 2: 514-20, 549-54; Charles Ingrao, *The Habsburg Monarchy 1618-1815* (New York: Cambridge University Press, 2000), 200-01.

192 Gerhard Ammerer, *Das Ende für Schwert und Galgen? legislativer Prozess und öffentlicher Diskurs zur Reduzierung der Todesstrafe im Ordentlichen Verfahren unter Joseph II. 1781-1787* (Innsbruck: Studien Verlag, 2010), 183-88.

193 Strakosch, *State Absolutism*, 159.

194 Strakosch, *State Absolutism*, 160-61.

195 LRRA, P 17/31, LK to EL, Vienna, 21 October 1785.

196 Blanning, *Joseph II*, 81.

197 Hock, *Der österreichische Staatsrath*, 312.

198 Joseph Pfundheller, ed., *Die schwarze Bibliothek: eine Sammlung interessanter Criminalgeschichten mit Benützung authentischer Quellen* (Vienna: Zamarski and Dittmarsch, 1861), 3: 195-97, 235; LRRA, P 17/28, LK to EL, Vienna, 23 August 1782 and 31 August 1782.

199 Mitrofanov, *Josef II.*, 1: 107-11.

200 LRRA, P 17/29, LK to EL, Vienna 14 July 1783.

201 Ammerer, *Das Ende für Schwert und Galgen?*, 434-35.

202 LRRA, P 17/28, LK to EL, Vienna, 10 August 1782; Gugitz, *Lieder der Strasse: die Bänkelsänger im josephinischen Wien* (Vienna: Brüder Hollinek, 1954), 70; Friedrich Hartl, *Das Wiener Kriminalgericht: Strafrechtspflege vom Zeitalter der Aufklärung bis zur österreichischen Revolution* (Vienna; Köln, Graz: Böhlau, 1973), 360.

203 Hock, *Der österreichische Staatsrath*, 315; Ammerer, *Das Ende der Schwert und Galgen?*, 361-64.
204 HHStA, HA SB 16-1, "Relatione del Viaggio . . . 1784," 98-99. The importance of this approach for a ruler who claimed to be enlightened is explored in Strakosch, *The Problem of Enlightened Absolutism* (Melbourne, Australia: F. W. Cheshire, 1970), 25-26.
205 Bernard, *The Limits of Enlightenment: Joseph II and the Law* (Urbana, IL: University of Illinois Press, 1979), 73-77; Strakosch, *State Absolutism*, 129-30; Hock, *Der österreichische Staatsrath*, 150-60.
206 The details of this case have been variously reported. Bernard, *Limits of Enlightenment*, 93-95; Wilhelm Weckbecker, *Von Maria Theresia zu Franz Joseph: zwei Lebensbilder aus dem alten Österreich* (Berlin: Verlag für Kulturpolitik, 1929), 44-50; LRRA, P 17/28, LK to EL, Vienna, 14 August 1782, 18 August 1782, and 25 August 1782.
207 LRRA, P 17/38, EL to Josephine Harrach, Laxenburg, 9 June 1786 and Vienna, 15 July 1786; Rebecca Gates-Coon, *Landed Estates of the Esterházy Princes* (Baltimore, MD: Johns Hopkins University Press, 1994), 48-50.
208 LRRA, P 17/41, EL to Josephine Harrach, 3 June 1786; Johann Siebmacher, *Die Wappen des böhmischen Adels*, reproduction of Siebmacher's Wappenbuch, vol. 4, Nürnberg, 1886 (Neustadt an der Aisch: Bauer und Raspe, 1979), 156; Eva Macho, *Joseph II., die "Condemnatio ad poenas extraordinarias": Schiffziehen und Gassenkehren* (Frankfurt am Main: P. Lang, 1999), 32, 38-39.
209 HHStA, KA ZT, Band 31, 10 March 1786; Bernard, *Limits of Enlightenment*, 48-51; Beales, *Joseph II*, 551.
210 William Wright, *Serf, Seigneur, and Sovereign: Agrarian Reform in Eighteenth-Century Bohemia* (Minneapolis: University of Minnesota Press, 1966), 71-77.
211 Beales cites a letter written by Prince Georg Starhemberg (Leopoldine Liechtenstein's uncle and former Habsburg minister in Brussels) in September 1783 to Mercy, the Habsburg ambassador to France, in which Starhemberg reports that income from his own estates and those of other grandees has been reduced by Joseph's reforms. In his statement Starhemberg does not specify which reforms he blames for these losses. Beales, *Joseph II*, 2: 344-45.
212 For summaries of agrarian reforms during the 1780s, in addition to sources mentioned in connection with agrarian reform of the coregency: Beales, *Joseph II*, 2: 239-70; Roman Rozdolski, *Die Grosse Steuer- und Agrarreform Josefs II.* (Warsaw: Państwowe Wydawnictwo Naukowe, 1961).
213 Szabo, "Perspective from the Pinnacle: State Chancellor Kaunitz on Nobility in the Habsburg Monarchy," in *Adel im "langen" 18. Jahrhundert.* (Vienna: Austrian Academy of Sciences, 2009), 252-54; Friedrich Lütge, "Die Robot-Abolition und Kaiser Joseph II.," in *Wege und Forschungen der Agrargeschichte: Festschrift zum 65. Geburtstag von Günther Franz*, ed. Heinz Haushofer and Willi A. Boelcke (Frankfurt a. M.: DLG-Verlag, 1967), 167-70.
214 Wright, *Serf, Seigneur, and Sovereign*, 147; Charles Ingrao, *The Habsburg Monarchy* (New York: Cambridge University Press, 2000), 204-05.
215 Beales, *Joseph II*, 2: 596.
216 LRRA, P 17/29, LK to EL, Vienna, 5 July 1783.
217 LRRA, P 17/33, LK to EL, Vienna, 10 July 1789 and 12 July 1789.
218 LRRA, P 17/28, EL to LK, Kromau, 24 July 1782.
219 The work of Kaschnitz is described in Wright, *Serf, Seigneur, and Sovereign*, esp. 89-92, 96-98.
220 LRRA, P 17/29, EL to LK, Kromau, 10 August 1783; Wright, *Serf, Seigneur, and Sovereign*, 80-82.

221 LRRA, P 17/29, EL to LK, Kromau, 22 August 1783.
222 LRRA, P 17/31, EL to LK Kromau, 1 October 1785.
223 LRRA, P 17/33, EL to LK, 27 August 1786.
224 LRRA, P 17/33, EL to LK, Meseritsch, 17 July 1789.
225 Strakosch, *State Absolutism*, 132; LRRA, P 17/33, EL to LK, Meseritsch, 6 July 1789.
226 SOAL-D, RACA, carton 67, JC to daughter Countess Wilczek, 14 February 1788.
227 LRRA, P 17/33, EL to LK, Meseritsch, 26 June 1789.
228 Wright, *Serf, Seigneur, and Sovereign*, 162.
229 LRRA, P 17/33, EL to LK, Meseritsch, 27 July 1789.
230 Szabo, "Ambivalenzen der Aufklärungspolitik," 28-30; Ingrao, "The Problem of 'Enlightened Absolutism,'" S174.
231 Wright, *Serf, Seigneur, and Sovereign*, 158-59.
232 Beales, *Joseph II*, 2: 595-597; Ingrao, *The Habsburg Monarchy*, 205.
233 Jonathan E. Israel, *Democratic Enlightenment: Philosophy, Revolution, and Human Rights 1750-1790* (Oxford: Oxford University Press, 2011), 290.
234 R .J. W. Evans, "Introduction: State and Society in Early Modern Austria," in *State and Society in Early Modern Austria*, ed. Charles W. Ingrao (West Lafayette, IN: Purdue University Press, 1994), 11-13.
235 Hock, *Der österreichische Staatsrath*, 131-35, 151.
236 Volker Press, "The Habsburg Court as Center of the Imperial Government," *Journal of Modern History* 58, Supplement: Politics and Society in the Holy Roman Empire, 1500-1806 (Dec. 1986): 44-45; Godsey, "Adelsautonomie, Konfession und Nation," 216. The persistence of the nobility's power even to 1848 is a theme touched on in essays in *Bündnispartner und Konkurrenten der Landesfürsten? Die Stände in der Habsburgermonarchie in der Neuzeit*, Veröffentlichungen des Instituts für Österreichische Geschichtsforschung, Bd. 49 (Vienna: R. Oldenbourg, 2007), 13-41, and also in the volume's introduction, "Die Stände in der Habsburgermonarchie: eine Einleitung," by the editors Gerhard Ammerer, William D. Godsey, Jr., Martin Scheutz, Peter Urbantisch, and Alfred Stefan Weiß. Also of interest is Henry E. Strakosch's *The Problem of Enlightened Absolutism* (Melbourne, Australia: F.W. Cheshire, 1970), 15-17.
237 Both Eleonore and her sister Leopoldine Kaunitz referred to French developments as "les fruits de l'esprit du philosophisme." LRRA, P 17/46, EL to Josephine Harrach, Vienna, 14 September 1791; LRRA, P 18/47, EL to Josephine Harrach, 25 August 1792.

Chapter 6

Joseph II's Foreign Policy and the End of an Era

In contrast to his mother, Joseph II believed that the experiences and informativeness of travel were vital to him as ruler, both for domestic affairs and even more in the shaping of foreign policy. During the coregency Joseph had found the superior authority of his mother Maria Theresia to be galling. As Bled has noted in his biography of Maria Theresia, a massive program of travel, which occupied fully one quarter of Joseph's time during the coregency, had been one of the emperor's unique responses to his awkward situation. Freeing himself from the complications of his mother's court and officials and eager to inform himself about the lands and subjects he would one day rule alone and the European powers with which he would one day join issue, Joseph had recourse to extensive independent traveling, usually in a modest fashion as "Count Falkenstein." Within Habsburg lands, his travels had included Bohemia (1766, 1769, 1770, 1771), the Banat (1768), Lombardy (1769), and Galicia and Transylvania (1773). He also routinely traveled to locations selected for military maneuvers. Beyond the monarchy's borders he visited Italy (1769), France (1777), and Russia (1780).[1] Two of his trips, in 1769 and 1770, included personal meetings with Frederick II, his mother's archenemy. Joseph far surpassed all contemporary heads of state in both the extent of his travels and in his efforts to observe firsthand the conditions in which his subjects lived. During his entire reign as emperor from 1765 to 1790, he logged over 30,000 miles of travel.[2] Travel was a serious preoccupation for Joseph, a strategy for obtaining direct feedback from subjects. His journeys outside the monarchy he approached systematically both as informative episodes and as foreign policy initiatives. But the emperor also enjoyed his journeys. Among the benefits of being intimates of the emperor, not least were the privileged and exclusive communications the *Dames* received from this indefatigable imperial traveler as he visited foreign lands. Eleonore Liechtenstein remained a special favorite, but the emperor wrote to each of the other women individually as well. At times the letters were addressed to Lacy or Rosenberg but included greetings and descriptive material intended for the *société*.

Evidently Joseph put substantial thought into composing these lively missives to the *Dames*. He made an effort to notice and record circumstances he observed that the women would find interesting. Leopoldine Kaunitz described for Eleonore a letter she received from Joseph during his journey to France in summer 1777. She did not wish to send it to her sister through the postal service, "although there are no secrets"; "it is as civil and friendly as possible, but I would say along with the journalists that it is not susceptible of extract, there are a multitude of things of every nature and color, but also indescribable wit." In addition to details about his travel schedule, he sent compliments to the chancellor, gallant remarks for Eleonore, and other messages to friends. Josepha Clary too had received a billet from the imperial traveler. "I think," Leopoldine commented, "that it is the turn of all the Swabians."[3] The *Dames* had been aware that the emperor's route on this journey would take him close to Voltaire's residence. They had learned that while in Paris for his visit to the French court Joseph II had attended a session of the Academy and visited Rousseau, Buffon, and other luminaries of the Enlightenment. He called on Tissot in Lausanne and the poet Haller in Bern.[4] The women assumed, as did most interested contemporaries, that the emperor would not pass up this opportunity to meet Voltaire as well. "He says nothing about Voltaire," Leopoldine wrote, "I would so like to have known if he [Joseph] saw him."[5] Leopoldine Liechtenstein reported to the other *Dames* from Feldsberg that the empress had learned that Joseph had bypassed Ferney "and deliberately did not see M. de Voltaire." The women's hostility to the French Enlightenment, most particularly in matters of religion, caused them to rejoice. They received their own firsthand account of the emperor's *visite manquée* in Joseph's letter to Leopoldine Liechtenstein. Eleonore found the story hilarious; "this blow will certainly kill him [Voltaire], and one will be able to say that the father of philosophy died of rage [*mort de rage*, rabid]."[6] In comments that may have been intended for broader dissemination, Leopoldine Kaunitz reported that the chancellor thoroughly approved of the emperor's decision and had assured his daughter-in-law that Maria Theresia had no part in it, although she would certainly be pleased. According to Chancellor Kaunitz, Joseph would have felt it was unseemly to visit an individual who would not be tolerated within Habsburg borders and who was "the head of a sect that is so destructive of society and of all good government." And yet, Leopoldine added, if Joseph had visited Voltaire, "he would have been not only pardoned but also praised, applauded."[7]

Having regaled the *Dames* with written accounts during his travels, after returning to Vienna the emperor invariably treated them to lively descriptions at evening soirées. At the conclusion of the trip to France and Switzerland, for example, the *Dames* who were present in Vienna to meet with Joseph received detailed accounts about the most intimate details of the French royal couple's joint life and characteristics of other French personages. Leopoldine Kaunitz admitted to her sister Eleonore how very anxious she was to hear Joseph's additional travel stories. She tried not to appear too eager lest the emperor should treat her as he had the former French minister Choiseul, victim of Count Falkenstein's second notorious *visite manquée*. Misled by his associates, the duke had expected the emperor to stop at his palace in Chanteloup. The emperor only passed close by, making a particular show of examining a new bridge under construction in the vicinity. Writing from Kromau, Eleonore confessed herself baffled by this omission. Observers concluded that Joseph had deferred to the wishes of Louis XVI and his new minister Maurepas, for whom Choiseul was persona non grata. For public consumption, the constraints of the travel schedule were adduced as causing the emperor's haste.[8] In contrast to Joseph's treatment of Voltaire, this humiliation of a former official who had staunchly supported the French alliance with Austria did not please Maria Theresia, and it seriously annoyed Marie Antoinette. Choiseul had been instrumental in engineering her French marriage.[9] Leopoldine Kaunitz wrote to Eleonore, "I am dying [to see JII], I am rather afraid that he will play the same trick on me that he did on Voltaire, although I am not going to post peasants in the trees, or as he did with Choiseul, although I certainly have not sent out relays."[10]

The French court, its personalities and politics, did receive a thorough airing in Joseph's subsequent evenings with the *société*. He returned home with a reasonably favorable opinion of Marie Antoinette. When Leopoldine Kaunitz ventured uncomplimentary comments concerning the French queen, Lacy rebuked her, although the emperor himself did not react: "as I ventured to make two or three minor remarks that were perhaps slightly critical of her [Marie Antoinette], the Marshal objected and said to me, what have you to do with the queen."[11] Prior to Joseph's French visit, Maria Theresia had urged Marie Antoinette to confide in the visiting emperor the details of her marital problems, assuring the French queen that Joseph would be circumspect. Marie Antoinette had done so. "I know well his discretion, and will speak frankly to him," she had written.[12] During Joseph's conversations with Louis XVI and Marie Antoinette in Paris and Versailles the king's difficulties in producing an heir with Marie Antoinette had been thoroughly analyzed. Joseph's "discretion" did not prevent him from detailing these problems in evening gatherings with the *Dames*. The women were delighted with the coregent's travel tales. Leopoldine Kaunitz fantasized about how congenial the group of *Dames* would be if conversation could always be so easy and pleasant. In August 1777 she wrote to Eleonore, who was in the countryside, "I would wish that we could be with him [Joseph] as St. Francis de Sales urges us to be while at table, refusing nothing, demanding nothing, regarding as good everything that is decent and reasonable, letting him praise Paris, Versailles, all with that degree of friendliness so to speak that is midway between indifference, which would be offensive, and too much sensibility, which he would interpret precisely as he chose; but this is easier to write about than to carry out."[13] In his private travel descriptions for the *Dames* Joseph was able to convey affection and interest in a manner that was often missing from daily intercourse. The women received quite personal messages from the emperor even during the military exercises he held at various locations in the monarchy, not to mention his letters from the field of battle, mentioned in a previous chapter. In a note that demonstrated considerable sensitivity, Joseph wrote to Leopoldine Kaunitz from exercises at Leitmeritz (Litoměřice) in September 1779 condoling with her over the deaths of her young children: "what would I not give for you to have all your children once again."[14]

During his decade of sole rule the emperor continued to maintain an active schedule of travel, both within the monarchy's borders and outside them, in spite of the frenzied pace of his reform program. Now that he was sole ruler, all visits to foreign courts were in truth serious foreign policy projects. As during the coregency the *Dames* enjoyed Joseph's accounts of his adventures. But now they were more critical of his actions than they had been during the previous decade, when the stakes had not seemed so high. He remained a remarkably ambitious traveler, as a list of his principal destinations makes clear. In early 1781 the emperor visited the Austrian Netherlands (Belgium), the Dutch Republic, and France. In 1783 he traveled to Hungary, Transylvania, and Galicia. In spring 1784 he journeyed to Italy. He visited Italy again in 1785. During the summer months of 1786 he was in Galicia, Transylvania, Upper Austria, and Styria. In spring 1787 he returned to Russia for a second meeting with Catherine II.[15]

Joseph still relished these journeys. As he visited Belgium in summer 1781 Leopoldine Kaunitz noted rather drily that the emperor was more forthcoming toward his subjects when traveling. "My wishes are for his happiness," she wrote, "and since he certainly causes more people to be happy and is happier himself away from Vienna, I believe I can, forgetting myself, wish that he would not come back." Leopoldine's husband had been told that the emperor had sent back "many more petitions with the *Placet* . . . than when he was here."[16] Eleonore considered Joseph's 1781 stopover in the Dutch Republic, a country that was by its very nature an object of some distaste for the *Dames*, to be imprudent in the extreme. The Dutch Republic and England, which was a major player in European politics and erstwhile ally of the republic, had taken opposing sides in England's war with her American colonies and relations between the two were hostile. Leopoldine Liechtenstein reported from Spa (in a letter to Josepha Clary that would be passed along to Eleonore Liechtenstein) that the "fermentation" in Holland was such that according to report "one should not be surprised to see a complete change in the form of government." She too was startled by the emperor's visit to Holland given these conditions.[17] Eleonore characterized Joseph's trip to Holland as "one of those peculiar things that no longer surprise us, for we know the author. To go to Holland at this time, to pay a visit to the stadholder seems to me something that I cannot fathom; I believe it is ill-advised, imprudent, disrespectful, both for them and for the English, for one or the other, for I have no idea what he intends by doing this."[18]

Joseph visited the French capital before returning to Vienna in summer 1781, hoping to elicit more active support from his French ally and to benefit from his sister Marie Antoinette's influence in his favor. To the *Dames*, the emperor again expressed admiration for the French queen. Visiting Leopoldine Kaunitz after his return, the emperor spoke of his sister with affection and enthusiasm. "He talked to me a great deal about his trip to France, the Queen has captivated him more than ever, her conduct in everything and with the King is admirable, little dinners in the society of Madame de Polignac, in a word everything is just as fine as can be." Very likely the emperor wished the *Dames* to pass along his optimistic report to their wider circle of associates. Leopoldine Kaunitz doubted that the French court was functioning so smoothly as Joseph claimed. Joseph predicted that Leopoldine Liechtenstein, who was then visiting Paris, would be delighted with the queen ("very satisfied").[19] A favored destination for aristocratic travelers from all over Europe, Paris was naturally attractive to Viennese visitors since France had a Habsburg queen. How cordially that queen received individual visitors from Vienna was the subject of much gossip and jealousy among them.[20] Leopoldine Liechtenstein expressed gratification concerning her sojourn in Paris and the welcome accorded her by the French court, describing enthusiastically to Josepha Clary her visit to Count Artois's "Bagatelle" in the Bois de Boulogne as well as to Marly.[21] But she did not share the emperor's ostensible complacency concerning the queen. Eleonore reported that Leopoldine Liechtenstein "is nowhere near as enchanted as he is with the Queen, and all of Paris is dissatisfied with her [Marie Antoinette]." The queen was sociable with only a select group and planned to reside at the Château de la Muette, a palace on the edge of the Bois de Boulogne, until her pregnant friend Madame de Polignac gave birth (actually not until December 1781). As Eleonore reported, "this is considered to be quite disrespectful. But she (Françoise) says in public and before the Emperor that the Queen treated her well, and she praises her a great deal."[22]

The emperor launched several diplomatic initiatives during the early 1780s, with varying degrees of success. To enhance the prestige of his own court and bolster his personal standing in diplomatic circles, even the businesslike emperor

Joseph needed to stage impressive events on those occasions when important visitors came to Vienna. Interestingly enough, when he chose to make the effort this utilitarian emperor was capable of sponsoring well-organized, magnificent court functions, as impressive as those of earlier Habsburg reigns.[23] Helping to orchestrate and populate these occasions remained an obligatory court function for families who were wealthy or influential and for individuals who were closely associated with the dynasty, as were the *Dames*. As during previous reigns, court aristocrats served as select company, as tour guides, or at least as admiring spectators. Major court events during Joseph II's decade of sole rule, in addition to the papal visit, included the visits of Grand Duke Paul and his relatives in 1781 and 1782 and the visit of the Moroccan ambassador who came to ratify a friendship treaty promoting free trade in 1783. The latter was a personage intensely interesting (and exotic) to the Viennese public. Later there was the brief stay of Joseph's sister Marie Christine and her husband Prince Albert, governors in Brussels, in 1786; and finally the celebration of the marriage of Archduke Franz and his Württemberg bride, an event upon which Joseph II lavished immense resources.

A new, closer Habsburg relationship with Russia was fundamental to Joseph II's foreign policy plans. Specific terms of a new Austrian-Russian alliance, ratified by exchange of letters in 1781, did not become known publicly until 1783. According to Eleonore only one member of the *société*, Marshal Lacy with his Russian military background, applauded the closer relationship with Russia (Lacy was "so Russophile [*si Russe*]," she observed).[24] Throughout her reign, Maria Theresia had considered Prussia to be her principal enemy and other considerations, such as Russia's expansion southward into former Ottoman territory, had received less attention. Chancellor Kaunitz had generally shared this orientation. Although Maria Theresia disliked what she knew of Catherine II, she had acquiesced in Joseph's visit to the Russian empress in 1780 and viewed the greater cordiality between Austria and Russia as some compensation for the disappointing results of Kaunitz's French alliance.[25] Like Maria Theresia the *Dames* deplored what they knew of the czarina personally (Leopoldine Kaunitz referred to Catherine as "this she-devil") but the Russian empress's moral character was not the women's main concern.[26] In practical terms, the alliance bound Russia to support the Habsburg monarchy if the latter was attacked by any power outside Italy. For his part Joseph II was obliged to assist Russia if Russia should be attacked by any power outside Asia. However, an additional provision called for prompt, massive mutual assistance if either power was attacked by the Ottomans, actually Catherine's principal preoccupation.[27] Joseph was called upon to support Russian demands for reforms in the behavior of the Turks toward Balkan Christians and Russian commerce. If the Turks proved unwilling or unable to comply, further collaboration between the empress and Joseph was mandated, including eventual joint armed intervention. The Turks might well choose to resist Russian diplomatic pressure militarily, raising the specter of Habsburg military action to support Russian claims. A Prussian attack on the Habsburg monarchy, certainly still viewed as a possibility by the monarchy's leaders, was not to be anticipated from one day to the next. But Catherine fully expected, and indeed desired, a misstep by the Turks that would justify Russian military action. Thus there was continual danger that the new alliance between Joseph and Catherine II would pull the monarchy into a war with the Ottoman Empire.[28] No doubt Joseph had concluded that he had few other options if he did not wish to leave the monarchy entirely bereft of effective allies. The advantages of the alliance for Russia were obvious but far from clear for the Habsburg monarchy, which had no interest in provoking the Turks. Observers found it difficult to imagine commensurate profit for the Habsburg monarchy, with its fear of an ascendant Prussia to its north.[29]

At his first meeting with Catherine II, prior to Maria Theresia's death, the emperor also had started planning a marriage alliance between Leopold's eldest son Franz, heir-in-waiting to the Habsburg possessions, and Princess Elisabeth of Württemberg, sister of the wife of Grand Duke Paul, Catherine's heir. Joseph pursued this goal with characteristic energy. Already during summer 1781 the *Dames* learned that the Russian couple (under the names Count and Countess "of the North") and Elisabeth's Württemberg parents would visit Vienna in the fall.[30] During the visit arrangements for the marriage were to be finalized. Joseph organized a lavish program for his Russian guests, sharing the itinerary and the ambitious schedule of entertainment with the *société*. As court functionaries Prince Clary and Ernst Kaunitz were at once mobilized. Prince Clary would orchestrate the hunting events that would be staged.[31] Ernst Kaunitz prepared living quarters for the guests in the Hofburg. He also selected and furnished rooms for the Württemberg princess at the Visitation convent where the emperor hoped she would reside after the departure of her relatives.[32] Josepha Clary reported to Eleonore Liechtenstein that Rosenberg had been deputed to greet the Württemberg guests and to urge them to leave the bride in Vienna after their departure, still a point of contention.[33] In the event Rosenberg fell ill in November, and his place was taken by the *Oberststallmeister* (master of the horse) Prince Dietrichstein. For her part, Eleonore reported from Feldsberg that the emperor had opposed a stopover there by the traveling Württemberg couple. The emperor, it seemed, preferred to have the travelers approach their final destination by way of Brod, obviating unfavorable comparisons between the palatial accommodations of the Liechtenstein family at Feldsberg and the living arrangements available in the Hofburg in Vienna ("lest Feldsberg should seem to them more beautiful than the apartments he has allotted to them").[34]

Careful attention to imperial representation and showmanship notwithstanding ("all the lodgings, the days of rest, the length of the visits, the objects to see, everything is indicated," in Eleonore's words), attendance upon the Russian visitors by members of the court aristocracy in Vienna was not recreational, or even optional.³⁵ According to Leopoldine Liechtenstein, participation in the scheduled events was a duty (*devoir d'état*) for the *Dames*.³⁶ Josepha Clary referred to the approaching Russian travel contingent as a horde of locusts (*Heuschrecken*); and the following year, when the Russians returned to Vienna, Eleonore spoke with foreboding of joining "the Russian free-for-all [*la bagarre Russe*]."³⁷ From Feldsberg in October 1781, as the moment of the Russians' arrival neared, Eleonore jested that few of her contemporaries would be sufficiently courageous "to expose themselves to the fiery furnace, like the three children."³⁸ In reality, elite Viennese society including the *Dames* would not let slip an opportunity to participate in the important visit, strenuous as such activity might be.

By all accounts, the Russian sojourn was a public relations success for the emperor. The Württemberg family including the young princess arrived in early November 1781, followed later in the month by Grand Duke Paul and his grand duchess, who stayed until early January 1782. The activities with which Joseph entertained his guests during their first visit and again briefly when they returned in October 1782, recounted in some detail in the contemporary *Wiener Zeitung* and most recently in a useful summary by Joseph's biographer Derek Beales, offer a striking example of eighteenth-century eclecticism. Events included a demonstration of a mechanical writing machine; visits to the imperial *Naturalienkabinett*, the porcelain factory in the Rossau, and the *Medaillenkabinett* in the Hofburg; a lecture by Abbot Maximilian Hell, imperial astronomer, about his trip to Lappland; tours to the imperial menagerie at Schönbrunn and the botanical garden in the Rennweg under the management of Joseph von Jacquin; tours of the veterinary hospital and the military hospital at Gumpendorf. Buildings of special note were visited: Schönbrunn palace, where the late Maria Theresia's special elevator was noted; Joseph II's new house in the Augarten; Trattner's printing establishment with its sixty presses; various hospitals and schools; Saint Stephan's cathedral, the Karlskirche and naturally Vienna's Russian Orthodox Church. There were wild boar and pheasant hunts, plays, balls, operas, visits to the court library and the Belvedere picture gallery, and promenades on the city ramparts and in the Prater. The guests witnessed a ceremony of the Order of the Golden Fleece and saw artillery maneuvers at Simmering. They watched an exhibition of the famous chess-playing machine at the residence of *Hofkammerrat* Baron Kempelen. For female guests a trip to the Visitation convent was arranged. Receptions were held for the grand duke by select personages including Charles Liechtenstein (who also sponsored a tour of the city's military barracks), *Obersthofmeister* Prince Schwarzenberg, Prince Colloredo, Prince Auersperg, and Chancellor Kaunitz. Leopoldine Liechtenstein sponsored a gathering for the most important Viennese and foreign ladies.³⁹ From contemporary reports and from comments made in their letters prior to the events, it is evident that the *Dames* participated actively in many of these events.

By the time the Russian guests were expected in Vienna for their projected second visit, in autumn 1782, observers had concluded that relations between them and Joseph had cooled. One possible factor was Grand Duke Paul's persistent and open predilection for Prussia. Leopoldine Liechtenstein reported to Eleonore that guests and host had come to cordially detest each other. Josepha Clary, usually quick to overlook the quarrels and pettiness of her contemporaries, confirmed the rift. She even predicted that the irritated Russian party would not return for the second stage of their visit in the autumn to transfer custody of Archduke Franz's future bride, who would have to be fetched from Prague. The emperor assured Leopoldine Kaunitz and Josepha at a soirée that the Russians would return, however, and Grand Duke Paul and his wife did spend two additional weeks in Vienna in October.[40] The prospective bride Elisabeth took up her residence at the Visitation convent as planned. Her conversion from Lutheranism to Roman Catholicism took place 26 December 1782 in the court chapel of the Hofburg.

The Russian alliance threatened to destroy any remaining cordiality that subsisted between the monarchy and its ostensible ally France, traditionally a protector of the Turks. In late 1782, in an effort to match a Russian plan to advance into Ottoman territory, the emperor prepared his forces for action on the frontier in the east, imposing a serious burden on the monarchy's finances. The Turks, however, yielded to demands made by the Russian empress, and military action was averted. When in spring 1783 Joseph asked his ambassador to France Count Mercy to speak frankly to the French foreign minister Vergennes in Paris about the evolving Habsburg relationship with Russia, the French response made it clear yet again that despite Marie Antoinette's best efforts Joseph could not expect support from France, and certainly not assistance in offsetting Russian acquisitions of Turkish territory.[41]

In spring and summer 1783 a full-blown diplomatic crisis unfolded when it seemed that Austria might be pressured to join Russia in open warfare against the Turks. Citing ongoing Turkish violations of the terms of their treaties with Russia, Catherine demanded intense Austrian diplomatic pressure or, failing that, military support to punish the Turks. In late spring 1783, Catherine simply took possession of Crimea outright. At a soirée in July 1783, conversation turned to the monarchy's relationship with Russia and a much anticipated manifesto by which Catherine would declare that Russia had annexed Crimea in order to preserve peace, claiming that the territory would otherwise become an "apple of discord" (*la pomme de discorde*). To the *Dames* the emperor disclaimed foreknowledge of this Russian advance. Leopoldine Liechtenstein made soothing remarks, Leopoldine Kaunitz reported to her sister: "Among other things Françoise, who said she was not at all Russophile, and that she found them insufferable, added that in reality they could not have been prevented from taking Crimea." But as soon as

Leopoldine Kaunitz was confident that Lacy had left the gathering, she herself observed that Catherine's next move would no doubt be to take Polish territory as well, again for the sake of peace. "It was decided that I was talking nonsense." The emperor was being disingenuous, Leopoldine Kaunitz thought: "how can he say that the Empress did not talk to him about Crimea when he negotiated with her? Did she not tell him that she wanted to expel the Turks from Europe, was she supposed to begin with Constantinople and leave Crimea untouched behind her?"[42] As usual Eleonore was disgusted with the monarchy's stance and the imperial ineptitude that, in her opinion, had worked so obviously to Catherine's advantage. The Habsburg government with its commitments to Russia was occupying its customary position, she sighed from Kromau: "In other words, advancing too fast, letting ourselves be caught, and then wanting to retreat when the mousetrap has been sprung, we will gain no credit at all and the hatred of everyone." The Russian empress alone would profit from this Austro-Russian relationship, using fully every advantage for "one cannot with impunity commit oneself to partnership with her." Soon the Habsburg monarchy would be forced to go to war "and the result of this tender friendship that we have purchased at such great cost will be to be forced to fight for her, until she is in a position to fight against us."[43]

The Russian crisis of 1783 defused itself, since the emperor accepted Russia's acquisition of Crimea from the Turks without seeking a counterbalancing gain. Back in Vienna at a soirée in September, Eleonore remarked sarcastically that the Russian empress had reason to be grateful to Joseph, since he had quite simply enabled her to become mistress of Crimea and Kuban. The emperor's reply suggested smugness, even hubris, to Eleonore: "that is true, he said, but she acknowledges it, I have been able to manage, to plan all of that." Eleonore was unconvinced. "As for me," she wrote to her sister, "I was full of wonder at hearing how vanity can blind one, so that for the sake of bragging one takes glory in one's disadvantages." Leopoldine Liechtenstein suggested then that some sort of profit for the Habsburg monarchy would surely be desirable as well. "I myself asked," Eleonore reported, "if it was then to our advantage to make the Russians stronger and to open the way for them to advance further, I am not sure what he had to say to that."[44]

Leopoldine Kaunitz's opinion concerning this Russian alliance was shared by many contemporaries and has often been echoed by historians. "What can we gain from the Turks that would compensate for the enlargement and proximity of the Russians," she had wondered in July 1783, "even without considering the loss of the alliance with France that our enterprises against the Turks will bring in their train sooner or later."[45] Eleonore echoed this view: "we have . . . nothing but risk and inconvenience to expect, to be evasive, to disgust, to betray everyone, and in the end to take our decision in a pique of jealousy, what misery, what pettiness, what a triumph for her [Catherine II], even greater perhaps to her way of thinking than the defeat and overthrow of the Turks. In truth we are in every sense of the word pathetic people, the more so because we believe ourselves rich, great, and powerful."[46] At meetings with the *Dames* the emperor exuded confidence, even swaggering belligerence, insisting that if aided by this Russian alliance the Habsburg monarchy could help itself to Bosnian and Serbian lands. One night in August 1783 the three women in attendance—Leopoldine Kaunitz, Leopoldine Liechtenstein, Josepha Clary—were astonished by the emperor's unusually bellicose pronouncements and his appetite for territory then under Turkish control. At first they surmised that a particularly rousing missive had arrived from Moscow. Instead, it seemed, the emperor was simply exulting in the consciousness that he had an army of 140,000 men available in Hungary, hundreds of cannons, "and all that without counting the regiments that are on a war footing, he believed himself to be backed by such a strong force that it frightened me," wrote Leopoldine Kaunitz, "although he assured us that we should just rely upon Joseph, then we would find that all will go well." The women urged caution, in their customary discreet manner. "We told him we remembered," Leopoldine Kaunitz reported to Eleonore, "that it was not so long ago that he himself acknowledged that we have so many neighbors on all sides who from one moment to the next could become our enemies."[47] No doubt the emperor enjoyed his sabre rattling sessions with the *société*. But in reality he was relieved that no military action had been required. In a letter to his brother Leopold at the end of July, he noted, "A foolhardy action is easily begun, but then to finish it well, that takes skill [*art*]."[48]

Certainly Joseph was more cautious than his friends, and the public, allowed. Deservedly or not, when he began his sole rule many diplomats and foreign rulers had already concluded that he was an expansionist, an aggressive and unpredictable sovereign with a penchant for military action.[49] These tendencies were enthusiastically publicized by Frederick II. Frederick's own record had demonstrated astute acquisitiveness; and Catherine II was far more aggressive than her Habsburg ally.[50] But several initiatives undertaken by the emperor in the 1780s certainly reinforced unfavorable perceptions of him. The *Dames* found it difficult to gauge the emperor's willingness to risk war in support of various positions he took, and so did foreign rulers. In 1782 the emperor successfully pressured the Dutch to dismantle the outmoded fortresses they still maintained within Belgian territory, a relic of the Treaty of Utrecht (1713). Originally the fortresses had acted to block a possible revival of French aggression. As noted previously, in the early 1780s Holland was embroiled in a conflict with its erstwhile ally England and in no position to counter Joseph's demands. In the same year, the margrave of Ansbach became seriously ill. In the Treaty of Teschen of 1779 the Habsburg government had acknowledged Prussia's future claims to Ansbach and Bayreuth. But Leopoldine Kaunitz reported to her sister Eleonore that at a soirée with Joseph there was much talk about war because Prussia might seek to obtain in exchange Lusatia or Mecklenburg instead of Ansbach. Josepha Clary had spoken of this prospect of hostilities "with real terror," no doubt recalling the nightmarish fate of her husband's estate Teplitz during the Bavarian war.[51] Eleonore, far from Vienna for the summer, counted on Joseph's previous military disappointment to cool his ardor: "the attempt the emperor already made reassures me, for I believe him to have been disgusted by it to the depths of his soul, and if he should begin again he will tackle only an easily managed enemy and be supported by his good allies the Russians."[52] Eleonore may have overrated the emperor's revulsion against military adventures. Certainly at the outset of his sole rule he was more preoccupied with repairing the monarchy's finances after the expensive Bavarian Potato War.[53] The margrave lived on, and the Ansbach crisis passed uneventfully. But clumsy diplomatic forays strengthened the public's belief in the emperor's bellicosity.

In 1784 the emperor sought to force Holland to open the Scheldt estuary and thus the port of Antwerp, so as to foster Belgian commercial development. Twice Joseph sent a ship up the Scheldt, in April and October. The Dutch, no longer at war with England, had the temerity to fire on the second vessel at Saftingen. Their active resistance, which included opening dikes to flood their borderlands, checkmated Joseph's move.[54] After months of blustering and maneuvering, during which the emperor was repeatedly disappointed by the lack of support he received from his French ally (the French even threatened to defend Holland against the Habsburg monarchy), the emperor obtained from the Dutch the evacuation of the antiquated fortress at Lillo, minor border adjustments, and an indemnity payment.[55] The Scheldt remained closed. In September 1785, when the emperor, Lacy, and Rosenberg came to Baden to visit Leopoldine Kaunitz, Leopoldine asked the emperor if he had brought with him the "olive branch" he had promised, but Joseph did not yet know the outcome of negotiations.[56] At a soirée that took place soon after news concerning the settlement had arrived, Leopoldine Kaunitz played devil's advocate, lightly teasing and goading the emperor as was her wont. When Joseph observed that, under the peace terms, navigation of the Scheldt would be free at least as far as Saftingen, Leopoldine replied, "but not further? He said no, the rest of the Scheldt remains theirs, but at least with the cession of the forts and surrounding lands one is no longer exposed to the vexation of their tariffs in moving from one locale to another." Lacy had expressed his satisfaction too, Leopoldine Kaunitz wrote, "and I understood that we were not to speak further about the Scheldt and must be or appear to be satisfied." After all, Leopoldine added, at least war had been avoided. She found that the misguided Viennese public believed the Dutch had been humiliated. When Leopoldine Kaunitz complimented the emperor on the applause he had received at the theater, he displayed annoyance. He claimed to have believed the plaudits were for the Princess Elisabeth, who had accompanied him. As always, according to Leopoldine, he was at pains to flaunt his supposed disdain for public opinion. As Leopoldine Kaunitz and Rosenberg left this gathering at Leopoldine Liechtenstein's residence and descended the stairs together, Rosenberg had spoken frankly to her about the Dutch fiasco and what was in fact a rebuff for the Habsburg side, remarking "for shame, to get ourselves paid off after all the noise we have made, and what are 10 millions, this affair is costing us much more."[57] Again the emperor's reputation suffered. He had blustered and threatened but achieved modest results. Although in the end he had shown restraint and distaste for the shedding of blood, Joseph's noisy gestures had strengthened the belief among diplomats, rulers, and the European public at large that he was both ambitious and belligerent. In Belgium itself, where some of the populace had supported this initiative as being favorable to the region's interests, there was disappointment and a sense of betrayal.[58]

Simultaneously the emperor made another attempt to trade Belgium for Bavaria in 1785, replicating the failed attempt of the coregency. In his mind the Dutch and Bavarian ventures were linked, since both the prosperity and status of Belgium could be expected to interest France, the ally whose support was essential for the Bavarian acquisition. This time peace was preserved. Joseph could not act in the face of French opposition and without the active backing of Russia. Neither Habsburg ally was willing to assist Joseph, although each was eager to broker a diplomatic settlement in the event of a quarrel. The dismay that was generated broadly within the Holy Roman Empire when news of this renewed effort to trade the Belgian Netherlands broke in early 1785 enabled Frederick II to sponsor a "League of Princes" (*Fürstenbund*) including Hanover, Saxony, and a number of lesser German princes to oppose Joseph's territorial ambitions. Frederick cast himself in the role of guardian of the integrity of the Empire (despite his own transgressions of the 1740s), and he reinforced this claim with a willingness to resort to military force. Joseph's plans for Bavaria were effectively blocked by the failure of his allies to provide support, not by Frederick's dramatic action. Nevertheless the *société* had lively autumn discussions about the *Fürstenbund*, a new phenomenon and certainly testimony to the elderly Frederick II's skill as a diplomat.[59] From Kromau Eleonore noted that Frederick's statement as published in the *Gazette de Leyde* had justified his position so effectively that it almost persuaded even her ("the declaration of the King of Prussia concerning the German league I fear could win him many supporters, it is so well written that one is greatly tempted to think that he is right").[60] The emperor gave Leopoldine Kaunitz a copy of a Habsburg response to Frederick's declaration, too bulky and too dull to send to her sister Eleonore, in Leopoldine's estimation.[61]

Once again the Bavarian scheme was dropped, and it was Joseph's final attempt to orient Habsburg policy toward the German lands of the Holy Roman

Empire.⁶² The existence of a hostile coalition within the Holy Roman Empire led by Frederick II could only lower even further Joseph's valuation of the worth of his imperial title. Briefly he had even considered offering that title, increasingly deemed to be largely symbolic, to the Bavarian elector in an effort to sweeten the deal by which the Habsburg monarchy would have acquired some Bavarian territory, thereby augmenting the monarchy's real power within German lands.⁶³ An indirect result of Joseph's efforts to counter Frederick II within the Empire was the cordial reception he gave to his visiting brother Archduke Max, Archbishop-Elector of Köln and Bishop of Münster, in 1785. The emperor had scant respect for his siblings, even for Leopold, who had demonstrated aptitude as a ruler in Tuscany. Joseph considered Max's abilities to be particularly modest. The machinations of Frederick II, Leopoldine Kaunitz believed, were the reason "that the elector [Archduke Max], who continues to have influence, is treated so well."⁶⁴ As the historian Blanning suggests, possibly a simple failure of imagination prevented the emperor from seeing any practical value in his imperial role. Frederick II, whose earlier disregard for imperial borders had imperiled and impaired Maria Theresia's inheritance, now found the Empire to be increasingly useful to his own interests. Joseph's policies increased the insecurities of the member states and weakened Habsburg influence.⁶⁵

As the decade passed and a number of Joseph's foreign policy initiatives came to grief, the *Dames* still reserved their sharpest criticism for Joseph's Russian policy. In 1787 yet another Russian-Turkish crisis occurred, and this time the outcome was less fortunate. In spring and summer the emperor had traveled to Crimea to consult with Empress Catherine for a second time, confirming the terms of their earlier alliance. Eleonore was convinced that Catherine II would take advantage of Joseph's favorable disposition toward Russia and would provoke the Turks, and her predictions were accurate.⁶⁶ The Turks had felt seriously threatened by Russia's expansion in Crimea and the Caucasus. Goaded into action by Russian provocations, the Turkish regime declared war on Russia in August 1787, hoping to regain territory it had recently lost. The emperor had pledged his assistance if Turkish forces attacked Russia, and that situation had now come to pass. Catherine called upon the emperor to fulfill the commitments he had made, to enable to her to punish the Turks. The emperor, without much enthusiasm, agreed to comply, hoping to further cement the Russian alliance and thus further secure himself against Prussia. Chancellor Kaunitz affirmed both the necessity and the desirability of Habsburg participation in the conflict.⁶⁷

While the emperor was away from Vienna for his second meeting with Catherine II, he received news about growing unrest over the reform measures he had introduced in Belgium. Joseph's initial comments to Chancellor Kaunitz suggest that the Belgian disturbances came as something of a surprise to him.⁶⁸ His reign in Belgium had begun auspiciously enough. Back in July 1781, at the time of the formal entrance of Archduchess Marie Christine and her husband Albert into Brussels, Leopoldine Liechtenstein, taking the cure with her own husband in Spa, had reported that the visiting emperor was quite popular with his Belgian subjects: "the enthusiasm they have for him there [Brussels] at present is apparently quite extraordinary."[69] But even during these early months, as he toured Belgium, Joseph upset prominent groups and offended the sensibilities of his devoutly Catholic Belgian subjects, sometimes rather gratuitously. He refused to participate in traditional ceremonies or to acknowledge the time-honored symbolic gestures of fealty offered to him, reluctant as he was to endorse what he considered to be old-fashioned notions concerning his own position as sovereign. Already in 1781, Archduchess Marie Christine was uneasy about her role as Habsburg representative in Belgium. According to Leopoldine Liechtenstein, Marie Christine was "extremely anxious about her future situation, her reflections on the matter are quite perceptive [*les reflexions les plus sensées*]."[70] The emperor's lack of confidence in his regents Marie Christine and Albert was already obvious at that early date. In a letter to Leopoldine Kaunitz Joseph referred disparagingly to the regents' inauguration as "the pompous arrival of the new governors."[71]

For several years the emperor had focused his attention elsewhere, less interested in reforming Belgian institutions since he still meditated trading at least some portion of Belgium for Bavarian territory. He delayed implementation of some religious reforms, although they were promulgated for Belgium as for other Habsburg lands. Belgian priests ignored those measures that they deemed especially irksome.[72] Joseph's attempt to open the Scheldt, a change that would have benefitted Antwerp, was viewed less favorably by other towns. In 1786 unrest caused by the establishment of one of Joseph's new reformed general seminaries for the training of priests in Louvain prompted Joseph's minister Count Belgioso to use troops to restore order among the students. When the emperor announced that reforms affecting the entire judicial and administrative system of Belgium would be enforced in 1787, standardizing and limiting the authority of the traditional, decentralized institutions of Belgium's cities and provinces, resistance stiffened particularly in the important Brabant province. These changes, which attacked the privileges of leading groups, brought to a head the seething but previously unorganized discontent. Opposition in Belgium rose to a dangerous level, its focal point being the state-approved seminaries and the administrative reforms that destroyed regional political autonomy. Already increasingly inclined to rein in expressions of public discontent that could thwart his goals, the emperor clamped tight new restrictions on the Belgian press in an effort to still the uproar. The opposition argued that the emperor had overstepped his authority in Belgium, violating fundamental constitutional laws and giving his oppressed subjects the right to resist the despotic measures. While Joseph was still traveling back from Russia, Marie Christine and Prince Albert unilaterally acceded to many of the demands of the recalcitrant Belgian estates, always with the proviso that the changes would require eventual imperial approval. Chancellor Kaunitz approved these conciliatory measures.[73]

The emperor hurried home from Russia, determined to deal firmly with the renitent Belgians and unwilling to ratify the concessions urged by Kaunitz and the governors in Brussels. Back in Vienna on June 30, he spent several days reading reports and deliberating on a course of action. In a conversation with the emperor at her residence during this period Eleonore, like others around the emperor, urged a moderate, conciliatory approach that might accomplish more with the Belgians than coercion. Eleonore Liechtenstein had recently received letters from Marie Christine, who was convinced that if no concessions were made the Belgian lands would be lost to the monarchy. In all likelihood Eleonore's suggestions to the emperor echoed those he was hearing from his sister Marie Christine directly, a circumstance that could only have increased his ill humor. Forbearance was anathema to Joseph. The almost unhinged, fanatical manner in which he insisted to Eleonore that a policy of harsh reprisal was necessary thoroughly unnerved her; in his anger the emperor brought to mind a raging lion that might devour her, she reported.[74] Belgian representatives who met with Joseph in Vienna in October 1787 found the emperor unwilling to treat with them. Archduchess Marie Christine and Duke Albert, ordered to appear in Vienna, met with stern imperial disapproval. And so opposition leaders in Belgium turned to active civil disobedience.

The conflict in Belgium sharpened and escalated during the remaining two years of Joseph's life and reign. In late 1788 he revoked all historic privileges of the rebellious Belgian estates. When Joseph dispatched troops to restore order, the opposition groups organized an armed insurrection from the safety of nearby Liège, beyond the reach of Habsburg authorities. Concerning the imperial use of force Leopoldine Kaunitz wrote, "We will have to see how it turns out in the long run, but even if not a single person makes a disturbance, what sad consolation after having trampled underfoot subjects who did not rebel, and thus so gratuitously to take with one to the very grave their hatred and unhappiness."[75] She was nonetheless indignant about the insolence of the Belgian opposition (from a Habsburg point of view) and alarmed for the safety of Count Trautmannsdorf, Habsburg minister in Brussels: "My God, how loathsome a creature is man, he is harsh, cruel, insolent when he has power, and if he is subjugated and oppressed he is vile, groveling, and contemptible. But I would not want to be in Trautmannsdorf's position. I think he must sometimes feel of his neck to see if his head is still attached there."[76] By late 1789, Belgian forces had chased the Habsburg army out of western Belgium, leaving only Luxemburg officially loyal.

The Belgian rebellion forced the emperor to deal with serious domestic and foreign crises simultaneously beginning in mid-1787. Not one to despond, the zealous emperor still expected to master both situations, convinced of the rectitude of his choices. As diplomatic and military events unfolded, Leopoldine Kaunitz found the emperor's preoccupation with the impending Turkish conflict to be a useful conversational resource. When the emperor unexpectedly showed up at her residence one evening in late August 1787 and the two of them, both drowsy, cast about for a congenial subject for conversation, the geography of the Turkish conflict was their choice. "I confess that I need to be seconded somewhat by another person to be at my ease with him, and so when finding myself perplexed for ways to entertain him, I quite luckily thought of having my Hoffmann atlas brought in, where we found quite delightful maps of Serbia, Bosnia, Turkey in Europe, the Black Sea, the course of the Danube and the Po, the theater of the last war of the Russians and Turks." It was a felicitous selection of topic for their conversation, Leopoldine told her sister. "It was my guardian angel who gave me this idea, there was so to speak no other possible choice, ecclesiastical matters touch me too closely and I find myself too weak to speak of them on my own, and moreover I do not like to initiate topics."[77] Leopoldine Kaunitz's buoyant mood soon darkened. At a soirée in early September 1787, attended only by Leopoldine Kaunitz, Rosenberg, and the emperor, she learned more about the double threat that loomed for the monarchy, famine as well as war, since harvests were so meager.[78] In late 1787 Josepha Clary communicated her growing fear of war to her daughter Thérèse Wilczek, who having married Habsburg diplomat Count Johann Josef Wilczek now lived in Italy. Josepha asked her daughter to pray for peace: "Signs of war are growing more serious by the day, it appears that no one is willing to get involved to save us from it."[79]

Duly honoring the terms of the Russian alliance, Austria declared war on Turkey on 8 February 1788, having already tried and failed to capture Belgrade before hostilities had officially begun. Historians with benefit of hindsight have noted the larger geopolitical situation in which the Habsburg monarchy found itself and the long-term imperative felt by Joseph and his advisors to match strength with both Prussia and Russia through *arondissement* of Habsburg borders including expansion into Ottoman territory, after Joseph's efforts to obtain additional German territory proved abortive. Dismissed by some historians as willful or foolish aggressiveness on Joseph's part, the war effort has received higher marks or at least greater understanding from other historians who believe it was driven by complex reasons of state.[80] By and large, at its outset the war did enjoy the enthusiastic support of the Viennese public. Joseph departed for the front in Croatia on February 29. His nephew Archduke Franz, recently married to Elisabeth, left for the army 14 March.

The *société* continued to expect attention, loyalty, and information from Joseph even as his situation became increasingly difficult and fraught with danger. He repaid the women's expressions of concern with friendly greetings, taking the trouble to express gratitude for their interest in his welfare even as he was preoccupied with trying circumstances at the front. During his momentous Russian trip earlier in 1787, he had remembered to send messages by way of Lacy to "the dear society," affirming that those times he spent with his friends were "the only sweet moments in life" and asking the *Dames* to think of him and pray for him as he played the courtier in Cherson.[81] When the alarming news of rebellion in the Belgian territories infuriated him and hastened his return to Vienna, Joseph had nevertheless taken the trouble to send word through Lacy of the joy and comfort he anticipated from his approaching reunion with his circle of *Dames*. "All my satisfaction depends upon the pleasure of embracing you and the *société* again," he wrote to Lacy in June 1787 from Leopol; "my sore heart and busy agitated mind will not prevent me from savoring this pleasure."[82] Now in the crush of the military conflict, he still recalled his companions. The Liechtenstein archive in Vaduz contains a note from Joseph to all the *Dames*, apparently written just as he was departing for the front in 1788. Explaining that his early morning departure and his many worries made him unwilling to face the poignancy of a farewell, he told the women how highly he valued the "gentleness [*douceur*] of your society" and "constancy in your friendship, of which I hope none of my actions will render me unworthy, which for so many years has made me forget the troubles and duties of my position, to which I have devoted myself all the day long." He thanked Eleonore in particular for giving him *pain d'épices* to take along, a form of high-energy gingerbread that remained edible and salubrious for some time (Leopoldine Kaunitz also sent this comestible as a gift after Joseph was already in the field).[83] Messages for the women came from the theater of war as well.[84] From Semlin in May 1788 the emperor took pains to encourage Leopoldine Kaunitz as she prepared for her daughter's smallpox inoculation. He referred reassuringly to the procedure, "this method that has been brought to almost perfect reliability," and added that he wished he could be as confident of the success of his military operations against the Turks as he was of the favorable outcome of the medical procedure.[85]

The Habsburg army painstakingly positioned itself in a dispersed fashion along the entire border with Turkey, setting up Lacy's now familiar defensive cordon and spreading out from the Adriatic coast to Wallachia. When Frederick II's successor Frederick William, newly energized by a victorious incursion into Holland the previous year, diverted some of Catherine's troops by encouraging the Swedes to attack Russia, the Turks broke into the Austrian-controlled Banat. The emperor had joined Lacy and took personal command of his troops, but he was ineffectual against the difficult conditions of the campaign. Joseph and Lacy had labored for decades to build and equip a strong, functional army. The Habsburg soldiers now proved to be tenacious fighters. However, Habsburg forces became bogged down, enervated by disease and poor nutrition. The Turks for their part were unexpectedly resilient. Heedless of his health as he tried to force a favorable military outcome, the emperor became seriously ill at the front. Although Joseph did not have sufficient humility or realism to accept responsibility for the monarchy's precarious situation, many of his statements from this time do convey the pathos and desolation of a heartsore ruler. In a letter to Leopoldine Kaunitz from the front, the emperor described his physical ailments in detail: "my health has been very disordered, and still is, there is a dry cough and difficulty in breathing to which is added an almost continual and intensifying quartan fever, wasting and loss of sleep, strength, and appetite. The latter have come back and the fever has left me; but the cough and pressure in my chest, such that in taking 100 steps I lose my breath and have palpitations, are still here and will probably persist more or less for the rest of my life."[86] His reports to his brother Leopold were bleak. "In short I do not know what to say to you, dear friend," he wrote, "but that I am the most unfortunate of beings, morally and physically suffering as much as possible, I would sooner die under a tree than to abandon things in the condition in which I find them, for the Marshal is in such despair himself that he no longer knows what to do."[87] Joseph urged his brother Leopold to come to Vienna. Joseph's old preoccupation with his bachelor status resurfaced; "as for me, without wife and children, I am nothing but a broken pane of glass that you could replace superbly."[88]

In Vienna, popular enthusiasm for military action had given way to disillusionment as the military initiative stalled. Eleonore predicted to her soldier husband in spring 1788 that the war would be prove to be ruinous, and so it was during the 1788 campaign, as the effort against Turkey flagged.[89] Hardship on the battlefield and at home made the Russian alliance odious to the public. More serious was the emergence of another source of acute domestic unrest, this time in Hungary. As noted previously, there the emperor had confounded the Magyar nobility and traditionalists by proceeding with his full array of administrative and legal reforms as well as the land tax or rectification. To obtain the recruits and provisions he needed for war, Joseph permitted the convening of the county assemblies of noblemen, moribund and largely prohibited during Joseph's heyday. The emperor refused as always to call for a diet or for the raising of troops through the *insurrectio*, the traditional method favored (and controlled) by the nobility. Although disaffection increased as months passed in 1788, the Hungarians eventually complied with most imperial requests, possibly in part because an unsuccessful campaign against the Turks could have had obvious, and ominous, consequences for the kingdom. Still, Hungary's increasing unreliability, both actual and potential, was a liability in the Habsburg war effort, although it was not until fall 1789 that many Hungarian counties actually refused to furnish more resources. In addition, Prussian agents and Prussian money were said to be fomenting unrest in the Hungarian kingdom, where the example of Belgian resistance attracted admiring attention from the restless nobility.[90]

During the military campaign of 1788, as Charles Liechtenstein fell ill and was forced to leave his post at Dubicza (described in chapter 1), Eleonore felt particular bitterness toward the emperor because even at this late date he failed to gratify Charles with words of commendation to accompany the promotion that Charles at last received, so long in coming. As before, the rift between Eleonore and the emperor was not permanent, and again Eleonore summoned sufficient patience and discretion to maintain amicable relations with the emperor. Soon after Charles's disappointing performance at Dubicza the emperor had sent a letter to Leopoldine Kaunitz from his camp at Semlin, dated 9 May 1788, in which he did speak generously about Charles's misfortunes, no doubt certain that his statements would reach Eleonore: "The action at Dubitza is distressing, as it always is to lose good men and that without gaining the object one had in view, but certainly Prince Charles and all those who carried out his orders did all that one could wish them to, and as captain and as a man of standing and spirit the Prince made the only reasonable choice."[91] The emperor worried when Eleonore traveled to Agram to care for her sick husband, fearing that she herself would fall ill.[92] She succumbed to illness only after her most taxing job was done and she and Charles had returned to Vienna. Writing to Leopoldine Kaunitz while still with the army in Illowa, Joseph had been almost frantic when he learned of Eleonore's sickness; "what terrible news you send me, your sister has putrid fever, she has been administered [the sacraments]." He had not even known Eleonore was ill, Joseph said; "I leave you to judge all the effect of the pain, fear, desire, hope that I feel, it is also a critical moment for an action with the Grand Vizier could take place from one day to the next, the signs are there. Add to that the asthma that makes breathing difficult for me, I confess to you my good friend, who at least have been fair to me and have had the kindness two times already to remember me [i.e., by sending letters or messages], that if among three things I could choose [I would wish] that your sister would recover, the Turks would be defeated, and I would willingly remain asthmatic for all my life."[93] Eleonore must have responded graciously to the emperor's expressions of concern, for subsequently he believed that he had justified his conduct toward Charles. Writing to Leopoldine Kaunitz from Lugos (Lugoj) in the Banat, he noted that Eleonore "does me justice a little. Her letter gave me a moment of gratification such as I thought was not possible for me, in the disagreeable situation in which I find myself through the failings of others, and with the scene of horror and misery that is continually before my eyes." He added, "Your good prayers at Mariazell will be efficacious, I hope, at least I am greatly relying upon that, and we have great need of them."[94]

The emperor was forced to retire to Vienna at the end of the campaign season in late November 1788, his strength failing from the effects of tuberculosis and malaria. As he prepared to leave the front in November he had reported to Leopoldine Kaunitz, after reciting his litany of woes, that he expected to see her soon, adding: "If I could transport the small number of persons who bind me to Vienna, that steeple of St. Stephans would see me no more."[95] Once back in Vienna in early December, his physical condition fluctuated. As the historian Lorenz Mikoletzky has observed, Joseph had actually contracted his mortal illness earlier, certainly by the beginning of 1788.[96] He continued to work hard. His condition was poor throughout the winter of 1788–1789. Most often during these months he remained alone with Rosenberg or Countess Chanclos, although at times he was able to converse with the *Dames*. A few written communications attest to these ongoing contacts with the group during the period. In mid-March, for example, Joseph informed the women in a note to Josepha Clary that he was too sick to meet with them on his name day, 19 March 1789.[97]

Marshal Lacy's experiences in the Turkish war, while not fatal to him, were thoroughly disheartening. When the Habsburg army fell so far short of its ambitious goals, many contemporaries blamed Lacy's defensive system. Some held Lacy responsible for the execrable Russian alliance itself, noting in particular his earlier service in the Russian military.[98] Archduchess Elisabeth, now wife to Archduke Franz, wrote to her husband in October 1788 that Lacy was afraid to return to Vienna because of popular resentment against him ("I believe he would meet with very serious affronts"). The capital resounded with lampoons, and there were reports of vandalism at Dornbach, Lacy's cherished villa and park in the Viennese suburbs. Yet when the more popular Laudon was leaving for the front in August 1788, Archduchess Elisabeth reported that because of the great public enthusiasm, his departure occurred at night, to avoid overly enthusiastic crowds.[99] According to Lacy's biographer, the opprobrium broke Lacy's spirit and destroyed his belief in Joseph's abilities as a leader.[100] Lacy refused to return to the field as commander of the main army for the 1789 campaign, pleading ill health. And so Lacy too came home a disappointed and bitter man. Like Charles Liechtenstein, he watched his replacement enjoy the success that had eluded him. The campaign of 1789, led first by Hadik and then by Laudon, was one of the most successful ever prosecuted by the Habsburg army. The announcement that Laudon would take command had elicited renewed enthusiasm for the war in the public and in the army, where he was known fondly as "Father [*Vater*] Laudon."

For the 1789 military campaign season the emperor remained in Vienna owing to his illness. Habsburg troops, although debilitated by typhus, malaria, and dysentery, rallied under the commanders Laudon, Coburg, and Hohenlohe. They captured Bosnia, Serbia, and most of Moldavia. Combined Russian and Habsburg forces conquered Wallachia as well. In surveying the results of this second year of the war historians have given the emperor some credit in recent studies for the improved military situation in 1789, noting also that the ample funding and careful preparation the army had received played a role in the eventual success of the Habsburg campaign. Contemporaries, perhaps unfairly, ascribed the successes to Laudon and to Joseph's own withdrawal from the field of battle. At the end of the campaign season came the most spectacular successes of all, the capture of Belgrade in October 1789 and Bucharest in November.[101]

Even as the monarchy's military fortunes improved, the conflict dragged on. Now Prussia openly made common cause with Turkey. The army required additional manpower and provisioning. Discontent, growing also because of unusually poor harvests and high food prices, produced a grim, almost surreal environment in Vienna, as Leopoldine Kaunitz's observations suggest. Because the army needed recruits so urgently, laborers and shopkeepers' assistants were being conscripted. Leopoldine described "terrible wailing"; and furthermore, she added, meat prices were set to rise "which will result in yet more wailing." At the same time, she observed, the usual Viennese diversions continued: "theaters and promenades are overflowing with people, it is an inconceivable contrast; since Friday it has rained every day but that is said to be too late for they are already harvesting the wheat." A week later Leopoldine remained concerned about popular unrest. She wrote to Eleonore, "They say the discontent of the people over the recruiting and the increase in the price of meat is extreme; there are some who state that they wish to pray for peace and that therefore they cannot pray for the health of the Emperor."[102]

To complicate matters further, in mid-1789 the first news of serious popular unrest in France arrived. The emperor and the Habsburg government were concerned but not unduly alarmed. France had been an unreliable ally for the Habsburgs. After decades of disappointment, Joseph and his advisors no longer valued the French relationship, even though a Habsburg queen shared the throne with Louis XVI.[103] The emperor absorbed the unsettling reports from France with remarkable calmness, according to Leopoldine Liechtenstein. Eleonore was surprised that the news did not worsen Joseph's condition. "I think he gives great proof of better health if it does not suffer from the effect this terrible affair must have on him," she wrote. After all, she reasoned, it was the emperor's government against which the French railed, "he is the one they hate, as they insult this unfortunate and imprudent Queen."[104] Only a few years earlier the fundamental soundness of the French polity had been taken for granted, even though the kingdom's financial weakness was public knowledge. Back in 1783 Leopoldine Kaunitz had blithely observed that the French "with their fickle superficiality and their immutable foundation are still the most solid and perhaps the wisest monarchy that exists." She had contrasted the French monarchy's solidity with the flightiness of the English, whose unfortunate king George III was saddled with a feckless Prince of Wales.[105]

Among the literate public in Vienna, events in France in 1789 generated strong reactions, both positive and negative. The *Dames* had acquaintances who welcomed the apparent liberalization of French political life. Observers of moderate views were willing to find positive traits in the developments and to hope for a satisfactory outcome. Progressives such as Zinzendorf and Eleonore's son-in-law Johann Harrach concluded that France had made a peaceful transition to constitutional government. Thus even scions of established, elite aristocratic families could be sympathetic to the initial limits imposed upon the French king by the National Assembly. Many aristocrats, like their French counterparts, viewed limitations on central power as an accretion to—or perhaps restoration of—the traditional authority of their own class. They opposed the "despotism" of monarchical power with its accelerating encroachments on the corporate identity and liberties of the nobility. But before long activists in France, no longer just critiquing the nobility's leadership and seeking to limit class prerogatives, wished to replace the class with a new ideal, the *citoyen*, an individual who might but need not be of noble birth. The growing radicalism of French political life weaned all but the hardiest supporters in the Habsburg monarchy from their initial enthusiasm.

Reports from France produced alarm and hostility among the *Dames* from the start, in contrast to the reactions of Joseph II and his advisors. Already in August 1789, Eleonore wrote to her daughter, "I must confess that if this is liberty I shall take the side of tyranny, despite the oppression with which it burdens us and the natural aversion that it has always inspired in me."[106] With regard to their friend Zinzendorf's views, Leopoldine Kaunitz remarked in late July after attending a soirée at Chancellor Kaunitz's, "Zinzinet came over to join the conversation, as for him, he is enchanted with the good fortune of France, I hope that it [France] may be as happy as he thinks, he is a very good man but he judges matters according to principles he has adopted, the consequences of which are far from being as certain in reality as he thinks them." Zinzendorf was outspoken, she continued, and "this assembly seems to him to be the most beautiful, most estimable thing, he would like to be at Versailles to see and hear it, he is sure that they do not at all oppose the privileges of the Nobility, particularly since it has joined in, that if this union [of the Estates] had not been accomplished then they might have suffered loss, that the king will forfeit nothing except the power to command arbitrarily, that all executive power will remain to him, in a word he finds all this so charming that I accorded him my vote to elect him Deputy to our first assembly." Leopoldine had demurred, arguing that "there are many objections to which he responded only by becoming angry because I had such a low opinion of the human race."[107] When Leopoldine Kaunitz heard reports of the storming of the Bastille, at once she feared that the French example would make the Belgians even more restless. She viewed these dire events as "the fruits of the enlightened luminaries [*lumières*] of this execrable century." In her opinion, lack of respect for religion had undermined the social and political order. "The Gospel, as Fénelon says, is that pearl, that stone rejected by the architect, which renders sovereigns good, gentle, compassionate, and subjects submissive and patient, thus it is that far from disputing with others what they have, one gives to them also one's own possessions."[108]

Although they detested and feared trends in western Europe, the women wanted to remain informed. They helped each other identify and obtain reliable sources of news. In August 1789, Eleonore commented to her daughter Josephine Harrach that a good source of information about events in France was the *Gazette de Leyde* (although in July she had suggested to Leopoldine Kaunitz that this newspaper was "completely devoted to the Third [Estate], speaking of nothing else and saying not a word about other news from the rest of the world, I think that I will subscribe to another newspaper in order to stay informed"). Strongly opinionated, Eleonore was indignant when she encountered any acquaintance who sympathized with the aims of the French National Assembly. She voiced the suspicion that freemasonry lay behind the activities of the revolutionaries. "For a long time I have thought," she told her sister, "that freemasonry is the great motivator behind the spirit that reigns in the General Assembly . . . it is an influence as singular as it is secret, but one can detect it there readily, they want only liberty and equality, which is to say, a situation where each is a law unto himself and where there is nothing but trouble, confusion, and misfortune, and especially destruction of religion, which is the only bond that makes us love and comply with our duties and makes us behave unto others as we would like them to behave towards us."[109]

All five women had known Joseph's sister Marie Antoinette, the French queen. As noted previously, Leopoldine Liechtenstein had visited with her and Louis XVI as recently as 1781, during a French voyage. The women took a personal interest in the French king and queen, although they had no illusions about the pair's wisdom or strength of character. They sensed almost immediately the peril facing the royal couple. Moreover, they appear to have discerned very early an implicit threat to the status of their own class and their way of life even though the menace of social upheaval seemed to be confined to France. Summering in Meseritsch in July Eleonore eagerly read reports from both Leopoldine Kaunitz and Leopoldine Liechtenstein, and she bombarded her sister with questions. "With regard to the affairs of France," she wrote, "just tell me what they want to do with the King, I remember the question that the Queen asked of Mr. Necker and which was more reasonable than people thought at the time."[110] In August the queries continued: "first I would like to know what it is that they want to do, and whom do they dislike so? Do they no longer want a king? Is Mr. Necker to become that under another title? What grievance do they have, who has done them wrong? Is it the king, or this ancient Nobility that has always been valued and respected and that has constituted the glory of the nation? Is there a conspiracy? Is all of this premeditated? Who is leading it, and where is it to go? How was it possible to corrupt this nation so quickly, how can they see their king in such extreme abjection?" Subsequently she remarked, "I wonder if there is a man in the world who would want to be in the situation of the King of France. Not to mention that of the Queen."[111]

The portentous nature of French events did not become fully apparent to the monarchy's leadership until after Joseph II's death.[112] Habsburg attention was focused on the monarchy's international standing, giving primacy to foreign affairs rather narrowly defined.[113] The harsh views expressed by Eleonore and her sister were partisan and relatively unnuanced, passing easily over the larger difficulties facing French society and the French government, but it must be conceded that at some level the women quickly recognized the seriousness of events. Their response to the onset of what soon became an international crisis was not entirely unidimensional. Their concerns for the preservation of family and "house" obliged each *Dame*, like earlier generations of aristocrats, to adapt to changing conditions in spite of substantial ideological repugnance toward international events and current political agents; and indeed when in due course Napoleon's brilliant military successes gave him mastery over much of Europe's land and compelled the Habsburg and imperial aristocracy to curry favor and compete for possessions and status under these new conditions, the *Dames* and their families would focus their attention not so much on ideology or the old world that was perishing as on maintenance of each family's well-being amid fluctuating fortunes and a new environment. On an individual level, it might even be argued, they put into practice their own form of the "primacy of foreign policy," affording yet another example of the persistent, traditional aristocratic will to survive.[114]

Throughout 1789 the *Dames* followed with concern the course of Joseph's illness. When no gatherings could be held with the ailing emperor for weeks at a time, Leopoldine Liechtenstein through her association with Lacy was the best informed among the women and could report conditions in the sickroom. Rosenberg also kept the friends apprised. In April 1789 Joseph was so ill that he received publicly the church's last rites. The *Dames* were in attendance. Zinzendorf reported in his diary that although he himself had not been present, he understood that Leopoldine Liechtenstein and Leopoldine Kaunitz had wept openly.[115] Rosenberg, who sent health updates to Leopold, remarked in May 1789 that Joseph's ills were as much "moral" (i.e., psychological or spiritual) as physical.[116] In a note to Leopoldine Kaunitz in May 1789, Joseph noted sadly his own lingering bad health and the likelihood that he would remain an invalid: "In descending the ladder, you always flatter yourself that you may climb up again."[117] In late June 1789 Rosenberg showed Leopoldine Liechtenstein a note from Joseph's doctor Brambilla that was full of foreboding ("that this illness is the hydra of the legend, with this difference . . . that it is real, to our very great misfortune"). Relaying Brambilla's remarks to Eleonore, Leopoldine Kaunitz exclaimed, "Domine salvum fac regem nostrum." Rosenberg predicted that the emperor would survive a few more months. Leopoldine Liechtenstein thought he would die in a few weeks.[118]

Briefly during late spring and summer of 1789 Joseph rallied, so much so that he even dreamed of rejoining his army.[119] He was able to move to Laxenburg in May 1789. Taking the waters nearby in Baden, several of the women visited him. Leopoldine Kaunitz sent relatively optimistic health bulletins to her sister. "According to reports the Emperor is doing as well as possible," she reported, "and I myself believe he will survive to the winter; one might say that gracious God is permitting him to live so that he can see with his own eyes the excessive confusion that has been produced by all his projects."[120] At the end of August 1789 Joseph moved to Schönbrunn. Leopoldine Kaunitz and her daughter visited with him there. Joseph appeared convalescent except for his persistent cough. He strolled with Leopoldine and they conversed for fully two hours about his health and Eleonore's family, about the army's status, the siege of Belgrade, and prospects for peace. The conversation then turned to France, concerning which, Leopoldine Kaunitz told her sister, "to me he had the air of a man to whom one gives a description of what he has done and who sees the effect with astonishment, and yet also with self-congratulation." Like some other contemporaries Joseph apparently believed that his own reform program had already accomplished in the Habsburg monarchy most of the more reasonable goals of the French malcontents. Joseph told Leopoldine that he did not believe the assembly could survive long, as it was chaotic and unable to produce a constitution. He had read the scurrilous publications circulating in Paris about members of the Habsburg family and pronounced Louis XVI to be "in every sense a most pitiful sovereign [*Sire*]," too easily cowed by the slightest menace to his own safety. The emperor appeared to believe that Belgium was growing calmer.[121] Eleonore too visited the emperor in Schönbrunn in September after her return from Meseritsch.[122] Rosenberg reported to Leopold in September that there was no longer any danger that Joseph would succumb to his illness. "At last we may flatter ourselves with having nothing further to fear concerning the health of the Emperor," Rosenberg wrote. Joseph had rewarded his doctors "in a manner worthy of his generosity."[123]

Joseph moved back to Vienna from Schönbrunn in early October 1789 and promptly fell ill again.[124] As noted previously, by this time news from the front had improved greatly. In August 1789, as the Habsburg army registered significant victories in the Banat, Eleonore had written to Leopoldine Kaunitz, "Here we are then with victories and Te Deums, God grant that this brings us peace and that we have one plague fewer."[125] Now after Laudon's capture of Belgrade, Joseph's appearance at the service held in St. Stephan's cathedral was accompanied by great pomp and mass acclamation in the streets (a circumstance that supports the historian Blanning's contention that the war itself had not been unpopular, only its failures).[126] The Viennese celebrated the fall of Belgrade for three days, with illuminated houses and dancing and singing. While Vienna rejoiced, Joseph wrote to Leopold on 15 October, "as for me, unable to enjoy anything in my miserable condition, I went to bed at 8 o'clock, without being able to sleep because of my coughing, this is how I miserably spend my life, not a moment without pain and also difficulty in breathing, I can have no pleasure, my physical pain blots out every other feeling."[127] Despite his fragile health, Joseph directed Rosenberg to invite "our *Dames*" to come for an evening's celebration of Belgrade's fall with him, as they had done after Ochakov was taken in December of the previous year.[128]

The stoic emperor soldiered on, clinging to his plans and his ideals. As Blanning has noted, even on his deathbed this courageous ruler displayed a "vigorous combination of resistance and concession" as he sought to restore stability to the monarchy and its international position. To rescue and salvage was the policy he chose and he took the necessary steps with skill despite his desperate physical condition, but it was also a policy that was forced upon him by the disarray of his domestic initiatives.[129] Economic hardship and the strains of war, although both were temporary phenomena, played their part in alienating the populace and undermining the work of a decade. The emperor's own words expressed a sense that the world and all its problems were closing in around him. It is possible that Joseph's expressions of exasperation, at least as late as 1788, somewhat overstated the catastrophe and were partially attributable to his penchant for melodrama. But he had become increasingly estranged from his brothers Leopold and Maximilian and his sister Marie Christine, who opposed many of his programs and corresponded with each other behind his back. Chancellor Kaunitz too had parted company with the emperor over the coercive policies adopted toward Belgium and Hungary. The elderly chancellor felt betrayed and disparaged. The chancellor's remarks in early 1790 were particularly bitter, in a letter to ambassador Mercy. He wrote, "It is dreadful that despotic obstinacy should have left this fine monarchy in the position where it is."[130] Zinzendorf, himself a progressive but antithetical to Joseph's new system of taxation and embittered by the treatment he received at the emperor's hands, had left his post in summer 1788. He had recorded in his diary at that time the sympathy Leopoldine Kaunitz had expressed with his predicament: "Madame Kaunitz conveyed to me very obligingly how sorry she was to learn that I was planning to resign. She thinks this reign is God's punishment on the nation."[131]

In early July 1789 Eleonore Liechtenstein had written to her sister from Meseritsch, "What is the poor Emperor doing now? At a distance one wants even more to have news of him, people here cannot comprehend his determination to push forward this terrible rectification, which will ruin so decidedly people of every status, without bringing relief or assistance to anyone."[132] In her reply Leopoldine Kaunitz had hinted to Eleonore that the emperor was beginning to feel regrets about measures he had promoted during his reign, mentioning his "anxieties and qualms concerning many things he has done."[133] A careful reading of Joseph's letters to his brother Leopold during the last months of his life suggests that Leopoldine Kaunitz's tidings were premature. Joseph's own illness and the fearful course of international events worried him, but he was by no means prepared to concede, much less rectify, any misjudgments in his own policies merely because of his weak physical condition. Joseph blamed the blunders or laziness of his officials and officers for unfortunate outcomes. Eventually discouragement was unavoidable even for the strong-willed emperor. In mid-November 1789 Leopoldine Kaunitz received a note in which there sounded a note of despair: "You will understand how in these critical and important moments a body that does not admit of activity and the necessary strength of mind is intolerable."[134] Even as his debilitating illness weakened him, Joseph's will remained strong. The indomitable emperor appeared to believe that had he been well he might still have mastered events. He continued to work, dictating letters to officials, friends, relatives, associates. Joseph's words conveyed anger or discouragement rather than remorse.[135] Zinzendorf recorded Rosenberg's account of a conversation with the ailing emperor even as late as mid-January 1790 about the land measurement and taxation, just a month before Joseph's death: "He [Rosenberg] talked to the emperor about the universal ferment caused by the cadaster, who repeated several times, If only I could speak!"[136]

Surviving correspondence of the women from Joseph's final year of life is fragmentary, particularly for the winter of 1789–1790, since the women were together in Vienna. However, occasional billets provide evidence of the group's activities during the emperor's final months and their communication with him, which was ongoing if sporadic. During this final year, when the emperor was sick and plagued by crises in Belgium and the Balkans—and by which time he had surely proved his loyalty to these friends—the women still noted with displeasure any real or imagined neglect on his part, although they did not communicate this dissatisfaction to the emperor. In July 1789 Leopoldine Kaunitz remarked with some irritation upon "this intimacy of ours at some times and our detachment without estrangement at others, for we are not better informed than people who do not know him; he thinks of us as old books in a library, when he has nothing better to do he leafs through them if they come to hand, and then he leaves them there without thinking further about it."[137] The longevity of the group no doubt owed much to this willingness of the *Dames* to make shift with the unpredictable relationship. They had not pressured the emperor for attention in the past and had adopted a stance that blended independence and accessibility. They did not alter their behavior as the end approached.

The winter of 1789–1790 was a grim season in Vienna, as the English ambassador Sir Robert Keith reported to his sister: "Our winter here is uncommonly melancholy, owing to the declining state of the Emperor's health, and the sickness which a great number of officers of the first families have brought back with them from the unhealthy climate of the Lower Danube . . . The Emperor's malady grows, alas! every day more alarming; but as the spring advances, some hopes are entertained of the salutary effects of a more favourable season." Sir Keith felt pity and sympathy for Joseph, and not only because of the emperor's frustrations in both domestic and foreign politics. "I am greatly afflicted at the sufferings of the monarch," Keith wrote, "and I will add that the enemies he may have can wish no aggravation to his present distress—; amidst a Turkish war, the near prospect of a quarrel with Prussia and Poland, the Netherlands lost, a general discontent among the lower classes of the people in many provinces, an incurable disease,—and, alas! no female hand near his pillow, to administer some comfort in every cup of those medicines he must take, though ever so inefficacious! . . . He has been kind, very kind to me for twenty years."[138]

By mid-November 1789 Joseph acknowledged that his illness prevented him from confronting the great array of threats facing the monarchy. By early December he was truly miserable, having great difficulty speaking. And by January 1790 Joseph knew he was dying. To attend to the monarchy's business, he appointed Rosenberg, Lacy, and *Obersthofmeister* Starhemberg to a special conference for foreign affairs. The group was to meet in the Hofburg, so that Joseph could be present when possible. Chancellor Kaunitz, who rarely came to court, was to send a representative.[139] Concerning this very small council's composition it is noteworthy that the principals actually in attendance were not state officials, although each did bear the old, largely honorific title of "conference minister." Starhemberg and Rosenberg were both court functionaries, and Lacy, although a close advisor of the emperor, really had no official position in government. Thus the functions of court and state still overlapped in a very fundamental sense even at the end of Joseph's innovative reign.[140] Always diffident and reluctant to assume too much official responsibility, Rosenberg required some persuading. According to Zinzendorf, the emperor told Rosenberg that he (Joseph) would die more tranquilly if Rosenberg agreed to participate in the arrangement.[141] Rosenberg had written to Leopold describing his own surprise at the appointment. "I did not expect such a mark of esteem," he remarked, "the more so after having been far removed from all affairs of state for so many years, I know that I am less competent than I was at the period of my greatest energy."[142]

Rosenberg remained the dutiful servitor to the end, even as he sent frank and confidential status reports concerning Joseph's health to his former (and future) master, the emperor-in-waiting Leopold in Florence. The emperor's friend Lacy did not attempt to defend the Joseph's reputation and legacy as the latter lay dying. Lacy told Zinzendorf "that the new sovereign will have to obliterate all traces of this reign of nine years, that he had never known Joseph the Second to make a moderate decision, always extreme, taking on everything himself, in such a manner that now no one knows what to do."¹⁴³ The marshal was heard to make caustic observations about the Joseph's competence in military as well as civil affairs. Though fundamentally loyal to the emperor the elderly Chancellor Kaunitz communicated with the emperor only in writing, as had been his practice during roughly the final two years of Joseph's life.¹⁴⁴

An undated note from Leopoldine Kaunitz to Eleonore, apparently written during Joseph's final illness in early 1790, describes how she and the other *Dames* went to court to inquire about the emperor's condition as he lay near death. On 15 February 1790 the women prayed in the Hofkapelle and accompanied the priest with the sacrament to Joseph's antechamber for the emperor's second public anointing and extreme unction. Leopoldine Kaunitz reported to her sister the grim assessment of the doctors (Eleonore had been absent on this occasion, detained at home by illness): "I have come back from the court . . . and if I was not afraid of inconveniencing you, with the medicine you have taken, I would have come myself to tell you the story of what happened."¹⁴⁵ Countess Chanclos, Leopoldine Liechtenstein, Sidonia Kinsky, and Josepha Clary with one of her daughters had attended. Leopoldine Kaunitz learned that the doctors had told the emperor he was now very near his end and that no remedy was possible. "He did not seem at all upset, and he made all sorts of arrangements as a result and among them that of having the Grand Duke come here, the courier is leaving now." The little group of friends had adjourned to Rosenberg's residence. "He [Rosenberg] told us generally the same things, but with fewer details, he wanted to have us come into his chamber, but la Kinsky [Sidonia Kinsky] made up her mind to go away, and I myself followed her example, for the unbelievable lamentations of Françoise [Leopoldine Liechtenstein] just were not to be borne any longer." Joseph had ennobled his principal doctor, Joseph Quarin (1733–1814), and had given him 10,000 florins (quipped Leopoldine Kaunitz, "never has someone been better compensated for worse services.").¹⁴⁶

In his final months one humiliation followed another in quick succession for Joseph. On 29 December 1789 the elderly Chancellor Kaunitz wrote formally to Vienna's ambassador at the papal court in Rome seeking Pius VI's assistance in reestablishing Habsburg authority in Belgium through instructions to the Belgian bishops. Kaunitz's communication conceded the pope's right to have his nuncio present in Brussels, reversing an order of February 1787 that had required the previous incumbent Antonio Felice to leave Brussels after he had published the papal condemnation of a pamphlet by Eybel (the publication entitled *Was ist der Papst?*) that attacked the pope's authority.¹⁴⁷ Weakened politically by external stresses and finding that his efforts to persuade or intimidate the opposition in Belgium, Hungary, and the increasingly restless hereditary provinces were unsuccessful, Joseph finally countermanded many of his controversial reform measures. Already in late 1789 he had suspended implementation of the land rectification in Hungary. Now in early January 1790 Joseph restored the administrative status quo ante in the various provinces and returned the crown of Hungary to its Hungarian repository in Budapest.

Newspapers were no longer as exuberantly unrestrained in their reporting as they had been early in Joseph's reign. But reporters evidently still felt free to discurse on both the emperor's declining health and the uncertain fate of the army. According to Leopoldine Liechtenstein, one report in mid-1789 had predicted openly that once Joseph was dead there could finally be a truce and then peace, since the new emperor Leopold would readily foster cordial relations with the interested powers. The Spanish fleet in the Mediterranean would intimidate the Turks ("make the Divan tremble") should they refuse peace terms. Rosenberg reported that the emperor read these remarks "and . . . it gives him pain, but that is the consequence of freedom of the press."[148] Now Joseph began the process by which the Habsburg monarchy would reach an accommodation with Prussia (completed by his successor Leopold at Reichenbach), and he obtained Russian consent to open separate negotiations with the Ottoman Empire.[149] Of his ambitious reform program, Joseph salvaged in toto only the decrees abolishing serfdom and broadening religious toleration. These were solid achievements, but the emperor had expected to accomplish so much more. He had clung to his reform plans, trying to drive the changes forward even as his own prospects for survival dwindled and the war drained both resources and the good will of his subjects. Formal repeal of the land conscription and new tax system in non-Hungarian lands was not completed until Leopold II had taken power after Joseph's death.

When Joseph neared death, the strength of his religious faith became apparent. In 1785, when the new papal nuncio Caprara had arrived in Vienna to replace Garampi, who had been such a good friend of the *Dames*, Caprara had told Leopoldine Kaunitz that he pitied the emperor who possessed a foundation of religious belief but had such extensive plans for aggrandizement of his own power.[150] Joseph had often been harsh and impatient in carrying out church reform.[151] But he apparently remained convinced to the end that his actions had promoted the health of the church and the Catholic religion even as they also benefitted the state.[152] Preserved among Leopoldine Liechtenstein's family letters was one, its addressee not clearly stated but bearing the date "the 17th" (no doubt February 1790), in which Leopoldine Liechtenstein detailed the emperor's actions and statements. Close to death, he feared his final agony and had asked for the crucifix that had been at the deathbed of earlier Habsburg monarchs, on which their names were inscribed. The emperor was much preoccupied with the childbed of Franz's wife the Archduchess Elisabeth, of whom he had grown very fond. She died soon after giving birth, just two days before Joseph himself died. Leopoldine Liechtenstein's letter dated 18 February 1790 then confirmed the death of the archduchess and Joseph's anguish over the loss. She wrote, "We are absolutely stunned by this unexpected blow that makes the tragedy complete; never has there been such a time." Joseph endured this final heartbreak with sad resignation. According to report he told his confessor, "Believe me, Father, I am well reconciled with my God." Leopoldine Liechtenstein wrote to her sister about the courage with which the emperor was facing his death: "I love . . . to speak of the object of my grief, and at the same time about the glory of him who concerns me so much, by virtue of the Christianity and the genuine heroism that he demonstrates." She praised in Joseph the same Christian resignation that she had recognized in his mother Maria Theresia ten years earlier. Providence had truly blessed Joseph, she wrote.[153] In her own farewell message to the emperor, even Eleonore Liechtenstein spoke of her gratefulness to God for the great examples of virtue and Christianity that the emperor's strength had permitted him to set before the world. Had she truly doubted his fundamental loyalty to Catholicism, Eleonore would not have volunteered this heartfelt acknowledgment at such a solemn moment.[154] On his deathbed the emperor obediently accepted the ministrations of the church. Like his mother before him, Joseph steadfastly fulfilled all religious obligations as his end neared.

The evening prior to his death Joseph composed a number of final, valedictory messages to his army and to his particular friends, rather melodramatic but surely sincere.[155] These included letters for both Lacy and Rosenberg. His letter to Lacy credited this friend and mentor for any greatness he had achieved as emperor, by which as always the emperor meant his efforts to improve the monarchy's military and diplomatic standing.[156] To Rosenberg Joseph expressed thanks for his friend's steadfastness during this final illness. "The wisdom and kindness of your counsel, in short the attachment you have shown me on every occasion unto the last moment of my life," Joseph continued, "fill me with gratefulness and friendship; accept these assurances and believe that the only thing I regret in parting from this world is that very small number of friends whom I must leave and to whom I am causing pain. Farewell then, I embrace you with all my heart. Keep me in remembrance."[157]

As the emperor lay near death the small group of friends convened at the residence of Leopoldine Liechtenstein or Eleonore Liechtenstein and quietly discussed his fate. Joseph composed an especially poignant final message for his Five Princesses, addressed to "five *Dames* joined together in society who tolerated me." Dated 19 February 1790, it was delivered to them by Lacy at Leopoldine Liechtenstein's residence in the evening.[158] "*MesDames*, it is time, my end approaches, to acknowledge to you once more here through these lines all my appreciation and gratitude for the kindness, patience, and friendship, and even flattering concern that you have been good enough to show me and to bestow on me during the many years that we have been together in society [*en société*], I miss each of those days, not once were there too many for me, and never to see you again is the only meritorious sacrifice that I make in leaving this world, be so good as to remember me in your prayers, I cannot be sufficiently grateful for the grace and infinite mercy of providence to me, in complete accord therewith I await my hour, farewell then, you will be unable to read this scribbling, the handwriting attests to my condition."[159] Joseph II died in the early morning on 20 February 1790.

At the time of his death the emperor's prestige and popularity had reached their nadir, as Joseph himself was painfully aware. As the work of Joseph's preeminent biographer Derek Beales has made clear, reassessment of many aspects of Joseph's reign is warranted. The traditional summaries that emphasize the total collapse of his programs are overdrawn. Although a great many historians have judged Joseph's reign as a whole to be a failure, the result of his "impatience, tactlessness, and needless military adventures" (in the words of Padover) and "a classic example of the primacy of foreign policy" (according to Blanning) that was flawed and undermined the earlier achievements, historians have also identified lasting accomplishments amid the wreckage of Joseph's dreams.[160] Padover noted with justice that if Joseph's policies were often "violent and crude," in this regard they were not fundamentally different from those of contemporary rulers such as Frederick II and Catherine II. More than one historian has suggested that Joseph's reform efforts very likely saved the Habsburg monarchy from the civil war and revolution that erupted in France—hardly the legacy of a failed regime.[161] In the same way, Joseph's careful attention to the monarchy's army during his reign helped Emperor Franz II to outlast Napoleon in the end.[162]

Contemporaries did not have the luxury of distance. In 1790 many judged Joseph's reign to be a tragic failure. After attending Joseph's funeral service, Count Zinzendorf reflected sadly upon "this man [Joseph II] to whom so few people dared to speak the truth, who recognized no other law than his own will, who, imbued with certain preconceived notions, never took the trouble to examine them thoroughly, there he lies lifeless, now a resident of the crypt, requiescat in aeternum. He would have been an amiable and good individual if he had always respected justice and morality and if he had been less arrogant."[163] Archbishop Migazzi, whom Joseph had often criticized and even mocked, presided over the emperor's memorial service, after which Joseph's remains were transported to the Capuchin crypt, traditional resting place of the Habsburgs. When the archbishop had visited Leopoldine Kaunitz and Ernst in Baden in summer 1786, Leopoldine had marveled at how youthful he seemed, "in spite of everything they have done to kill him."[164] Weathering his humiliations, Migazzi emerged from the Josephinian decade in good health and spirits, nearly reaching the age of ninety before he died in 1803. Former papal nuncio Garampi who, named a cardinal in 1785, had returned to Italy from Vienna and, in an interesting parallel to the emperor's situation, had been stricken by a near-fatal illness in early 1790, reported his own recovery in a letter to Eleonore Liechtenstein and expressed his hopes for an improvement in the status of the church under the new sovereign Leopold II. "And then I would wish for wings to fly, to be witness to such consoling events after having seen the most fatal catastrophes," he wrote. "For now I pray, I hope, and I wait."[165] At the time of Joseph's death observers saw only a stricken and broken emperor whose domestic program was discredited and whose foreign distractions had offered Prussia an opportunity to weaken the monarchy's fragile cohesion. And in the background there loomed an undisciplined, turbulent France where revolutionary ideas and social unrest were a growing menace.

One day before the National Assembly in Paris ceremoniously ended the feudal rights of the nobility in France in August 1789 Eleonore Liechtenstein had exclaimed to her sister Leopoldine Kaunitz, "What changes have we not seen pass before our eyes in these times!"[166] Yet just ahead, all unknown to the women, lay truly cataclysmic changes. For Europe a new era was beginning. Joseph's successor Leopold did not arrive in Vienna until March 1790, after Joseph's death. Leopold found the monarchy seething with discontent. Even the hereditary provinces had grown restless under the harsh economic conditions and high taxes necessitated by the Turkish war. Overextended militarily and increasingly distracted by the predicament of the French king Louis XVI and Marie Antoinette, Leopold II moved quickly to defuse the major trouble spots. Negotiations with Prussia resulted in the Reichenbach convention in July 1790, in which Prussia pledged to stay out of the internal affairs of the Habsburg monarchy and to support Leopold's candidacy as Holy Roman Emperor in return for a Habsburg commitment to make peace with the Turks based on the status quo ante bellum.[167] With external peace assured, Leopold was able to quell domestic unrest, partly by playing the various sides against each other and partly by repudiating Joseph's most unpopular reforms while making constitutional concessions similar to those allowed by his mother, Maria Theresia.

Like Joseph II, Emperor Leopold urged the French king and queen to cooperate with the National (subsequently Constituent) Assembly, initially hoping in this way to preserve any residual value France could have as an ally. The flight of the French royal couple in June 1791, intercepted at Varennes, precluded such an outcome. Eleonore and Leopoldine Kaunitz were beside themselves with horror and anger as they learned that the escape attempt had been frustrated. Leopoldine had used subterfuge to discover the true extent of the disaster quickly from Rosenberg. Not being well informed herself, she had merely remarked to him that "severe blows are being dealt in France; he regards me with a surprised air and says: you know already? And I was a bit dishonest in what I said . . . something that led him to believe that I was informed, and so he tells me that the King and Queen fled and were arrested not far from Metz, but that Monsieur [the king's brother Count de Provence] escaped. That evening he explained in greater detail that it was the son of the postmaster who recognized the King, took to horseback with all speed, and alerted the next post station that it was the King."[168] Eleonore wrote to her sister, "I thought I would fall from my chair . . . as I read your letter, and I can understand that opera scenes appear ridiculous and intolerable when one considers such terrible things [Leopoldine Kaunitz was visiting Baden and Laxenburg, where court festivities were being staged]. My God, into what depths of misfortune is it possible to fall? What this family has endured in coming to such a pass." Eleonore wanted immediate retribution. "This son of the postmaster, I would have him beaten mercilessly. What will the Emperor [Leopold II] do? Would it not be better to defend the righteous cause, his own, that of all sovereigns, of all the universe, and to exterminate this infernal Assembly and all its supporters, Illuminati, Rosicrucians, Masons of all genuses and species both real and imaginary." The Habsburg monarchy's leadership was passive, lethargic, she complained. "The indifference, the apathy, the lethargy of us all beginning with the Emperor, the Empress, the Archduchesses, conference ministers and ministers of all types, in short everyone in general, and I do not except even myself, seems to me to bode ill for what lies ahead, for when God wishes to destroy he first blinds."[169]

As noted earlier, the *Dames* had known Marie Antoinette as a lighthearted young archduchess in Vienna and recognized both strengths and flaws in her character. The women and their family members, male and female, had maintained friendly contact with her during her years as dauphine and French queen.[170] Marie Antoinette's execution in 1793, while no longer a surprise to them when it occurred, was a calamity of the first order for the women. According to the Prince de Ligne, writing in later years, Sidonia Kinsky owned a statuette (a small bust) of the unfortunate deceased French queen. When Sidonia learned that the prince had lost the portraits of the queen he had owned and treasured, she offered this object to him as a sort of legacy during her lifetime, telling the prince that she might not remember to make this gift at the time of her own death; receiving the statue would comfort him both for the loss of the queen and for his loss of the royal portraits.[171]

With each passing year after Joseph II's death, the international situation grew more perilous for the Habsburg monarchy. Leopold II's response to the French challenge was to join with Prussia in the Pillnitz Declaration of August 1791, which conjured up the vague threat of a hostile coalition of governments that would defend and then avenge the French royal couple. An unintended byproduct of this declaration, so famous in history, was a thoroughly aroused and belligerent French legislature that declared war on Leopold in April 1792. Leopold had not planned to start a full-scale war, but he assumed that France, in such disarray, would not be difficult for a coalition of powers to defeat in any case. His goal had been simply to gain leverage over against an expansionist Prussia, which was greedily eyeing French and Polish territory. Almost off-handedly on the Austrian side there began the first of the series of French wars that preoccupied the monarchy and its ministers for more than two decades until the definitive Congress of Vienna in 1815, inflaming passions throughout Europe as boundaries fluctuated. Ahead lay years of desperate, destructive warfare with the new French Republic and subsequent French Empire and with its dynamic leader Napoleon Bonaparte (whom Eleonore Liechtenstein referred to as "this Devil incarnate," "our terrestrial Devil").[172] The French Revolution and wars brought with them wrenching change, painful to older members of Europe's elites who had looked to Paris as cultural lodestar throughout their lives. In 1796, Josepha Clary noted the paradoxical but continuing importance of the French language, "for we must resign ourselves to keeping this language, much as we detest everything else."[173] Years later, in 1812, when newspapers published a false report that Napoleon had died in Paris, Eleonore commented to her daughter that the French, possessors of such a lovely country, were a people as ferocious as the Russian barbarians. In the absence of Napoleon, they would relapse into "the days of Robespierre."[174]

The *Dames* remained close friends, and for a number of years they met as a group with some frequency. During summers in the 1790s, the women met at Leopoldine Liechtenstein's villa in Hütteldorf, where they discussed with consternation the worsening military situation and their discontent with Chancellor Kaunitz's principal successor Baron Thugut. Josepha Clary remarked to her son in summer 1794 that an upcoming dinner at Hütteldorf would not be cheerful; "there are continual reports of new worries, for we are brought so low, so low, and we shall never recover." And in fact, Josepha Clary's next letter to her son related news concerning the "Jacobin" plot against the Habsburg emperor Franz that, according to Rosenberg's report to the women, had resulted in the arrest of 300 individuals. In July 1798, staying with Sidonia Kinsky in Weidlingau, Josepha Clary told her son that she rather dreaded her weekly meetings in Hütteldorf (a location also easily reached by Lacy) with Leopoldine Liechtenstein and Eleonore because the war news was always bad.[175]

Under the new regime of Leopold and in 1792 that of his son Franz, individuals with whom the *Dames* had been proud to associate became marginalized and faced difficult readjustments. After Emperor Leopold's death in 1792, the older generation of Habsburgs, siblings of the hapless Marie Antoinette, became at once less influential and more approachable. Marie Christine and Prince Albert, driven from the Belgian provinces where they had served as governors, moved once more to Vienna. The chastened archduchess became more of a friend to the *Dames* and, after all the trials she had endured, met with genuine sympathy from them. Eleonore Liechtenstein in particular had not trusted the friendly overtures of Marie Christine in earlier years, believing her to be an ambitious intriguer. Now Eleonore warmed to the archduchess.[176] Shorn of political significance, Marie Christine lost her health as well, probably to cancer, and died in 1796. Prince Albert withdrew to private life after the death of his wife, devoting himself to his artistic and collecting interests, but he remained a good friend of the *Dames* and actually outlived them all, dying 10 February 1822 at 83 years of age. The ebullient Maria Carolina, chased out of Naples by Napoleon, also came home to Vienna and lived there from 1800 to 1802 (and again in her final year of life, 1814). The remaining *Dames* resumed their contacts with her as well.[177] She continued to claim legitimacy as queen of Naples in the face of Napoleon's aggression, just as her estranged husband Ferdinand insisted that he was still its king.[178]

Friendly association with both Rosenberg and Lacy continued. All the women relied on their old friend Rosenberg for political information. After Joseph II's death, Rosenberg was confirmed in his offices by Leopold, including his post as *Oberstkämmerer* and "conference minister." He accompanied Leopold to Frankfurt for the imperial coronation, where he learned of his own elevation to the rank of prince. In 1792 the new emperor Franz likewise confirmed Rosenberg in his honors and offices. According to a political rival, Count Philip Cobenzl, Leopold II's widow Marie Louise recommended Rosenberg's services with great earnestness to her son Franz shortly before her death, which followed her husband Leopold's by only a few months.[179] Rosenberg served the court in his accustomed unobtrusive manner until his death in the Hofburg in 1796. He worked effectively with successive regimes, offering his sovereigns the counsel of an experienced courtier but expecting in return few signs of deference or special attention. When he traveled, first to the Frankfurt coronation and then to Florence and Pisa in 1793 and 1794 (already more than 70 years of age), all of the *Dames* corresponded with him, and Rosenberg wrote letters to them as a group and also individually, complaining when he did not hear from them. In a letter to Josepha Clary from Pisa in September 1794 he described the piteous situation of the French émigrés ("If they stay at home, sooner or later they are guillotined, if they emigrate they are refused hospitality") and then noted pointedly that although he had written to each of the *Dames* in order, he had not yet received a single reply.[180] When Rosenberg was in Vienna the women could obtain political news before it reached the interested public through conversation with him. That the women's friendship went beyond expediency was demonstrated by the loyal attendance of these comrades at Rosenberg's bedside during the months of his final illness. On one occasion, arriving at Rosenberg's residence for a visit, Zinzendorf reported that he had found Rosenberg in bed, surrounded by "les Princesses" and Lacy. Sidonia Kinsky, Lacy, and the invalid were singing the popular French song "Quand on sait aimer et plaire," followed by another ditty "Je vous adore." Rosenberg found the solicitude of the aging princesses exasperating at times. Speaking to Zinzendorf in October and November 1796 just days before he died, Rosenberg referred to them as "these tiresome Princesses" and remarked that a visit from Eleonore Liechtenstein had bored him.[181]

Marshal Lacy's advice was still sought occasionally by the Habsburg emperor and his councilors. Lacy retained his official position as member of the ministerial conference under both Leopold II and Franz, but he no longer had much influence. His legacy to the army, the methodical defensive cordon system (which was recalled by the interested public long after Lacy's tireless organizational work was forgotten), offered few advantages with the advent of the citizen army in France. Lacy's system restricted the autonomy of commanders in the field and discouraged initiative.[182] Lacy accompanied Leopold to his meeting with the Prussian king at Pillnitz in 1791, where the critical situation of the French royal family was discussed and the ill-timed warning dispatched to the French revolutionary government. Lacy did not readily abandon or amend his convictions. Yet it is interesting to note that alone among the top Habsburg military advisors, he warned in 1792 that the optimistic, almost nonchalant Austro-Prussian plans for a quick march on Paris would prove difficult to execute.[183] In contrast to many around him, as well as Austria's new-found ally Prussia, he advocated assembling a major strike force to counter France in Belgium. His counsels were not heeded. Always distrustful of the populace at large, Lacy could not countenance a *Volksbewaffnung* or arming of "the people," urged by some advisors as the monarchy's military situation grew desperate. Throughout his career Lacy had exhibited a certain petulance. Previous sovereigns had humored him despite this unfortunate trait because of his valuable organizational abilities and his otherwise genial nature.[184] Even as he grew old and infirm, contemporaries still believed Lacy to be devious and ambitious, a reputation that mortified a man so sensitive about his honor. By the mid-1790s Lacy's knowledge of actual events was limited. Requests for his input often came too late for his opinions to have an impact on affairs. He complained to no avail about the secretiveness of the regime of Baron Thugut, selected by Franz II to serve as chancellor in 1794. Lacy received one new appointment in 1794 that gave him both pleasure and occupation, the chancellorship of the Maria Theresia Military Order, formerly held by the elderly Kaunitz. He took satisfaction in this role and was a diligent, conscientious administrator. His health eventually forced him to keep to his house for many days at a time. But like his former sovereign and friend Joseph II, Lacy stayed in harness virtually until his death in 1801.[185]

Leopoldine Liechtenstein remained Lacy's loyal friend. Of the five women, she continued to be the most active and ambitious after Joseph's death, busily attending social events and hosting evening gatherings. She shored up her diminished position and indirectly enhanced the status of the other *Dames* as well through her ongoing association with Lacy and through the growing importance of her second son Johann, an outstanding military officer who excelled during this period of incessant warfare. Leopoldine Kaunitz likewise did not mellow with age. Her father-in-law, the chancellor, remained a political force and thus a potential source of political information for her after Joseph II's death, but his health was failing and his counsels, always unpunctual, were rarely heeded by emperors Leopold or Franz. Leopoldine Kaunitz's special relationship with him no longer yielded a rich harvest of news. In the face of alarming news from abroad, his reactions and advice to his emperors remained moderate. Even during his final months Kaunitz continued to defend the state's independent stance vis-à-vis the Catholic clergy.[186]

The former chancellor did become more devout, as both domestic and foreign events prompted a backlash against liberal Catholicism and Enlightenment thought. In this personal evolution he was not alone.[187] It is also probable that a core of basic theological orthodoxy had persisted throughout his adult life.[188] His disdain had been (and remained) for the overweening, wealthy church hierarchy, jealous of its power, and for ill-educated, superstitious priests and monks. In other words, he was more anticlerical than antireligious. When at last the elderly Kaunitz knew that his death was imminent, it was gratifying to both Leopoldine Kaunitz and Eleonore Liechtenstein, with their steadfast orthodox beliefs, to see the old reprobate chancellor exhibit respect for the precepts of the Catholic faith. It seems unlikely that as he neared death he made frivolous or hypocritical religious gestures simply to please his more conservative relatives and friends. Leopoldine Kaunitz and Eleonore were relieved when the ailing chancellor accepted the ministrations of priest and confessor during his first serious crisis in April 1794.[189] According to Josepha Clary administration of the church's last rites in early June 1794, when the elderly statesman was indeed dying, was carried out without publicity and even without the notification and presence of Kaunitz's eldest son Ernst. Josepha described an exchange Kaunitz reportedly had with his friend Casanova concerning the ritual: "he [Kaunitz] said to Casanova: Well, what do you say to this; it is well done replied the latter—it is a duty, the Prince responded." Josepha also reported that the elderly chancellor expressed regrets on his deathbed: "He is said to have asked his confessor to tell his household that he has set a bad example for them, that he is sorry for it."[190] Even after her father-in-law's death Leopoldine Kaunitz, opinionated as ever, remained an avid collector of political news and gossip. Zinzendorf recorded many lively conversations with Leopoldine Kaunitz, usually on political or economic topics: at Rosenberg's residence, "[conversing with] Madame de Kaunitz alone, still arguing"; at Eleonore Liechtenstein's gathering, "Madame Kaunitz attacked me, but in an amiable way." Leopoldine Kaunitz and Eleonore accused Zinzendorf of being a "democrat" during the 1790s.[191] Zinzendorf relished these exchanges, which could become informal debates.

By the 1790s there were many social gatherings in Vienna that were far livelier than the soirées of these old friends. The *Dames* tried to follow events, to discuss and debate them, but their sources of news were limited and unreliable.

Censorship controls, tightened in the Austrian and Bohemian lands during the final years of Joseph II's reign and then progressively stricter under emperors Leopold II and Franz, discouraged free-wheeling political discussions. News was particularly difficult to obtain in time of war, and the monarchy was often at war after Joseph's death. During crises, even letters from sons and other relatives who were serving in the army became extremely scarce. And all news reports were worthless when Vienna itself was threatened because the government invariably sought to suppress the worst tidings. After recording in his journal the latest news he had obtained, the realistic Zinzendorf often added a caveat. Concerning rumors circulating at Leopoldine Liechtenstein's about ambassadorial and court appointments in 1806 he commented after his visit, a "hotbed of lies . . . And of all of this probably nothing is true."[192]

By the late 1790s the women no longer met as a group, but they remained loyal friends for the rest of their lives, staying in touch through visits and solicitous inquiries. It was really only through death that the *Dames'* fundamental cohesion and friendship was weakened and destroyed. Leopoldine Kaunitz died in 1795 at the age of 53, a devastating loss for her sister Eleonore Liechtenstein. Rosenberg died in 1796. Lacy and Josepha Clary followed in late 1801, within days of each other.[193] Eleonore described for her daughter Leopoldine Liechtenstein's dramatic, public grief over the death of Lacy, so typical of her sister-in-law, as Eleonore thought. Sidonia Kinsky was overwhelmed with grief by the death of her cherished sister Josepha.[194] Even as their numbers dwindled, the political interest of the remaining *Dames*—most obviously Leopoldine Liechtenstein and Eleonore Liechtenstein—remained keen, a habit impossible to break. The biographer of Eleonore Liechtenstein, Adam Wolf, observes that as the women aged they became more pious and focused their attention less on the larger political world and more narrowly on the interests of their families. Certainly one can find affirmations of pious resignation and disinterest in Eleonore's later letters, such as her assertion to her daughter in 1792 that happiness could not be found in the noise and diversions of the world, or in rank and riches, but only in oneself. She had never found any consolation, Eleonore wrote, except in the familiar words "gloria in excelsio deo et in terra pax hominibus bonae voluntatis." The women were deeply religious individuals and conscientious family matriarchs.[195] However, Wolf's dismissive observation about their political interests is belied repeatedly by remarks in the diary of Count Zinzendorf, who usually visited the soirées of Leopoldine Liechtenstein several times a week until her death and then became a more regular visitor at Eleonore Liechtenstein's evening gatherings. Throughout his life Zinzendorf remained a sober, industrious individual, serious about his career and not fond of light social chatter. He preferred the offerings at Leopoldine Liechtenstein's, where there would usually be a greater number of men in attendance ("The society at Princess Françoise's is better, there are fewer women"). At Eleonore's, he complained, very often the women were excessively talkative ("These women chatter like magpies"), without knowing much about current events (he described an "evening at Princess Charles's, where no one knew anything").[196] Both Liechtenstein soirées were small, staid affairs, but they were determinedly political in focus. Leopoldine Liechtenstein managed to attract to her gatherings individuals who could provide current, if not always strictly accurate, political reporting. Eleonore described a typical evening gathering with her sister-in-law in October 1805, during which political topics were aired and exhausted. When the conversational sands ran out, Leopoldine would generally interject, "It is certain that we are in a very critical situation" (doubtless true in those weeks leading to the battle of Austerlitz), and the politicking would begin anew.[197] Eleonore remarked to her daughter in 1808, "the passion of my sister-in-law for news passes all description."[198] Leopoldine continued to collect and retail political news at her own soirées until she died in 1809 at her beloved Feldsberg.

The Prince de Ligne recorded in his memoirs that after the deaths of Emperor Joseph, Lacy, and Rosenberg, he himself visited Eleonore Liechtenstein virtually daily.[199] Her letters to her daughter demonstrate her eagerness to be au courant concerning political events. Clemens Metternich, who married Leopoldine Kaunitz's daughter Lorel, reported in his memoirs that in the mid-1790s it was gatherings at Eleonore Liechtenstein's residence that he most often attended. But the guests clearly reflected the advancing age of the hostess. "Princess Charles gathers together the residue of the society of earlier days," Metternich wrote, "adding to this what Vienna considers individuals whose conversation is agreeable."[200] Eleonore Liechtenstein died in Vienna in late 1812, surviving just long enough to sense that the eery silence and dearth of news from the Russian front in 1812, where Austrian troops including two of her sons were fighting as reluctant allies of the French, at long last portended a permanent reversal in the fortunes of the "great Satan." Initially she like many contemporaries had simply hoped that an inevitable French victory over Russia would occur quickly so that peace could be restored. But at last she began to suspect that a seismic change was coming. She had learned that Napoleon's client King Bernadotte of Sweden had defected, and at her soirée there had been talk about a possible turn in Napoleon's fortunes, fatal, decisive, and lasting. Just a month before her death Eleonore wrote to her daughter, "The silence about what is happening at Moscow is beginning to worry me, it is not natural."[201] The last *Dame*, Sidonia Kinsky, survived until April 1815, dying while the Congress of Vienna was meeting. She alone of the five women was alive when the glittering array of diplomats and courtiers assembled in Vienna to celebrate Napoleon's defeat and to fashion a peace settlement.

Of the five *Dames*, only Josepha Clary and Leopoldine Kaunitz were spared by their early deaths from witnessing the destruction of the Holy Roman Empire and the spectacle of their beloved Vienna twice occupied by French troops, in 1805 and 1809. Emperor Joseph's disgust with its unwieldiness notwithstanding, the Holy Roman Empire had been an important institution for aristocratic families in much of the Habsburg monarchy and in the German lands. It had established ground rules (very imperfectly enforced) in the jostling for property, position, and alliances of sovereigns and aristocratic families.[202] When he attended Leopold II's coronation in Frankfurt in 1790, not long after Joseph's death, Leopoldine Kaunitz's husband Ernst voiced enthusiasm for the imperial ceremony and the ancient institutions quite unlike the reputed discouragement and skepticism of many contemporaries noted by historians. Although thoroughly fatigued by his activities, Ernst wrote, he was overwhelmed by "this splendor, this magnificence, indeed this dignity, long live the Empire."[203] Despite the constraints the Empire imposed on its nominal head and the caustic remarks Joseph II let fall quite publicly about the Empire, despite his own frustrating role within it and his recognition that the future of the Habsburg dynasty lay in developing and defending Habsburg interests and dependencies, the imperial title and institutions had been of symbolic importance even to Joseph, if Eleonore Liechtenstein's recollections in 1804 are to be credited. When the ramshackle Empire was in its final months of existence and Napoleon made his triumphal entry into Mainz to receive the homage of the German princes, Eleonore thought of Joseph, remarking to her daughter: "In such a matter one must do justice to Emperor Joseph, he felt these sorts of things keenly, and quite differently from the present one [Emperor Franz]."[204]

The fate of the Empire had consequences for the families of the *Dames*. Four of them hailed from the southwestern lands of the Empire, and Leopoldine Liechtenstein's family too had strong imperial links because of its new principality and the alliances of her brother and son with the Manderscheid family. The Kaunitz family with its territory of Rietberg, the Öttingen family, and the Sternberg-Manderscheid family were all mediatized by Napoleon's orders, shorn of their proud status as diminutive but sovereign entities. The Hohenzollern-Hechingens were spared, for their territory was admitted as member state to Napoleon's new Confederation of the Rhine, along with lands of other branches of the larger Hohenzollern family, through the support of their Prussian Hohenzollern relatives. Leopoldine Liechtenstein's family too received gentle, even favorable treatment from Napoleon, a move calculated to lessen the hostility of this important clan at least temporarily. The family's small principality in the defunct Empire was admitted to Napoleon's Confederation as a sovereign state, apparently because the French emperor admired Leopoldine's son Johann Liechtenstein as a gifted military leader and hoped to groom him as a friendly client. As head of the Liechtenstein clan Johann declared his young son to be the titular ruler of the principality and member of the new Confederation. Thus Johann avoided a personal conflict in loyalties for himself; but Eleonore considered her nephew's ploy to be a humiliating stunt. The two branches of the Liechtenstein family thus diverged somewhat in their attitude toward the French emperor, with Eleonore and her sons implacably hostile while Leopoldine Liechtenstein and her sons accepted the evolving political situation and tried to accommodate the family's actions to the new reality without betraying the old order. Concerning Leopoldine Liechtenstein's stance, Eleonore wrote to her daughter in 1806, "she [Leopoldine Liechtenstein] is pleased about an affair that would vex me, to be among those whom Bonaparte distinguishes, to owe him anything, and to become his dependent, and all of this in order to have the misfortune of signing the peace of Pressburg [one of Johann Liechtenstein's accomplishments], all that humiliates me to such an extent that I am very sorry that such favor has come to be bestowed upon my name."[205]

The scramble for territory let loose by Napoleon's ascendancy in the old imperial lands seemed demeaning to many families, even as they fought for status and survival.[206] Leopoldine Liechtenstein wrote to her brother that the new, fluctuating situation in the Empire was "absolutely a case of might makes right [*la loi du plus fort*]."[207] Eleonore was ashamed of the spectacle unfolding in Regensburg in 1803, as German princelings rushed to pay court to the French emperor and stole, plundered, and sold themselves. She told her daughter about the late Lacy's prediction that it would be only after peace was concluded that the misery of the Habsburg monarchy's situation would be truly understood. Eleonore was convinced that Napoleon would never be satisfied; poor Germany would be completely destroyed.[208] She viewed the new Confederation, formally inaugurated in 1806, as a wretched creature of Napoleon's. Zinzendorf reported with equal distaste on 20 July 1806 his conversation with Leopoldine Liechtenstein, Eleonore Liechtenstein, and Josephine Harrach about the new political entity: "We talked there about this so-called new Constitution of Germany." Eleonore sincerely mourned the passing of the Empire that had existed since the age of Charlemagne. She believed that Emperor Franz had made an unworthy choice when he relinquished his position as Holy Roman Emperor.[209] The Empire had shored up private and class interests of the aristocracy; but the women believed it had also been a stabilizing force offering at least some protection for weaker states from the predations of larger ones.[210] In 1807 after conversing with a visitor from the formerly independent but now mediatized principality of Thurn and Taxis, Eleonore wrote to her daughter sadly about the formerly independent entities of the old imperial realm, "which from the great to the smallest are without recourse and lack any means to avenge themselves."[211]

It was a newly configured Habsburg monarchy that emerged victorious from the French Revolutionary and Napoleonic wars, very different from the realm of Maria Theresia and Joseph II that the *Dames* had known and loved. Belgium was permanently lost, a land with which the women had acknowledged ties of affection and interest. The flawed but familiar Holy Roman Empire was lamented by those who had lost lands and prestige and who found in the German Confederation established in 1815 a paltry and ineffective replacement. The prospect of a nationalistic, armed German *Volk,* so enticing for pamphleteers and publicists during the French wars, was not attractive to the *Dames,* whose sympathies had lain with their own ruling class, with its idiosyncrasies and complex loyalties and the institutions that preserved its status. The generation of the 1760s, 1770s, and 1780s, and Emperor Joseph II himself, could not have foreseen that their political world, while it could accommodate dramatic reforms of enlightened despots and could tolerate limited aggressions by individual German states such as Prussia and the Habsburg monarchy, would be fractured beyond repair in a few years by the military force and ascendant ideology of an outside power.[212] Had the women lived longer, beyond Napoleon's defeat and exile, they would have found the resurgent German Confederation to be an alien environment, not a restoration of the old order in which they and their kind had flourished and their particular friend the emperor had been overlord.

Notes

1. Bled, *Marie Thérèse,* 332-37.
2. Beales, *Joseph II,* 1: 242.
3. LRRA, P 17/24, LK to EL, Vienna, 26 July 1777.
4. Wolf, *Fürstin Eleonore Liechtenstein,* 145-46.
5. LRRA, P 17/24, LK to EL, Vienna, 26 July 1777.
6. LRRA, P 17/24, EL to LK, Kromau, 26 and 30 July 1777.
7. LRRA, P 17/24, LK to EL, Vienna, 30 July 1777.
8. LRRA, P 17/24, EL to LK, Kromau, 26 July 1777; Ch. de Larivièra, "L'Empereur Joseph à Paris en 1777 et en 1781," *Revue politique et parlementaire* 28 (1901): 623-24.
9. Gaston Maugras, *La disgrâce du duc et de la duchesse de Choiseul* (Paris, Plon-Nourrit, 1903), 353-57.
10. LRRA, P 17/24, LK to EL, Vienna, 2 August 1777.
11. LRRA, P 17/24, LK to EL, Vienna, 6 August 1777.
12. HHStA, HA SB 3, MT to Marie Antoinette, Vienna, 2 January 1777 and Marie Antoinette to MT, Versailles, 16 January 1777.
13. LRRA, P 17/24, LK to EL, Laxenburg, 21 August 1777.
14. SÚA, RAM AC, 11/22, JII to LK, Leitmeritz, 29 7bre 1779.
15. There is a helpful map showing Joseph's routes of travel during the 1780s in Beales, *Joseph II,* 2: 134-35.
16. LRRA, P 17/27, LK to EL, Vienna, 4 July 1781.
17. SOAL-D, RACA, carton 64, LL to JC, Spa, 8 July 1781.
18. LRRA, P 17/27, EL to LK, Kromau, 25 July 1781.
19. LRRA, P 17/27, LK to EL, Vienna, 18 August 1781.
20. An example was the case of Josepha Clary's daughter Countess Hoyos who visited Paris and felt herself to be somewhat slighted. LRRA, P 17/31, LK to EL, Baden, 26 September 1785.
21. SOAL-D, RACA, carton 64, LL to JC, Paris, 14 August 1781.

22 LRRA, P 17/27, EL to LK, Vienna, 31 August, 1781.
23 Beales, *Joseph II*, 2: 132.
24 LRRA, P 17/28, EL to LK, Kromau, 21 August 1782.
25 Guglia, *Maria Theresia*, 2: 310.
26 LRRA, P 17/27, LK to EL, Vienna, 21 July 1781.
27 Matthew Z. Mayer, "The Price for Austria's Security: Part I. Joseph II, the Russian Alliance, and the Ottoman War, 1787-1789," *International History Review* 26, no. 2 (2004): 262.
28 Michael Hochedlinger, *Austria's Wars of Emergence: War, State and Society in the Habsburg Monarchy 1683-1797* (London: Pearson Education, 2003), 378.
29 Beales, *Joseph* II, 2: 117-23; Isabel de Madariaga, "The Secret Austro-Russian Treaty of 1781," *Slavonic and East European Review*, 38 (Dec. 1919): 114-45.
30 Elisabeth's parents were Duke Friedrich Eugen, 1732-1787, and his wife Sophia Dorothea of Brandenburg-Schwedt, a niece of Frederick II.
31 LRRA, P 17/27, EL to LK, Feldsberg, 27 September 1781.
32 LRRA, P 17/27, LK to EL, Vienna, 16 August 1781, 25 September 1781, and 16 October 1781.
33 LRRA, P 17/27, EL to LK, Feldsberg, 21 October 1781.
34 LRRA, P 17/27, EL to LK, Feldsberg,19 September 1781.
35 LRRA, P 17/27, EL to LK, Feldsberg,19 September 1781.
36 LRRA, P 17/27, EL to LK, Kromau, 5 August 1781.
37 LRRA, P 17/27, LK to EL, Vienna, 28 and 29 October 1781 (Josepha's remarks were quoted by Leopoldine Kaunitz); LRRA, P 17/28, EL to LK, Kromau, 28 August 1782.
38 LRRA, P 17/27, EL to LK, Feldsberg, 15 October 1781.
39 Gutkas, *Kaiser Joseph II.*, 259-64; Beales, *Joseph II*, 2: 127-32; *Wiener Zeitung*, issues from 1781 and 1782.
40 LRRA, P 17/28, LK to EL, Vienna, 14 August 1782, 18 August 1782, 21 August 1782, and 25 August 1782; EL to LK, Kromau, 17 August 1782.
41 Beales, *Joseph II*, 2: 386.
42 LRRA, P 17/29, LK to EL, Vienna, 22 July 1783.
43 LRRA, P 17/29, EL to LK, Kromau, 6 August 1783.
44 LRRA, P 17/29, EL to LK, Vienna, 30 September 1783.
45 LRRA, P 17/29, LK to EL, Vienna, 10 July 1783.
46 LRRA, P 17/29, EL to LK, Kromau, 19 July 1783.
47 LRRA, P 17/29, LK to EL, Vienna, 12 August 1783.
48 *Joseph II. und Leopold von Toscana: ihr Briefwechsel von 1781 bis 1790*, ed. Alfred von Arneth (Vienna: W. Braumüller, 1872), 1: 164-66; JII to Leopold, 31 July 1783.
49 Beales, *Joseph II*, 1: 490-91; 2: 104, 373.
50 Mayer, "The Price for Austria's Security: Part I," 259.
51 LRRA, P 17/28, LK to EL, Vienna, 18 August 1782 (reported by Leopoldine Kaunitz).
52 LRRA, P 17/28, EL to LK, Kromau, 21 August 1782,
53 Beales, *Joseph II*, 2: 374.
54 Paul P. Bernard, *Joseph II and Bavaria: Two Eighteenth Century Attempts at German Unification* (The Hague: Martinus Nijhoff, 1965), 189; Beales, *Joseph II*, 2: 390-93.
55 Beales, *Joseph II*, 2: 396-97.
56 LRRA, P 17/31, LK to EL, Baden, 23 September 1785.
57 LRRA, P 17/31, LK to EL, Vienna, 29 September 1785; Beales, *Joseph II*, 2: 397.
58 Wolf, *Marie Christine*, 1: 219-21.
59 Bernard, *Joseph II and Bavaria*, 214.
60 LRRA, P 17/31, EL to LK, Kromau, 18 September 1785.

61 LRRA, P 17/31, LK to EL, Vienna, 10 October 1785.
62 Bernard, *Joseph II and Bavaria*, 215.
63 Hans Rall, *Kurfürst Karl Theodor: regierender Herr in sieben Ländern* (Mannheim: B.I.-Wissenschaftsverlag, 1993), 246-47.
64 Braubach, Max. *Maria Theresias jüngster Sohn Max Franz, letzter Kurfürst von Köln und Fürstbischof von Münster* (Vienna: Herold, 1961), 212-18; LRRA, P 17/31, LK to EL, 8 October 1785.
65 Blanning, *Joseph II*, 9, 148-50.
66 LRRA, P 17/32, EL to LK, Kromau, 1 September 1787.
67 Beales, *Joseph II*, 2: 557-58. For a summary of the course of the war: Hochedlinger, *Austria's Wars of Emergence*, 382-86.
68 Beales, *Joseph II*, 2: 516-17.
69 SOAL-D, RACA, carton 64, LL to JC, Spa, 14 July [1781].
70 SOAL-D, RACA, carton 64, LL to JC, Spa, 8 July 1781.
71 SÚA, RAM AC, 11/22, JII to LK, Brussels, 21 July [1781].
72 Janet L. Polasky, *Revolution in Brussels, 1787-1793* (Brussels: Académie Royale de Belgique; Hanover: University Press of New England, 1987), 35-51.
73 Wangermann, *The Austrian Achievement*, 161-62; Oskar Criste, *Kriege unter Kaiser Josef II. Nach den Feldakten und anderen authentischen Quellen* (Vienna: L. W. Seidel, 1904), 230.
74 LRRA, P 17/42, EL to Josephine Harrach, Vienna, 2 and 24 July 1787; Wolf, *Marie Christine*, 1: 256-57, Marie Christine to EL, 27 June 1787.
75 LRRA, P 17/33, LK to EL, Vienna, 29 June 1789.
76 LRRA, P 17/33, LK to EL, Vienna, 29 July 1789.
77 LRRA, P 17/32, LK to EL, Vienna, 31 August 1787.
78 LRRA, P 17/32, LK to EL, Vienna, 2 September 1787.
79 SOAL-D, RACA, carton 67, JC to daughter Countess Wilczek, 3 December 1787.
80 Mayer, "The Price for Austria's Security: Part I," 257-99; Mayer, "The Price for Austria's Security: Part II. Leopold II, the Prussian Threat, and the Peace of Sistova, 1790-1791," *International History Review* 26 no. 3 (Sept. 2004): 507-09; Beales, *Joseph II*, 2: 641-47. Mayer's article explores the motives behind Joseph's foreign and military policy, avoiding the usual blunt judgments that his Russian alliance and its results were a foolish failure.
81 HHStA, HA SB 72-4, JII to Lacy, Leopol, 5 May [1787].
82 HHStA, HA SB 72-4, JII to Lacy, Leopol, 25 June 1787.
83 Hausarchiv der regierenden Fürsten von Liechtenstein, Vaduz, carton 489, Joseph II to "Damenrunde" [February 1788].
84 LRRA, P 17/32, LK to EL, Vienna, 27 July and 5 August 1788.
85 SÚA, RAM AC, 11/22, JII to LK, Semlin, 9 May 1788.
86 SÚA, RAM AC, 11/22, JII to LK, Illowa, 4 September [1788].
87 HHStA, HA SB 9, JII to Leopold, Illowa, 20 September 1788.
88 HHStA, HA SB 9, JII to Leopold, Semlin, 29 October 1788.
89 LRRA, P 17/35, EL to husband Charles Liechtenstein, Vienna, 28 March 1788 and 20 April 1788.
90 Beales, *Joseph II*, 2: 583, 626-27.
91 SÚA, RAM AC, 11/22, JII to LK, Semlin, 9 May 1788.
92 SÚA, RAM AC, 11/22, JII to LK, Morva, 4 September [1788].
93 SÚA, RAM AC, 11/22, JII to LK, Illowa, 11 September 1788.
94 SÚA AC, 11/22, JII to LK, Lugos, s.d. [1788].
95 SÚA, RAM AC, 11/22, JII to LK, Semlin, 15 November [1788].

96 Lorenz Mikoletzky, "'Der Bauern Gott, der Bürger Not, des Adels Spott liegt auf den Tod': Kaiser Josephs II. langes Sterben aus eigener und fremder sicht," *Mitteilungen des Österreichischen Staatsarchivs* 39 (1986): 16.
97 Wolf, *Fürstin Eleonore Liechtenstein*, 214.
98 Edith Kotasek, *Feldmarschall Graf Lacy: ein Leben für Österreichs Heer* (Horn, Austria: F. Berger, 1956), 168.
99 "Briefe an Erzherzog Franz (nachmals K. Franz II.) von seiner ersten Gemahlin Elisabeth, 1785-1789," ed. H. Weyda, *Archiv für österreichische Geschichte* 44 (1871), 131 (13 August 1788), 162-63 (12 October 1788). Kotasek, *Feldmarschall Graf Lacy*, 179.
100 Kotasek, *Feldmarschall Graf Lacy*, 180.
101 Blanning, *Joseph II*, 182, 203; Beales, *Joseph II*, 2: 642.
102 LRRA, P 17/33, LK to EL, Vienna, 28 June 1789 and 4 July 1789.
103 Michael Hochedlinger, "Who's Afraid of the French Revolution? Austrian Foreign Policy and the European Crisis 1787-1787," *German History* 21, no. 3 (2003): 304.
104 LRRA, P 17/33, EL to LK, Meseritsch, 31 July 1789 and 3 August 1789. Eleonore cites Leopoldine Liechtenstein.
105 LRRA, P 17/29, LK to EL, Vienna, 17 July 1783.
106 LRRA, P 17/44, EL to Josephine Harrach, Meseritsch, 1 August 1789.
107 LRRA, P 17/33, LK to EL, Vienna, 25 July 1789.
108 LRRA, P 17/33, LK to EL, Vienna, 26 July 1789.
109 LRRA, P 17/33, EL to LK, Meseritsch, 7 September 1789.
110 LRRA, P 17/33, EL to LK, Meseritsch, 20 July 1789.
111 LRRA, P 17/33, EL to LK, Meseritsch, 3 August 1789 and 10 August 1789.
112 Ingrao, *The Habsburg Monarchy*, 220-21.
113 Hochedlinger, "Who's Afraid of the French Revolution?" 313-14, 316-17.
114 LRRA, P 18/52, EL to Josephine Harrach, Meseritsch, 26 April 1797.
115 HHStA, KA ZT, Band 34, 16 April 1789.
116 HHStA, HA SB 9, Rosenberg to Leopold, Vienna, 4 May 1789.
117 SÚA, RAM AC, 11/22, JII to LK, 8 May 1789.
118 LRRA, P 17/33, LK to EL, Vienna, 29 June 1789.
119 HHStA, HA SB 9, JII to Leopold, Laxenburg, 17 August 1789 and Rosenberg to Leopold, Vienna, 9 September 1789.
120 LRRA, P 17/33, LK to EL, Vienna, 10 July 1789.
121 LRRA, P 17/33, LK to EL, Vienna, 10 September 1789; Hochedlinger, "Who's Afraid of the French Revolution?" 301-02.
122 Wolf, *Fürstin Eleonore Liechtenstein*, 220-21.
123 HHStA, HA SB 9, Rosenberg to Leopold, Vienna, 9 September 1789.
124 Wolf, *Fürstin Eleonore Liechtenstein*, 221.
125 LRRA, P 17/33, EL to LK, Meseritsch, 17 August 1789.
126 Blanning, *Joseph II*, 186-87.
127 HHStA, HA SB 9, JII to Leopold, 15 October 1789 and in *Joseph II. und Leopold von Toscana: ihr Briefwechsel von 1781 bis 1790*, 2: 280.
128 KLA, FAR, fasc. 64-355a, JII's note to Rosenberg, s.d.
129 Blanning, *Joseph II*, 189. Joseph's retraction of many of his reforms was forced upon him, but it is reasonable to credit the emperor with tactical skill as he sought to save what he could of his life's work. Certainly many of Joseph's reforms were acutely unpopular among a number of vocal groups, and a clear threat of foreign intervention menaced Habsburg power in Belgium and Hungary. Friedrich Engel-Jánosi, "Josephs II. Tod im Urteil der Zeitgenossen," *Mitteilungen des Österreichischen Instituts für Geschichtsforschung* 44, nos. 2/3 (1930): 324-46.

130 *Correspondance secrète du comte de Mercy-Argenteau avec l'empereur Joseph II et le prince de Kaunitz*, 2: 291-92, Chancellor Kaunitz to Mercy, Vienna, 6 January 1790.
131 HHStA, KA ZT, Band 33, 10 July 1788.
132 LRRA, P 17/33, EL to LK, Meseritsch, 3 July 1789.
133 LRRA, P 17/33, LK to EL, Vienna, 17 July 1789.
134 SÚA, RAM AC, 11/22, JII to LK, 15 November 1789.
135 *Joseph II. und Leopold von Toscana: ihr Briefwechsel*, vol. 2; letters from November 1789 to JII's death are found on pages 283-22.
136 HHStA, KA ZT, Band 35, 16 January 1790.
137 LRRA, P 17/33, LK to EL, Vienna, 23 July 1789.
138 Sir Robert Murray Keith, *Memoirs and Correspondence*, ed. Mrs. Gillespie Smyth (London: Henry Colburn, 1849), 2: 248, 259, Keith to his sister, 23 January 1790 and 11 February 1790.
139 L. Wiener, "Kaiser Josef II. als Staatsmann und Feldherr," *Mitteilungen des K.K. Kriegs-Archivs*, 1885, 143.
140 Beales, *Joseph II*, 2: 53, 630-31.
141 HHStA, KA ZT, Band 35, 31 January 1790.
142 HHStA, HA SB 9, Rosenberg to Leopold, Vienna, 1 February 1790.
143 HHStA, KA ZT, Band 35, 23 February 1790.
144 Szabo, "Between Privilege and Professionalism: the Career of Wenzel Anton Kaunitz" in *Social Change in the Habsburg Monarchy* (Bochum: Winkler, 2011), 150-51; Gutkas, *Kaiser Joseph II.*, 450.
145 Eighteenth-century doctors prescribed purgatives of one sort or another for many ailments, obliging the patient to remain at home until the effects wore off. Wolf, *Fürstin Eleonore Liechtenstein*, 226.
146 This event, coupled with Leopoldine Kaunitz's description of Joseph's ennoblement of Quarin and his gift to the doctor, indicate that the note was written during the first week of February 1790, within days of the emperor's death, when his doctors informed him that he would not survive this illness. LRRA, P 17/34, LK to EL, s.d.; Vehse, *Geschichte der deutschen Höfe*, 14: 282-85.
147 Chancellor Kaunitz to Cardinal Hrzan, 29 December 1789 in Alphonse Sprunck, "Vizekanzler Johann Philipp von Cobenzl und der belgische Aufstand von 1790 nach seinen Berichten an Kaunitz," *Mitteilungen des Österreichischen Staatsarchivs* 9 (1956): 102-05.
148 Rosenberg's remark was reported by Leopoldine Kaunitz. LRRA, P 17/33, LK to EL, Vienna, 17 and 18 July 1789.
149 Beales, *Joseph II*, 2: 590.
150 LRRA, P 17/31, LK to EL, Vienna, 20 October 1785.
151 Hoppe, *Predigtkritik*, 48.
152 Friedrich Engel-Jánosi, "Josephs II. Tod im Urteil der Zeitgenossen," *Mitteilungen des Österreichischen Instituts für Geschichtsforschung* 44, nos. 2/3 (1930): 333.
153 NM, RAŠM, carton 93, LL to her "sister," Vienna, 15 February 1790.
154 Rodinný Archiv Ditrichštejnů (Dietrichstein), Moravský Zemský Archiv, Brno, G 140, K. 570 Inv.-Nr. 2425, EL's farewell response to JII (copy),
155 Beales, *Joseph II*, 2: 635.
156 Kotasek, *Feldmarschall Graf Lacy*, 248-49.
157 KLA, FAR, fasc. 64-352c, Vienna, 19 February 1790; HHStA, KA ZT, Band 35, 20 February 1790.
158 Wolf, *Fürstin Eleonore Liechtenstein*, 225.

159 A copy of the emperor's letter can be found in Leopoldine Kaunitz's papers (SÚA, RAM AC, 11/22) and in Josepha Clary's papers (SOAL-D, RACA, carton 66). The texts vary only slightly in spelling and punctuation. Eleonore Liechtenstein reported to her daughter Josephine in November 1811 that Sidonia Kinsky's daughter-in-law had had the text printed in the "Gazette." LRRA, Q 1/65, EL to Josephine Harrach, Hietzing, 3 November 1811.
160 Padover, *Joseph II*, 9; Blanning, *Joseph II*, 202.
161 For example, Strakosch, *State Absolutism*, 104. A more general discussion of this interesting issue can be found in Charles Ingrao, "The Problem of 'Enlightened Absolutism' and the German States," *Journal of Modern History* 58, Supplement: Politics and Society in the Holy Roman Empire, 1500-1806 (December 1986), esp. S178-S180.
162 Blanning, *Joseph II*, 203; Beales, *Joseph II*, 2: 647.
163 HHStA, KA ZT, Band 35, 22 February 1790.
164 Gutkas, *Kaiser Joseph II.*, 452-53; LRRA, P 17/32, LK to EL, Baden, 19 September 1786.
165 Archivio Secreto Vaticano. Fondo Garampi 283 27rv. Correspondence of Giuseppe Garampi with Eleonore Liechtenstein and Leopoldine Kaunitz. Garampi to EL, Cometo, 14 April 1790 (draft). Copy provided by the Vatican Archive.
166 LRRA, P 17/33, EL to LK, Meseritsch, 3 August 1789.
167 Ingrao, *The Habsburg Monarchy*, 210.
168 LRRA, P 17/33, LK to EL, Laxenburg, 1 July 1791.
169 LRRA, P 17/33, EL to LK, Vienna, 1 July 1791.
170 The following examples document these many connections: HHStA, HA SB 3, Marie Antoinette to MT, Choisy, 14 May 1774 (Lacy); HHStA, HA SB 3, MT to Marie Antoinette, Vienna, 5 March 1775 (Rosenberg). HHStA, HA SB 3, Marie Antoinette to MT, 16 August 1776 (Dominik Kaunitz); HHStA, HA SB 3, Marie Antoinette to MT, Versailles, 16 March 1780 (LL's oldest daughter); HHStA, HA SB 3, Marie Antoinette to MT, Versailles, 13 April 1780 (Joseph Kaunitz); Leopoldine Liechtenstein's visit in 1781; *Marie Antoinette, Joseph II und Leopold II.: ihr Briefwechsel*, ed. Alfred von Arneth (Leipzig: K. F. Köhler, 1866), 98-100, Marie Antoinette to JII, 20 October [1785] (Josepha Clary's daughter Christine Hoyos); *Marie Antoinette, Joseph II und Leopold II.*, 139, Marie Antoinette to Leopold II, 7 November [1790] (Charles Liechtenstein); also Wolf, *Fürstin Eleonore Liechtenstein*, 229.
171 Charles Joseph Ligne, *Fragments de l'histoire de ma vie* (*L'âge de lumières* 6), ed. Jeroom Vercruysse (Paris: H. Champion, 2000-2001), 2: 356.
172 LRRA, P 18/59, EL to Josephine Harrach, 1 October 1804; LRRA, Q 1/65, EL to Josephine Harrach, 31 August 1811.
173 SOAL-D, RACA, carton 76, JC to her son Prince Clary, 20 August 1796.
174 LRRA, Q 1/66, EL to Josephine Harrach, Vienna, 4 November 1812.
175 SOAL-D, RACA, carton 65, JC to son Prince Clary, 23 and 29 July 1794; SOAL-D, RACA, carton 66, JC to her son Prince Clary, Weidlingau, 4 and 22 August 1798.
176 Wolf, *Fürstin Eleonore Liechtenstein*, 52-53.
177 Friedrich Weissensteiner, *Die Töchter Maria Theresias* (Vienna: K & S, 1994), 103, 206.
178 SOAL-D, RACA, carton 64, LL to JC, Hütteldorf, 20 [August] 1800; LRRA, P 18/55, EL to Josephine Harrach, 19 August 1800.
179 Alfred Arneth, "Graf Philipp Cobenzl und seine Memoiren," *Archiv für österreichische Geschichte* 67 (1886): 41.
180 Rosenberg reported to them about political events and the military turbulence in Naples. SOAL-D, RACA, carton 66, Rosenberg to JC, Florence, December 1794 and Pisa,

20 September 1794; additional letters to JC or to *la société*, April and December 1793 and September 1794.
181 HHStA, KA ZT, Band 41, 2 December 1795, 18 October 1796, and 2 November 1796.
182 Gunther E. Rothenberg, *Napoleon's Great Adversary: the Archduke Charles and the Austrian Army, 1792-1814* (Bloomington: Indiana University Press, 1982), 27.
183 According to Sir R. M. Keith, British envoy, reporting from Vienna in May 1792, Lacy "who, for twenty years, held the sole direction of military matters, is extremely tenacious of that plan he himself established. Yet he now feels that he must, in the end, submit to many and great alterations in that system." Keith, *Memoirs and Correspondence*, 2: 512; Gerda Mraz and Gottfried Mraz, *Österreichische Profile: Maximilian I., Wallenstein, Prinz Eugen, Maria Theresia, Kaunitz, Franz II., Erzherzog Carl, Metternich, Radetzky, Franz Joseph I.* (Königstein: Athenäum, 1981), 128.
184 Kotasek, *Feldmarschall Graf Lacy*, 222-23.
185 H. R. von Zeissberg, "Zur Geschichte der Räumung Belgiens und des polnischen Aufstandes (1794). Nach Lacy's Vorträgen an den Kaiser," *Archiv für österreichische Geschichte* 72 (1888): 5-11.
186 Hochedlinger, "'... Dass Aufklärung das sicherste Mittel ist, die Ruhe und Anhänglichkeit der Unterthanen zu befestigen': Staatskanzler Kaunitz und die 'franziszeische Reaktion' 1792-1794," *Aufklärung—Vormärz—Revolution* 16/17 (1996/1997): 62-65, 76; Hochedlinger, "Who's Afraid of the French Revolution?" 313.
187 Alexander Novotny, *Staatskanzler Kaunitz als geistige Persönlichkeit: ein österreichisches Kulturbild aus der Zeit der Aufklärung und des Josephinismus* (Vienna: Hollinek, 1947), 145-52, 158-71.
188 Szabo, *Kaunitz and Enlightened Absolutism 1753-1780* (New York: Cambridge University Press, 1994), 32.
189 LRRA, P 17/34, LK to EL, s.d.
190 SOAL-D, RACA, carton 65, JC to her son Prince Clary, 14 June 1794 and 18 June 1794.
191 HHStA, KA ZT, Band 38, 16 January 1793, 17 July 1793, and 10 November 1793.
192 HHStA, KA ZT, Band 51, 30 June 1806.
193 Leopoldine and her husband were buried in a new chamber they constructed at the *Spitalkirche* in Austerlitz. Josepha Clary's death occurred in Vienna but her remains were moved to Teplitz. Leopoldine Liechtenstein died at Feldsberg (according to Zinzendorf she had "a very peaceful death") but was laid to rest at the parish church of Hütteldorf. Eleonore died in Vienna and her final resting place was beside her husband Charles in the crypt of the "Gruftkapelle" in Kromau. When Sidonia Kinsky died in 1815, she was buried (along with her canoness sister Marianne) at Mariabrunn. LRRA, P 17/33, LK to EL, Austerlitz, 16 September 1794; LRRA, Q 1/62, EL to Josephine Harrach, Vienna, 28 May 1807; HHStA, KA ZT, Band 54, 25 June 1809 and 5 July 1809.
194 LRRA, P 17/56, EL to Josephine Harrach, 24 November 1801 and 3 December 1801.
195 Leopoldine Kaunitz and Eleonore Liechtenstein were reported to have experienced particularly edifying deaths. According to Zinzendorf, Leopoldine Kaunitz had complained about darkness during the last days of her life but "In dying she cried out Now there is light." Several weeks later Zinzendorf noted, "It is said that people [probably LK's household staff in particular] consider Madame de Kaunitz to be a saint." HHStA, KA ZT, Band 40, 3 January 1795 and 5 March 1795. Concerning Eleonore, Zinzendorf reported a conversation he had while visiting at the Countess Buquoy's (an aunt of Eleonore's grandson Charles): "We spoke much about the dear departed Princess Charles, whose confessor was so satisfied with her that Madame de B. believes her translated at once to heaven without having to pass through purgatory." In Eleonore's case too close

acquaintances wished to invoke her as a saint. Wolf, *Fürstin Eleonore Liechtenstein*, 337; HHStA, KA ZT, Band 57, 27 November 1812 and 1 December 1812.
196 HHStA, KA ZT, Band 54, 24 June 1809, 5 August 1809, and 22 August 1809.
197 LRRA, P 18/60, EL to Josephine Harrach, 3 October 1805.
198 LRRA, Q 1/63, EL to Josephine, Vienna, 12 October 1808.
199 Ligne, *Fragments de l'histoire de ma vie*, 1: 414.
200 Clemens Lothar Wenzel Metternich-Winneburg, *Mémoires, documents et écrits divers laissés par le prince de Metternich, chancelier de cour et d'état* (s.l., R.C.L. Metternich, 1879), 1: 24-25.
201 LRRA, Q 1/66, EL to Josephine Harrach, Vienna, 24 October 1812.
202 Ingrao, "The Problem of 'Enlightened Absolutism,'" S172.
203 SÚA, RAM AC, 11/19, Ernst Kaunitz to LK, Frankfurt, 10 October 1790. For the growing interest of historians in the Holy Roman Empire in recent decades see the introduction written by Peter H. Wilson and Michael Schaich in *The Holy Roman Empire, 1495-1806*, ed. R. J. W. Evans, Michael Schaich, and Peter H. Wilson, German Historical Institute (London. Oxford: Oxford University Press, 2011), 3-8; Blanning, "The Holy Roman Empire of the German Nation Past and Present" *Historical Research* 85 no. 227 (Feb. 2012).
204 LRRA, P 18/59, 17 September 1804; Wolf, *Fürstin Eleonore Liechtenstein*, 282. Blanning has pointed out that Joseph II's predecessors had increasingly placed dynastic interests ahead of their concerns as emperors. Blanning, "The Holy Roman Empire of the German Nation Past and Present," 67.
205 P 18/59, EL to Josephine Harrach, 14 June 1804; LRRA, P 18/61, EL to Josephine Harrach, St. Veit, 1 August 1806.
206 LRRA, P 18/57, EL to Josephine Harrach, October 1802.
207 NM, RAŠM, carton 93, LL to her brother, Vienna, s.d.
208 Wolf, *Fürstin Eleonore Liechtenstein*, 282.
209 HHStA, KA ZT, Band 51, 20 July 1806; LRRA, P 18/60, EL to Josephine Harrach, Saint Veit, 1 and 13 August 1806.
210 Jeroen Duindam, "Early Modern Europe: Beyond the Strictures of Modernization and National Historiography," *European History Quarterly* 40, no. 4 (2010): 613-14.
211 Eleonore's guest had been court doctor. Q 1/62, EL to Josephine Harrach, Vienna, 2 May 1807.
212 Blanning, *The French Revolution in the Rhineland 1792-1802* (Oxford: Clarendon Press, 1983), 20.

Conclusion

Eleonore Liechtenstein's biographer Adam Wolf observes that as Joseph II's star set in the late 1780s, so too did Eleonore's, with the loss of her imperial friend and her special role.[1] Wolf's comments apply to the other *Dames* as well, who found themselves relegated to the sidelines of political life. Without question the high point of these women's lives was their unique association with the emperor and his two close advisors Lacy and Rosenberg. Even as it was for the Habsburg monarchy as a whole, in a more immediate, personal sense for the five women the year 1790 constituted a watershed. Their continuing enthusiasm for political life notwithstanding, with Joseph's death their special preeminence ended abruptly. Now the *Dames* were aging. They assumed roles more typical for their ages, family positions, and gender. Jerzy Lukowski's comment concerning high-achieving women of the eighteenth century is apt in this case: "The place that individual women carved out for themselves, or even had thrust upon them, remained just that—a matter of individuals."[2] Habsburg emperors had no tradition of established female favorites, although romantic dalliances especially with lower-class women had not been rare and Joseph himself had a reputation for promiscuity. There had been no model after which the women could pattern themselves as imperial associates; no precedent had existed for such a relationship with a Habsburg emperor. And there was no successor to the *société*. A new generation of political and social elites would face the challenges of the 1790s and the century beyond. The seeming familiarity of circumstances during Leopold II's brief reign masked the acceleration of change. Conflicts that followed upon the revolution in France led to the remapping of Europe and a wholesale attack on "legitimate" traditional governments. Leopold II was his dead brother Joseph's contemporary, but a younger generation of men and women moved quickly to the fore.

The most striking characteristic of the small *société* of the Five Princesses had been its stability: the group had weathered both the disharmonies of the coregency and the disruptive changes of Joseph's sole rule. The *société* did not create a new or expanded public space for the women, or even a quasi-public space on the model of Parisian salons of prerevolutionary France—concepts difficult to apply to the political life of the late eighteenth-century Habsburg monarchy in any case, although active, astute hostesses and diverse forms of sociability abounded in Vienna as elsewhere.[3] Just as many of Joseph's specific reforms had an ad hoc character and were the products of expediency rather than system, so the women's reactions reflected in part their personal experiences and unusual association. The sources examined for the present study do not make possible a systematic comparison of these special women's political interests with those of fellow aristocratic women and men. But if the outlook and reactions of this small group of women cannot be generalized without further study to apply to their fellow aristocrats, certainly a disparate group with political and religious views ranging across a broad spectrum, the "Five Princesses" can nevertheless serve as a case study in the aristocratic response to the coregency and the Josephinian decade that followed.

Like other aristocratic matrons, each of the *Dames* had as a matter of course to represent and promote within elite society the family interests of her great "house."[4] Even as they became part of a chosen circle of imperial favorites the women neglected neither ongoing stylized activities of the Habsburg court, with their symbolic affirmations concerning rank, prestige, and fealty of participants, nor the less constrained associations with their peers that were equally important for the welfare and prosperity of their houses. They joined enthusiastically in events of the capital as well as more bucolic social pursuits. Their association with the emperor was certainly an object of respect and envy, and they occasionally cadged minor favors from him for family members. But the women were aware of the emperor's sensitivity about favoritism and they refrained from overt petitioning for substantive imperial largess. Available evidence suggests that the *Dames* did not wield direct powers of influence or patronage much beyond those generally typical for their rank and wealth, fielding requests for help from impecunious relatives and craftsmen or aspiring soldiers and officers, often from individuals who might have multigenerational ties to the families of the women or their husbands. At least in part the women's relative restraint, even as they enjoyed direct and frequent access to the emperor, was very likely a response to the emperor's strict and much-vaunted views about the need to separate public goals from private whims.[5]

The rewards of membership in the *société* for the women were principally of an intangible nature. As noted earlier in this study, in recent decades historians of politics have adopted a more nuanced approach that examines not just the formal influences of ministers and officials but also the informal associations that involved courtiers and politically savvy contemporaries, including women. It has become easier to perceive that the boundaries between public and private spheres of politically interested individuals and their families in the late eighteenth-century Habsburg monarchy (as in ancien régime Europe at large) and between the various functions of "court" and "state" were permeable. This insight, in combination with a broader definition of political life in general, has helped to underscore the significance of social as well as political concerns for members of the aristocracy, not to mention the sovereign. Participation in their special group certainly afforded the *Dames* enhanced standing within the politically interested first and second *noblesse*, where their unique imperial connection was known, and it prompted the women to self-identify as persons of some political importance.

The *Dames* were never servile flatterers. From their earliest years of association with the emperor, they noted personal characteristics in Joseph II that they felt were weaknesses in a ruler. His sensitivity about his public image, well documented by historians, made them fearful that his decisions would be affected by unworthy considerations. They believed that he was inordinately eager for "glory," preferably of the military type enjoyed by Frederick II. They found the emperor to be moody, uneven in his relationships, bombastic in his language, and inconsistent in his choices. Joseph II himself disclaimed the status of "philosopher." But he enjoyed being deemed clever and perhaps a bit risqué. The women feared his wish to shine and to win the praise of international literate society.[6] They were disappointed by his performance during the War of the Bavarian Succession, having themselves favored expansion into Bavarian territory if the cost in lives and treasure was not great. They had joined the chorus of detractors who distrusted Joseph's attempts to work in partnership with Catherine II toward poorly delimited goals of conquest to the southeast. The women's most persistent, repeated criticisms, however, targeted Joseph's religious reforms and, in a more diffuse manner, Joseph's treatment of their own social class, the Habsburg aristocracy. With regard to measures applied to the church, the reactions of the *Dames* were direct and largely hostile. Their responses to reforms that affected the nobility are less easily categorized, being both less explicit and more varied.

Not antireligious himself, the emperor nonetheless laid profane hands on hoary, sacred traditions and, of greater significance, on the underpinnings of the church's status, wealth, and even doctrinal competency. The women's critical stance toward the whole of Joseph's reign was determined and colored above all by his approach to the church. Thus their principal objections to Joseph's loosening of censorship practices focused on the likely religious ramifications. Most of all they feared the impact of public attacks on Catholic orthodoxy, although they also voiced uneasiness about popular loss of respect for secular institutions and their leaders. Unmistakably, Joseph wished to harness church resources for his rational, utilitarian state ideal. With considerable astuteness, and far more acutely during the 1780s than during the coregency, the women came to identify the primary issue as that of authority, church versus state, in religious matters. Joseph's religious reforms were carried out before the more coercive example was set by France in the 1790s, and thus in gentler times. Still, on a number of occasions the *Dames* contested point-blank Joseph's right to decide and act in vital matters of religion. The *Dames*, although not of a single mind as a group on all specifics, parted company with their imperial friend over this fundamental question.

Certainly individual clerics and aristocrats enthusiastically supported Joseph's church reforms. Many moderately liberal Catholics and Jansenist-leaning individuals initially viewed Joseph's initiatives with favor. But the emperor's increasingly ambitious goals, which seemed always to recede into a distance of uncertain measure, left even his supporters baffled and uneasy. Throughout the life of their *société* these women remained unable to make peace with Joseph's most ambitious reforms. Segments of Viennese aristocratic society were in greater sympathy with church reform even in its more radical guises than were these women. However, the women's stance does roughly mirror the tendency of the literate Habsburg aristocracy as a whole, noted by Ivo Cerman, to reject or ignore those elements of contemporary French, German, and English thought that offered trenchant criticism of Catholic doctrine and emanated from "freethinkers" and skeptics, while remaining open to other products of Enlightenment thought.[7] Clearly the Habsburg monarchy was not fertile ground for the planting of a secular republic on the lines of France's experiment, which lay only a few years in the future. For the *Dames*, and especially for convent-educated Eleonore Liechtenstein and Leopoldine Kaunitz, Joseph quickly appeared to move beyond the proper limits of his authority as secular ruler. Eleonore, Leopoldine Kaunitz, and Josepha Clary habitually encouraged each other, avowing that outspoken opposition was absolutely essential. Other points of disagreement could be finessed and glossed; for the *Dames* the fight for the faith was the good fight.

Toleration for non-Catholics was a particularly distasteful innovation for these *Dames*, but it was only one issue of many. It is noteworthy that over time the focus of the women's criticism, and the source of their greatest uneasiness, was dissension and change within the Catholic church rather than the greater latitude granted to Protestants and Jews outside the church. They reserved their strongest expressions of disapproval for Catholics whose criticism might undermine the unity of the church under the pope. To all appearances this preoccupation with the church's internal enemies was in no wise lessened by the affirmations of the emperor, repeated formally in his new regulations, that the Catholic religion retained its supremacy in his lands. It is possible that the women's urgings played a role in what progressives of the time, and historians since then, have seen as Joseph's tendency to backslide on issues such as toleration and censorship over the course of the 1780s, his directives becoming noticeably more restrictive (noted in chapter 5). The sentiments expressed by the women at the time of the emperor's death suggest that their greatest fears concerning his spiritual welfare had been assuaged somewhat. Possibly an additional factor was the women's gradual, implicit recognition—without approval—of the church's altered status as a fait accompli. A direct, substantive link between the emperor's vacillations and the admonitory counsels of the *Dames* (or other specific groups and individuals) cannot be demonstrated by reference to the women's letters.

In a character sketch of Joseph ostensibly written for Catherine II, the Prince de Ligne affirmed, "He demanded greater nobility from the nobility [*plus de noblesse de la part de la noblesse*], and was more contemptuous of them than of other classes when they did not possess it; but it is untrue that he wished to harm them. He wanted to have the greatest authority so that others would not have the right to do harm."[8] Possibly these comments overstate Joseph's forbearance, since his reforms deliberately curtailed the nobility's legal prerogatives and reduced the share of wealth that could be requisitioned by landed proprietors. Certainly the *Dames* resented what they viewed as Joseph's cavalier treatment of the nobility and the injurious measures found in both his legal and his economic reforms. But the emperor did not launch a frontal assault on the nobility's corporate existence.[9] He offended the great magnates of his realm and attempted to circumscribe their wealth and authority, but he did not set out to destroy the class. The recent work of Duindam and Lukowski suggests that at base all European sovereigns and nobilities were aware of their mutual dependence, an alliance unarticulated but presumably descried clearly by Joseph. He was himself, after all, a hereditary monarch, for whom the application of revolutionary tenets to a broad restructuring of society could have little appeal. As Blanning notes, the young Joseph appeared to be unconcerned about the fact that he, like the overmighty aristocrats he criticized, enjoyed his position largely through an accident of birth and inheritance.[10]

Like most of their peers, the *Dames* were inclined to see Joseph's most radical agrarian reforms, culminating in the "rectification," as an attack on the aristocracy and by extension malfeasance against the monarchy and its economy as a whole. The *Dames* were not inhumane. Those who traveled to their family estates were aware of the widespread poverty in the countryside; Eleonore Liechtenstein in particular often commented on the poor condition of agriculture as she traveled to her summer residence in Kromau. But while willing to consider the merits of gradual reforms such as regulation of compulsory labor or even its redemption, they were evidently pessimistic about prospects for a total, beneficial transformation of society. The women were not well equipped to envision anything beyond minor ameliorative changes; and in this outlook they were no doubt joined by many, though not all, of their peers. Like most of their peers they did not welcome the radical social critique of the French Enlightenment, with its antifeudal pronouncements.[11] In their communications, there is little evidence of an evolution in their valuation of the peasant population as subjects or citizens or a new moral tone, such as one might find in the case of a discerning aristocrat like Chancellor Kaunitz.[12] Joseph II perceived a direct relationship between the prosperity of agriculture and the effective power of his state and was thereby motivated to enforce changes. The women were less likely to draw this connection, although they recognized the peasantry's importance to society at large.

To the *Dames*, Joseph's measures and his dramatic gestures that humiliated members of the aristocracy and other leading figures, religious as well as secular, appeared to be haphazard and even contradictory in nature, the opportunistic, misguided products of a fertile, quick mind. The high standards against which the emperor was wont to measure his aristocratic servitors were intelligible to the women, however, if not always welcomed by them. Eleonore's frequent references to the old-fashioned views of her military husband regarding his service to the person of the emperor signaled her recognition that noble roles were evolving and could be deliberately recast by a resolute sovereign. Leopoldine Kaunitz more than once expressed her fear that her own husband Ernst lacked the requisite education and the physical strength to withstand the demands of constant travel that the emperor expected of him in his role as inspector of buildings. When Ernst received his appointment under Maria Theresia, it will be recalled, Leopoldine Kaunitz had been uneasy because at the time the post was widely regarded as a sinecure. In the 1780s under the reforming emperor the job required considerable exertion on the part of its incumbent. In the case of Prince Clary, *Oberstjägermeister*, Joseph apparently spared the feelings of the ailing courtier but, as noted previously, simply shut down much of the imperial hunt department's operations immediately after Prince Clary's death.[13] The emperor wanted a service-oriented aristocracy, dedicated to the common good and thus, in Joseph's view, to that all-important abstraction the state. In their own way, the women themselves can be said to have responded to this imperative, even as they disapproved of Joseph's specific actions. Participation in the *société* was a source of pride and prestige for them. But it was also much more. The women assured each other that their friendly association with the emperor was a form of duty. They spoke in terms of Christian morality rather than enlightened aristocratic reformation. Most assuredly they spoke with reference to a wider environment, not just family interest. Their seriousness of purpose, their diligence, their untiring interest in political, social, and diplomatic events within the monarchy, can perhaps be seen as a form of female equivalent to the ethos of state service and seriousness of purpose that increasingly informed the professional activities of a segment of the male Habsburg aristocracy.[14] Perhaps this generalized sense of a high calling, of duty, communicated itself among the members of the group and enhanced its attractiveness for all members, the emperor included.

Fulfilling this obligation was irksome at times, given the emperor's prickly personality and the occasional clumsiness of even his friendliest overtures. The emperor had a self-righteous, condescending manner of expressing himself that offended even well-disposed contemporaries. Certainly he larded his decrees with tiresome preaching about his lofty goals. Beales notes Joseph's habit of "preening himself on . . . his intellectual superiority" or, in another context, using a style that was "at once self-pitying and self-glorifying."[15] In 1779, irritated by the emperor's intrusive concern about her health, Eleonore Liechtenstein had exclaimed to her sister, "My God, in truth he is a difficult [*incommode*] person and we would all be happy if he had stayed on his throne!"[16] Still, it is really only Eleonore Liechtenstein's expressions of exasperation that support the notion that the *société* was not really a circle of well-disposed, willing companions. Possibly one should not exaggerate even Eleonore's irritation, since her connection with the emperor survived many turbulent episodes.[17] With considerable self-knowledge, she once wrote to her sister, "And so I ask of God only gentleness and patience, but all my life I have had the misfortune to lose my temper any time someone has wanted to annoy me, it is incredible, and yet it never fails."[18] In an undated letter (probably from 1787) Eleonore described how she so readily lost her temper especially with the emperor: "I do not know what demon possesses my tongue, that makes me speak when I ought to keep quiet without any effect except to turn people against me and bring me anxiety and remorse. Yesterday it was with the emperor, and on the subject of this voyage to Cherson, about which especially our good Clary [Josepha Clary] made such a singular fuss and which in reality is a matter of such indifference to me." Against her better judgment, she reported, "without thinking first, I began to get involved, I spoke truths that were incontrovertible and so much the more offensive because they were unanswerable, and moreover I said all of this with that unfortunate passion that spoils everything; and the result was much ill humor."[19] Eleonore's frequent use of hyperbole and exclamations of outrage or despair were matched by the emperor's melodramatic statements and inflated convictions about his own rectitude and importance. Such outbursts, and the occasional discomfort of an especially contentious evening gathering, did not seriously dampen the women's enthusiasm for their important roles. A cheerful confidence and conviction that their company was valued by the emperor pervades the letters of the Five Princesses. And there is an engaging, artless candor in the women's assessments and forthright acknowledgment of their remarkable standing.

Joseph's protestations notwithstanding, the women's unstudied reports about their imperial contacts are indisputable evidence that issues of governance and policy were liberally aired at their meetings with the emperor. In view of these close friends' hostility to some of his most cherished objectives, the cohesion of the group and Joseph's striking loyalty to it are extraordinary. Biographers have noted Joseph II's disparaging remarks about the intellectual capacity of women and the futility of serious conversation with them. In practice, the emperor discussed the vicissitudes of his métier as ruler with women friends more frequently and earnestly than did his mother Maria Theresia, the quintessential female ruler.[20] The company of the *Dames* provided relaxation and entertainment for the emperor. He did not view them as advisors. But they served a more serious purpose as well, as a sounding board for his ideas. One is forced to conclude that he took these companions seriously and wished to witness their reactions to his ideas and plans as well as the reasons (or *déraison*, the term used dismissively by the emperor to describe the ideas of women in general, as noted previously) underlying their responses.

If Joseph was to all appearances dismissive of opinions the women expressed during meetings of the *société*, in a basic sense the small *société* simply received the same treatment as that meted out to most of the emperor's male aristocratic servitors.[21] Looking back after the emperor's death, Zinzendorf observed that Joseph had refused to consult in earnest with his servitors or to give careful thought to the implications of his plans, rushing to dictate unripe instructions and inundating his officials with decrees and billets.[22] Most of Joseph's top officials and advisors were aristocrats, and in his relationship with the aristocracy the apparent failure to consult was perhaps the emperor's besetting sin. Joseph doubted the capabilities and the motives of all his ministers. To the aristocracy, a ruler who refused the counsel of his supportive aristocracy and acted without regard to its interests, who undermined the traditional intermediate powers within his lands and adopted an uncompromising statist approach to governance, was a despot.[23] Contemporaries, including the *Dames*, viewed Joseph as an arbitrary ruler who generally discounted the advice of even his closest collaborators and drove them away with scornful remarks and humiliating gestures.

Beales affirms that Joseph generally did give advisors a hearing of sorts, and there were cases in which he retreated from his most ambitious plans as a result.[24] That the *Dames*, wives and friends of military leaders and courtiers, chosen by the emperor as companions consistently and repeatedly over the course of two decades, did not have some informal influence on imperial choices with regard to both policy and personnel is not credible. The *Dames* recognized the perils of Joseph's hastily organized programs and the strong tincture of sophistry and superficiality in his approach, shortcomings also deplored by well-informed advisors such as Zinzendorf. However, the women neither could nor would offer a systematic critique of policy. This circle of aristocratic women was not able to steer the well-intentioned but headstrong monarch toward circumspection and caution with any greater success than could his official political advisors, ministers, and male courtiers. Until the very end of his life, Joseph typically did hold to a course of action once he had chosen it. Setbacks in his final years and his own ill health did not soften the tone of the emperor's discourse, nor did they break his will or compel him to alter his course until the very last weeks of his life.²⁵ Joseph was arguably the most diligent and energetic of all Habsburg rulers. His biographer Padover is surely correct when he concludes that, compared and contrasted side by side with contemporary German princes, Joseph II stood out "as a man of decency and principles."²⁶ The women had been a friendly voice of caution in this ruler's ear. Except during the most heated discussions concerning religious affairs they had spoken carefully, couching their expressions of concern in words of praise and encouragement that could preserve the emperor's regard and retain his attention. In 1778, when Leopoldine Liechtenstein asked Eleonore Liechtenstein to scold the emperor (*gronder*) about the press's crabbed treatment of Lacy's generalship, which Leopoldine Liechtenstein ascribed to the emperor's own misplaced restraint and modesty, Eleonore said she would do so "with that air of concern and zeal for him that still seems to me to be the best way to induce him to do decent and sensible things."²⁷

Although initially many dismissed his reign as an overall failure the dead emperor's contemporaries, with benefit of hindsight and much like later historians, soon gave Joseph II greater credit for sincere efforts to improve the lives of his subjects, even if all agreed that he tried to do too much too fast.²⁸ Statements of the *Dames* after the emperor's death show how very quickly they recognized the remarkable nature of his reign and his unremitting efforts to better his lands. Leopoldine Liechtenstein, loyal to the emperor despite the ill humor of her friend Lacy, predicted this change in public sentiment very soon after Joseph's death. She believed that harsh feelings would fade quickly, and she defended "the opinion I have always had concerning this dear departed one, concerning his heart, his solid foundation of religion, yes, it has been well demonstrated." She was convinced that already people increasingly regretted his passing. "His intentions were invariably good," she affirmed, "but unfortunately they were often abruptly or badly carried out."²⁹ Leopoldine Liechtenstein saw to it that her daughter, the *Landgräfin* of Hesse-Rheinfels, who was in Paris at the time of the emperor's death, conveyed a message of condolence and esteem to Marie Antoinette, by then a virtual prisoner in the Tuileries. The landgravine reported Marie Antoinette's response: "she commissioned me to tell you [Leopoldine Liechtenstein] that she was quite grateful for the concern you express for her, that it is a consolation to her to know that there are others who share her feelings about her brother."³⁰ Before many years had passed the bungling and inexperience of subsequent Habsburg leadership prompted many additional Habsburg subjects to revise their assessments of Joseph, or at least to express themselves more charitably. As early as June 1791 Eleonore Liechtenstein, who had often found fault with both the style and the substance of her imperial friend's governance, looked back with respect and regret to Joseph's reign. She deplored the inertia and timidity of the new regime, which caused it to stifle discourse among its subjects. "The influence of the government," she wrote to her sister, "must be a great deal stronger than I could ever have imagined, stronger than during the time of this poor departed emperor." The emperor had provoked and exasperated them, but he had also given them "such activity, such spirit, such abundance." "One could not write or speak enough, one was never finished, always a thousand topics remained for another time," Eleonore recollected. "Now there is nothing, there is a sort of general apoplexy, and I who could never stop talking to you . . . I have nothing more to say."[31]

The Five Princesses had not acted as political hostesses fostering discourse and the formation of interest groups among their associates, although they were certainly very active socially, nor had they served as policy advisors. Rather they are best viewed as confidantes to the emperor. The concern that the emperor demonstrated repeatedly to retain the good opinion of these companions, though not necessarily their concurrence in his plans, was evidence of his continuing need to unburden himself before this reliable, sympathetic, and far from sycophantic audience. Joseph's steadfast loyalty to Eleonore and the other *Dames* is so unmistakably evident in letters dating from both the coregency and his sole rule, as well as in his actions, that it really is not open to question. For their parts, even as they excoriated his policy choices the *Dames* often ended by expressing compassion for the temperamental emperor's predicaments, and not only to his face. These relationships withstood the test of time and overcame misunderstandings too numerous to describe. Certainly this was a circle of friends. When Joseph, deathly ill, asked Rosenberg how the little group was faring, Rosenberg answered honestly that it was like a candle that no longer had a wick.[32] In their farewell message to the dying emperor the *Dames* assured him that he had been the soul (*âme*) of the small *société*, whose members would pray for him every day, "a solemn engagement that each of us will keep to our last breath."[33]

Notes

1 Wolf, *Fürstin Eleonore Liechtenstein*, 205.
2 Lukowski, *European Nobility*, 168.
3 A study that focuses on the public-private distinction and the varieties of "sociability" in prerevolutionary Europe is James Van Horn Melton's *The Rise of the Public in Enlightenment Europe* (Cambridge: Cambridge University Press, 2001).
4 Heide Wunder, "Herrschaft und öffentliches Handeln von Frauen in der Gesellschaft der Frühen Neuzeit," in *Frauen in der Geschichte des Rechts*, ed. Ute Gerhard (Munich: C. H. Beck, 1997), 27-54; Katrin Keller, *Hofdamen: Amtsträgerinnen im Wiener Hofstaat des 17. Jahrhunderts* (Vienna: Böhlau, 2005), 9-14; Corinna Heipke, "Landgräfin Karoline of Hessen-Darmstadt: Epistolary Politics and the Problems of Consort Biography," *Biography* 27, no. 3 (2004): 535-36.
5 Concerning traditional aristocratic patronage systems, see Dewald, *The European Nobility*, 41-47; Lutkowski, *European Nobility in the Eighteenth Century*, 38-40.
6 This penchant for favorable publicity is noted in Joseph Karniel, *Die Toleranzpolitik Kaiser Josephs II.* (Gerlingen: Bleicher, 1985), 327, among other sources.

7   Cerman, *Habsburgischer Adel und Aufklärung*, 24.
8   Ligne, *Mémoires et mélanges historiques et littéraires*, 1: 239. "Portrait de Joseph II.," in letter to Catherine II dated 21 February 1790.
9   William D. Godsey, Jr., "Adelsautonomie, Konfession und Nation im österreichischen Absolutismus ca. 1620-1848," *Zeitschrift für historische Forschung* 33, no. 2 (2006): 219-22.
10 Blanning, *Joseph II*, 101; Lukowski, *European Nobility*, 52-56.
11 Cerman, *Habsburgischer Adel und Aufklärung*, 451.
12 Szabo, "Perspective from the Pinnacle: State Chancellor Kaunitz on Nobility in the Habsburg Monarchy," in Gabriele Haug-Moritz, Hans Peter Hye and Marlies Raffler, eds., *Adel im "langen" 18. Jahrhundert* (Vienna: Austrian Academy of Sciences, 2009), 239-60
13 Various reforms summarized in Blanning, *Joseph II*, 107.
14 Leopoldine Kaunitz's father-in-law was the most striking example. James Van Horn Melton, "The Nobility in the Bohemian and Austrian Lands, 1620-1780," in *The European Nobilities in the Seventeenth and Eighteenth Centuries* (New York: Longman, 1995), 2: 110-43.
15 Beales, *Joseph II*, 2: 485, 487.
16 LRRA, P 17/25, EL to LK, Kromau, 9 October 1779.
17 Eleonore's distaste for court life in general began prior to her association with Joseph. As noted by both Wolf and Beales, her outbursts of anger or annoyance were frequent; but she did not withdraw from court life or from the *société*. Beales, *Joseph II*, 2: 443; Wolf, *Fürstin Eleonore Liechtenstein*, 53, 67, 226; LRRA, P 17/26, LK to EL, 28 August, 24 October, and 1 November 1780.
18 LRRA, P 17/27, EL to LK, Meseritsch, 8 August 1781.
19 LRRA, P 17/34, EL to LK, s.l., s.d.
20 Two of Maria Theresia's biographers have even described her as a "man's woman." Edward Crankshaw, *Maria Theresa* (1969; New York: Atheneum, 1986), 110; William J. McGill, *Maria Theresa* (New York: Twayne, 1972), 59.
21 Beales, *Joseph II*, 2: 653; Bérenger, *Joseph II*, 540.
22 Cited in Wolf, *Geschichtliche Bilder aus Österreich*, vol. 2, *Aus dem Zeitalter des Absolutismus und der Aufklärung* (Vienna: Braumüller, 1880), 288-89.
23 Cerman, *Habsburgischer Adel und Aufklärung*, 449.
24 Beales, *Joseph II*, 2: 32, 650-52.
25 HHStA, KA ZT, Band 35, 16 January 1790; Frank Huss, *Die Wiener Kaiserhof: eine Kulturgeschichte von Leopold I. bis Leopold II.* (Gernsbach: Casimir Katz, 2008), 350.
26 Padover, *Joseph II*, 202.
27 LRRA, P 17/24, EL to LK, [Kromau], 3 October 1778.
28 Padover, *Joseph II*, 232.
29 NM, RAŠM, carton 93, LL to unspecified family recipient, Vienna, 1 March 1790.
30 Hausarchiv der regierenden Fürsten von Liechtenstein, Vaduz, carton 234, s.n., Leopoldine von Hesse to LL, [Paris] 17 March [1790].
31 LRRA, P 17/33, EL to LK, Vienna, 4 June 1791.
32 LRRA, P 17/33, LK to EL, Vienna, 23 July 1789 and 28 June 1789. Leopoldine Kaunitz reported Rosenberg's comment.
33 Rodinný Archiv Ditrichštejnů (Dietrichstein), Moravský Zemský Archiv, Brno, G 140, K. 570 Inv.-Nr. 2425, response of the five *Dames* (copy).

Bibliography

Archival sources

Brno, Czech Republic. Rodinný Archiv Ditrichštejnů, Moravský Zemský Archiv. Notes and letters concerning the five *Dames*. G 140, K 570 Inv-Nr. 2425.

Děčín, Czech Republic. Rodinný Archiv Clary-Aldringenů (Teplice), Státní Oblastní Archiv v Litoměřicích, Pobočka Děčín. Personal papers and correspondence (Boxes 54, 64–68, 76).

Edinburgh. Douglas Home Papers, National Archives of Scotland. Lady Mary Coke's journal, volumes 485–501 (1775–1799); personal papers and correspondence of Lady Mary, Boxes 104, 196–97, 199.

Klagenfurt, Austria. Familienarchiv Rosenberg, Kärntner Landesarchiv. Letters to Rosenberg from Maria Theresa and Joseph II, Leopold (as grand duke and emperor). Carton 76, 77, 78, 86.

Nelahozeves, Czech Republic. Lobkovicové Roudničtí Rodinný Archiv. Formerly in the custody of the Státní Oblastní Archiv v Litoměřicích, Pobočka Žitenice. Correspondence of Eleonore Liechtenstein, her family, and her acquaintances (some in fair copies). P 16/4, 7, 11, 18–23, P 17/24–46; P 18/47–61; Q 1/62–74, 85, Q 3/118.

Prague. Rodinný Archiv Metternichů, Státní Ústřední Archiv. Acta Clementina 11/19–24. Letters to Leopoldine Kaunitz from family and acquaintances (including Maria Theresa and Joseph II). Francisco Georgicum 2566 (Leopoldine Kaunitz's audiences with Popes Clement XIII and Clement XIV)

Prague. Rodinný Archiv Šternberk-Manderscheid, Národní Muzeum. Family correspondence of Caroline Liechtenstein *née* Manderscheid (carton 47), Leopoldine Liechtenstein *née* Sternberg (carton 93), papers of Philip Sternberg (cartons 150–55).

Rome. Archivio Segreto Vaticano. Fondo Garampi 282 529r-53lv, 283 21r-23v, 27rv. Correspondence of Giuseppe Garampi with Eleonore Liechtenstein and Leopoldine Kaunitz. Scanned copies provided by the Vatican Archive.

Sigmaringen, Germany. Fürstlich Hohenzollernsches Haus- und Domänenarchiv, Staatsarchiv Sigmaringen. Depositum 39. Bestand: HH1. Rubrik/Nr.: A878, A542, A491. Communications concerning major family events and genealogical documents. Copies provided by Staatsarchiv Sigmaringen.

Vaduz, Liechtenstein. Hausarchiv der Regierenden Fürsten von Liechtenstein. Family documents from cartons 79, 230, 231, 234, 239, 292, 489, 518, 521, 566, 570, 637. Marriage contracts, testaments, correspondence. Copies provided by Liechtenstein Archive in Vaduz.

Vienna. Haus-, Hof- und Staatsarchiv, Österreichisches Staatsarchiv. Habsburgisch-Lothringische Hausarchive (12. Jh.-1918), Hausarchiv, Sammelbände 3, 4, 6, 7, 8, 9, 14, 15, 16, 72; Kabinettsarchiv, Staatsrat, Nachlaß Franz M. Lacy (1741–1795); Grosse Korrespondenz. Kaunitz 405 b, c.

Vienna. Haus-, Hof- und Staatsarchiv. Kabinettsarchiv, Kabinettskanzlei. Zinzendorf Tagebücher, Band 1–57, 1757–1812. Reprosammlungen [microfilm].

Published sources

Arneth, Alfred. "Graf Philipp Cobenzl und seine Memoiren." *Archiv für österreichische Geschichte* 67 (1886): 1–182.

Arneth, Alfred, ed. *Joseph II. und Katharina von Russland: ihr Briefwechsel.* 1869. Osnabrück: Biblio-Verlag, 1973.

Arneth, Alfred, ed. *Joseph II. und Leopold von Toscana: ihr Briefwechsel von 1781 bis 1790*. Vienna: W. Braumüller, 1872.

Arneth, Alfred. "Maria Theresia und der Hofrath von Greiner [with correspondence]." *Sitzungsberichte der Kaiserlichen Akademie der Wissenschaften, Philosophisch-Historische Klasse* 30 (1859): 307–378.

Bystrický, Vladimir. "Zprávy vyslanců Rýnské Falce a Bavorska ve Vídni o nevolnickém povstání v Čechách roku 1775." *Sbornik Archivnich Praci* 42, no. 1 (1992): 3–32.

Chesterfield, Philip Dormer Stanhope. *The Letters of Philip Dormer Stanhope, 4th Earl of Chesterfield*, edited by Bonamy Dobrée, vols. 5 and 6. New York: AMS Press, 1932.

Coke, Lady Mary. *The Letters and Journals of Lady Mary Coke*. 4 vols. 1889–1896. Reprint. Bath: Kingsmead Reprints, 1970.

De Luca, Ignaz. *Das gelehrte Oesterreich*. Vienna: Ghelen, 1776.

De Luca, Ignaz. *Topographie von Wien*. Vol. 1. Facsimile reprint. Vienna: Promedia, 2003. Originally published Vienna: Thad. Edlen v. Schmidbauer, 1794.

Du Montet, Alexandrine. *Souvenirs de la baronne du Montet, 1785–1866*. Paris: Plon-Nourrit, 1914.

Elisabeth of Württemberg. "Briefe an Erzherzog Franz (nachmals K. Franz II.) von seiner ersten Gemahlin Elisabeth, 1785-1789." Edited by H. Weyda. *Archiv für österreichische Geschichte* 44 (1871): iii–xviii, 1–262.

Esterházy, Valentin. *Mémoires du Cte Valentin Esterházy.* Edited by Ernest Daudet. Paris: Plon-Nourrit, 1905.

Esterházy, Valentin. *Lettres du Cte Valentin Esterházy à sa femme, 1784–1792.* Edited by Ernest Daudet. Paris: Plon-Nourrit, 1907.

Esterházy, Valentin. *Nouvelles lettres du Cte Valentin Esterházy à sa femme, 1792–1795.* Edited by Ernest Daudet. Paris: Plon-Nourrit, 1909.

Georgel, Jean François. *Mémoires pour servir à l'histoire des événemens de la fin du dix-huitième siècle depuis 1760 jusqu'en 1806–1810 par un contemporain impartial (feu M. l'abbé Georgel).* Paris: Alexis Eymery, 1817.

Guibert, Jacques Antoine Hippolyte. *Journal d'un voyage en allemagne fait en 1773.* 2 vols. Paris: Treuttel et Würtz, 1803.

Hamilton, William. *The Hamilton Letters: The Naples Dispatches of Sir William Hamilton.* Edited by John A. Davis and Giovanni Capuano. London: I. B. Tauris, 2008.

Karajan, Theodor Georg von. *Maria Theresia und Joseph II. während der Mitregentschaft: ein Vortrag gehalten in der feierlichen Sitzung der Kaiserlichen Akademie der Wissenschaften* [Letters of Maria Theresa, Joseph II, Chancellor Kaunitz]. Vienna: K. K. Hof- und Staatsdr., 1865. 28–39.

Kaunitz, Wenzel Anton. "Denkschriften des Fürsten Wenzel Kaunitz-Rittberg." Edited by Adolf Beer. *Archiv für österreichischen Geschichte* 48 (1872): 1–162.

Keith, Robert Murray. *Memoirs and Correspondence.* 2 vols. Edited by Gillespie Smyth. London: Henry Colburn, 1849.

Khevenhüller-Metsch, Johann Josef. *Aus der Zeit Maria Theresias. Tagebuch des Fürsten Johann Josef Khevenhüller-Metsch.* 7 vols. Vienna: Adolf Holzhausen, 1907–1925.

Khevenhüller-Metsch, Johann Josef. *Aus der Zeit Maria Theresias. Tagebuch des Fürsten Johann Josef Khevenhüller-Metsch. 1774–1776 und Nachträge.* Edited by Maria Breunlich-Pawlik and Hans Wagner. Vienna: Adolf Holzhausens, 1972.

Kotasek, Edith, ed. "Die Privatkorrespondenz des Feldmarschalls Grafen Lacy mit Maria Theresia und Joseph II." *Mitteilungen des Österreichischen Staatsarchivs* 4 (1951): 167–183.

Lacy, Franz Moritz. "Les correspondants du Prince: le Maréchal de Lacy," *Annales Prince de Ligne* 4, no. 14 (April-June 1923), 140–141; 4, no. 15 (July-September 1923), 175–180; 4, no. 16 (October-December 1923), 223–229; 5, no. 17 (January-March 1924), 30–33; 5, no. 18 (April-June 1924), 98–104; 6, nos. 22-23 (April-September 1925), 259–262; 6, no. 24 (October-December 1925), 322–324.

Lacy, Franz Moritz. "29 lettres inédites du maréchal de Lacy au prince de Ligne." Edited by Georges Englebert. *Nouvelles annales Prince de Ligne* 4 (1989): 7–72.

Lamberg, Max. *Casanova und Graf Lamberg. Unveröffentlichte Briefe des Grafen Max Lamberg an Casanova aus dem Schloßarchiv in Dux.* Edited by Gustav Gugitz. Vienna: Bernina, 1935.

Leopold II. *Leopold II. und Marie Christine: ihr Briefwechsel (1781–1792).* Edited by Adam Wolf. Vienna: Carl Gerold's Sohn, 1867.

Ligne, Charles Joseph. *Fragments de l'histoire de ma vie. L'âge de lumières, 6.* 2 vols. Edited by Jeroom Vercruysse. Paris: H. Champion, 2000–2001.

Ligne, Charles Joseph. *Mémoires et mélanges historiques et littéraires.* 5 vols. Paris: Ambroise Dupont, 1827–1829.

Maaß, Ferdinand. *Der Josephinismus: Quellen zu seiner Geschichte in Österreich 1760–1790.* Fontes rerum Austriacarum, 2. Abt., Diplomataria et acta 72 (1953).

Maria Theresia. *Maria Theresia und Marie Antoinette.* Edited by Alfred von Arneth. 2nd ed. Leipzig: K. F. Köhler, 1866.

Maria Theresia. "Zwei Denkschriften der Kaiserin Maria Theresia." Edited by Alfred von Arneth. *Archiv für österreichische Geschichte* 47 (1871): 267–354.

Maria Theresia. *Politisches Testament.* Edited by Josef Kallbrunner. Vienna: Verlag für Geschichte und Politik, 1952.

Maria Theresia. *Briefe der Kaiserin Maria Theresia an ihre Kinder und Freunde.* Edited by Alfred von Arneth. 4 vols. 1881. Reprint, Osnabrück: Biblio Verlag, 1978.

Maria Theresia. *Maria Theresia und Joseph II.: ihre Correspondenz sammt Briefen Joseph's an seinen Bruder Leopold.* Edited by Alfred von Arneth. 3 vols. Vienna: C. Gerold's Sohn, 1867–68.

Marie Antoinette. *Marie Antoinette, Joseph II. und Leopold II.: ihr Briefwechsel.* Edited by Alfred Arneth. Leipzig: K. F. Köhler, 1866.

Marie Antoinette. *Correspondance secrète entre Marie-Thérèse et le comte de Mercy-Argenteau, avec les lettres de Marie-Thérèse et de Marie-Antoinette.* 3 vols. Edited by Alfred von Arneth and A. Geffroy. 2nd ed. Paris: Firmin-Didot, 1874–1875.

Mercy-Argenteau, Florimond-Claude. *Correspondance secrète du comte de Mercy-Argenteau avec l'empereur Joseph II et le prince de Kaunitz.* 2 vols. Edited by Alfred Arneth. Paris: Imprimerie Nationale, 1889–1891.

Metternich-Winneburg, Clemens Lothar Wenzel. *Mémoires, documents et écrits divers laissés par le prince de Metternich, chancelier de cour et d'état.* Vol. 1. R. C. L. Metternich, 1879.

Moore, John. *A View of Society and Manners in France, Switzerland, and Germany.* 2 vols. 5th ed. London: W. Strahan and T. Cadell, 1783.

Olaechea, Raphael. "Kaiser Joseph II. vor der Frage eines Schismas." *Zeitschrift für katholische Theologie* 80 (1958): 410–420.
Die österreichische Zentralverwaltung. Abteilung 2, Band 4. Die Zeit Josephs II. und Leopolds II. (1780–1792). Edited by Friedrich Walter. Veröffentlichungen der Kommission für Neuere Geschichte Österreichs 36. Vienna: Adolf Holzhausens Nachfolger, 1950.
Paget, Arthur. *The Paget Papers: Diplomatic and Other Correspondence of the Right Hon. Sir Arthur Paget, G.C.B., 1794–1807.* Edited by Augustus B. Paget. 2 vols. London: Heinemann, 1896.
Perey, Lucien. *Histoire d'une grande dame au XVIIIe siècle: la Princesse Hélène de Ligne.* Paris: Calmann Lévy, 1888.
Podewils, Otto Christoph von. *Friedrich der Grosse und Maria Theresia: Diplomatische Berichte von Otto Christoph Graf v. Podewils.* Edited by Carl Hinrichs. Berlin: R. V. Decker, 1937.
Swinburne, Henry. *The Courts of Europe at the Close of the Last Century.* Vol. 1. 1841. London: H. S. Nichols, 1895.
Tanucci, Bernardo. *Epistolario, 1723–1768.* Vol. 12. Rome: Edizioni di storia e letteratura, 1997.
Thürheim, Lulu. *Mein Leben: Erinnerungen aus Österreichs grosser Welt, 1788–1819.* Vol. 1. Munich: Georg Müller, 1913.
Toegel, Miroslav, et al., eds. *Prameny k nevolnickému povstání v Čechách a na Moravě v roce 1775.* Prague: Akademia, 1975.
Trench, Melesina Chenevix.. *Journal Kept During a Visit to Germany in 1799, 1800.* London: Savill and Edwards, 1861.
Wienerisches Diarium and *Wiener Zeitung*, 1760–1790.
Wraxall, Nathaniel W. *Memoirs of the Courts of Berlin, Dresden, Warsaw, and Vienna, in the Years 1777, 1778, and 1779.* Vol. 2. London: T. Cadell Jun. and W. Davies, 1799.
Zinzendorf, Karl. *Aus den Jugendtagebüchern: 1747, 1752 bis 1763.* Edited by Hans Wagner, Maria Breunlich, and Marieluise Mader. Vienna: Böhlau, 1997.
Zinzendorf, Karl. *Europäische Aufklärung zwischen Wien und Triest: die Tagebücher des Gouverneurs Karl Graf Zinzendorf, 1776–1782.* 4 vols. Vienna: Böhlau, 2009.
Zinzendorf, Karl. *Journal, chronique belgo-bruxelloise, 1766–1770.* Edited by Georges Englebert. Brussels: Hayez, 1991.
Zinzendorf, Karl. Wagner, Hans, ed. *Wien von Maria Theresia bis zur Franzosenzeit: aus den Tagebüchern des Grafen Karl von Zinzendorf.* Vienna: Wiener Bibliophilen Gesellschaft, 1972.
Zorn von Bulach, Anton Joseph. *L'ambassade du prince Louis de Rohan à la cour de Vienna 1771–1774.* Reprint. Strasbourg: G. Fischbach, 1901.

Select Secondary Sources

This select list is confined to works that were particularly useful in depicting the activities of the women and their associates or the political and social background against which these activities occurred. A fuller list of literature consulted can be found in the endnotes.

Ammerer, Gerhard. *Das Ende für Schwert und Galgen? legislativer Prozess und öffentlicher Diskurs zur Reduzierung der Todesstrafe im Ordentlichen Verfahren unter Joseph II. (1781–1787)*. Innsbruck: Studien Verlag, 2010.

Ammerer, Gerhard, and Hanns Haas, eds. *Ambivalenzen der Aufklärung: Festschrift für Ernst Wangermann*. Munich: R. Oldenbourg, 1997.

Arneth, Alfred. *Geschichte Maria Theresia's*. 10 vols. Vienna: Wilhelm Braumüller, 1863–1879.

Asch, Ronald G., ed. *Der europäische Adel im Ancien Régime: von der Krise der ständischen Monarchien bis zur Revolution (ca. 1600–1789)*. Köln: Böhlau, 2001.

Austria in the Age of the French Revolution, 1789–1815. Edited by Kinley Brauer and William E. Wright. Minneapolis: Center for Austrian Studies, University of Minnesota, 1990.

Barton, Peter F., ed. *Im Lichte der Toleranz: Aufsätze zur Toleranzgesetzgebung des 18. Jahrhunderts in den Reichen Joseph II., ihren Voraussetzungen und ihren Folgen*. Vienna: Institut für Protestantische Kirchengeschichte, 1981.

Barton, Peter F., ed. *Im Zeichen der Toleranz: Aufsätze zur Toleranzgesetzgebung des 18. Jahrhunderts im Reiche Joseph II*. Vienna: Institut für Protestantische Kirchengeschichte, 1981.

Beales, Derek. *Enlightenment and Reform in 18th-Century Europe*. London: I. B. Tauris, 2005.

Beales, Derek. *Joseph II*. 2 vols. Cambridge: Cambridge University Press, 1987–2009.

Bérenger, Jean. *Joseph II: serviteur de l'état*. Paris: Fayard, 2007.

Bernard, Paul P. "The Emperor's Friend: Joseph II and Field Marshal Lacy." Pt. 1. *East European Quarterly* 10, no. 4 (1976): 401–408.

Bernard, Paul P. *Jesuits and Jacobins: Enlightenment and Enlightened Despotism in Austria*. Urbana, IL: University of Illinois Press, 1971.

Bernard, Paul P. *Joseph II*. New York: Twayne, 1968.

Bernard, Paul P. *Joseph II and Bavaria: Two Eighteenth-Century Attempts at German Unification*. The Hague: Martinus Nijhoff, 1965. http://dx.doi.org/10.1007/978-94-015-7575-1.

Bernard, Paul P. *The Limits of Enlightenment: Joseph II and the Law*. Urbana: University of Illinois Press, 1979.

Blanning, T. C. W. *Joseph II and Enlightened Despotism*. London: Longman, 1970.
Blanning, T. C. W. *Joseph II*. Profiles in Power. London: Longman, 1994.
Bled, Jean-Paul. *Marie-Thérèse d'Autriche*. Paris: Fayard, 2001.
Bodi, Leslie. *Tauwetter in Wien: zur Prosa der österreichischen Aufklärung 1781–1795*. Schriftenreihe der Österreichischen Gesellschaft zur Erforschung des 18. Jahrhunderts 6. 2nd ed. Vienna: Böhlau, 1995.
Cerman, Ivo. *Habsburgischer Adel und Aufklärung: Bildungsverhalten des Wiener Hofadels im 18. Jahrhundert*. Stuttgart: Franz Steiner, 2010.
Cerman, Ivo, Rita Krueger, and Susan Reynolds, eds. *The Enlightenment in Bohemia*. Oxford: Voltaire Foundation, University of Oxford, 2011.
Chadwick, Owen. *The Popes and European Revolution*. Oxford: Clarendon Press, 1981.
Clary-Aldringen, Alfons. *A European Past: Memoirs*. Translated by Ewald Osers. London: Weidenfeld and Nicolson, 1978.
Criste, Oskar. *Feldmarschall Johannes Fürst von Liechtenstein. Eine Biographie*. Vienna: Gesellschaft für Neuere Geschichte Österreichs, 1905.
Criste, Oskar. *Kriege unter Kaiser Josef II. Nach den Feldakten und anderen authentischen Quellen*. Vienna: L. W. Seidel, 1904.
Dewald, Jonathan. *The European Nobility, 1400–1800*. New Approaches to European History 9. New York: Cambridge University Press, 1996.
Dickson, P. G. M. (Peter George Muir). *Finance and Government under Maria Theresia, 1740–1780*. 2 vols. New York: Oxford University Press, 1987.
Diemel, Christa. *Adelige Frauen im bürgerlichen Jahrhundert: Hofdamen, Stiftsdamen, Salondamen 1800–1870*. Frankfurt am Main: Fischer Taschenbuch, 1998.
Duffy, Christopher. *The Army of Maria Theresa: The Armed Forces of Imperial Austria, 1740–1780*. New York: Hippocrene Books, 1977.
Duffy, Christopher. *The Instruments of War*. Vol. 1. The Austrian Army in the Seven Years War. Rosemont, IL: Emperor's Press, 2000.
Duffy, Christopher. *The Military Experience in the Age of Reason*. 1987. Ware, Hertfordshire: Wordsworth, 1998.
Duindam, Jeroen. *Myths of Power: Norbert Elias and the Early Modern European Court*. Amsterdam: Amsterdam University Press, 1994.
Duindam, Jeroen. *Vienna and Versailles: The Courts of Europe's Dynastic Rivals, 1550–1780*. New Studies in European History. New York: Cambridge University Press, 2003.
Eberhart, Helmut. "Magna Mater Austriae: zur Wallfahrtsgeschichte von Mariazell von der Gründung bis in das 19. Jahrhundert." In *Schatz und Schicksal: Steirische Landesausstellung 1996: Mariazell und Neuberg an der Mürz, 4.*

Mai bis 27. Oktober. Edited by Ileane Schwarzkogler. Mariazell: Kulturreferat der Steiermärkischen Landesregierung, 1996, 23–34.

Ehalt, Hubert Christian. *Ausdrucksformen absolutistischer Herrschaft: der Wiener Hof im 17. und 18. Jahrhundert.* Vienna: Verlag für Geschichte und Politik, 1980.

Elias, Norbert. *The Civilizing Process.* Translated by Edmund Jephcott. 1939. Revised edition. Malden, MA: Blackwell, 2000.

Eltz, Erwein H., and Arno Strohmeyer, eds. *Die Fürstenberger: 800 Jahre Herrschaft und Kultur in Mitteleuropa.* Korneuburg: Ueberreuter, 1994.

Evans, Robert John Weston. *The Making of the Habsburg Monarchy, 1550–1700.* New York: Oxford University Press, 1979.

Falke, Jacob von. *Geschichte des fürstlichen Hauses Liechtenstein.* 3 vols. Vienna: W. Braumüller, 1868–1882.

Feigl, Helmuth, and Willibald Rosner, eds. *Adel im Wandel: Vorträge und Diskussionen des elften Symposions des Niederösterreichischen Instituts für Landeskunde, Horn, 2.-5. Juli 1990.* Studien und Forschungen aus dem Niederösterreichischen Institut für Landeskunde 15. Vienna: NÖ Institut für Landeskunde, 1991.

Fejtö, François. *Joseph II: un Habsbourg révolutionnaire.* New edition. Paris: Quai Voltaire, 1994.

Folkmann, Josef Erwin. *Die gefürstete Linie des uralten und edlen Geschlechtes Kinsky: ein geschichtlicher Versuch.* Prague: K. André, 1861.

Gampl, Inge. *Adelige Damenstifte: Untersuchungen zur Entstehung adeliger Damenstifte in Österreich unter besonderer Berücksichtigung der alten Kanonissenstifte Deutschlands und Lothringens.* Wiener Rechtsgeschichtliche Arbeiten 5. Vienna: Verlag Herold, 1960.

Godsey, William D. "Adelsautonomie, Konfession und Nation im österreichischen Absolutismus ca. 1620-1848." *Zeitschrift für historische Forschung* 33, no. 2 (2006): 197–239.

Godsey, William D. "Nobles and Modernity [review article]." *German History* 20, no. 4 (2002): 504–521.

Godsey, William D. "Vom Stiftsadel zum Uradel. Die Legitimationskrise des Adels und die Entstehung eines neuen Adelsbegriffs im Übergang." In *Eliten um 1800: Erfahrungshorizonte, Verhaltensweisen, Handlungsmöglichkeiten,* edited by Anja Victorine Hartmann, Malgorzata Morawiec, and Peter Voss. Mainz: Philipp von Zabern, 2000, 371–391.

Goodman, Dena. "Public Sphere and Private Life: Toward a Synthesis of Current Historiographical Approaches to the Old Regime." *History and Theory* 31, no. 1 (1992): 1–20. http://dx.doi.org/10.2307/2505605.

Goodwin, Albert, ed. *The European Nobility in the Eighteenth Century: Studies of the Nobilities of the Major European States in the Pre-Reform Era*. New York: Harper and Row, 1967.

Grünberg, Karl. *Die Bauernbefreiung und die Auflösung des gutsherrlich-bäuerlichen Verhältnisses in Böhmen*. 2 vols. Leipzig: Duncker & Humblot, 1894.

Guglia, Eugen. *Maria Theresia: ihr Leben und ihre Regierung*. 2 vols. Munich: R. Oldenbourg, 1917.

Gutkas, Karl. *Kaiser Joseph II.: eine Biographie*. Vienna: Paul Zsolnay, 1989.

Habermas, Jürgen. *The Structural Transformation of the Public Sphere: An Inquiry into a Category of Bourgeois Society*. Translated by Thomas Burger. Cambridge, MA: MIT Press, 1984.

Hassenpflug-Elzholz, Eila. *Böhmen und die böhmischen Stände in der Zeit des beginnenden Zentralismus: eine Strukturanalyse der böhmischen Adelsnation um die Mitte des 18. Jahrhunderts*. Munich: R. Oldenbourg, 1982.

Haug-Moritz, Gabriele, Hans Peter Hye, and Marlies Raffler, eds. *Adel im "langen" 18. Jahrhundert*. Vienna: Austrian Academy of Sciences, 2009. 239–260.

Hersche, Peter. "War Maria Theresia eine Jansenistin?" *Österreich in Geschichte und Literatur* 15, no. 1 (1971): 14–25.

Hersche, Peter. *Der Spätjansenismus in Österreich*. Veröffentlichungen der Kommission für Geschichte Österreichs 7. Vienna: Österreichische Akademie der Wissenschaften, 1977.

Höbelt, Lothar. "The Discreet Charm of the Old Regime." *Austrian History Yearbook* 27 (1996): 289–302. http://dx.doi.org/10.1017/S0067237800005919.

Hochedlinger, Michael. *Austria's Wars of Emergence: War, State, and Society in the Habsburg Monarchy 1683–1797*. Modern Wars in Perspective. London: Pearson Education, 2003.

Hochedlinger, Michael. "'. . . Dass Aufklärung das sicherste Mittel ist, die Ruhe und Anhänglichkeit der Unterthanen zu befestigen': Staatskanzler Kaunitz und die 'franziszeische Reaktion' 1792–1794." *Aufklärung—Vormärz—Revolution* 16/17 (1996/1997), 62–79.

Hochedlinger, Michael. "'La cause de tous les maux de la France': die 'Austrophobie' im revolutionären Frankreich und der Sturz des Königtums 1789–1792." *Francia: Part 2 Frühe Neuzeit* 24, no. 2 (1997): 73–120.

Hochedlinger, Michael. "Who's Afraid of the French Revolution? Austrian Foreign Policy and the European Crisis 1787-1797." *German History* 21, no. 3 (2003): 293–318. http://dx.doi.org/10.1191/0266355403gh286oa.

Hock, Carl von and Hermann Ignaz Bidermann. *Der österreichische Staatsrath, 1760–1848*. Vienna: H. Geyer, 1879, reprint, Vienna: W. Braumüller, 1972.

Hoppe, Bernhard M. *Predigtkritik im Josephinismus: die 'Wöchentlichen Wahrheiten für und über die Prediger in Wien' (1782–1784)*. St. Ottilien: EOS, 1989.

Hunt, Margaret R. *Women in Eighteenth-Century Europe*. Harlow, UK: Pearson Longman, 2010.

Ingrao, Charles W. *The Habsburg Monarchy 1618–1815*. New Approaches to History. 2nd ed. New York: Cambridge University Press, 2000.

Ingrao, Charles W., ed. *State and Society in Early Modern Austria*. West Lafayette, IN: Purdue University Press, 1994.

Israel, Jonathan E. *Democratic Enlightenment: Philosophy, Revolution, and Human Rights 1750–1790*. Oxford: Oxford University Press, 2011.

Jäger-Sunstenau, Hanns. "Über das Hineinwachsen des Hauses Liechtenstein in den höchsten Fürstenadel Europas." *Adler. Zeitschrift für Genealogie und Heraldik* 17 (1993–1994): 289–296.

Kallenberg, Fritz, ed. *Hohenzollern*. Schriften zur politischen Landeskunde Baden-Württembergs, 23. Stuttgart: Kohlhammer, 1996.

Kann, Robert A. "Aristocracy in the Eighteenth-Century Habsburg Empire." *East European Quarterly* 7, no. 1 (1973): 1–13.

Karniel, Joseph. *Die Toleranzpolitik Kaiser Josephs II*. Translated from Hebrew by Leo Koppel. Gerlingen: Bleicher, 1985.

Kerner, Robert. *Bohemia in the Eighteenth Century: A Study in Political, Economic, and Social History, with Special Reference to the Reign of Leopold II, 1790–1792*. New York: AMS Press, 1969.

Klingenstein, Grete. *Der Aufstieg des Hauses Kaunitz*. Schriftenreihe der Historischen Kommission bei der Bayerischen Akademie der Wissenschaften, 12. Göttingen: Vandenhoeck & Ruprecht, 1975.

Klingenstein, Grete. "Modes of Religious Tolerance and Intolerance in Eighteenth-Century Habsburg Politics." *Austrian History Yearbook* 24 (1993): 1–16. http://dx.doi.org/10.1017/S0067237800005233.

Klingenstein, Grete, and Franz A. J. Szabo, eds. *Staatskanzler Wenzel Anton von Kaunitz-Rietberg 1711–1794: neue Perspektiven zu Politik und Kultur der europäischen Aufklärung*. Graz: Andreas Schnider, 1996.

Koschatzky, Walter, ed. *Maria Theresia und ihre Zeit: eine Darstellung der Epoche von 1740–1780 aus Anlass der 200. Wiederkehr des Todestages der Kaiserin*. Salzburg: Residenz Verlag, 1979.

Kotasek, Edith. *Feldmarschall Graf Lacy: ein Leben für Österreichs Heer*. Horn, Austria: F. Berger, 1956.

Kovács, Elisabeth. "Am Schisma vorbei. Zu den Ergebnissen der Reise Pius' VI. im Jahre 1782." *Österreich in Geschichte und Literatur* 28 no. 3 (1984): 149–154.

Kovács, Elisabeth, ed. *Katholische Aufklärung und Josephinismus*. Vienna: Verlag für Geschichte und Politik, 1979.

Kovács, Elisabeth. *Der Pabst in Teutschland: die Reise Pius VI. im Jahre 1782*. Munich: R. Oldenbourg, 1983.

Kovács, Elisabeth. *Ultramontanismus und Staatskirchentum im theresianisch-josephinischen Staat: der Kampf der Kardinäle Migazzi und Franckenberg gegen den Wiener Professor der Kirchengeschichte Ferdinand Stöger*. Vienna: Wiener Dom-Verlag, 1975.

Krueger, Rita. *Czech, German, and Noble: Status and National Identity in Habsburg Bohemia*. New York: Oxford University Press, 2009. http://dx.doi.org/10.1093/acprof:oso/9780195323450.001.0001.

Küppers-Braun, Ute. *Frauen des hohen Adels im kaiserlich-freiweltlichen Damenstift Essen (1605–1803)*. Quellen und Studien 8. Veröffentlichungen des Instituts für kirchengeschichtliche Forschung des Bistums Essen. Münster: Aschendorff, 1997.

Küppers-Braun, Ute. *Macht in Frauenhand: 1000 Jahre Herrschaft adeliger Frauen in Essen*. Essen: Universität Gesamthochschule Essen, 2002.

Landes, Joan B. *Women and the Public Sphere in the Age of the French Revolution.*. Ithaca: Cornell University Press, 1988.

Lebeau, Christine. *Aristocrates et grands commis à la cour de Vienne (1748–1791): le modèle français*. Paris: CNRS Éditions, 1996.

Lettner, Gerda. *Das Rückzugsgefecht der Aufklärung in Wien 1790–1792*. Frankfurt am Main: Campus Verlag, 1988.

Link, Edith Murr. *The Emancipation of the Austrian Peasant, 1740–1798.* 1949. New York: Octagon Books, 1974.

Lukowski, Jerzy. *The European Nobility in the Eighteenth Century*. New York: Palgrave Macmillan, 2003.

Lütge, Friedrich. "Die Robot-Abolition und Kaiser Joseph II." In *Wege und Forschungen der Agrargeschichte: Festschrift zum 65. Geburtstag von Günther Franz*. Edited by Heinz Haushofer and Willi A. Boelcke. Frankfurt am Main: DLG-Verlag, 1967. 153–170.

Macartney, Carlile Aylmer, ed. *The Habsburg and Hohenzollern Dynasties in the Seventeenth and Eighteenth Centuries*. New York: Walker, 1970.

Macho, Eva. *Joseph II., die "Condemnatio ad poenas extraordinarias": Schiffziehen und Gassenkehren*. Frankfurt am Main: P. Lang, 1999.

Die Manderscheider: eine Eifeler Adeslfamilie. Herrschaft, Wirtschaft, Kultur. Katalog zur Austellung, Blankenheim, Gildehaus, 4. Mai-29. Juli 1990. Manderscheid, Kurhaus, 16. August-11. November 1990. Köln: Rheinland-Verlag, 1990.

Mansel, Philip. *Prince of Europe: The Life of Charles-Joseph de Ligne, 1735–1814*. London: Weidenfeld and Nicolson, 2003.

Mat'a, Petr, and Thomas Winkelbauer, eds. *Die Habsburgermonarchie 1620 bis 1740*. Stuttgart: Franz Steiner, 2006.

Mayer, Matthew Z. "The Price for Austria's Security: Part I. Joseph II, the Russian Alliance, and the Ottoman War, 1787-1789." *International History Re-*

view 26, no. 2 (2004): 257–299. http://dx.doi.org/10.1080/07075332.2004.9641031.

Mayer, Matthew Z. "The Price for Austria's Security: Part II. Leopold II, the Prussian Threat, and the Peace of Sistova, 1790-1791." *International History Review* 26, no. 3 (2004): 473–514. http://dx.doi.org/10.1080/07075332.2004.9641037.

Melton, James Van Horn. *The Rise of the Public in Enlightenment Europe*. New York: Cambridge University Press, 2001. http://dx.doi.org/10.1017/CBO9780511819421.

Meyer, Jean. *Noblesses et pouvoirs dans l'Europe d'Ancien Régime*. Paris: Hachette, 1973.

Mikoletzky, Lorenz. "'Der Bauern Gott, der Bürger Not, des Adels Spott liegt auf den Tod': Kaiser Josephs II. langes Sterben aus eigener und fremder Sicht." *Mitteilungen des Österreichischen Staatsarchivs* 39 (1986): 16–30.

Mitrofanov, Pavel. *Josef II. Seine politische und kulturelle Tätigkeit*. 2 vols. Vienna: C. W. Stern, 1910.

Nosinich, J. "Kaiser Josef II. als Staatsmann und Feldherr. Österreichs Politik und Kriege in den Jahren 1763 bis 1790; zugleich Vorgeschichte zu den Kriegen Österreichs gegen die französische Revolution." *Mitteilungen des K.K. Kriegs-Archivs*, 1882. 219–288, 349–416; 1883, 1–109, 131–179. Fifth and concluding part by L. Wiener, *Mitteilungen des K.K. Kriegs-Archivs*, 1885. 74–145.

Novotny, Alexander. *Staatskanzler Kaunitz als geistige Persönlichkeit: ein österreichisches Kulturbild aus der Zeit der Aufklärung und des Josephinismus*. Vienna: Hollinek, 1947.

O'Brien, Charles H. "Jansenists and Josephinism: 'Nouvelles ecclésiastiques' and Reform of the Church in Late Eighteenth-Century Austria." *Mitteilungen des Österreichischen Staatsarchivs* 32 (1979): 143–164.

Oberhammer, Evelin, ed. *Der Ganzen Welt ein Lob und Spiegel: das Fürstenhaus Liechtenstein in der frühen Neuzeit*. Vienna: Verlag für Geschichte und Politik, 1990.

Österreich zur Zeit Kaiser Josephs II.: Mitregent Kaiserin Maria Theresias, Kaiser und Landesfürst. Ausstellung, Stift Melk, 29. März-2. Nov. 1980. Vienna: Amt der Niederösterrischen Landesregierung, Abt. 3/2, Kulturabt., 1980.

Padover, Saul K. *The Revolutionary Emperor, Joseph II of Austria*. Rev. ed. Hamden, CT: Archon Books, 1967.

Pangerl, Irmgard, Marin Scheutz, and Thomas Winkelbauer, eds. *Der Wiener Hof im Spiegel der Zeremonialprotokolle (1652–1800): eine Annäherung*. Innsbruck: Studien Verlag, 2007.

Pasteur, Claude. *Le prince de Ligne: l'enchanteur de l'Europe*. Paris: Librairie académique Perrin, 1980.

Pawlik, Hans. *Orsini-Rosenberg: Geschichte und Genealogie eines alten Adelsgeschlechts*. Klagenfurt: Geschichtsverein für Kärnten, 2009.

Pekacz, Jolanta T. *Conservative Tradition in Pre-Revolutionary France: Parisian Salon Women*. New York: Peter Lang, 1999.

Pfeifer, Wilhelm. *Das Fürstenhaus Liechtenstein in Nordböhmen*. Backnang: Niederlandverlag H. Michel, 1984.

Plaschka, Richard Georg, Grete Klingenstein, Otto Drischel, Gernot Heiss, Karlheinz Mack, Helmut Reinalter, Karl Vocelka, Erich Zöllner, eds. *Österreich im Europa der Aufklärung: Kontinuität und Zäsur in Europa zur Zeit Maria Theresias und Josephs II. Internationales Symposion in Wien 20.-23. Oktober 1980*. 2 vols. Vienna: Verlag der Österreichischen Akademie der Wissenschaften, 1985.

Pohl, Nicole. "'Perfect Reciprocity': Salon Culture and Epistolary Conversation." *Women's Writing* 13, no. 1 (2006): 139–159. http://dx.doi.org/10.1080/09699080500436265.

Press, Volker and Dietmar Willoweit. *Liechtenstein, fürstliches Haus und staatliche Ordnung: geschichtliche Grundlagen und moderne Perspektiven*. Munich, Vienna: R. Oldenbourg Verlag, 1988.

Reinalter, Helmut. *Am Hofe Josephs II*. Leipzig: Edition Leipzig, 1991.

Roider, Karl A. "Kaunitz, Joseph II and the Turkish War." *Slavonic and East European Review* 54, no. 4 (1976): 538–556.

Roos, Harke de. *Mozart und seine Kaiser*. Berlin: Ries und Erler, 2005.

Rozdolski, Roman. *Die Grosse Steuer- und Agrarreform Josefs II*. Warsaw: Państwowe Wydawnictwo Naukowe, 1961.

Sashegyi, Oszkár. *Zensur und Geistesfreiheit unter Joseph II: Beitrag zur Kulturgeschichte der habsburgishen Länder*. Budapest: Akadémiai Kiadó, 1958.

Schlitter, Hanns. *Pius VI. und Josef II. von der Rückkehr des Papstes nach Rom bis zum Abschlusse des Concordats: ein Beitrag zur Geschichte der Beziehungen Josefs II. zur römischen Curie von 1782 bis 1784*. Fontes Rerum Austriacarum. Dipomataria et Acta 47 pt. 2. Vienna: F. Tempsky, 1894.

Schlitter, Hanns. *Die Reise des Papstes Pius VI. nach Wien und sein Aufenthalt daselbst: ein Beitrag zur Geschichte der Beziehungen Josefs II. zur römischen Curie*. Fontes Rerum Austriacarum. Diplomataria et Acta 47 pt. 1. Vienna: F. Tempsky, 1892.

Schmal, Kerstin. *Die Pietas Maria Theresias im Spannungsfeld von Barock und Aufklärung: religiöse Praxis und Sendungsbewußtsein gegenüber Familie, Untertanen und Dynastie*. Mainzer Studien zur Neueren Geschichte 7. Frankfurt am Main: Peter Lang, 2001.

Schöpfer, Gerald. *Klar und Fest: Geschichte des Hauses Liechtenstein*. 2nd. ed. Graz: Arbeitsgemeinschaft für Wirtschafts- und Sozialgeschichte, 1996.

Scott, H. M., ed. *The European Nobilities in the Seventeenth and Eighteenth Centuries*. 2 vols. New York: Longman, 1995.

Smíšková, Helena. "Rodinný archiv Clary-Aldringenů, Teplice." *Archivní časopis* 55, no. 2 (2005): 117–126.

Stekl, Hannes. *Österreichs Aristokratie im Vormärz: Herrschaftsstil und Lebensformen der Fürstenhäuser Liechtenstein und Schwarzenberg*. Munich: Oldenbourg, 1973.

Strakosch, Henry E. *State Absolutism and the Rule of Law: The Struggle for the Codification of Civil Law in Austria 1753–1811*. Sydney: Sydney University Press, 1967.

Szabo, Franz A. J. "Between Privilege and Professionalism: The Career of Wenzel Anton Kaunitz." In *Social Change in the Habsburg Monarchy*, edited by Harald Heppinger, Peter Urbanitsch, and Renate Zedinger, 137–153. Bochum: Winkler, 2011.

Szabo, Franz A. J. "The Center and the Periphery: Echoes of the Diplomatic Revolution in the Administration of the Habsburg Monarchy, 1753-1773." In *Nation, Nationalitäten und Nationalismus im östlichen Europa: Festschrift für Arnold Suppan zum 65. Geburtstag*, edited by Marija Wakounig, Wolfgang Mueller, and Michael Portmann, 473–490. Vienna: LIT Verlag, 2010.

Szabo, Franz A. J. "Competing Visions of Enlightened Absolutism: Security and Economic Development in the Reform Priorities of the Habsburg Monarchy after the Seven Years War." In *Miscellanea fontium historiae Europaeae: emlékkönyv H. Balázs Éva történészprofesszor 80. születésnapjára*, edited by János Kalmár, 191–200. Budapest: ELTE, 1997.

Szabo, Franz A. J. *Kaunitz and Enlightened Absolutism 1753–1780*. New York: Cambridge University Press, 1994. http://dx.doi.org/10.1017/CBO9780511523489.

Szabo, Franz A. J., Antal Szántay, and István György Tóth, eds. *Politics and Culture in the Age of Joseph II*. Budapest: Institute of History, Hungarian Academy of Sciences, 2005.

Tanzer, Gerhard. *Spectacle müssen seyn: die Freizeit der Wiener im 18. Jahrhundert*. Vienna: Böhlau, 1992.

Vanysacker, Dries. *Cardinal Giuseppe Garampi, 1725–1792: An Enlightened Ultramontane*. Brussels: Institut Historique Belge de Rome, 1995.

Wandruszka, Adam. *Leopold II., Erzherzog von Österreich, Grossherzog von Toskana, König von Ungarn und Böhmen, römischer Kaiser*. 2 vols. Vienna: Herold, 1963–65.

Wangermann, Ernst. *Die Waffen der Publizität: zum Funktionswandel der politischen Literatur under Joseph II*. Vienna: Verlag für Geschichte und Politik, 2004.

Weissensteiner, Friedrich. *Die Töchter Maria Theresias*. Vienna: K & S, 1994.

Wolf, Adam. *Aus dem Hofleben Maria Theresia's: nach dem Memoiren des Fürsten Joseph Khevenhüller*. Vienna: Carl Gerold's Sohn, 1858.

Wolf, Adam. *Fürstin Eleonore Liechtenstein, 1745–1812*. Vienna: Carl Gerold's Sohn, 1875.

Wolf, Adam. *Marie Christine, Erzherzogin von Oesterreich*. 2 vols. Vienna: Carl Gerold's Sohn, 1863.

Wright, William E. *Serf, Seigneur, and Sovereign: Agrarian Reform in Eighteenth-Century Bohemia*. Minneapolis: University of Minnesota Press, 1966.

Wunder, Heide. "Herrschaft und öffentliches Handeln von Frauen in der Gesellschaft der Frühen Neuzeit" in *Frauen in der Geschichte des Rechts*. Edited by Ute Gerhard. Munich: C. H. Beck, 1997, pp. 27-54.

Zöllner, Erich, ed. *Österreich im Zeitalter des aufgeklärten Absolutismus*. Vienna: Österreichischer Bundesverlag, 1983.

Index

administrative reforms
    during Maria Theresia's reign, 111–12
    under Joseph II, 254–55
agrarian reform
    abolition of compulsory labor (*robot*), 262
    abolition of serfdom, 261
    and Joseph II, 152–56, 266–67
    during Maria Theresia's reign, 112, 152–56, 159–61
    "rectification" (land tax system), 263–66, 309
Albert of Saxe-Teschen, 213, 314–15
alliance with France. *See* French alliance
alliance with Russia. *See* Russian alliance
American Revolution, 194
Ansbach, 187, 289, 290
Antwerp, 290, 293
Arnstein, Fanny, 52n127, 63
Augarten, 70
Austerlitz, 75–76, 139, 157, 170
Austrian Netherlands. *See* Belgium (Austrian Netherlands)

Baden (bei Wien), 7, 69, 76–77, 136, 290, 304, 311, 313
balls, 60, 64, 86, 214, 245, 286
Banat, 296
barge-hauling (as punishment), 259
Barton, Peter (historian), 252–53
Bavaria, 156, 176–78, 191–94, 217, 291–92, 293
Bayreuth, 187
Beales, Derek (historian), 5, 120–21, 140, 141, 311
Beethoven, Ludwig van, 21, 93
Belgium (Austrian Netherlands), 176–77, 255, 291–92, 293–95, 308, 321–22

Belgrade, 304–05
Binder, Friedrich, 234
Blanc, Franz Anton, 159
Blanning, T. C. W. (historian), 168, 179–80, 198, 199, 210, 292, 304–05, 311, 335
Blarer, Melchior, 232, 234–35, 251
Blumauer, Alois, 228
Bohemia, 25, 153
Bosnia, 299
Brambilla, Giovanni, 258, 303
Brigittenau, 240
Brünn, 31, 75, 83, 116, 119, 161, 174, 232, 234–35
Brunner, Otto (historian), 53
Buchau, 77
Bukovina, 176
Buquoy, Johann Nepomuk, 247–48, 249

cannibalism, 258
capital punishment. *See* death penalty
Carinthia, 153
Casanova, Giacomo, 317
Catherine II, 195–96, 218, 335
Catholicism
    baroque, 161–62
    and Quietism, 162–63
    reform, 162–63
censorship, 167, 219–23, 223–25, 317–18
Cerman, Ivo (historian), 39, 55, 63, 334
Chanclos, Countess, 142, 192, 299, 308
chapels, contemplative, 237
charitable institutions, 246–49
Charles VII (Wittelsbach, emperor), 19
Chotek, Rudolf, 91–92, 266
civil service reforms, 253–54
Clary-Aldringen, Christine, *née* Ligne, 91
Clary-Aldringen, Franz Wenzel
    elevation in rank, 20, 61–62

as grand master of the hunt, 29–30, 61–62, 211, 285, 336
and Teplitz, 77, 191–92
Clary-Aldringen, Johann (Josepha's son), 39–40, 91
Clary-Aldringen, Josepha, *née* Hohenzollern-Hechingen, 1, 35
birth and early life of, 14
and censorship reforms, 230–31
and convents, 242, 243
death of, 318
and Joseph II, 197, 214–15
personal characteristics, 35
quarrel with Leopoldine Kaunitz, 192
receptiveness to reforms, 214–15
and the "rectification," 265
and religious reforms, 227
role in *société*, 135–36
son and daughters of, 38, 39, 91–93
and *Stift* at Nivelles
and tolerance edicts, 226
and Turkish war, 295
and the War of the Bavarian Succession, 191–93
Clary-Aldringen family, 5, 19–20, 28
elevation in rank (for head of family), 20, 61–62
and theater, 68
Cobenzl, Philip, 115, 315
Coke, Lady Mary, 35, 53, 64, 75–76, 116, 131, 139, 167, 170–71
Cologne (Köln), 59
compulsory labor (*robot*), 112, 261, 262
Congress of Vienna, 7, 314, 319
Constantinople, 288
convents and monasteries, 171, 240–44
cordon (defensive), 179, 296, 316
coregency
nature of, 2, 112–14, 138–39, 151, 199, 218
foreign policy during, 175, 279–82
court, Habsburg
under Joseph II, 59–60
during Maria Theresia's reign, 56–59
service at, 57
Spanish influence, 60
Crimea, 287–88

Dames (as a group), 1, 2, 3–5, 8, 127, 340
and agrarian reform, 155, 158–59, 160–61, 335–36

opinion of coregency and coregent, 198
and censorship, 309
and charity, 247
and convents, 241–44
at court, 56–57, 60, 216, 285–86
discretion of, 78–79, 81
and French Revolution, 301–03, 312–13
and general seminaries, 245–46
and the Holy Roman Empire, 319–24
during Joseph II's final illness and death, 305–06, 308, 310–11
and Maria Theresia, 116–17
and papal visit to Vienna, 251
religious practices of, 69, 89, 165, 166–67
and religious reforms, 227–29, 333–35
and religious tolerance, 222–23, 253, 334
and Russian alliance, 284, 287–89
and the theater, 67–68
and Turkish war, 304–05
during the War of the Bavarian Succession, 180–94, 333
Daun, Leopold, 128
death penalty, 256–57, 260–61
demesne. *See* dominical lands
dominical lands, 152
Dornbach, 59, 70, 71–72, 120
Dubicza, 298
duels, 41
Dutch Republic. *See* Holland

Eisgrub, 72, 182
Elias, Norbert (sociologist), 54
Elisabeth of Württemberg, 226, 242, 284, 285–87, 295, 309
Emancipation Patent (abolition of serfdom), 261
enlightened despotism, 218
Enlightenment, 55, 65, 163, 239, 252
Eskeles, Eleonore, 259–60
Esterházy, Marie, *née* Liechtenstein, 85–86
Esterházy, Nicholaus I, 61, 85, 86, 260
Esterházy, Nicholaus II, 85–86
Esterházy, Valentin, 141
Esterházy family, 61, 85–86, 90
Evans, R. J. W. (historian), 18–19, 266
Eybel, Joseph Valentin, 231, 233–34, 308

Index ♦ 361

famine, 153
Fast, Patrizius, 229–30
Febronius (Johann Nicholas Hontheim), 165
Feldsberg, 23, 29, 72–74, 85, 125, 217, 285, 319
Feller, François-Xavier, 229–30
Fénelon, François, 43, 162, 165, 166, 301
Ferdinand (archduke), 11, 58
Ferdinand (king of Naples), 116, 117–19, 315
"Five Princesses," 1, 80, 310, 331–32, 337, 340. See also *Dames*
foreign policy
    during coregency, 175, 194, 195–96
    during Joseph's sole rule, 283–86, 287–92
Frankfurt, 57
Franz (archduke, later emperor) 7, 15, 284, 295, 311, 316
Franz Stephan (emperor), 19
    death of, 57, 112
Frederick II, 21, 110, 111, 114, 157, 177–78, 183, 191, 192, 218, 279, 289, 291–92
freemasonry, 236, 302, 313
French alliance, 25, 111, 287, 300
French language, 66
French Revolution, 7, 300–03, 304, 312–13
Friedel, Johann, 229
Fürstenberg, Josepha, *née* Sternberg (Leopoldine Liechtenstein's sister), 133, 190
Fürstenberg, Karl Egon I, 190, 262

Gabrielli, Katharina, 82–83, 117–18
Galicia, 175, 176
gallantry
    strictness of Maria Theresa, 77–78
    tolerance of aristocratic society, 78–79, 81–82
gambling and card games, 34, 64, 137
Garampi, Giuseppe, 230, 309, 311–12
general seminaries, 245–46
German language, 66
"golden patent," 157
Goodman, Dena (historian), 109
Greiner, Caroline, 63
Grimm, Friedrich Melchior, 226
Günther, Valentin, 259–60

Haller, Albrecht von, 66, 151, 280
Harrach, Johann, 88–89

Harrach, Josephine, *née* Liechtenstein, 5, 21, 64, 68, 85, 88–89, 93, 125, 302, 321
Harrach family, 88–89
Hatzfeld, Karl Friedrich, 159
Haugwitz, Friedrich Wilhelm, 111
Henry of Prussia (Frederick II's brother), 177, 188, 225
Hertzberg, Ewald Friedrich, 187
Hofburg, 57
Hoffmann, Leopold Alois, 228–29
Hohenzollern-Hechingen family, 13–14, 16, 320
Holland, 222, 289
Holy Roman Empire, 16–18, 140, 176, 179–80, 312, 319–22
honor, 12
hospitals and poorhouses. *See* charitable institutions
"house" (aristocratic), 12, 37, 332
Hungary, 152, 254–55, 258, 297, 308–09
hunting, 72–73
Hütteldorf, 74, 237, 314

In coena Domini (papal bull), 226, 235
Isabella of Parma, 56–57, 134

Jacobin plot, 314
Jansenism and Jansenists, 89, 163–65, 224, 231, 234, 242
Jesuits (Society of Jesus), 162, 169–71
Jews, 223
Joseph II (emperor)
    as bachelor and widow, 134–35
    and Catherine II, 195–96, 284–85, 292
    Catholicism of, 173, 222–23, 252
    as coregent, 112, 151, 197
    and *Dames*, 142–43, 212–13
    death of, 309–11
    and Eleonore Liechtenstein, 115–16, 120–22, 124, 126–27, 337
    failure of reform program, 308–09
    foreign policy of, 219, 283–97, 303, 311
    governing style of, 59–60, 113–14, 138, 143, 338
    health of, 210
    illness and death of, 297, 298–99, 303–11
    and Leopoldine Kaunitz, 118, 133, 135
    and Maria Theresia, 114, 209
    married life of, 56–57, 134–35
    as military leader, 114, 177–79, 296–97

and the nobility, 109–10, 253–54, 258–61, 266–67, 335, 336
personal characteristics of, 115, 138–40, 197, 198, 210–11, 212
and public opinion, 222
reputation of, 178–79, 221–22, 289, 291, 305, 309, 311–12
as ruler, 113–14, 139, 198–99, 210, 211, 218
travels of, 218, 279–83
and women, 109, 115, 122–24, 127, 134–35, 138–40
Josephinism, 168

Kauffman, Angelika, 212–13
Kaunitz, Bernardine, *née* Plettenberg, 39, 79
Kaunitz, Dominik, 157
Kaunitz, Eleonore ("Lorel"), 37, 238–39
Kaunitz, Ernst, 30–31
    affairs, 82–83
    in Brünn, 119
    fondness for Vienna, 80–81
    in Naples, 116–19
    as *Obersthofmarschall*, 211
    and papal visit to Vienna, 250
    as superintendent of buildings, 119, 211, 336
Kaunitz family, 23–25, 28
Kaunitz, Leopoldine, *née* Öttingen-Spielberg, 1, 4, 36
    as advisor to Eleonore Liechtenstein, 79–80, 121
    and agrarian reform, 263
    and Baden, 76–77
    birth and early life of, 16–17
    and censorship reforms, 230–31
    daughter of, 38–39
    death of, 318
    and Joseph II, 135, 305–06, 339
    and legal reform, 257
    as moderating influence, 124
    in Naples, 82–83, 116–19
    personal characteristics, 36
    quarrel with Josepha Clary, 192
    receptiveness to reforms, 215–16
    and religious reforms, 227, 230–31, 232, 235–36, 334
    role in *société*, 135, 216
    and street sweeping, 258
    and Turkish war, 300

and the War of the Bavarian Succession, 184–89
Kaunitz, Franz Wenzel (Ernst's brother) 30, 250
Kaunitz, Wenzel (chancellor), 16, 24–25, 30–31
    agrarian reforms of, 190, 262, 336
    Belgian policy, 292–93
    criticism of Joseph II's policies, 211, 305
    during coregency, 151–52
    education and early life, 54–55
    final illness and death of, 317
    and French alliance, 25
    and legal reforms, 259
    and nobility, 110
    and papal visit to Vienna, 250–51
    and religion, 317
    and religious reforms, 163, 227, 228
    and religious tolerance, 222
    and the War of the Bavarian Succession, 187–88
Keith, Robert Murray, 53, 57, 62, 64, 72, 91, 187, 306–07
Khevenhüller-Metsch, Johann Joseph, 6, 56, 68, 133, 137
Kinsky family, 12, 20–21, 27–28
Kinsky, Ferdinand, 21, 93
Kinsky, Franz Ulrich, 27–28
    generosity to Clary-Aldringen family, 193
    generosity to Sidonia Kinsky, 70–71
    military career, 31–32
Kinsky, Philip, 21
Kinsky, Sidonia, *née* Hohenzollern-Hechingen, 1, 35
    birth and early life of, 14
    death of, 319
    as hostess, 115
    and Kaunitz (chancellor), 35
    marriage, 81
    personal characteristics of, 35
    and religion, 167
    and religious reforms, 227
    role in *société*, 136
    son and daughter of, 38, 39
    and the War of the Bavarian Succession, 82, 194
    and Weidlingau, 70–71, 82
Klingenstein, Grete (historian), 54–55
Kromau (Mährisch Kromau), 74–75, 125, 157, 159, 235, 244, 247–48, 263–64

Lacy, Moritz, 1, 3
  cautions *Dames*, 215, 281
  criticism of Joseph II, 307–08
  during coregency, 152
  as described by Eleonore Liechtenstein, 129
  as described by Nathaniel Wraxall, 129
  and Dornbach, 70–72
  and Franz Wenzel Clary, 29–30
  and Joseph II, 3, 129
  and Joseph II's final illness and death, 310
  later life and death of, 316–17, 318
  and Leopoldine Liechtenstein, 128, 130–31
  and Liechtenstein family, 128
  and Maria Theresia, 128–31
  military career of, 128, 311
  personal characteristics of, 128–31
  and Turkish war, 296, 299
  and the War of the Bavarian Succession, 182, 184, 185, 186, 189–91
land reform. *See* agrarian reform
Langendonck, Franz, 87
Laudon, Ernst Gideon, 177, 179, 182, 184, 189, 190, 299, 300
Laxenburg, 69–70, 217, 304
legal reforms
  administration of justice, 255–56
  civil, 227, 255–56
  criminal, 255, 256–57
  impact on nobility, 256, 259–61
  under Maria Theresia, 255
Leopold II (grand duke, emperor), 11
  and criticism of Joseph II, 107, 122–23, 214, 217, 290–91, 305
  as Joseph II's successor, 41, 312, 313–14
  opinion of Leopoldine Kaunitz and Ernst Kaunitz, 118
  and religious reforms, 229, 252–53
Liechtenstein, Caroline, *née* Manderscheid, 85
Liechtenstein, Charles (Eleonore's husband), 23
  affairs, 83–84
  and court, 32–33, 126, 211–12, 286
  illness and death, 298
  as Louis Liechtenstein's guardian, 43–44
  and military barracks in Vienna, 125–26
  military career of, 32–33, 125–26, 180, 211–12, 298
  religion, 166
Liechtenstein, Charles (Eleonore's son), 40–41, 89–90
Liechtenstein, Eleonore, *née* Öttingen-Spielberg, 1, 4, 36–37
  and agrarian reform, 159–60
  birth and early life of, 16–17
  at Frankfurt, 57
  and the French Revolution, 267, 302–03
  illness, 298
  and Joseph II, 108, 115–16, 120–22, 124, 125–26, 126–27, 212, 337, 339
  and Joseph II's death, 310
  later life and death of, 318–19
  personal characteristics of, 36–37
  and the "rectification," 263–65
  and religious reforms, 227, 334
  sons and daughter of, 38, 40–42
  and the War of the Bavarian Succession, 181–84
  as widow, 75
Liechtenstein, Franz Joseph I, 16, 23, 28, 43, 81
Liechtenstein, Johann, 44, 87, 316, 320
Liechtenstein, Karl I, 22
Liechtenstein, Leopoldine, *née* Sternberg, 1, 36
  and convents, 243
  early life of, 16
  and Feldsberg, 72–74
  as hostess, 115, 286
  and Joseph II, 215, 309, 339–40
  personal characteristics of, 36
  and Kaunitz (chancellor), 36
  and Lacy, 81, 316–17
  later life and death of, 316, 318, 319
  marriage, 16, 28, 81
  and papal visit to Vienna, 251
  in Paris, 283
  receptiveness to reforms, 214–15
  and religious reforms, 227–28
  role in *société*, 135, 216
  sons and daughters of, 38, 42–44, 339
  in Spa, 213–14
  and the War of the Bavarian Succession, 189–91
  as widow, 43–44, 73–74
Liechtenstein, Louis (Alois I), 28, 66, 74, 85–87, 189, 193, 259

Liechtenstein, Maria Anna, *née* Khevenhüller-Metsch, 90–91
Liechtenstein, Wenzel, 23, 32, 128
Liechtenstein family, 12, 22–23, 27, 86–87
Liechtenstein (principality), 23, 176, 320
Ligne, Charles Joseph de, 68, 83, 91, 142, 166, 175–76, 313, 319, 335
Lobkowicz family, 5, 90
Lombardy, 171, 249, 255
Loretto Chapel (Augustinerkirche, Vienna), 240
Louis XVI (French king), 281, 304

Manderscheid-Blankenheim family, 16
Maria Carolina (archduchess, queen of Naples), 11, 117–19, 315
Maria Josepha (archduchess, Joseph II's sister), 117
Maria Theresia (empress)
  agrarian reforms of, 152–156
  Catholicism of, 164–65, 171–72
  death of, 196, 209, 310
  early reforms of, 111–12
  governing style of, 59, 113–14, 143
  and Joseph II, 113, 114
  loyalty of, 119, 143
  personal characteristics of, 213
  political testaments of, 111–12
  religious intolerance, 171–72
  religious reforms, 157, 161, 163, 168–69
  and women in politics, 108
Maria Theresia Military Order, 31–32, 58, 316
Mariabrunn, 250
Mariahilf, 70, 250
Mariazell, 237–40, 298
Marie Antoinette (French *dauphine*/queen), 58, 281, 283, 300, 302–03, 313, 339
Marie Beatrix of Modena, 58, 59
Marie Christine (archduchess), 59, 83, 192–93, 213, 293, 305, 314–15
marriage law (*Ehepatent*), 1783, 227
Maximilian Franz (archduke, Joseph II's brother), 59, 194–95
Maximilian Joseph of Bavaria, 177
Mercy-Argenteau, Florimond Claude, 199, 251, 287
Meseritsch (Gross Meseritsch), 69, 157, 158, 159, 263–64, 265
Metternich, Eleonore, *née* Kaunitz, 38, 93–94, 319

Metternich family, 5, 94
Migazzi, Christoph Anton (archbishop), 174–75, 228, 229, 230, 232, 253, 311
Moldavia, 299
Mons, 55
Moravia, 18, 22, 24, 27, 72, 88, 119, 153, 157, 158, 160–61, 172, 183, 234, 264
Muratori, Ludovico Antonio, 162–63, 230

Naples
  Ernst Kaunitz's assignment to, 30, 75, 81–83, 116–19
  Joseph II's visit, 1769, 118, 151
  and Leopoldine Kaunitz, 82–83, 116–19
Napoleon Bonaparte, 7, 314, 315, 319, 320–21
National Theater (Burgtheater), 67
neo-Adamites, 157
Nicolai, Christoph Friedrich, 220
nobility, 109–10, 253–54
  and agrarian reform, 266–67, 335
  Bohemian, 18–19
  economic strategies of, 25–28, 37–38
  education of, 37, 65–67
  extramarital affairs of, 78–83
  and marriage, 12, 39, 40–41, 83–94
  ranks and distinctions of, 60–62
  political roles, 110, 253–54
  regional differences of, 55–56
  "seconde noblesse," 63
  social life of, 62–65, 77–78
  as subject for historical study, 53–54

O'Donnell, Carl, 79–80
Order of the Golden Fleece, 58, 140, 286
Ottoman Empire. *See* Turkey
Öttingen-Spielberg family, 11–12, 16–19, 26, 320
Öttingen-Spielberg, Johann Alois I, 16–18, 140

Paar, Josepha, *née* Öttingen, 59, 114, 115–16, 119, 142
papacy, 224
parfilage, 64
Paris, 56
Paul (grand duke of Russia), 284, 285–87
peasants. *See* land reform
peasant unrest
  in Bohemia and Moravia, 156–60
  in Transylvania, 261–62

Philibert (Jean-Antoine Gazaignes), 174–75, 231
philosophes and "philosophy," 58, 65
pilgrimages, 164, 169, 238
Pillnitz, 316
Pius VI (pope), 249–52
Pochlin, Joseph, 230
Podstatzky-Liechtenstein, Count, 260
Poland, 313
    partitions of, 175–76, 265, 313
politics and women, 3–6, 107–09, 142, 214, 332–33
poor relief. *See* charitable institutions
Prague, 20, 22, 55, 77, 81, 82, 136, 172, 177, 182, 190–91, 233
private sphere. *See* public and private spheres
Protestantism, 13, 17, 22, 157, 171, 172–73, 222
Prussia, 300, 312, 313
public and private spheres, 108–09, 144n6, 332–33

Quarin, Joseph (doctor), 308

Raab, Franz Anton, 156
Raab system, 156, 159, 261, 263
Rautenstrauch, Franz Stephan, 232–33
Raynal, Guillaume Thomas (*Abbé*), 225–26
reading and books, 65–66
"rectification" (land tax system). *See* agrarian reform
reforms (of Joseph II), repeal of, 309
religious reforms
    during coregency, 161–62, 163, 164–65, 168–71
    under Joseph II, 222–39, 240–46, 333–34
religious tolerance
    during coregency, 171–74
    under Joseph II, 219, 223, 224–25, 226, 252, 334
"representation"
    at imperial court, 58
    among nobility, 62
reversal of alliances. *See* French alliance
robot. *See* compulsory labor
Rosenberg, Franz Xavier, 1, 3
    career of, 131–32
    criticism of Joseph II, 291
    early opinion of Leopoldine Kaunitz and Ernst Kaunitz, 117–18
    illness and death, 315
    and Joseph II, 3, 132
    and Joseph II's final illness and death, 306, 307, 310
    liaisons of, 132–33
    and Leopold II, 131
    and Maria Theresia, 131–32
    and Marie Christine, 193
    and papal visit to Vienna, 250–51
    personal characteristics of, 131–33
    as reformer, 132–33
    and religious reforms, 228
    role of, 57, 299, 303, 307, 307–08, 315
    as theater manager, 67, 133
Rossau, 70
Rousseau, Jean-Jacques, 71, 130, 215, 219, 280
Russia, 157, 175, 176, 178, 179, 195–96, 222, 226, 284–90, 292, 295–300
Russian alliance, 195, 284–85, 287–89
rustical lands, 152–53, 261, 262

Saftingen, 290
Saint Stephan, Order of, 58
Salburg, Rudolf Ferdinand, 93
salons, 63
Saxony, 110, 111, 158, 177, 182, 192–93, 291
Scheldt, 290
Schneller, Joseph, 230
Schönbrunn, 69, 286, 304
science (popular), 68–69
"season" (social), 108
seminaries, general. *See* general seminaries
Serbia, 299
serfdom, abolition of. *See* Emancipation Patent
Seven Years War, 111
Sévigné, Marie de Rabutin-Chantal, 65
Silva-Taroucca, Emanuel, 56
Sinzendorf, Philip, 81, 139
Sinzendorf, Wenzel, 93
social life and women, 62–63, 77–79, 108
société, 2, 10n10, 34, 37, 53, 69, 94, 109, 142
    characteristics of, 199, 331–33, 336–38
    composition of, 133–34
    during Joseph's sole rule, 212–13, 216
    Joseph II's role in, 134
    longevity of, 143–44, 180, 194, 213–14, 216, 295, 331–32

roles of male members, 127–28
roles of women, 135–37, 180, 336. See also *Dames* (as a group)
Sonnenfels, Joseph, 55, 66, 188
Spa (Belgium), 64, 213–14, 225
Starhemberg, Georg, 15
Sternberg, Leopoldine, *née* Starhemberg, 15–16
Sternberg, Philip, 15–16, 56
Sternberg family, 5, 14–16, 320
Sternberg(-Manderscheid), Christian, 16, 56
Steuben, Friedrich Wilhelm, 14
Stift (female foundation)
    at Buchau, 14
    eligibility for, 16, 85, 87–88, 92–93
    at Essen, 85, 87–88
    at Hall, 14
    Joseph II's reforms of, 244–45
    lifestyle in, 87–88
    at Mons, 55–56, 244
    at Nivelles, 92–93, 194, 244, 258–59
street sweeping (as punishment), 259–60
Styria, 131, 133, 153, 237, 282
Swabia, 176
Swieten, Gottfried van, 166, 220–21, 232, 267
Swinburne, Henry, 30, 55, 134, 135
syphilis. *See* venereal disease
Székely, Samuel, 260

Teplitz, 19–20, 68, 77, 191
Teschen, treaty of, 289–90
theater, 58, 66–68, 82, 86, 122, 134, 140, 164, 214, 234, 235, 290, 300
Thirty Years War, 13
Thugut, Johann Amadeus, 177–78, 186, 314, 316
toleration edicts. *See* religious tolerance
torture, prohibition of, 255
Transylvania, 153, 261
Trattner, Joseph Thomas, 65, 187, 220, 286
travel (Joseph II), 218, 279–83
Turkey, 33, 176, 195, 295–97, 284–89, 292, 295–97, 312
Turkish war, 295–300, 304–05

Unigenitus (papal bull), 163–64, 226, 235
urbaria, 158
Utraquists, 20

Van Swieten, Gottfried. *See* Swieten, Gottfried van
venereal disease, 33–34, 212
Vetter, Anton Maria, 234–35
Vienna (as social and political center), 54–57, 62–63, 69, 74, 76, 81, 94, 108, 184–85, 219–20, 249, 283–84, 317–18, 332
Vienna, Congress of. *See* Congress of Vienna
Visitation convent
    in Strasbourg, 57, 165, 242
    in Vienna, 226, 242, 243–44, 287

Waldstein family, 19, 191
Wallenstein, Albrecht, 19
Wangermann, Ernst, 252
War of the Austrian Succession, 110
War of the Bavarian Succession, 32–33, 71, 82, 155–56, 176–90, 191–94, 333
Weidlingau, 35, 70–71, 143, 194, 216, 314
White Mountain, battle of, 18–19, 20
Wiesenthaler, Josef, 257
Windischgrätz, Joseph Nicholaus, 115
Windischgrätz, Josepha, 115, 123
Wittola, Mark Anton, 231–32
Wolf, Adam (historian), 4, 5, 127, 141, 198, 318, 331
women. *See* politics and women; social life and women
Wraxall, Nathaniel, 37, 64, 72, 77–78, 108, 113, 121, 129, 132, 137, 166, 173, 178, 192, 219

Zahlheim, Franz, 260–61
Zahradisch, 74, 265
Zinzendorf, Karl, 6, 35, 142, 165–66, 261, 262
    criticism of Joseph II, 266, 305, 311, 338
    and French Revolution, 301
    affairs, 78–79
    and Eleonore Liechtenstein, 37
    and Leopoldine Kaunitz, 36, 215–16, 301, 317
Zippe, Augustin, 231, 233
Zips, 175

www.ingramcontent.com/pod-product-compliance
Lightning Source LLC
Chambersburg PA
CBHW070009010526
44117CB00011B/1484